The Rise & Fall of the Zulu Nation

'The Zulu nation
is a collection of tribes,
more or less autonomous,
and more or less discontented;
a rope of sand
whose only cohesive property
was furnished by the presence of
the Zulu ruling family and
its command of a standing army.'

Memorandum by
Sir Theophilus Shepstone,
12 August 1887
(*British Parliamentary Papers* [C. 5531], enc. in no. 13).

The Rise & Fall of the Zulu Nation

John Laband

ARMS AND
ARMOUR

This edition published in 1997 by
Arms and Armour Press
An imprint of the Cassell Group
Wellington House, 125 Strand, London WC2R 0BB

Distributed in the USA by
Sterling Publishing Co. Inc., 387 Park Avenue South,
New York, NY 10016-8810.

First published 1995 by
Jonathan Ball Publishers (Pty) Ltd
under the title *Rope of Sand*
P O Box 33977, Jeppestown 2043
Republic of South Africa.

British Library Cataloguing-in-Publication Date:
a catalogue record for this book is available from the British Library

ISBN 1-85409-421-1

Design by Michael Barnett, Johannesburg.
Typesetting and reproduction of text, picture sections and dust jacket by Book Productions, Pretoria.
Maps by cartographic unit, University of Natal, Pietermaritzburg.
Printed and bound by National Book Printers, Drukkery Street, Goodwood, Western Cape.
Republic of South Africa.

Contents

List of Maps

Preface

Since 27 April 1994 'the institution, role, authority and status' of the Zulu monarch in the province of KwaZulu-Natal have been recognised and protected in the constitution of the post-apartheid South African state.[1] This acceptance of an historic reality marked the culmination of a remarkable resurgence in the fortunes of the Zulu royal house after over a century of eclipse under white rule. The precise nature of the revitalised Zulu monarchy within a late twentieth-century developing country has naturally still to be worked out in practice. That process, in the overheated political environment of KwaZulu-Natal, where deep personal and party rivalries are still so pronounced, promises to be a troubled one. But whatever form it eventually takes, the new 'kingdom' will inevitably be very different from its precursor, the kingdom founded by King Shaka in the early decades of the nineteenth century.

That kingdom lasted only a little over six decades before being overthrown in war, broken into pieces, consigned to bitter civil war and eventually annexed piecemeal by its rapacious white-ruled neighbours. But short as was its history as an independent state, the original Zulu kingdom still figures large as a potent symbol, and bestows its legitimacy on its modern inheritor. In its time, it was the most politically sophisticated, administratively integrated and militarily powerful black polity in all of south-eastern Africa, and its stern shadow spread over the entire region. It was brought to its knees only after a spectacular war with imperial Britain, which still commands the imagination. Zululand's subsequent and progressive degradation during a period when colonial rule was extended over its people, when its king and chiefs were reduced to petty functionaries in the pay of the colonial state, and when most of its land was given over to white farmers, is a poignant tale of humiliation and loss which summons up pity and calls for redress. But the image of the kingdom which remains the most striking, which still serves most expressively as an emblem of Zulu nationalism and unity, is that of the great kings of the nineteenth century, in all their majesty and might.

Memories of the old Zululand – kept alive in a people's proud traditions and in their national consciousness, and given visible substance and continuity in the unbroken line of the royal house of Shaka – provide a constant inspiration for the present. That is why, to comprehend KwaZulu-Natal today, it is essential to understand the course of Zulu history in the nineteenth century.

ix

Acknowledgements

It is the historian's demanding task to understand cultures and periods different from his own through the techniques of empathy and intuition, in which an effort of the imagination must be made to relinquish present-day values in order to apprehend previous ages on their own terms. Such an enquiry turns on the interpretation of the evidence which the historian converts into a coherent, causal narrative which differs from the novelist's creation in that it tries as faithfully as it can to be a reconstruction of real events.

In order to achieve this, the historian must attempt to immerse him or herself as fully as possible in the available primary evidence. Nevertheless, in a work of the scope of *Rope of Sand*, which traverses a time-span from the Stone Age to the late nineteenth century, an historian such as I has no option but to avail himself of the scholarly work of others in those areas which he has not made his own research speciality. Inevitably, therefore, *Rope of Sand* is a work of synthesis, in which fifteen years of my research among the primary sources and in the field is augmented by the scholarship of historians and archaeologists like Jeff Guy, Tim Maggs, Paul Thompson, John Wright and others of similar stature. The footnotes and bibliography should make it sufficiently clear where I am relying on their work, rather than on the fruits of my own original research.

The Anglo-Zulu War of 1879 has been my particular area of interest, and it is consequently unavoidable that the section of this book dealing with that conflict should be based upon a number of my earlier, more academically specialised articles and books, particularly *Kingdom in Crisis* (Manchester and New York, 1992), notably chapters 4, 6, 7, 9, 10 and 12. I am very grateful to Manchester University Press for their generous permission to draw upon this work.

Begun in Pietermaritzburg while I was still fully engaged in teaching in the Department of Historical Studies at the University of Natal, and pursued there during the first phase of a period of sabbatical leave, the manuscript of this book was completed at Clare Hall, Cambridge, where I was a Visiting Fellow during the Easter Term of 1994. I am deeply mindful of the constant support and encouragement offered me by Professor Bill Guest and my other colleagues in the Department of Historical Studies. Clare Hall proved the perfect environment for concentrated writing, and I am sincerely appreciative of the friendly welcome extended me by the President, Professor Anthony Low, the Fellows and other members of the College community, and of the companionship and intellectual stimulus they unfailingly provided.

Research and writing require both money and release from mundane duties. I am properly grateful to the University of Natal and its generous Research and Travel Grants for providing me with the necessary funding and breathing-space for undertaking a project of these sprawling dimensions.

Colleagues and associates have, over the years, helped form my perspectives and judgements. Foremost among them was the late Professor Colin Webb, the doyen of the present generation of Natal historians, whose untimely death robbed the profession of his wisdom and extensive knowledge. Professor Bill Guest has been a constant and much appreciated guide, while Professor John Wright has opened up many new vistas for me and given willingly of his specialist advice, including his knowledge of Zulu orthography. Dr Adrian Koopman has also helped me with his expert knowledge of the Zulu language. Professor Paul Thompson and Dr Jeff Mathews have been both my companions in the field and co-authors, and working with them has ever been stimulating and rewarding. Ian Knight has proved a generous and helpful plougher of the same furrow as I, as have S.B. Bourquin and the late Frank Emery. Nevertheless, the burden of responsibility for historical reconstruction and interpretation in this book must be mine alone.

I have been fortunate in the help I have received over the years from the dedicated staffs of various archives, museums and libraries in South Africa and the United Kingdom, particularly the Natal Archives Depot, the University of Natal Library and the Natal Society Library, all of Pietermaritzburg; the Killie Campbell Africana Library, Durban; and the National Army Museum, London. To the staffs of the many institutions left unnamed here – some of which figure in the bibliography and picture credits – I also extend my sincerest thanks, as I do also to the many individuals who have offered a stray researcher hospitality.

Helena Margeot has, as she has unfailingly done in previous books of mine, created the accurate and elegant maps. Once again, it is a pleasure to thank her and her assistant, Toni Bodington.

I am particularly grateful to my publisher, Jonathan Ball, for beguiling me into attempting this project, and then, with Francine Blum, the Production Manager at Jonathan Ball Publishers, for supporting and encouraging me over the many succeeding months of writing and polishing. I am most appreciative of the meticulous and sensitive care with which my editor, Frances Perryer, has tidied up and improved my manuscript.

No set of acknowledgments would be complete without special reference to my wife, Fenella, and our children, Felix and Zoë. They are the ones who have had to bear the tedious and dislocating burden of my constant mental abstraction and frequent physical absences. For their almost unfailing patience and understanding, I thank them with true sincerity.

University of Natal, Pietermaritzburg
Clare Hall, Cambridge

PROLOGUE

The Killing of a King

King Shaka, while taking his usual sleep during the heat of midday, dreamed that he was a dead man.[1] The spirits of the ancestors spoke through dreams, so he took his sleeping vision as an urgent warning. There had been attempts on his life before.

Himself a usurper, his path to power washed with a brother's blood, he suspected his surviving brothers of conspiring against him. He confided in some of the more favoured women of the royal household at his kwaDukuza homestead, a great circle of a thousand huts or more lying in the pleasant coastal lands near the banks of the Mvoti River. One of the women who learned of the king's ominous dream was the sister of Mbopha kaSithayi of the emGazini people, Shaka's trusted personal attendant who shared his very food. She went immediately to her brother, for she feared that Shaka, alerted by the spirits, would strike out at all those he suspected might be planning his death, and it seems that in his dream Shaka had seen the supposedly devoted Mbopha compromisingly serving another king.

Indeed, Mbopha, tall, stout and dark,[2] was deeply involved in a plot with two of Shaka's ambitious half-brothers, Mhlangana and Dingane, to assassinate him. His motives were mixed and not altogether praiseworthy. Mbopha's mother, so it was said, had been put to death on Shaka's directions, a deed calling for revenge that would have festered in her son during all his years of close attendance on the king;[3] while Mhlangana and Dingane played on his cupidity and thirst for power by promising to make him a chief with wide lands to rule over.

Mbopha and his two royal accomplices, who had returned unbidden on pretence of illness from the army campaigning to the north, met clandestinely in the veld outside kwaDukuza to discuss the news of the king's inauspicious dream. They decided they must act immediately, while they still had the chance. Mnkabayi kaJama, Shaka's formidable king-making aunt, encouraged them in their resolve, for she felt Shaka's incessant campaigning was beginning to endanger the kingdom he had created.

The opportunity was orchestrated the very same day, on 24 September 1828. A party of travel-weary men arrived at kwaDukuza from the Mpondo country far to the south, beyond the Mthamvuna River. They carried with them the rare and valuable crane feathers and skins of monkey, genet and otter that were worn by the king and other favoured men of high distinction. Shaka, who had long been expecting them, and was extremely dissatisfied with the time they had taken, ordered them brought before him at sundown to the relative privacy of a small homestead called kwaNyakamubi (or Ugly Year), which was fifty metres distant from kwaDukuza itself. There they sat cowering in the open before the angry king, who harshly reprimanded them for taking so long about their errand, while at the same time casting a proprietorial eye over the extensive herds of cattle being driven home from pasture for milking.

Mbopha, as was customary, reiterated his master's words, energetically berating the tardy travellers from Mpondoland for troubling the king, then suddenly threw his stick at them. This they not unnaturally interpreted as the signal for their immediate execution and, leaping to their feet, they rushed away in an attempt to cheat their fate. Shaka severely asked Mbopha why he had taken it upon himself to drive them off in that insubordinate manner. And there was indeed a reason, but unsuspected by the king. Mhlangana and Dingane had hidden themselves behind a small fence near which Shaka was seated on his pile of mats, each with a spear concealed under his skin cloak.

Seeing the party from Mpondoland run out of the homestead in panic, leaving the king alone in the gathering darkness, except for the treacherous Mbopha and two or three aged and harmless councillors not privy to their plot,[4] Mhlangana seized the moment. He drove his spear into Shaka, but because of the skin cloak the king was wearing, misjudged his aim and stabbed him through the back of the left shoulder. Perhaps Mbopha threw his spear at his master at the same time, for, as Shaka's confidential servant, he alone had enjoyed the privilege of carrying a spear in the close presence of the king.[5]

Stunned with pain, Shaka only had time to look behind him before Dingane also thrust in his spear. 'What is the matter, children of my father?' he cried in agonised disbelief. He then threw off his hampering skin cloak and, with a last accession of strength, pulled the spear with which Dingane had stabbed him out of his side. Maybe he intended to defend himself with it, for Mbopha had taken the precaution of hiding the king's own weapons in one of the huts.[6] His overriding instinct, however, was to escape his assailants, and the grievously wounded Shaka tried to make for the open ground and the cover of the night. But after a few steps he stumbled and fell just outside the gate of kwaNyakamubi. There, he called out piteously for mercy, humbling himself as he pleaded, 'Leave me alone, sons of my father, and I shall be your menial.'[7] But his assassins scoffed at that unlikely pledge, and finished off his life in a flurry of spear thrusts.

Once Shaka lay dead and bleeding on the earth before them, Mhlangana jumped over the corpse of his brother in a ritual of victory, as Shaka in his triumph had once leaped over the body of Phakathwayo of the Qwabe. Nor could Dingane misinterpret what was meant. Mhlangana was giving his brother an unmistakable sign that he, Mhlangana, was laying claim to his right to succeed Shaka as king of the Zulu.[8]

There were complex but well-defined procedures governing succession in Zulu society. These were made necessary by the large number of wives and male children in the household of a man of substance, and by the desire to prevent the bloody process of inheritance by fratricidal elimination that would otherwise ensue. On the other hand, the automatic succession of the eldest son was considered far too dangerous to the continued well-being of an aging father, so the naming of an heir was delayed as long as possible to lessen the possibility of usurpation. If such dangers stalked a mere chief, how much more so did they trouble the king of the land, who knew the whole process of succession to be a hazardous business at best, and one that could rend the kingdom into warring factions before a clear successor emerged.

Shaka's response to the problem of the royal succession had been only partial, and therefore unavailing. He never acknowledged any child he might have sired as his own, thus precluding any threat from an impatient heir. As the Zulu said, their kings were like male leopards or lions, who would kill their male offspring unless they were spirited out of their way.[9] But Shaka was still surrounded by ambitious brothers, whose only concern with the customs of inheritance was that the crown should fall to the strongest. In fact, no settled principle of royal succession would ever become firmly established in the Zulu kingdom. As his ancestors were believed to have reminded Shaka's nephew King Cetshwayo in a dream, 'you of the Zulu are always killing one another in disputing the kingship'.[10] And so it was. From the very beginning, regicide and civil war characterised the Zulu kingdom, helping sap its ability to withstand the flowing tide of white colonialism which, before the century was out, would sweep over Zululand.

PART I

The plaiting of the rope

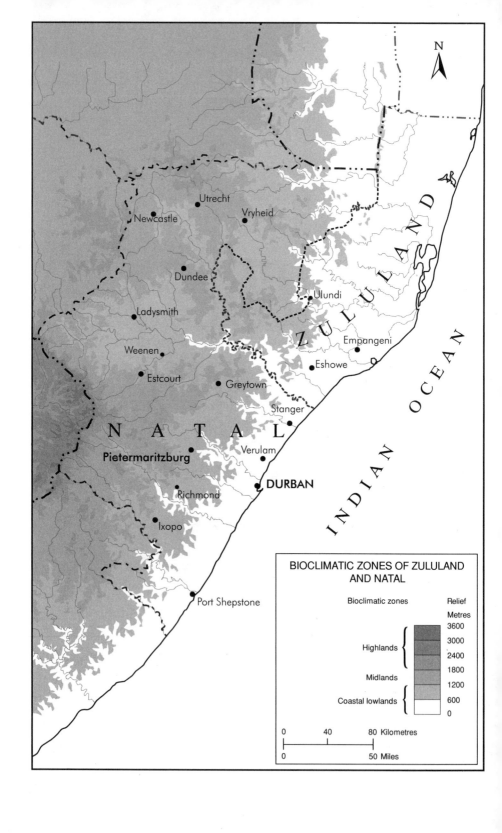

N

BIOCLIMATIC ZONES OF ZULULAND AND NATAL

Bioclimatic zones

Relief
Metres
3600
3000
2400
1800
1200
600
0

Highlands

Midlands

Coastal lowlands

0   40   80 Kilometres

0   50 Miles

Utrecht

Vryheid

Newcastle

Dundee

Ulundi

Ladysmith

Empangeni

Weenen

Eshowe

Estcourt

Greytown

Stanger

N A T A L

Pietermaritzburg

Verulam

DURBAN

Richmond

Ixopo

Port Shepstone

Z U L U L A N D

I N D I A N   O C E A N

1

A Land and its People

The links between the Zulu people and the land upon which they depended for their livelihood were immediate. And the Zulu were fortunate, because their physical environment was particularly well suited to their needs as keepers of herds and tillers of the soil.[1]

It is difficult to say what territory precisely comprises Zululand, for its boundaries have changed substantially over the years. At its furthest extent, when in the first decades of the nineteenth century the power of the Zulu kings was at its mightiest, Zulu influence extended from the majestic scarp of the Drakensberg Mountains in the west to the Indian Ocean in the east; from the southern regions of what are now Swaziland and Mozambique in the north, across modern-day KwaZulu-Natal to the borderlands of the Transkeian territories to the south.

But Zululand has an essential core, and the mighty Thukela River marks its southern limit. Steep hills, often covered with bush, rear up commandingly on either side of the ample valley through which the Thukela winds, the greater part of its course forming a succession of rapids and pools. In the rainy season, during the time of heavy thunderstorms, when the waters from its vast catchment area come down without warning in flood, it is passable only at a few well-known drifts. These flood-waters form new channels every year near its mouth, where the Thukela spreads at last over the level ground before smearing its brown, silt-laden stain over the brilliant waters of the Indian Ocean. The troughs and long narrow pools of the Phongolo River define Zululand to the north; to the west flows the Mzinyathi River, the home of the buffalo. The valley of the White Mfolozi (named after the light-coloured sands and rocks of its bed and the wild fig that grows in large quantities in certain places along its bank) is at its very heart.

These rivers, with the additional major river systems of the relentless Mhlathuze and the violent and unrestrained Mkhuze, have incised wide, deep, open valleys. Their tributaries and smaller streams, though, are precipice-sided and very sinuous. The courses of these rivers are comparatively short, so that during the rainy season all can rise several metres with great suddenness and come down in torrent, churning through their narrow channels and flooding the surrounding lands. For the rest of the year they are insignificant streams, wandering through wide, sandy beds. On reaching the coastal plain the rivers become sluggish, and their mouths are closed by sandbars, producing lagoons and marshes bordered by beds of high, thick reeds.

The countryside through which they flow characteristically undulates and swells in gentle, rounded ridges, rather than in distinct mountain ranges. Not that there are not enormous variations in the Zulu landscape. The low-lying coastal strip, subtropical, hot, humid and enjoying a considerable rainfall, rises a few kilometres inland to well-watered, boldly modelled hills. As the rains borne off the Indian Ocean steadily decrease, the terrain changes. The midlands are characterised by great mountainous spurs thrown out from the high, dry, open tablelands further inland, whose plains are dotted with solitary, abruptly rising, flat-topped mountains, their rocky coronets full of rugged caves. Between the wooded midland spurs, which form the watersheds of numerous streams, are extensive valleys, giving the region its characteristic broken aspect.

Game once abounded in great variety and unimaginable quantity, from the prized elephant, lion, leopard, buffalo, rhinoceros and hippopotamus, to crocodile, giraffe, zebra, wildebeest, baboon, monkey, jackal, hyena, hare, mongoose, snakes and myriads of birds. By the 1870s, even though the Zulu kings tried to restrict the areas in which Europeans could hunt with their devastating firearms, the fauna was diminishing rapidly, especially elephant, hippopotamus and buffalo, which were the focus of commercial hunting and trading. By that period elephant, for example, could still be found only north of the Phongolo. Nevertheless, wild animals survived in far greater numbers in nineteenth-century Zululand than in any of the territories to its south.[2] Perhaps the reason was that, despite the depredations of the commercial hunters, and the much more limited hunting by the Zulu monarchs of certain designated species of royal game, like elephant, most Zulu took only a limited interest in hunting, whether for amusement or as a means of subsistence. For in truth, the Zulu of the early historic period held all animal food, except beef, in varying degrees of aversion.[3] Thus, for them, the successful rearing of cattle was the vital thing. Fortunately, the grassess of Zululand provided the means.

The great variations in rainfall in Zululand have created a number of different vegetation types. Naturally, these are constantly being affected by human activities such as burning, agriculture and stock grazing, which drive back the forest and bush and permit the grasses to flourish in their place. At the time of the formation of the Zulu kingdom in the early nineteenth century, the low-lying coastal alluvial plain was still extensively covered with bush. In between flourished the luxuriant sourveld grasses, which occur in the rainy coastlands (and in the midlands in areas once covered by forests). They are good for cattle only after the spring rains, for once sourveld matures, it ceases to be nutritious. Inland, with less rain and a more temperate climate, there was progressively less bush and wider tracts of grass.

The rainfall was low along the great river valleys, which sheltered savanna or lowveld vegetation, with its scattered thorntrees and grassy understory. These grasses are 'sweet', and provide palatable and nutritious grazing for cattle even during the dry winter months. Fortunately, the tsetse fly, so devastating to stock and normally associated with sweetveld conditions, was confined to the deepest valleys or to the north-eastern margins of Zululand; moreover, unlike many other parts of southern Africa, the relatively dry sweetveld of Zululand generally had sufficient surface water from the many streams rising in the forest-covered hills to support a high density of stock. Between the sweetveld and sourveld regions were belts of mixed veld, which can be grazed for about half the year. Zululand was thus well suited to raising stock. So long, that is, as the herds could move to take advantage of both the spring sourveld grazing and the sweetveld in the winter.

The Zulu were essentially pastoralists.[4] The paramount importance of cattle in their lives was symbolised by the position of the cattle-fold, or *isibaya*, in the centre of every homestead, or *umuzi*. All ceremonies and rituals were performed there, and many taboos related to this special area. The deep pits, where grain was stored during the winter, were also dug in the *isibaya*, with their funnel-shaped mouths carefully disguised. A Zulu man was never happier than when contemplating his cattle, every one of which was known by its distinctive horns, colourings and markings. Indeed, the Zulu language contains hundreds of terms by which to distinguish the visible attributes of cattle. So familiar would even a chief be with his prized herd, that it was held as a measure of his great affluence when it could be said of him that he did not recognise every beast.[5]

Wealth (in a society that had little other means of storing it) was counted in terms of cattle. Marriage was only legalised – and its issue legitimised – with the transfer of cattle to the father of the bride in exchange for the loss of the valued domestic labour of his daughter. This was known as the *ilobolo* system. Cattle were of ritual significance, for it was only through their sacrifice that the spirits of the ancestors could be propitiated, for one was giving them what was still theirs. They were of basic material importance too, as providers of milk and meat and hides for garments and shields. So great was the value of cattle, that war in Zulu society often had as its primary purpose the enrichment of the victor with the captured herds of his enemy.

The Zulu also tilled the soil in small, scattered fields of irregular shape, enclosed only when protection was needed against animals. Climatic variations permitted some choice in the cultivation of appropriate crops. Indian maize appears to have become established by the eighteenth century, and by the early nineteenth had supplanted sorghum and millet as the favoured food crop. When grown in a suitable environment it has a high yield and is more pest resistant and less labour intensive than other corn. Yet the relatively inferior status of agriculture in a strongly patrilineal society is shown by the fact that it was normally the woman's task to cultivate and reap the crops (though men of low rank might help their wives with sowing, hoeing and weeding).

Routine domestic duties were also the woman's responsibility. These included fetching wood and water, cooking, and making matting for covering huts and to sleep on. Grandmothers would do the housework, and the younger children would be looked after by the older ones when their mothers were working in the fields. To men fell the more prestigious activities of caring for the cattle, building and repairing the homestead, digging holes for the storage of grain, making spoons and baskets, clearing the ground about to be cultivated, self-importantly discussing affairs of moment, and going out to hunt or fight.[6]

Dress was minimal, if distinctive, and regulated by the person's status in society. By it, an unmarried man or woman could be distinguished from a married one, while there were definite characteristics which differentiated a boy or girl who had reached puberty from one who had not. Children wore no dress except a string of beads about the waist, but after puberty loincovers were worn. An unmarried girl would have an oblong piece of beadwork or leaves as a frontal covering, or a fringed waistband of skin. A boy's loincover was a frontal covering of strips of skin or tails and a backflap of leather. On marriage, a woman would wear a short leather skirt, and a skin concealing her breasts until the birth of her first child, or when pregnant. The loincovering of a man was similar to a youth's, but of more generous proportions, with the skin at the back often replaced with strips similar to the frontal tails. Before Shaka's time, it seems men had worn long, skirt-like loincovers, of the sort old men continued to prefer.

The style of hair-dressing was intricate and varied, changing in fashion from district to district and from period to period. A differentiation in terms of sex and status was always maintained, though, from the shaved head of the child, to the intricate top-knot of the married woman. Ornamentation was similarly complex. In the early days, before beads were much available, ornaments consisted chiefly of grass necklaces, strings of snail shells, armlets of gall-bladders and so on. Those who could afford them wore ornaments of imported beads, copper or brass. Ornaments were favoured especially by young men and women, particularly at the time of courting, and were not much worn in married maturity. Certain ornaments were indicators of rank, and only the great, for example, could wear the skin of leopards and their claws as necklaces. Men of standing used to allow their nails to grow long, though women were not allowed to do so. In the days of Shaka and his brothers the most prestigious ornament of all was the *ingxotha*, or brass armlet, which the king alone could confer on his favourites, men and women alike. It reached from wrist to elbow, and was split along its length. Taking it off was a painful exercise, and wearing it could be most uncomfortable, especially on a hot day, when water was kept handy to pour over it and cool it down.

By the early nineteenth century circumcision had ceased, though young men and women always pulled out their pubic hair, which was considered disgusting. In some places scarification of the body was practised, for purely ornamental reasons.

The Zulu day, which they divided into various stages by the movement of the sun and the change of light, started at dawn when the herdboys took the cattle out to the fields, and the women and girls went to the stream to fetch water and set about their agricultural and domestic chores. At mid-morning the boys brought the cattle back to milk, and the first meal of the day was taken, usually lighter than the second one in the evening. What a Zulu liked above all was meat and beer. The meat was roasted or boiled in large chunks and apportioned in terms of the complex rules governing the status of the individual parts, ranging from the sirloin which went to the chief, down to the spleen with which the boy who minded the calves had to be content. There were also made-up dishes in which fat, blood-clots, minced meat and grains were turned into various forms of sausage or broth. The tasty and nutritious beer was brewed essentially from fermented sorghum and was pinkish in colour. Its alcoholic content was low, hardly more than two per cent.

Meat and beer might have been the favourite foods, but they were luxury items, so that ordinary people had far less of them than persons of rank. What a Zulu mostly got was sour clotted milk and vegetables. The sour milk, *amasi*, was prepared in gourds. The Zulu never drank milk fresh from the cow, except in special circumstances. Maize, prepared in various forms, was the principal staple: boiled, roasted or ground and turned into various consistencies of dry or runny porridge. Boiled vegetables such as pumpkin, sweet potato, beans, ground-nuts and *idumbe* tubers *(Colocasia)* would accompany it, spiced with leaves of the pumpkins and other plants, which made a herby sort of spinach.

After the morning meal, the cattle would be taken back to pasture, the women would resume their duties, and the men would set about theirs. Just before sunset the cattle would be brought home, and the women would return from the fields and begin cooking the evening meal. There would then be dancing, riddles and storytelling around the fire, and the playing of intricate games akin to chess to the light of torches of grass or reeds.

In its fundamental aspects, the daily life of the Zulu people, as described here, continued practically unaltered from long before the days of Shaka until the late nineteenth century. This is neither to ignore that there have been considerable changes over the years, nor to claim that an absolute uniformity of custom has existed over all of Zululand. It was noted in the 1820s, for example, that the powerful Ndwandwe people, then living in what is now north-eastern Zululand, were more agriculturalists than pastoralists, and that the men habitually joined their women in the labours of the field, contrary to the general practice elsewhere.[7] Again, in the mid-nineteenth century, most baskets were made by men, though that task is now undertaken almost exclusively by women, demonstrating that the roles of men and women in Zulu society have never remained static. Nevertheless, there was a basic constancy in pre-industrial Zulu life, which would have made the daily routine of someone living in the time of Shaka as familiar and explicable to his great-grandparents as to his great-grandchildren. This continuity applied equally well to the typical Zulu habitation.

Tens of thousands of scattered *imizi*, looking like so many tiny villages, dotted the rolling countryside, supported by their own grazing and agricultural land. Each was the home of a married man *(umnumzane)* and his two or three wives and their children, though a man of wealth and status might have as many as a dozen wives. Every *umuzi* was circular, and built on dry, sloping ground with the main entrance at the bottom. The huts *(izindlu)* – which should really be regarded as separate rooms in a single home, rather than as distinct houses –

were arranged in a crescent around the central *isibaya*. Charles Maclean, who spent several years in Zululand as a child in the 1820s, described this cattle-fold as made from a double row of posts, the space between being compactly filled up with branches of thorn to create a solid fence about a metre and a half high, neatly arranged and evenly cropped to give a very pretty appearance like a natural hedge. A protective palisade, constructed on similar lines, enclosed the huts on their outer side.[8]

All Zulu huts were alike in both construction and furnishings, and had been so for many centuries. But as the hunter and naturalist Adulphe Delegorgue pointed out in the 1840s, those of the great were distinguished (as in any society) by their luxury in the choice of materials and in their workmanship.[9] Grass huts are successfully insulated dwellings, being cool in summer and warm in winter. Those in nineteenth-century Zululand were circular and domed, much in the shape of a beehive, constructed from thousands of curved intersecting saplings and sticks, rather like compact wicker work, tied together with grass where they crossed. The average hut was three metres in diameter, but those occupied by chiefs were double the size with several poles (rather than a single one) supporting the structure. A neat thatch of long, tough grass covered the huts. Sometimes the thatch was bound on with tightly drawn grass ropes, though the best huts were made waterproof by layers of grass matting fixed over the thatch.

The floor was made of a mixture of the earth from ant-heaps compressed with cowdung, and polished to a blackish dark-green, glossy smoothness, not unlike marble. The hearth was a circular cavity in the centre of the floor with a raised, flattened edge, and pots were placed on three cooking stones. Fires were lit from the glowing dust created by a dry stick being rapidly rotated in a hole made in another piece of wood. There was no chimney through which the smoke could escape, and it seeped out through the hemispherical doorway, forty-five to sixty centimetres high (often with a reed or grass windscreen placed before it), or through the thatch. This had the beneficial effect of fumigating the hut of the many insects which made their home in the dried grass and wooden supports (and whose persistent susurrations could be heard throughout the stillness of the night), but it also meant that a dense cloud of smoke constantly floated within a metre of the floor.

The right-hand side of the hut was traditionally reserved for the men, and the left for the women. At the back was a special area, the *umsamo*, where the ancestral spirits were thought to dwell (as also in the cattle enclosure). There would be kept the pots of maize and beer, eating utensils and wooden platters, agricultural implements, the special spear for sacrifice, and other valuables. The *umsamo* was strictly reserved for the *umnumzane* and his wife when working there. Little was to be seen on the floor of a hut during the day, for the sleeping mats were rolled up and hung on the walls, as were the wooden headrests, baskets of supplies and the bundles of spears and sticks. Various small oddments would be thrust into the thatch for safekeeping. A wickerwork partition might form a pen for a calf or goat. Fastidious cleanliness was usually the intention of the Zulu housewife, though in the crowded circumstances of a hut it was not

always easy to maintain. William Humphreys, when staying in 1851 in the homestead of no less a personage than King Mpande's commander-in-chief, was 'a good
deal bothered by rats, cockroaches and other vermin' crawling over him during
the night.[10]

The *umuzi*, with its internal arrangements, was nothing less than the whole
Zulu social system in miniature. This was manifested, though, in its fullest
intricacy in the households of chiefs and royal functionaries, rather than in the
simpler and much smaller ones of commoners. The hut at the centre, in the top-
most position of the *umuzi*, was that of the great wife *(inkosikazi)*, who bore the
son and heir. Each of the other wives had her own hut, positioned according to
her rank, where she lived with her children, and received her husband. The
inqadi (right-hand wife), or supplementary great wife, had her hut (and, in a rich
household, those of other wives assigned to her section) to the right of the
entrance, facing the main hut; while the *ikhohlo*, or left-hand wife, who very often
had been the first wife the *umnumzane* had loved and married, had hers (and those
of other, older wives, if there were any) on the opposite side of the entrance. This
section of the homestead could never produce the heir, though the eldest son in
the family often was born to it.

The *umnumzane*, if he wished to defuse the tensions and jealousies endemic
in a polygamous household, divided his attentions as equitably as possible between
his wives. If he was a man of importance, he had a hut of his own, where he could
withdraw to be alone or with his friends, away from the women and children.
Sons who had not yet left to establish their own *imizi* had their own huts near
the gate. There was often also a special hut for the adult girls, and another for
the boys. Also near the gate would be huts for retainers and dependents. Each
section of the *umuzi* had its own storage huts for beer, vegetables and grain, usually built between the dwelling-huts and the outer fence.

Every *umuzi* was essentially self-sufficient, supported by its own labour (divided
on sexual lines) and resources. The household fed itself off its own cattle and agricultural produce. There was still sufficient wood in Zululand, except in the western highlands, to provide fuel and the materials for building huts. Basic items of
clothing were made from hides of slaughtered cattle (more decorative furs came
from hunted wild animals), while cooking and eating utensils were manufactured
from grass, wood and clay. Iron for weapons and agricultural tools (such as
hoes) was mined, smelted and forged within the country. But the working of iron
was increasingly a matter for specialist smiths, and most households had to
obtain their metal implements through trade, as was the case with luxury items,
such as beads.

On the death of an *umnumzane*, his household would break up, or segment,
and each of the sons would establish his own umuzi. In the special case of
chiefs, this would occur during his lifetime, when the *ikhohlo* section would
move off once the heir borne by the great wife had reached maturity. All the men
and women who believed that they, through this process of segmentation, had
descended from a common ancestor strictly through the male line, formed a
social unit which anthropologists call a clan. Marriage within the clan was

prohibited, and wives had to be taken from other clans in exchange for cattle, or *ilobolo*.

The clan was not an egalitarian social unit. The chief son of an *umuzi* inherited the bulk of his father's property, including the cattle, which he could use to obtain more wives. This in turn allowed him to produce more children, which meant productive workers in his household and *ilobolo* in exchange for his daughters. In this way, a particular lineage, tracing direct descent from its founder, would increase in size and wealth over its competitors, and eventually became dominant within the clan, forming the chiefly house.

By the eighteenth century, if not long before, clans did not form political units as such. Rather, the major political unit was the chiefdom. A number of clans – or some elements of these clans – formed part of a chiefdom, where political power was vested in the dominant lineage of the strongest clan. Thus, while membership of a clan was an immutable matter of ancestry, being part of a chiefdom involved a political choice – or necessity. It was always possible (if hazardous) to tender allegiance to another chief, and in this way chiefdoms grew and contracted or disappeared altogether. Chiefdoms were consequently never territorially discrete units with clear-cut boundaries. A chief's adherents might present a fairly solid core clustering around the *imizi* of the ruling house, but those living towards the fringes of a chief's sphere of influence might be more dispersed and uncertain of their allegiance, so that their *imizi* would be intermingled with those of people recognising other chiefs. Thus, in a sense, the wars of the late eighteenth and early nineteenth centuries, which saw the rise of the Zulu kingdom, were nothing more than the consequence of attempts by the more aggressive chiefdoms of the region to acquire wealth and power through the capture of cattle and land, and to incorporate adherents at the expense of their rivals.

2

Climbing the Long Rope

The people who built the Zulu kingdom, and the way in which they lived and or-ganised their lives at the time, have just been described. But it had not always been so in Zululand, for humans have lived there for many, many thousands of years, and their ways were not the ways of the Zulu of the nineteenth century.

Stone Age sites (those, at least, known to archaeologists) are widely distrib-uted throughout the entire Natal region, including Zululand. They date back to the Early Stone Age, which began one and a half million years ago.[1] Today, most is known about the more recent inhabitants of these sites, the hunter-gath-erer people of the Later Stone Age, which began about 30 000 years ago. These hunter-gatherers lived in rock shelters and probably temporary encampments in the open. It would seem that they migrated seasonally between the Drakens-berg (which they occupied in the summer months) and the coast, following the movements of game.

Their way of life came under threat between 2 000 and 1 500 years ago when Iron Age people entered the region. The interlopers lived in fairly large vil-lages, cultivated crops, kept domestic stock, made pottery and worked metal. Up to about 1000 AD it seems that the Stone Age and the Iron Age people lived fair-ly equitably together, trading and even intermarrying. However, the progressively more sophisticated social and political structures of the pastoralist and farming communities put the hunter-gatherers at an increasing disadvantage. Attitudes of the Iron Age people towards the original inhabitants of the land changed too over time, so that by the nineteenth century they were characterising them as cunning and thieving, with an unnatural ability to climb cliffs like baboons, or to sleep in the open without fires like dogs or antelopes. They were chary too of the magical powers attributed to the little people (whose very physical appear-ance was becoming a matter of mistrust), and contemptuous of their clicking language.[2] In King Dingane's praises, the Stone Age people are commemorated as holding their mouths in amazement at the sight of a Zulu army on the march, and saying in their incomprehensible tongue: '*gqa, bo bo bo bo bo bo!*'[3]

The Stone Age people survived nevertheless into the mid-nineteenth centu-ry and the period of white settlement. But the farmers and keepers of cattle, first black and then white, drove them further and further out of their hunting-lands into the inaccessible fastnesses of the Drakensberg, from where they were

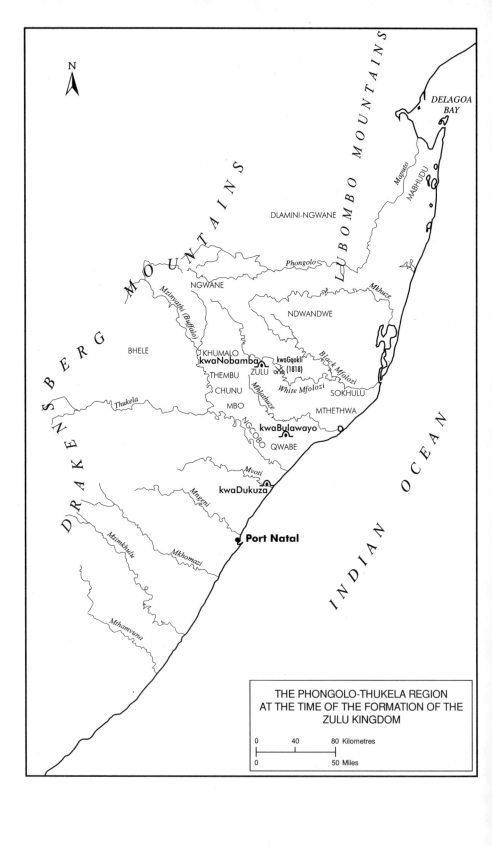

THE PHONGOLO-THUKELA REGION
AT THE TIME OF THE FORMATION OF THE
ZULU KINGDOM

reduced to raiding the settler livestock. To the colonising whites, the 'Bushmen', as the Stone Age or San people were once called, were vermin to be shot on sight. The upshot was that by the 1880s the San, who were the region's oldest inhabitants, had become extinct. Their most obvious legacy is the paintings with which they adorned their rock shelters. Today, 516 sites have been properly surveyed, containing a total of 29 874 paintings.

Archaeologists believe that the Iron Age people, who reached Natal and Zululand at least by the third century AD as part of a migration down the eastern side of Africa, were certainly black and probably Bantu-speaking.[4] They were related to an eastern coastal and lowland cultural tradition with links as far north as eastern Kenya, known as 'Matola'.

After about AD 1500 the evidence indicates that the Iron Age people of the Natal-Zululand region were culturally, linguistically and physically the direct ancestors of today's black population, and that their distinctive Nguni-speaking culture had developed within their own region. Customary practices described in the previous chapter, such as small settlements of hemispherical huts built of poles and thatch, pits for the storage of grain, the initiation of young men, bridal exchange for cattle *(ilobolo)*, the sacrifice of cattle to the ancestors – all were recorded by visiting white sailors in the sixteenth century and remained essentially unchanged down to the nineteenth. Trade, especially in small items, had developed over long distances during the first millennium AD. By the sixteenth century ivory was being exported to Islamic and white traders at the coast, while beads, brass rings and cloth were being imported. These were items of value and high status, and had an undoubted (if unquantifiable) effect on political developments in the region, as rulers increasingly coveted the goods and attempted to control the trade.

There were no large, centralised political units in the region until the end of the eighteenth century.[5] Until then, chiefdoms ranged in structure from those in which the ruling chief exercised a light and mainly ritual authority over the people who paid him tribute (who could be as few as 1 000 or less), to paramountcies, extending over thousands of square kilometres, in which the dominant chief ruled over subordinated chiefs who recognised him as an overlord. But, because the paramount chief had insufficient military force at his disposal to incorporate the subordinated chiefdoms fully under his direct rule, their vassal chiefs continued to enjoy considerable autonomy. Consequently, such paramountcies stopped short of being fully fledged states, and were liable to fall apart into their constituent chiefdoms.

In the last quarter of the eighteenth century, between Delagoa Bay and the Thukela River, there began a process of political centralisation and expansion, which brought these budding states into conflict one with another. The reasons may have been environmental, connected to the developing imbalance between the growing population density (which had been sustained by the introduction of maize as a staple since the early eighteenth century, if not before) and resources made more limited through unscientific and destructive farming and grazing methods. It has been suggested that a chiefdom's survival depended on the defence or extension of control over a variety of sweet, sour and mixed veld types. This would have provided effective year-round grazing and, in an economy based on cattle, would have given a chiefdom the economic and political strength to withstand or overcome its competitors.[6]

Some historians, recently downplaying such speculation, have claimed instead that the rapidly expanding international trade in ivory and slaves at Delagoa Bay (which they date from the 1760s and attribute to growing European demand), had the effect of destabilising the whole region. A number, led by Julian Cobbing, have gone so far as to blame the turmoil of the period on the impact of the demand in the Cape Colony for labour, and the consequent penetration of whites into the interior in search of slaves. Indeed, Cobbing and his adherents perceive a three-pronged slaving system in operation, based around Delagoa Bay, the north of the Orange River and, eventually, the Natal-Zululand region. Yet, however points of emphasis might differ, and the empirical evidence be in dispute, most recent scholars are in fundamental agreement. They would argue that the attempts by various chiefdoms in south-eastern Africa to establish control over the lucrative trade routes and the valuable commodities carried along them (and, debatably, to organise an effective defence against slaving) led not only to territorial expansion, but to the necessary strengthening of state structures and the enhanced power of ruling social groups.[7]

This last necessarily involved major social and political changes. The most significant of these concerned the transformed functions performed by the bodies of young men known as *amabutho*. The *amabutho* seem originally to have been circumcision schools which a chief would periodically form by banding together a number of young men under his authority, all roughly the same age, in order to conduct them through the rites that marked the transition from youth to manhood. These *amabutho*, with their own special names and distinct *esprit de corps*, were under the chief's ritual authority. They could thus be put to the chief's service and turned, for example, to hunting ivory on his behalf. The chief could then use the wealth they brought in to reward both them and his influential subordinates, so extending his range of patronage. As control over their *amabutho* extended, chiefs were increasingly able to use them as instruments of internal force to extract tribute and obedience, as well as armies to fight their external rivals. And as the dependence of certain ruling houses on the institution of *amabutho* grew, so did the necessity of acquiring additional cattle and luxury items for rewards, or 'payment'. These limited resources could only be gained at the expense of other chiefdoms, which had consequently to be raided. And, since additional cattle required grazing land, raids for booty turned into wars of territorial conquest to bring suitable grazing land under control.

In the early years of the nineteenth century, conflicts over cattle and land were sharpened by the effects of a major drought, still remembered as the *Madlathule* ('let him eat and remain silent'). The ensuing series of wars and migrations which wracked the whole of south-eastern Africa have conventionally been conceptualised as the *'mfecane'*, or the crushing. The *mfecane* has always been specifically connected to the spectacular and savage rise of the Zulu kingdom during this period. However, the latest scholarship has been at pains to demonstrate that the upheavals of the time were not the result of the aggressions of the Zulu alone, but were a product of the struggles between all the emergent rival states north of the Thukela. This does not mean, though, that the destructive effects of the *mfecane* should be underrated, even if the white settler myth of a landscape swept entirely clear by the *mfecane* of its original inhabitants should be discounted. Rather, people migrated from their original homes, took up their abodes elsewhere and tried to sink new roots. This inevitably involved enormous suffering and a considerable number of deaths. As Shaka's praise-poem puts it:

The newly planted crops they left still short,
The seed they left among the maize-stalks,
The old women were left in the abandoned sites,
The old men were left along the tracks,
The roots of the trees looked up at the sky.[8]

The evidence of the 'crushing' was there for the first whites travelling in Zululand-Natal to see, though it should also be kept in mind that certain regions would inevitably have suffered worse than others, and that the devastation would not have been absolutely universal. The young Charles Maclean, journeying in 1825 north from Port Natal (now called Durban) across the Thukela, passed through what he called 'comparatively depopulated country'. People still lived there, but they were the battered remnants who had escaped the widespread destruction, or who had not moved off in search of more tranquil parts. Some of those who remained survived by banditry, operating from isolated fastnesses in the more wooded and broken countryside. Indeed, as Maclean put it, there was 'no evidence wanting in our travels by the wayside to show what the fate of the many had been. The heaps of human skulls and bones blanching the plains were sad monuments of the fearful conflicts that had annihilated whole tribes'.[9]

Of the emerging rival states, the Mabhudu chiefdom in what is now southern Mozambique, the Ndwandwe to the south-west of them between the Mkhuze and Black Mfolozi rivers, and the Mthethwa to their south, between the lower Mfolozi and the Mhlathuze, were the first to grow appreciably in size and power, to develop the *amabutho* system, and to establish centralised institutions of government. Their ambitions and rivalries came inevitably to affect their neighbours. In particular, the steadily intensifying war between the Ndwandwe chiefdom, expanding southward across the Mkhuze, and the Mthethwa chiefdom, pushing west up the valley of the White Mfolozi, boiled over in the late 1810s to scorch their neighbours. Thus threatened, their choice was either to abandon their homes and move away in search of greater security, or to stay and strengthen themselves to resist the aggressors.

On the one hand, therefore, Ndwandwe raids for cattle and captives caused the Ngwane under Matiwane kaMasumpa, living at the headwaters of the White Mfolozi, to flee west. During the course of their violent migration the Ngwane shattered the Hlubi paramountcy on the upper Mzinyathi, which lay across their path, killing its chief, Mthimkhulu kaBhungane. Continuing to the south-west, the Ngwane settled in the valley of the upper Thukela, among the foothills of the Drakensberg. There they dislodged some unfortunate smaller chiefdoms who had held the land before them, and incorporated others under their paramountcy. The Qwabe, on the other hand, who dwelt between the Mhlathuze and the Thukela rivers to the south of the Mthethwa, responded rather differently to the latter's aggressions. They dug themselves in and consolidated their position through some 'crushing' of their own at the expense of their weaker rivals along the Thukela. First the Thuli and then the Cele were pushed across the Thukela into the coastlands and midlands of what is now Natal, there to set up loose paramountcies under weak central authority, rather as the Ngwane were doing to the west.

North of the Thukela, it was the Ndwandwe who were succeeding best in creating a centralised and militarised state, ferociously expanding under their chief, Zwide kaLanga. Zwide is remembered for his violent and cunning nature:

He who crouches over people that they might be killed...
Ford with the slippery flagstones...[10]

The Mthethwa state under Dingiswayo kaJobe was less tightly controlled. Dingiswayo, praised as a straightforward, upright ruler, 'Strongly built beast of the royal line',[11] allowed the ruling houses of chiefdoms subject to the Mthethwa to retain a considerable degree of autonomy. So long as they ruled in the interests of the Mthethwa, they were even permitted to keep some control over their armed men. This became increasingly important as Ndwandwe ambitions grew, with the Mthethwa facing them across an uneasy frontier that stretched north-west from the mouth of the Mfolozi to the region of the present town of Vryheid. Indeed, Dingiswayo encouraged some of the more strategically placed subordinate chiefdoms to expand their own military capacity. One of these clients was the Zulu chiefdom on the middle White Mfolozi. There Dingiswayo had set up Senzangakhona, who was born in about 1757 and succeeded his father Jama in about 1781, to secure the western marches of the Mthethwa territory. And because it was under Senzangakhona that the Zulu first rose from obscurity, he is commemorated in his praises as

He who plaited a long rope, son of Jama,
Who plaited a rope and climbed up,
There even the ancestral spirits of Mageba[12] could not come...[13]

In 1817 the Mthethwa-Ndwandwe rivalry reached a terrible termination. The Ndwandwe pushed south in force, defeated the Mthethwa army, and killed Dingiswayo. It is said this was only made possible because Zwide of the Ndwandwe achieved supernatural mastery over Dingiswayo through the possession of his rival's sperm, which his sister had been able to obtain through feigned love of the deluded Mthethwa chief. Dingiswayo was bewitched into wandering alone into the hands of his enemy, leaving his army leaderless.[14]

Victorious over the Mthethwa, all that still stood between Zwide and Ndwandwe dominance of the whole region between the Phongolo and the Thukela was the little Zulu state, once tributary to Dingiswayo. The Zulu ruler was Shaka kaSenzangakhona, who had succeeded his father in 1816.

Shaka was born in about 1787 to Senzangakhona and Nandi. Senzangakhona (he who acts with good reason), was the son of Jama (he of the stern countenance) and grandson of Ndaba kaPhunga (the man of affairs), who in turn was probably the great-grandson of Zulu, founder of the clan. The early history of the Zulu people was handed down by word of mouth, chiefly by the kings themselves and men of importance. As King Cetshwayo admitted in 1880, very little was remembered of Zulu and his heirs before Senzangakhona, except that they lived in the valley of the White Mfolozi, bred cattle, and were believed to have been of peaceful disposition and to have made no wars.[15] Senzangakhona himself was commemorated for his personal beauty, and his praises pile up his perfections:

Tree with fragile trunk;
He whose body was beautiful even in the great famine
Whose face had no fault,
Whose eyes had no flaw,
Whose mouth was perfect,
Whose hands were without defect...[16]

Nandi was a daughter of Mbhengi (or possibly Bhebhe, his father),[17] a chief of the Langeni who lived by the Mhlathuze River between the Zulu and Mthethwa.[18] Nandi conceived shortly after she was betrothed to Senzangakhona, but before she had been officially taken as a wife. So when it was reported that she was pregnant, the Zulu unconvincingly tried to refute the claim by insisting that she had swollen up only because she was afflicted by a 'shaka', or intestinal beetle. When the baby was born, that was the name duly given him. The consequence of her inopportune conception was that Shaka, although Senzangakhona's eldest son, was not recognised as his heir. That honour subsequently fell to Sigujana (otherwise known as Mfokazana or Nomkwayimba), the son of Senzangakhona's eighth wife, Bhibhi, whom he recognised as his 'great wife'. Nandi, meanwhile, became Senzangakhona's third wife, and Shaka's position was regularised. His mother was clearly of a most difficult, aggressive temperament, however, and Nandi's praises refer to her physical unattractiveness and sexual frigidity, as well as to her violent temper:

She whose thighs do not meet,
They only meet on seeing her husband.
Loud-voiced one...[19]

In about 1794 Senzangakhona eventually drove both Nandi and Shaka into exile after she had reputedly struck one of his leading advisers a severe blow over the head with a knobkerrie. Nandi returned to the Langeni, where she married a commoner, Ngendeyana of the Qwabe people, by whom she had a son, Ngwadi. After Ngwadi's birth, Shaka left and placed himself under the protection of Jobe of the Mthethwa. The colourful tradition concerning Shaka's departure from the Langeni has it that the people were becoming concerned at the distress he was always causing their chief's son by aggressively breaking his toy bull while at play, and wished him gone.[20]

Jobe died in about 1807, and Dingiswayo assumed the Mthethwa chieftainship after deposing and killing his younger brother, Mawewe, who had initially succeeded Jobe. The new chief swiftly recognised Shaka's extraordinary military aptitude and courage. He placed him under the special care of Ngomane, his commander-in-chief, who became in effect Shaka's adoptive father and confidant.

Shaka continued high in Dingiswayo's favour. So, when Senzangakhona died in 1816 at his esiKlebheni homestead, Dingiswayo supported Shaka's claim to the chieftainship, even though Senzangakhona should rightfully have been succeeded by his favourite son and designated heir, Sigujana. The situation, after all, precisely mirrored the circumstances in which Dingiswayo himself had seized his throne. So, with the backing of his overlord, Shaka employed his half-brother Ngwadi to assassinate Sigujana while he was bathing in the river. Then, supported by a military force sent by Dingiswayo, Shaka grasped the chieftainship.

He returned to kwaNobamba, his father's chief homestead, which had been Jama's before him, to be welcomed by Mnkabayi kaJama, Senzangakhona's domineering elder sister, who had acted as effective regent of the Zulu until he could take up his inheritance.[21] Mnkabayi's support had been crucial in Shaka's usurpation. She evidently had a ruthless taste for political power, which she had first indulged when she ruled as co-regent during the interregnum caused by Jama's death in about 1781. It was a taste she was never to relinquish, for not only had she encouraged Shaka's ambitions while in exile, but there are strong grounds to believe that when she eventually lost confidence in him, she inspired the plot that was in turn to bring him down.[22] She is thus appropriately recognised in her praises as one who determined the course of Zulu history:

Little mouse that started the runs at Malandela's[23]
And thought it was the people of Malandela
Who would thereby walk along all the paths.[24]

3

He Who Thunders as He Sits[1]

As a usurper, Shaka was faced by strong opposition from within the Zulu ruling house, and was forced to secure his position through tighter political control and success abroad. In the words of his praises, which celebrate his conquests:

> The young viper grows as it sits,
> Always in a great rage,
> With a shield on its knees...
> He has not let them settle down, he keeps them in a state of excitement,
> Those among the enemy and those at home.[2]

It is said that the initial act of his reign was to revenge himself on those responsible for the afflictions of his childhood, and the Langeni, who had cast him out, were the first to suffer a cruel fate.[3] Under him, the Zulu soon became a new regional power which, though still small, was relatively centralised and militarily effective. But Shaka remained a tributary of Dingiswayo, and his territorial successes were really no more than welcome sub-imperialism for his Mthethwa lord. Shaka had, moreover, to tread warily. His position as Zulu chief was by no means secure, and the threat hung over him that Dingiswayo, grown suspicious of his burgeoning power, might depose him as an over-mighty subject.

When in 1817 the Ndwandwe struck their fatal blow at Dingiswayo, Shaka held his army back, perhaps intentionally as a means of finally breaking loose from Mthethwa tutelage. If this was his plan, he succeeded. But he now stood painfully isolated as the Ndwandwe launched several raids against the Zulu in 1818, determined to remove the last obstacle in the way of the consolidation of their control over the former Mthethwa territories. With his army intact and fresh, Shaka was strong enough to beat the Ndwandwe off, traditionally repulsing them at kwaGqokli hill in the valley of the White Mfolozi, and killing five of Zwide's sons. But the battle had been desperately close, with the left wing of each army victorious, and Shaka himself at one stage finding himself hemmed in and in immediate danger of death or capture.[4]

The victory at kwaGqokli hill was crucial for the fledgling Zulu state, but all knew it to be no more than the first round in a lethal struggle for survival. The valley of the White Mfolozi was laid waste by the retiring Ndwandwe, and for a

19

time Shaka had to fall back on the coastal country with his people and cattle. To recoup his losses and to ensure that he had the resources to withstand the Ndwandwe in future, Shaka set about increasing the size of his army and improving its capability. Once he had achieved that fundamental objective, and with his increasingly intimidating instrument of war firmly under control, he proceeded through skilful diplomacy and military might to extend and consolidate his position over the whole region between the White Mfolozi and the Thukela:

Strong stick with a knob at the end,
Which struck the water and mud appeared.[5]

As Magema Fuze, the first Zulu historian, later put it: 'And there was wild confusion amongst the people, who began to lift their ears and say, "What sort of king has now arisen?" And he conquered everywhere.'[6] Fuze, whose writing reflected the popular tradition, continued: '[T]he country was greatly disturbed by refugees, but some remained behind with their heads bowed low, finding it hard to abandon their homes. They who lacked courage fled.'[7]

Smaller chiefdoms who submitted to Shaka gained Zulu protection against Ndwandwe raids in return for providing manpower for the Zulu *amabutho*, and yielding up cattle as tribute. Larger chiefdoms might baulk at the sacrifice involved in becoming part of a Zulu-dominated political and military alliance, and resist. But, as in the case of the powerful Qwabe between the Mhlathuze and Thukela, who had successfully resisted the Mthethwa, Shaka had the military power to overthrow and kill their chief, Phakathwayo kaKhondlo. Moreover, he was able to ensure future Qwabe acknowledgement of Zulu overlordship through replacing Phakathwayo as chief with the grateful Nqetho, a member of the Qwabe chiefly house who had been living in exile. For while Shaka might put to death recalcitrant chiefs and most of their close relatives, he still needed malleable puppets with sufficient legitimacy to provide the men, cattle and women necessary to build up the Zulu state. He was in the habit of summoning compliant tributary chiefs and receiving them well. The judicious disposal of gifts and compliments only bound them closer to him.[8]

There were options open to chiefdoms neighbouring the Zulu besides submission or resistance. Some of the lesser chiefdoms of the lower Thukela valley, who did not wish to accept Zulu rule, but who were too weak even to contemplate armed defence, preferred to migrate south or west out of the range of Shaka's authority. Since it was Shaka's policy to try and incorporate such chiefdoms rather than to eject or destroy them, the flight of coherent chiefdoms like the Bhele, Chunu and Thembu was effectively a setback. Some, like the Chunu, had good reason to flee south, though. Their aggressive chief, Macingwane kaLubhoko, 'Croucher like a beast sneaking into a maize-field',[9] was a contemporary of Senzangakhona, and had harassed his little chiefdom constantly. Now the tables were turned. Shaka enjoyed more success with those who, like the Qadi, Sibiya, Zungu and remnants of Mthethwa, submitted and, in return for the usual tribute, were left in occupation of their territory.

20

The control of these chiefdoms meant not only that the Zulu could exploit their resources, but also that they were faced by no threat from the south. So, by the time that the still hostile Ndwandwe to the north began to renew their raids, the rapidly consolidating Zulu state was able to put up a successful resistance. A second Ndwandwe expedition was beaten off, thanks to a night march by the outnumbered Zulu which caught the Ndwandwe army unprepared between kwa-Magwaza and the north bank of the Mhlathuze River. The engagement was not decisive, and though the Ndwandwe withdrew, they managed to drive off a considerable number of Zulu cattle and left the region devastated once more.

In 1819 Zwide mounted what he hoped would be the final blow against the Zulu. Shaka retired south of the Mhlathuze before the superior Ndwandwe host, and took up position in the wooded country of the Nkandla range. The broken country favoured the superior discipline of his men and, in a pitched battle that lasted from early morning until after midday, the Zulu routed and scattered the Ndwandwe. Shaka immediately followed up his victory and counterattacked, advancing into Ndwandwe territory and destroying Zwide's capital.[10] Zwide consequently shifted his chiefdom's centre of gravity north-west across the Phongolo into what is now southern Swaziland. As Shaka's praise-song puts it:

I like him when he pursued Zwide son of Langa,
Taking him from where the sun rises
And sending him to where it sets;
As for Zwide, he folded his two little shoulders together,
It was then the elder was startled by the younger...[11]

Though worsted, the Ndwandwe remained powerful beyond the Phongolo. They continued to play a central role in the Delagoa Bay hinterland, biding their time until they could try conclusions once more with the Zulu. But for the moment, they left the field south of the Phongolo to Shaka. As for the Zulu chief, he emerged from a grim war of survival a king indeed. All at once he found himself ruling a larger territory, with a greater population, than had any chief in south-eastern Africa before him. It was a daunting prospect.

Shaka the man has long since become a myth. Celebrated in his praises as

The voracious one of Senzangakhona,
Spear that is red even on the handle,[12]

he remains a potent symbol of Zulu national pride, and as such is beyond rational appraisal. He remains the 'black Napoleon', who deployed superlative military and organisational skills in building up the nation. Awesome, potent, he is

The Thunderer while seated, son of Menzi[13]
The bird that devours other birds...[14]

21

To others, however, he was the savage tyrant who, with inhuman cruelty, ordered a pregnant woman slit open while living to see if her baby lay in her womb as in that of a cow.[15] The tone was set by Nathaniel Isaacs, one of the first white traders in Natal. He charged Shaka with being 'a monster, a compound of vice and ferocity', and eagerly quoted Lieutenant King, one of his companions, who characterised him as 'a most cruel, savage and despotic king'.[16] Among Shaka's own subjects, people like the dissident Qwabe, who suffered under his inveterate suspicion, also preserved traditions of the king's callous bloodthirstiness. Thus Baleka kaMpitikazi of the Qwabe, who heard most of her tales from her grandmother, in 1919 repeated this popular anecdote about Shaka:

Seeing vultures flying above, he cried, 'Wo! The birds of the king are hungry!' People were then killed and put out on a hill to be eaten by the vultures. And wu! the vultures were all on the hill![17]

Certainly, Shaka was commemorated among the Zulu as always talking of war, and people said that when he killed, as he frequently did, it was simply brushed off as the king having his sport, especially since he never seemed much troubled by the death of his victims.[18] Yet there was inevitably another side to Shaka. It is remembered that he frequently went to sit by the sea, when he was lost in contemplation of the Indian Ocean's great breakers inexorably pounding the white-sanded shore. More in character, perhaps, is the further insight that when at sunset he started off for home from the seashore, he did so at a run without any pause for rest, forcing his gasping entourage to keep up with him as they might.[19]

Perhaps Charles Maclean, who spent nearly three years at Shaka's court and, as a child, was permitted a degree of intimacy that would have been denied an adult, summed him up more equitably than most. 'Shaka', he wrote in 1875, 'was a man of great natural ability, but he was cruel and capricious; nevertheless, it is possible that he has left behind something more than the terror of his name.'[20]

And indeed, the Zulu kingdom itself was his monument. It must be recollected, however, that Shaka was a product of his time, one chief among the many who were attempting to seize the opportunities proffered by the period of change and dislocation through which they were living. Chance and circumstance played their part, but clearly so too did extraordinary personal ability. For had Shaka not been skilful and aggressive, decisive and ruthless, he would not have succeeded over his many rivals and bitter enemies.

Shaka's appearance, like his character, remains something of a mystery. There seems general agreement, though, that Shaka's was a good, strong, muscular body, and that as a man of war he never allowed it to run to fat. His buttocks were small and well shaped, of the sort that are drawn in. He was of medium height, and his skin was a handsome dark brown, being neither yellow nor black. Like his father, he had never been circumcised.[21] Jantshi, who had his information from his father, Nongila, who had earned his living as a spy for Shaka and his brothers, recounted in 1903 that Shaka spoke the Mthethwa dialect.[22]

However, there were other, hostile, traditions which described Shaka most un-

flatteringly. Baleka of the Qwabe, for example, whose people had no reason to admire the Zulu king, recollected that her father had said Shaka had a large nose,
and was ugly. Besides, he spoke with an impediment, mouthing his words, as if
his tongue were too big for his mouth and pressed on his teeth.[23] And indeed, there
might well have been some truth in these aspersions. It was generally held that
Shaka had two prominent front teeth,[24] and Jantshi also testified that Shaka was
supposed to have lisped or stuttered.[25] Mayinga described very precisely in 1905
how Shaka's nose used to perspire, and how he was in the habit of taking hold
of it from above and giving it a twist as if to blow it and to get the sweat off at
the same time.[26] Mtshebwe, whose father Magaye had been a great favourite of
Shaka's, recounted in 1910 how once the king had declared that he would be
laughed at should he kill Magaye, for all would say it was because he was jealous, since Magaye was outstandingly handsome, while Shaka himself was ugly,
with a protruding forehead.[27]

The dominance of the Zulu ruling house headed by Shaka (who was undoubtedly able, although, it would seem, questionably good-looking) depended
on its ability to maintain its tight control over the *amabutho*. These had been
strengthened during the emergency of 1818-19, and were to remain the central pillar of the Zulu state.

The *amabutho* (or military) system, was brought to its fully articulated form
by Shaka and it endured, with modifications, until the eventual destruction of
the Zulu state.[28] By the 1870s, when its functioning was fully described, Zulu boys
between the ages of fourteen and eighteen would gather at *amakhanda*, or enormous military homesteads, which were the centres of royal authority in each locality and the mobilisation point for local elements of the *amabutho*. These circular or elliptical *amakhanda* consisted of various elements. At the upper end, where
the great wife's hut would have been in an ordinary *umuzi*, was the *isigodlo*, or
royal enclosure. There resided the king himself, or his representatives in the
form of members of the royal family (often women of character and political acumen) or trusted royal officers. They presided over the *amabutho* who lived in the
two great wings of huts *(uhlangoti)* – up to a thousand or more – which surrounded
the large parade ground and cattle enclosures.

Youths might serve in their local *ikhanda* for two to three years as cadets,
herding cattle, working the fields and practising military skills. Once enough boys
of an age-group were congregated at the various *amakhanda* around the country, they would all be brought before the king, who formed them into an *ibutho*
with orders to build a new *ikhanda*, often bearing the name the king had given
the ibutho. Charles Maclean saw the 'young, active, cheerful fellows' of a newly
formed *ibutho*, but perceptively commented that, like the 'juvenile sons of Mars'
elsewhere in the world, they considered themselves a privileged class above the
common herd, and 'seemed to despise their more humble brethren whose pursuits were those of peace and utility'.[29] And indeed, the ideal warrior was thought
of as one who combined courage and loyalty with a desperate eagerness for battle. Take the praises of Zulu kaNogandaya of the Zungu, a famous hero in
Shaka's army:

Storm that thundered in the open,
Where there was neither thorn-tree nor wattle for shelter...
Trampler across the burnt grass of the enemy...[30]

In terms of internal formation – as certainly was the case by the mid-nineteenth century – each *ibutho* was divided up into a number of sections *(amaviyo)*.
Each *iviyo* consisted of men of the same age-group, drawn from a particular
locality, who had been formed into the section during their days as cadets at one
of the *amakhanda*. Each *ibutho* was commanded by an *induna*, or royal official,
who might be a member of the royal house. His was a position of great power
and prestige. Under him were a second-in-command and two wing officers, as
well as a number of junior officers. There were at least two of these to each *iviyo*,
and they had been chosen by their contemporaries in their days as cadets. It is
not possible to put a firm figure to the strength of an *iviyo*, as this depended, as
did the number of them comprising any particular *ibutho*, on the degree of
royal favour conferred. Thus an *iviyo* by the 1870s could vary on average between
forty and sixty men, and an *ibutho* could muster between a few hundred and a
few thousand.[31]

Women too were inevitably part of the military system, in that as those primarily engaged in agricultural labour, they produced the food to feed their male
relatives while away serving the king. Shaka stepped in to regulate their lives in
service of the state more fully, and so institutionalised a practice that was already
developing in the region. Marriage had traditionally only taken place when fathers received *ilobolo* from their daughters' prospective husbands. Shaka now
formed girls into *amabutho* for the purpose of marriage. At intervals the king gave
the members of a female *ibutho* leave to be married, but only to suitors from those
male *amabutho* who had received royal permission to put on the headring *(isicoco)*, a privilege usually not granted until about the age of thirty-five or forty.

It seems that the custom of the headring (which was a circlet of tendons or
fibres sewn into the hair, coated with beeswax or gum and then greased and polished) was a substitution for the defunct circumcision ceremony. This had
marked a male's attainment of adulthood, full incorporation into communal life
and the right to marry and set up his own homestead. Shaka did not institute
the headring, which is known to have gone back to at least the sixteenth century,
and he himself assumed it when he left Dingiswayo and came among the Zulu.
But it was he who turned it into an instrument of royal control throughout the
Zulu kingdom. By withholding the headring until middle age, the king was pro-
longing the period in which the men of the *amabutho* would be regarded as
unmarried youths *(izinsizwa)* in Zulu society, and consequently remain more
thoroughly under the authority of their elders and, through them, the king.

Another significant way in which the king controlled the women of Zululand
was through his royal establishments of women, or *izigodlo*. Shaka, it seems, did
not institute the *izigodlo*, for Dingiswayo reputedly already had such households, and this type of institution doubtless preceded him too. But, as with so much
else, they received a definitive form and function in Shaka's time.

Izigodlo consisted of young women, some of whom the more important men of the kingdom had presented to the king as tribute, others who had been seized from men who had committed crimes punishable by death, or who had been captured in war. They were kept physically secluded in the royal enclosures at his *amakhanda*. A few of the favoured among them served as royal concubines, but their importance lay in the fact that they were all regarded as the 'sisters' and 'daughters' of the king, and thus his to dispose of in marriage to rich or powerful men, who valued the connection to the royal house. Thus they were not only an important instrument of patronage and political control, but also a source of wealth. For the *ilobolo* went to the king, not to their real fathers; and, by the 1860s, if not before, this was fixed at ten times the normal amount.

Men performed specific tasks while serving the king at an *ikhanda*. This could be while they were cadets before being formed into an *ibutho*, during the continuous training period of seven to eight months immediately after formation, for the short stints thereafter of a few months a year as fully fledged warriors, or when gathered together for the annual national ceremonies. They kept the *ikhanda* in repair, tended the royal cattle attached to it and cultivated the king's land. Daily dancing and praise-singing effectively doubled as military exercises. An *ibutho* might be called upon to participate in great hunts; to supply the king with exotic foodstuffs and items of apparel like feathers and skins only obtainable from specific locations in distant parts of the kingdom; to collect tribute from outlying subordinated chiefdoms; to exact fines from offenders against the king or to punish them with death and the destruction of their homes and families; to assist in the national ceremonies; and, not least, to go out to war against the king's external enemies.

The cattle and commodities of value which the *amabutho* accumulated for the king on their forays, or as a result of their labour at the *amakhanda*, provided a vital source of royal power. By redistributing a portion as rewards to the *amabutho* themselves and to the great men of the kingdom, the king was able constantly to consolidate his position and to ensure the loyalty of his subjects.

The *amabutho* system, in fine, as applied to both the men and the women of the kingdom, formed the basis of the king's power and authority, for it was an instrument of both internal control and external defence. Essential was the way in which it enabled the king to exercise a real degree of social and economic control over his subjects, and to divert their productive and military potential away from their own *imizi*, localities and chiefs and to harness it to the service of the state. But besides operating as a system of taxation, where labour was substituted for money or goods, the *amabutho* system served also to integrate the men and women of the various chiefdoms subsumed into the Zulu state, and to make them recognise the Zulu king as their leader, in both the actual and the ritual sense.

The required aura of religious and ritual leadership, or what might be described as the ideological basis of Shaka's position as head of state, was obviously a vital element in his construction of the new Zulu monarchy.

Religion played its part in almost every aspect of Zulu life, and everywhere the spirits of the ancestors *(amadlozi)* were looked to for help and guidance and propitiated with offerings.[32] This was only their due, since living and dead were not separate, but intimately associated in one community. The Zulu did believe in a vague and abstract First Cause who created all things; his daughter, who was related to fertility; and a Lord of Heaven who was responsible for thunder and rain. These figures were distant, however, and could only be approached through sacrifice to the ancestral shades. Indeed, the real, vital religion of the Zulu concerned the shades, who were not worshipped as such, but were consulted in everything.

The *amadlozi* lived underground and maintained the status they had enjoyed while alive, having power over inferior spirits. They were interested in every aspect of their descendants' lives. In this way, the strict kinship and lineage system of the Zulu was maintained after death. When an *idlozi* wished to revisit the world, it did so in the form of a snake (a chief, for example, turns into a black or green mamba), spoke through dreams, or revealed its wishes through omens and illness. In turn, the living made contact with the ancestral spirits through sacrifice, the officiator always being the head of the family or the chief, the direct representative on earth of the *amadlozi*.

The sacrifice always took place in the *isibaya* or cattle kraal, and the instrument was an ancestral spear, handed down from father to son. The officiator, wrapped in a large skin cloak, praised the ancestors and reported to them, dancing before the animal which he patted and rubbed, for he loved and valued it. He then stabbed the beast in the neck and exhorted it to bellow, to cry out to the shades as it died to signify their approval. The onlookers, after a moment's holy silence during the act of sacrifice, then shouted and cheered with joy. Before anyone could partake of the meat, though, the spirits had to have their share, the parts which were traditionally their special food. These were presented to the lineage shades present in the *umsamo* (the sacred place of the spirits in the hut). Most was in the form of a burnt offering, though meat was also set aside for the spirits to 'lick'.

Since the Zulu were convinced that an overlap existed between this world and the world of spirits, there was dangerous scope for a mystical force, *umnyama*, which was darkness, or evil influence. Misfortune was therefore either the consequence of spirits being offended, or of malicious action by wizards, or *abathakathi*. This is where the *isangoma*, or diviner, played a crucial part. Such a person was considered the most direct link between the ancestors and the living, having the greatest ability to interpret their messages. The powers of the *isangoma*, who could be a man or a woman, were derived from the ancestors themselves, who possessed the diviner. The *isangoma* was thus quite different from the *inyanga*, the traditional healer or herbalist, who claimed no special relationship with the spirits, but treated people without ceremony through a knowledge of the properties of roots and herbs. The *isangoma*, who dressed differently from ordinary people according to individual taste, and who could thus always be identified by a weird appearance (plaited hair, painted body), was the protector of society. When disorder in the natural or social world broke out, the *isangoma* was called on to use his or her spiritual powers to identify the reason and to prescribe the ritual remedy. For illnesses and calamities were understood as having an essentially supernatural cause, as being the consequence of *umnyama*.

It could be that misfortune was the expression of the ancestors' legitimate anger. The victim might have neglected to honour the *amadlozi* by failing to perform basic rituals, or have antagonised them through unseemly behaviour, particularly in terms of proper relations in the family. Ritual pollution and the shades' disapproval might also have been incurred, for example, though committing a crime or shedding blood. In such instances the victim was responsible for his own misfortune. The *isangoma* might divine this, and advocate sacrificial rituals to propitiate the ancestors.

On the other hand, the victim might have been blameless if the agent of misfortune were a malicious witch, or *umthakathi*. *Abathakathi* were men or women who had harnessed the powers of the universe by magic to work against the welfare of society. Such a person operated in secret, and his or her magic potions included parts of the human body and its waste products, such as nail-clippings or urine, for the Zulu believed that the most potent medicines contained such things. The Zulu were thus always very careful lest their *insila*, or body dirt, come into the hands of those who wished to do them harm. The correctly prepared medicine, placed in an appropriate spot, such as buried along the path to a homestead, could do infinite damage, calling down disease, lightning or death. What made an *umthakathi* even more terrifying was his or her familiar, often an animal, who carried out the witch's evil commands. Besides, a wizard or witch employed various medicines as protection against possible discovery.

When it seemed to the *isangoma* that an *umthakathi's* machinations were at the root of the problems besetting his or her client, then it was necessary to strengthen and protect the victims of the harmful magic with magical countermedicines. In addition, it was desirable to 'smell out' or track down the wicked person who had acquired the evil power to bring down disaster on the community.

Since only the *izangoma* had the ability to detect the invisible and intangible force that was 'witchcraft', and to 'smell out' the evil-doers who were practising it, this gave them enormous powers over even the greatest in the land. By 'smelling out' Shaka's favourites they could interfere even with his exercise of authority. Shaka consequently set out to break their hold. Once he had demonstrated that he could bloodily prune the ranks of the 'witchdoctors' with impunity,[33] Shaka convinced his subjects that it was his supernatural powers alone which were dominant in the land. Henceforth, the ritual authority of the Zulu kings went unchallenged, and their beneficent ancestral spirits were regarded as those looking after the interests of the whole nation.[34]

At a more mundane level, however, in order to maintain the *amabutho* system and command obedience, it was necessary for a king constantly to obtain sufficient cattle for redistribution as douceurs to the politically influential of the kingdom, to feed the *amabutho* themselves and to reward warriors of distinction. These demands made the continuing expansion into new territories imperative for Shaka.

27

It was inevitable, therefore, that once the Ndwandwe had been driven away northwards, Shaka should attempt to impose Zulu authority over the chiefdoms north of the Black Mfolozi which had previously been Zwide's tributaries, and to extend the centralising *amabutho* system to this potentially rebellious region. But the Zulu lacked the resources to bring the newly subordinated chiefdoms under immediate direct rule. Shaka therefore permitted control of the northern territories to be exercised through a viceroy, Maphitha kaSojiyisa, the senior member of a lineage closely related to the Zulu chiefly house. Maphitha was both ruthless and shrewd, as his praises attest:

Jackal that escaped the trap,
When others had been caught the previous day.
Stabber that cannot be denied...[35]

He established his homestead near the upper Mona River to the south of the region formerly dominated by Zwide, and ruled with a considerable degree of autonomy, though his people served in Shaka's *amabutho*.

In the mid-1820s the Zulu were drawn into intervening further north in the politics of the Mabhudu and Thembe chiefdoms to prevent their monopolising the Delagoa Bay trade. Shaka laid claim to suzerainty over the coastal region north of the Mkhuze River and periodically extracted tribute. But this was not the same as exercising political domination, which did not extend effectively beyond the Mkhuze. Indeed, the essential weakness of the Zulu in the northern reaches of their kingdom was demonstrated by chiefs like Bheje of the Khumalo. He lived in the difficult hilly terrain of the Ngome forest, and successfully beat off repeated Zulu attacks. In the north-west, the Zulu did not attempt to expand their power beyond the Phongolo for fear of the migrant Ndwandwe, who were consolidating themselves in what would become the eastern Transvaal.

Instead, Shaka set up two *amakhanda* and attached *amabutho* to guard this vulnerable frontier, not only from raids by the Ndwandwe, but also from people like the Swazi and Khumalo. These *amakhanda* were vital centres of royal influence and developed a particular place in the Zulu kingdom. The ebaQulusini *ikhanda*, for example, situated near the present town of Vryheid, Shaka placed under the authority of his father's formidable sister, Mnkabayi. The political power this gave her suited her well for, having helped Shaka to the throne, she had remained unmarried, preferring to retain her independence and influence. The people attached to ebaQulusini came to dominate the surrounding region and to regard themselves as a separate group with a special connection to the royal house. The men formed a distinct *ibutho* drawn only from the specific locality. On Mnkabayi's death the Qulusi would come directly under King Mpande, her nephew. Thereafter, the Qulusi regarded themselves as the Zulu kings' particular followers, and stood by them through all the tribulations that befell the royal house.[36]

Beyond his southern frontier, Shaka sought to drive away chiefdoms which posed a possible threat, or, alternatively, to set up clients like Jobe of the Sithole, Zihlandlo of the Mkhize and Magaye of the Cele who would serve his interests. But Zulu influence, though predominating by the early 1820s in a broad belt south of the Thukela and west of the Mzinyathi, continued to be contested by the Ngwane to the west and the Chunu to the south.

It was at this stage that internal opposition to Shaka's rule, combined with increasing pressure from the Ndwandwe in the north, fused to set off a further chain of conquests. Despite his victory over the Ndwandwe and the dynamic expansion of the Zulu kingdom, Shaka had continued to face considerable, if muted, opposition from within the chiefly house. There was nothing unusual in a chief's being rivalled for power by his close male relatives. But being a usurper made Shaka's legitimacy questionable, and festering jealousies and divisions within the ruling house continued to threaten his position to the end. Moreover, important sections of the Qwabe chiefdom resisted Zulu efforts to incorporate them more closely.

The assassination attempt of 1824 on Shaka may well have been the work of Qwabe dissidents, though it could just as possibly have been the execution of a plot concerted by his family. Shaka is said to have recognised the spear as being of the kind he had distributed to the isiPhezi *ikhanda*, where some of his brothers were in charge. The name of his assailant has come down as Ntintinti kaNkobe. He stabbed the king, under cover of the uncertain light of torches that illuminated the dancing, through the left arm above the elbow, which prevented the blade from penetrating sufficiently deeply between his ribs to be fatal. Shaka himself drew out the spear and ran into a hut. There was wild panic among the people and several days of extreme consternation before it was clear Shaka was out of danger. The Qwabe were officially blamed for the assassination attempt, and many were hunted down and killed, being stabbed in the left side in retaliation for the wound inflicted on Shaka.[37]

Resistance to Zulu overlordship and a desire to regain independence ran deep too in some quarters of the Mthethwa, where former greatness was not easily forgotten. Moreover, persistent raiding from the north, where the Ndwandwe were again flexing their muscles, helped to destabilise the internal situation further.

Shaka's solution to these problems was in 1824 to shift his capital, kwaBulawayo, from the White Mfolozi and the heartland of the Zulu chiefdom to within Qwabe territory between the Mhlathuze and lower Thukela. Thereby Shaka was able more effectively to suppress dissidence among the Qwabe, besides putting distance between himself and the unstable northern border. Furthermore, he positioned himself to take firmer control of the rich territories south of the Thukela with their resources of cattle, manpower and agricultural land.

A necessary preliminary was the destruction of the rival Ngwane and Chunu chiefdoms. Accordingly, the Chunu were broken up and pushed as far south as the Mzimkhulu River. The Ngwane put up a stouter resistance, striking back unexpectedly at Shaka's army after an initial attempt at flight. But their courage availed them little. They managed to save their women and children but lost their cattle to the Zulu and took refuge over the Drakensberg[38] – their destructive peregrinations set once more in motion.

The Ngwane and Chunu campaigns of the mid-1820s brought the Zulu to the mountain barrier in the west and to the vicinity of the Mzimkhulu River in the south. However, they did not occupy these territories. For in the far west and south, as in the Phongolo region to the far north (threatened by the Ndwandwe), the Zulu did not have the capacity to set up a permanent presence. In the west, they had to contend with the Griqua and other mounted gunmen who were increasingly raiding across the southern highveld to the Mzinyathi; in the south, they had to contest the ground with powerful chiefdoms such as the Thembu and Mpondo, who were struggling for dominion.

So, in the western and southern margins of the region which was to become Natal, the Zulu confined themselves to periodic raids for cattle, especially against the Mpondo, whom they first attacked in 1824. On the other hand, they consolidated their hold on the coastland region already controlled by proxy through Magaye, the client Cele chief, and broke up the Thuli paramountcy. This they achieved through quartering *amabutho* in the region and establishing a string of royal cattle posts. Territorially, the Zulu kingdom was approaching its apogee, its solid core centred in the valley of the White Mfolozi shading off into client chiefdoms and shadowy tributaries.

4

Go Every One to War!

Almost unnoticed at first, in 1824 an entirely novel element intruded itself suddenly into the world dominated by the emergent Zulu kingdom. In that year the first permanent white settlement in south-east Africa was established at Port Natal, enmeshing the unsuspecting Zulu kingdom in the toils of the political economy of imperial Britain. This involvement was destined to transform the region. Raw materials would be produced for the industrial order in Britain, and in turn Natal and Zululand were fated to provide markets for British manufactured goods. European material culture would be introduced, accompanied by Christianity and the capitalist ethos. This transmission would be effected as traders, missionaries, officials and settlers made progressive contact with the indigenous inhabitants, sometimes through peaceful interchange and conversion, more often through war, dispossession and subjugation.

These momentous developments had the most trifling of beginnings. British traders and hunters from the Cape Colony, with the backing of Cape commercial interests and the colonial authorities, had begun to take an interest in the possibilities of the Zulu region.[1] In May 1824 the twenty-one-year-old Henry Francis Fynn, son of the owner of the British Hotel in Long Street, Cape Town, arrived at what they called Port Natal with five others on the tiny sloop *Julia*. They were the advance party of a larger group of twenty-six prospective settlers under Lieutenant Francis George Farewell, born in 1791 in an English country rectory and a naval veteran of the Napoleonic wars. He had secured the support in Cape Town of J.R. Thompson & Co. for a permanent trading post at Port Natal. He and Fynn were to act as agents for these Cape Town merchants, who sought a market among the Zulu, from whom they intended to obtain ivory, hides and maize. They hoped especially to develop a flourishing trade along the northern marches of the Zulu kingdom, and so capture some of the trade that was flowing through the Portuguese settlement at Delagoa Bay.

Farewell's party arrived in the brig *Antelope* at the Port in July 1824. The hardships of the situation soon caused most of the party to return to Cape Town, so that by December 1824 the settlement was reduced to six men: Farewell, Fynn, John Cane, Henry Ogle, Joseph Powell and Thomas Halstead. They were reinforced in October 1825 by James Saunders King, who had been born in Halifax, Nova Scotia in 1795, and had taken his discharge as a midshipman from the Royal Navy in 1815. He had subsequently entered the merchant navy, and had vainly been attempting to drum up support in England for the Port Natal project. He brought with him his seventeen-year-old assistant Nathaniel Isaacs, who had spent two years in St Helena in the counting-house of his uncle. Isaacs's memoirs of his time at Port Natal, like those of Fynn and Charles Rawden Maclean (the nine-year-old who arrived with King), though published many years after the events they described, have remained the standard – if problematical – sources for subsequent knowledge of the traders at Port Natal.

The place itself was magical in European eyes, and remained so in the memory of Charles Maclean, writing in 1853. The wonder of his first impressions suffuses his pages. He describes the sandbar impeding the entrance to the great natural bay, with its several small, wooded islands; also its deep channels that allowed passage for vessels between the sandy flats and their flamboyant population of flamingoes, which at a distance reminded him of a grand parade of soldiers arrayed in their scarlet. The channels abounded with hippopotami, turtles and enormous quantities of fish. Endless troops of monkeys frolicked in the surrounding trees and dense bush. In the gently undulating valley of the Mngeni River north of the bay, wooded heights bounded the extensive, grassy plain with their scattered clumps of stately trees. Herds of buck grazed peacefully in this park-like setting to the songful accompaniment of numberless birds.[2]

This Eden was, however, beyond the protection of Britain, whose authority terminated at the frontier of the Cape Colony. Fynn and Farewell's attempts to force British involvement through petitions for annexation, and ceremonies involving the hoisting of the Union Jack, fell on unreceptive official ears. The government at the Cape made it clear that it would sanction no attempt to lay claim to the area in the name of the Crown, and that the traders were on their own in their dealings with Shaka. So in August 1824 Fynn and Farewell opened communications on their own account with the Zulu king.

Shaka initially welcomed the traders for a number of reasons. He saw them as suppliers of goods – such as brass and copper beads, woollen and cotton blankets, calico and salempore cloth and various trinkets – that previously he had only been able to obtain from the Portuguese at distant Delagoa Bay; he divined their use as potential allies against his enemies; and he realised how they might form the conduit through which he could establish contact with the British at the Cape, whose importance he had begun to recognise since Zulu involvement in the Mzimkhulu region. He therefore granted Fynn and Farewell permission to occupy the land surrounding Port Natal and to exercise authority over it, as well as giving them permission to trade.

In no sense did he cede the territory to the traders or renounce his sovereignty over it. Rather, he regarded the white traders as client chiefs, and expected them to render service to the Zulu state, like other tributaries. Indeed, without the desired intervention of the British government, the traders had to accept Shaka's overlordship and abide by his terms, which included attempts to control them through restrictions placed on their commercial operations. The traders, inevitably, played the delicate game of doing their best to evade the curbs without going so far as to alienate Shaka.

Within six months of the establishment of the settlement at Port Natal, the traders were adopting local customs and setting themselves up as petty chiefs under Shaka. The local people living in the vicinity of the bay, as well as destitute refugees from Shaka's campaigns, were organised along typically Nguni lines with separate homesteads acknowledging individual traders as their chiefs. The hunting, fishing and agricultural activities of these people freed the traders from having to import supplies from the Cape, and allowed them to devote their time and energy to trading and hunting for commercial gain. The absence (with the occasional temporary exception) of white women at Port Natal meant that the traders took wives and concubines from the local people, and also from among the 'Hottentots' brought with them from the Cape. One such was the redoubtable Rachel who, in her European dress, may have been a manumitted slave. She confidently exercised authority for Farewell when he was up country.[3]

Many of the traders – in this context, they would be better referred to as chiefs – legitimised their marriages through the payment of *ilobolo*, and situated their wives' huts around their residences in conformity with the layout of the *umuzi* of a local man of status. Indeed, they became distinctly assimilated into the local culture. As late as 1835 only one dwelling at the Port had the semblance of a European house, and this was built of reeds and mud. European-style furniture, such as tables or chairs, were generally lacking. The traders were characteristically attired in a picturesque costume that was a combination of the local with several tattered, European flourishes, like Fynn's crownless straw hat.

Charles Maclean has left a vivid description of his first impressions in 1825 of the settlement of Port Natal and its denizens. Farewell's fort, which was situated on the north side of the bay in what is now the centre of the business district of modern Durban, he characterised as a 'very primitive, rude looking structure'. It consisted of a quadrangular palisaded enclosure, protecting a barn-like wattle-and-daub structure of a type 'in common use among the Hottentots', and two or three diminutive clones. The 'fort' was surrounded by numerous beehive huts. The proprietors of the fort Maclean described as a 'motley group' of whites, Hottentots and Africans, the latter in a state of nudity and the rest in an indescribably tattered condition. Of the three groups, Maclean declared, the Africans certainly had 'the advantage of appearance'.[4]

Shaka was not concerned with the sartorial condition of the Port Natal traders. As his tributaries, liable to render service to their lord, he drew them from 1826 onwards into the politics of his kingdom. The displaced Ndwandwe had remained a threat, and the danger they posed was growing during the 1820s because, after several shifts, they had settled near the Phongolo on the kingdom's north-western borders. Besides this uncomfortable proximity, it seems that Sikhunyana, who succeeded Zwide as chief of the Ndwandwe early in 1825, was giving support to Shaka's insidious internal rivals. But, appropriately, it was similar rivalry within the Ndwandwe ruling house which was to give Shaka his opportunity.

Somaphunga, Sikhunyana's main rival for the succession, defected to Shaka in the early part of 1826 with a number of adherents, thus weakening his brother's position. The moment seemed opportune for Shaka to make a preemptive strike, especially as he had at his disposal the Port Natal traders and their firearms. A combination of royal pressure and the promise of booty induced Farewell, some of his white employees and a number of African retainers trained in firearms to join the Zulu army in their final battle with their longstanding foe. At the izinDololwane hills, north of the Phongolo, Shaka's soldiers and his white mercenaries finally routed Sikhunyana in September 1826 and shattered the Ndwandwe chiefdom.

Henry Francis Fynn witnessed the battle,[5] and though his notes recording his experiences were not written up until some thirty years later,[6] his account is nevertheless of great importance. For not only was it a first-hand description of one of the first occasions in which whites participated as auxiliaries in the wars between African antagonists in Zululand – a baleful role that was to grow in significance over the years; it also drew a vivid picture of how a Zulu army under Shaka went on campaign. Even more crucially, Fynn inadvertently demonstrated that by 1826 the methods employed by the Zulu army were already essentially set in the form they were to maintain until the end of the nineteenth century. Zulu military thinking was thus revealed to have been of the most conservative kind: Shaka's winning formula, once it had proved its worth, was not to be tampered with, and the *amabutho* marching against the British in 1879 might just as well have been those attacking the Ndwandwe in 1826.

Because of the strong continuities in the way in which, from the time of Shaka, the Zulu went about fighting their wars, it is worth investigating the campaign of 1826 as a templet for all those that were still to come in the course of the history of the kingdom.

Fynn and his party were at kwaBulawayo when Shaka summoned his army for the coming campaign against the Ndwandwe. Although he did not describe the rituals through which the *amabutho* were prepared for war, their 'doctoring' would have conformed with age-old practices which were maintained as long as the kingdom lasted, and beyond.[7]

As has been mentioned, the Zulu believed in an overlap which existed between this world and the world of the spirits. This was expressed by a mystical force, *umnyama*, which was darkness, or evil influence, and was represented by the colour black. It reduced resistance to disease, created misfortune and, in its worst form, was contagious. Because such pollution was a mystical rather than organic illness, it could be cured only by symbolic medicines. Deaths by violence, expressed as *umkhokha*, were an especially virulent form of *umnyama*, as the killer himself was polluted. In consequence, warriors about to go to war were in particular danger of pollution, and needed to be purified of evil influences and strengthened against them through treatment by black medicines (which symbolically represented death) in a ritual context.[8]

On the first day of the essential rituals, the *amabutho*, who were mustered at their *amakhanda*, collected great heaps of firewood and green mimosa. A black bull from the royal herds, upon which all the evil influences which had accumulated in the land were symbolically cast, was caught on the second day and killed bare-handed by a favoured *ibutho*. War-doctors cut strips of meat from the bull *(umbengo)*, treated them with the black medicines intended to strengthen the warriors and bind them together in loyalty to their king, and then roasted them in a fire of the wood collected the previous day. They then threw the strips up into the air and the *amabutho*, who were drawn up in a great circle, caught and sucked them.

Meanwhile, the war-doctors burned further medicines and made the warriors breathe in the smoke, sprinkling them with the cinders. Then, in order finally to expel all dangerous influences from the body, each warrior drank a mouthful from a pot of medicine, and a few at a time vomited the contents into an especially dug hole close by a running stream. This ritual vomiting took all day to complete, and occurred when hostilities were supposed to be imminent.[9] Its purpose was once again to bind all the people together in loyalty to their king, and some of the vomit was added to the great *inkatha* of the Zulu nation, the sacred grass coil which was the symbol of the nation's unity and strength.

On the third day the warriors went down to any running stream to wash, but not to rub off the medicines with which they had been sprinkled. Once these rituals were completed, the warriors (who had undergone a symbolic death) withdrew from society and, like bereaved persons, abstained from all pleasurable experiences *(ukuzila)*. They could no longer sleep at home or on their mats, nor could they have anything at all to do with girls or women. For all who had participated in the rituals were now set aside from ordinary life and were in an intensified and contagious state of *umnyama*.[10]

When ritually preparing for a campaign, the king would call a few favoured pairs of *amabutho* who were *uphalane* (or of nearly the same age and numbers, and who regularly accompanied each other into battle)[11] into the cattle enclosure. There, in a ceremony that would continue until sunset, one individual after another would leap and *giya*, shouting ritual challenges to the rival *ibutho*, or responses to those hurled by its representative. His own *ibutho* would praise him all the while. The effect of the ritual harangues was to spur the rival *amabutho* on to outdo each other in deeds of valour during the coming war. During battle itself *izinduna* would remind their men of their rivals' challenge, and after the campaign there would be a close accounting.

It was also important that the spirits of the king's ancestors should approve of the decision to go to war, and they were formally addressed through the customary sacrifice of cattle and accompanying rituals.[12] Moreover, cattle were sent to the spirits to ask them to go with the army when it set out, and they answered through the bellowing of the oxen late at night. Thus reassured, the king could issue his orders for the coming campaign.[13]

There is contradictory evidence regarding what the Zulu wore on campaign.[14] The ceremonial attire of the *amabutho* that distinguished them one from another was lavish and intricate, and contained many rare and fragile items which were supplied through the king's favour.[15] Members of an *ibutho*, who were expected to be smart, upright and active in their movements, were also responsible for keep-

35

ing their dress neat, clean and in conformity with their *ibutho's* regulations. Should a member of an ibutho be found to be improperly dressed, he would be set upon by his companions who would thrash him with light sticks and send him home in disgrace.[16]

The festival attire consisted of various basic elements, with particular details differentiating the various *amabutho*. Over time, of course, certain changes did occur in ceremonial costume, clearly related to the continuing availability of materials. When it is seen that a festival dress consisted of at least twenty skins of various kinds, and sometimes as many as fifty, it can be understood why substitutions had to be made in later years as hunting depleted game. Thus, it was obviously impossible for amabutho in the later nineteenth century to continue to wear the two cords across the breast – as described by Fynn – from which were suspended the skins of genets and monkeys cut into strips fifteen centimetres long and twisted to resemble tails.[17]

Later descriptions, drawings and, ultimately, photographs, show that white ox and cow tails were fastened around the neck to hang down the back as far as the knees, and down to the waist in front. Others were tied below the knees and above the elbow. Flaps of the skin of rare animals such as leopard were worn as part of the headdress (held together by a thick, padded skin headband), either to hang down either side of the face or down the back of the neck. Various sorts of skin tassels could also form part of the headdress, as invariably did combinations of valuable feathers. These could be arranged in bunches or in single plumes, worn upright or pointing backward.[18]

The loincover originally consisted of a kilt of strips of fur twisted together to resemble tails, though by the 1830s this had changed to a bunch of tails in the front and an oblong of cowskin behind, sometimes supplemented with further tails. As Maclean noted, the king and important men wore the same style of festival dress as ordinary *amabutho*, but differences in status were marked by the costliness or profusion of the materials used. Thus only the great of the realm or especially favoured *amabutho* could wear leopard-skin, and Maclean observed that the king's brother, Dingane, though dressed in the same manner as Shaka, could not boast so large a display of beads.[19]

It seems that only an abbreviated form of this precious and constricting costume was worn to war, and that it was a matter of some personal taste as to which items were retained.[20] Men of status apparently wore more regalia than ordinary warriors as a distinguishing mark. Armies that had less distance to march generally kept more of their costume than those which had to strike further afield, and it seems generally that in the time of Shaka men preferred to retain more of their ceremonial garb on campaign than was the custom in later years. Even then differences continued, and during the Anglo-Zulu War it was evident that the more conservative men of the older *amabutho* preferred to wear more than the younger men, who laid most decorative pieces aside.

The basic traditional weapon was the spear (today still popularly called the assegai, after the Arab term for the weapon), of which there were some ten varieties.[21] The most deadly was the short-handled stabbing-spear *(iklwa)*, reputedly introduced by Shaka, though, like all military so-called innovations, probably a refinement on a weapon already in use by the Mthethwa and other people of the region. Undoubtedly, it gave those *amabutho* who wielded it a terrifying advantage over opponents who clung to the traditional practice of throwing their spears and avoiding hand-to-hand conflict. For the *iklwa* was only used at close quarters, when an underarm stab – normally aimed at the abdomen – was followed without withdrawing by a rip. This methodical operation requires considerable skill and practice, and this is probably where Shaka's intervention was most important, for he had the military foresight and authority to insist that his *amabutho* become proficient in the *iklwa's* use.

The undoubted success of the *iklwa* did not mean, though, that all other forms of weapons were discarded. The *ibutho* still carried in addition two or three throwing-spears with long shafts *(izijula)*. Used also for hunting, they were well balanced in flight, and could find their target at up to thirty metres.[22] Some warriors might also carry a wooden knobkerrie *(iwisa)* for close fighting,[23] or perhaps a few might have a battle-axe with a crescent blade *(isizenze)*, of Swazi or Pedi origin.[24] The making of spears was a skilled and increasingly specialised craft that was eventually concentrated among the blacksmiths in the regions of the Nkandla forest and Black Mfolozi. The spears, as a national asset, were handed over to the king, who distributed them to his *amabutho*.[25]

The war shield of cattle-hide *(isihlangu)*, which took great care and patience to manufacture, and was a most valuable item, since a hide produces only two shields,[26] was also supplied by the king (whose property it remained) and was kept in a special hut in the *ikhanda* on account of its ritual properties.[27] By the 1860s the shield had generally shrunk to two-thirds of the man-height size originally stipulated by Shaka, though there are indications that full-size ones continued to be carried by chiefs and perhaps some veterans of the older *amabutho*.[28] The uniformity of shield colours and patterns, which distinguished the different *amabutho* in Shaka's time – Charles Maclean saw separate *amabutho* of black shields, and of white with black spots, white with brown spots, brown and pure white[29] – ceased gradually to be observed as sufficient cattle with the required markings became unavailable. There is evidence that by the mid-nineteenth century many *amabutho* carried shields of no particular hue,[30] although the convention (which dated from Shaka's time) seems generally to have been observed that younger *amabutho* should carry predominantly black or reddish shields, and married *amabutho* white ones.

Once the *amabutho* had been ritually cleansed of and protected against evil influences, the king decided which *ibutho* would have the honour of leading the army against the enemy, or of 'drinking the dew'.[31] The others followed according to their status.[32] In 1826, the departure of the army took Fynn and his men by surprise, and they did not catch up with it until they reached kwaNobamba in the emaKhosini valley, which had been Senzangakhona's principal homestead. There the army rested some days before continuing its march north-west towards the Phongolo. Until it reached enemy territory, a Zulu army marched in one great column, and Fynn recollected the great cloud of dust as the packed formation moved forward, each *ibutho* headed by its *izinduna*, the praise-singers in the van loudly reiterating the heroic accomplishments of Shaka. The day was hot, and every man was ordered to roll up his shield and carry it on his back, a custom that was still being observed fifty years later when the enemy was known still to be at a distance.

Boys, few of them over twelve and some not more than six years of age (by the 1870s they would generally be over fourteen), accompanied the army as *udibi*, or carriers,[33] moving in the rear (as in 1826) or some kilometres off on its flanks. These *udibi* were attached to the chiefs and principal men, and carried their mats, head-rests, tobacco and the like, as well as driving the cattle required for the army's consumption. Some of the *izinduna* were accompanied by girls carrying beer, corn and milk. After a day or two, when these stocks had been exhausted, the girls returned to their homes, as did those *udibi* boys who could no longer keep up with the army's advance.[34] When this happened, even the *izinduna* would have to carry their own belongings. All the men carried iron rations in a skin sack (a cooked cow's liver and maize grains were the favourites), but these soon began to give out.

The hungry *amabutho* tried to spare their own civilian population as far as possible, slaughtering the cattle they brought with them, and camping at *amakhanda* where there were stores of food. But as an army left friendly territory behind and entered that of the enemy, it began to forage ruthlessly as it advanced.[35] Fynn remembered that once they reached Ndwandwe territory, *amabutho* were sent off to *imizi* deserted by the enemy to raid their grain-pits. The loads of corn they brought back were a great luxury to an army that had been subsisting for several days on scanty rations of inferior meat. Naturally, all comforts progressively dwindled on campaign, and Fynn recollected camping in the open plain under stunted bushes, and men dying of exposure from the excessive cold of the frosty nights. Water became a problem. There were scenes of ugly confusion when the desperately thirsty army came upon a stream and trampled some of the weaker men and boys to death in its rush to reach the banks of the rapidly muddied water, ignoring pleas to help the victims.

Increasing lack of firewood in the uplands of northern Zululand meant that food had to be cooked as best it might with dry grass. As was the practice in very open country, Shaka's army occasionally moved in extended skirmishing order across the plain, driving wild game towards its centre to be killed for consumption. In 1826 they drove hartebeest, rhinoceros, pheasant and partridge in great numbers, in contrast to the army marching in 1879 on Rorke's Drift, which started only rietbuck and duiker – a sad comment on the progressive depletion of game.[36]

Several pervasive myths concerning a Zulu army's advance should be dispelled. An army might continue its march after darkness fell (Fynn recorded moving forward until nine at night), but it did not undertake night marches as such. Nor did it cover up to sixty kilometres in a day's march, regardless of this oft-repeated claim by astonished and admiring white commentators. In the advance on Isandlwana in January 1879, the Zulu army covered no more than nineteen kilometres a day, and usually went only about fourteen kilometres.[37] Similarly, Shaka's men in 1826 advanced by easy stages, resting on one occasion for two whole days, and on another for a day and two nights. Zulu mobility was supposed to have been enhanced as a result of Shaka insisting that his men throw away their sandals and harden their feet. Indeed, the British reported in 1879 finding Zulu corpses with the soles of their feet as hard and indestructible as horn. What are we to make, then, of Fynn's statement that once the Zulu army reached hard and stony ground in 1826, Shaka ordered sandals of ox-hide to be made for himself?

The Zulu army rendezvoused in 1826 at inqaba kaHawana (or Hawana's fastness, a mountain cave where this chief had traditionally taken refuge). It was close by Khambula, where, in March 1879, the British were to defeat the Zulu in the battle that marked the turning-point of the Anglo-Zulu War. Shaka's army had been marching in several divisions, for it was the custom to split it into at least two on nearing the enemy, both to ease the problem of supply and to confuse the enemy.[38]

Scouts, especially selected for their courage, preceded each division in extended order by about eighteen kilometres. These bodies of scouts were intentionally substantial (each about 500 strong). They were supposed to trick the enemy into thinking they were the main body, and so if attacked to draw him onto the rest of the army – with which they were in close contact by runner and which would have been given time to prepare for action. Besides these advance-guards, which moved provocatively in the open as decoys, sometimes driving cattle to tempt the enemy,[39] the Zulu also sent out spies in twos and threes to locate the enemy and help give the army the advantage of surprise.[40]

Such scouts brought news of the Ndwandwes' whereabouts to Shaka in his bivouac at inqaba kaHawana. The Ndwandwe had concentrated in the wooded country of the izinDololwane hills. There, on a mountainside, their armed men were gathered, surrounding their cattle, with their women and children in a body higher up the mountain.

Once the enemy had been located, it was up to the Zulu commander, in consultation with his subordinates, to take the decision whether or not to engage. If just a general appointed by the king were in command of the army, this could be a matter for lengthy debate. (At the battle of Khambula in 1879 the British had to wait for a full hour before the Zulu, halted in sight of their camp, decided at last to attack.) But, as Fynn saw, where the king himself was present, such consultation was purely nominal. No officer with his future in mind would dare contradict Shaka.

The decision to attack once taken, the army was drawn up in a circle *(umkhumbi)*. War-doctors, who had accompanied the army, stirred up the medicines they had carried with them in a basket, and sprinkled them over the circle of warriors.[41] The commander gave his instructions, and took up position with his staff on suitable high ground at some distance from the coming engagement. From this eminence he was able to direct operations by runner, to despatch a high-ranking officer to rally his men at a crucial moment, or even to retire unscathed should the battle go against the Zulu.[42] At the izinDololwane hills Shaka remained in the forest, and Fynn climbed a hill to view the action, and saw the Ndwandwe all sitting down awaiting the Zulu assault.

The habitual Zulu tactical intention was to outflank and enclose the enemy in a flexible manoeuvre, evidently developed from the hunt, that could be readily adapted to either a formal battle or a surprise attack. At the izinDololwane hills the Zulu army tried just such an outflanking movement, though it seems the Ndwandwe did not. For the purpose of executing this standard manoeuvre, the army was divided into four divisions in a formation likened to an ox. The 'chest' or centre *(isifuba)*, which consisted of the veteran *amabutho*, advanced slowly, while the flanking 'horns' or wings *(izimpondo)* of younger, more agile *amabutho* were rapidly sent out. One horn made a feint, while the other, concealed as much as possible by the terrain, moved with greater speed to effect a junction with the less advanced horn. The chest then charged the surrounded enemy and destroyed him in close combat, where the stabbing-spear came into its own. The 'loins' or reserve *(umuva)*, traditionally kept seated with their backs to the enemy so as not to become unmanageably excited, had the task of supporting an engaged unit in difficulty, or pursuing the defeated enemy.[43] Similarly, a reserve of youths was sometimes held back from joining in an attack, but was later sent in for support, in pursuit, or to round up captured cattle. A very young *ibutho* might be confined to this role.[44]

Contrary to the now generally accepted impression, the Zulu did not attack shoulder-to-shoulder in a solid body. In fact, they utilised ground with skill and rapidity, advancing in what European commentators would describe in 1879 as open skirmishing order.[45] They only concentrated when upon the enemy and about to engage in hand-to-hand fighting, and this they prefaced with a shower of throwing-spears to distract the foe as they rushed in at close quarters.[46]

It was not quite thus at the battle of the izinDololwane hills, for Shaka's forces marched slowly and with much caution, until within twenty metres or so of the Ndwandwe. Then the course of the battle followed the form later familiar to European observers. Flights of spears and insults were exchanged, until musket shots from Fynn's men brought on a Zulu charge. Fynn recollected that both sides met with a tumultuous yell, clashed together stabbing furiously in individual combats for about three minutes, and then fell back, temporarily exhausted. Each *ibutho* had its own songs, and its battle-cry was uttered three times on setting off to engage the enemy. When battle was actually joined, and especially when the spear was being thrust into the enemy, the national war-cry was shouted.[47]

It was customary for the Zulu to renew the engagement if the first encounter proved inconclusive. At the izinDololwane hills the Zulu charged again after a short rest. They remained engaged for about twice as long as at the first onset before again retiring. It was now apparent that the Ndwandwe were taking heavy casualties, and the Zulu charged a third, and final, time in an overwhelming rush. The Ndwandwe warriors were too mauled simply to fall back, and broke in flight. The fugitives sought shelter in the nearby woods, from which they were soon driven. The shrieks and screams were now terrible, for those of the surrounded Ndwandwe women and children who could not escape were killed on the spot. This heartless action was common, for among the Zulu in historic times no quarter was usually given to the defeated foe, who was pursued to his complete destruction. With Shaka, intent on building up his kingdom, it was sometimes different. Perhaps on this, certainly on other occasions, he extended amnesty to those brave survivors who would accept his rule, and drafted them into his army.[48]

The enemy's cattle usually fared better than the enemy did themselves, for cattle were the prized booty of war, and the Zulu hardly ever slaughtered them indiscriminately. At the izinDololwane hills, the cattle taken by the different *amabutho* were driven to the *umuzi* lately occupied by Sikhunyana, the now fugitive Ndwandwe chief who, Shaka told Isaacs, hid from his conquerors in a pit deep in the woods.[49] The battle itself had not lasted more than an hour and a half, but night fell while the cattle (which Fynn rather over-enthusiastically reckoned at 60 000) were being rounded up, and the whole valley remained a scene of dreadful confusion. Cattle taken in war were the sole property of the king, who gave away large numbers to chiefs and favourites, and the ordinary *amabutho* had little expectation of such favours. But normal procedures clearly broke down after the climactic battle against the Ndwandwe, and Fynn saw groups of men going about killing the captured cattle or simply cutting the tails off others to make into their war attire.

Meanwhile, the Zulu wounded were crawling about in the hope of attention. Spear wounds, unlike bone-crushing bullet wounds, could be healed with the simplest of treatment. For flesh wounds the Zulu had a poultice made from the leaves of the ubuHlungwana herb *(Wadelia natalensis)*, or the powdered bulb of the uGodide *(Jatropha hirsuta)*, which prevented inflammation. Open wounds could be tied up with grass. Fractures were set with splints, and certain herbs – particularly the powdered root of the uMathunga *(Cyrtanthus obliquus)* – were rubbed into incisions made at the point of breakage. Some *izinyanga* had the ability to open skulls smashed by knobkerries and remove harmful blood clots.[50] But many of the wounded would not have survived the long march home, and their bodies would have been disposed of in dongas, antbear holes and grain-pits by friends or relatives, who had the obligation to see to their decent burial. Otherwise, the Zulu dead might be left where they had fallen, simply covered with a shield. The Ndwandwe wounded, on the other hand, had no hope of survival, for they were put to death as soon as the Zulu located them, and their bodies left to the wild animals.

When a Zulu killed in battle (or ritually stabbed an enemy who had already been slain in fulfilment of a custom related to overcoming a fierce beast like a lion in the hunt, and so honouring its courage), it was necessary to perform certain rites. The object was the removal of the contagious ritual pollution that followed homicide and the consequent dangerous identification with death and the other world. A Zulu thus considered it essential to disembowel his slain enemy lest *umnyama* should follow and he swell up like the dead. Equally part of the rites was the stripping of the dead man's apparel so that the slayer might *ukuzila*, or observe the customary abstention after a death. He put on an item from each man he had stabbed in place of his own (which had been polluted by the harmful influences of his victim's blood), and wore them until he had been ritually cleansed.

Warriors who had killed in battle, or had ritually stabbed the dead, were polluted by the evil and dangerous influences of homicide. This meant they could not present themselves before the king, rejoin their companions or resume normal domestic life until they had first been ritually purified and correctly ornamented with *iziqu*, or amulet necklaces or bracelets of small pieces of willow-wood. Shaka conferred these strings, with their ritual properties of warding off the evil effects of killing, in recognition of deeds of valour done in battle. Each row, whether worn around neck or arm, represented a particular heroic action. Consequently, these *iziqu*, though inconvenient to wear, were borne with considerable pride.[51]

For four days the ritually contaminated were separated from their companions and fed with cattle captured from the enemy. Daily, they went out to wash ritually in a stream, and then returned to *ncinda*, or suck medicine from the fingertips and squirt it in the direction of their foes. In this way they hoped to ward off *umnyama*, and to obtain occult ascendancy over the spirits of their vengeful victims, the blood from whose fatal wounds formed a dangerous bridge between the living and the dead. Because many of the warriors had carried the medicines necessary to *ncinda* with them, a war-doctor was not required, except to sprinkle medicines on the final day.[52]

Once they were ritually clean, those who had stabbed in battle presented themselves with their own weapons before the king, carrying as many additional captured spears as they had victims. With the king seated in their midst, and fortified against *umnyama* by having his face and body well smeared with appropriate medicines, the *amabutho* exchanged accounts of the fighting and renewed the challenges they had made before setting off to war. Fynn reflected that praise or thanks were the last thing they expected of Shaka, who habitually found fault with his *amabuthos'* performance. Already, each *ibutho* had picked out its cowards. They were mockingly told, 'Just feel the spear which you tried to avoid',[53] and were stabbed through the armpit like a goat or similar inferior beast. Fynn surmised that the commanders, for fear that Shaka might suspect them of favouring their men unduly, had picked out a quota to kill, regardless of their actual performance in battle. In later years, supposed cowards were not dealt with so arbitrarily and ferociously. Shaka's successors held extensive discussions to discover who had distinguished themselves on the campaign, and who had revealed themselves as cowards. Subsequently, when the brave were rewarded with cattle, the cowards (those who had run away, or held back in the fighting, or failed to stab an enemy, even ritually) were publicly humiliated at the same time. While the king looked on, the cowards would be ordered to eat roasted meat which had been set aside and soaked in cold water. Meanwhile, their more courageous comrades, seated in a semi-circle, would enjoy their meat crisp and warm.[54]

With his victory at the izinDololwane hills, Shaka had at last removed the most powerful and persistent single threat to the emerging Zulu kingdom. As it is expressed in his praises:

As for Zwide, you have made him into a homeless criminal,
And now today you have done the same to the son.
The people of Zwide, Shaka, you have leapt over them...[55]

A few months later, in early 1827, the firepower of James King's party was crucial in permitting the Zulu finally to subdue Bheje of the Khumalo, who had held out for years against Shaka's rule in the rugged Ngome region of the northern borderlands.

These military success destroyed the main external threat to Shaka's rule. Yet it seems that internal difficulties were nevertheless increasing. It is in this context that the extraordinary events following on the death in August 1827 of Nandi, Shaka's mother, must be understood. Nandi had returned to live with Shaka as the Queen Mother in 1816. She held imperious and reputedly cruel sway over his household, as well as exercising great influence in the affairs of the kingdom. Fynn declared she died of dysentery, but the persistent Zulu tradition has it that Shaka killed her. There is the possibility that it was Mnkabayi, Shaka's king-making aunt, who first spread that malicious story in order to turn people against Shaka, whose assassination she had in mind.[56]

In any case, the widely believed details are as follows. Shaka was said to have habitually put to death any of the women of his *isigodlo* he made pregnant to prevent the birth of a rival to the throne. (It seems, in actual fact, that pregnant women were immediately sent away to live in obscurity, and their children were never recognised as being of royal blood.[57]) Be that as it may, the disposal (by death or oblivion) of such children was a sensitive one. It would appear that on this particular occasion Shaka believed that his mother, who had charge of the women, had not informed him of a girl of the Cele people whom she had permitted to leave the *isigodlo* with her newly born son. Enraged with Nandi over her denials of being at fault, he stabbed her with the sharp shank of a spear through her leather skirt and up her anus, as she stooped to feed the fire.

Whether or not this was really what occurred, Shaka suffered great remorse when his mother died and 'cried like a little girl'.[58] He came out of his hut in full dress, laid down his shield, and stood sobbing before his silent people. They knew only too well that tears such as these portended a remorseless desire for scapegoats. Shaka suddenly gave a loud scream, 'Alas for my mother', and all took their cue from his wild, unrestrained grief, trying to outdo each other in ostentatious mourning as proof of innocence of any complicity in Nandi's death.[59] Various personal attendants, women as well as girls, were killed and buried with her, for it was said that a person of her rank could not die alone, but must have people to serve and cook for her down below.[60]

Yet the general hysteria which ensued, the herds of cattle driven from all over the country to Shaka to console him,[61] the widespread killings (in which many a private grudge was indulged), and the enforced public mourning of a year's duration, must all be viewed in terms of their political dimensions, rather than simply as expressions of Shaka's growing mental instability and the mounting terror of his subjects. For it appears clear that Shaka deliberately used the opportunity to rouse popular feeling against his enemies and political opponents – as always, the Qwabe featured high on his list – in order to justify eliminating them. Besides, as Fynn (who had attended Nandi in her last illness and witnessed the consequences of her demise) speculated, Shaka doubtless wished his people – and any aspirant assassins – to absorb the lesson that if such an extravagant letting of blood followed on his mother's death, 'how frightfully terrific' must be that which his own would require.[62] Not that Shaka's ruthless actions succeeded in damping down political tensions within his kingdom. Execution of one set of rivals simply raised exaggerated fears among another, and fresh conspiracies inevitably followed in its bloody train.

Meanwhile, at the end of 1826, Shaka had established his new capital at kwaDukuza, near the lower Mvoti River and only seventy kilometres from Port Natal.[63] The reasons were manifold. His old residence, kwaBulawayo, was in the heart of the Qwabe country, and he knew them still to be deeply hostile to his rule, and suspected they were devising plans to kill him. By moving closer to the white traders, he could more readily depend on their potent firepower for protection, while at the same time exerting more effective supervision over these independent-minded and potentially dangerous allies. Besides, by coming to kwaDukuza, Shaka was signalling the shift of gravity of the whole Zulu kingdom to the coastlands south of the Thukela, and the tightening of control over the client chiefdoms of the region, like the Cele.

But increased reliance on the traders was no solution to Shaka's problems, for they were now falling out between themselves, and he was inevitably drawn into their disputes. Shaka, as we have seen, had allowed them to set up what amounted to new chiefdoms at Port Natal and in the coastlands to the south by permitting them to accept the allegiance of the local people. As commercial, political and personal rivalry developed between the leaders of the two main parties – Farewell and King – each tried to build up his adherents into a private army, and to win the king's favour at the expense of the other. By the end of 1827, King had gained Shaka's ear by promising to lead a mission to the Cape to establish good relations between the Zulu and British. Shaka desired British support as a weight against continuing opposition to his rule within Zululand. He also realised he needed British sanction to expand Zulu influence (or raiding range) southwards over the Mzimkhulu into a region which the imperial power, concerned with the volatile situation on the Cape eastern frontier, considered particularly sensitive.

King and his embassy got no further than Port Elizabeth. The Zulu element was led by Sothobe kaMpangalala of the Sibiya, a giant of a man who wore his headring on the back of his head and was a favourite chief of Shaka. He was subsequently celebrated in his praises for his heroism in sailing out to sea in a ship:

Splasher of water with an oxtail,
Great ship of the ocean,

The uncrossable sea,
Which is crossed only by swallows and white people...[64]

But while the embassy was pleading Shaka's cause, the Zulu king undid all their efforts. In May 1828 he lead a major raid south into the Mpondo country, reinforced once again by a strong contingent from Port Natal:

Buffalo that stood glaring with a spear on the banks of the Mzimvubu,
And the Pondos feared to come down to it...[65]

Shaka's reason for this inopportune, but technically successful, foray against the cowed Mpondo was probably to muffle internal opposition by seizing sufficient cattle to redistribute to his most important chiefs. But it is also evident that he was egged on by an unscrupulous faction among the Port Natal traders. For they were in hope that a confrontation between the Zulu and the British authorities, which the Zulu armed presence so near the Cape frontier was calculated to induce, would expedite British intervention in the affairs of Port Natal. Thus the way would be opened for increased trade, for the loosening of Shaka's control over the settlement at Port Natal and, ultimately, for British protection.

The effect of the Mpondo raid was indeed to scuttle Shaka's attempt to open up friendly relations with the British. King returned in August 1828 carrying the stern message that any future Zulu expansion to the south would be sharply resisted. And in July 1828, just after Shaka's army began withdrawing northwards, the Cape authorities sent their own expedition 300 kilometres deep into African controlled territory. The purpose was to warn the Zulu to stay north of the Mzimkhulu, since everything to the south of it was to be considered within the British sphere of influence. In earnest of their power, and as a dire warning to those who might in future dispute their claim to be the dominant factor south of the Mzimkhulu, the Cape forces turned on the Ngwane of Matiwane in August 1828. They broke up the chiefdom which, after all its wanderings since it was driven from its lands, first by the Ndwandwe and then by the Zulu, had finally come to rest beyond the Mzimkhulu.

The failure of King's mission proved catastrophic for Shaka, since it provided added incentive for Shaka's enemies to move against him. A conspiracy among prominent members of the royal house to kill him – in which some of the Port Natal traders may well have been involved in hope of a future relaxation of Shaka's trading regulations, and the ending of the personal influence of their trading rivals – had been brewing for some time. Shaka, it seems, had wind of the plot. In a desperate attempt to put distance between himself and the plotters, he ordered his army – even before it had returned from the expedition against the Mpondo – to raid Soshangane kaZikode, the founder of the Gasa kingdom, who lived far away along the Olifants River in the hill country to the north-west of Delagoa Bay.

The army was severely disgruntled at being given no respite, and grudgingly obeyed its king. A war-song made up for the occasion was still remembered fifty years later:

> Go every one to war!
> Old bird and young!
> He says this –
> Who is as big as the whole country.
> You who stayed at home yesterday
> Won't stay at home today.[66]

The army's absence on this unpopular and bootless campaign over inhospitable terrain, against an elusive enemy, provided the conspirators with their opportunity. Mhlangana and Dingane, whom Shaka clearly mistrusted, submitted to his orders to accompany the army. But large parties were deserting the disintegrating host as it advanced, and this gave the royal plotters the confidence to believe they could do the same with impunity. When they got as far as Ceza mountain just north of the Black Mfolozi, both discovered that they were indisposed and must return home. They left behind their half-brothers Mpande (whom they considered too soft to be an assassin) and Nzibe (who was still a lad) to continue with the demoralised army.

So it was that Mhlangana and Dingane found their brother Shaka at kwaDukuza, almost bereft of loyal warriors who might have protected him to the last, or have instantly avenged his death. The assassins struck on 24 September 1828 and, as has been related, butchered their brother with Mbopha's help.

Fittingly, the king who had bound together the Zulu state and led it to pre-eminence in south-east Africa, is widely believed to have uttered last, prophetic words. One suspects the many versions of these to have been pervaded with subsequent hindsight. Most have Shaka accurately cautioning his brothers that it is not they who will rule in the land, but 'white people who will come up from the sea.'[67] But one variant surely reflects how the Zulu royal house itself saw the matter. Shaka's last words, as they were remembered in his family, were repeated in 1921 by Mkebeni kaDabulamanzi, King Cetshwayo's nephew and the grandson of King Mpande: 'Are you stabbing me, kings of the earth? You will come to an end through killing one another.'[68]

46

PART II

The breaking of the rope

5

Black Horn that Devours Men[1]

Shaka's corpse lay unattended where it had fallen the whole night through, but no hyena came near it. Other scavengers might have been less reluctant, and Mhlangana suggested it be fed to the crocodiles. But fraternal respect seems to have been stronger in Dingane than in his brother. He was willing to be persuaded by Sothobe and other men of influence under the old regime that at the very least so mighty a king as Shaka deserved a proper burial.

Great personages in Zululand were buried little differently from commoners, only their graves were larger, with a special niche in the side for placing the body, which was wrapped in the supple hide of an ox and tightly bound with cords. All the attire a king had worn and all the articles he had used were placed by his side, and Shaka was surrounded by heaps of beads, food vessels, weapons and the like. Kings were 'planted' in the homestead they had been occupying when they died, so Shaka lies in the *isibaya* at kwaDukuza, over which has been built the modern town of Stanger. The precise position of his grave has consequently been entirely lost. But it never fared well. A king's grave was fenced off, and men were posted every year in the grass-burning season to ensure that the enclosure was preserved from the flames. These overgrown, tree-filled spots were places of sanctuary where game could not be hunted, and where malefactors could flee for refuge and subsequent immunity. Yet, only sixteen years after Shaka's assassination, the British rulers of Natal parcelled out his grave-site to one T. Potgieter when allocating farms in Natal, and so it was lost to the Zulu people.[2] In a sense, though, that did not much matter. Dingane rebuilt kwaDukuza in the emaKhosini, the valley of the kings, close by the homesteads of his father and grandfather. It was intended as a spirit home for Shaka, whose shade thereafter dwelt there in the company of his ancestors.[3]

Ritual purification was necessary for all those involved in a burial to ward off the effects of *umnyama*. Shaka's guilty killers not unnaturally expected his vengeful spirit to attempt reprisals, which made appropriate ceremonies of propitiation particularly needful. Nevertheless, Shaka's obsequies were scamped and hurried since other matters were proving exceedingly pressing. The succession remained undecided, there were disaffected members of Shaka's court and family to be dealt with, and the acquiescence of the army had to be secured once it returned from its campaign against Soshangane.

49

The first direct challenge the assassins faced came from Mxhamama ka-Ntendeka, Shaka's main *inceku* (personal attendant) and *imbongi* (praise-singer). A special favourite of Shaka's and second only to Mbopha at court, he had been away on a mission and returned to find his master dead. Taking advantage of an *imbongi*'s usual privilege of speaking the truth with impunity, he broke into furious lamentations, cursing Mhlangana and Dingane as dogs. He flung himself upon Shaka's grave and begged to be allowed to follow his king into death. Stung by his fierce rebukes, the royal fratricides obliged. So Mxhamama became food for vultures, which was only fitting, for his had been the vile habit of praising Shaka with the observation that the king's hungry vultures had come to the assembly, and must be fed with flesh from fresh executions.[4]

Mxhamama had been an embarrassment to the royal brothers, but a much greater danger was their lack of military force to sustain their precarious position.[5] Since the army (which they hoped to win over) was still away, they assembled a force from the men they had to hand. These were the iziYendane, tributary people from south of the Thukela and the western marches, who were not members of the regular *amabutho*, but who guarded the royal cattle posts, especially in the coastal country. Playing on their desire for full acceptance into the kingdom, the royal brothers formed them into a single new *ibutho*, known as the Hlomendlini, or Home Guard, with a status now equal to those *amabutho* away on campaign.

Units of this new force, including the equally newly constituted and inexperienced iziNyosi *ibutho*, which was formed prematurely from young cadets, were ordered to round up all the royal cattle in the southern districts and bring them north lest the Mpondo and others take advantage of Shaka's death to raid them. Yet these rescued cattle brought problems of their own. They had been Shaka's, but whose were they now? Mhlangana and Dingane quarrelled over their allocation, yet neither dared be seen openly arrogating royal powers until actually recognised as king by the great men of the nation and the army. Since both their positions were clearly so uncertain, Dingane and Mhlangana handed over the running of affairs to Mbopha, their fellow assassin, until the army's return. So Mbopha had an early reward for his treachery, though the charm of his position of power was doubtless tempered by his consciousness of its vulnerability.

He was evidently both ruthless and decided, and he was swift to advise Dingane and Mhlangana that they must eliminate Ngwadi, Shaka's half-brother. Ngwadi had helped Shaka seize the Zulu chieftainship, and had consequently been high in the murdered king's favour. Shaka had permitted him to rule his chiefdom in semi-autonomous fashion, maintaining his own small army. The brothers were agreed that he must harbour ambitions of his own and posed a real challenge to their position. So they listened to Mbopha and despatched him to destroy Ngwadi. With the iziNyosi under his command, Mbopha surprised Ngwadi at daybreak in his kwaWambaza homestead. But Ngwadi was a man of real mettle, and the iziNyosi only overcame his loyal warriors after a desperate fight in which the assailants suffered considerable casualties and none of the defenders survived. Ngwadi himself fell after reputedly killing eight of his enemies with his own hand, stabbed in the back by one of the iziNyosi, no more than a boy.[6]

With Ngwadi and their most obvious rival dead, Mhlangana and Dingane inevitably eyed each other with increasing suspicion. Mhlangana persisted in considering himself Shaka's rightful heir and was confident the returning army would recognise him as such. Dingane, on the other hand, seemed to have been the more greatly favoured by Shaka during his lifetime. This would no longer have counted for much had it not been for the vital support of his influential, king-making aunt, Mnkabayi, who insisted that Dingane was genealogically Senzangakhona's proper heir.[7]

Mbopha, too, played a crucial, though treacherous, part in the mounting crisis, in which he finally came down on the side of Dingane. Being in the confidence of both brothers, he went between the two, fanning their fears and jealousies with tales of plots and concealed weapons, until in about November 1828 Dingane was at last persuaded he must act before he himself was killed. With Mnkabayi's approval he had Mhlangana seized and executed. Mhlangana's death was most likely by drowning in a deep, shady pool in the Mbozamo River near kwaDukuza where he (all unsuspecting) and Dingane had gone to bathe.[8] Realising at the last how he had been duped and brought to his death, Mhlangana turned on Mbopha and cried: 'Nhi! Son of Sitayi, have you done this to me?'[9]

About two weeks after Mhlangana had been betrayed to his death, the army began to straggle back from its campaign against Soshangane in a most sorry, demoralised state. It had suffered heavily from hunger and fever, had failed to win any military successes or capture any cattle, and had been severely harried as it withdrew. The situation now became extremely delicate for Dingane. On the one hand, there was great relief among the returning *amabutho* that Shaka was dead, for if he had still been alive they would doubtless have been punished, as all were gloomily anticipating, for their unsuccessful campaign. Yet there was inevitably great consternation and confusion among the *amabutho* on finding their great king murdered. Dingane's fate might well have been otherwise if he, the usurper, had had to face an army confident and aggressive after a victorious war. As it was, he was able to project himself as *Malamulela*, The Intervener, because he had stepped between the people and Shaka's growing madness.[10] He could promise a popular new policy which would call a halt to the incessant military campaigning under his brother's rule, and which would put an end to his increasingly arbitrary and bloody regime, which were exposing the Zulu people to hardship and uncertainty. And in Mnkabayi he had a powerful advocate.[11]

Nevertheless, the matter of the succession could only be decided upon by the great men of Zululand in assembly, when they discussed the merits of the heir presumptive before summoning him to accept the kingship. Mnkabayi again wielded her influence, and the assembly concurred that Dingane should indeed rule over them. To legitimise his position further, and remove any taint, the assembly disingenuously declared that it was Mhlangana, rather than Dingane, who had Shaka's blood on his hands, which would in any case have debarred him from the kingship.[12]

Dingane was now king, at the age of about thirty, but he had at first to tread

51

softly, and not antagonise the great men of the realm and Shaka's favourites until he felt his position secure. Here the attitude of the *amabutho* was crucial. Dingane did his best to conciliate them by undoing some of Shaka's more onerous obligations and sexual prohibitions, and by assuring his war-weary warriors that he preferred the dancing stick to the spear. Thus he inaugurated his reign by allowing all the *amabutho* freely to enjoy premarital intercourse, and by permitting several of the older *amabutho* to marry. Moreover, he relaxed military discipline and ensured his *amabutho* such a superabundance of meat when they came up to serve at the *amakhanda* that it was said they could rub themselves clean with it.[13]

Once he felt himself firmly in position, however, Dingane moved swiftly and mercilessly. Himself a usurper, he considered it essential to eliminate as many potential challengers from within the royal house as possible. Shaka had distributed his family far and wide in the kingdom as effective viceroys. Dingane knew from his own experience that, with their political power, great herds of cattle and many adherents, they might be tempted to assert their independence; they could also form focal points around which discontented elements might coagulate. Accordingly, he killed off almost all his half-brothers, some dozen of them, even though this ultimately weakened his own kingship through his future inability to use his own lineage to extend his authority.

Dingane purged his royal brothers, if the memory of the deed is to be credited, in a particularly calculating manner. He invited them and other men of importance to make free with his *isigodlo* – where, under Shaka, it would have been death merely to have been found. While they joyfully disported themselves with the maids-of-honour he stood impassively by, apparently in approval. But this was no dawn of a new, free-and-easy era. The next day Dingane appeared in a black blanket and ordered his *amabutho* to seize those miscreants who had fallen for the bait and defiled his *isigodlo*. As the king named each transgressor he was bludgeoned in the parade ground at uMgungundlovu (his new capital) with straight, thick, short sticks, and dragged out dying to the place of execution to feast the waiting vultures. The guilty maids-of-honour were taken out and killed in the bed of the steep-sided Nzololo stream.[14]

Dingane's only siblings to escape the massacre were his half-brothers Mpande, the twenty-four-year-old son of Senzangakhona and Songiya kaMgitsha of the Hlabisa, Gqugqu, who was still a small boy, and Ngqojana. Mpande had indeed feared for his life, but Dingane spared him, why it is not really known. He has been variously described as weak in the legs or mind, and therefore harmless.[15] On the other hand, he had held high military command under Shaka, who had also presented him with his first two wives, Nqumbazi and Monase, whose sons in years to come were destined to fight each other for the succession. In any event, Dingane permitted him to live in relative retirement and to build up a personal following between the Mhlathuze and Thukela rivers. Ngqojana, whose adherents were also concentrated in the vicinity of the Thukela, survived until 1835. Dingane then had him strangled for alleged intrigue, and all his dependents (as happened when a chief was executed) were summarily put to death. The horrified evangelist, Allen Gardiner, who witnessed Ngqojana's tragic end, described him as a man of open and engaging countenance, intelligent conversation and unassuming manners. His crime was to have stood next in succession to Dingane, a most hazardous proximity.[16] Nzibe, Mpande's promising young full brother, of whom he was very fond, had died of malaria during the Soshangane campaign.

Shaka had built political allegiances by placing hitherto obscure men in positions of political importance. Since they owed everything to the king, their loyalty could be depended upon. Consequently, to secure his own position, Dingane had to move against Shaka's trusted friends and their families, those who had built up large followings and herds of cattle, but who could not be relied upon to exercise their considerable political weight in favour of the new regime. His praises grimly pile name upon name of those whom he 'devoured'. In all, King Cetshwayo later estimated that in his purges his uncle Dingane had executed at least eighty people of high position and dubious loyalty, and confiscated their accumulated wealth.[17] They included Ndlaka kaNcidi, Shaka's famous commander-in-chief, who dared to lament his late master, and who made it plain that he had preferred Mhlangana's claim to the succession. Clearly, a disaffected chief of such influence could not be allowed to survive, especially since he wielded such influence among the *amabutho*.

Among other prominent men eliminated were the key figures in the structure of authority which Shaka had set up south of the Thukela when he moved the centre of gravity of the kingdom to kwaDukuza. Dingane intended to shift the focus of his power back to the heartland of Zululand (in 1829 he began the construction of his capital, uMgungundlovu, in the emaKhosini valley), and it was essential to ensure that his authority was secure over the southern parts of his kingdom. The events of 1829 demonstrated the necessity. Nqetho kaKhondlo and a large section of the Qwabe, whose disaffection had always troubled Shaka, revolted against his still insecurely established successor. Nqetho led his people south, out of the orbit of Zulu power, to between the Mzimkhulu and Mzimvubu rivers. The Qwabe drove their great herds with them, including many royal cattle.

Furious at the loss of such resources of manpower and wealth, and conscious that the defection of the Qwabe might inspire others to break free of the Zulu yoke, Dingane took stern measures. Chief Magaye of the Cele, whom Shaka had set up as his client to control the country south of the Thukela, should (Dingane believed) have done more to prevent the escape of the Qwabe. He was in any case a marked man for being such a favourite of Shaka's, and Dingane killed him in about February 1829 for conniving at the Qwabe's migration through his territory. Dingane replaced him with his son Mkhonto, who could be expected to be loyal to his benefactor and to prevent the further flow of refugees out of the kingdom. It was an uneasy elevation for Mkhonto, and he did not long survive Dingane's suspicions.

Early in 1830 Dingane attacked the satellite Mkhize chiefdom of Zihlandlo, who had also stood high in Shaka's favour and continued unreconciled to the new dispensation. Zihlandlo and his brother Sambela were surrounded at night in their *imizi* by Dingane's forces and killed. His people, who had lived between the middle Thukela and upper Mvoti, fled south. At the same time, Dingane attacked and

53

eliminated Mathubane, regent of the Thuli, and another of Shaka's die-hard favourites.[18] Others against whom Dingane took punitive measures because he perceived them as a threat to his authority or to the security of the Zulu state included Matiwane kaMasumpa of the Ngwane, who returned a suppliant in 1829 after the destruction of his following by the forces of the Cape Colony. Dingane did not trust his intentions and he was put to death on a small stony hill across the Mkhumbane stream from uMgungundlovu, a place of execution known ever afterwards as kwaMatiwane.

Dube kaSilwane, the Qadi chief, who also suffered execution, is remembered as having excelled Dingane in a dancing competition. Dingane took great pride in his own ability, and even such an antipathetic witness as Captain Gardiner conceded that, for so heavy a man, the Zulu monarch danced with 'much natural grace and...no ordinary ease and agility'.[19] Predictably, therefore, it is said that Dingane was provoked by his public humiliation into demonstrating to the world at the cost of the tactless Dube's life that, if not the best dancer in Zululand, he was nevertheless the most powerful.[20] A more prosaic explanation for Dube's fate is that the Qadi (who lived on the left bank of the Thukela opposite Kranskop) were purged, like the Hlubi in the strategic Mzinyathi frontier zone and the Khumalo on the upper reaches of the Mkhuze, precisely because they and their leaders were members of powerful chiefdoms where royal authority remained alarmingly uncertain.[21]

One of Shaka's most prominent favourites, however, proved a fortunate survivor. This was Sothobe kaMpangalala, once Shaka's ambassador to the Cape, who had ventured across the salt sea for his sake, and who had advised Dingane to give his old master a decent burial. He was one of the few of the old guard Dingane considered trustworthy, and who, for his part, was sensible enough to adhere wholeheartedly to the new regime. It was he whom Dingane set up as his viceroy over the country south of the Thukela, now largely purged of Shaka's creatures, and whom he entrusted in 1831 with the final elimination of Mkhonto and the Cele.[22]

Ngomane, Shaka's chief adviser, was not likewise recalled to office, but Dingane at least allowed him to die quietly in retirement. On the other hand, Mbopha, the regicide, was permitted to enjoy his ill-earned chiefdom south of the Mhlathuze for no more than a few months. How could such a creature be allowed to live? A trusted courtier, he had conspired to kill his king, and could never thereafter be trusted by his successor, whatever the debt that was owed for such treason. Besides, the unsavoury part Mbopha played in the death of Mhlangana proved how easily he might betray his co-conspirator in the future.[23]

Dingane replaced his brother's eliminated favourites with his own, chief among them Ndlela kaSompisi of the Ntuli, the brother of Bhibhi, who had been Senzangakhona's favourite wife and the mother of Sigujana, whom Shaka had eliminated on his way to the throne. Ndlela, therefore, had close connections with the royal house, despite not being a member of the Zulu clan, and had already risen to prominence under Shaka as a general of note and a much-wounded warrior of acclaimed courage:

54

Rattler of spears!...
Hornbill that is reluctant to set out,
Long-tailed leaper like a leopard,
Reedbuck that escapes again and again.
Daily they stab the Rattler but he retaliates...[24]

Dingane raised him to became his chief councillor and commander-in-chief. He was older than the king, dark-complexioned, about 1,73 metres tall and rather stout. He wore a slight beard. Clear-headed and a good orator, he was considered a kindly man who only admonished people in a temperate way. But Dingane always remained somewhat wary of him, not least because Ndlela persuaded him to spare Mpande – a mercy Dingane would live bitterly to regret.

Nzobo kaSobadli (also known as Dambuza) had also pleaded Mpande's cause, and he too Dingane raised to particular eminence, second only to Ndlela. Dark in colour and portly, he had a terrible temper and was in the habit of rebuking people angrily.[25] Indeed, Nzobo seems to have had a particularly baleful influence on Dingane, stiffening his master's backbone whenever he showed signs of idealism and weakness he considered unbecoming in a Zulu king. Thus, when at the beginning of his reign Dingane apparently wished to abolish the institution of the royal *isigodlo*, because it was the unnecessary cause of numerous people being put to death for daring even to look at the king's women, Nzobo sternly reminded him that he could not presume to be called a king without one. Nzobo clinched his case with a chilling and, to him, incontrovertible argument, which revealed his bleak conception of the Zulu monarchy. 'The killing of people is a proper practice', he insisted, 'for if no killing is done there will be no fear.'[26] Dingane took his admonition to heart. It was not long before he, like Shaka before him, was declaring that the vultures had come to attend the assembly and must therefore be given the human flesh they required.[27]

There is, though, the strong imputation that it was Dingane's favourites (particularly Ndlela and Nzobo), rather than the king himself, who were most responsible for the arbitrary execution of people and the appropriation of their cattle. In this way they entrenched their political power and enriched themselves, thinking it necessary to report their actions only after the event for the king's formal approval.[28] Indeed, as Dingane's praises express it:

Goat of Dambuza and Ndlela,
Which they held by the ear and it was patient...[29]

This is hardly the image of Dingane which has been preserved in the popular mythology. To complete the picture, the king's character, the powers of the Zulu monarchy and the nature of the royal court will be held up to scrutiny in the next chapter.

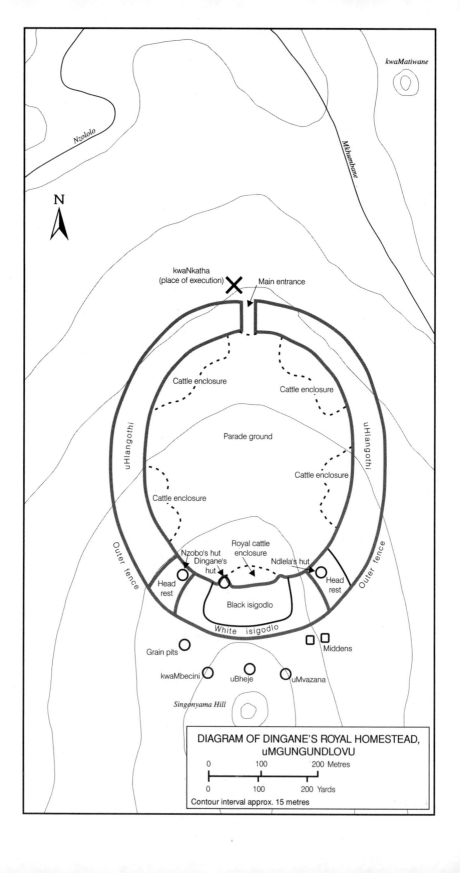

DIAGRAM OF DINGANE'S ROYAL HOMESTEAD,
uMGUNGUNDLOVU

6

You are the Quiet One, O Great Elephant![1]

Dingane's notorious reputation was sealed in 1964 by Peter Becker's lurid biography, *Rule of Fear*. Yet this book was only the culmination of a long tradition which grew out of the disapproving portrayals of Dingane's character and conduct by the Port Natal settlers and missionaries, and fed on the furious denunciations of the Voortrekkers. The picture that emerged was one of a capricious, untrustworthy, cruel, blood-thirsty, self-indulgent and indolent despot with none of the intellectual or physical abilities of his brother Shaka.[2] Even his physical appearance was counted against him. White observers dwelt scathingly on his corpulent and fleshy build, short neck and heavy foot, and drew attention to the banality of his not unpleasant countenance, which they believed belied his vicious disposition.[3]

Zulu have remembered him rather differently, and his praises make reference to his generosity and his possession of 'a good heart among men'.[4] In 1909 Lunguza kaMpukane described him as tall and dark brown in colour. He had very fat thighs with prominent buttocks, a large neck and a double chin off which he constantly wiped the sweat with a snuff-spoon. Yet, despite his bulk, Dingane was not flabby, but firm and tough. He had the slightest show of whiskers and sported a small beard. His teeth were very small and short and were barely visible. They embarrassed Dingane who avoided exposing them and tried not to laugh out loud, contenting himself with a close-mouthed grunt of amusement. He spoke in the particular style of the Qwabe people because, when as a young man he left his father Senzangakhona's homestead, he gave his allegiance to the Qwabe (as Shaka did to the Mthethwa) and lived among them. He wore the headring.[5]

Dingane's apparent contradictions have baffled historians and the Zulu themselves. They have pointed out the contrast between his initial attempts at conciliation, which included the undoing of some of the more extreme aspects of Shaka's regime, with his manifest scheming and unpredictability, which went with his growing willingness to shed blood. That is why, in his praises, he is commemorated as

Ford of Ndaba,
That has slippery rocks;
...Ox that encircles the homestead with tears;

Mamba who when he was down he was up!
...Deep One, like pools of the sea![6]

These images of shrewdness, cruelty, resilience, implacability and fathomless-ness nevertheless celebrate the necessary attributes of the successful states-man. As king, Dingane was concerned above all with the preservation of his own throne and the integrity and strength of his kingdom, and was prepared to take whatever actions necessary in their pursuit. Even so, it must also be recognised that, as king, Dingane operated within definite constraints.

The *ibutho* system, as institutionalised by Shaka and integrated into the whole fabric of the nation's life, formed the basis of the king's power and authority. Through it he was theoretically able to exercise a real degree of social and eco-nomic control over his subjects, to harness their productive and military potential to the service of the Zulu state, and to undermine the regional power-bases of over-mighty subjects. Nevertheless, despite hardening colonial opinion during the nineteenth century which characterised the Zulu state as despotic and ar-bitrary,[7] the kingdom was never as centralised, nor the king's power as effective, as supposed. Not only was the king constrained by traditional laws and custom,[8] but it seems that there remained considerable scope for independent action by the leading men of the kingdom. Forces of decentralisation, which had always to a degree neutralised the political integration of the Zulu state – even in Shaka's time – were to become steadily more evident during the reigns of his brothers Dingane and Mpande, and particularly apparent in that of his nephew Cetshwayo. The latter especially, through the many interviews he accorded his captors in 1880-1, provided a detailed and necessarily informed picture of how the Zulu monarchy operated in his time.

Most fundamental in terms of unavoidable decentralisation was the basic social unit of the kingdom, the *umuzi* itself, which, as has been shown, was an almost self-sufficient productive unit.[9] The state depended on the homestead for part of its labour potential through the *ibutho* system, as well as upon its surplus production. Cattle, so absolutely central to Zululand's political economy – though in theory belonging to the nation and so, by extension, through the chiefs to the king (as did the land itself)[10] – were in reality part of the *umuzi* unit. Individuals' private control over ordinary cattle was almost complete, while even the king's own cattle, for reasons of pasture availability, were entrusted with right of usufruct to *amakhanda* or *imizi* through the custom of *ukusisa*.[11] These realities were inevitably a force militating against political cohesion, for as large numbers of the Zulu people were not ultimately dependent on centralised authority for the economic functioning of their *imizi*,[12] their way of life was secured as long as the *umuzi* structure survived. And, as events were repeatedly to prove, this consid-eration all too frequently came before a commitment to the centralised political structure.

The patrilineal segmentary lineage system was the basis of Zulu social or-ganisation (as the *umuzi* unit was the basis of the economy), and with similar con-sequences to state integration. Political power in the chiefdom was vested in the dominant lineage of the strongest clan, where wealth too was concentrated. Chiefdoms, where they had survived the Shakan revolution relatively intact, were a force for decentralisation which the Zulu kings were unable to overcome. Despite centralising institutions such as the *amabutho*, there was always the danger that members of a chiefdom would give their first loyalty to their hereditary chief and kinsman, rather than to the king. The kings found it difficult to counter this check to their authority without resorting to military action against the dissident chiefdoms. Dingane, as we have seen, did so on numerous occasions, but a king such as Cetshwayo was more likely to seek accommodation and avoid violent confrontation. The way he managed this (and it was an option also often employed by his royal predecessors) was to confirm powerful local personalities with strong claims of illustrious lineage and hereditary authority as district chiefs. The king often consulted these district chiefs and, if he was sensible, would take their views into account before adopting decisions that would affect their districts or the kingdom as a whole.

Such consultation might take place on an individual basis, or in assemblies (known as *amabandla*), whose composition might vary depending upon the issue under consideration. Consequently, many subordinated pre-Shakan chiefdoms still maintained a measure of political cohesion and influence through their hereditary chiefs, whom the king recognised as territorial chiefs since they were too powerful to be disregarded, and whose influence was accepted in the highest councils of the land.[13]

This meant, in effect, that the central state authority was in the habit of delegating powers to existing political hierarchies who ruled the land in the king's name. Thus authority ran from the king, through the greater chiefs, to those chiefs of diminishing degree under them, until it reached the individual homestead heads, the tens of thousands of *abanumzane*. In this sense, the political structure of the kingdom reflected that of the *umuzi*, with the king at the apex of the hierarchy exercising his authority through descending layers of rank and responsibility, just as the head of any homestead would do on a smaller scale.[14] Such delegation must have been unavoidable, considering the structure of Zulu society and the problems of distance and communications in the far-flung Zulu kingdom with its broken terrain and many rivers.

Nor, considering the nature of the economy and the social structure, was there the means to support anything approaching a developed bureaucracy. This was a common problem in African kingdoms,[15] but the disadvantages were grave. It placed in the hands of the great chiefs, already enjoying the advantages of a personal following and a developed power-base, additional authority vested in them through royal recognition. Inevitably, it tempted them to exercise powers over life and death, and to settle disputes over land, without due reference to the king.[16] Their privileged position gave them considerable political power and the opportunity to amass wealth through tribute and fines from their adherents, in addition to frequent gifts from a king anxious to retain their loyalty. Similarly, *abantwana*, or princes of the royal clan, with whom the king could not avoid sharing a degree of power, and who possessed a status that was a reflection of his own, were naturally very high in the hierarchy of power. (Female members of the royal house could function as chiefs, though on their death their chiefdoms reverted to the king.)[17]

Powerful men in the kingdom, such as have been described, were known as *izikhulu*. This was the term for high-ranking persons who were distinguished by the great advantages of noble birth and royal favour, as well as by a necessary degree of competence. In other words, while it was usually a prerequisite for an *isikhulu* to be a royal prince or an hereditary chief, not all chiefs or princes were *izikhulu*. For *izikhulu* were the select 'great ones' through whom the king ruled. This inevitably put them in a position to build up an extensive personal following of clients, and even small armed forces of their own. Such assets, as with the great hereditary and territorial chiefs (some of whom might also be acknowledged as *izikhulu*), could serve as the basis for a movement towards regional autonomy, especially in those parts territorially remote from the king's capital. Conscious of their great powers, *izikhulu* habitually stood up for their rights before the king, resisting, for example, his attempts to place people on land they had allocated to their own adherents.

There was also a class of men known as *izilomo* who, though holding no official position, were nevertheless accepted as leading people at court on account of their personal friendship with the king and their ability to entertain him. Sometimes the sons of important chiefs were recognised as *izilomo* if they could not hold any official position because of physical shortcomings or lack in ability. The king would on occasion reward these courtiers with land, so allowing the *izilomo* to attract their own followings. However, because *izilomo* were relatively weak, they would generally attach themselves to the train of influential *izikhulu*. So while such royal favourites gained a more secure footing by tendering their allegiance to men more powerful than themselves, their action also fed the power of the *izikhulu*, always anxious to build up the network of their adherents.[18]

Considerably more tightly under the king's control than the *izikhulu* and *izilomo* were the *izinduna*, state officials whom he appointed (with the approval of the other chiefs) to perform various administrative functions. These could include commanding the *amabutho*, presiding over the *amakhanda*, or ruling in his name over a district where they had no strong claims of hereditary authority but where they were empowered to allocate land and administer justice like a chief. If they performed their jobs well, they were rewarded from time to time with presents of cattle from the royal herds.[19] Similarly amenable to the royal will were the collaterals of chiefly houses who, with royal support, had displaced the former ruling line. They, with the *izinduna*, owed their elevation to royal favour rather than right of birth, and knew that it lay equally within the king's power to disgrace them, should they in some way displease him. The same applied to the *izinceku* who, as confidential royal officials, wielded considerable influence through being close to the king's person and in his confidence. They functioned as his attendants, saw to his personal needs, and undertook delicate missions on his behalf. Although the position of *izinduna* was less secure than that of the great chiefs and *izikhulu*, the more prominent among them frequently joined the 'great ones' in the *amabandla* when the king wished to consult them on matters of policy.

No king, it is clear, could make great decisions involving the future of the state without prior consultation with its leading men,[20] though during the reigns of Shaka and Dingane they did not often venture to question their king's wishes. In Mpande's and Cetshwayo's time, however, the king found increasingly that the opinion of his leading advisers had to be taken into account. An inner core of these advisers, known as the *umkhandlu*, determined policy.[21] One among them was pre-eminent, and he was the one the king had appointed as his chief *induna*, or prime minister and commander-in-chief. He generally resided in the royal homestead, and was the king's voice and hand throughout the land. He may have been a commoner by birth, though this became increasingly unlikely. His was a position of considerable power and influence, though dependent on royal favour.[22]

By King Cetshwayo's time, between four and six of the most influential advisers, including the chief *induna*, would typically hold a confidential conclave in the royal cattle enclosure to concert their plans before proceeding to consult the king. Only after the king had considered their proposals would other great men of the realm be summoned to hear the royal decision. An even larger meeting, which would include the *izinduna*, might then be called to air the issue. But, effectively, the vital decisions of state were in the hands of the king and his inner council, known by Cetshwayo's time to ordinary people as the *amanqe* (or vultures) from the grey military blankets they wore.[23] Once a decision of state was taken or a new law was framed, it was announced to the people at a general assembly, preferably during a great national festival. It was then left to *izikhulu* to put it into effect.[24]

With the king lay the ultimate decisions over life and death, and he was always the final court of appeal. The king could, and did, overrule the decisions of his advisers and officials.[25] The Revd Francis Owen witnessed Dingane over several days in 1837 trying an *induna* charged with slaughtering some of the royal cattle for his own use. The council sat on the ground in a semi-circle with the offender in the middle. Dingane was seated in a chair as judge in his own cause, an attendant shading him from the sun with a shield. Normally rather sparing with his words, Dingane became very animated. Rising from his chair, he paced about snapping his fingers, clapping his hands, throwing about his arms, sticking out his chin and speaking rapidly. His council agreed slavishly with all he had to say, and before long the *induna*, whom none dared defend, was ordered away to execution.[26]

The execution of those the king sentenced to death took place at a special place outside the royal homestead, and was usually effected by braining the victim with a heavy stick, or through breaking his neck. Women were not bludgeoned to death. Rather, a rope was tied around the neck with a slip-knot, and the rope struck with a stick until the woman's eyes came out of her head and she was throttled to death.[27] In Shaka's time, the victim was often first stunned and then impaled, being left afterwards to die transfixed in the bushes where he had been thrown.[28] This particular practice fell into disuse, but not the whole purpose of sudden and terrible royal justice.

Unpredictable violence, as opposed to executions that were the outcome of a judicial procedure, were a most effective means of helping the king maintain a degree of control over the unmanageable 'great ones' of his kingdom. By destroying some in an apparently indiscriminate and arbitrary fashion, the rest were intimidated, for a while at least, into toeing the line. Shaka, and Dingane too (after his restrained beginning), were most noted for constantly employing violence with this objective in mind. Mpande and Cetshwayo after them certainly did not abandon the practice, even if they exercised more restraint.

Shaka, when he eliminated a chief, destroyed also his wives and whole family, so that none would be left alive to avenge him.[29] Dingane was noted, to his ultimate cost, for not being so thorough, though on a number of occasions he struck terror in the hearts of his subjects through mass executions in the style of Shaka. R.B. Hulley, who accompanied Owen to Zululand in 1837, was horrified to witness the killing of sixty unsuspecting young women from the homestead of a chief whom the king accused of showing disrespect. Their deaths were a sign of royal disapproval and a warning to all uppish chiefs which they could hardly ignore.[30]

The king, then, certainly exercised great powers, even if they were curtailed by the norms of Zulu society and the residual powers of the great chiefs. There was, however, another aspect to his authority, and this was a ritual one of great potency.

The symbol of Zulu national unity and strength was the *inkatha yezwe yakwa-Zulu*,[31] a circular grass coil about a metre in diameter and the thickness of a man's calf, wrapped in a python skin and securely bound with grass rope by the leading men of the nation. The Zulu believed it to have the mystical power of collecting up, rejuvenating and protecting the king and the nation, and joining the people so together in loyalty to their king that they would neither be scattered nor pay homage to other rulers. Important chiefs had personal *izinkatha* to bind their own adherents, as did the king himself, but his was incorporated into the national *inkatha* when he died.

The composition of the *inkatha* ensured its power, for it included all sorts of body parts, or the soul-essence of the living nation, from which great magic could be made and the enemies of the nation confounded. It consisted of grass from the paths brushed by people and cattle as they passed, and from the doorways of huts which people had rubbed when entering. Into it went the *insila*, or body-dirt, of the king, his predecessors and relations. Shaka had incorporated bits from the *izinkatha* of vanquished chiefdoms and particles from the bodies of their slain chiefs. The litter from the ground where the leading men used to sit and discuss affairs of state was added, as was grass from the pits into which the *amabutho* vomited when they were ritually purified before going on campaign. The hair and teeth of fierce and powerful wild animals like lions were included, as well as special plants and medicines prepared by the *izangoma*. The powerful, occult properties of the sacred coil were believed to be transferred to the people by the king and the spirits of his royal ancestors. Thus, when a king squatted on the *inkatha*, a force was supposed to emanate from him which boosted the courage of his army in battle and prevented the spirits of dead chiefs and their subjects from aiding the enemy.

The *inkatha* was handed down from king to king, growing in size as it was added to. It was always carefully hidden away and guarded in the great hut of the royal family, where it was entrusted to the keeping of one of the elder queens. Shaka kept it at kwaBulawayo, but Dingane removed it to the esiKlebheni homestead in the emaKhosini valley, where it remained until burned by the British in 1879. This was a hallowed place for, on reaching manhood, Senzangakhona had built esiKlebheni close by his father Jama's kwaNobamba homestead (meaning the place of unity and strength), which gave its name to the whole locality. Langazana, Senzangakhona's fourth wife, who died only in 1884, presided over esiKlebheni until its destruction. Senzangakhona's burial place, however, still marks its site, making it the most sacred spot in Zululand.

Alongside the *inkatha* was preserved the sacred royal spear, which the king used for sacrificing to his ancestors. It was an ancient throwing-spear, its shaft black with smoke and age, its blade covered with rust. In 1879 King Cetshwayo took the sacred spear with him in flight, and on his death it was handed on to his son, Dinuzulu.

The king was also the great rain-maker, and the fruitfulness of the crops depended upon him. At crucial times, such as at the sowing of the seed and the eating of the first-fruits, he was strengthened with ritual medicines to ensure a good harvest. This ritual function was seen most clearly at the national *umKhosi*, or first-fruits festival, where other aspects of his mystical powers were also manifested. Then, the ancestral spirits were invoked and their favour courted, the king and the army were ritually strengthened, and the allegiance of the people to their king renewed.[32]

During Dingane's reign the *umKhosi* was reputed to have been celebrated in its greatest magnificence. The ceremony was divided into two, the Little and Great *umKhosi*, always held when the moon was at its full and about to wane. The date was decided upon by the king after making country-wide enquiries concerning the state of ripeness of the coming harvest. The Little *umKhosi* took place about a month before the Great, in late November or early December, when the green mealies were ready and the new grass was covering the paths. Before the festival was held, no one could taste the new crops on pain of death. It was a relatively private ceremony, in which the king was ritually strengthened by special medicines. These he sucked from his fingers and squirted out of his mouth at sunrise to drive out evil influences from his people and to send confusion among his enemies. Cattle were then sacrificed to the ancestors, who were also praised when the king went to visit the graves of the former kings in the emaKhosini valley. There was much rejoicing among the people at this auspicious time.

Preparations were then immediately set on foot for the Great *umKhosi*, and the *amabutho* began to gather at the district *amakhanda* preparatory to proceeding to the king's 'great place' for the ceremonies. When the festival began, the king was kept in seclusion while he was ritually purified and fortified against evil influences with powerful black medicines. These, it was believed, would have killed a commoner instantly. Early on the morning of the appointed day, he emerged from the Great Hut in the *isigodlo* to the entreaties and singing of his *amabutho* and women. His aspect was considered terrible. He was dressed in the skins of uncanny animals such as baboons, and his mystical, fructifying role was emphasised by greenish, fibrous coverings which made him look like a tree. His right cheek was painted white and his left black, while his forehead was red. These were the symbolic colours of Zulu ritual medicine. He was also smeared with the powerful black medicines. In his hand he carried the ancestral spear of sacrifice. He was greeted by the great swelling sound of the national song-dance peculiar to the *umKhosi*.

As at the Little *umKhosi*, the king spurted medicines at the rising sun and dashed a bitter *uselwa* gourd to the ground. The purpose was to exorcise all evil spirits, pestilences and diseases from the nation. The *amabutho* too were purified of evil influences and strengthened in three days of ceremonies that followed the same pattern and purpose as those they underwent when being prepared for war, as has been described in Chapter 4. Afterwards, king and *amabutho* ritually bathed and were treated with white medicines. These rendered them fit to re-enter normal society after their period of mystically dangerous treatment by the black medicines.

Next day there was feasting on cattle killed as offerings to the ancestors, and a grand review of the *amabutho* in their fullest regalia, attended by the king in all his finery. The *amabutho* would compete in various military manoeuvres and dancing competitions to honour the king and to wish him well in managing the kingdom. The king, if the mood took him, might join in the dancing and singing. Afterwards, the *amabutho* would form a crescent round the king, while the chief *induna*, in his name, proclaimed the laws the king and his council had decided upon. When the laws were announced the people would sing the praises of the king and his ancestors.

The setting for the great ceremonies and rituals of the nation was the king's 'great place', or royal homestead. There were always a number of these, and the king would move from one to another, the women of his household carrying all his goods and chattels.[33] The favoured one, where he spent most of his time, must be regarded as his capital. Shaka's was initially kwaBulawayo, and them kwaDukuza. Dingane's was uMgungundlovu, which he established in 1829 in the emaKhosini valley on the slope of the stony Singonyama, or Lion hill, in the fork between the Mkhumbane stream to the east, and the Nzololo stream to the west, which flow into the White Mfolozi. uMgungundlovu's situation is in fairly high and cool lowveld country with both sweet and mixed grazing. Acacia bush, aloes and euphorbias abound.

The inner workings of this royal homestead must be described, for they formed the background to Dingane's daily life and that of his household and principal advisers, and were the context in which the decisions of state affecting the Zulu people and their neighbours were made.

uMgungundlovu means 'the place that encloses the elephant'. Since the king was honorifically referred to as 'the elephant', the name boils down in prosaic terms to 'the royal capital'.[34] We are fortunate in our extensive knowledge of uMgungundlovu, which is based on the detailed observations of white traders and missionaries who visited the place, the mass of Zulu oral testimony concerning it which James Stuart collected at the beginning of this century, and on the archaeological excavation of the site (hampered though it is by lack of funds).[35]

In its layout, uMgungundlovu was like any other *ikhanda*, though perhaps the greatest of them all in size, too large for a man to be heard if he tried to shout from one side to the other. It was more or less oval in shape and consisted of between 1 400 and 1 700 grass huts. These stood in rows six to eight deep, enclosing a huge open area known as the large cattle kraal or parade ground, where the king inspected his *amabutho* and cattle, and officiated during rituals. A strong palisade of stout timbers protected the sweep of huts on the outside, though the inner palisade was not as robust, and would have consisted in part of reeds or thatching grass. Naturally, such a vast concourse of huts was very vulnerable to fire, and *amakhanda* regularly fell prey to runaway veld-fires, domestic accidents with cooking-fires, and even arson.[36]

Inside the great cattle kraal were smaller cattle enclosures which bordered on the inner palisade. Access was through narrow entrances at several places in the palisade, though the main entrance was on the northern, or lower, side of the slope on which the *ikhanda* was built. This entrance was divided into two sections by a central pillar to control the traffic, and was closed by laying long wooden poles across. Directly opposite the main entrance, towards the foot of Singonyama hill, 600 metres away across the great cattle kraal (which was 500 metres across from east to west), was the *isigodlo*, or royal enclosure.

There, Dingane kept approximately 500 women, divided into two groups. About a hundred women formed the black *isigodlo* under the charge of Mjanisi, one of Senzangakhona's widows. They consisted of the king's 'mothers', or the widows of his predecessors, and the favoured maids-of-honour, or *umndlunkulu* girls, who waited on them and were at the disposal of the king as concubines. If Dingane had had any wives, they too would have lived in the black *isigodlo*. The only outsider who could freely enter the black *isigodlo* was the king; the lives of others were forfeit unless they had been summoned. This restriction applied even to the king's closest advisers and brothers. The remainder of the royal women lived in the white *isigodlo* in the charge of Bhibhi, once Senzangakhona's favourite wife and the sister of Ndlela, Dingane's senior *induna*. These were the younger or more unattractive girls who had not drawn the attention of the king, as well as a number of female servants. Should there have been royal children, they too would have lived in the white *isigodlo*.

All the gates to the *isigodlo* were shut tight at night, and the king was the only male to sleep within its precincts. Such circumstances might be expected to give rise to lubricious fantasies, and what are we to make of the French naturalist Adulphe Delegorgue's description in 1839 of King Mpande's sleeping arrangements, which he swore was the very truth? Entering the king's hut early one morning, his envious eyes (so he claimed) beheld Mpande lying with ten naked young women on their sleeping mats, their soft and delicious limbs entwined with those of the king, their bodies forming his living pillow and mattress.[37]

The huts of the black *isigodlo* formed the central core of the royal enclosure at the head of uMgungundlovu, and were divided into numerous compartments of about three huts each, demarcated by two-metre-high hedges of intertwined withies. Dingane's great hut where he held audience stood in one such triangular compartment, with its three or four entrances, in the extreme north-western corner of the black *isigodlo*. It was unusually large and lofty, with ten pillars to support it, and could accommodate as many as fifty people. Appropriately, it was a supreme example of the hut-builder's art, and was kept exquisitely neat with the floor as bright as polished marble. The king also had a small, private bachelor hut on the eastern side of the black *isigodlo*, where he normally ate and slept. It had one pillar, made beautiful by the maids-of-honour who had entwined it from top to bottom with intricate patterns of red and white beads. Such was the custom in the royal *isigodlo*. Elsewhere it was forbidden. The huts of the white *isigodlo* surrounded those of the black *isigodlo* on all sides except the northern, which abutted the royal cattle enclosure at the top of the parade ground.

Higher up the slopes of Singonyama hill, just behind the *isigodlo*, were three small homesteads. From east to west, these were the uMvazana, uBheje and kwaMbecini *imizi*. The largest, uBheje, was connected to the *isigodlo* and was where its women could isolate themselves, bask in the sun and relax. If children had been born to Dingane, this is where they would have been kept until they could walk. A number of men stayed at uBheje to cook for the women in huge pots, and there were special servants to wait on them. The kwaMbecini *umuzi* was near the site of a coppersmith, and probably housed these specialist workers. Some grain-pits have been excavated fifty metres to the south-west of the *isigodlo*. While the *ikhanda*'s main grain-pits were in the great cattle kraal, these were most probably dug in a small cattle kraal related to the *isigodlo* and supplying it with both milk and grain.

The maids-of-honour wore nothing except a few strings of opaque red and amber beads (which no one except the king and his household were permitted to wear) and wristlets of pure white ones. These special beads were imported by sea from Cape Town through Port Natal. Favoured maids-of-honour and the king's wives might also wear heavy, broad brass armlets, and brass coils around their necks and upper arms. When they left the *isigodlo* to bathe in the stream, they were always accompanied by armed men. Anyone who met them on the road had to move quickly aside and fall face down in the grass lest he should look at them and be killed for his temerity. Similarly, anyone summoned into the *isigodlo*, including servants, kept his eyes carefully averted. People also gave the area to the rear of the *isigodlo* a wide berth, for that was where the women went out to relieve nature.

The women themselves, kept secluded and unoccupied, since servant girls and widows did all the domestic chores, grew exceedingly stout and unfit, perspiring heavily onto the mats where they spent their days, anointing themselves the while with fat from the heavy tails of sheep. Dingane particularly favoured the fat young women with pretty faces, and of an evening especially enjoyed it when about a hundred of them sang loudly to him, their animated songs filling the air for many kilometres around. Because of their corpulence they did not stand or dance as did other women when they sang, but sat on the ground and went through the usual actions with their arms only, becoming increasingly exhausted as Dingane demanded one song after another.

The main entrance to uMgungundlovu was the dividing line between the left-hand (or eastern) and right-hand (or western) sections of the *uhlangoti*, the two great wings of huts that accommodated the *amabutho*. Each wing was itself divided up into a number of sections, connected by openings in the fences. On the left were the four *amabutho* commanded by Ndlela, whose hut was at the top, at the 'headrest' against the fence of the *isigodlo*. The fifty or so male attendants to the king, who served him in the *isigodlo*, and who had been specially selected for their confidential task by the king's advisers, slept at the 'headrest' too. They were lavishly and regularly rewarded with food and cattle. These arrangements were exactly mirrored on the right, where Nzobo was in command. uMgungundlovu, when full, as it would have been for the celebration of the *umKhosi*, would probably have held between 5 000 and 7 000 people.

Since chiefs and *amabutho* were constantly coming and going to uMgungundlovu to serve the king, pay their respects and attend the national festivals, their huts were periodically left empty during their absences at home. Untenanted huts ran the risk of being filled with ash and filth by comrades jealous of the pleasures the absent ones were enjoying at home, where they were presumed to be making love to girls and drinking beer at their ease. Family members and friends of absent *amabutho* had to be relied upon to look after empty huts. But even if huts were not vandalised, they became very dirty after some months of neglect, and returning warriors' *udibi* boys would have to clean them before they became habitable again.

It was easy for *amabutho* to become lost among the confusing maze of deceptively similar huts, and they often resorted to marking their own by means of a stick inserted into the thatch in a recognisable way. But when a man did become lost, and wandered into the wrong section, he ran the risk of having a bone or similar missile thrown at him and being beaten up and chased away by *amabutho* jealous of their own particular bit of turf. Indeed, neighbourliness does not seem to have been a mark of the *ikhanda*. If, for example, an *ibutho* left firewood near the door of his hut (and a long walk had been necessary in the first place to fetch it), it would be stolen as soon as his back was turned.

When not away on campaign, the work regularly performed by those *amabutho* staying at uMgungundlovu included finding suitable materials for the construction and repair of the huts and palisades, ploughing, weeding and harvesting the king's fields, and looking after his cattle. Their shields, which belonged to the king, were placed in storage huts raised on wooden stilts to preserve them from rats. To prevent their being infested by worms and rotting away, these shields were frequently taken down, dusted and left to lie in the open air.

If the king wished to speak to one of the men then residing at uMgu-ngundlovu, his name would be repeatedly shouted out over the *ikhanda* until he heard and responded. He than ran up towards the *isigodlo*. If he was ordered to enter the enclosure and go to the king's hut by the men guarding the entrance, he advanced singing the king's praises as loudly as he could, and stooping as a sign of respect. If more than one had been summoned, the senior would do the praising. A man did not enter the king's hut until specifically ordered to do so. He was then given meat, which would most likely have been 'high', since they preferred it that way in the *isigodlo*. However, he did not eat sitting down. Rather, he would eat the food on the tray in front of him lying on his belly like a dog, nib-bling and chewing, but never touching it with his hands. He would be given beer to drink out of a basket held by a servant or maid-of-honour. If he were offered *iwili*, blood-clots and fat cooked into a rich soup (the staple diet of the *isigodlo*), the accompanying drink would be whey instead of beer. Dingane, meanwhile, who might be reclining on a mat at the left side of the door, or be seated on a pile of rolled-up sleeping mats or on his carved chair, would be chatting and laugh-ing with the thirty or so maids-of-honour who were shuffling about on their knees in attendance. A visitor to the *isigodlo* did not dare laugh, lest his mirth be mis-construed. When somebody left the royal hut, he did so backwards, so that he always faced the king. Once back among his comrades he was a figure of awe, for he had been in the terrible presence of the king.

Certain customs were observed regarding the king's person. The king was shaved and had his hair dressed in the *isigodlo* or in the royal cattle enclosure on the upper side of the parade ground in front of the *isigodlo*, where a section was divided off for his ablutions. Every time his blade touched the king, the barber, Manokotsha kaPhangisa (who had also tended Shaka) would jump back as if in fright at his own temerity in touching the royal person, and stand at a distance for a moment. He would then stealthily creep back towards the king, who would be engaged meanwhile in conversation with one of his councillors. Manokotsha would shave a little more (no more than three or four strokes) and then repeat the pan-tomime until the operation was finally complete. All the royal hair and stubble would be caught in a little basket, burnt, and the ash poured into a running stream. In this way it could not fall into the hands of a malevolent magician and be turned against the king. Similarly, if the king squirted saliva or coughed up phlegm, a servant would rub it into the ground so that it could no longer be found.

The king's meat was cooked by his male attendants in the royal cattle enclo-sure, out of the sight of ordinary people, while maids-of-honour prepared his veg-etables and porridge in the white *isigodlo*. A manservant served his sour milk. While the king was at dinner, alone except for his attendants, a maid-of-honour would rapidly and continuously knock two iron hoe-heads together. Their ringing would be heard throughout the *ikhanda*, warning everybody that they could not spit or cough until the sound had ceased, signifying that the king had done and rinsed his mouth. The king touched neither milk nor meat from any cow that had been captured in foreign parts. The water he and his household drank came from the pure spring of the Mkhumbane, which rose on the Mthonjaneni heights, and had to be fetched every day by the women.

Dingane had a number of dogs, which Shaka's army had brought back from their Mpondoland campaign in 1828 and which were a feature of uMgungundlovu. Three particularly favoured animals stayed and slept in the *isigodlo* like the king their master, and no one ever dared beat them. Another, which had been neutered and had long hair, was an excellent watchdog and would pounce on anyone foolish enough to raise a stick to it. There were a further half-a-dozen or so who went out with the herdsmen, and yet a few more who preferred to stay with the *amabutho*. They were all greatly feared, and Dingane is reputed once to have set his dogs on a man whom they savaged to death.

When the king left the *isigodlo* for the royal cattle enclosure at the top of the parade ground to hold a general assembly (as distinct from a confidential meeting with his councillors), a general cry of summons went up. The people hurried out of their huts, singing praises as they went. Dingane seated himself on a chair carved out of marula wood and decorated with spotted poker-work, which was placed on a specially raised mound in the royal cattle enclosure. This ensured that the king could be seen by the people assembled in the parade ground in a half circle immediately outside the enclosure. Dingane's court arranged itself around him. His personal attendants and *izilomo* flanked him, one of them (a son of Nzobo) holding up a shield attached to a long pole to shade him from the sun, and another carrying his calabash snuff-box in a basket. Members of his council sat in front of him, with the most important advisers, such as Ndlela and Nzobo, a little apart and nearer the king. The approaching people saluted and acclaimed the king before seating themselves. Only the king and the *izikhulu* would speak. Whenever the king said anything, the *izikhulu* would ask the assembly, 'Do you hear the King?' The king's words would then be passed on until all had heard them. Whereupon the whole crowd would cry out in agreement, declaiming 'Yes Father, yes Lion!'

When matters of war were discussed and deeds of valour remembered and praised, the men of renown would dance before the king. Such dancing was a regular occurrence at uMgungundlovu, as was praise-singing. The *izikhulu* danced daily to encourage the cows when they were brought back to be milked by their crowd of herdsmen, all carrying spears and shields. These herdsmen were members of the youngest *amabutho* and slept near the entrance to the *ikhanda*. They too would join the *izikhulu* in the dance. Attracted by the sound of bellowing cattle and the stamp of feet, other young *amabutho* would pour into the great cattle kraal and join the dancing and singing. This was the signal for the king to appear at the fence of the *isigodlo*, where he would stand on a convenient anthill and watch his councillors and *amabutho* displaying their highly disciplined and intricate dancing skills. Dozens of servants would now appear to do the milking of the cows, of which there were about 800, standing in their allotted places all over the great cattle kraal. With arms outstretched these servants carried high the milking vessels of marula wood, covered with basketwork.

Once the milking began, the councillors and *amabutho* went back to their huts to eat, loudly chanting Dingane's praises and shaking their hands with fingers extended in sign of gratitude for the piles of meat (which had generally been stewed in great, black earthenware pots) being distributed for their consumption. The *amabutho* clustered in dense circles, two or three deep, about each carver, who apportioned a helping to every second or third man, who took first bite before passing on the gobbet to his neighbour. Dingane was undoubtedly generous with his councillors and *amabutho*, and was always presenting them with cattle to eat. When a beast was slaughtered at uMgungundlovu, the herdsmen and gate-keepers always received their particular perk, which was the kidneys. While the beast was being skinned the kidneys were removed and placed in a glistening, purple heap for them to collect and take away.

Something of the pageantry and excitement that attended ceremonial life at uMgungundlovu was captured by Captain Gardiner when, in February 1835, he witnessed Dingane's state progress between uMgungundlovu and esiKlebheni, only five kilometres away to the north.[38] About 900 *amabutho* marched out of uMgungundlovu accompanied at some distance on either flank by the king's servants and camp followers, who carried his household items. Dingane, followed by Ndlela and Nzobo at the head of all the inhabitants of uMgungundlovu, walked a little way to the high ground, his two main praise-singers volubly and tirelessly within earshot. On reaching the heights, Dingane rested in his chair and reviewed his people as they filed past in dignified and splendid show, all bedecked with their ceremonial finery. As they approached their king, each bent almost double and maintained this respectful posture until well past the royal station. Dingane at length called a halt and resumed his position at the head of the column.

On nearing esiKlebheni, Dingane seated himself under the shade of a great mimosa tree, with his favourite dog, Magilwana, at his feet. From this position of comfort he savoured the impetuous reciprocal mock charge and other military exercises between the *amabutho* stationed at esiKlebheni and his own military escort, basked in the cries of welcome from all the *ikhanda*'s inhabitants, and graciously received the deputation of women from its *isigodlo*, led by his father's widow Langazana, who came out dancing in stately fashion to greet their lord. Prominent warriors then *giya*'d before him, competing in their exertions for his approbation.

At length, preceded by all his people, Dingane made his way forward. Once inside the main cattle enclosure the people formed a circle about him, and Dingane witnessed a further exhibition of dancing before retiring to the seclusion of the *isigodlo*. Adulphe Delegorgue described just such a dance which was performed in 1839 for Mpande, Dingane's successor.[39] The warriors formed a circle in most orderly manner about him, intoning meanwhile warlike chants in deep-throated unison which they accompanied with the heavy rhythmical stamping of their feet and the raising and lowering of their fighting-sticks. Their movements and facial expressions became ever more frenzied, though their singing retained its solemn, measured tone. Renowned warriors then danced solo in turn, while a praise-singer kept up his ceaseless *obbligato*. The women, who were enclosed within the circle of men, sang shrilly at the same time as the men, harmonising in strict time with their bass voices, stamping their feet and clapping their hands to a rhythmic beat. It was an experience which deeply moved the visiting Frenchman with its controlled power and aesthetic force.

Yet, for all its glamour as the seat of power and royal munificence, uMgungundlovu was a place of which to be wary. Living conditions, except for the denizens of the *isigodlo* and the men directly connected to the court, were distinctly uncomfortable. Worse than that, it was a place of uncertainty and fear for all who entered it. The chiefs and *amabutho* who came to do the king homage could not breathe freely again until they left for home. For nobody could have been unaware that just outside the main gate, on the western side of uMgungundlovu, was kwaNkatha, the place of execution. Most of those Dingane condemned to death were killed there, and their bodies were then dragged across the Mkhumbane to kwaMatiwane, where executions sometimes also took place to prepare a feast for the vultures.

7

'You Thrust in an Evil Spear!'

At King Mpande's court, when the entire line of Zulu kings was praised, the royal bard, Magolwana kaMkhathini, always recited the following dirge for Dingane:

Alas, O Hairy one of Mgungundlovu!
You killed the Boers!
You thrust an evil spear into Zululand!
You thrust in an evil spear!
You thrust it into your own stomach, did you not?
What measure of courage is this?[1]

And truly, Dingane's dealings with the emigrant farmers from the Cape proved his personal nemesis and the undoing of his kingdom. Yet the Voortrekkers' alarming arrival in 1837 at the passes over the Drakensberg, in sight of the spreading plains of their promised land, was not an entirely unforeseen event. Throughout his reign Dingane had had to contend as best he could with various forces impinging on Zululand and threatening the edifice which, raised by his brother Shaka, it was his obligation to maintain.

Dingane was not a soldier before all else, like Shaka. He lacked his brother's overweening urge for conquest, and avoided the hardship of accompanying his armies on campaign. Nevertheless, his *amabutho* regularly took the field against his neighbours. In Zulu eyes, the boundaries of their kingdom were determined by the extent of the territories occupied by those people who had tendered their allegiance to the Zulu king.[2] Borders were thus fluid, and military expeditions served the varied purposes of keeping peripheral tributaries loyal, gaining the submission and tribute of additional adjacent chiefdoms and, most important of all, keeping the *amabutho* employed and rewarded with captured cattle.

However, Dingane's *amabutho* were not operating in quite the same open arena as had Shaka's. The presence of restless white communities, hungry for land and profit, was increasingly being felt within the Zulu sphere of influence, and Dingane soon learned that no action could be taken without including them in his calculations. Already, by the last years of Shaka's reign, the affairs of Zululand had become interlocked with those of the colonial world, and in particular with those of the traders at Port Natal. Involved too, though less direct-

72

ly, were the Portuguese at Delagoa Bay and the British in the Eastern Cape. After 1835 the presence of Christian missionaries would complicate interaction between the Zulu king and the settlers. But it was the arrival of the Voortrekkers in 1837 which would pose a direct challenge to the kingdom's continued existence. Particularly dangerous for the Zulu was the way in which these disparate groups of whites, regardless of their often deep differences, would co-operate against their common foe in times of crisis.

On seizing the throne, Dingane tried to reduce the Zulu presence south of the Thukela.[3] He was uneasy with the way in which Shaka had moved the centre of gravity of the kingdom southwards to the Port Natal coastland, for this gave the Port Natal settlers an inordinate degree of influence over the affairs of Zululand. Nor were these settlers faithful subjects, for they were clearly trying to establish the port and surrounding region as an autonomous base for the unrestricted commercial penetration of the hinterland. So Dingane, as we have seen, moved his capital back to the emaKhosini in the traditional heart of the kingdom, abandoned the Zulu advance posts far to the south, and turned his eyes back to Delagoa Bay.

There was considerable commercial rivalry between Port Natal and Delagoa Bay, and Dingane exploited this to obtain the commodities he desired at favourable rates, or to acquire from the one port what was denied him by the other. And if the traders proved recalcitrant, Dingane could always resort to force, for he still held the distinct edge in that regard. Thus, in 1833 he sent an army to attack Delagoa Bay, kill the uncooperative governor and replace him with a more compliant substitute. This highly successful military expedition (which gives the lie to the popular impression of Dingane's unassertiveness in matters of foreign policy) also consolidated Zulu sway over the Mabhudu-Tsonga chiefdoms of southern Mozambique, and brought Zulu influence in the region to its highest pitch.

The expedition against Delagoa Bay demonstrated that more – rather than less – involvement was necessary to keep the Portuguese traders in line. The same lesson applied equally to their British rivals at Port Natal. Dingane soon found that he could neither relax his hold on the southern peripheries of his kingdom, nor weaken the close commercial, political and military links with Port Natal forged by Shaka. Control of the one could not be divorced from exploitation of the other.

Consequently, Dingane rapidly reversed his initial policy and set about re-establishing his authority over the area and, like Shaka before him, making a show of strength in the Zulu sphere of influence beyond it. The flight of the Qwabe in 1829 and their involvement in the conflicts of the Mzimkhulu-Mzimvubu region provided the opportunity. The Mpondo successfully attacked the migrant Qwabe at the end of 1829 and scattered them, while their cattle (which included many beasts from the Zulu royal herds) fell into the hands of the Bhaca. Dingane sent an expedition in 1830 to recover the cattle.[4] It failed, but the attempt showed his determination to remain the dominant power of the region. Port Natal, however, continued to be the key to the territories south of the Thukela.

The traders possessed firearms and related military skills. Shaka (as we have seen) had commandeered them in a number of his campaigns, and Dingane reluctantly found himself constrained to do the same. The problem was that some of the peoples the Zulu army continued to raid over ever-longer distances and harsh terrain were adept counter-tacticians. The Swazi, for example, who lived to the north over the Phongolo River, habitually took to the natural defences of their mountainous country when threatened, and neutralised superior Zulu numbers. In this way they thwarted Zulu raids despatched by Shaka in 1827 and 1828. Dingane fared no better when he mounted a major campaign in 1836 to recapture cattle the Swazi had been raiding for some time from the Zulu in the northern reaches of the kingdom. He had eventually to recruit mercenaries from Port Natal, and in 1837 their guns frightened the Swazi into disgorging some 15 000 head of cattle.[5]

The lesson was obvious: to maintain their dominance in the region, the Zulu must have firearms, and Dingane became importunate in his demands that the traders supply him with what he required and train his men in their use. But, because firearms were so desirable, equated as they were with power, the traders limited the sale of them to the king (and sometimes stopped supplying them altogether) in order to maintain a lever in trade relations with him. Yet trade, the rulers of Zululand were coming to understand, could undermine their authority if it did not remain a monopoly of the crown. Once the settlers traded directly with the people, luxury goods and the prestigious firearms would no longer remain within the gift of the king to favoured subjects and *amabutho*, but would become instruments of political power for over-mighty chiefs and tributaries as well. Thus, Dingane attempted to impose restrictions on what the settlers might trade, and to dictate the terms on which they might do so. They, in turn, did their best to evade them and expand their trade, which meant that the blacks living near Port Natal became increasingly involved in the new economy despite Dingane's wishes.

Meanwhile, Port Natal was growing. Though James King died in 1828, and Francis Farewell was killed by the Qwabe in 1829 on suspicion of being a Zulu spy when he tried to travel through their country, after 1832 other traders from British settlements in the eastern Cape came to the Port, so that by 1838 the white population had increased to about forty. Some, like Alexander Biggar and his two sons, brought numerous Khoikhoi with them, and employed them like their counterparts in the Cape and Orange River regions as hunters, interpreters and transport-riders. What made the burgeoning settlement particularly threatening, as far as Dingane was concerned, was the flight to it of refugees from his rule. There was nothing new in that, and Shaka had been prepared to countenance the effective setting up of white chiefdoms within the vicinity of the Port. But under Dingane the number of refugees was swelling to about 2 500 by the mid-1830s, which meant that Port Natal was fast becoming a significant nest of Zulu malcontents. Many of these entered the traders' service and were trained in musketry, so that by the mid-1830s the Port was able to field an army of nearly 300 men carrying firearms. This force clearly constituted a danger, especially since the traders were hardly content to remain in their earlier role of subordinate chiefs.

Dingane was in a dilemma as to how best to maintain control over Port Natal. One way was to remind the traders that they were there only under his sufferance. In April 1831 he sent an impi under Zulu kaNogandaya, a famous commander, to punish John Cane for failing to report back after leading an unsuccessful diplomatic mission to the Cape on Dingane's behalf. The Zulu force seized Cane's cattle and, in fear for their lives, the Port Natal settlers took to the bush. It was only several months later that they felt safe enough to return. Two years later another incident, in which John Cane's clients attacked a passing Zulu army as it returned in a disorderly state after a second unsuccessful campaign against the Mpondo and Bhaca to recover the Qwabe cattle,[6] led to the traders' flight to Mpondoland in anticipation of Dingane's retaliation. Again, as in 1831, they returned on Dingane's assurances that no harm would come to them.

In guaranteeing their safety, Dingane was flouting the advice of many among his councillors who were urging him to deal drastically with Port Natal and the refugees harboured there. Their deep suspicions of white ambitions at the Port were being fuelled by Jacob Msimbithi. Jacob was a Xhosa who had come to Zululand in 1823 as interpreter for the first whites at Port Natal. He had found the power and prestige denied him by his white masters through attaching himself first to Shaka, and then to Dingane, and gaining their confidence. His eventual fall from grace and execution in January 1832 was the consequence of his theft of royal cattle, rather than because the king had ceased to believe his tales and suspected him of treachery. For Jacob's information concerning the ruthless British expansion along the Cape's eastern frontier, which fanned Dingane's fears of white intentions around Port Natal, was essentially accurate, if lurid.[7] And indeed, the powerful interests in the Cape which backed Port Natal were increasingly bearing down on the territories south of the Thukela.

The Cape government was beginning to pursue a more interventionist policy beyond its boundaries, while white and coloured freebooters were becoming involved in the conflicts of the Mzimvubu-Mzimkhulu region. Missionaries were also on the advance. The Wesleyan Missionary Society in the Cape had established a chain of missions north up to the Mpondo people by 1830. Merchants followed. By 1829 a wagon route had been opened up from the eastern Cape via the mission stations to Port Natal. Various Cape merchants, who saw the region as a promising field for commercial enterprise on a far wider scale than originally envisaged, were starting to call for the increased settlement of Port Natal and for effective British protection. In 1834 they went so far as to petition the British government to annex Port Natal. Their petition was unsuccessful, but it was clear that the country south of the Thukela was inexorably being pulled out of the orbit of the Zulu kingdom into that of the Cape. An alarming portent was a visit overland in 1834 to Port Natal by thirty Boers from the eastern Cape under Petrus Lafras Uys – the *Kommissie* Trek – to investigate whether the region was suitable for establishing a farming settlement.

Yet, despite these disquietening signs, Dingane had little option but to treat the Port Natal traders with circumspection. Strong-arm methods, he realised, were becoming more risky. Besides, while he mistrusted the whites at the Port and feared growing Cape involvement, he valued the goods they brought – especially firearms – and appreciated their potential as mercenaries. Consequently, despite frequently strained relations with the Port, he did not again intervene militarily as he had in 1831. Instead, he adopted a policy of disengagement and containment.

The people living on the southern side of the middle reaches of the Thukela were brought under close supervision from 1832 by Sothobe, while the inhabitants of the coastal lands were ordered to withdraw north across the Thukela. The Hlomendlini, or Home Guard units, were stationed in southern Zululand to guard the Zulu heartland from Port Natal, and to prevent the seeping away of any more refugees seeking asylum there. But their flight continued, and in 1834 an entire *ibutho* is reported to have defected. Provoked, Dingane resolved in 1835 that the right of Port Natal to continue as a trading settlement must be conditional upon the repatriation of all future refugees. Only thus would the Port cease to promote the disintegration of his kingdom through providing sanctuary for disaffected elements. The traders' agreement to these terms, in return for Dingane's promise to respect their lives and property, was brokered through Allen Gardiner, a retired captain of the Royal Navy turned missionary.

Gardiner, the first Christian evangelical to attempt to convert the Zulu, had arrived in Port Natal in 1835, and proceeded straight to uMgungundlovu. There, his knowledge is remembered to have 'amazed the people'.[8] Gaining Dingane's confidence, he had struck his deal with the king on the traders' behalf. In addition, Dingane gave permission for the admission of missionaries into his kingdom. The Revd Francis Owen of the Church Missionary Society, accompanied by his wife and children, was duly to arrive in October 1837 to set up his mission in some huts on the ridge overlooking uMgungundlovu from the east, while agents of the American Board of Commissioners for Foreign Missions were to begin their work on the coast. In return for this concession (for Dingane was more concerned that his people should learn to use firearms, drive ox-wagons and sew clothes than that they should learn the alien Gospels, and none dared take Christian instruction without the king's permission[9]), Gardiner agreed to assume charge of Port Natal and bring order to the settlement. To give Gardiner the necessary weight, on 13 July 1835 Dingane proclaimed him chief over all the country between the Thukela and Mzimkhulu rivers, the same territory that would later comprise the Colony of Natal.[10] In earnest of his good faith, Gardiner even returned some recent fugitives to Dingane for summary execution.

But the agreement of 1835 did not hold. Gardiner's authority was not generally recognised in the Port, and some traders failed to honour the terms of the agreement by continuing to encourage Zulu – particularly young women – to move to the settlement. Dingane, incensed but mindful of the traders' firepower, stopped short of launching an attack on the Port, but retaliated by prohibiting all commerce between it and his subjects, and by forbidding any white (with the exception of Gardiner) to cross north over the Thukela. The traders responded with shrill indignation, and they and their patrons in the Cape called more urgently than before for British annexation to protect their interests. The

Cape of Good Hope Punishment Act of 1836, which made British subjects at Port Natal liable to punishment in Cape courts, but which gave them no other support, was hardly what they required, however, and the traders declared themselves independent of British authority. This threw them back onto greater dependence on Dingane's good will. Realising this, the king reopened commercial relations in 1836. For their part, the traders co-operated with the Zulu state, and in 1837 John Cane led a party of some thirty whites from the Port to aid Dingane in his latest raid against the Swazi.[11] But matters between the Zulu king and the whites at Port Natal were still at an essentially unsatisfactory pass when the appearance of the Voortrekkers at the passes over the Drakensberg transformed the situation, casting the entire region into the melting-pot.

The Great Trek was, in a sense, a continuation of a long tradition on the part of the white stock farmers and hunters of the Cape frontier, who were habitually trekking into the wide lands of the interior in search of grazing and game. But these *trekboers* were not attempting to throw off British authority, irksome as they often found it, and colonial rule followed in their wake. This is where the Voortrekkers, who deliberately left the Cape forever to set up independent republics free from British interference, were so different. The Great Trek was an organised movement of resistance against British rule that took a form hallowed by the limited migrations of the *trekboers*. Yet, paradoxically, when the emigrants (as they called themselves) threw off what they regarded as colonial oppression, they themselves were embarking on an act of colonisation that was significantly to affect the lives of all the black peoples of the interior.[12]

About 15 000 Dutch-speaking settlers from the Cape eastern frontier left for the interior between 1834 and 1840 to set up their own states. Their reasons were many, but interrelated. Conflict between the white stock farmers and the Xhosa across the Cape frontier was steadily escalating, but while the British administration was attempting to limit settler habits of independence, especially in the military sphere, it did not have the means adequately to safeguard their lives and property. The Sixth Frontier War of 1834-1835 caused considerable loss to the frontier farmers and increased their disenchantment with the British. Another issue was that the consolidation of the eastern Cape frontier by the 1820s, and the government allocation of farms, meant that there was a perceived shortage of land for a growing settler population. Certainly, land prices were sharply rising. To make matters worse in the eyes of the settlers, Ordnance 50 of 1828 and the emancipation of slaves led to a shortage of labour and financial losses, and exacerbated the emotive problem of vagrancy.

Emigration seemed an ever more attractive alternative to these difficulties, especially since the Dutch-speaking settlers lacked the political means to protect themselves from the pervasive climate of British rule and humanitarian sentiment. British attitudes failed, in the settlers' view, to recognise the naturally privileged position of the whites in relation to the blacks, and British insistence on the equality of both before the law was quite contrary to the convictions of the frontier farmers, who distinguished sharply between black and white in terms of religion, race and class. In the interior, it was believed, free from the British, the settlers could regulate society as they desired.

The decision to emigrate was no light one, even if it seemed the obvious solution to an intolerable situation. It meant abandoning homes built up over
years, and selling farms and other fixed property, often at great financial loss. Nevertheless, thousands of Boers, their families and coloured servants, left their homes
to escape the detested British administration and find their Promised Land. They
did not go simultaneously, but in several spurts over a number of months between
early 1835 and late 1836. They trekked in their covered, ox-drawn wagons, which
contained all their belongings: their agricultural implements and domestic
tools; their small pieces of furniture, Bibles, guns and bullet moulds; their precious items of silver and porcelain from their forsaken homes in the Old Colony;
their clothing and supplies of tobacco, coffee and sugar.[13]

Reared in the traditions of the *trekboer*, they were physically and psychologi-
cally accustomed to loading up their possessions and living in their wagons in
the open veld. They accepted the slow pace of travel dictated by the plodding draft
oxen and the pasture and water requirements of their extensive flocks and
herds. Accordingly, the Trekkers moved spread out in small groups to accommodate
the grazing needs of their livestock. These parties each consisted of several families and their equally numerous coloured dependents, who had left the Cape together. In turn, these various trek parties each accepted the leadership of some
man of proven ability and experience among them.

The emigrants were not travelling into the complete unknown, for traders,
hunters, missionaries, *trekboers* and the *Kommissie* Trek had shown them the way.
The British authorities let them go in peace for the moment, not yet quite realising the scope and implications of the emigration. But if, unlike the Children of
Israel, the Voortrekkers did not have Pharaoh hard on their heels, they had
their own Canaanites to overcome before they could enter their Promised Land.
This meant they had to impose some discipline on their movement if they were
successfully to combat the various black communities who might bar their
progress across the highveld.

Necessary as some sort of administrative institutions were to hold the Trek
together, the truth was that Voortrekkers were individualists, with no traditions of political organisation beyond the strictly local. This meant that they found
it very hard to forge any effective unity among the various groups. Attempts to
create a single community with a hierarchy of officers constantly foundered on
the disappointed ambitions of some group leaders and (in this contentious
Protestant society) on disputes over a suitable minister. The most earnest dispute,
however, concerned the direction of the Trek.

Initially, the emigrants spread out across the wide grasslands between the Mod-
der and Vaal rivers, but they required access to the sea, beyond the control of the
British, where they could replenish their stocks of sugar, coffee, tea and, above
all, gunpowder and shot. Those under the leadership of Andries Potgieter, an experienced commando leader who had been voted out of his former position as
Chief Commandant in April 1837, favoured the lands across the Vaal and the
development of trade with Delagoa Bay. Piet Retief, who had been brought up

in the sophisticated milieu of a wine farm in the western Cape, though he had later abandoned Cape Town for Grahamstown and the Winterberg, where he had won considerable reputation as a commandant on the eastern frontier, preferred Natal and the closer outlet to the sea at Port Natal. It was he who had supplanted Potgieter as Chief Commandant on the Burgher Council, when he was also elected Governor.

Retief was supported by Gert Maritz, a superior wagon-maker from Graaff-Reinet with a reputation as a good businessman and competent administrator, who had been elected President and Judge. Piet Uys, a farmer from Uitenhage, who had led the *Kommissie* Trek to Port Natal in 1834 to investigate the region's potential, agreed with Retief and Maritz, even though, like Potgieter, he was distinctly put out at holding no office on the Burgher Council. These differences and personal animosities were never completely reconciled but, towards the end of 1837, most of the Voortrekker groups drifted towards the Drakensberg, Retief's group in the lead. Potgieter's group, meanwhile, continued north into the lands beyond the Vaal River.

The Drakensberg-bound emigrants knew they might well have to face the military might of the Zulu kingdom. Over thirty years of almost continuous warfare on the Cape eastern frontier had hardened many of them, and they knew how to comport themselves in battle. For defensive purposes they had developed the laager of wagons lashed together end-to-end, with the shaft of each wagon fitting under the chassis of the next. Drawn up thus into a circle, the wagons formed an improvised fortification, from which the Boers could keep up a devastating all-round fire with their muskets, supported sometimes by small cannon. Once they had broken the enemy's attack by these means, it was their practice to sally out on their horses and turn a retreat into a rout. This *commando* of armed horsemen was most effective in other ways as well, for it could travel long distances to take the enemy unawares, while its mobility and firepower enabled it to scout, skirmish, disengage and pillage with great effectiveness and minimal casualties to itself.

Members of a commando often dismounted in action for more effective firepower, and had perfected a vital technique for breaking off an inconclusive skirmish and regaining their horses before being cut off by the enemy. As soon as the front rank of dismounted men became too hotly pressed, it mounted and cantered to the rear, where it again dismounted. The second rank thus became the first, and the procedure was repeated, with the ranks retiring alternately and keeping up a good fire. Long experience along the Cape's frontiers had proved the military techniques of the laager and commando against the enemies encountered there, but their efficacy against a nation of soldiers like the Zulu remained to be tested, though recent events had served to bolster the emigrants' confidence, just as they had shaken Dingane's.

Mzilikazi kaMashobane had been a chief of a branch of the Khumalo living near the Black Mfolozi in a region being contested between the Ndwandwe and Mthethwa. Initially a troublesome vassal of Zwide of the Ndwandwe, in about 1819 he had transferred his allegiance to Shaka. However, his continuing independent-mindedness (he had refused to accept the prestigious post of *induna* at kwaBulawayo) came to a head in 1821 over his refusal to hand over to Shaka cattle he had captured in a raid against the Sotho. Shaka proceeded to attempt to 'eat him up', and Mzilikazi fled in 1822 to the highveld of the northern Drakensberg with the survivors of his people, 'Splinter which the Zulus splintered and left lying'.[14] There he built up a new chiefdom, augmenting his original Khumalo from among the Sotho and Pedi people in the vicinity, and from other refugees from Shaka's wrath, including remnants of the Ndwandwe.

To put distance between himself and Shaka's growing power, and to find better watered territory, Mzilikazi moved south-west in about 1825 to the Magaliesberg hills in the vicinity of modern Pretoria. There he built up an even larger kingdom from the chiefdoms he subjugated, raiding north across the Limpopo into the Shona country, west against the Tswana, east against the Pedi, and as far south as the Caledon River valley. Through these raids he acquired vast herds of cattle, and created a defensive barrier of devastated territory. But even so he was not yet out of the reach of the Zulu, and in 1830 an *impi* sent by Dingane, clearly benefiting by good intelligence, successfully raided him while much of his own army was absent on campaign. A further, though much less successful, Zulu attack in 1832, compounded by constant mounted Griqua and Kora raids from the south-west, persuaded Mzilikazi in 1833 to move further westwards, to Mosega on the Marico River, displacing the Tswana chiefdoms already in the area. From Mosega, rather like Dingane, he ruled autocratically over a highly developed state in which the *ibutho* system was a central feature of political, social and economic organisation.[15] In company with the Zulu monarch, whose raiding armies still continued to trouble him, he attempted to obtain firearms from traders and missionaries.

The Ndebele state was militarily superior to the other chiefdoms of the highveld, but it was no real match for mounted men armed with guns. From 1836 the advance of so many parties of Voortrekkers towards the Vaal was of mounting concern to Mzilikazi, especially as they were so similar in style to the dreaded Griqua and Kora raiders and, moreover, evidently intended to settle.

On 16 October 1836, after a number of skirmishes in which the Ndebele surprised Voortrekker groups who had crossed the Vaal, about 6 000 Ndebele under Mkhaliphi (Mzilikazi's leading general) attacked Andries Potgieter's laager of fifty wagons at Vegkop, just south of the Vaal. Employing chest and horn tactics that were in all essentials the same as the Zulus', and carrying similar stabbing-spears and shields, the Ndebele failed to penetrate the laager, which was defended by only about forty men. The effectiveness of an all-round defensive position, held by men with firearms against assailants who relied upon bare steel, was again confirmed. The Ndebele lost about 500 men killed to the Voortrekkers' 2. The emigrants did not attempt a sally when the Ndebele began to retire, which allowed Mkhaliphi's men to drive off all their livestock. This was poor compensation, though, for an ignominious defeat administered by a mere handful of men, and the implications were clear, not merely throughout the highveld, but east across the Drakensberg.

In January 1837, reinforced by fresh arrivals from the Cape, Potgieter and Gert Maritz led a commando of 107 Boers and 40 Griqua and Rolong against Mzilikazi. They succeeded brilliantly on 17 January when they took Mosega by surprise, with their firepower breaking up every Ndebele attempt to rally. They killed over 400 of the inhabitants of Mosega, who fled north, and then retired with 7 000 captured cattle, many of which had been Pretorius's.

Word of the Ndebele's discomfiture reached Dingane, who decided to take advantage of his old adversary's misfortune. By June 1837 a Zulu army under the command of Ndlela was again campaigning in Ndebele territory. Indecisive if bitter fighting took place, and the Zulu army eventually returned home in September, driving with them considerable numbers of captured long-horned Afrikander cattle and sheep. Significantly for the future, some of this livestock had originally belonged to the Boers, who continued to lay claim to it.

The very conception of this campaign displayed a fatal shortsightedness on the part of Dingane, though it was all too typical of the response of rulers of the black polities of southern Africa when facing up to the challenge of the white advance into the interior. Instead of combining to withstand the invader, they seized short-term advantages against old rivals, and so compromised the ability of any to survive as independent states. Thus, when in November 1837 a commando of some 360 Boers with their Griqua and Rolong auxiliaries under Potgieter and Uys struck again at the Ndebele, it was against a foe further weakened by the recent Zulu invasion. The nine-day battle at eGabeni to the north of Mosega, in which the slowly retreating Ndebele lost heavily against the Boers, reaffirmed the superiority in the open field of mobile, mounted gunmen against the classic horn formation and mass frontal attacks. Indeed, the battles of the emigrants against the Ndebele had thoroughly vindicated the effectiveness both of their defensive wagon laagers and of their offensive mounted commandos.

The Ndebele could devise no means capable of offsetting these traditional Boer tactics and, thoroughly worsted, Mzilikazi and the remnants of his people migrated out of range of Boer and Zulu alike. They crossed the Limpopo and created a new capital in the Matopo hills which they named Bulawayo, in defiant emulation of King Shaka's capital.[16]

The Ndebele defeat at eGabeni was not known to Dingane until January 1838. But he knew enough of their previous rough handling at the hands of the Boers to see in their fate the palimpsest of his own should the Voortrekkers, now moving steadily towards the Drakensberg under Retief's leadership, attempt to settle in his lands. If he were not to be forced to retire north with the Zulu, like Mzilikazi and the Ndebele, and re-establish his migrant kingdom somewhere in the interior, he had two options, both of them extremely risky. Either he must accommodate the emigrants, in which case his throne might not survive the blow to his prestige, or he must attempt to destroy them, which promised to be a bloody, if not impossible, undertaking. The Zulu had failed to overcome the already weakened Ndebele in June 1837, so what chance had they against their white conquerors in open battle?

For his part, Retief, who reached the Drakensberg passes in early October

1837, understood that if the emigrants were to settle securely in Natal, it was necessary to come to an understanding both with the Port Natal traders and with Dingane. Accordingly, Retief left his main group in laager at Kerkenberg near Oliviershoek, and took a small party by wagon to Port Natal. He was gratified to discover that the traders were prepared to welcome the Voortrekkers as allies and neigbours. Indeed, the traders hoped that with Boer aid they would be released both from Dingane's economic and political control and from the Cape's wavering interference.

Assured of the traders' enthusiastic support, Retief next opened communications with Dingane through the missionary Francis Owen at uMgungundlovu. He set out in a letter of 19 October the Boers' wish to live at peace with the Zulu, though at the same time ominously referring to Mzilikazi's defeat at Boer hands.[17] Indeed, with its veiled threat of the use of force, this superficially conciliatory missive set the tone for Retief's ambiguous dealings with Dingane.

Retief and his party of fifteen Boers and two traders (Thomas Halstead acting as interpreter) arrived in uMgungundlovu on 5 November 1837, at the very moment that Potgieter and Uys were preparing their *coup de grâce* against Mzilikazi. What would Dingane have made of Retief and his companions? Were they much different in his eyes from the Port Natal traders and missionaries he knew? They would have been dressed in their characteristic broad-brimmed, flat-crowned felt hats, workaday clothes of tweed or moleskin, and hand-made leather shoes. They did possess finer clothes for special occasions, and perhaps 'Piti' (as Retief was known to the Zulu) would have put on a rich waistcoat of satin, silk or velvet.[18] Adulphe Delegorgue, the young French naturalist, who saw the peoples of southern Africa with a sophisticated, articulate stranger's eye, was in no doubt that the Boers were singular in their own way. His description of a party of them in 1839 was not to their advantage, however: '...great, gangling, long-limbed fellows, with clumsy gestures, awkward bearing, dull faces, faltering speech, gaping mouths, men made to drive oxen and to hold converse with them'.[19]

Dingane was probably not critical of the Boers for the same reasons, but he certainly would have known them to be dangerous men. Over the following days he did his best to impress the emigrants with displays of his military might and great wealth in cattle.[20] There were magnificent displays of dancing and military exercises, first by 2 000 young *amabutho*, and on the following day by 4 000 older ones. Dingane himself, arrayed in all his finery, took part in the review. A great herd of 2 224 red cattle with white backs (which Dingane had deliberately collected to astonish the Boers) was driven before them and counted.

Getting down to business only on 8 November, Dingane assured Retief that he was 'almost inclined' to grant him territory. What land he meant, he did not specify precisely. He knew the Boers wanted the cession of all the territory south of the Thukela, for Retief had told him that if he could choose, he would like 'the tract of Country near the Natal Bay, as we white people need many things that come from over the sea.'[21] But he had already settled the territory on Gardiner as chief. In any case, it is clear that what he actually had in mind for Retief was the country lately vacated by Mzilikazi and occupied by Potgieter's party, and no part of the Zulu kingdom at all.

Owen hastened to warn Retief that Dingane was being duplicious, but the Boer leader felt he must nevertheless play along and show good will. In particular, he reasoned that he must fulfil a precondition Dingane set on any further negotiations concerning land. Dingane explained that 'a people having clothes, horses and guns', and therefore suspected as Boers, had recently stolen cattle belonging to the Hlubi, who acknowledged Dingane as their king. If Retief recovered these for Dingane, he would prove that the Boers had not been involved in their theft.[22]

In fact, Dingane knew well that the culprits were the Mokotleng Tlokwa, the predominant people in the Caledon River valley, who raided and fought in the same style as the Boers and Griqua. Their chief, Sekonyela, had already refused Dingane's request for the return of the cattle (which he had actually raided a full two years before) and had grievously insulted the Zulu king to boot. With reference to the Zulu custom since Shaka's day of no longer circumcising boys to indicate their admission to the status of manhood, Sekonyela had contemptuously declared to Dingane's messengers: 'Tell that impubescent boy that if he wants to be circumcised let him come and I'll circumcise him.'[23]

Retief also knew the Tlokwa to be the real cattle thieves, but was prepared to perform the labour of recovering the stolen cattle to prove the Boers' good intentions. Nevertheless, he could not forbear from adding some sanctimonious words of clear intimidation to remind the Zulu king that, for all his ostentatious display over the previous days, superior military power lay in the hands of the Boers:

> The great Book of God teaches us that kings who conduct themselves as Umsilikazi does are severely punished, and that it is not granted to them to live or reign long; and if you desire to learn at greater length how God deals with such bad kings, you must enquire concerning it from the missionaries in your country.[24]

Dingane could hardly have relished such harsh and threatening words from Retief, whose frank, open manners and mildness of demeanour[25] clearly belied his true sentiments. He allowed him to leave uMgungundlovu in mid-November, but there is evidence that he ordered his death on the way back to Port Natal. According to Chief Silwebana, who fled to Port Natal with the remnants of his people after being 'eaten up' for disobeying his commission, Dingane instructed him to invite Retief and his party to his homestead and, while entertaining him with dance and food, to put them to death.[26] This plot, as reported, prefigured the circumstances of the actual death of Retief and his companions at uMgungundlovu three months later. If Silwebana's account was true, it is an indication that Dingane had already made up his mind to destroy the Voortrekkers rather than to accommodate them. At the *umKhosi* on 22 December 1837, the *amabutho* made clear and repeated reference before their king to fighting the Boers when they cried, 'Who can fight with thee; no king can fight with thee! They that *carry fire* cannot fight with thee.'[27]

Retief was not blind to simmering Zulu animosity and the dangers it held for his people, but he thought that straight and firm handling of Dingane could still produce the fruits the emigrants desired. So while he returned to Port Natal to confer with his new allies the traders, he sent word to the laager at Kerkenberg of his not unsuccessful negotiations. The emigrants thereupon brought their wagons down the Drakensberg passes. Delegorgue, who was a fair if critical commentator, praised the Boers' uncommon ability in this sort of difficult operation:

> ...the Boers are the finest wagon drivers in the world. Their boldness in the management of their teams is exceptional...while negotiating mountain passes. They will frequently drive their teams along a ridge bordering on a precipitous drop of perhaps 1 200 feet, where a single unexpected stone could send a wagon and oxen crashing to destruction...They make light of these dangers which fill me with trepidation.[28]

By the time Retief arrived back from Port Natal at the end of November, the various parties – his own, Maritz's and even some of Potgieter's people – were laagered in small groups across the lovely, well-watered countryside around the headwaters of the Thukela and its tributaries. But the emigrants, several thousand strong, had descended onto land Dingane still considered within his kingdom before Retief had fulfilled his side of the bargain struck with the Zulu king. Moreover, they were in laagers, which the Zulu knew to be extremely effective defensive formations, and, even more provocatively, they were soon seizing grain from neighbouring *imizi* as if they were conquerors and the land their own. Dingane and his councillors must have had the sour satisfaction of finding their fears realised. It had been possible to contain the traders at Port Natal, but here, in the person of these aggressive pastoralists, was a mortal threat to Zulu hegemony.

Meanwhile, at the end of December 1837, Retief led a commando back over the Drakensberg to recover the stolen cattle from the Tlokwa. He persuaded their chief, Sekonyela, to meet him at Mparane in the garden of James Allison, the Wesleyan missionary. There by a ruse, he placed handcuffs on Sekonyela, who in fear of his life admitted to taking 300 head of cattle from the Zulu. Retief refused to release him until his people had handed over their cattle and paid further compensation. Allison tried to instil in Retief some shame for his act of treachery, but the Boer leader held firm. Sekonyela's mother, MaNthatisi, who had for many years been regent of the Tlokwa and had acquired a ferocious reputation as a merciless marauder, was now a drunken old lady, and capitulated. She ordered her people to bring in their cattle and, with 700 head, plus 63 horses and 11 guns, bought her son's freedom.[29]

Retief arrived back at his laager on 11 January 1838 with his booty, and wrote to Dingane informing him of his success. He intended to leave immediately for uMgungundlovu to claim his reward, which he hoped would be Zulu permission to settle in Natal. But Retief was running into trouble with his factious compatriots. Maritz protested at his high-handed actions, while Uys criticised his rejection of any possibility of accepting British authority in Natal. In particular, Retief was condemned for desiring a large force to accompany him on his return to uMgungundlovu, for Maritz and others deeply suspected Dingane's intentions, and wished to limit possible casualties.

Retief, in what was to prove a catastrophic miscalculation, was confident that a large, well-armed commando would intimidate Dingane and persuade him to carry out his part of the bargain struck in November. Besides, he felt he knew Dingane's passionate love of warlike displays, and was sure that the military exercises he planned to perform in his honour would have the effect of mollifying him and making the pill easier to swallow. Since there were so many objections and apprehensions, however, he called for volunteers to accompany him into the lion's den. So at length 69 emigrants and 30 coloured attendants eventually left under Retief's command for uMgungundlovu, which they reached on 3 February 1838 with the 300 Zulu cattle recovered from Sekonyela.[30]

Had Dingane already made up his mind to kill the importunate Boers? He and his advisers had been considerably unsettled since Retief's departure in November by detailed intelligence of the apparently invincible Boers' latest victory over Mzilikazi at eGabeni.[31] Then Retief's letter outlining his successful expedition against Sekonyela, which arrived on 22 January 1838, must have put Dingane uneasily in mind of Retief's earlier warning concerning the fate of 'bad kings'.

At the same time, Dingane was incensed that Retief was not handing Sekonyela over to him for punishment, and indignant that the captured guns and horses were not being sent to him either. For as Owen realised, he coveted the dreaded muskets and had in mind the formation of a force of mounted gunmen along the same lines as a Boer commando.[32] Dingane could have been nothing but deeply affronted, moreover, at Retief's response to his messengers when they demanded the guns and horses. Pointing to his grey hairs, Retief scathingly told them to remind their master that he was not dealing with a child.[33]

Undoubtedly, there was mounting pressure on Dingane from his advisers to deal with the Boers before the fate of Mzilikazi or Sekonyela overtook him. If Retief and his party could be killed while at uMgungundlovu, and the rest of the Boers taken by surprise and annihilated in their laagers, then perhaps the kingdom might be saved. Only unexpected blows such as these – 'treachery' if you will – could outweigh the proven military excellence of the Boers.[34] Yet much would still depend on how the Boers comported themselves at uMgungundlovu, and killing them was not Dingane's only option. He might well have continued to negotiate, and have allowed Retief to depart unharmed, if Gardiner and John Cane had been at uMgungundlovu to advise him when Retief's commando rode in. But, fearful for their own safety, they had declined the king's invitation to be present to mediate.[35]

On 2 February 1838 large number of *amabutho* in war-dress began gathering at uMgungundlovu in anticipation of the Boers' arrival, and were crammed into the huts.[36] The Boers appeared the following morning, heralding their coming with an unsettling *feu de joie*, and riding provocatively right into the *ikhanda* with their guns in their hands. Dingane had challenged them the previous day to compete with his *amabutho* in dancing, and the Boers immediately set about demonstrating their skill in 'dancing' their horses. They charged each other on horseback in sham combat, making the air resound with their firing and filling uMgungundlovu with the unfamiliar smell of exploded gunpowder.[37] The Zulu had never experienced anything like it, and Dingane's forebodings must have been accentuated. The *amabutho* responded with their own war dances and military manoeuvres, and over the next two days they continued to entertain the emigrants with their displays of singing and dancing. Retief's party, who were encamped at the Mkhumbane stream, even forwent Sabbath service on 4 February to demonstrate their goodwill by attending the festivities.

All seemed amity and accord, and on that same Sunday Dingane put his mark to a previously prepared document written in English. In the words of the dubious surviving copy, it gave

> Retief, Gouvernour of the Dutch emigrant South Afrikans ... and his Countrymen ... Port Natal, together with all the land annexed, that is to say from Dogela [Thukela] to the Omsoboebo [Mzimvubu] River westward and from the Sea to the North, as far as the land may be usefull in my possession.[38]

Three Zulu, designated 'Great Councillors', also put their marks to the paper of cession. Their names are not met with elsewhere among prominent men of the time, and it seems that they were simply royal attendants, and not councillors at all.[39] In this way, it would seem, Dingane was indicating the invalidity of the document extracted from him under duress. For their part, the Boers did not seem to find it strange that Dingane was apparently so willing to cede his own territory. Simply, they rejoiced that they had gained what they had come for without the trouble or violence they had been half anticipating. All that remained was to observe the proper courtesies over the next day, and then to depart.

On the morning of 6 February, as Owen sat in the shade of his wagon reading the Bible, a messenger came from Dingane to tell him not to be alarmed, but that it was his master's intention to kill the Boers since they were going to kill him. Overcome by horror, Owen turned his telescope on kwaMatiwane, and spied a great crowd on the hill, with groups of nine or ten Zulu each dragging a Boer or one of their coloured attendants to its summit. Owen and his terrified wife set up an appalled cry and threw themselves trembling and fainting to the ground. They only roused themselves when they heard the exultant cries of acclamation when the crowd returned to the great cattle kraal at uMgungundlovu to praise their king, who sat in earnest conversation with Ndlela and Nzobo, his chief advisers. The following morning two *izinduna* came to Owen to explain further the execution of Retief and his party. Dingane declared through them that he could live in peace with the Port Natal traders and the missionaries, for they were few in number, but that the Boers had come in such force, like an army, and had been bent on settling on his lands whether they received his permission or not.

It seems clear that the Boers' behaviour while at uMgungundlovu finally decided Dingane that he must kill them, and in this he was strongly urged on by Ndlela, who mistrusted their intentions entirely.[40] In his own suspicious state, Dingane soon found sufficient evidence that the Boers intended to kill him while he slept. On successive nights the guards stationed at the top end of the *ikhanda* reported that the Boers had been seen moving around the outside of uMgungundlovu with the apparently sinister intention of surrounding the *ikhanda*. Hoofmarks and horse-droppings discovered in the morning proved their point. The Boers insisted that they had simply been in search of their horses which had broken loose and strayed in search of grazing. But they were not believed, and in Zulu tradition their supposedly hostile attempt to encircle uMgungundlovu has been taken as sufficient justification for their subsequent execution.[41]

On the day of their departure the Boers antagonised Dingane further by peremptorily demanding the return of those livestock which the Zulu had brought back from their last campaign against Mzilikazi, and which the Boers claimed had originally belonged to them. The proud Zulu reply was that 'no cattle ever left Zululand after once getting here'.[42] The Boers then added to Dingane's resentments and suspicions by declaring that they wished to fire a parting salute with blank cartridges, as they had done on their arrival. This was also construed as a plot to kill Dingane, and was confirmed afterwards to the Zulu's satisfaction when their muskets were found to be loaded with shot.

It was in these circumstances that Dingane held a meeting of his inner council to discuss what should be done with the Boers, and how their hostile ambitions could be nipped in the bud. Nzobo put forward the suggestion that they should be invited to a display of dancing and killed while unprepared and unsuspecting. Otherwise, to attack them while they were armed and mounted would lead to terrible casualties.[43] The conclave required little convincing, and Dingane accordingly invited the departing Boers and their servants, whose horses were already saddled up, into the great cattle kraal to take leave of him.

After their satisfactory meeting on the 4 February and the lavish hospitality of the succeeding day, the Boers were congratulating themselves on their success, and suspected no treachery. They ignored young William Wood, Dingane's interpreter, who warned them to be on their guard since he perceived from Dingane's manner that he 'meditated some mischief'.[44] Not even when they were requested to pile their arms outside the *ikhanda*[45] did they smell perfidy, for all seemed friendliness. They were invited to sit and drink beer with the king and receive the cattle assigned them for their journey. If the Boers had known – or recollected – the fate of Dingane's brothers, invited to taste the pleasures of his *isigodlo* and then put to death for their temerity, they would have been less trusting of their apparently jovial host.

Dingane, who was seated in his chair at the top of the great cattle enclosure, ordered two crack *amabutho* drawn up either side of him (the younger of which were the iHlaba)[46] to dance and sing to entertain his guests. Forming themselves into the customary half moon, they performed an *inkondlo*, which was a spirited dance with a gradual forward and backward movement.[47] They came closer and closer to their unsuspecting victims, while a mass of other *amabutho* looked on, until Dingane suddenly clapped his hands and cried out 'Seize them!' The *amabutho*, who were only armed with sticks, since they could not have danced before the king with their spears, rushed upon the Boers before they could even get to their feet. The dust rose as some Boers desperately slashed at their assailants with their long knives, killing some. But they were swiftly overwhelmed and, beaten senseless or with their necks broken, dragged off to kwaMatiwane with their feet trailing on the ground.[48] Dingane, still seated, called out 'Kill the wizards!'[49]

Retief was held and forced to witness his comrades being finished off before he too was clubbed to death. Only Lomana, a coloured attendant who had been left with the guns outside the gate, succeeded in escaping on his horse. He was still alive and living near Weenen in 1909.[50] Young Thomas Halstead, their interpreter from Port Natal, died with the Boers despite his despairing attempts to plead with the king. His death alone Dingane regretted somewhat, for he had no wish as yet to alienate the traders at Port Natal, or the distant British. But the Boers were now his unreconcilable enemies, and he ordered Retief's heart and liver to be placed in the path of the emigrants to make strong magic against them.

Richard Hulley, Owen's interpreter, arrived back at uMgungundlovu from Port Natal on 9 February to observe a large flock of vultures hovering over kwaMatiwane, and to find a pile of saddles at the entrance to uMgungundlovu. With these signs, he needed no one to spell out to him what had occurred.[51] On 11 February Owen and all his party were permitted to leave in safety for the coast. But they knew that the situation was more than perilous for the emigrant parties bivouacked in the foothills of the Drakensberg. For later on the very day Retief was killed, Owen had seen Dingane reviewing several *amabutho* who, at about noon (or some two hours after the execution), had set off at a run in the direction from which the Boers' commando had come. There had been no doubt in Owen's mind that they intended to surprise the emigrant encampments, and his fears were confirmed on 8 February when he noticed more *amabutho* leaving on campaign.[52] Dingane was confident that his decisive action had secured his kingdom. But, as Hulley dourly warned the king, he had begun a war whose end none could predict.[53]

8

Blood River

'We will go and kill the white dogs!'[1] the *amabutho* ferociously promised Dingane on 6 February 1838 before setting out to surprise the Voortrekkers in their scattered encampments. What they were about to do was no different in essence from the usual comprehensive 'eating up' of a disgraced and executed chief's homestead, family, adherents and livestock. But this second element in the Zulu plan to wipe the country clean of the Voortrekkers was a failure.

The Zulu forces advanced south-west from uMgungundlovu, over the Mzinyathi River near what is now Rorke's Drift, along the Helpmekaar heights and towards the confluence of the Bloukrans and Thukela rivers.[2] The unsuspecting Voortrekkers lay in their camps pitched under the groups of large, flat-topped trees in the grassy valleys of the Bloukrans and Bushman's rivers. Because no attack was anticipated, the encampments were scattered over considerable distances and not organised for defence. Many of the men were away hunting or assisting other parties of emigrants down the Drakensberg, so their families and dependents were left unprotected.

The right and centre divisions of the Zulu army began their onslaught before midnight on 16 February, striking the camps along the Bloukrans and its tributaries (later tellingly named the Great and Little Moord (Murder) rivers). Taken completely by surprise – Daniel Bezuidenhout, for one, thought his dogs were barking at a leopard, and was dumbfounded to see them baiting Zulu – these camps were rapidly overrun, and whole Voortrekker families were wiped out before they could offer any resistance. Others managed to make something of a stand. The Bothmas, for example, trying to retreat down the Great Moord to other camps, were overwhelmed on a small koppie by Zulu who advanced using captured cattle as a shield.

Hearing firing from the east, the inhabitants of camps further away thought at first that the volleys were welcoming back Retief and his party. The arrival of desperate fugitives and the sight of flames from burning wagons soon disabused them. But at least they were granted some time in which to improvise their defence. The very dispersion of the Boer encampments came to their aid, for the Zulu, involved in an unaccustomed night attack, and having underestimated the sheer size of their target, soon lost cohesion and control. Laden with booty, and driving captured livestock, they began to break up into small groups, and the

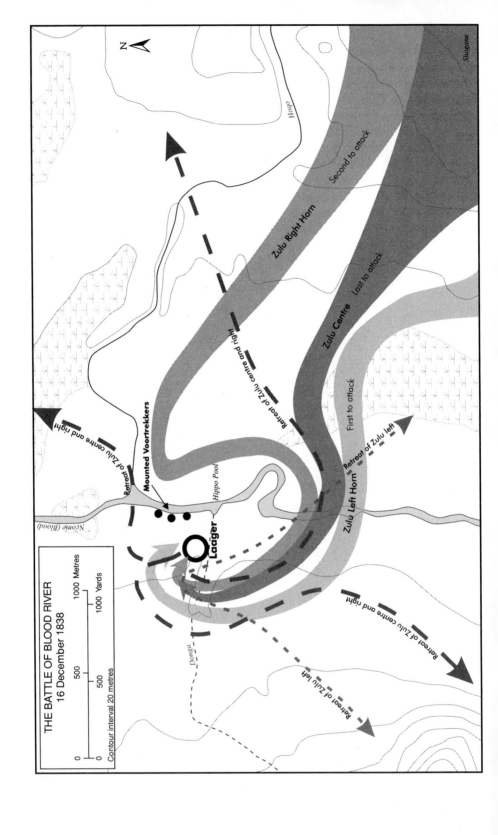

THE BATTLE OF BLOOD RIVER
16 December 1838

Contour interval 20 metres

0   500   1000 Yards
0   500   1000 Metres

impetus of the attack steadily waned, petering out beyond the Little Moord.

The attack of the Zulu left wing, meanwhile, had not even succeeded to the extent of that of the centre and right. Here Gert Maritz and Hans Dons de Lange had had the foresight to establish proper laagers, from which they threw back the Zulu. Commandant Johannes van Rensberg's family and several other family groups were able to make a successful stand on a koppie behind their camp on what was dubbed the Rensburgspruit. The Boers rallied in Maritz's and De Lange's laagers, and also in those of A. Greyling and Sarel Cilliers beyond the Bloukrans River towards Doornkop, which the Zulu right horn had not reached. On the afternoon of 17 February the Voortrekkers launched a mounted counter-attack from the four laagers. Heavy casualties were inflicted on the exhausted Zulu, and by evening they were in full retreat, but driving 25 000 head of cattle and thousands of sheep and horses before them. At dawn on 18 February a commando of about fifty mounted men under Maritz set out in pursuit and caught up with the Zulu as they were crossing the Thukela with their captured livestock. The river was in spate, however, and the Voortrekkers turned back after inflicting further casualties, tears of frustration and grief pouring down their faces.

That day the shocked Trekkers conducted a search of the whole region attacked by the Zulu, which was bitterly to be known as Weenen (Weeping). It was a scene of terrible devastation. Overturned wagons were literally awash with blood, the grass was matted with gore, household possessions were scattered in all directions, and vultures and crows were gathering, greedy for the feast. Some 40 white men, 56 white women, 185 white children and 250 coloured servants lay dead, and there were many more wounded. But Dingane and his advisers had underestimated the Voortrekkers' gritty determination to survive, and their thirst to avenge their slaughtered families, which their bitter tears and lamentations could not slake. The Zulu had lost up to 500 men in the affray, far too many in a surprise attack against a scattered and unprepared prey. Moreover, their withdrawal had been a fatal strategic error, though very much in the tradition of the punitive raid. The enormous amount of booty taken back to Dingane could not compensate for the plain fact that the Boers, though badly damaged, had been far from eliminated, and that the Zulu had now expended the advantage of surprise and lost the military initiative.

The emigrants had drawn together in laagers for mutual protection following the massacre. They still had about 1 000 wagons, and numbered about 640 men, 3 200 women and children and 1 260 black retainers. Despite their losses, they were rich yet in livestock, having 40 000 cattle, 300 000 sheep and 3 000 horses.[3] But life under canvas in a large muddy camp full of flocks and herds in the midst of a particularly rainy season was hard to bear. Many had been left quite destitute when the Zulu destroyed their belongings and drove off the livestock. Daniel Bezuidenhout, a wealthy man who had owned 7 000 sheep, was left with nothing but his shirt and pantaloons, four orphans in his care and a wounded arm. People's health began to give way, as did supplies of food. There was no grain available, and those whose cattle the Zulu had carried off had to depend almost entirely on hunting game. The Trekkers desperately felt they could not go on like this.

The arrival of Piet Uys, with a small body of men who had remained to the west of the Drakensberg, infused fresh courage. Negotiations were opened in March with the settlers at Port Natal for joint action against Dingane, both to exact revenge and to recapture some of the cattle the Zulu had driven off. It was agreed that a force from Port Natal would advance on uMgungundlovu from that direction, while a retaliatory Voortrekker commando would attack from the southwest.

On 6 April a commando of mounted men set off from the Voortrekker laagers, soon dividing into two sections as rivalry between the leaders made a single command unacceptable.[4]Andries Potgieter commanded 200 men, and Piet Uys a further 147. No wagons accompanied the force, for the intention was to move as rapidly as possible to surprise the Zulu, as they previously had the Ndebele in 1837. So, taking only such stores as could be carried on their horses, Potgieter's and Uys's men crossed the rugged and precipitous valley of the Thukela and set off in the direction of uMgungundlovu. But the Zulu were fully appraised of their coming, and Dingane had ordered all cattle to be driven out of their reach. On 10 April, on the other side of the Mzinyathi, near the source of the Mhlathuze River and the eThaleni Hill, the Zulu laid their ambush. The advancing commando sighted a herd of cattle being driven over a long, narrow nek between two hills leading into a large, rocky basin, seamed with deep dongas. With too little caution they gave pursuit.

The Zulu, numbering several thousand made up from the umKhulutshane, iziGulutshane and smaller elements of other *amabutho*, under the command of Nzobo himself, were divided into three. One division was on each of the two hills commanding the nek, and a third was posted at some distance to cut off the commando's retreat. Uys and his force impetuously attacked the largest of the Zulu divisions, which had remained sitting among the rocks on the northernmost of the two hills, waiting for the Boers to commit themselves. Uys's men dismounted, scrambled up the hill and fired a couple of volleys.

The Zulu, who had taken some casualties, then deliberately fell back, drawing Uys's men, who had remounted, into the broken terrain of the basin. In their reckless pursuit, the Boers broke up into small parties. These were then attacked on all sides by the Zulu who had rallied and been reinforced by more of their comrades who had been concealed in the dongas.

Meanwhile, Potgieter had led his men gingerly halfway up the southern hill, and then withdrawn again to the valley. Seeing that he was sensibly reluctant to attack over the treacherous, broken ground, the Zulu in their turn charged down the hill with such a rattle of shields and shouting of war-cries that Potgieter's force turned tail and fled, believing it better to live and fight another day. The third Zulu division manoeuvred to cut them off, but Potgieter managed to evade them and, keeping up a good pace, outdistanced the pursuit. The small party under Field Cornet Landman which volunteered to stay back and cover Potgieter's retreat had at least the satisfaction of shooting an *induna* mounted on a horse which they recognised as having belonged to Piet Retief. But Uys's force, left in the lurch and surrounded, had to fight their way out. For nearly two hours they conducted a fighting retreat over the broken country, alternately dismounting, firing and retiring in classic Boer fashion, changing directions many times under Zulu pressure, until they were able at last to join up again with Potgieter's men.

They did not extricate themselves unscathed. Uys was mortally wounded in the loins by a thrown spear, and fell from his horse from loss of blood. His gallant son Dirk, aged fourteen, could not bear the sight of his father abandoned on the ground and surrounded by Zulu. He turned his horse and rode back to suffer certain death at his dear father's side. Eight other Boers also fell, only one of whom was of Potgieter's division. On top of this, the Zulu captured sixty of the commando's pack horses and a considerable amount of baggage.

The Zulu must have suffered considerable casualties themselves – probably several hundred – since they had been compelled to brave heavy gunfire to get close enough even to throw their spears with any effect. But the Voortrekkers could not disguise the fact that they had been defeated, and exaggerated word of the extent of their reverse caused terrible consternation in camp. The commando itself began to be referred to derisively as the *Vlugkommando* or Flight Commando. Under this renewed adversity the old Voortrekker dissensions flared up again with new intensity, and Potgieter was openly accused of cowardice. Indignant at what he considered the unfounded criticism, and impressed moreover with the military strength of the Zulu, he withdrew across the Drakensberg, taking with him his invaluable group of horsemen, and resumed his endeavour to achieve his ideal of liberty on the highveld.

The temporary destruction of the Port Natal community that followed on the Zulu strikes against the Boers was not an obvious corollary, but a consequence of opportunistic and exceedingly ill-advised intervention by the more bellicose of the Port Natal settlers.[5] In March John Cane, known as Jana to the Zulu, with a force of 2 100 coloured retainers and black adherents from Port Natal, took advantage of the disturbed state of the country to strike a blow in support of the beleaguered Boers. Revenge for their own compatriots killed with Retief was a motive too, but they also acted shamelessly for the sake of their own pockets.

In a successful raid in the vicinity of Kranskop (Ntunjambili), where a great spur of the Drakensberg ends precipitously on the southern side of the middle Thukela, Cane and his men destroyed several large and populous *imizi*. These belonged to the great chiefs Sothobe and Nombanga kaNgidli, and considerable numbers of royal cattle were kept there. Cane's attack was well timed, for the cattle guards had all been summoned away by Dingane to prepare to repel the Voortrekker attack that was in the offing, and which would be repulsed at the battle of eThaleni. The raiders, meeting almost no opposition, carried off nearly 6 000 head, and a few hundred women and children besides. The women were as great a prize as the cattle, for their captors would have the benefit of their labour, and later receive *ilobolo* for them when they duly married them off.

In April, thinking to repeat their earlier success, and in support of Potgieter and Uys who were mounting their own punitive expedition against the Zulu, Robert Biggar, Cane and John Stubbs led forth a force even larger than the one which had struck at Ntunjambili. Those armed with guns were a further 16 Port Natal settlers, 30 coloureds and 400 blacks. Several thousand black levies carrying spears and shields were in support. Counsel was divided among the leaders of this so-called 'Grand Army of Natal', and strategy hazy. On reaching the lower Thukela, scouts reported the hilly, bush-covered country on the opposite bank to be full of unattended cattle. After much rancorous debate the Port Natal leaders resolved to make a sudden foray across the river. But, as some of the more perceptive had feared, this only meant falling for the Zulu ruse.

This time the Zulu were ready for the insolent ragtag and bobtail of Port Natal, and several *amabutho* under the nominal command of Mpande, Dingane's half-brother, awaited them. Biggar's force crossed the drift early on the morning of 17 April and surrounded and attacked Ndondakusuka, the large *umuzi* belonging to the famous warrior Zulu kaNogandaya, who was himself with the army lurking nearby. Biggar's men burned Ndondakusuka to the ground and killed its inhabitants, but their victory was shortlived. It is said that one of their dying victims exclaimed, 'Kill me right now, but the great elephant is coming, and it will trample you underfoot.'[6] And indeed, the Zulu army under the effective command of Nongalaza kaNondela and Madlebe kaMgedeza then advanced rapidly from the north. Moving in two columns to the east and west of the hill above Ndondakusuka, it cut Biggar's force off from the Thukela. Those of his men with firearms stood firm near the *umuzi* they had just destroyed, and their steady fire did much execution among the Zulu who charged them. But the Zulu fell back only to come on again from different directions over the broken terrain. The black Port Natal levies, after some initial success, found themselves being cut off by the Zulu from the division with firearms, and panicked. They cast off the white calico which had distinguished them as being on the settlers' side, and caused utter consternation among the armed men who could no longer distinguish friend from enemy. Fierce hand-to-hand fighting ensued. Biggar, Cane and all except four of the settlers, two or three coloureds and a handful of the black levies were stabbed where they stood or herded down to the river to be speared or drowned as they tried to make for the opposite bank.

For a decade or more the heaps of bleached bones lay thick on that terrible killing ground, and Prince Mpande could claim a great victory. Little could he know that eighteen years later, in this very place, his own sons would pit their armies against each other in a furious and deadly struggle for the succession to the Zulu crown.

Several survivors from the battle of the Thukela gave warning to Port Natal of their disaster and the approach of the Zulu. The Zulu took their time, however, in following up their victory, and encamped for a while near the Mngeni River to recoup and perform the necessary rituals of purification. So it was not until 24 April that they swept down on Port Natal from the Berea Heights above the settlement. Panic and lamentations had engulfed the place for days, but providentially the brig *Comet* was anchored in the bay. The white settlers and their families were able to take refuge on board on 17 April, but their black adherents were left to face the Zulu as best they could.

For nine days the Zulu occupied Port Natal and comprehensively sacked it. They set fire to the buildings and huts, killed any fugitives they found hiding in the bush, slaughtered domestic animals such as dogs, cats and fowls, destroyed household furniture, books and clothing – anything, in fact, that had belonged to the whites. At night they danced and celebrated to the light of the burning settlement, some dressed derisively in looted clothing, while the horrified settlers looked on helplessly (but safely) from the *Comet*. The Zulu sometimes approached the shore near the ship and shouted to those on board that Dingane intended to kill all the whites living in his domain, Boer and Briton alike. When they at last withdrew, driving away the useful livestock and carrying anything of value to them, like calico cloth, there was nothing left of Port Natal but debris and the walls of some of the houses. One at least of Dingane's endemic difficulties seemed to have been eliminated, but the permanence of its removal was only illusory.

In August Dingane's *amabutho*, encouraged by their April successes against the Voortrekkers and Port Natal, took the offensive in a second campaign aimed at completing their destruction of the emigrants.[7] Under the command of Ndlela, about 10 000 of the older, more experienced *amabutho* left uMgungundlovu on about 10 August, crossed the Mzinyathi and marched towards the Bushman's River. Because the Voortrekkers were in great fear of being caught unawares again, they had decided to institute larger and better defended laagers. A number of parties had come together in a laager on a low ridge in the valley of the Bushman's River, called the Gatsrand, some eight kilometres west of the present town of Estcourt. Hans Dons de Lange and J. Potgieter were recognised as the leaders.

The Gatsrand laager was shaped in a rough triangle because of the dictates of the lie of the ridge, and consisted of a double line of 290 wagons, lashed together with thorn-bushes filling all openings. A 75 mm black iron cannon was sited at the north-western apex of the laager, but was sufficiently light to be easily repositioned on its two wheels. There was a generally good field of fire, but dongas to the east and west of the position offered cover to assailants. Because the Voortrekkers had dug pits, or *trous-de-loup* as they are called in the technical language of siege-craft, in which to entrap an enemy crossing the river on the south-eastern side of the laager, the Zulu would call the coming battle emaGebeni, or Place of the Pits.

The Zulu were unable to take the laager by surprise, as they had hoped to do, because on 13 August some of Potgieter's herdboys caught sight of Zulu scouts in the close vicinity. Potgieter and De Lange immediately led out a patrol, sighted the advancing Zulu force, and galloped back to the laager to give the warning. At about 10 a.m. the Zulu came in sight of the laager, and halted to deploy out of column into their traditional attacking formation. The Bushman's River was in flood, so while one division forded the river below the laager, the greater part came direct from the east and swung around to the west, cutting the Boers off from any possible retreat. Thus the Zulu soon had the laager entirely encircled. Those in the leading ranks wore items of clothing taken from the Voortrekkers in earlier engagements. They came on in waves, probing one point of the defences after another. As soon as the front line was exhausted it fell back, immediately to be replaced by another.

Conditions in the laager were difficult. The large number of anxious women and children, many of them widows and orphans, took cover in a spear-proof shelter constructed of wagons and boards in the middle of the laager. Some of the more intrepid women, however, stayed out in the open to deal out powder and bullets to the mere seventy-five fighting men who had to move position repeatedly to reinforce different sectors of the perimeter as they came under attack. The Voortrekkers carried no standard weapons, but most would have been armed with muzzle-loading muskets. If charged with sufficient powder they had a range of 200 metres, but they were tolerably accurate only up to about 80 metres. The rate of fire was slow, even in practised hands, being no more than two to four shots a minute. But the Voortrekkers fired and loaded in rotation, so that there was always a constant wall of fire. Consequently, the Zulu could not find a vulnerable spot and, subdued by the persistent and telling fire, began to falter at about midday. De Lange decided this was the moment to make a mounted sally, and the Zulu withdrew out of range to dead ground downstream, where they encamped for the night. The Voortrekkers' livestock, which had been left grazing in the veld round about, were at the mercy of the Zulu, who that evening made a great feast of some of them, both to satisfy their hunger and to taunt their anguished owners.

Early on the morning of 14 August De Lange made a mounted sortie, and then fell back, drawing the Zulu into the laager's zone of fire. The Zulu again retreated under the unremitting fusillade, having failed to set the wagons alight with burning grass plaited around the spears which they cast. The impregnable wall of wagons was not to be broken. While their futile assault was under way, other parties of Zulu were more productively engaged in rounding up all the emigrants' livestock. These they drove east over the hills into Zululand, having set the long grass on fire behind them. That night the defenders again stood to arms, lit by the burning veld and the lanterns bound to whipsticks all around the laager.

On the third day the Zulu made no real attempt to storm the laager, and gave up the enterprise. They performed a war-song and withdrew, harried by the Voortrekkers who rode out to pursue them. But the latter's horses were so thin and weak from being kept inside the laager without fodder, and were so few besides, that the chase could not be kept up for long. So the Zulu were able to retire unscathed with most of the Trekkers' livestock, leaving the wagons stranded, just as the Ndebele had done at the battle of Vegkop in 1836.

The lessons of this battle were many. The Veglaer, as it became known to the Boers, had succeeded as spectacularly as the Vlugkommando had failed. The laager, the all-round defensive position, was clearly the key to military success. On this occasion the Zulu had carried the few guns they had captured in previous engagements, but they so lacked training in their use that they failed to hit a single person, despite keeping up a constant fire. Only one Boer, Hans Froneman, who was caught out of camp tending his sheep, was cut off and speared in the pool where he had tried to hide. The Zulu, moreover, had failed over three days to find a means of breaching the laager, and had retired baffled. This failure caused them once more to abandon the initiative, and to wait on the emigrants to make a move.

During the cold winter of 1838 disease and hopelessness continued to strike at the Voortrekkers, still crowded together in their laagers, which were now concentrated together and strengthened with deep earthworks, so they became veritable forts. On 23 September the Trekkers lost another leader when Gert Maritz died. Now, of all the principal Natal leaders, only Carel Landman, the Chief Commandant, was left. The Trekkers were short of food, ridden with illness and suffering from low morale. In their plight they turned to Andries Pretorius, whom a deputation approached for help in August 1838.

Pretorius was a gifted organiser and an experienced commando leader from the Graaff-Reinet District, where he was born in 1798. In 1837 he had made a reconnaissance of the regions occupied by the emigrants, and had taken part in the fighting against the Ndebele. He had then returned home and organised a trek of his friends and relations to Natal. So when Pretorius arrived in Natal on 22 November with sixty mounted men and a small ship's cannon, ahead of his party of trek wagons, he already enjoyed a considerable reputation. The Natal emigrants accordingly elected him their Chief Commandant on 26 November at Sooilaer (Sod Laager), which the veterans of the battle of Veglaer had formed across the Little Thukela from Gert Maritz's laager.

Pretorius, adept at irregular frontier warfare and a prudent if personally gallant commander, began immediately to make preparations for a counter-attack against the Zulu. In his planning he took full account of the lessons of both the disaster at eThaleni and the victory at Veglaer. It was clear to him that to seek out the Zulu on their own ground with only a mounted commando was too dangerous. He therefore decided to advance with sixty-four wagons, carrying only supplies and ammunition, which could be drawn up into the proven defensive formation should the Zulu attack. The horsemen of the commando would be used for scouting, to defend the laager and to follow up any victory.

Pretorius planned the punitive expedition with great thoroughness. He concentrated on developing obedience and alertness among the undisciplined and disheartened men he commanded. A proper chain of command was established, officers were kept informed of his plans, insubordination was punished, sentries were posted, scouting parties sent out and a laager formed every evening when the commando halted. Above all, Pretorius exhorted and inspired his men. Religious services were held every morning and evening, and in true Calvinist style they were encouraged to believe that they were the chosen servants of the Lord in a just and holy cause. The related idea of a covenant vow, the purpose of which was to strengthen the commando spiritually, originated with Pretorius and Sarel Cilliers (a veteran of Vegkop acting as chaplain to the commando). The covenant was made on 9 December at Danskraal on the banks of the present Wasbankspruit, and was subsequently repeated every evening:

Here we stand
Before the Holy God of heaven and earth
To make him a vow that
If He will protect us
And deliver our enemies into our hands,
We will observe the day and date each year
As a day of thanks, like a sabbath,
And that we will erect a church in His honour
Wherever He may choose
And that we will also tell our children
To join with us in commemorating this day,
Also for coming generations.
For His name will be glorified
By giving Him
All the honour and glory of victory.

The *Wenkommando* (Winning Commando), as it would soon be known, advanced by way of what are now the towns of Winterton, Ladysmith and Dundee, and reached the west bank of the Ncome River on 15 December.[8] The Zulu were naturally fully informed by their scouts of the progress of the commando. Dingane had time to mobilise his army of between 12 000 and 16 000 men, ritually prepare it for war, and send it out to confront the invaders before they had penetrated too close to the heart of the kingdom. The command was entrusted to no less than Ndlela and Nzobo, for the king fully comprehended the gravity of the threat and the need to throw in every resource to stem it.

Voortrekker patrols first made contact with the Zulu army east of the Ncome River where it was bivouacked in two rocky ravines of a mountain. Pretorius (or Potolozi, as the Zulu called him) himself went forward to assess the situation and, despite the urging of some of the more hot-headed commandants, refused to attack that day. It was already afternoon, the country was broken, and the fate of the Vlugkommando, which had gone heedlessly into the attack in similar circumstances, was doubtless present in his mind. So Pretorius firmly decided to stick to pre-planned tactics, and ordered the construction of a laager.

The sixty-four wagons were formed up on a spit of land near the west bank of the Ncome. There they were protected from an attack from the east by the river, which had formed a long, deep reach (or 'sea-cow hole') which could not easily be crossed, and from the south by a deep donga with banks some four metres high. This meant, effectively, that the laager could only be attacked from the north and west, which would allow the defenders to concentrate their resources. Normally, as at Veglaer, branches from thorn trees would have been dragged between and under the wagons to close any gaps. But since Pretorius had known that he would be advancing through the open veld, he had had hurdles (*veghekke*, or fighting gates) made in anticipation to replace the thorns, and ox-skins prepared to stretch over the wheels. Since a dawn attack was anticipated, Pretorius had lanterns hung from whipsticks placed in the gaps between the tops of the wagons to make the loading of the muskets easier in the poor early morning light. The force defending the laager consisted of Pretorius in command, his deputy, Carel Landman, 6 commandants, 464 Voortrekkers and 3 settlers from Port Natal. One of the latter, Alexander Biggar, had about 120 Port Natal blacks with him. It would seem that these were also armed with muskets, and probably helped with the defence. Besides these combatants, the laager was crammed with other personnel and animals which, after the heavy stock losses at Veglaer, could hardly be left outside to be driven off by the Zulu. But the number of animals, probably about 700 oxen for drawing the wagons and 750 horses (most of the mounted men would have had two horses each), constituted a real threat. If left unattended they would have stampeded during the fighting and dangerously dislocated the defence. That is why it seems that the 130 or so wagon drivers and leaders tied their teams of oxen forehead to forehead and pegged them to the ground with *rieme* (oxhide thongs), and talked soothingly to them throughout the battle. Similarly, the approximately 200 grooms with the commando held the terrified horses in fours until they were required for the pursuit.

The defenders knew they should man the gaps between each wagon with about eight men, firing in ordered rotation to keep up a constant and uninterrupted rate of fire. Pretorius supplied them with small leather cartridges of buckshot (*loopers*) which would burst at about forty metres with the devastating effect of a shotgun blast. He also had three muzzle-loading cannon to deploy: his own ship's gun with a range of several thousand metres, and two smaller guns, each with a range of about 300 metres. They too fired grapeshot and variety of small, hard projectiles such as stones or metal potlegs.

Once the laager had been formed, the Voortrekkers held evening service and renewed the Vow. The lanterns were lit, the *veghekke* pulled to and the guards posted. The night was misty and without a moon. The Zulu advance parties, with superstitious dread, heard the eerie singing of psalms, while it is said that the main army looked on the distant circle of light with foreboding, convinced that they were being called upon to attack an unearthly army of spirits.

The Zulu moved into the attack on the morning of Sunday, 16 December, from the south-east. There appeared to be some disorder among the *amabutho* as they deployed with their left horn considerably in advance of the chest and right. The reason for this disjuncture could well be put down to traditional tactics, for it was the objective of one wing rapidly to surround the enemy and cut off any possibility of their retreat while the rest of the army moved up to engage them. And indeed, the Zulu left was made up of the younger, fleeter *amabutho* like the uDlambedlu. But young *amabutho*, avid for glory, were notoriously difficult to control, and it could well be that the left horn surged out well before dawn in disregard of plans for a more co-ordinated attack. Some 3 000 strong, they stealthily crossed the Ncome below the laager and circled around it well to the west. The defenders could hear the shuffle of their feet, and the experienced Port Natal contingent warned of an imminent attack. Once they had reached the open plain to the north-west of the laager, the left horn quietly sat down some 160 metres away, neatly formed up by *ibutho* in a semicircle 100 metres deep, to await the dawn.

When the early morning mists began to rise at about 6.30, and the Voortrekkers first caught sight of the Zulus' menacing presence, they nearly lost their nerve. They had little time for reflection, however, for the Zulu left sprang suddenly to their feet, rattled the hafts of their spears on their raised shields, whistled, shouted their war cry, and stormed up at a run. Fortunately for the defenders, the day dawned clear and their powder remained dry. The *loopers* fired from the muskets and the grape from the cannons did terrible execution at short range – sometimes no more than ten paces – gouging holes in the tightly packed Zulu ranks as they converged on the laager. There was no wind, and the north-western side of the laager was soon completely enveloped in thick black smoke, rising straight up in the air, from the exploding gunpowder.

Despite terrible losses, the Zulu repeatedly attempted to press home their assault. So rapidly did the defenders have to fire that they had no time even to ram their charges home down the barrels of their muskets. The *amabutho*, realising to their dismay that they could find no gap in the wall of deadly fire, at length no longer heeded their commander's orders to charge. Instead, they withdrew out of range and began to manoeuvre in a vain attempt to find a less well-defended sector. Losing their nerve under the unremitting hail of fire, many began to take cover in the deep donga to the south of the laager. Pretorius, seeing them bunched up there and clearly demoralised (for they were lying under their shields), ordered a mounted sally to drive them out. The Zulu left were no longer in any mood to withstand this counter-attack, and they broke and ran, hotly pursued by the mounted Voortrekkers. Some fled towards the drift across the Ncome, while others broke off in the opposite direction, where a hill, lying to the south-west of the laager and later named Vegkop by the Boers, offered some illusory sanctuary. The Boers called off their pursuit at about 8 a.m., by which time some 500 Zulu lay dead on the plain and in the donga.

The Voortrekkers had no respite, however, for the main body of the Zulu army was now advancing to the attack. The umKhulutshane and iziGulutshane *amabutho* of the right horn (who were in the prime of life), streamed forward somewhat in advance of the older but more experienced uDlangezwa and iziNyosi of the chest. The uKhokhothi, a young *ibutho* carrying only knobbed sticks, was kept back in reserve east of the Ncome, to be thrown in only if the attack was a success. When the chest reached the Shogane, a low range of hills about one and a half kilometres south-east of the laager across the Ncome, it formed up on the lower slopes, while the commanders took up position on a conical hill at the northern extremity of the range. The right horn, meanwhile, continued its advance across the open plain towards the laager. Until close by the river it was protected from Voortrekker fire by the dead ground. Realising this, Pretorius despatched mounted horsemen to line the banks of the river. They opened up a withering fire and deflected the Zulu right from their intention of crossing the Ncome just to the north-east of the laager. Meanwhile, cannon-fire from the laager found the Zulu commanders on their hill and caused them to scatter after sustaining casualties.

Prevented from flanking the laager from the north-east, the right horn veered south to cross the Ncome by the same drift as the left horn earlier. The chest followed the right horn across at the same place. This change of direction meant the Zulu were unable to employ their usual tactics and attack the laager from several directions at once. Instead, the younger *amabutho* of the right horn rushed at the north-west side of the laager between the donga and the river, while the less impetuous older *amabutho* of the chest moved up in support. Now began the most crucial stage of the battle. The right horn made repeated and determined onslaughts, but were mown down like the left horn earlier in the day by the concentrated musket and cannon fire. As their attack faltered, the older *amabutho* behind began to taunt their young rivals, and to make attempts to break through their ranks in order to come to grips with the Voortrekkers themselves. Fighting even broke out between elements of the disorganised right and the impatient men of the centre. Such unruly behaviour only increased the confusion and packed the Zulu even tighter, making them a better target than ever. Sensing victory, the Boers tried to goad the Zulu into coming on again into the deadly zone of fire. But as discipline and cohesion began to evaporate, the Zulu assault broke down in futility, and at about 11 a.m. some units began to withdraw in confusion.

This was the moment for which Pretorius had been waiting. With a mounted force of about 160 men he sallied out in small groups of 5 or 6 and struck the Zulu (as they recalled) like a swarm of bees, breaking their army in two. Some warriors were driven towards the river, where, to avoid their relentless pursuers, they hid among the rushes or plunged into the deeper water of the sea-cow hole. There, like veritable hippopotamuses, they remained submerged except for their noses. Their relentless pursuers soon discovered the subterfuge, and carefully searched the river, making a sport of picking off their helpless prey. Soon the semi-stagnant river looked like a pool of blood. Henceforth the victorious Voortrekkers would know the stream as the Bloed, or Blood, River.

Perhaps 1 000 Zulu gave up their lives in the blood-stained waters. Others from the routed army fled – as had the left horn earlier – to Vegkop or the drift. The fugitives tried to hide themselves in antbear holes, in dongas and under the heaps of bodies to be found everywhere. But the Boers fired even at supposed corpses to make doubly sure. Soon, as Charl Cellier expressed it in his homely simile, the Zulu dead 'lay on the ground like pumpkins on a rich soil that had borne a large crop'.[9] The commando was relentless in its pursuit which continued east across the Ncome until the horses were too exhausted to go on. Over 1 000 Zulu more died in the plain of bones, as the Zulu called it afterwards. In all, the Zulu dead numbered more than 3 000, according to the Boer body-count, excluding those wounded who got away but would subsequently have died. Lunguza, a member of the uKhokhothi *ibutho*, remembered how over thirty elders of the Thembu people alone surrendered their lives in the battle. The only losses the Voortrekkers sustained were three men wounded. One of these was Pretorius himself, who was stabbed through the left hand during the pursuit.

After a thanksgiving service for their great and astonishing victory against over-whelming odds, which had left the *Wenkommando* miraculously whole, Pretorius sent out another commander to follow up the flying Zulu. But their enemies had scattered and fled, and for the moment there was no organised force left to oppose the commando's advance.

The Covenant and the battle of Blood River still arouse strong emotions in many Afrikaners, for they see in them God's hand and the justification for their sub-jugation of the black people. The battle has been remembered more prosaically by the Zulu as one in which they suffered a severe, though not terminal, defeat. Yet, however it may be viewed, the battle was undoubtedly a classic exemplar of the devastating superiority of controlled fire by resolute men from an all-round defensive position over warriors armed with spears, whatever their numerical superiority and courage. It was also a lesson in the fatal dangers of insubordi-nation and unconcerted strategy, a text, unfortunately for the Zulu, which they were never to learn. For at the battle of Khambula in 1879, which was to prove the crucial turning-point of the Anglo-Zulu War, an identically uncoordinated attack on a fortified position would permit the British to deal with the Zulu horns and chest in detail. Indeed, though some forty years separated the two bat-tles, they followed precisely the same pattern, the only difference being the improved firepower of the whites.

The defeat at Blood River and the dispersal of their army temporarily crippled Zulu ability to carry on the war. They were unable to offer any resistance to the forced march of the *Wenkommando*, by which it reached uMgungundlovu on 20 December. The Voortrekkers could be forgiven for believing the victory to be com-plete. No force opposed them, and Dingane's capital lay at their feet. But it was already in flames, and not theirs to do with as they pleased. Before he withdrew out of range of the *Wenkommando* across the White Mfolozi, Dingane ordered uMgungundlovu and two neighbouring *amakhanda* set on fire, and dismally watched the conflagration from the hills across the Mahlabathini plain.[10] But he had not entirely succeeded in denying the Boers the satisfaction of looting his principal *amakhanda*. The victors held an auction at uMgungundlovu of elephant tusks, beads and other valuable items they had come across poking among the half-burnt ruins. Pretorius himself bought a handsome silver goblet, fit for a king.

On the following day, 21 December, the members of the Wenkommando found the mortal remains of Retief and his party, lying exposed to the sky on the slopes of kwaMatiwane. It was a harrowing moment, in which grief and rage were intermingled. Fathers, brothers, friends were identified by means of the frag-ments of cloth, such as Retief's glossy waistcoat, still adhering to the poor bones. In a leather shooting-bag belonging to Retief the searchers purported to find the document signed by Dingane on 4 February 1837 ceding Natal to the Voor-trekkers. It was in a remarkable (if not miraculous) state of preservation, con-sidering that the other papers with it were in a deplorable condition. The Voortrekkers based their legal claim to Natal on this document, but its status can-not be other than problematical, if not entirely spurious. True, Andries Pretorius, Carel Landman and three others vouched for its authenticity under oath, and a tracing was made of it in about 1891 and the facsimile lithographed. But the original disappeared in 1900 during the Second Anglo-Boer War, allegedly out of the trunk in which it was stored when it fell into British hands. Two further copies have indeed been preserved, but the original can never now be verified. Not, in a sense, that this even matters, for Dingane clearly held no store by the paper he signed and the Voortrekker claim to Natal has long since lapsed.[11]

Pretorius's men collected all the bones of Retief and his party which they could find and buried them in a mass grave at the base of kwaMatiwane. The Zulu, however, have long insisted that, after they were killed, the bodies of Retief and his companions were secretly dragged 200 paces north-east of kwaMatiwane, thrown in a heap into a donga and then covered over with earth and stones. The corpses of their servants, however, were left lying in the open near kwaMatiwane, and it was the remains of these, they say, which Pretorius interred. In 1956 an attempt was made to verify the Zulu account, but no bones could be found in the donga, and the matter must remain unresolved.[12]

One of the objectives of the Wenkommando's punitive expedition was to recover the thousands of cattle and other livestock captured from the Voortrekkers by Dingane's men. It was almost to lure Pretorius's men to disaster, just when they thought there was no more to be feared from the defeated Zulu.[13] On Christmas day, near by their camp at uMgungundlovu, the Boers seized an apparent spy. His name was Bhongoza kaMefu of the Ngongoma people, and he had his home near the Mzinyathi River. No commoner in the Zulu kingdom has attained such fame as he. For Bhongoza was a decoy, and he played his part to perfection. With every sign of mortal terror, he blurted out a plausible tale to the effect that Dingane had left his cattle behind in the valley of the White Mfolozi in the hope that the Boers would be content with capturing them, and give up their pursuit of the king. Some members of the commando disbelieved this likely tale, but the majority were duped, and Bhongoza allowed himself to be induced to show them the place so that they could fetch away the cattle they so desired.

On 26 December the Boers moved their camp to the Mthonjaneni heights, which disclosed a breathtaking view of the valley of the White Mfolozi below. The next day Bhongoza, mounted on a spare horse and secured by a rope halter, guided about 300 mounted Boers under Carel Landman (who took over the command from Pretorius, who was in pain from the wound in his hand), as well as some 70 Port Natal blacks on foot under Alexander Biggar, towards the edge of the heights. At the eastern brow a small body of Zulu fell back on being fired at, confirming Bhongoza's prediction that the Zulu would no longer stand and fight. Looking down over the side of Mthonjaneni, the commando saw forms moving far below which they mistook for cattle. In fact, they were Zulu with shields on their backs, creeping among the rocks and bushes. Quite fooled by this stratagem, the commando descended a steep path along the narrow back of a spur, and reached the floor of the valley close to where the uPhathe stream flows into the White Mfolozi through a rocky gorge. Stunted mimosa trees and aloes dotted the rocky slopes, unnervingly resembling human sentinels. Only once they had entered the kloof, however, did the Boers fully recognise the peril into which they had been lured. And indeed, on a sharp, rocky, bush-covered hill to their right sat a look-out called Xwana, waiting to give the signal. In high-pitched clear tones that carried for a great distance, he suddenly called out that the enemy was enclosed. The trap was sprung, and from all sides the *amabutho* emerged from among the rocks and advanced. Bhongoza, his heroic task complete, took advantage of the confusion to slip his halter and escape.

Carel Landman was in command of the commando, but the man who saved it was Hans Dons de Lange. Hemmed in on all sides, Landman suggested standing back-to-back and fighting it out. But De Lange saw that they must fight their way out of the trap since they had insufficient ammunition for a prolonged stand. Because it was hardly practicable to scramble back up the mountain, the only way lay forward to the level ground where the horsemen could manoeuvre, away from their camp on the heights above. The going was at first extremely difficult, being strewn with jagged rocks, overgrown with thorns and aloes and cut by many steep dongas. It was hardly country the commando could gallop over, which suggests that the Zulu surging about them on their flanks and to their front were cautiously keeping their distance. In any event, led by De Lange, the commando eventually extended line and broke clean through the Zulu.

The relieved men crossed the White Mfolozi and reached the open ground on the opposite bank without suffering any losses. Thereafter they could keep better order and adopt their customary tactics of alternately firing and retiring. In this fashion they fell back across the Mahlabathini plain towards the west, arriving again at the White Mfolozi where the Mkhumbane stream flows into it from out of the emaKhosini valley. There, the young uDlambedlu *ibutho*, who had been following the Trekkers' movements from the south bank, were waiting for them in the narrow bed of the stream and among the crags on either side. Four Boers died in the ambush; so too did Alexander Biggar, who refused to abandon his toiling group of horseless retainers, most of whom were cut off and killed. Once over that treacherous crossing, the commando was pursued for a further twenty-four kilometres through difficult terrain in the overwhelming heat of a summer's day. The uDlambedlu at last gave up the chase, and the exhausted and demoralised horsemen regained their camp. They had probably covered sixty kilometres since setting out over five hours before. In recompense for their fright and humiliating withdrawal, they put about that they had killed 1 000 Zulu, an obviously outrageously inflated figure.

The next day the chastened commando went for safer, but dramatic, effects and burned three great *amakhanda* in the emaKhosini. On New Year's day, 1839, it at last captured some of the livestock that had been eluding it. A far-flung raid netted 5 000 head of cattle and 1 500 sheep. This was far, far short of the numbers the commando had hoped to take, but it had to do. The horses were too out of condition to attempt any further raids or aggressive action of any sort, while the Zulu were making sure that they and their herds stayed out of reach. So on 2 January 1839 the commando retired unmolested the way it had come.

Interestingly, Boer and Zulu accounts of the Wenkommando's withdrawal differ sharply. The Voortrekkers recorded that they had remained in their camp on

Mthonjaneni, sending out patrols in the hope of drawing the Zulu on to attack it. According to them, they then retired deliberately slowly over the Mzinyathi with the intention of enticing the shadowing Zulu into a final battle which would end the war. The Zulu insisted, on the other hand, that so precipitate was the Wenkommando's retreat after the affair at the White Mfolozi that the pursuing Zulu found it impossible to overtake it, try as they might.

It is true that the commando did arrive back at the Sooilaer on the Little Thukela on 8 January, which shows that it had hardly dallied on the way home. But this was hardly a helter-skelter flight. Thus, the Zulu version of events must be dismissed as an attempt to give the false impression that the Voortrekker invasion had been successfully repelled. Nevertheless, extensive Zulu casualties and their temporarily damaged morale must not be allowed to obscure the fact that the Voortrekkers had in fact failed to break Dingane's power or conquer his kingdom. Their punitive expedition had been just that, and had done no more than deliver the Zulu king a crushing lesson while slaking their desire for vengeance. What the Voortrekker's great victory at Blood River did mean, however, was that they were no longer on the defensive as they had been since Retief's death. Henceforth, they would be able confidently to negotiate their future in the lands east of the Drakensberg from a position of undoubted strength.

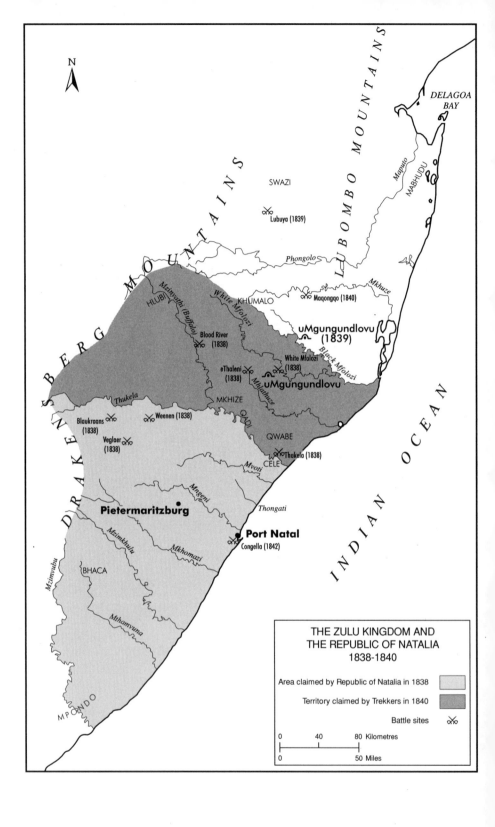

N

DELAGOA
BAY

SWAZI

✂ Lubuya (1839)

Phongolo

Maputo

MABHUDU

LUBOMBO MOUNTAINS

Mkhuze

HLUBI

Mzinyathi (Buffalo)

White Mfolozi

KHUMALO

✂ Maqongqo (1840)

MOUNTAINS

BERG

Blood River
(1838) ✂

eThaleni
(1838) ✂

White Mfolozi
(1838) ✂

uMgungundlovu
(1839)

Black Mfolozi

uMgungundlovu

Mhlathuze

Thukela

MKHIZE

QADI

Blaukraans ✂
(1838)

✂ Weenen (1838)

Veglaer
(1838) ✂

QWABE

✂ Thukela (1838)

CELE

Mvoti

DRAKENSBERG

Pietermaritzburg ●

Mngeni

Thongati

Mzimkhulu

●**Port Natal**

✂ Congella (1842)

INDIAN OCEAN

Mkhomazi

BHACA

Mzimvubu

Mthamvuna

MPONDO

THE ZULU KINGDOM AND
THE REPUBLIC OF NATALIA
1838-1840

Area claimed by Republic of Natalia in 1838

Territory claimed by Trekkers in 1840

Battle sites ✂

| 0 | 40 | 80 Kilometres |

| 0 | | 50 Miles |

9

The Maqongqo Hills

The battle of Blood River no more destroyed Dingane's power than the battle of
Mosega did that of Mzilikazi. Like the Ndebele king, Dingane had suffered a severe, but not irremediable, setback at the hands of the Boers. Though battered,
royal authority and the Zulu army were still intact, and the Boers were hardly
in a military position to press home their advantage. It was consequently still possible for Dingane to contain the damage through negotiation and the cession of
territory. Besides, the option theoretically existed of relocating the focus of Zulu
power further north should the Boers prove impossible neigbours. Mzilikazi,
after all, was to put sufficient distance between himself and the white interlopers when he set up a new and stable kingdom north of the Limpopo. Yet, in the
end, what was to pull Dingane down was not so much the machinations of external foes like the Boers and Swazi, as the civil war ignited by the flight of his
brother Mpande.

The Zulu might claim after the rapid Boer withdrawal across the Thukela following the battle of the White Mfolozi on 27 December 1838 that they had repelled the Boer invaders. But they could not disguise the extent of the blows they
had suffered earlier. Dingane did not return to the emaKhosini and the Mkhumbane stream, which he so loved, to rebuild uMgungundlovu.[1] Instead, he
tarried for a while in the Mahlabathini plain, twenty-four kilometres north
across the White Mfolozi, where he was still supplied with the sweet water
drawn from the lovely spring on the Mthonjaneni heights. He then removed north-
east to the valley of the Hluhluwe River, where he began rebuilding a smaller
uMgungundlovu in the country of the Mdletshe chiefdom. But malaria was
prevalent in this low-lying countryside of dense valley bushveld, and Dingane
moved the site of the new uMgungundlovu inland to higher, more healthy
ground, just south of where the Vuna stream twists westward before flowing into
the Black Mfolozi, some thirteen kilometres from the present town of Nongoma.
From this region, which once had been the Ndwandwe heartland, Dingane set
about reconfirming his authority and building up his army.

The Boers, meanwhile, were attempting to consolidate the position they had
won. They had begun to spread out between the Mzinyathi and Thukela rivers
to the north, and the Mzimkhulu to the south, carving out enormous farms wherever good pasture and perennial water were to be had. By October 1838 a town-

ship had been laid out on the banks of the Msunduze River, in the centre of the area the Boers occupied, to function as their seat of government. It was named Pietermaritzburg in honour of Piet Retief and Gert Maritz.[2] The Boers also established their own village of Congella, westwards round the bay from the wreckage of Port Natal, to challenge the traders' settlement.

Some form of government was necessary for the fledgling state they were creating, and the key institution adopted was an elected Volksraad of twenty-four men with executive and legislative powers. But 'scarcely two' of the members of the Volksraad could agree upon any matter.[3] Debilitating in any circumstances, such lack of accord was particularly serious since the Boers were not in any case entirely free to arrange matters to their own liking. They were still technically British subjects and, though the British response to the Great Trek had been vacillating and half-hearted, the Boers' own actions were soon responsible for a firmer British line. The wars between the emigrants and the Ndebele and Zulu activated the evangelical lobby in Britain, which feared the Boers would annihilate and enslave the blacks, while the Cape authorities were concerned that turmoil in the interior would rebound on the frontiers of the Cape Colony.

Sir George Napier, Governor of the Cape, was consequently persuaded that he must assert his authority over the Boers and check their mischievous proceedings. On 4 December 1838 a detachment of a hundred British soldiers (men of the 72nd Highlanders and the Royal Artillery), under the command of Major Samuel Charters, occupied Port Natal and declared martial law. Charters's orders were to prevent any further 'hostile aggression' by the Boers of the sort that had recently led to 'the slaughter of the Zulus and the unwarranted invasion of their country'.[4]

In keeping with his instructions, Charters sent to the Boer camp at the Thukela on 6 December, warning Andries Pretorius not to proceed with the campaign that was to culminate in the battle of Blood River. But the commando had already left and, in any case, the Boers did not admit the right of the British government to interfere with their proceedings. Yet, despite the potential for conflict between the Boers and the British detachment at the Port, affairs between the two parties were conducted most amicably. Charters left Natal on 7 February 1839, and the extraordinarily tactful Captain Henry Jervis remained in command. Though his authority was not accepted by the Boers, his presence was at least tolerated, and his good offices welcomed. Understanding (so far as the incoherent orders of the Colonial Office permitted) that the purpose of his mission was to facilitate negotiations for a lasting treaty between the emigrants and the Zulu, he immediately set about achieving that objective.

Dingane's possible reaction to negotiations had already been informally sounded by Theophilus Shepstone, the son of an 1820 settler turned Wesleyan missionary in the Cape, who had accompanied Charters's force to Port Natal. The thrusting young Shepstone had acquired a mastery of the Xhosa language on the mission stations where he had been reared, which permitted him to make himself understood in Zulu; he also had experience as interpreter for Sir Benjamin D'Urban during the frontier war of 1835.[5] He was to return to Natal in 1845, when his growing influence was to have the profoundest effect on the future of the Zulu people. Now, in February 1839, his report indicated that Dingane's situation was such that he was willing to treat.[6]

The Boers were equally anxious to make peace, but Dingane's invariable execution of their messengers was provoking many into advocating a fresh campaign to compel him to reach a settlement. To stave off this threat, Jervis despatched fresh peace messages through Henry Ogle, a leading figure among the Port Natal traders and personally well known to Dingane. The British requested to negotiate through Sothobe, familiar as Shaka's emissary and Dingane's chief official south of the Thukela.

Dingane did not see fit to send Sothobe to the Port, possibly because his loyalty was already in doubt, and instead despatched a trusted *inceku* called Gambusha. The king admitted through him that he was 'on the brink of ruin', and indicated his willingness to accept any terms the British might make for the Boers. However, it was clear from what else he had to say through Gambusha that he looked to the British to assist him in sending the Boers 'out of the country'. Never, he made it quite plain, would he be prepared to acknowledge their presence. Yet, without adequate means to dislodge the hated interlopers, Dingane had to be content with British assurances that no further Boer aggression would be permitted.

On 23 March, a month after he had returned to Dingane with the British response, Gambusha arrived back at the British camp at the Port with two chiefs, Gikwana and Gungwana, who had Dingane's full authority to negotiate on his behalf. The two chiefs brought with them in confirmation of their serious intentions about 300 horses the Zulu had captured from the Boers during the fighting of 1838. Jervis brokered a meeting between the Zulu envoys and Andries Pretorius, 'Chief Commandant of the Right Worshipful the Representative Assembly of the South African Society at Natal', and peace was concluded on 25 March 1839. The terms were that Dingane would restore all the arms, cattle, sheep and remaining horses taken from the Boers, and would allow them to live unmolested south of the Thukela River. In return, the Boers would assist the Zulu if they were attacked unjustly by another party. Loaded with presents of beads and snuff, the Zulu delegation returned home, leaving the Boers sceptical of Dingane's intention of fulfilling the terms of the treaty, but with no alternative but to hope for the best. As for the British government, they considered the object accomplished for which troops had been sent to Natal, and began considering arrangements for their withdrawal.[7]

During the months succeeding the conclusion of the treaty, neither Boer nor Zulu breached its terms. Dingane, though, fell short of full compliance in that he returned less than a hundred head of the 40 000 cattle the Boers claimed had been stolen from them. Even so, he tried to avoid an open breach through apparently earnest promises of an imminent handover of the missing cattle, and through *douceurs* like the delivery of 2 000 pounds of ivory to the rapacious Boers.[8] The truth was that his attention was focused elsewhere, and he wanted no inconvenient entanglements along the new Thukela frontier.

Apprehensive about the future of his kingdom in such uncomfortable proximity to the belligerent and land-greedy Boers (temporarily sated though they might be, and reined in by the British military presence), Dingane was seriously attempting to secure his future position by 'building two countries' through expansion across the Phongolo River into the southern parts of the Swazi domain. Dingane hoped that, if he succeeded in carving out a trans-Phongolo kingdom, he would be able to defy the Boers indefinitely, for even if he lost the rest of Zululand to their renewed aggression, he would still have his additional kingdom to sustain him.[9]

The Swazi campaign of the winter of 1839 was therefore no mere side-show: it was a full-scale attempt at conquest and occupation involving the full mobilisation of Dingane's remaining military resources. Its failure was to have devastating repercussions. As a first step in the proposed conquest of the new kingdom, Dingane dispatched four *amabutho* (the Mbelebele, uNomdayana, umKhulutshane and imVokwe) to clear the bush and establish an *ikhanda* called Mbelebele on the Nguthumeni Ridge, north of the sources of the Ngwavuma River. Their commander was Klwana kaNgqengelele of the Buthelezi, one of the most powerful and influential men in the northern part of the kingdom.

Sensing the gravity of this preliminary step of Zulu conquest, the Swazi did not retire as was their wont to their mountain fastnesses when threatened by the Zulu, but 'rose to a man' to drive out the invader. Under the leadership of Mngayi Fakudze, the Swazi forces met the Zulu in battle in the valley of the Lubuye stream. The battle of Lubuye is justly famed in the annals of Swazi tradition, for after a hard fight the Zulu were forced to withdraw, leaving two *amabutho* dead in the field behind them. Dingane was constrained to hurry two further *amabutho* north to sustain the foundering campaign, but continued Swazi resistance resulted in its being abandoned as a failure.[10]

This severe reverse at the hands of the Swazi, coming hard on the heels of his worsting by the Boers and the humiliating territorial concessions wrung out of him, did Dingane's authority as king inestimable damage. To compound matters, no northern bolt-hole had been opened up for him, and he would have in future to stand and die in Zululand. Immediately, though, an unanticipated consequence of his attempt to mobilise his subjects for the doomed Swazi campaign presented him with the greatest crisis of his reign, more damaging even in its implications than the threat of renewed Boer aggression.

In September 1839 Mpande, Dingane's half-brother, fled from Dingane across the Thukela with some 17 000 of his adherents and 25 000 cattle to seek the protection of the Boers. Forces loyal to Dingane, with orders to bring the people back, hotly pursued them over the border as far south as the Mvoti River, but fears of a confrontation with the Boers caused them to give up the attempt. The way was thus laid open for dynastic conflict within the Zulu royal house to combine with Boer ambitions to bring civil war and ruin upon Zululand. So fraught with repercussions was the event that it has always been known to the Zulu people as 'the breaking of the rope that held the nation together'.

Mpande has traditionally been dismissed as the obese, indolent, ineffectual and therefore unworthy successor of Shaka. Yet he lived and reigned with not inconsiderable success through a period of profound change and difficulty. To underestimate him, as have so many commentators in the past, is to disregard the real abilities of a shrewd and determined survivor; to understand him is to know something of the context in which he moved.

Mpande was born to Senzangakhona and Songiya between 1795 and 1798.[11] As a boy, he was sent to be reared by the Cele chief, Dibandlela, who ruled the coastal plain between the Thukela and Mdloti rivers, in order to foster good relations between the Zulu and the Cele, who were close allies of Dingiswayo, Senzangakhona's overlord. Mpande thus spent his childhood at Dibandlela's kwaGqikazi *umuzi* on the northern side of the Mdloti River, only a few kilometres from the sea. Like any other boy in Shaka's evolving kingdom, Mpande served as an *udibi*. In 1819 he became a member of the newly formed umGumanqa *ibutho*, stationed at the kwaKhangela *ikhanda*, which was ruled over by Nandi. KwaKhangela, which was a few kilometres south-east of the present-day town of Eshowe, was in the rich grazing country of Nqetho's Qwabe chiefdom. As a member of the umGumanqa *ibutho*, Mpande took part in various campaigns, and was rewarded by Shaka with at least two wives.

Mpande was in great danger following Shaka's assassination but, as we have seen, Dingane permitted him almost alone among his many brothers – and potential rivals – to live. The reason seems to have lain principally with the influential Ndlela, who did his best to protect and promote Mpande's interests with the king. Perhaps this support stemmed from political affiliation and developing bonds of lineage, for Ndlela's Ntuli chiefdom was built up in the territory abandoned by the Qwabe after their flight from Dingane, close to Mpande's *imizi* in the south-eastern corner of the kingdom between the Mlalazi and Thukela rivers. More importantly, Mpande had fathered sons, and it seems Ndlela persuaded Dingane that Mpande's legitimate offspring could alone guarantee the continuity of the royal line, for neither Shaka nor Dingane had married or sired acknowledged heirs.

For his own part, Mpande always made known his lack of kingly ambitions and sedulously attended to his royal brother's interests, always maintaining his loyal and unassuming demeanour. But, while he lived, Mpande could never be other than a potential threat to Dingane. As an *umntwana* or royal prince, he maintained an *isigodlo* and lived in regal and self-indulgent style while inevitably building up a following of his own in the south-east of the country. His adherents gradually increased further as the remnants of the Qwabe and Cele chiefdoms (both of which Dingane broke up) searched for a new chief to attach themselves to, for Mpande had strong ties with the people amongst whom he had grown up.

Naturally, Mpande knew he was as vulnerable as any of his royal brothers whom Dingane had put to death, so he did his best to build up useful alliances as insurance. Thus, he sent Cetshwayo, his son by Ngqumbazi, to be brought up by the influential Sothobe of the Sibiya chiefdom along the middle Thukela in order to create a firm personal and political bond of the sort that had been formed when he had been placed as a child among the Cele. In addition, he assiduously polished his confidential relations with Senzangakhona's wives, those formidable and influential matrons who continued to supervise *amakhanda* and the royal cattle. It is also clear that he forged significant contacts with Chief Maphitha kaSojiyisa of the Mandlakazi branch of the royal house.

Maphitha was the dominant force in north-eastern Zululand, the former country of the Ndwandwe, and ruled it for the king, even assuming the king's prerogative of placing *izinduna* on the land. He also had charge over the tributary chiefdoms around and beyond the Lubombo mountains. Indeed, these people never even assembled at the king's great place, but rather at Maphitha's, who might in turn transmit any matters of importance to Dingane.[12] This independent-minded northern baron was not inclined to accept much royal control, and Mpande would find it difficult in future when he was king to keep him in check. But while he was in his exposed position as putative crown prince, Maphitha was an ally of significant weight.

The extent to which Mpande and Dingane were secretly working against each other is unclear. There are reports that Dingane made an unsuccessful attempt on Mpande's life in 1832 and again in early 1838, for Mpande stood accused of doing his best to sabotage the 1837 campaign against the Swazi by withholding *amabutho* living in his domain until it was too late. Be that as it may, the fact remains that Dingane continued to permit Mpande to live in peace until the time of the failure of the Swazi campaign of 1839.

During mid-1839 Dingane summoned Mpande to furnish reinforcements to make up for losses at the hands of the Swazi and, in addition, to prepare to move north with all his people to help colonise the territories the king still hoped to conquer across the Phongolo.[13] Such a migration would have scattered Mpande's adherents and destroyed his power-base. He therefore stalled and temporised, and ceased paying Dingane the customary visits of respect. With the patent excuse that he was ill he stayed at home at his emLambongwenya homestead just north of the Thukela at Middle Drift. This behaviour inflamed Dingane's suspicions that his brother was conspiring to seize his throne, and he resolved to cut Mpande down before the putative plot matured. So he sent his supposedly sickly brother a gift of a hundred heifers which, according to the accepted rules of etiquette, should have compelled Mpande to visit the king to express his gratitude. Once safely in the king's hands, it would have been an easy matter to put him to death like Matiwane before him and many another. But the *izinduna* who drove the cattle to Mpande, Nxagwana kaZivalele and Mathunjana kaSibaca, were in Ndlela's service, and warned Mpande to be on his guard.[14]

Mpande urgently consulted with his *izinduna* and his mother, Songiya. They, despite their terror of Dingane, advised him that he had no choice but to flee for his life. So Mpande sent out messengers throughout southern Zululand, and they had little difficulty in persuading the people to cross over the Thukela and seek sanctuary among the Boers.[15] With their families and livestock they left their homes and went with the prince, whom they hailed as 'You who crossed all the rivers on the way to restoring yourself'.[16]

112

Those who accompanied Mpande in his flight consisted of most of the inhabitants of the country between the Mhlathuze and Thukela rivers and many
individuals of high lineage. One such was Manyosi kaDlengezele of the Mbatha people, a renowned praise-singer and notorious glutton with spindly legs and
an enormous stomach who 'could consume a calf as a python swallows a bush-
buck'. When people learned that even he was deserting Dingane to face an uncertain future, they laughed and said in reference to his great stomach: 'It will
subside, Manyosi!'[17]

The motives of Manyosi and his fellow refugees were mixed, however, for not
all were Mpande's loyal adherents, who would follow obediently where he led.
Many were those whom Dingane had ordered in the mid-1830s to evacuate the
coastal areas south of the Thukela when he attempted to stop the flow of refugees
to Port Natal. Such people wished simply to return to their ancestral homes and
to break free from Dingane's arbitrary and increasingly discredited rule. Certainly,
they had no wish to be resettled even further away from their familiar coastlands
to feed Dingane's Swazi ambitions. Others, besides these exploited coastal tributaries, were disenchanted with Dingane after his long string of defeats, and wished
to avoid further conflict with the Boers. Many more would have been aware that
simply by being Mpande's adherents they were guilty by association of the treason for which he stood accused, and were in real danger of being 'eaten up' unless they moved out of range of Dingane's retribution. It seems clear that Mpande
too had initially little other purpose but to secure his personal safety in flight,
though scope for his ambitions through a political and military alliance with the
Boers rapidly presented itself.

Once across the Thukela, Mpande and his host moved down along the coast
and encamped near the Thongati River within striking distance of Port Natal.[18]
Mpande then opened up communications with the Boers, professing his peaceful intentions. Accompanied by the experienced and travelled Sothobe, who
had joined him in his flight, and other prominent men of his party, he first met
Boer representatives on the south side of the hippopotamus-filled Mlazi River. It
must have been a strange encounter for the Zulu prince. The conference took place
in a wattle and daub hut. Mpande sat on a chair, while Sothobe and the other
izinduna knelt down in front of him, facing the Boers and leaning on their
sticks. A table was placed between them and Wessel Wessels, the principal Boer,
on which were arrayed plates, spoons, forks and knives. Young Dinya ka-
Zokozwayo, who remembered these details nearly fifty years later, interpreted for
them.

Since only the Volksraad could properly deal with such matters, Mpande
agreed to proceed to Pietermaritzburg to consult its members. He walked the whole
way there and back, though his belongings were carried in a wagon. An entourage
that included his young son, Cetshwayo, accompanied him.[19] Pietermaritzburg,
which was then only a stockaded camp with a collection of wattle and daub
shanties,[20] could not have impressed one used to the scale and order of great
amakhanda. At his meeting on 15 October with the Volksraad he requested only
that he be allowed to settle on the territory between the Mvoti and Mhlali rivers,

the southern half of the former Cele chiefdom and the home of his childhood. There he undertook to settle peacefully as a Boer subject, and to allow his heir to be educated by Christian missionaries.[21]

Yet, despite Mpande's pliable and unaggressive projection of himself, the Boers were overcome by the deepest suspicions. They knew little of Mpande except what he chose to tell them and, by crossing the Thukela, the prince had broken the terms of the March treaty with Dingane. The Boers understandably feared that what they were seeing was a ruse by which Dingane's army had gained entrance to their territory. Voices were raised at Congella, which stood in most immediate danger if such suspicions proved true, advocating a surprise preemptive attack on the so-called 'refugees' to hurl them back across the Thukela. The same did not apply to their great herds of cattle, for many Boers were as anxious to lay their hands on them as they were to secure their own safety. More temperate counsels eventually prevailed over the advocates of butchery and cattle theft. It was agreed that a deputation be sent to treat further with Mpande, despite the fearsome precedent of Retief's fate in similar circumstances, and the reservations of Captain Jervis, who did not want to see his developing good relations with Dingane jeopardised.

The Boer deputation of twenty-eight men under the elderly but resolute F. Roos, dressed as for hunting, set off on 21 October 1839 in thirteen wagons to beard Mpande in his hastily erected homestead, which had been built according to the pattern of a royal *ikhanda*.[22] Mpande received the Boers with all the panache of a royal prince, entertaining them with great exhibitions of dancing by his warriors and with extravagant feasting. Mpande's noble but easy bearing and obvious intelligence much impressed Delegorgue (who had accompanied the Boer delegation), and he admiringly described his shining, stout body, jutting brows, high, square forehead, generous mouth and firm, square chin. Yet what he noticed above all were Mpande's brilliant eyes, large and well-shaped, which shone 'like black diamonds'.[23] It was only in his later days that Mpande became so fat that he could not walk, and had to be taken to the assembly in his cart.[24] Even in his prime, though, Mpande had breasts, so stout was he. He had an ordinary voice and spoke fluently, keeping his speech measured and controlled even when angry and excited. What people particularly remembered about his appearance was his extreme fondness for ornaments, and the profusion and ostentation of his dress.[25]

On 27 October 1839, in a long tent erected for the occasion, the Boers struck an alliance with Mpande, whom they formally recognised in a ceremony as the 'Reigning Prince of the Emigrant Zulus'. The parties agreed upon a combined attack on Dingane, his overthrow, and the establishment of Mpande as king. For this assistance, Mpande undertook to pay the Boers the cattle still owed them by Dingane and to cede them the bay of St Lucia. In addition, he promised not to allow any military action against Zululand's neighbours without the prior consent of the Volksraad.

Before they left Mpande, the Boers witnessed an incident which filled them with horror. A great restless, swaying crowd, murmuring and shouting, coiled its way

114

to a particular spot where a man was being mauled and pushed from hand to hand as he was bludgeoned to death with fighting-sticks, the blue cotton cloth he was wearing fluttering among the heaving mass. The victim was Mpangazitha kaMncumbatha of the Ndwandwe, formerly an influential and notoriously blood-thirsty *induna* of Dingane's at uMgungundlovu, whom Mpande had just appointed as one of his own principal *izinduna*. His killing seems to have been an expression of popular feeling against Mpangazitha's unabated overbearing manner, and Mpande certainly denied any complicity.[26] But Mpangazitha's death must have filled him with concern, for it indicated that many of his followers considered him a weak ruler whose will could be flouted. To rule, Mpande would have to make his authority felt and shed his cultivated image of an indolent and complaisant prince.

Over the next few months Mpande kept in close touch with the Volksraad at Pietermaritzburg. But while the British troops were still at the Port, with their instructions to prevent further conflict between the Boers and Dingane, the Boers felt that the treaty with Mpande to overthrow Dingane could not be implemented. The Zulu king, meanwhile, had received the news of Mpande's defection with the greatest consternation.[27] He bitterly reproached Ndlela for advising him against killing Mpande while he had the chance, and for harbouring that venomous snake.[28] Yet he could do little except pin his hopes on British mediation, and attempt to discredit Mpande with the Boers in order to prevent their acting in concert against him. So he sent an envoy to the Volksraad who declared of Mpande:

He is not a man; he has turned away his face; he is a woman. He was useless to Dingaan his master, and he will be of no use to you. Do not trust him, for his face may turn again.[29]

The Boers were not persuaded. And although Captain Jervis felt the country still to be most unsettled and a clash imminent between Mpande and Dingane,[30] Sir George Napier was satisfied that the task of the small Port Natal garrison was done, and that it could be withdrawn. Jervis and his redcoats sailed away on the *Vectis* on Christmas Eve 1839, and the jubilant Boers fired a derisive salute, hoisting the diagonal red, white and blue flag of their Republic of Natalia.[31]

Freed (if only temporarily, as it turned out) from unwelcome British tutelage, they immediately decided to embark on their delayed joint campaign with Mpande against Dingane. To set their legalistic minds at rest, on 4 January 1840 the Boers repudiated their treaty of 25 March 1839 with Dingane on the grounds that he had failed to deliver the cattle stipulated. Having justified their intended aggression, the Boers opened the campaign on 14 January 1840. It was agreed that Mpande's army would advance on the new uMgungundlovu by way of the lower Thukela and the coastal route under the command of Nongalaza kaNondela, chief of the Nyandwini and Mpande's general. Mpande himself (to ensure his full co-operation) marched with the Boer commando, following the path of the Boers' 1838 campaign across the Mzinyathi and Ncome rivers.[32]

Dingane was placed in a terrible situation. He doubted if he could hold his own against the forces combined against him, yet he could not realistically flee out of their way. Since the failure of his Swazi campaign the way north was barred. What could be done, he did. He sent no less a personage than Nzobo to Pietermaritzburg with a gift of 200 cattle to make what terms he could with the Boers. But Nzobo, whom the Boers associated directly with the killing of Retief, was to them a criminal, deserving of the direst punishment. So, instead of receiving him with the honours appropriate for an ambassador and one of the king's closest advisers, the Boers immediately threw him and his associate, Khambezana, into chains.

The advance of the combined forces thus proceeded unswayed by diplomatic attempts to halt them, and Dingane soon felt uncomfortably exposed in his new uMgungundlovu at the Vuna River. He therefore moved forty-eight kilometres north, himself occupying Magudu Mountain, which stands conspicuously in the plain about thirteen kilometres south of the Phongolo River. His army, which he entrusted to Ndlela, that veteran commander of so many campaigns, took up a defensive position just a few kilometres south-west at Maqongqo, an unassuming group of round knolls in the open plain, destined to be of lasting significance in the annals of Zululand.

The Boer commando, which reached the banks of the Thukela on 18 January, consisted of 308 armed men, nearly 500 coloured and black attendants, 50 wagons, some 600 horses and 700 oxen. Most of its Boer members looked on it as a glorified hunting expedition, and were far more concerned to make their fortune in captured cattle than to take on the Zulu in battle. In nominal command of this rather chaotic expedition was the ineffably conceited Commandant-General Andries Pretorius who, to Delegorgue's astonished amusement, seemed to compare himself favourably with conquerors like Napoleon.

On 27 January the commando, after struggling slowly over the rain-sodden ground, reached the Sundays River. There, they were informed by messengers sent by Nongalaza (wearing the identifying marks of Mpande's adherents, which consisted of two thongs of white cowhide, suspended from the neck and hanging over the back and chest) that Mpande's army had reached the vicinity of the Magongqo hills, and that battle was imminent. The Boers were still nearly 200 kilometres away, and sent back orders that Nongalaza was not to engage the enemy until they had arrived to reinforce him.

The commando passed the site of the battle of Blood River on 29 January, where a large number of whitened bones and many skulls lay scattered in the long grass. What the Boers did not know was on that very same day, even as they stood upon the scene of their victory over Dingane's army, Mpande's forces were engaging Dingane's in a great battle, spear against spear and shield to shield, as in the old days before the coming of the white men and their guns.

The numbers of both sides at the Maqongqo hills were probably about equal, about 5 000 men each. But the morale of Mpande's men was higher than that of Dingane's, for it was dispiriting for the latter to know that even if they defeated Nongalaza's men they would still have to face Pretorius's commando.[33] Even so,

Nongalaza was surely somewhat rash to stake everything in battle without waiting for the Boers and their invincible firearms. It could be, though, that he was acting on Mpande's instructions, for it was surely the desire of the Prince of the Emigrant Zulus to win the battle without Boer aid so as to loosen their hold over him.

Nongalaza's confidence must in any case have been boosted by the presence in his army of Mahlungwana kaTshoba, the premier *isangoma* of the Zulu kings. Mahlungwana had abandoned Dingane's cause, and he was there to doctor Mpande's army before the battle. He burnt a patch of grass and treated it with special medicines (which doubtless included some of Dingane's *insila*), so that Dingane's men would be defeated the moment they stepped upon it.[34]

The battle was fiercely contested, and for a long while the issue hung in doubt. At one time Ndlela's men believed the victory would be theirs, and the uDlambedlu *ibutho* in particular surged triumphantly forward. But Nongalaza's men rallied, especially the iziBawu *ibutho*, and forced Ndlela's men back. Dingane's army started to take heavy casualties, and increasing numbers of discomfited warriors began to go over to the enemy. These defections conclusively turned the tide, and Nongalaza's men eventually prevailed. Dingane's army withdrew, worsted and in no condition to fight further, leaving two *amabutho* dead on the field behind them. The hero among Ndlela's men had been Nozitshada kaMagoboza of the Nzuza people, the *induna* of the uDlambedlu. He stabbed and stabbed until his fighting arm became so tired and swollen that he had to transfer his spear to his left hand. At last, overwhelmed, he sank to the ground crying out: 'Stab me! Woh! The king is dead. Come, stab me.'[35]

Ndlela's losses were considerable, though unknown. Nongalaza also suffered significant casualties – the Boers observed 1 200 wounded men in his camp – and was reluctant to pursue the remnants of Dingane's forces with any vigour. His men did scavenge the surrounding plain, however, finishing off the wounded and killing members of Dingane's household who had not made good their escape when the battle turned against them. One such unfortunate was no less a personage than Bhibhi, Senzangakhona's widow and Ndlela's sister, who had been high in favour with Dingane. She tried to take refuge in the bush at the bottom of a small stream near a little sharp-pointed hill called uVe, but Nongalaza's men caught up with her, flushed her out, and killed her without mercy, regardless of her distinguished royal status.[36]

Ndlela fared no better than his sister. In the closing stages of the battle he was wounded on the outside of his right thigh by a spear-thrust as he tried to take cover in the bush.[37] He nevertheless succeeded in joining his now fugitive king, who had found temporary sanctuary with the remnants of his household in the *imizi* of Klwana kaNgqengelele's people. But no welcome awaited him. Dingane had been raging against his defeated commander-in-chief, crying out:

Woh! Where is Ndhlela? He too must die. It was he who used to say that Mpande was less than nothing. I see that it is he who has ruined my army as well.[38]

So Ndlela was forthwith strangled to death upon the king's orders with an ox-hide thong and his body declared unworthy of burial, his failure at the Maqongqo hills outweighing in Dingane's eyes all his many years as chief *induna*.[39] But Mpande did not forget the numerous services Ndlela had rendered him, despite the personal risks involved. He honoured his promise to Ndlela to care for his orphaned children, and once he became king he lavished cattle upon them, raising Godide and Mavumengwana, Ndlela's eldest sons, to great prominence in the kingdom.[40]

The Boers were still nearly a hundred kilometres away from the Maqongqo hills, just south of the White Mfolozi, when on the evening of 30 January they received word from Nongalaza that Dingane was in flight with the intention of trying to join up with Mzilikazi. Since the war seemed to have been won without their intervention, the Boers decided it was time to clean their slate. They did not yet know of Ndlela's fate, nor of Dingane's, whom they intended to execute if captured. But they decided the moment had come to proceed against the hated enemy already in their hands, naked, in chains, and exposed to the freezing rain. Nzobo was doubly unfortunate that Mpande was accompanying his Boer captors, for the prince hated him for repeatedly advocating his death to Dingane, and was as determined as the Boers on his destruction. Nzobo must have known he had no hope when he was first brought a prisoner to the commando, and Mpande addressed him with cool malice:

Son of Somidhli, give me some snuff from your snuffbox, the snuff you used to take when you sat at the gate at Mgungundhlovu, remarking as you did so that the king had no younger brothers left'.[41]

Legalistic as ever, the Boers convened a court martial on 31 January to try Nzobo and Khambezana, his fellow envoy. Sentence was a foregone conclusion, for judges and counsel for the prosecution were one, and the hostile witnesses were Mpande himself and several of his *izinduna*. All accused Nzobo of advising Dingane in his various bloody acts against his own family, his subjects and Retief and his party. Mpande wept as he told the Boers, 'All that has been done to you stemmed from this fellow, who, when he spoke, was never contradicted by the king.'[42]

Throughout this sham trial, the impassive Nzobo comported himself with the utmost dignity. His simple and honourable response to the accusations against him was not to deny them, but to state that he had always attempted to act in his master Dingane's interests. All that he requested was that Khambezana, who was innocent of the charges against him, Nzobo, be shown mercy. But the court was not swayed by this admirable selflessness, and sentenced both men to immediate death by firing squad. Pretorius tried to talk to Nzobo of the redemptive powers of Christ, but Dingane's great *induna* silenced him with his reply. He had only one master, he declared, and it had been his duty to remain faithful to him. If there were some other master in heaven, then he 'could not fail to be grateful to him for having performed this duty'.[43]

118

Nzobo and Khambezana were taken, still tied together, to the place of execution. Both fell at the first volley of the firing squad, but Nzobo was only wounded. Despite his pain, he struggled valiantly to his feet, steadfastly to face his executioners. He died at the second volley, having given his judges and executioners a memorable lesson in courage, both moral and physical. The Zulu generally did not credit that Nzobo had been simply shot, and believed that the Boers must have imposed a much more spectacular revenge upon their great enemy. The widespread tale had it that he had been tied by the feet, face downwards, from the brake of a wagon and dragged to his death; or, alternatively, that he had been lashed to the spokes of the wheel of a moving wagon, and kept there until he died.[44]

On 3 February, 201 Boers set out from their camp to join in the pursuit of Dingane. Delegorgue, as ever, was not impressed:

What a strange sight these men made, setting off in the greatest confusion, riding up the hills in disorderly fashion, their long guns slung clumsily over one shoulder. No distinction was made between the dress of commandant or veld-cornet, corporal or simple horseman, and there was no formality in the execution of orders...[45]

The heavy rain and mist were against the commando, and Dingane's broken following rapidly scattered and took shelter in inaccessible caves and forests. A few inconclusive skirmishes took place, and the Boers, with sickness ravaging their horses, were soon looking for an excuse to call off the unprofitable operation. On 6 February they made contact with Nongalaza, who informed them that Dingane had already crossed the Phongolo with only a few followers and that his *amabutho*, disgusted at his craven flight, had dispersed. Most significantly too, Klwana of the Buthelezi and Maphitha of the Mandlakazi signified their desire to make their peace with Mpande. Dingane had tried to keep them by him, since they were the greatest chiefs of the north, and their decision to break loose signified that he had lost all hope of support.

Indeed, the Boers encountered numerous parties of the king's erstwhile followers trying to make their way back south. All these signs told them that Dingane had fled friendless into the country of his enemies, 'who gladly await[ed] him as an old rotten enemy, like the cat expects the mouse as his prey'.[46] So, driving 10 000 captured cattle before them, the Boers turned back on 8 February from the mimosa-covered banks of the Phongolo, leaving Nongalaza to keep an eye on Dingane's movements. Nongalaza pursued Dingane fifty kilometres across the Phongolo in a north-easterly direction, but succeeded only in capturing the king's old mother, Mphikase, who, too exhausted to walk any further, had been callously abandoned. Fearing the fevers that raged in that district, Nongalaza withdrew, satisfied that nothing more was to be feared from Dingane.

As the Zulu said, 'a king who left his home and went to the mountains was finished'.[47] So it proved with Dingane. Once he had crossed the Phongolo, he fled north-east with diminishing forces towards the Lubombo mountains. On reaching them, he ordered a makeshift homestead to be built in the dense bush on the slopes of the Hlathikhulu hill which he called eSankoleni, or the 'secluded spot'.[48] Even in these abject circumstances Dingane attempted to keep up the observance of his royal state. Esankoleni was designed as a typical royal residence with an *isigodlo* at its head; moreover, when crossing the Phongolo, Dingane had one of his attendants instantly executed for so far forgetting the respect due to the king as to let his eyes stray upon the exhausted women of the *isigodlo* wading across the river.

Esankoleni was in the territory of Silevana, the regent for Sambane, the heir to the Nyawo chieftainship. At first, Silevana gingerly welcomed Dingane, for he still had a relatively considerable following, and it would have been dangerous to oppose him. Yet the very number of his adherents rapidly proved a problem for Dingane, since it was no easy matter to find sufficient food in the Lubombo mountains to sustain them. Most of the *amabutho* had therefore to be dispersed to forage. And, since Dingane was determined to keep up the show of royalty, he sent other *amabutho* back to Klwana's *umuzi* near Magudu hill to fetch the valuable brass rings, genet skins and other necessary props he had left behind in his precipitate withdrawal after the battle of the Magongqo hills. For his personal protection he kept by him only the iziToyatoyi, a young lads' *ibutho*, but one which had seen action.

The Nyawo began to become impatient with their unwelcome guest. Not only were his people consuming all their precious stores of grain, but they were failing to hand over the cattle they had promised in return. Besides, Dingane's continuing presence was calculated to draw hostile armies into the area. Silevana decided that he must get rid of Dingane while he only had the iziToyatoyi to guard him. He made contact with a Swazi patrol under Sonyezane Dlamini, and confided that the great enemy of the Swazi people lay unsuspecting in his territory. Sonyezane hastily moved south with his forces and, with Nyawo support, surrounded Esankoleni at night.

A picked force crept into the *isigodlo* where Dingane slept, avoiding the guards at the main gate. One of the king's great dogs, Magilwana, who lived only on beef and milk, and who slept at the door of his royal master's hut, barked and gave the alarm. It was too late. As Dingane emerged from his hut, resolutely grasping his spear, Silevana cast his throwing spear at him with all his force. The blade passed through the king's thigh and the point penetrated his lower intestines. Streaming blood, Dingane nevertheless managed to escape into the bush, protected by a few personal attendants roused during the attack. These included Makhanda, who had the office of sewing on the royal headring, but who now valiantly fought off the pursuers. Some of Dingane's *isigodlo* women succeeded in joining him in the dark woods, but his sister, Nozilwane, was caught and killed, as was the loyal dog, Magilwana.

Dingane's assailants made off before the surprised iziToyatoyi could rally. The iziToyatoyi fanned out in search of the king and his few attendants in the dense, dark forest, but it was not until dawn was breaking that they came across them. It is perhaps not too much to suppose that Dingane had lain, fearful and in pain, reflecting among other things on the assassination of his brother Shaka, while his two attendants, Ndikili and Ndlebeyemkhonto, failed to staunch his blood. His young guards carried him back to Esankoleni where they inspected his wound and saw it was fatal. To hasten his inevitable end and shorten his death agony, they enlarged the terrible wound with a spear. The lurid and oft-repeated tale concerning Dingane's death, concocted for the Boers' special delectation – in which he was said to have been tortured to death by being pricked from head to toe with sharp spears, bitten by dogs, blinded and starved – was simply a fabrication.[49]

The dead king's faithful attendants buried him at Esankoleni. Silevana, Sambane and Silevana's brother Zulu (all members of the ruling Nyawo house) each ritually placed a stone on the royal grave. But, since the Nyawo feared the Zulu royal house might in future exact revenge for the killing of one of its leading members, they persistently tried to smother their part in the deed, and kept the place of Dingane's burial a closely guarded secret, known only to a few.

With his last, laboured breaths Dingane is believed to have whispered to those about him:

I am now dead. Go and return to Mpande and pay homage to him. But there is one thing that is painful to me, and that is our people will always be maligned at Songiya's [Mpande's mother] as evil-doers.[50]

As soon as Dingane was dead, the women of his *isigodlo* did indeed make their way back to Mpande, though some of his now leaderless adherents gave their allegiance to chiefs living about the Lubombo. On the way, the women passed through Maphitha's territory, and he kept half of them for his own *isigodlo*. This provocative deed (which was to be emulated thirty-nine years later by Maphitha's son, Zibhebhu, when he retained some of King Cetshwayo's *isigodlo* women after the battle of Ulundi) incensed and perturbed Mpande. Nor was he pleased to learn that others of Dingane's people, who had followed him to the end but were returning to their own country to submit, were being (as Dingane had predicted they would) treated with derision and contemptuously referred to as 'the rectum of Ndlela'. Mpande ordered that such provocative talk must at once cease, since it was his purpose to weld the riven nation together again. It was no simple undertaking, though, to heal the rift between those who had followed Mpande across the Thukela and sought the assistance of the Boers, and those who had resisted them and stood by Dingane to the last.[51]

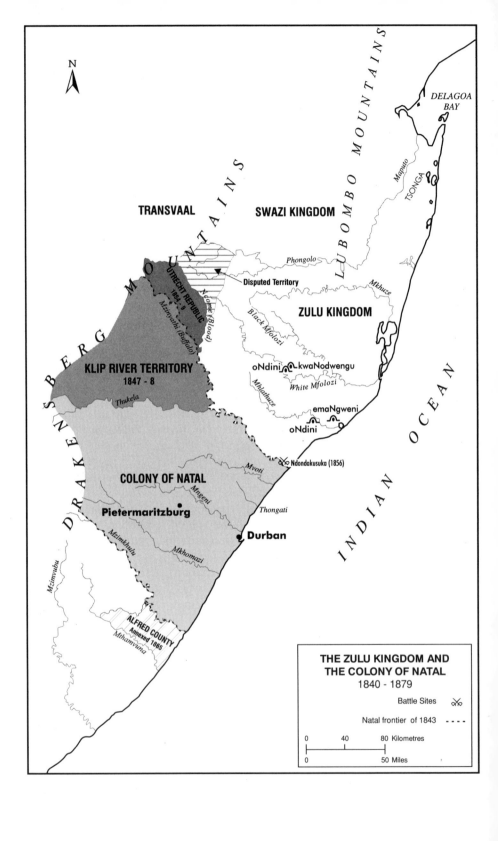

N

TRANSVAAL

SWAZI KINGDOM

DELAGOA
BAY

L U B O M B O   M O U N T A I N S

Maputo

TSONGA

Phongolo

Disputed Territory

Ndome (Blood)

Mkhuze

ZULU KINGDOM

UTRECHT REPUBLIC
1854-3

Mzinyathi (Buffalo)

Black Mfolozi

KLIP RIVER TERRITORY
1847-8

oNdini kwaNodwengu

White Mfolozi

Mhlathuze

Thukela

emaNgweni

oNdini

M O U N T A I N S

D R A K E N S B E R G

I N D I A N   O C E A N

Ndondakusuka (1856)

Mvoti

COLONY OF NATAL

Mngeni

Thongati

Pietermaritzburg

Mzimkhulu

Durban

Mkhomazi

Mzimvubu

ALFRED COUNTY
Annexed 1865

Mthamvuna

**THE ZULU KINGDOM AND
THE COLONY OF NATAL**
1840 - 1879

Battle Sites

Natal frontier of 1843 - - - -

0   40   80 Kilometres

0   50 Miles

10

Between the English and the Boers

On the morning of 10 February 1840, Andries Pretorius, Chief Commandant of the Boer commando encamped on the south bank of the Black Mfolozi, called Mpande and his chief *izinduna* before him.[1] The Boers, he complacently informed Mpande, had been 'instruments in the hands of God to put an end to the indescribable cruelties and murders committed by Dingaan', and to deliver the Zulu people from his tyranny. Accordingly, in the name of the Volksraad, he proclaimed Mpande 'king or chief of the Zulus'. In return, Mpande was to undertake to be the Boers' 'great ally'. These terms had, in fact, been those of the agreement Mpande had entered into with the Boers on 27 October 1839, but the new Zulu king diplomatically pandered to his allies' sense of self-esteem. Accordingly, in the words of the official chronicle of the commando, Mpande 'was filled with excessive joy from head to heels' and offered the most profuse thanks.

Pretorius had not done, however. Mpande had effectively been obliged to recognise titular Boer overlordship; now he was to be deprived of half the kingdom that had remained to Dingane. On the morning of 14 February, the Chief Commandant ordered the flag of the Republic of Natalia raised, and P.H. Zietsman, the Secretary of War, read a proclamation. Mpande learned to his dismay that the Volksraad seized all the land from the Thukela to the Black Mfolozi (including St Lucia Bay) bounded to the west by the Drakensberg, and to the east by the ocean. After this announcement the Boers fired a salute of twenty-one guns and gave a general cheer. Mpande, considerably put out, told Pretorius he could not stand the 'violent roaring' of the guns. Stooping every time a gun was fired, he and his *izinduna* withdrew to their own camp.

Delegorgue, who witnessed the scene, could not help reflecting critically on the extraordinary conceit of colonising Europeans, whether Boer or Briton, who lightly annexed already populated country, not to settle there, but simply to prevent their rivals from laying claim to it. Not only was it unjust, he concluded, but foolish too, for in this case the Boers had no means of occupying or controlling the lands between the Thukela and Black Mfolozi.[2]

Having settled Zululand to their satisfaction, and engraved the date of their proclamation on two large stones (one of which they buried) on the banks of the Black Mfolozi, the Boers withdrew south of the Thukela. They drove with them an enormous herd of 31 000 cattle, not quite the 40 000 they had demanded from Dingane, but quite large enough. To placate Mpande, who was hardly content to see the wealth of his new kingdom being driven away, the Boers distributed a remaining 15 000 head among the great chiefs who had forsaken Dingane in good time for Mpande.[3]

To all appearances, Mpande was left by the Boers in a weak position, the vassal king of an impoverished and diminished kingdom, bleeding from the unhealed wounds of civil war.[4] But Mpande (as we have seen) was no fool at all, despite the ever-green myth to the contrary. And he still possessed several real assets, particularly the continuing Zulu acceptance of the whole institution of the monarchy, as created by Shaka. This meant he continued, like Dingane and Shaka before him, to enrol the *amabutho* and so control marriage and homestead formation; to officiate at the national ceremonies, where he expressed his ritual powers; to maintain the *isigodlo*; to administer justice and hand out both punishment and reward; to head the councils of the land; to obtain wealth through the levying of fines and the sending out of raids against neighbouring chiefdoms; to derive profit from trade with the whites; and, in all, to enjoy the respect and deference accorded a king. Potential threats to his power still lay, as they ever had, in the hands of other ambitious members of the royal house, and in those of powerful and independent-minded chiefs like Maphitha. Undoubtedly, the civil war with Dingane had opened up interesting vistas of possibility for such men. It would be necessary in the years ahead to control or eliminate such potential rivals if they were not to form rallying points for rebellion, as Mpande himself had done.

Initial acceptance of Mpande's rule in his reduced kingdom might well have been related to continuing Zulu fears of Boer interference. And indeed, with the ending of the first British occupation of Natal in December 1839, the Boers were pushing forward with plans for their ideal republic. The Volksraad registered claims to farms north of the Thukela, and hunters like Johannes de Lange ranged far and wide in the game-filled plains and valleys of Zululand, providing the hides and ivory desired by the traders at the port. Nevertheless, Boer writ did not really run in the territory north of the Thukela, and Mpande, regardless of whether the Boers had officially annexed it or not, still governed there as *de facto* ruler and expelled Boers guilty of misdemeanours such as cattle-rustling. Over the next few years, renewed British intervention and Mpande's undoubtedly adroit diplomacy would ensure that the frontiers of the Zulu kingdom were pushed firmly back to the Thukela.

The British authorities became increasingly unhappy with the Republic of Natalia as its policies became evident.[5] Blacks were to have no rights in those parts of Natal settled by the Boer pastoralists, except as servants or tenants of the whites. At first, the Boers experienced a shortage of labour, but very soon they were overwhelmed by a flood of refugees from Mpande's kingdom. Most of these were tributary people who had been moved north by Mpande's predecessors, and were returning home to be free from the obligations of being a Zulu subject. Their numbers have always been a matter for debate, but were certainly many tens of thousands. To cope with this unwelcome influx, with all its attendant problems of 'squatting' and cattle theft, the Volksraad decided in 1841 that all 'surplus'

124

blacks should be relocated between the Mthamvuna and Mzimvubu rivers in territory south of the Republic and in the Cape's sphere of interest. This decision (which was never in fact implemented), when combined with a severe Boer raid in December 1840 against Ngcaphayi's Bhaca, whom they accused of cattle theft, convinced the British authorities at the Cape that the activities of the Boer republic were threatening the stability of their entire eastern frontier. This fear fused with existing humanitarian concerns and long-term strategic and economic interests to persuade Napier to intervene once again in Natal's affairs.

On 4 May 1842, Captain Thomas Smith, a stolid veteran of Waterloo, who had marched overland from the Cape in command of a force of 237 men of the 27th Regiment and the Royal Artillery, raised the Union Jack once more at Durban (which had been Port Natal's irregularly used if official name since 1835). The Volksraad, determined to resist, defeated Smith's men in a night skirmish at Congella on 23 May, and besieged them in their fort. After Dick King's legendary ride of 960 kilometres to Grahamstown to summon aid, the garrison was relieved on 25 June by a strong force under Colonel Josias Cloete, which arrived on the frigate *Southampton*. Completely outgunned, the Boers retired on Pietermaritzburg, and on 5 July 1842 the Volksraad agreed to submit to the Queen's authority.

Protracted negotiations continued for a space, and Natal entered a curious stage of transition with shared rule between the British and Boer authorities. But by December 1842 the British government had reluctantly decided that Natal must be annexed to exert proper control over the Boers. The Republic of Natalia was finally extinguished on 31 May 1844 with the annexation of Natal as a separate District of the Colony of the Cape. However, it was not to be until 12 December 1845 that the first Lieutenant-Governor took his oath of office in Pietermaritzburg, and only on 15 July 1856 would Natal be created a separate colony of the British Crown.

Mpande displayed considerable acumen during the period of gradual British take-over, and his grateful people praised him as

He who crossed afterwards
Of the house of Shaka;
The swallow that gets lost in the sky,
He who appears in his feather head-dress
Between the English and the Boers.[6]

The new king realised very early on that the best way to counterweigh the persistent Boer threat to his kingdom was to enlist British support. He cultivated the goodwill of the British community in Durban, and after the arrival of British troops in 1842 pledged his military support against the Boers.[7] That proved unnecessary, but confidence in future good relations with the Zulu encouraged the British to proceed with their annexation of Natal.

Mpande reaped immediate dividends when Her Majesty's Commissioner in Natal, Cape lawyer and parliamentarian Henry Cloete, younger brother of

Colonel Cloete, journeyed into Zululand in September 1843 to fix the boundaries between Natal and Zululand.[8] Cloete found Mpande firmly ensconced in his esiKlebheni *ikhanda* in the emaKhosini valley, right in the middle of the territory annexed by the Boers in 1840. Mpande received him in state in the cattle enclosure in front of the *isigodlo*, surrounded by his councillors. Over the next few days the king publicly entertained the Commissioner (as was customary) with exhibitions of dancing by his *amabutho*. He also did him the enormous honour of inviting him into the *isigodlo*, where twenty of the women, 'decked out with beads in the most profuse and gorgeous manner from head to knees', sang and danced for his pleasure – though Cloete did not appreciate their 'monotonous chorus' and 'abject submission' before their lord. What struck Cloete most was Mpande's reluctance to enter into any treaty without the presence of Maphitha, which testified to his cousin's great influence.

Maphitha did not arrive from his northern domain, however, and on 5 October 1843 Mpande assented to the document written in English, which Cloete had translated word for word for the king. By it, Mpande was recognised as 'King of the Zulu Nation', and Pretorius's annexation of the territory between the Thukela and Black Mfolozi was cancelled. The new boundary line between Natal and the Zulu kingdom was recognised as being the Thukela River from the sea until its junction with the Mzinyathi River, and then north along that river until the foot of the Drakensberg. Mpande agreed that all of his adherents finding themselves on the Natal side of the border would move their *imizi* north into Zululand, as now defined.[9] This boundary-line was to remain the Zululand-Natal border until Zululand was incorporated into Natal in 1897. Significantly, Zululand's north-western and northern boundaries were not laid down, and this omission would prove a fertile source of conflict in the years to come.

It must be questioned, though, just how seriously Mpande took the boundary agreement of 1843 with the British. After all, he had never observed the Black Mfolozi as his southern boundary, regardless of his treaty of 1840 with the Boers. This understandably cavalier attitude to boundaries as defined on pieces of paper by visiting white dignitaries led to the farcical episode of the Klip River Republic.

As the British hold tightened over Natal, Boer resentment was inflamed daily. They had trekked from the Cape to Natal to escape unacceptable British rule, had suffered many hardships and tragedies (and victories too) along the way, but now, disconsolately, they prepared to move again. By the end of 1848 most had trekked over the Drakensberg to the interior. There, independent Boer republics were eventually recognised by Britain, the fledgling South African Republic (or Transvaal) by the Sand River Convention in 1852, and the Orange Free State by the Bloemfontein Convention of 1854. The few Boers in Natal who did not emigrate were soon swamped by nearly 5 000 British immigrants who flowed in between 1849 and 1852, and gave the settler society of the new colony its distinctive British cast.

There were a few Boer settlers, however, in the great wedge of land between the Thukela and Mzinyathi rivers and the Drakensberg, who wished neither to trek, nor to accept British rule.[10] Andries Spies, sometime landdrost of Weenen (the administrative district centred on the Bushman's River and the little settlement of the same name), 'bought' the territory from Mpande in January 1847 in 'perpetual ownership' for a derisory £75 – which was never paid. The Klip River insurrection, as it is called, did not last very long, and ended in January 1848 when the British exerted their authority.

Mpande must soon have realised that he had allowed himself to be placed in an untenable position, and that British boundaries (unlike those of the Boers) were meant to be observed. Doubtless, it had been a gratifying turnabout to assume overlordship over a Boer republic, no matter how unlikely its chances of survival. Besides, it is quite possible that he had never become reconciled to the loss of the territory in 1843, for it was one of rich grazing lands that had previously rendered considerable tribute. But, in permitting the creation of a client Boer state, he had 'sold' territory that was no longer his to dispose of, and his rash action imperilled his good relations with the government of Natal. A stern message in July 1847 from Martin West, the Lieutenant-Governor, caused Mpande hastily to repudiate his agreement with Spies. Subsequently, even a visit by no less a personage than Andries Pretorius failed to shake him in his reinforced determination to cleave to the British cause.

The episode finally confirmed Mpande in his earlier foreign policy of the closest co-operation with Britain. Henceforth, it was axiomatic with him (as his son Cetshwayo was later to explain) that, while never at any time acknowledging British authority over him, he nevertheless would treat his British neighbours in Natal 'like relations', keeping them informed – as he would his own family and great chiefs – of everything that transpired in his kingdom. In that way he hoped to ensure constant British support against the Boers, for he simply did not trust them not to renew their territorial demands on Zululand.[11] That was certainly the case after 1852, for the boundary between the new South African Republic and Zululand was not defined, and Mpande confidently anticipated Boer infiltration into the good, open grazing-lands of the north-western parts of his kingdom.

Close, frank relations with his British neighbours to the south, which were calculated to frustrate Boer ambitions in the north-west, promised Mpande the freedom he required in Zululand itself to secure his own position, and to rebuild his kingdom after the ravages of the Voortrekker invasion and the civil war with Dingane. He assimilated Dingane's *amabutho* into his own, and confirmed Nongalaza as his commander-in-chief. Nongalaza, now an elderly man, continued to thrive under Mpande. Humphreys, a trader-hunter, described his great homestead near the Mhlathuze River with considerable admiration, and was astonished at the size of his herds and household, which he estimated at over 2 000 head of cattle (besides sheep and goats), 200 women and almost 400 children.[12]

Mpande raised up other personal favourites, as had Dingane in his time. Mbilini kaCungeya of the Mthethwa, the *induna* of kwaNodwengu, seems initially to have been Mpande's pre-eminent *induna*. When he died (some say of mysterious causes), he was succeeded as sole principal *induna* by Masiphula kaMamba of the emGazini, who had already shared some of Mbilini's official functions during the latter's lifetime, such as summoning the *ibandla* and making announcements to it in the king's name. Dingane had raised Masiphula to the chieftainship of the emGazini over Sitshaluza, the rightful heir, and the grateful Masiphula had served his king as an *inceku* at uMgungundlovu. He was to remain Mpande's principal *induna* until the king died, despite – or perhaps because of – his ferocious personality and widespread unpopularity. For it could be that precisely because Mpande (whose name meant he was the 'root' of his nation) nurtured his reputation as a benevolent and modest monarch, loath to punish a single subject, that he required a merciless and much-feared agent to take public responsibility for the more unpopular, but nevertheless necessary, actions of government. Still, it does seem that Masiphula was excessively cruel, sending people without compunction to their deaths for the smallest misdemeanours. He was likened in his frequent and violent rages to a wild animal, and when he was in fury's thrall even the king and the royal children feared him. One day, it was said, Masiphula went so far as to kill his own son, Ziyankome, to the helpless grief of the princes who had been his companions and friends, because this cruel, unbending father suspected his boy of sleeping with a girl of the *isigodlo*.[13]

As one of the means of consolidating his authority, Mpande liberally *sisa*'d (loaned) royal cattle, so creating an extensive network of dependents. His committed maintenance of the *isigodlo* was similarly of crucial importance, for the daughters of men of wealth and power entered it, and were married again out of it, so building up valuable alliances for Mpande, and increasing his wealth. Mpande's *isigodlo* was by all accounts extremely large, for he combined his existing one with the remnants of Dingane's, and was continually adding to it. There were no fewer than 500 women living in the *isigodlo* at kwaNodwengu, Mpande's principal *ikhanda* after 1843, built across the White Mfolozi from the emaKhosini in the centre of the Mahlabathini plain. Others were dispersed among the various *ikhanda*, which continued to be ruled over as before by members of the royal family (including prominent women) and dependable *izinduna*, like Nongalaza, and still functioned as nodes of royal authority. Those who infringed on Mpande's prerogatives or challenged his authority in any way courted heavy fines, if not destruction, and he regularly clipped the wings of over-mighty or rich subjects by confiscating their herds on charges of witchcraft.[14]

The exchange of goods between Zululand and Natal was steadily intensifying during Mpande's reign, and white traders and hunters were penetrating the country in ever-growing numbers. The days were fast disappearing when the wives and children of a great chief like Nongalaza would scatter in fright like hares at their first sight of a white man.[15] Mpande's power was sufficient, though, for him to keep tight control of the external trade in valuable commodities such as ivory, and to insist that white traders, in exchange for permission to trade in his kingdom, must provide him with firearms (those ultimate instruments of power), rather than common-or-garden beads and blankets. (Blankets, it should be mentioned, had been brought by increasing trade to within the reach of all in Zululand, and were no longer a luxury reserved for the king and his chiefs.)[16]

Mpande ensured that white traders and their goods were protected, and any of his subjects who harmed or stole from them were put to death. On the other hand, if traders did not keep to the king's rules, he expelled them, as he did other whites whose activities appeared to challenge his authority. Thus in mid-1842 he attacked those of his subjects who had settled near the mission at Empangeni of the American Board missionary, the Revd Aldin Grout, compelling him to abandon his evangelising in Zululand. To Mpande, these Christian converts, or *amakholwa*, by accepting Grout's authority, had compromised their allegiance to him and constituted an unacceptable fifth column in his kingdom.

Inevitably, though, Mpande's most dangerous potential rivals came not from the ranks of his few Christianised subjects, but from within his own family. Only one other son of Senzangakhona still survived, the king's half-brother Gqugqu, who had only been a child at the time of the death of Shaka. Gqugqu not only kept up his own *isigodlo* in royal style, but raised his own *amabutho* like an independent chief. What made him particularly dangerous was that his power-base was in the north of the country, where the king's grip was relatively tenuous, and he had become a rallying-point for the opposition, very much as Mpande himself had been in Dingane's time.

Those who clustered about Gqugqu included some important people who had fallen out of favour with Mpande. Such a one was Sothondose of the Nxumalo, who had strong ties with Somaphunga of the Ndwandwe, who had been alienated by being placed under Malanda of the Mkhwanazi, a protégé of Mpande's and husband of his sister. Various others of great influence were part of the circle, including Mawa, the daughter of Jama and sister of the formidable Mnkabayi, and thus Mpande's aunt. Her homestead was at Ntonteleni in the south-east of the kingdom.

Gqugqu's undoubtedly growing popularity and power induced Mpande to act. The catalyst, according to tradition,[17] was a small event which occurred when Gqugqu was paying his respects to Mpande, as custom demanded. As he was sitting in the assembly, Gqugqu sneezed, and his attendants exclaimed, '*Thuthuka Mageba!*' Now, these words were reserved solely for the reigning monarch when he sneezed, and by uttering them Gqugqu's people were giving public notice of his aspirations to the crown. Mpande mulled over the situation, for it gave him scant joy to kill Senzangakhona's only other surviving son, the second to last of that once numerous progeny. But Masiphula urged him on to commit the unpalatable deed, and in June 1843 Mpande ordered the massacre of his half-brother and all his household in his homestead among the Sigubuthu hills to the north of the Black Mfolozi, including even his children still in the womb. The executions extended to those of the supposed conspirators on whom the king's *amabutho* men could lay their hands. Mawa, Sothondose and others of note, including Makobosi, the executed Ndlela's former principal *induna*, managed to flee across the middle Thukela with a large following and take refuge with the British in Natal. Only the izinGulube *ibutho*'s determined pursuit of the fugitives to the border prevented the exodus from being larger than it actually was.

The 'Crossing of Mawa' was one of those memorable events which the Zulu used to employ as markers when calculating dates.[18] Mawa and her associates crossed the Thukela with 2 000 to 3 000 adherents and as many cattle. They were part of a steady stream that passed into Natal in the 1840s, debilitating Zululand's resources. Figures are most unreliable, but it does seem fairly certain that by the end of the 1840s the population of Natal had surpassed that of the Zulu kingdom, and its herds of cattle were also considerably greater.

The balance of cattle shifted to Natal not only because of the great herds the Voortrekker commandos and refugees brought out of Zululand, but on account of the increasingly brisk trade in cattle across the border in return for manufactured goods. Mpande heartily disapproved of his subjects selling their cattle to Natal traders, but found it impossible to halt the practice. What made this steady depletion of Zululand's cattle even more serious was the introduction in the mid-1850s of cattle 'lung-sickness' (bovine pleuro-pneumonia), which was to reach serious proportions by the 1860s.

Part of the reason for the population haemorrhage lay in the restrictions of the *ibutho* system, for young men in Zululand could not fail to notice that it was possible to marry considerably earlier in Natal, where they were not obliged to serve the king as they did at home, while the fathers of girls realised that they could obtain a much higher *ilobolo* if they married off their daughters in cattle-rich Natal. Mpande did his best to staunch the flow, and received the co-operation of the British, who wished to limit the black population of the new colony to manageable proportions. He assigned the territory between the Thukela and Mhlathuze rivers to Nongalaza, his commander-in-chief, who temporarily depopulated the strip along the southern frontier by destroying the people's *imizi* and erected military posts to control their movements. For their part, the Natal authorities repatriated refugees' cattle to Zululand, and introduced new regulations making it more difficult for people from Zululand to settle in the colony.

The British, then, allowed Mpande an almost completely free hand within Zululand, only becoming involved if the tranquillity of Natal itself was affected by developments north of the Thukela. Mpande discovered, though, that the British were not prepared to allow him to pursue whatever foreign policy he desired if this entailed stirring up conflicts which might involve a reluctant Britain in the affairs of the interior. This restriction posed a problem for Mpande because, like his royal predecessors, he needed to send the *amabutho* out on campaign to hone their military skills and to bring back the spoils of war. Such booty was a vital instrument of royal power, for by judiciously distributing it the king would ensure the loyalty of the army and of individuals of influence. Two raids in 1851 against the Mabhudu chiefdom, for example, brought in 500 cattle, 4 000 sheep and 120 firearms. If there were a cessation of similar raids the crown would be weakened by the loss of essential resources, and the inactive *amabutho* might well be tempted to transfer their loyalty to a prince more prepared to indulge their thirst for military action and its rewards. Mpande was therefore obliged regularly to raid his neighbours, but he found that he was no longer able to do so quite with the frequency and on the scale of Dingane, though in the early years of his reign his armies were certainly active.

For Mpande, as for Dingane, Swaziland was the obvious source of booty and the place to develop a territorial refuge in case Zululand proper should be lost.[19] At first, though, he avoided attacking Swaziland because of the disturbingly good relations between the Boers and the Swazi, dating from the last days of Dingane; and then because the British disapproved. Instead, beginning in 1842, he raided a number of tributary kingdoms to the north-west of his kingdom, along that sensitive frontier where not only the interests of the Zulu and Swazi collided, but where those of the Boers settling the highveld were becoming increasingly involved. In particular, he attacked Langalibalele kaMthimkhulu of the Hlubi, who was exhibiting increasingly independent pretensions and usurping the royal function of rainmaking, and required to be knocked into proper submission.

A dynastic dispute in Swaziland at length gave Mpande the opportunity to intervene militarily. Mswati had been installed as king in 1839 or 1840, but he was still young and Swazi affairs remained for some years in the hands of regents. Mswati was circumcised in 1845, and thus attained the status of manhood, but his brother, the senior regent Malambule, attempted to hang on to power. Malambule gained Mpande's backing, for the Zulu king hoped to set up a client chiefdom under him in southern Swaziland, and by July 1846 the Zulu army was being mobilised for active intervention. But both Malambule and Mpande overlooked a new element in the scenario. In August 1845 the community of Ohrigstad Boers under A.H. Potgieter was established to the north-west of Swaziland, and strengthened in 1846 by an influx of Voortrekkers from British Natal. Mswati turned to these Boers for assistance and protection, and on 27 July 1846 ceded them a massive stretch of land between the Crocodile and Olifants rivers in the hope of their future military assistance. Mpande, meanwhile, was being hamstrung by the Natal authorities' strong objection to a Zulu invasion of Swaziland, and realised that he would require a watertight *casus belli* to overcome them.

Malambule provided the means when, in September 1846, he was defeated by Mswati and a small contingent of Ohrigstad Boers. He fled with Mpande's connivance into the north-western marches of Zululand, drawing his brother's victorious troops after him. Mpande could now notify Natal that he was obliged to repel a Swazi invasion, and the uneasy British authorities were persuaded to condone an act of 'self-defence'. Free now to act, by late 1846 Mpande had massed his *amabutho* on the Swazi border. Early in 1847 the Zulu army swept across the Phongolo in several divisions and, advancing as far north as the Crocodile River, initially brought great swathes of southern Swaziland under Zulu control. The Swazi adopted their conventional tactics of taking to their caves with their families and livestock, and bogged the Zulu *amabutho* down in irregular warfare. This time, though, they and their herds could also take refuge with the neighbouring Boers, whom they called upon for assistance. Baffled by a combination of hit-and-run Swazi tactics and Boer firepower, the Zulu army retired from Swaziland in July 1847.

Mpande had not yet given over his Swaziland ambitions, however. In 1848, to obtain a secure bridgehead for a renewed attack on south-western Swaziland, he struck again at Langalibalele of the Hlubi, driving him and his ally, Phutini of the Ngwe, over the border into Natal, where the authorities settled them in the foothills of the Drakensberg, between the Bushman's and Little Thukela rivers. Their rear thus secured, Mpande's *amabutho* launched a new invasion of Swaziland, where Mswati was embroiled in conflict with yet another over-mighty brother, Somcuba, who had gained the support of the Boers.

This time, unable to call on the Boers for help, and receiving no assistance from the British to whom he appealed, Mswati was forced to submit, even apparent-ly becoming Mpande's tributary for a time. It seems Mpande had to stop short of outright conquest, however, because of British concern and his desire to avoid provoking Natal to the extent of open conflict. He tried nevertheless to in-crease his effective control over Swaziland, and this led to Mswati's attempt in 1852 to break free of Zulu overlordship. Mpande responded with a full-scale invasion of Swaziland in July 1852, which in its magnitude took the Swazi by surprise. In this last of Mpande's campaigns, the Zulu army swept the country at will, driving off vast herds of cattle.

Swaziland faced disintegration as its people fled before the invaders. Para-doxically, it was the very flight of these starving refugees which saved the coun-try, as Mswati desperately begged the Natal authorities to give them asylum. Since the last thing the British in Natal desired was a massive influx of displaced Swazi, the Natal government put pressure on Mpande to withdraw his army. He complied at length, not merely because the British were voicing their disap-proval, but because many of his own leading chiefs were becoming opposed to the recurring Swazi venture. Mswati used the breathing space to consolidated his hold over his kingdom. Becoming more secure in his knowledge of Zulu in-ternal divisions and in his hope of support from Natal and possibly the Boers, he even started to reassert Swazi control over the disputed borderlands at the head-waters of the Phongolo. Mpande responded to this insolence in 1858 and again in 1860 with plans for another invasion of Swaziland, but it was never to ma-terialise, thanks primarily to internal conflicts within the Zulu kingdom.

Yet, even if Mpande failed ultimately to conquer Swaziland and turn it into a second kingdom and place of refuge, it must surely be conceded that his major campaigns in Swaziland had been crowned with considerably more success than had Dingane's. He was militarily active too along his kingdom's north-east-ern borders, where the Tsonga people had long provided valuable tribute to the Zulu kings. When in the early 1850s a dynastic dispute flared up in the Mabhudu chiefdom, Mpande intervened to ensure that his candidate, Noziyingili, he of the enormous hands and feet, became both chief and subservient ally.[20] Mpande's armies campaigned even further afield, and in 1851 conducted an inconclusive campaign against Chief Sekwati of the Pedi in the mountainous country of the north-eastern Transvaal. Like the Swazi, the Pedi retired to their fastnesses, but one *ibutho* made an unexpected night march and captured a large herd of cat-tle, permitting the army to return with a respectable haul of booty.[21]

The intensity and frequency of these campaigns – at least in the earlier part of Mpande's reign – reveal the fallacy of his carefully fostered reputation as a ruler of 'peaceful disposition...averse to war',[22] at odds with the military predilections of his predecessors. What had changed was not the nature of the Zulu monarchy, but its situation. Neighboured by mistrustful white polities to the south and north-west, Mpande no longer possessed the freedom to launch campaigns at will, but was inhibited by fear of white disapproval and possible hostile intervention. Only when British objections in particular were overcome, usually through the exercise of considerable diplomatic skill, could he embark on the military adventures both appropriate to a Zulu monarch and essential for his survival.

Mpande's considerable catalogue of successes, both internal and external, gives the lie to the accepted historian's wisdom that his reign saw the perceptible diminution of royal power and the steady decline of Zululand's position as a great power in south-eastern Africa. By the early 1850s Mpande was firmly in the saddle, assured in his relations with his new white neighbours, unchallenged at home, and militarily dominant over the black polities along his northern marches. He could justifiably live at peace and, as his son Cetshwayo later said, encourage the breeding of cattle and amuse himself (as he preferred) with dancing and lavish costumes.[23]

Filled with confidence, in 1850 Mpande even permitted Christian missionaries, expelled in 1842, to resume work in his kingdom. Thus began his relationship with Hans Schreuder of the Norwegian Missionary Society, a tall, sandy-haired man of immense physical strength and explosive temperament.[24] Schreuder was an accomplished classical scholar, with considerable practical skill in trades such as carpentry. He succeeded in winning the king over through his medical knowledge, for he was able to ease Mpande's many minor ailments. The grateful king permitted him to establish a mission station within calling distance of kwaNodwengu, at Empangeni near the mouth of the Mhlathuze.

A visiting white hunter-trader has left a description of Schreuder conducting a Sunday service there in 1851. As preliminary, a Zulu boy was sent out to the surrounding hills with a gong to summon the converts. When they had assembled (163 of them, and mostly comely young women), and were squatting together on the grass in front of his hut, Schreuder first prayed and then read to them in Zulu from the Bible. Afterwards they all sang a hymn together (Schreuder had written a hymn-book in Zulu), and then he took them through their alphabet, for he was determined to educate his flock as well as instruct it.[25]

Over the next two decades Schreuder set up seven mission stations in Zululand, and acted both as adviser to Mpande and as his chief conduit with the colonial world. Schreuder was consequently there to witness the dramatic reversal in Mpande's fortunes within a few years of his own arrival in Zululand, a change which had at its core the festering succession dispute between two of Mpande's sons.

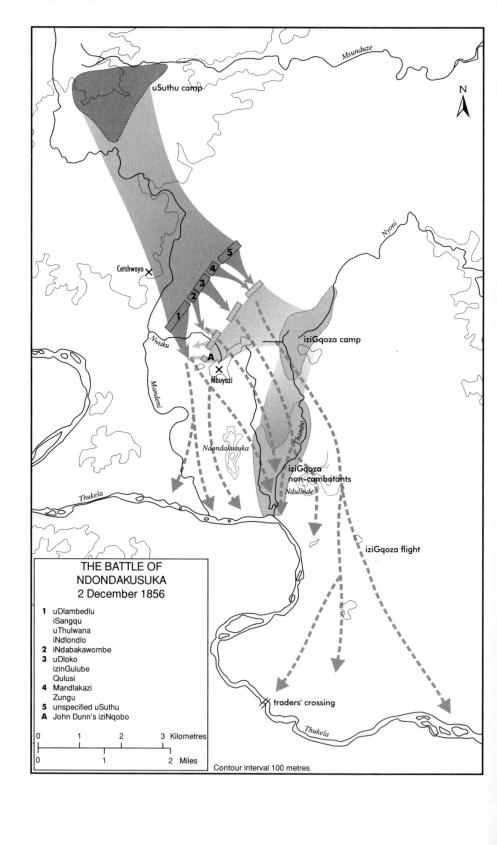

THE BATTLE OF
NDONDAKUSUKA
2 December 1856

1 uDlambedlu
  iSangqu
  uThulwana
  iNdlondlo
2 iNdabakawombe
3 uDloko
  izinGulube
  Qulusi
4 Mandlakazi
  Zungu
5 unspecified uSuthu
A John Dunn's iziNqobo

0   1   2   3 Kilometres
0   1   2 Miles

Contour interval 100 metres

uSuthu camp

Cetshwayo ✗

Msunduze

Nyoni

iziGqoza camp

Nyaku

Mandeni

A
Mbuyazi ✗

Ndondakusuka

Thambo

iziGqoza
non-combatants

Ndulinde

Thukela

iziGqoza flight

traders' crossing ✗

Thukela

11

And the Thukela Turned Red

The battle fought on the northern bank of the Thukela on 2 December 1856 is known as Ndondakusuka after the highest hill in the area. The hill, in turn, was named to commemorate the *umuzi* of Zulu kaNogandaya, the famous warrior and 'storm that thundered in the open',[1] which had stood there in Dingane's day.[2] As for the battle itself, it was, in terms of the numbers involved, one of the greatest battles ever fought on the soil of Zululand. If casualties are to be the measure of its frightfulness, it was certainly among the most deadly. What made it all the more horrible was that so many lives were lost, not in the country's defence against an invading army, but in civil strife, in the cause of one or the other of two of King Mpande's sons, rivals for recognition as his heir to the kingdom. It is insufficient, though, to reduce an explanation of a civil war simply to a matter of personal animosities and ambitions, for much wider issues were involved.[3]

As we have seen, the most fundamental defect in the constitution of the Zulu kingdom was the lack of a settled principle of succession.[4] The heir to the king (or any other chief) was the first-born son of his great wife, whom he usually wedded or designated only relatively late in life to minimise the risk of usurpation by an adult son. In practice, the rules of succession could be manipulated or simply set aside, though the field of competitors was effectively limited to those with a sufficiently legitimate genealogical claim. Thus, while Mpande had overthrown Dingane, Dingane had assassinated Shaka, and Shaka had eliminated Sigujana, and not one of them had been able to claim the throne by simple right of seniority, all were nevertheless princes, the sons of Senzangakhona. For as Mpande was sorrowfully to concede, in the wake of the disastrous war of succession between his sons, 'Our house did not gain the kingship by being appointed to sit on a mat [i.e. by being appointed heir]...Our house gained the kingship by stabbing with the assegai.'[5]

What gave Mpande particular cause for regret was that he had possessed the opportunity to break the Zulu monarchy free from its destructive cycle of succession by usurpation. Unlike either Shaka or Dingane, he had legitimate sons, and was in a position to designate one of them his heir. At the time of the 'breaking of the rope', when Mpande journeyed to Pietermaritzburg to seek assistance from the Boers, he presented his little boy Cetshwayo to the Volksraad as the son of his great wife, and thus his heir. The Boers thereupon took a snip

135

out of the child's ear (as if he had been nothing more than some calf) so as to be sure of his identification as Mpande's heir should his father be killed by Dingane.[6]

It might have been a political necessity for Mpande in 1839 to acknowledge Cetshwayo as his heir, but the premature act stored up trouble for the future. Cetshwayo grew into young manhood confident of his grand destiny as the next king, and inevitably attracted an ambitious following about himself, eager to attach themselves to the rising star. The ageing Mpande became fearful that his own authority would in consequence be weakened. So, from the early 1850s, he began to foster the claims of Mbuyazi, another of his sons, over those of Cetshwayo, and to encourage him into believing that he would be the old king's heir. What Mpande was evidently trying to achieve by muddying the previously clear stream of the succession was to delay Cetshwayo's emergence as his unchallenged dynastic rival.

The king justified his new position regarding his successor by insisting that although Cetshwayo had been his heir before he had become king, Mbuyazi was better suited to succeed him on the throne. The reason presented was that Shaka had taken Mbuyazi's mother, Monase, from his own *isigodlo* and given her in marriage to Mpande with the specific purpose that his brother raise his seed on his behalf. Thus Mbuyazi was, as Mpande put it, 'the son of Tshaka, the king of the earth', and the rightful 'chief of the land'.[7] It should also be acknowledged that Mpande feared and disliked the vigorous Cetshwayo while, by contrast, he deeply loved Mbuyazi. Consequently, dynastic politics apart, it could be that he wished simply to further the cause of his favourite – and less threatening – son, a tall, light-skinned young man with distinctively fleshy eyelids, a large mass of head-hair and a tuft of hair growing low down on his back, which accounted for his praise-name, given to him by Mpande himself, 'the elephant [denoting his royal status] with a tuft of hair'.[8]

Despite his efforts, Mpande's genealogical gerrymandering failed to undermine support for Cetshwayo's candidature. A possible reason was that, among more solid considerations, Mbuyazi was offensively arrogant to the king's councillors and courtiers, whereas Cetshwayo always showed them proper and flattering respect. Mbuyazi, moreover, kept his own *inkatha*,[10] thus too blatantly advertising his aspirations. Sensing that not enough people were rallying to Mbuyazi's cause, Mpande set out to help it by becoming more provocatively open in its support. For example, at the annual *umKhosi* ceremony following the Swazi campaign of 1852, he singled out Mbuyazi to participate in the royal rituals with him, and left Cetshwayo out altogether;[11] while on another public occasion he humiliated Cetshwayo by praising the dancing of Mbuyazi's people at the expense of that of the former's followers.[12] Perhaps Mpande was hoping by these blatant signs of disfavour to intimidate Cetshwayo into withdrawing his claim to the succession. But Cetshwayo, the prince, was not prepared to back down.

Cetshwayo was born in about 1832 at Mpande's emLambongwenya homestead in south-eastern Zululand. His name signifies 'The Slandered One', and probably had reference to some unfounded accusation by Dingane at the time of his birth.[13] His mother was Ngqumbazi, a daughter of Mbhonde kaTshana of the chiefly house of the Zungu people. Shaka paid the *ilobolo* for her on Mpande's behalf, thus confirming her status as Mpande's chief wife.[14] According to Cetshwayo's own account, his mother's first-born, Mlanjwane, was killed on Shaka's orders.[15] He himself, as the eldest surviving son by a great wife of a prince of the Zulu royal house, was from birth a person of the highest standing, and consequently in as much danger as was his father from Dingane's suspicions. His conventional life as a princeling was disrupted in 1839 when Mpande 'broke the rope' and took his family with him into Natal. The boy's horizons must have been considerably broadened during the months of exile and novel contact with the strange-looking Boers, with their long beards and great hats, their horses, wagons and firearms.

Once Mpande became king in 1840, the young Cetshwayo's status burgeoned accordingly, and he grew into young manhood secure in the belief that he would one day succeed as king. Even a crown prince, however, conformed to the normal patterns of Zulu society, and in 1850 or 1851 Cetshwayo was recruited into the newly formed uThulwana *ibutho*. With his comrades of the uThulwana he took part in the Swazi campaign of 1852, and was blooded as the future war leader of his people. His membership of the uThulwana, with that of seven other princes of his age-group (including Mbuyazi), conferred great prestige on the *ibutho*, though it also encouraged it in arrogant and unruly behaviour. Its first *induna* was Sogweba kaMasekwana of the Ntuli, though he lost Mpande's favour and was soon replaced by Mnyamana kaNgqengelele of the Buthelezi, a man of sufficient wealth and wisdom to gain the natural respect and obedience of this fashionable and ill-disciplined *ibutho*.[16]

Mnyamana, who was destined to play so significant a part in the affairs of Zululand, was born in about 1813. His father was Ngqengelele, a confidant of Shaka, who raised his friend to great heights and made him the chief of the Buthelezi people in northern Zululand.[17] His mother was Phangela of the Sibiya people. When Ngqengelele died, he was succeeded by Klwana, a renowned warrior and the son of Mnyamana's deceased elder brother, Khoboyela. Soon after Mpande seized the throne, Klwana was killed, probably on Mpande's orders – but certainly on the ambitious Mnyamana's instigation. The new Buthelezi chief's evident high favour in Mpande's eyes and subsequent great riches in cattle and political power had much to do with his obvious abilities. Tall and of slight build, with a dark complexion, his face (which was perkily adorned with a slight pointed beard and little whiskers) bespoke his considerable intelligence.

Mnyamana was cautious, conservative and not easily swayed once he had decided on a course of action, yet he was also of logical, rational mind and extremely astute politically. His deep, resonant voice was always listened to with the greatest respect in the highest councils of the land. His measure can be gauged in his approach to Zululand's white neighbours. He was distinctly hostile to whites (and traders and missionaries disliked him thoroughly in return) precisely because of the threat he knew they posed. Yet, because he also fully appreciated their power, he always advised moderation when dealing with them, and the avoidance of conflict.

This was the man, then, who would influence Cetshwayo in his impressionable years, and in due course become his chief minister. As commander of the uThulwana, Mnyamana ate in the same hut as the princes, and became known as the 'father' of Mpande's children. This daily close personal contact with them was crucial for both Mnyamana and Cetshwayo. As they gained each other's friendship and confidence, they inexorably tied their joint futures together. In the coming conflict with his brother, Cetshwayo would enjoy Mnyamana's crucial support, while in return, Mnyamana would earn the prince's gratitude and secure his place at his right hand.

Cetshwayo, so determined to be recognised as Mpande's heir, took after his mother in appearance.[18] When still in his twenties, he was already a handsome, big, heavily built man, with a well-proportioned frame and great breadth of chest. He was slightly bandy-legged, but an extremely fleet runner. Later in life he became fat, but his flesh remained firm, not flabby like that of his brother Hamu, and he maintained his fit, hard condition, walking about ten kilometres every day for his health. There was never anything soft about him. Like so many other members of the Zulu royal house, he had immense thighs, clearly a family trait. In colour, he was darker than most other Zulu, and flushed deeply when angered or dismayed. His bearded face was broad, open and remained remarkably unlined. He possessed a very pleasant smile and his expression was habitually good-natured. Large, lustrous eyes indicated his restless energy, powers of observation and quickness of comprehension.

Never other than royally dignified and courteous in his demeanour, Cetshwayo held himself very erect, with his head thrown slightly back, clearly accustomed to looking on all those about him as his inferiors. Nevertheless, his manner towards them was consistently genial and engaging. A straightforward man, he generally said what he thought, speaking with a strong, deep voice. He was a master of the Zulu language, and would correct mistakes of speech made by his attendants. Although he could be very cheerful and extremely witty, his eyes twinkling as he related a comic incident and his smile lighting up his face, he also had a tendency towards a rather intimidating taciturnity.

Cetshwayo was passionately interested in the laws, customs and history of his people. Since he possessed a very retentive memory, he became a walking repository of Zulu lore. People always had ready access to him, and he was genuinely concerned with their affairs. When sitting in judgement he did his best to reconcile disputants and to try cases justly, and usually condemned people to death only after considerable deliberation. He was brave physically and courageous in battle, and as a friend he generally proved considerate and faithful. On the other hand, he could be autocratic, headstrong and obstinate, and reluctant to take advice. Although actively interested in all affairs of state, he was also an inveterate gossip, and could be seduced into chatting away the hours with his intimates. When he was in a fury none dared oppose him. He was also notorious in his *isigodlo* for his stinginess in distributing food among his women. This was a cheese-paring habit he had inherited from his mother, Ngqumbazi, and which he was to pass on to his son and successor, Dinuzulu.

Mpande, during the course of consolidating his hold over his new kingdom in the early 1840s, had set up Cetshwayo's mother, Ngqumbazi, as head of the kwaGqikazi *ikhanda*.[19] KwaGqikazi was built in the northern regions of the kingdom, in the undulating country between the Vuna River and the Nongoma hill, in the vicinity of Dingane's last capital at the time of the battle of the Maqongqo hills. It was particularly important that a strong royal presence be established in the north, since it was the regional base for both Maphitha and Masiphula, those immensely influential chiefs and councillors. However, Mpande did not allow Cetshwayo to accompany his mother to kwaGqikazi. He knew too well that the royal *amakhanda*, besides being vital for the spreading of royal influence, were also places where dynastic opposition could form and thrive. A prince living far away at kwaGqikazi would have the opportunity to cultivate a personal following and develop dangerous regional alliances. He himself, after all, had done precisely that when living as a prince in southern Zululand.

As Cetshwayo grew into manhood, however, Mpande found it impossible to prevent him from frequently visiting his mother at kwaGqikazi. Since the increasingly obese and ailing monarch never went so far from home,[20] he was unable to counteract Cetshwayo's growing influence there. And, as Mpande feared he would, Cetshwayo began building up a solid core of support centred at kwaGqikazi and at the associated ekuBazeni *ikhanda*, close by to the south, where a number of Mpande's other wives related to Ngqumbazi had their residence. It is here that the *ibutho* system played into an ambitious prince's hands. Cadets drawn from the same area undertook their initial training at a regional *ikhanda* like kwaGqikazi or ekuBazeni before being formed into a new *ibutho*; at the same time, members of various different *amabutho* living in the vicinity of the *ikhanda* fulfilled their annual period of service there, when they took their turn at keeping it in repair and serving the needs of the royal household. Inevitably, close bonds developed between the young cadets and the royal prince living at the *ikhanda* where they assembled, and these were consolidated during their annual stints of service. The upshot was that Cetshwayo was able to create an enthusiastic body of adherents who had a distinctive regional base, but were nevertheless drawn from most of the king's *amabutho*.[21] The Swazi campaign of 1852 simply affirmed their loyalty to Cetshwayo, and served to make the prince more popular in the army as a whole.

By the mid-1850s Cetshwayo was also beginning to count on the support of several leading chiefs. Most notable among these were his northern neighbours, with all their political influence and their solid body of followers. Masiphula and his emGazini were north of kwaGqikazi across the Mkhuze; Maphitha of the Mandlakazi was his direct neighbour to the east; Mnyamana and the Buthelezi lived across the Sikhwebezi River just to the west; while Chief Mfanawendlela KaManzini of the Zungu, from whose chiefly house Cetshwayo's mother had sprung, dwelt just to the south along the banks of the Black Mfolozi.

The reasons why such chiefs joined Cetshwayo's camp are not particularly clear. Perhaps they thought they would be able to manipulate a young king of their choice and restrict his power, thus creating more scope for their own regional ambitions. Maphitha, for example, already comported himself like a semi-independent prince. Possibly, like Mnyamana, they saw his success as the key to their own elevation. It could be that they personally resented Mpande's frequent expropriation of his more powerful subjects' cattle, or that they did not see eye-to-eye with him over his foreign policy. Certainly, there were sufficient popular grievances they could harness to promote Cetshwayo's cause against that of his unpopular father's candidate.

Despite the king's various campaigns, his generosity in *sizaing* cattle, and his regular redistribution of confiscated livestock, there were still insufficient cattle available to reward his *amabutho*. Partly to blame for the lack were the drain of cattle to Natal, the effects of lung-sickness, and the restraints imposed by Zululand's white neighbours on the king's freedom to raid nearby chiefdoms. Mpande's attempt to make good the shortfall by plundering the herds of his richer chiefs only placed the burden back on ordinary people, for in order to recoup their losses chiefs made increased demands on their own subordinates. Drought and famine in 1852-3 only made the situation worse. In these straitened circumstances, there were many – especially among the chiefs and *amabutho* – who saw in their support of Cetshwayo the opportunity for civil strife and the massive redistribution of cattle. For war meant losers, and rich rewards for the winners.

Thus, when Mpande began to champion Mbuyazi as his successor, and to attempt to pressure Cetshwayo into making way for him, his eldest son already had a dangerous weight of support behind him, as well as the capacity to raise even more. His adherents were known as the uSuthu, a name derived from the large 'Sotho'-type cattle his supporters in the Zulu army had captured from the Pedi in the campaign of 1851.[22] Mbuyazi's party became known as the iziGqoza, from the word meaning 'to drop down like drops of water from a roof'. This was in reference to the steady trickle of adherents willing to *khonza* to Mbuyazi.[23] But nothing could disguise the fact that Mbuyazi commanded considerably less support than Cetshwayo.

Mpande could not continue playing down this unpalatable reality. Realising to his regret that Cetshwayo had grown too popular and powerful either to sideline or to eliminate through assassination, Mpande had to devise a new strategy. Accordingly, he ordered an *ikhanda* called oNdini built for Cetshwayo on the southern bank of the lower Mhlathuze, some twenty-four kilometres southwest of Empangeni, and placed Mbuyazi north of the White Mfolozi near Nhlazatshe, a great flat-topped mountain thirty-two kilometres north-west of kwa-Nodwengu. In that way the king physically separated the rival princes with himself in the Mahlabathini plain between them, and Cetshwayo was pried loose from his territorial power-base around kwaGqikazi.

As a solution, Mpande's plan did not succeed. For one thing, Mbuyazi found to his discomforture that Masiphula actively supported Cetshwayo's objections to the leader of the iziGqoza settling in the northern part of the country.[24] For another, the rift between the two princes had already become too public to disguise, and the nation was already polarising in support of one or the other. Tempers were high, and any chances of a peaceful resolution had begun rapidly to fade. Both princes decided to have the issue out. They requested and received Mpande's permission to hold a joint hunt in the wild, game-thronged country at the confluence of the White and Black Mfolozi rivers where the Zulu kings traditionally pursued larger game. Everybody, though, must have known the purpose of the coming 'hunt', and both the uSuthu and the iziGqoza carried warshields to the rendezvous rather than the smaller ones normally used for hunting. It can only be surmised that Mpande approved of the venture because he banked on the iziGqoza being able to take the uSuthu by surprise in the dense bush. The uSuthu, however, were more than ready for any ambush the iziGqoza might attempt to spring on them, and gathered in significantly larger numbers than their rivals. Outfaced, the iziGqoza lost their nerve and withdrew without a blow being struck, singing these brave words to salve their pride: 'We almost got the buck, almost. We almost stabbed it.'[25]

The inconclusive 'mock hunt' only postponed a solution. Reluctantly realising that an armed clash could not be avoided for much longer, Mpande resolved to do what he could to help the cause of his favourite son. He refused Cetshwayo's challenge to discuss the matter of the succession in public before the full council.[26] Instead, in November 1856 he allocated Mbuyazi and the iziGqoza a tract of land in the south-east of the country, in the selfsame region where his own influence had been its greatest before 'breaking the rope' in 1839. Mpande's hope was that, securely established in this region with its tradition of loyalty to himself, Mbuyazi would not only be able to recruit adherents, but would be close enough to Natal to solicit decisive support from the neighbouring British. Conversely, if events turned against him, he would be positioned to flee into Natal for sanctuary, just as his royal father had done seventeen years before. Mpande's new plan was no better than his last, however, and it failed to save Mbuyazi and his iziGqoza.

On the arrival of the iziGqoza in their designated territory, Mbuyazi set provocatively about clearing homestead sites, levying tribute, 'eating up' opponents and lifting cattle belonging to Cetshwayo. Maphitha, who knew all about the exercise of power, bluntly advised Cetshwayo: 'You will never be king if you do not act at once.'[27] So with Maphitha's and Masiphula's urging and support, and Mnyamana's too,[28] Cetshwayo mobilised his uSuthu at oNdini to drive the iziGqoza out. His was still the majority party, and Cetshwayo had in his camp a significant proportion of his brothers, all of whom would become influential councillors during his reign. These were his full-brothers Ndabuko and Silwana, and his half-brothers Dabulamanzi, Shingana, Ziwedu and Hamu. The odds were distinctly in the uSuthus' favour, and Masiphula's advice to a southern chief who was considering heeding Mpande's orders to go to Mbuyazi's aid was simple and to the point: 'Wo! Do not go. You will die. Cetshwayo will kill you.'[29]

Gathering growing support as he marched south,

The restless black one moved on,
Leaning on his barbed spear[30]

and striking terror into the hearts of his opponents.[31] Alerted to his brother's inexorable approach, Mbuyazi gathered up his people – men, women, children and their livestock – at the iSangqu *ikhanda* near Schreuder's Entumeni mission, and moved southwards towards the drifts across the lower Thukela to Natal. Sixteen kilometers north of the Thukela lived E.F. Rathbone, a hunter-trader regularly moving between Zululand and Natal. He knew very well that civil war was brewing in Zululand, and was none too pleased when Mbuyazi compromised him by fetching up at his house on 23 November 1856 requesting advice and support. He turned down flat Mbuyazi's offer of half the coastal region under his control if he, and the various other traders gathered in alarm near his house, would but support the iziGqoza with their firepower. Instead, he relayed urgent messages to Captain Joshua Walmesley, the Natal Border Agent stationed just to the south of the Thukela.

Walmesley sent to Pietermaritzburg for instructions, but no reply had come before Mbuyazi and two of his brothers, conscious that Cetshwayo's numerically superior forces were fast approaching, crossed the Thukela and desperately requested British assistance. This Walmesley had no authority to give him, but he gave permission to his administrative assistant, John Dunn, a forceful and adventurous frontiersman with a preference for Zulu over European ways, to cross the Thukela with thirty-five of the frontier policemen he had trained in the use of firearms and horses, and a hundred of his African hunters. His avowed object was to broker a settlement between Mbuyazi and Cetshwayo. This hardly seemed a likely prospect, and Dunn's intervention must be regarded as purely self-serving. Like so many other greedy people in Zululand, he knew that war meant the prospect of rich booty.

On 28 November Dunn crossed into Zululand at the head of his policemen and hunters. Once there, he was joined by a few white trader-hunters and their Zulu assistants, and the whole force became known as the iziNqobo, or the 'Crushers', because of their firepower. Mbuyazi's host, of which about 7 000 were fighting-men, was camped near the source of the Nyoni River. Cetshwayo's army, which numbered between 15 000 and 20 000, was drawing perilously close. On 30 November the uSuthu encamped not far away from the iziGqoza, spread out among the low hills at the head of the valley through which flowed the Msunduze stream, and along the upper reaches of the Mandeni River.

Negotiations, Dunn's ostensible reason for being present at that dangerous moment, were clearly no longer feasible. Instead, he bent his efforts to saving the iziGqoza from the fate staring them in the face, and to rescuing five panicking white trader-hunters and their families who were caught with their wagons and livestock on the wrong side of the lower drift across the Thukela. Being rainy, early summer, with the young maize everywhere still growing its tassels, the great, broad river was relatively full and flowing fast, and could not be forded. The hunter-traders' women and children could be taken across by the ferry-boat regularly plying the treacherous waters, but the wagons and cattle could not. In an attempt to preserve their possessions from the impending battle, the trader-hunters drove them through a relatively shallow stretch of the river onto an extensive sand island about two-thirds of the way across. Further they could not go, for the final channel between them and the security of Natal was over four metres deep.

Acutely aware of the numerical superiority enjoyed by the uSuthu, whom he could see clearly through his telescope being drawn up in an enormous circle to be 'doctored' for battle, Dunn urged Mbuyazi on 1 December to try without delay to move his women, children and cattle across the river to safety. Mbuyazi considered the state of the river and refused to risk them in its swirling, yellow waters. Then the portly Mantantashiya, one of Mbuyazi's full-brothers, jeered at Dunn for his cowardice in even making the suggestion, and declared the iziGqoza were quite strong enough to face the uSuthu without his help. Rebuffed, Dunn then tried another tack, and advised Mbuyazi to take the offensive against the uSuthu, which would at least prevent the iziGqoza from being penned against the impassable river.

Although it was by now late in an afternoon of great thunderstorms, Mbuyazi agreed to follow Dunn's counsel. His men were ritually prepared, and the many fearful non-combatants and their cattle were ordered to take refuge before the fighting began in the various heavily wooded stream-beds leading down to the Thukela. Meanwhile, the uSuthu, taking note of the iziGqozas' preparations, had begun gingerly to advance. When they saw the iziGqoza *amabutho* also moving forward in battle-array they hesitated and halted. Dunn's mounted men then came up and opened fire on the uSuthu advance scouts. No further fighting took place, however, since the sun was about to set. Both sides of reluctant warriors retired to their respective camping-grounds, on high ground either side of the Mandeni stream. Outnumbered by nearly three to one, the iziGqoza *amabutho* spent a miserable night, disturbed by a number of false alarms.

The fateful dawn of 2 December broke raw, cold and drizzling, as often happens in Zululand's wet, early summers. It is not possible, from the very fragmentary evidence, to be particularly precise concerning the dispositions of the two sides and their movements during that day of battle. It would appear, nevertheless, that the uSuthu moved southwards along the Mandeni valley early that morning, and that Cetshwayo took up position with his commanders on a low rise to the west of the stream, called Masomongca. He carried a dark-brown or black shield with a small white patch at the side, and wore (by some accounts) his black loincover of silver jackal and a buttock-cover of genet skin. His headdress was the band of otter skin with tassels of blue monkey skin and the tall crane feather of the uThulwana, possibly with a bunch of eagle feathers as well.

Mbuyazi took his station on the Ngcono hill, south-east from Cetshwayo across the Mandeni valley. The uSuthu were formed up in the traditional chest and horns formation, with their most reliable and committed elements in the centre. Serving with one of the horns was Christian Groening, a young Boer, one of the only two men on Cetshwayo's side to carry a firearm.[32] The iziGqoza were drawn up in equally conventional fashion facing the uSuthu. To compensate for their inferiority in numbers, they had a considerable preponderance in firearms, mostly in the hands of Dunn's policemen and experienced hunters.

While the iziGqoza commanders were conferring just before battle joined, a gust of wind blew off Mbuyazi's proud ostrich plume. This unfortunate accident set up a murmur among his already less than confident men, who considered it a bad omen. Cetshwayo, for his part, 'He who stabs on bended knee like a sucking calf',[33] kneeled deliberately upon a shield which had belonged to his rival. His *amabutho* were cheered at the sight, for they knew this ritual action would enable their prince to achieve supernatural mastery over Mbuyazi in the coming battle.

The uSuthu plan was for their right horn to deploy rapidly and to get between the iziGqoza and the Thukela, cutting them off from escape across the river. The left horn and chest would then advance, and the iziGqoza would be encircled and destroyed. Accordingly, elements of the uDlambedlu, iSangqu, uThulwana and iNdlondlo *amabutho* serving with the uSuthu swung out towards the river. The iziGqoza left horn was commanded by Shonkweni, a half-brother of Mbuyazi, whom Mpande had fathered as Dingane's heir, as he had Hamu for Nzibe.[34] Dunn and his men, the iziNqobo, were also positioned on that flank, and the whole iziGqoza left resolutely advanced to frustrate the uSuthus' attempt to outflank them. Battle was joined near the Nwaku stream. Cetshwayo's men gave their great battle-cry of 'uSuthu!', and the iziGqoza answered with their 'Laba! Laba! Laba! Laba!' Although outnumbered ten to one, the iziGqoza left was considerably stiffened by Dunn's determined gunmen, and managed to throw back the uSuthu right. Cetshwayo reinforced his discomfited right horn with the iNdabakawombe *ibutho* from the chest, and sent it forward again. The iziGqoza and iziNqobo repulsed it once more. It was evident to the uSuthu commanders that the battle could be lost on their right, and they exhorted their men to stand fast, crying 'Where will you find refuge?'[35]

The uSuthu saved their cause, however, on their left. The iziGqoza right was not stiffened with gunmen as was their left, and the uSuthu commanders grasped that they must change their plan and attempt to turn that flank. So they fed their left with two of their best units from the centre. The experienced Mandlakazi contingent advanced in the lead, under the command of Matsheni and Sikizana. Two of Maphitha's sons, Hayiyana and Hlomuza, were with them. After the battle, the Mandlakazi force was commonly given the main credit for the uSuthu victory.[36] They were supported by the contingent of Zungu, Cetshwayo's mother's people.[37] Their determined attack proved irresistible, and the iziGqoza right horn was forced to fall back. Seeing them in retreat, the iziGqoza of the left horn lost courage and suddenly also gave way, retiring up the Nwaku valley. With their flanks gone and encirclement imminent, the iziGqoza centre lost all heart. Seeing them waver, the remaining uSuthu units of the centre, namely the uDloko, izinGulube and abaQulusi *amabutho*, raised their shields slightly, rattled the shafts of their spears against them, and charged. Mbuyazi's chest of picked men had burned a line of grass behind them, as was the custom, to indicate that their last stand would be before it. But, when it came to the point, Mbuyazi failed to rally them and they fell back across the line, their shields in the air to indicate that they would fight no more.

The iziGqoza initially conducted an orderly retreat, with the intention of falling back in a south-easterly direction across the rain-filled Thukela. But to maintain a measured withdrawal, over broken country, pursued by a victorious and numerically overwhelming foe, is extremely difficult. To do so when caught up with panicking civilians, who saw their shield of warriors falling apart and began wildly fleeing for their lives, is all but impossible. Thus, for the iziGqoza on 2 December, retreat turned into rout, and rout into massacre. At about 10 a.m. the anxious traders sheltering with their possessions on the sand island saw the first of the iziGqoza running for the river. Dunn soon also came into sight. He was still mounted on his horse, and was directing what was left of the iziNqobo in an attempt to cover the retreat. Their resolute rearguard action certainly allowed numbers of the fugitive iziGqoza to reach the river bank in safety. But the uSuthu were pressing the pursuit hard. Dunn was soon overwhelmed by a heaving; hysterical mass of men, women, children and livestock, through which the uSuthu moved, as he described it, 'with terrible earnestness, hard at work with the deadly assegai, in some cases pinning babies to their mother's quivering forms'.[38]

Prince Mantantashiya, the jeerer who had called Dunn a coward, but who had taken no part in the battle except to be caught up in the flight, begged him to take him up on his horse. But, coolly balancing the fat, breathless prince's weight against his horse's exhaustion, Dunn left him to his fate. He was himself then brought to a halt by the numbers of fugitives clinging to his horse. So he abandoned it, stripped to his shirt, and plunged into the turbulent Thukela. Dodging through the yelling, drowning mass of bodies and flailing limbs, by some miracle he encountered the ferry-boat in mid-stream, and was taken across to safety.

Dunn was fortunate, for most of his iziNqobo were killed. The terrified hunter-traders on their sand island escaped with their lives, though their wagons were plundered and a thousand of their cattle were carried off by the triumphant uSuthu. They could only have been left unmolested on Cetshwayo's orders, and Rathbone was astonished to be greeted in friendly fashion by many uSuthu as they passed by, bloodied spear in hand. For the iziGqoza there was no mercy. Harried and desperate, the survivors from the battle were hemmed up on the bank against the crocodile-infested river. They died where they stood, or tried to cross the rushing waters from the point where the Mandeni stream runs into the remorseless Thukela, downstream as far as the sea. The slaughter appears to have been particularly heavy on the bank opposite the sand island on which the hunter-traders were cowering. Great numbers were also killed in the valley of the Thambo stream below Ndulinde hill, just down from the Mandeni. It seems many of the non-combatants had been sheltering there, and that some of the defeated fighting-men had attempted to flee that way. The uSuthu spared neither man, woman nor child.

Cetshwayo himself mingled with his *amabutho*, and took part in the pursuit as far as the banks of the Thukela:

Red-winged loury of Menzi [Mpande] that set out from Ntumeni,
And the Ndulinde hills went red and the Thukela reddened;

145

Powerful bull of Ndaba whom they covered with tail tufts,
Which when it arose ate up the Zulu nation.[39]

It is impossible to know how many iziGqoza fell before uSuthu spear and club,
or drowned in the raging river, where the sandbanks were strewn with their bodies and the eddies choked with their floating corpses. At the very lowest estimation
they must have numbered many thousands. The Natal authorities later calculated that only 2 000 of their *amabutho* and a quarter of the non-combatants
succeeded in escaping into Natal. Cetshwayo was later praised as

He who caused people to swim against their will,
For he made men swim when they were old.[40]

Indeed, men of great status like Nongalaza, Mpande's elderly commander-in-chief
who had joined Mbuyazi, and the famous warrior, Matshekana, were among those
who had been compelled to brave the terrible river. A few of those left on the
Zululand bank had lucky escapes. Such a one was Nkukhu, one of Mbuyazi's
izinceku, who shammed dead in the reeds.[41]

Mbuyazi and five of his brothers were among the dead, namely his full brothers Mantantashiya and Madumba, and half-brothers Shonkweni, Somklawana,
and Dabulesinye.[42] Dead too were several sons of the venerable Sothobe. Mbuyazi's
body was never identified, which permitted rumours long to flourish that somehow he had escaped, and would one day return to claim his own.[43] But his
corpse most likely would have lain with the thousands which covered the banks
of the Thukela or were washed up during the succeeding weeks upon the beach-
es south of the sated river's mouth. Perhaps, though, his bones were among those
which for decades whitely littered the Thambo stream at the foot of Ndondakusuka hill; or maybe they are with those which are still being ploughed up
along the Nwaku valley.

The number of uSuthu losses cannot be computed, but it is known that
Dunn's men had done great execution with their firearms. There were certainly many wounded. R.C.A. Samuelson shuddered ever afterwards when he remembered seeing Cetshwayo and his victorious army pass by the Empangeni mission after Ndondakusuka on their way back to ekuBazeni. First came the
uninjured *amabutho*, driving thousands of captured cattle and joyously reiterating their short but telling song of praise in honour of their conquering prince:
'The one who remains silent and provokes quarrels with no one! O ya O!'[44] But
behind them dragged the walking casualties, 'with gaping wounds, groaning as
they went along'.[45]

12

The Young Tiger[1]

Not since the crossing of Mawa in 1843 had there been such a great exodus of people out of Zululand into Natal as there was after Ndondakusuka. The Natal government felt it necessary to issue what became known as the Refugee Regulations to staunch the flow. Even so, it was estimated that by the middle of 1857 at least 4 000 people and 10 000 cattle had entered the colony.[2] Yet, whatever the hardships and sorrows heaped upon the iziGqoza after Ndondakusuka, the truth was that their destruction in battle and the death of Mbuyazi had removed the greatest challenge to Cetshwayo's claim to the crown. Still only twenty-four years of age, his victory confirmed him as one of the most powerful men in the kingdom.[3] Mpande had to come to terms with that stark reality, and in November 1857 he and Cetshwayo reached a formal reconciliation. In return for Cetshwayo's promise to keep the peace, Mpande pledged to allow him a considerable part in ruling the nation, though on condition that the old king remain the ultimate authority.

Despite this accession of power, Cetshwayo's position as Mpande's heir was still not absolutely settled. For one thing, the uThulwana *ibutho*, of which he was a member, had not yet received the king's permission to put on the headring and marry. In other words, Cetshwayo was still a 'boy' in the eyes of the people, and until he had attained full manhood he could not aspire to become king. More significantly, there were still other rivals in the field from among Mpande's many sons. The one who was ultimately to prove the most insidious, persistent and destructive to Cetshwayo's house had been an ally during the Ndondakusuka campaign. He was Hamu kaNzibe.

Hamu was Mpande's first-born son by Nozibhuku, the daughter of Chief Sothondose of the Nxumalo people, who was the brother of Monase, Mbuyazi's mother. Despite his pre-eminence by age, Hamu was, through the *ukuvuza* custom, heir not to Mpande (his biological father) but to the king's full-brother Nzibe kaSenzangakhona, who had died in 1828 and for whose spirit Mpande was 'raising seed'.[4] Hamu thus inherited kwaMfemfe, his 'father's' great homestead in the north-west of the country on the hills sloping down from the Ngome forest to the Mkhuze River. There he ruled as chief over the Ngenetsheni people. This was a vulnerable region of the kingdom. The Swazi kingdom was just to the north across the contested line of the Phongolo River, while to the west lay the South

African Republic, its covetous eyes firmly fixed on the fine grazing lands over which Hamu held sway.

As a prince of the highest lineage, a recognised *isikhulu* (despite his relative youth), and an *induna* of the uThulwana, Hamu had built up a strong following and was already a considerable power in the land. Cetshwayo had thus welcomed his significant assistance during the war against Mbuyazi. But Hamu, self-indulgent, flabby, with the immense thighs of his family and impassive, sensual features, was a most ambitious man. It doubtless rankled in him that, despite his seniority in age, he ranked in the succession behind all the other sons of Mpande on account of being Nzibe's genealogical son. Perhaps it was in compensation that he made a conscious point of emphasising his royal lineage at every turn. Certainly, he lived in royal style at kwaMfemfe, maintained his own inordinately large *isigodlo* of 300 women, appointed his own *izinduna* and *izinceku*, and officiated at his own *umKhosi* festival, which was attended by the warriors from his chiefdom.

Not surprisingly, considering his pretensions, wealth and power, Hamu brooked as little royal interference as did Maphitha – his fellow northern baron – in the administration of his chiefdom. The king consequently never went to kwaMfemfe, and neither dared punished Hamu's adherents nor apportion others land in his domain. He was, besides, one of the most popular among the princes, and his admirers were prepared to overlook his genealogical inferiority. And, despite his violent and overbearing manner with subordinates (he knocked his own servants about, while his attendants, taking their cue from him, beat up those who did not show their master sufficient respect), they appreciated him as a liberal, plain-spoken and brave leader whom they might well be prepared to follow into a war of succession. His praises ably catch the complex character of this ambitious prince, burning with resentment at his exclusion from the highest place in the land:

> He who devours with his broad bladed spear...
> ...The favourite of Mpande!
> Scrubber of the vagina as if he does not like it
> While in reality he loves it
> Beast that encircles the reed bed of Mpande
> And then goes back to the reeds...[5]

Hamu, in fine, despite the conventions governing the succession, comported himself as nothing less than Cetshwayo's equal, and in the wake of Ndondakusuka he asserted himself. Cetshwayo could not accept this, and in late June 1857 their forces clashed. There was no conclusive outcome, and for a while thereafter the princes lived in relative harmony. But Hamu had given notice of his ambitions, and these Cetshwayo could never again ignore.[6]

As rivals to Cetshwayo, the surviving princes of the iziGqoza were of more immediate and pressing concern than was Hamu. Mbuyazi and five of his brothers might lie dead, but there were others of their house still living in Zululand.

The most prominent among these was Mkhungo, Mbuyazi's thirteen-year-old younger full-brother. Mpande tried to protect him, and put him into the safe-keeping the uMcijo *ibutho*. But in mid-1857 they abandoned Mkhungo without a fight on learning that Cetshwayo, intent on having done with his adolescent rival, was approaching their *ikhanda* with a large force.[7] Mkhungo managed nevertheless to elude Cetshwayo's men and reached the safety of Natal by way of Utrecht. His escape was made possible with the help of the Khumalo people under Mtezuka, whom Cetshwayo subsequently 'ate up' for their pains.[8]

In Natal, Mkhungo joined Sikhotha, another of Mpande's sons by his wife Masala, who had earlier taken refuge in the colony. Monase, Mbuyazi's and Mkhungo's mother, also made good her escape at much the same time, accompanied by her brother, Sothondose, the Nxumalo chief.[9] The Natal authorities were happy to harbour them, and to recognise Mkhungo and Sikhotha as royal princes and potential successors to Mpande.

The two princes were harboured by one of the most remarkable, if controversial, men in Natal's history, and educated at Ekukhunyeni (the Place of Light), his school for the sons of chiefs at Bishopstowe, just outside Pietermaritzburg. He was John William Colenso, first Anglican Bishop of Natal from 1853 until his death in 1883.[10] Colenso greatly desired to extend his missionary operations in Natal to Zululand, and welcomed the prospect of instructing the future (and 'civilised') king of Zululand under his own roof.

Colenso was a most handsome man, with chiselled, delicate features, a firm mouth in a determined jaw, a steady, fearless gaze from behind gold-rimmed spectacles, and luxuriant, curling hair and side-whiskers. As his looks might have portended, he was a liberal, if extremely stubborn, theologian, and altogether an incorrigible controversialist. He ardently desired his missionary work to be based on the idea that all people were members of one human family under God. His ideas concerning the doctrine of salvation and the doubts he expressed about the literal truth of the Bible were to lead to his excommunication in 1866. Thanks to a ruling in the civil courts he retained his bishopric (though not without creating a local schism). He finally lost the sympathy of the white colonists and the colonial administration when, in 1874, he campaigned against the irregular trial of Langalibalele, the Hlubi chief, who had been charged with treason and rebellion against the Natal government. Up to that time, Colenso had believed in the British government as the protector of the poor and weak, and the means by which truth and justice would prevail. Thereafter, he saw expediency and force prevailing at the expense of the people over whom God had set the government as protector. He was therefore to oppose the British invasion of Zululand in 1879, for he believed it was an unjust war which the local imperial authorities had deliberately provoked.

Yet, through all of his bitter disputes over theological, constitutional and legal issues his passion for truth and justice (as he saw them) never ceased to shine out. The Zulu recognised in him a true friend and champion, and called him *Sobantu*, 'Father of the people'. The pitiful plight of Zululand after 1879 was to turn him into the deposed Cetshwayo's staunchest champion. Colenso profoundly influenced his daughters, particularly his eldest, the plain and intense Harriette, who became known to the Africans as *uDlwedlwe*, the 'staff' of her father. As indefatigable a controversialist as her father, she was to spend most of her life in bitter dispute with the Natal authorities and the British government on behalf of the Africans of Natal and Zululand. On her father's death she continued to carry high the embattled standard of the royal cause in Zululand, first on behalf of Cetshwayo, and then for his son, Dinuzulu.

This was in the future. In 1857 Bishop Colenso was still content to act as the exiled iziGqoza princes' mentor and to fit them for the role the Natal government had in mind for them. Their potential value cut two ways, however. For if the Natal officials regarded the princes as useful tools in the event of their requiring leverage in the internal affairs of Zululand, then Mpande understood equally well that he could play Mkhungo, Sikhotha and their Natal patrons off against Cetshwayo to restrain his ambitions. As long as the two brothers were alive and safe in Natal, Cetshwayo could never be completely sure of the succession.

A complicating factor in the manoeuvres against each other by king and prince was the encroachment into Zulu territory of Boer farmers from the Utrecht District.[11] Following the collapse of the abortive Klip River Republic in 1848, numbers of the irreconcilable Boers, who would not remain under British rule, began in 1852 to lay out farms and build their dwellings in the wide, grassy plains between the Mzinyathi and Ncome rivers. These expanses were in Zululand proper, as recognised by the boundary agreement of 1843 with Natal. But the land had been left relatively empty when Langalibalele and his Hlubi fled to Natal in 1848 after being attacked by Mpande. By early 1854 the Boers in the narrow wedge of land between the two rivers numbered nearly 200 families, quite enough to discourage any Zulu attempt to dislodge them. Mpande decided to leave well alone, and in September 1854 ceded the farms to the Boers, who proclaimed their insecure and troubled little Republic of Utrecht. There, under Zulu sufferance, they apprehensively remained, always unsure of the security of their tenure.

Some of these land-hungry Boers, stifled in their pocket republic, nevertheless began to encroach east of the Ncome, and to lay claim to lands which Mpande categorically denied ever ceding them. Then, on 6 November 1859 the Utrecht Republic submerged itself into the larger South African Republic, becoming the Utrecht District under a landdrost appointed by Pretoria. Not only was the eastern border of the South African Republic shifted east thereby to the Ncome, but the Utrecht Boers' land claims across the Ncome were united under one political authority with those of Transvaal Boers, who were steadily infiltrating the hazy frontier zone about the headwaters of the Phongolo which was ruled by Hamu.

These Boers, with their eyes firmly on the eastern horizon and determined to spill over the borders deep into Zululand, began to play a subtle game. They knew of Cetshwayo's continuing insecurities and fear of rivals for the crown. By seeming to offer him their support against such claimants they hoped in return to win his backing for their land claims. There was, of course, nothing new in this strategy. It had worked with Mpande against Dingane in 1839 and, as we shall see, it was to work again with spectacular success in 1884.

Cetshwayo's recurrent nightmare that a new rival might yet emerge to challenge his hard-won position as heir was given uncomfortable reality by Mpande's growing favour for Mthonga, his son by a beloved junior wife, Nomantshali.[12] She was the daughter of Sigulana of the Bhele people, and as great a favourite of Mpande as Bhibhi, who was also a Bhele, had been of Senzangakhona. Nomantshali was of medium height and build, light-coloured, good-looking, and not fat. Mpande forsook all his other wives for her, and rumours soon abounded concerning her undue influence over the besotted king, stories which it was extremely convenient for the threatened Cetshwayo to credit. The aged king's growing physical and mental weaknesses (his inability to walk, his memory losses) were all put down to the love-charms with which Nomantshali was allegedly bewitching him. Touching Cetshwayo closely, it was also told that she had · gone so far in her spitefulness as to cast a spell on Ngqumbazi, his mother. Ngqumbazi, it was whispered, had begun to grow a beard like a man after having passed by emDumezulu, Nomantshali's homestead.

What does seem plain, in the midst of these extravagant tales of the *isigodlo*, is that Mpande, thoroughly uncomfortable with having to co-exist with his overmighty son, Cetshwayo, and encouraged by his sweet Nomantshali, was deliberately raising up a new 'bull calf' to challenge him. It was even sometimes said that Mpande had set Cetshwayo and Mbuyazi against each other to quarrel to the death so that the path to the throne would be cleared for this cherished son of his dearly loved wife. Cetshwayo could not brook this carefully nurtured threat to his succession indefinitely. Relations became increasingly strained between him and his father over the affair. Receiving no satisfaction, Cetshwayo decided to act.

In early March 1861 Bhejana kaNomageje, Cetshwayo's trusted *inceku*, who was of the same age as his master, was entrusted with the task. At the head of a reliable detachment of the iNgobamakhosi, Cetshwayo's favourite *ibutho*, he surrounded Nomantshali's emDumezulu homestead, which was in the Mahlabathini plain between the middle reaches of the White Mfolozi and kwaNodwengu. But Bhejana's intelligence was faulty, and he had seriously mistimed his coup. Their main quarry, the fourteen-year-old Mthonga and his younger brother, Mgidlana, were – fortunately for them – away. Nomantshali herself was also absent, for she was visiting esiKlebheni in the emaKhosini, where Langazana, Senzangakhona's revered widow, presided. Only her youngest son, Mpoyiyana, was at home. He managed to evade the ring of armed men, and tried to make his way to his mother at esiKlebheni. But Bhejana's men caught up with him in the valley of the White Mfolozi, and dragged the terrified boy back with them to kwaNodwengu, where they presumed Nomantshali to be sheltering with her doting old husband.

Mpande, badly shaken at the armed incursion and at the sight of Mpoyiyana a captive, denied she was there. Thereupon, Manyonyo kaZongolo, the officer in command of the detachment of iNgobamakhosi, quite forgot the respect due to

Mpande as king, and rudely berated the old man, demanding that he bring No-mantshali out of the *isigodlo*. Since she was not there, Mpande could not com-ply, and Bhejana's men had at length to accept that. But thwarted, angry, and fearful that their whole mission had miscarried, they then brutally turned on the weeping and quaking young Mpoyiyana, who had sought refuge in his old fa-ther's arms. Disregarding his pathetic entreaties, they dragged the little prince from Mpande's embrace and hurried him out of kwaNodwengu to his pitiful death. Mpande, who knew that he himself had barely escaped assassination, could do no more than break into tears. It is remembered that he cried out in impotent despair to Sonkehlenkehle, his *inceku*, 'Give me an assegai so that I may kill my-self.' He then turned for a last time to the party of killers, about to set out in search of Nomantshali and her surviving sons. Solemnly, he assured them, 'Since you have treated me in this way, you will never see my young sons, not until the stars shine during the day.'[13]

Bhejana was not deterred from his mission, however, and Manyonyo scattered his men into the hills in search of the fugitives. Nomantshali's hiding-place was eventually betrayed, some say by Langazana herself, who was currying favour with Cetshwayo. So Manyonyo's men tracked Nomantshali down in a little *umuzi* attached to esiKlebheni. She was engulfed in terrible grief, for she had al-ready learned of the murder of Mpoyiyana, her youngest boy. Knowing it was all over with her, she did not wait to be hunted down in her hut, but came out of the homestead to meet her killers. Pathetically she said to her executioners, 'Let me be killed in the wilderness, for everyone dear to me is dead.'[14] It is likely that they would not have stabbed her, but, as a woman, would have throttled her to death. She died without the knowledge that Mthonga and Mgidlana had managed to make good their escape to Utrecht by way of Khambula mountain.

Cetshwayo was mortified when he learned the details of this outrageous and botched affair. His orders had been that Nomantshali and her children were to be done away with without fuss at emDumezulu, and his men had quite exceeded their instructions by threatening and insulting the old king and causing an up-roar among the royal *amakhanda*. The whole unsavoury affair was now completely in the open and a matter of unfavourable general comment. It was said in ret-rospect that on the day of the foul deed 'the earth shook and the mountains thun-dered'.[15] Relations between Cetshwayo and Mpande were inevitably soured con-siderably further. Mpande was never to lose his sense of impotent grief and resentment, and was heard to say that he did not believe that the ancestral spir-its would ever allow Cetshwayo to become king after such an act.

Mthonga and Mgidlana, meanwhile, were still at large in the Utrecht District. The land-hungry Boers knew that they had been delivered a trump-card, and they were determined to play it for all it was worth. Within hours of receiving Mtho-nga and Mgidlana, representatives of the South African Republic were negoti-ating their extradition with Cetshwayo, who had marched on the Ncome River at the head of a large force. By the so-called Treaty of Waaihoek in March 1861, to which Cetshwayo and his brothers Ziwedu and Sitheku allegedly put their marks (though they subsequently vehemently denied that they had),[16] the

Boers handed the princes over, having first extracted a promise that Cetshwayo would spare their lives. In return, Cetshwayo made the concession – so fatal for the future – of recognising indeterminate Boer land claims east of the Ncome.

Thus was laid the basis for the future extensive Transvaal claims upon Zulu territory.[17] These very soon had a detrimental effect on the already strained relations between Hamu and Cetshwayo, because much of the Boer encroachment would occur at the expense of Hamu's lands in north-western Zululand. These were particularly tempting to the Boers because of the ideal combination of grazing grasses they offered. On the other side of the coin, the Treaty of Waaihoek gave Cetshwayo precisely what he wanted in the short term. Not only had he secured Mthonga and Mgidlana, but, in the course of the negotiations, the Boers had publicly recognised his claim to be Mpande's heir. This greatly strengthened his position within the kingdom, which was soon made unassailable when the Natal authorities, eager not to be upstaged by the Boers, also hastened to acknowledge him as heir.

In Natal and the Cape a number of British officials had long cherished their own designs on the western marches of the Zulu kingdom. Most significant among these was Theophilus Shepstone, the Natal Secretary for Native Affairs. *Somtsewu*, as he was known to the Africans, 'father of the white man',[18] was destined to have the most profound effect on the affairs of Zululand, and the fate of the Zulu royal house would one day be in his hands.

Shepstone was, in many ways, an extraordinary person.[19] H. Rider Haggard, who for a time was on his staff, described him as 'a curious, silent man, who had acquired many of the characteristics of the natives among whom he lived. Often it was impossible to guess from his somewhat impassive face what was passing in his brain. He had the power of silence, but he observed everything and forgot little.'[20]

Certainly, Shepstone was secretive and reticent, but this was in part the carapace of a person sensitive to criticism and cautious in making decisions. Yet he also shrewdly understood the power of silence, which he employed against those who attempted to control his activities. He was mistrustful of officials outside his department, and kept his vast fund of information on the black people of the region in his own mental armoury, to be brought out only if it served his purposes. His first loyalty was to the interests of Natal, as he perceived them; South Africa came next and the British empire only third. That is why the Boers considered him one of their own, despite his 1820 Settler and missionary background, and why an imperial administrator like Sir Bartle Frere thought of him as essentially un-British, 'a singular type of Africander Talleyrand'.[21]

Despite being widely credited in white circles with fully understanding black society, Shepstone's grasp was inevitably limited by his unquestioning belief in the superiority of western civilisation and Christian mores, which justified in turn his thoroughgoing paternalism. Yet it cannot be gainsaid that with his self-assurance, energy, great physical courage and simple dignity he cut a commanding figure. For many Africans in Natal this lantern-jawed white man, with his cleft chin and inscrutable gaze, became a sort of father-figure as he set about regulating their lives:

Pure of heart is he whose ears glow with the rays of the sun.
The young and hornless bull that has repeatedly silenced other young bulls.
The bird that devours other birds, some in one way and some in another.[22]

Shepstone first visited Natal in 1838 as a member of Major Charters's expedition to Port Natal. He returned in 1845 as Diplomatic Agent to the Native Tribes in Natal. In 1853 his position was upgraded to Secretary for Native Affairs, and he was to hold the post until 1875. For thirty unbroken years, therefore, from his poky office in Pietermaritzburg, he administered the lives of the black people living in Natal, maintained a network of diplomatic relations with black states throughout south-east Africa, and trained up a school of administrators in his own image. Through them, his 'Native Policy' would long survive his retirement. Basic to it was the location system, which was introduced in 1846. In an important sense it was an attempt by officials, and the British government whom they represented, to protect the African population from the settlers who wished to exploit them as cheap labour. Lack of funds meant, however, that the locations were never turned, as Shepstone had initially hoped they would be, into active agencies of western civilisation, with its attendant mechanical and agricultural skills. Instead, they remained places where Africans could continue to lead their own lives away from the land thrown open to white farmers.

This being the case, Shepstone improvised an expedient system of indirect rule to run the locations. He was conscious of the dangers inherent in a precipitate transition from an African to a colonial administration, and believed that hereditary chiefs should be left with a modicum of their former powers under the supervision of white officials. He intended that under this arrangement the chiefs' authority would gradually be undermined and eventually negated once their adherents came to realise that the effective source of power resided not with them, but with the white officials. The system was paid for by the imposition of a hut tax, which had the advantage of forcing blacks out of the locations onto the labour market. Here again, by preserving a certain continuity with the existing norms and practices of black society, and by maintaining the homestead as the basis of the system of production, it was possible, without eliciting much resistance, to divert a proportion of the homestead's surplus – whether as tax, rent or labour – from the chiefs to the colonial authorities. This expedient system, which gradually became elevated to a set of principles, would one day be introduced into Zululand when it became a British colony.

In the 1850s and 1860s, however, when Zululand was still an independent kingdom, the 'Shepstone system' impacted on it less directly, though still significantly. Shepstone had come to believe that the sparsely populated country along the western borderlands of Zululand could in time serve as an outlet for Natal's rapidly expanding African population. There, he hoped, free from interference from bigoted settlers, he could return to his earlier plans and create a 'civilised' black state under white administrators.

Other officials, thinking in geopolitical terms, wanted British rule extended over the area to create a buffer against the landlocked South African Republic's attempts to reach the sea and gain economic viability. Its way was blocked by the Portuguese at Delagoa Bay and by the Swazi kingdom, but the Boers clearly had a corridor in mind, to be driven through northern Zululand or along the Thukela.[23] Their diplomatic success in forging an alliance with Cetshwayo in March 1861 made the British fear that he might well be prepared to grant them such a concession. Shepstone was approached by Mpande, who invoked his mediation, and, alarmed at the various possible consequences of the recent rapprochement between Cetshwayo and the Boers, took it upon himself in April 1861 to visit the old king. He hoped that he would be able to shore up Mpande's authority and thereby reassert British influence at the expense of that of Cetshwayo and the Boers.

Shepstone arrived at kwaNodwengu on 8 May 1861 with a small escort, having made his presence felt in Zululand by moving with pompous deliberation along a meandering route.[24] At kwaNodwengu he immediately announced his full support for Mpande before the assembly of notables. Cetshwayo, who had accurately divined the purpose of Shepstone's visit, had refused his father's orders to be at the gathering. He eventually consented to attend only when Shepstone threatened that Natal would recognise Mkhungo as the next king, and when those about him advised him that it was in his own interests to be diplomatic.

But when Cetshwayo did arrive at kwaNodwengu, where thousands of Mpande's *amabutho* were already assembled, he came wearing a feather headdress ominously similar to the one he had worn at Ndondakusuka, and escorted by men of the uThulwana *ibutho* dressed in full regalia. The uThulwana then began to dance before Mpande, who was in his small hand-pushed wagon, flanked by Masiphula and the other Zulu dignitaries who were hosting Shepstone. As the uThulwana reached the climax of their dance, they began to shout, 'Iya! Ehe! Cover them with dust! Insignificant little fools!'[25] and for a terrible moment it seemed as if the massacre of Retief and his followers was to be repeated. The king, Masiphula and other chiefs desperately shouted at the frenzied uThulwana to hold back, though Cetshwayo made no move. At length the tumult died down, and Cetshwayo came face-to-face with Shepstone.

Throughout their stormy confrontation Cetshwayo was perpetually on the point of losing control, and his *izinduna* had periodically to intervene to quieten him down. The initial bone of contention was the prince's demand that Natal should return Mkhungo because, he insisted, the killing would never stop in Zululand until then. Shepstone countered with the suggestion that all Mkhungo's remaining close kin in the kingdom should be allowed to join him in Natal. The already heated discussion then threatened to go completely out of control when Cetshwayo brought up the subject of Ngoza kaLudaba of the Majozi, Shepstone's chief *induna*, in whose homestead in Natal Mthonga was living. It appeared that, with a crass disregard for Zulu etiquette, Ngoza (who was only a commoner) had accompanied his master into the *isigodlo* at kwaNodwengu when Shepstone was invited there for private consultations with Mpande. To make matters worse, it was quite likely that Ngoza's real purpose in penetrating the *isigodlo* had been to deliver a clandestine message from Mthonga to his sister, Bathonyile. Cetshwayo passionately required Ngoza's death, but Shepstone stolidly asserted his right to beat his own dogs.

The assembled *amabutho*, who had been listening to the exchange, then began to move menacingly in, all of them inflamed even more than before. Again, it seemed as if Shepstone, this interfering white outsider, was perilously close to suffering the same fate as Retief. But Shepstone was nothing if not brave and in command of himself. As his praises commemorated:

He bathes in a crocodile pool,
And the crocodile does not harm him,
It merely swallows the froth of his body-dirt.[26]

Thus, he sat on unflinching, with set face, surrounded by the great circle of gesticulating and shouting *amabutho*. Mpande's *izinduna* belaboured them with sticks in an effort to bring them to order, while the king himself berated them for their shameful behaviour and lack of respect to a guest. Once their joint effort had finally succeeded in quietening the *amabutho* down, Shepstone rose to face them. His sense of theatre did not desert him. Pointing in the direction of the ocean, he solemnly warned the restless *amabutho* of the bitter revenge that would come from across the seas should he be harmed. The turbulent assembly could not but respect his indomitable courage. Cetshwayo appreciated it too, and he was later to say of Shepstone: 'Somtseu is a great man; no man but he could have come through that day alive.'[27]

In the calm that followed the earlier homicidal excitement, the meeting proceeded. In a bid to make Cetshwayo more amenable to overtures from Natal, Shepstone had set about persuading Mpande during their earlier discussions to recognise Cetshwayo as his heir. Confronted by the irresistible combination of pressure from the uSuthu within the kingdom and the British from without, Mpande had at last capitulated. So, in the presence of his assembled councillors and *amabutho*, with Shepstone as witness, he proceeded formally to proclaim Cetshwayo his heir-apparent. It had taken nearly five years since the carnage at Ndondakusuka, but the succession was at last unequivocally Cetshwayo's, and the kingdom effectively in his hands. Shepstone returned to Natal with an elephant tusk with which Cetshwayo had presented him in half-apology for the insults and threats to his life, but it was the only really concrete thing he carried back from his mission.

The drama between Cetshwayo and his rival brothers was not yet altogether played out, however.[28] While they remained at large they would always pose a real, if considerably diminished, threat. Between October and November 1868, for example, Cetshwayo's scouts spotted Mkhungo, Sikhotha and Mthonga hovering provocatively near the confluence of the Thukela and Mzinyathi rivers, just south of the Zululand border. Cetshwayo over-reacted by massing an armed force at the border and protesting their presence to Natal. The princes were accordingly removed deeper into Natal. They had one last card to play, nevertheless, in the succession stakes. Just before Mpande's death, in mid-1872, Mkhungo and Mthonga braved death to visit their expiring father at kwaNodwengu. It made no difference to their cause. Cetshwayo sent an *impi* to seize them, and they were chased back to the border, only escaping after firing at their pursuers. Those homesteads which had received them – some thirty in number – were systematically destroyed with their inhabitants. The princes had quite ceased to be a serious threat to the heir, whose power daily became surer.

Mpande was old and ailing by 1861, increasingly desirous of enjoying what domestic pleasures he could after the murder of Nomantshali, and relieved to shed some of the many cares of state. The ambitious and energetic Cetshwayo was now his undisputed heir, exercising an increasing number of the royal prerogatives formerly wielded by his father. But Mpande was still the king, and Cetshwayo only the prince. The venerable king continued to officiate at the great national festivals, and only he could give permission for the formation of new *amabutho* or the marriage of existing ones. Since he was consequently more than a mere figurehead, Cetshwayo had to refer most important decisions to him for his approval, besides according him the proper deference in public. Moreover, Mpande could still keep his arrogant son in some check by playing the Boers and British off against him. He also found new allies in the missionaries, whom he let into the kingdom in increasing numbers after 1856. The most important new missions to be established were those of the Hermannsburg and Berlin Societies (both Lutheran), and those of the Anglicans, sponsored by the Society for the Propagation of the Gospel. Schreuder, whose Norwegian missions had previously been the only ones permitted, was enraged at the Anglicans for horning in on Lutheran territory.[29]

These confessional disputes were of no concern to Mpande. He was prepared to accept the presence of missionaries purely for the useful material benefits and contacts they might bring. By allowing greatly increased missionary activity he hoped to create a favourable impression in Natal, especially since he was able to use the missionaries as political advisers and intermediaries with the colonial authorities. It remained axiomatic with both him and Cetshwayo (who, for his part, actively distrusted the missionaries, not least on account of their connections with his father), that Christianity should not be allowed to disrupt the institutions of Zulu society. Consequently, both deliberately discouraged conversions. This was deeply frustrating for the missionaries. Robert Robertson, for example, who established his Anglican mission station among the tall trees on a hill-top at kwa-Magwaza in south-eastern Zululand, was progressively warped by his failure to win many conversions into becoming one of Cetshwayo's severest critics. Harping on Cetshwayo's adverse attitude towards converts, he was to play a considerable part during the late 1870s in moulding British opinion against him as a danger to Christianity and civilisation.

Cetshwayo was no slower than his father to seek support in the outside world. But in sharp contrast to the missionaries courted by Mpande, he turned to hunter-traders, precisely the class of whites most distrusted and disapproved of by the men of God – a dislike heartily reciprocated by the rough types of the frontier. When he set about making alliances with hunter-traders from Natal, it was specifically in order to acquire the vital firearms he had been lacking at Ndondakusuka. Chief and foremost among these new allies was John Dunn, or Jantoni as the Zulu called him, the neatly bearded hunter with his wide, visionary gaze, who had fought against him so effectively at Ndondakusuka.[30] Cetshwayo begged him in 1857 to come to Zululand because he wanted 'a white man as a friend to live near him and advise him'.[31] Cetshwayo settled him in the tract of coastal land from the lower Thukela drift north across the Matigulu River as far as the Ngoye forest. There Dunn accumulated wives (two of them sisters of the king and several from his *isigodlo*), adherents, cattle and land, and became one of the most influential chiefs in the country.

As Cetshwayo's 'white chief', friend and confidant, who kept the king spellbound with tales of the world across the seas,[32] Dunn became the main conduit through which his patron dealt with the Natal government and settlers, just as the missionary Schreuder was Mpande's. No messenger from Cetshwayo, Dunn later recalled, was ever sent to the Natal government without first consulting him, because he would write the letter to be carried. When the messengers returned, he always heard the verbal message, and read the written answer to Cetshwayo.[32] Significantly, Cetshwayo used Dunn's trading connections during the 1860s to obtain the firearms and gunpowder he wanted (together with luxuries like sugar, salt and coffee), and by the early 1870s several hundred of his adherents were armed with guns. Dunn tried to excuse this lucrative trade to the sceptical Natal authorities on the grounds that, by arming Cetshwayo, 'he would soon get all the nation on his side', and so prevent another civil war.[34]

During this period Cetshwayo spent much of his time at his emaNgweni *ikhanda*, just north-east across the Mhlathuze from oNdini. In 1867 Mpande gave the uThulwana permission to marry. Cetshwayo's first son, Dinuzulu, was born in 1868. His mother, Nomvimbi, a daughter of Msweli of the Nzimela people and one of Mbuyazi's *isigodlo* girls, had been captured at Ndondakusuka and taken to the *isigodlo* at emaNgweni, where she worked as a menial. There she was forced by Cetshwayo and made pregnant.[35] In later years he fathered another son, Manzolwandle, and six daughters, namely, Sililo, Simiso, Sabede, Siyele, Bekisile and Nomandlambi.[36] Mkebeni kaDabulamanzi, Cetshwayo's nephew, related a tradition in the royal family that, soon after Dinuzulu's birth, Cetshwayo had a dream in which the spirits of Ndaba and Dingane appeared to him. They dolefully reminded him that the members of the royal house were given to killing one another, so, to put an end to the customary slaughter, only this male child, Dinuzulu, would survive into manhood and reign.[37]

The tranquillity of the kingdom (disturbed in 1863 by an outbreak of smallpox)[38] continued to be compromised by the uncontrollable external forces Mpande and Cetshwayo had conjured up during the long-drawn-out succession crisis. The Boers proceeded as before to encroach on Zululand's western borders, and their land claims enjoyed some credence thanks to Cetshwayo's expedient, but ill-considered, cession of March 1861. Within a month of Shepstone's embassy of May 1861, both Mpande and Cetshwayo had repudiated any cession of Zulu territory east of the Ncome.[39] But Cornelius van Rooyen and other Utrecht Boers moved into the territory anyway, proclaimed a corridor down the Thukela to the sea, took up defensive positions in their laagers, and called on the South African Republic for military assistance.

Cetshwayo began mobilising his *amabutho* with the intention of preventing the Boers from making good their claims. The Natal colonists, however, extremely suspicious of Cetshwayo's intentions after Ndondakusuka and living in fear of a Zulu attack, leapt to the erroneous conclusion that he was planning an invasion of Natal to seize Mkhungo. What few regular British troops there were stationed in Natal were rushed to the border, while the frontier farmers trekked away to the security of the towns. Cetshwayo, in his turn, perceived this military activity as a prelude to a British invasion of Zululand in favour of his rivals. So he withdrew his *amabutho* preparing to clear the disputed territory of the Utrecht Boers, and deployed them instead to repel the British concentrating along the Thukela.

Since neither side actually wanted a confrontation the crisis subsided by August 1861, and both Zulu and British troops were withdrawn. But the 'invasion scare' of 1861 caused Cetshwayo to lose his crucial opportunity to deal decisively with the Boers in the disputed territory. Nor was it an opportunity to be repeated. The moment he turned away in July 1861 to face the Natal frontier, the Boers came out of their laagers and proceeded to occupy the territory they claimed east of the Ncome. They also reopened negotiations with Mpande, and in August 1861 the king promised to honour Cetshwayo's land concession of March 1861. Faced with such a combination, Cetshwayo hesitated to act and the moment was lost.

At the end of 1864 the confident Boers began to assert their land rights even more blatantly than before by beaconing off a boundary line between their farms east of the Ncome and what they conceded was still Zulu territory. Thoroughly provoked, Cetshwayo immediately ordered his people to tear down the offending beacons. But then, in December 1864, Mpande ceded the South African Republic an avenue down the Thukela to the sea in return for the promise of their military support.

This continuing Boer expansion, and Mpande's readiness to co-operate with them in order to exercise some control over his over-mighty heir, had the vital effect of compelling Cetshwayo to turn to Natal. In what was a major shift of policy on his part, he sent off messengers to Pietermaritzburg to request the Natal government to intervene in the boundary dispute. His previous, brief accommodation of convenience with the Boers was definitely over, and in future Cetshwayo would look ever more frequently to the British to counteract their insatiable expansionism, abetted as it was by his father's unfortunate scheming.

The prince's relations with the Natal authorities continued to improve during the late 1860s. Several times he made further requests for British intervention in the boundary dispute, which the Boers continued to press hard. In June 1869 the government of the South African Republic went so far as to allot farms east of the Ncome to Boer settlers, and in February 1870 Commandant Paul Kruger, the future president of the Transvaal, tried to browbeat Mpande at kwaNodwengu into making further concessions.[40] Pressured thus, Cetshwayo had reached the point by June 1870 of being willing to offer to cede Natal a buffer strip between the South African Republic and Zululand in order to bring the debilitating issue to an end.

If it had enjoyed a free hand, the Natal government, urged on by Shepstone who, for a brief moment, imagined his expansionist dreams were about to be realised, would probably have taken up Cetshwayo's offer. But the British government, anxious to avoid the increased expense and political responsibility, refused to give its sanction. Thus an important opportunity was lost for bringing this potentially very destabilising border dispute to an end. A fresh chance had presented itself in 1869 when, in response to yet another plea from Cetshwayo and Mpande, the Natal government agreed to arbitrate. This initiative came to naught in its turn when Boer-British relations broke down in 1871 over the Kimberley diamond fields dispute. So the question of the Disputed Territory, as it became known, remained a dangerous and unresolved quarrel between the Zulu and Boers, and it was allowed to simmer on with ultimately tragic consequences for the Zulu kingdom.

PART III

Warding off the falling tree

13

Mr Shepstone Crowns a King

Shepstone noted in his diary that King Mpande died on 18 October 1872 at kwa-Nodwengu. Since the Zulu did not officially acknowledge the king's death until several months after the event, the precise date will remain obscure, and it is possible that he breathed his last as early as September 1872.[1] In the kingdom itself, as the mealies ripened and harvest time approached, word spread from kwaNodwengu that the king was 'indisposed'.[2] The people understood this to mean that the old man had died, but dared not speak of it in so many words. For this was the period when, according to the old Zulu custom, the body of the dead king was bound up in a squatting position and, wrapped in the hide of a freshly slaughtered reddish-brown young steer, which left his head uncovered, was propped up against one of the wooden uprights of his hut. A fire of aromatic woods and bones was kept ablaze in the hearth to dry the corpse and disguise the foul stink of decomposition. All the great men of his inner council, and the women living in the isigodlo (who shaved their heads in mourning), had to endure the stench as best they could, stuffing their noses with the leaves of the umsuzwane shrub, whose disagreeable smell suppressed one even more vile. Only once the corpse had desiccated and become odourless would the late king cease to be 'indisposed' and his body be buried.

There was no crying or lamentation for Mpande in the isigodlo, for it was the duty of all at kwaNodwengu to conceal the king's demise until his successor made the fact public. Indeed, the major practical objective of the custom just described was to enable the king's successor to keep the great fact of his predecessor's death secret until he had securely gathered up the reins of authority in his own hands. Thus, when Cetshwayo learned that his father was at last on death's threshold, he did all he could to ensure that the semblance of normality was maintained. The young uMcijo ibutho, which was stationed at kwaNodwengu, was given strict orders not to leave when the king died, and precautions were taken to prevent the isigodlo girls from running away. On 22 October he summoned all the princes and important personages of the kingdom to appear before him and to accompany him to kwaNodwengu. There they all subjected themselves to the crown prince's authority, and the pervasive fear of a disputed succession was dissipated. Confident now that his word as king would be obeyed, Cetshwayo allowed def-

163

inite news of Mpande's death to seep out, and his corpse to be buried with full ceremony.

That had not been possible with his royal brothers, Shaka and Dingane, who had been hastily interred after their assassinations. The circumstances were more propitious for Mpande, who had expired of natural causes in the *isigodlo* of his favourite residence. It was customary for a king to be buried in the homestead where he had breathed his last, and Mpande's grave was accordingly dug by his household officers at kwaNodwengu, between the top end of the great cattle enclosure, on the left-hand side, and the *isigodlo*. It was about two and a half metres deep and shaped like a boot. There were few people at kwaNodwengu when, shortly after sunrise, Mpande's body was handed down into the grave, for the actual moment of burial had been kept secret among the principal members of his household. The body was placed in the 'toe' of the grave and propped up with stones. Personal articles last used by the deceased, such as his loincovers, arm rings, beadwork, blankets, sleeping mats, snuff boxes and eating utensils were interred with him. His pots were buried outside the *ikhanda*, and his four great chairs, each carved from a single piece of wood, were burned. Four of his spears were thrown into a hole among the rocks at the Ntukwini River nearby, rather than being laid beside his corpse with his other possessions. It was feared his spirit might use them to 'stab' people, so that they would be afflicted with sharp pains, blood would come from their mouths, and they would die.

The age-old custom was for a body-servant, one or two wives and several *isigodlo* girls to follow the king into the grave so that their shades might continue to serve his spirit, as they had done during life. Although it was announced, primarily for the consumption of the British who found such practices totally abhorrent, that this custom had not been followed at Mpande's burial, the fact was otherwise. Cetshwayo gave orders that the late king's body-servant and two of his wives should follow him into the spirit world. The victims had to be overpowered unexpectedly, their mouths sealed and their necks broken, for if they succeeded in crying out their lives had to be spared. Just before his death, Mpande had warned Makhanda, who had been his body-servant and Dingane's before him, to flee his impending fate. So Makhanda, who had sewn on the headrings of both kings, and who had been present at Dingane's miserable death, escaped to the Ngoye forest. His place in the grave was taken by Mpande's great *inceku*, the exceedingly stout Nhlangano kaLubaca of the Ntuli people, who became the 'mat' on which the royal body was placed. Rumour always had it that other attendants who quietly disappeared at that time must also have joined their late master.

Because his councillors insisted that he would be ritually polluted if he went near the corpse, Cetshwayo did not attend his father's burial in person, but remained at his oNdini *ikhanda* near the mouth of the Mhlathuze. Masiphula, the late king's chief *induna*, conducted the burial proceedings. Once the grave was filled with soil and covered with stones, it was thoroughly fenced off with branches and poles to prevent anyone getting near it. As was usual, kwaNodwengu was then soon abandoned, leaving the grave to be looked after by the head of a small *umuzi* in the immediate neighbourhood. The uDlambedlu *ibutho* was given the annual task of burning the grass in a wide radius around the grave, leaving a thick patch on it where the old grass could accumulate and a thicket of trees spring up. To burn the grass over the grave itself would have been tantamount to burning the king; likewise no person might touch the ground nearby with his stick on pain of being beaten for 'stabbing' the king. A royal grave such as Mpande's became a sanctuary for malefactors, and a special place of pilgrimage during national crises. Cattle would be sacrificed there, the ancient anthems sung and the king's spirit invoked.

Mpande's bones, if the allegations are true, were only allowed to rest in peace for seven years.[3] In September 1879, after the Zulu defeat by the British, various witnesses reported the exhumation of the king's body by a party of British soldiers. The soldiers were allegedly shown the site, which had been overgrown as intended by a thicket of bush, by John Dunn, though he did not wait for them to open the grave. They found four decayed blankets of different colours had been wrapped round the body, one inside the other. Outside there had been a kaross of jackal-skins, but this was quite rotten. Hospital orderlies packed the bones into a biscuit-box and put it in on a mule-wagon to be carried away. When questioned by members of the Natal Native Contingent concerning the fate of the bones, their white captain replied that they would be 'carried across the sea to be looked at'. Before they left, the soldiers put the stones back on the grave and covered it over. Such proceedings were not at all unusual in the early days of crass anthropological imperialism. Yet, even if the British did carry away some bones from Mpande's grave, there is no guarantee that they were those of the king, rather than one of the attendants buried with him. In any event, the site of the grave is marked today by a suitable funerary monument, and it is believed that Mpande's body still lies beneath the granite slabs.

After the royal burial, Cetshwayo ordered a small herd of oxen killed as food for the inhabitants of kwaNodwengu and sustenance for the shades of Mpande and his attendants in the spirit world. Only once this final ritual was completed did Cetshwayo feel he could officially inform the Natal government of his father's death. Yet, when his embassy left for Pietermaritzburg on 26 February 1873, it did not only carry word of the nation's mourning. It also conveyed a request that Shepstone visit Zululand both to cement the kingdoms's ties with Natal, and to demonstrate the colony's readiness to intervene on Cetshwayo's behalf in the matter of the Disputed Territory. Such overtures were necessary, for Zululand's circumstances had not changed simply because Cetshwayo was at last its sole ruler. In fact, his accession brought several matters to a head, both internal and external. Of these, internal problems took priority, for Cetshwayo had to establish himself firmly on his throne before he could deal effectively with his troublesome neighbours.

A major consequence of the festering succession dispute, and of the power-sharing arrangement between Cetshwayo and Mpande, had been to allow power to slip from the hands of the monarchy into those of the *izikhulu*, the great territorial chiefs. In effect, there had been two rival kings in Zululand since 1856, each bidding against the other for British or Boer support. The old king's councillors humoured him and gave him all the respect due to his exalted rank, meanwhile paying court to his heir. Cetshwayo, for his part, owed certain chiefs a special obligation for their support in the civil strife. The effect was to put more real power into the great chiefs' hands, so that by the time Cetshwayo came to the throne they were reasserting local prerogatives which had been lost in the time of Shaka and Dingane. The new king found that the great chiefs would brook little interference in the internal affairs of their own chiefdoms, and were even exercising the right of life and death over their adherents. The only real sway the king still exercised over them related to his control over the *amabutho* and marriage.

For Cetshwayo, what made the increasing independence of the great chiefs particularly alarming was his uneasy knowledge that pretenders to the throne were ready waiting in the wings, eager to throw in their lot with any coherent faction of great chiefs which might decide to overthrow him. Indeed, there were no fewer than five of Mpande's sons sheltering in Natal, of whom Mkhungo and Mthonga were the most active plotters. Mkhungo now lived in Weenen County, not far from the border, where he was gathering large numbers of iziGqoza refugees about him, while Mthonga, who had arrived in Natal in 1865, had moved to the Newcastle Division where he was close both to Zululand and the South African Republic.[4] When Cetshwayo invited Shepstone to Zululand, therefore, it was not only to elicit support against the Boers. It was also to discountenance these tenacious pretenders to the throne, and to undermine those ambitious territorial chiefs who were challenging royal power.

Shepstone, naturally, was following an agenda of his own when he responded to Cetshwayo's invitation, for he came not merely to demonstrate Natal's goodwill, but to give Cetshwayo British sanction by 'crowning' him. A personal love of power and intrigue certainly led him on, but his main purpose was to strengthen his influence over the kingdom and the territories beyond. This ambition was in line with his latest vision, which imagined tapping the vast wealth of central Africa (whether in terms of minerals or migrant labour) and funnelling it through the port of Durban. Safe corridors for this potentially rich commerce had still to be developed, and that is why the Zulu kingdom's compliance had to be secured.

Mindful of the very real dangers he experienced when he visited Mpande in 1861 and faced Cetshwayo down, Shepstone crossed the Thukela on 8 August 1873 with an armed escort of 110 officers and men of the settler Natal Volunteer Corps. This eager, if inexperienced, force incorporated detachments of the Natal Carbineers, the Richmond Rifles, the Weenen Yeomanry Cavalry, the Alexandra Mounted Rifles, the Victoria Mounted Rifles and the Durban Volunteer Artillery, with two field-guns. Some 300 Natal blacks under their *izinduna* also accompanied the expedition. This was the first time the Natal Volunteers had crossed their borders. They all knew they would be at Cetshwayo's mercy while in Zululand, and took precautions against a surprise attack. But they were also conscious that their object was to impress the Zulu with their military effectiveness, so every effort was made to maintain good discipline and efficiency, and to show off fancy drill manoeuvres and fire-power.[5]

Shepstone's expedition, carrying the paraphernalia with which to crown Cetshwayo, proceeded towards the Mahlabathini plain by way of Schreuder's mission at KwaMondi, flatteringly acclaimed by womenfolk and in receipt of presents and words of welcome from Cetshwayo. On the way, however, Shepstone learned to his chagrin and disquiet that Cetshwayo had not waited for him to give him his *imprimatur* as king, but had already gone through a form of coronation some time before.

Cetshwayo, who in July 1873 had been living in his oNdini *ikhanda* near the Mhlathuze River, declared the period of mourning for Mpande over, and made his arrangements to move up to the Mahlabathini plain, both to claim his throne and to meet Shepstone.[6] He mustered many thousands of his *amabutho* at oNdini and set off with them in full festival attire, though somewhat unsettled by the unlikely rumours that the long-dead Mbuyazi was coming with Shepstone to demand his rights. His *isigodlo* girls had to join the march to carry all his goods and chattels.

On the way, Cetshwayo thriftily combined the need to feed his host with the requirements of the purification ritual of the Great Hunt, or *iHlambo*. As the final ceremony connected with a king's obsequies, the *amabutho* had to wash their spears in blood to remove the evil influences that would have accumulated upon them during the time of mourning. The ritual hunt took place in the dense thornbush of the Mhlathuze valley. Cetshwayo's entire following formed an immense circle, about eight kilometres in diameter, and then closed in, killing so much game that it remained scarce in the vicinity for many years to come. The following few days the column continued to hunt for food as it went, Cetshwayo travelling comfortably part of the way in John Dunn's fine trap, drawn by four greys, and sleeping in the tent his considerate white chief had brought for him and his *isigodlo*.

There was a considerable undertow of anxiety to this triumphal progress, however, for no one was quite certain what would transpire when Cetshwayo reached the heart of the kingdom. Rumours abounded that the northern chiefs intended mischief, and Hamu's intentions in particular remained a matter for nervous speculation. These great northern magnates, whose support had been so vital for Cetshwayo in 1856, were apparently watching his progress towards the place of his ancestors with some resentment, and were derogatively enquiring who these people were who were bringing home the king. Cetshwayo knew he could not rule without the northerners' support, but it was also imperative that he leave them in no doubt as to where the real power lay. Consequently, when a contingent from northern Zululand joined up with his men while on the march, Cetshwayo collected all his followers who had been equipped with firearms through John Dunn, and had them fire two volleys to impress the newcomers. Word of this overwhelming technological superiority, he calculated, would rapidly filter back to the northerners' chiefs and dampen their belligerence.

When Cetshwayo reached Mthonjaneni, that great hill overlooking the White Mfolozi and the many *amakhanda* clustered in the emaKhosini valley and the

Mahlabathini plain below, he halted to await the arrival of the northern chiefs. Meanwhile, considerable discontent was mounting among Cetshwayo's senior councillors at the demeaning prospect of their new king having to receive the spurious sanction of a foreign dignitary. Led by Masiphula, they tried to persuade Cetshwayo, uncomfortably bivouacked in the rain and mist on the chilly Mthonjaneni heights, of the absolute necessity of securing the blessing of his ancestors on his reign. That alone would make him an authentic king. Their arguments were greatly strengthened by a favourable omen, which encouraged Cetshwayo to act. Lions were already extremely rare in those parts, but his men succeeded in cornering one in a thicket and slaying the royal beast. That sign from the spirits was enough for Cetshwayo, and he agreed to undergo the Zulu ritual of coronation before Shepstone arrived.

Cetshwayo accordingly led his entire force down into the emaKhosini valley and encamped at emaKheni, an ancestral *ikhanda* at the base of Mthonjaneni, six kilometres to the east of the site of uMgungundlovu. It had been built by Ndaba, used by his grandson Senzangakhona, and rebuilt by Mpande. Its name meant the 'Perfumery' because it was here that the king and his household were periodically annointed with sweet-smelling herbs. While he waited three days in this hallowed place for the northern contingents to arrive, Cetshwayo sacrificed to the ancestral spirits to make contact with them and to appease them. It was a tense time, for no one seemed quite sure what would happen. The situation lightened somewhat when the people from kwaNodwengu forded the White Mfolozi to greet their future king, bringing with them a large herd of cattle to feed his following, but anxiety returned as word came that the northern contingents were approaching, and the inevitable meeting must soon take place.

On the day, Cetshwayo and his followers arrived first at the open place near emaKheni selected for the ceremony. A much larger host then came threateningly into sight from the north-east. It was led by Zibhebhu, the new Mandlakazi chief, who had just succeeded his father, Maphitha, whose death had come soon after Mpande's.

Zibhebhu, with his cool, determined gaze, lop-sided little headring, and long nails of the Zulu aristocrat, was born in 1841.[7] In future years he would be hailed as the ablest general in Zululand. The British would come to recognise his intelligence, force of character and straightforwardness which, coupled with his undoubted courage and reserved mien, earned their sincere respect. They would approve too of his progressive admiration for western technology, while his trading interests and developed contacts with Natal would bring him into close working relationships with white traders and officials. These very abilities, interests and connections made Zibhebhu dangerous to Cetshwayo, especially since he maintained his late father's quest for greater political independence, and likewise resisted the exercise of royal authority in his chiefdom. As it was said, he practically looked upon himself as Cetshwayo's equal.[8] However, in 1873 he owed Cetshwayo a favour. Maphitha, towards the end of his life, suspected the cool and ambitious Zibhebhu (with what foundation it cannot be known) of planning to poison his decrepit father in order to accelerate his succession to the chieftainship. The old chief reported the matter to Mpande, who must surely have identified closely with his predicament, and received the royal permission to execute his over-eager successor. But the youthful Zibhebhu had stood by Cetshwayo in 1856, when the Mandlakazi turned the battle of Ndondakusuka in the prince's favour, and he intervened successfully on his behalf.[9] Would Zibhebhu, approaching the apprehensive Cetshwayo with his warlike Mandlakazi, remember his debt?

A kilometre from Cetshwayo's people the Mandlakazi began to form up into battle order, and the agitated word spread that they were going to take the king by force. Just then, to the west of the king, Hamu's Ngenetsheni and Mnyamana's Buthelezi took up position together on a small hill, placing him between the two forces. The Mandlakazi suddenly came on with a rush. Cetshwayo's panicked following began to prepare for flight, while Hamu's and Mnyamana's also took alarm. Cetshwayo, however, remained calm in the face of the mounting threat of violence, and sent forward some of his *izinceku* to calm the Mandlakazi down. Their powers of persuasion were greatly assisted by the presence of 200 of John Dunn's hunters, brandishing firearms, and by the number of Cetshwayo's men also carrying guns. The crisis, if it really had been one, passed off.

All the various parties came together peacefully and formed a great circle. Cetshwayo then met his obligations towards his ancestral spirits by sacrificing twenty head of cattle. These had first been driven to kwaNobamba, the Place of Unity and Strength built by Jama, Senzangakhona's father, where the *inkatha*, the sacred symbol of unity and strength, was kept. There, the cattle were imbued with the magical spirit of the birthplace of the nation. Through his sacrifice of these special cattle according to the prescribed rituals, Cetshwayo ensured that he, his throne and his people would be bound together in a mystic community under the favourable auspices of the royal ancestors. That night thousands assembled, both men and women, to celebrate the new reign. The following morning the assembly was much diminished, but it was then that Masiphula proclaimed Cetshwayo king. All the princes and great men of the kingdom took the opportunity to make speeches and affirm their loyalty to their new king. Hamu in particular, who had been suspected of making a bid for the crown, made a point of insisting on his fidelity and his sense of his royal brother's superiority.

Shepstone's arrival was still awaited, and Cetshwayo moved meanwhile to the emLambongwenya *ikhanda*, the home of Mpande's mother, Songiya, in the Mahlabathini plain. It was from this *ikhanda* that, on 16 August, Shepstone received the message that Masiphula had died, and that the court would be in mourning for four days. John Dunn later recalled that Masiphula, shortly before his death, found himself frozen out of a meeting between Cetshwayo and his other councillors at which Mpande's reign was the topic of discussion. The old *induna* understood the snub to mean his dismissal. He said to Dunn as he left his tent, where he had been sitting disconsolate, 'Good-bye, child of Mr. Dunn, I have finished my part and am now going to lie down...Look after your own affairs – I have no more a voice in matters.'[10]

But Masiphula was not to be allowed to retire in peace. Now that Cetshwayo was firmly in the saddle, he was determined to be rid of his father's old councillor. He could never forgive him for his ambivalence in the matter of the succession and his fluctuating support of Mbuyazi and Mkhungo, aimed at bolstering the position of his master, Mpande. His arrogant disregard of certain of Cetshwayo's orders at Mpande's funeral, coupled with his known ruthlessness, made the new king fear what he might yet do should he be allowed to live. Nevertheless, he dared not execute this renowned elder statesman publicly; the man, after all, had just proclaimed him king. So he went about his death by stealth. He brought into his confidence some of the women of his *isigodlo* who attended to the millet beer, and supplied them with poison to put in Masiphula's drink. Both Masiphula and Mnyamana (whom Cetshwayo already treated as Masiphula's equal,[11] and who would replace him on his death as chief councillor) kept their own personal drinking vessels, which were hollowed-out gourds, in the king's hut at emLambongwenya. One day at noon Masiphula drank deep in the king's presence, and at once began to sweat excessively and tremble. When he rose, staggering, to leave the king's presence, the girls sitting at the entrance mockingly called after him, 'Farewell, father!' Masiphula died before midnight, and Cetshwayo ordered his corpse to be taken to his homestead near the Mkhuze River for burial.[12]

Once Shepstone pitched camp on Mthonjaneni on 25 August,[13] a diplomatic game began, in which Cetshwayo was prevailed upon by his councillors to make many spurious delays as a calculated mark of disrespect to the pushy interloper, who responded with sharp threats to terminate proceedings. On 28 August Cetshwayo and Shepstone at last met, and their discussions continued throughout the following day at emLambongwenya, covering Natal-Zulu relations, Boer aggression, and certain 'laws' which Shepstone and Cetshwayo agreed to promulgate at the forthcoming 'coronation' ceremony. That grand pageant, orchestrated by Shepstone, duly took place on 1 September 1873 before a considerably smaller crowd than that which had attended Cetshwayo at emaKheni. A large marquee had been erected at the top of the great cattle enclosure at emLambongwenya. Cetshwayo and his councillors assembled before it, waiting to receive Shepstone. Somtsewu arrived on foot at the head of a procession consisting of a loudly playing military band, the two pieces of artillery and a long column of mounted Volunteers. All were in gala uniform and doing their best to impress. Jostling *amabutho* were ranged around the perimeter of the cattle enclosure.

Shepstone addressed the crowd in fluent Zulu, extracted the vocal assent of Cetshwayo and his councillors to the 'laws' he announced, and then led Cetshwayo, unattended except for a single *inceku*, into the marquee. There Shepstone invested him with a scarlet and gold mantle and placed an extraordinary crown, devised by the master-tailor of the 75th Regiment, on his head. He then led Cetshwayo forth, arrayed in all this trumpery finery, to take his seat upon a chair of state placed on a carpet in front of the marquee. The band struck up, the artillery fired a seventeen-gun salute, and Shepstone presented the king to his people. The following day he held further discussions with Cetshwayo and his council, and departed for Natal on 3 September.

What had this rather farcical 'coronation' actually achieved, besides providing the Natal Volunteers with some much-needed practical experience in the field? Zululand, after all, remained an independent kingdom. The British Colonial Office deprecated any suggestion that Shepstone's action might have pledged Britain to annexing the territory or even forming a protectorate over it, whatever nebulous degree of moral ascendancy Somtsewu might have gained over the Zulu. Cetshwayo's leading subjects, on the other hand, seem to have grasped its implications far more clearly than had the officials of the Colonial Office. Mnyamana, Hamu and other great chiefs had begun reproaching Masiphula shortly before his death for ever having countenanced Shepstone's coronation expedition. Doubtless, their anger was an element in his fall. And no sooner had Shepstone marched away to Natal, than many of the great chiefs also packed up and left for home as an indication to Cetshwayo of their displeasure with recent events. Mnyamana is reputed to have said to his abashed new king: 'So he is a good man, one who pisses with his legs apart; he plants one leg on the other side of the Thukela, and the other in the Zulu country!'[14]

Yet the chiefs' anger was not occasioned only by the insult of Shepstone's expedition to their monarch's dignity and the independence of his kingdom. Rather, they were put out by their realisation that Cetshwayo had used it to assert his power over them. The 'coronation laws' Shepstone had proclaimed had been agreed upon in consultation with Cetshwayo, and were loudly repeated to the common people present so that their purport could not be stifled by the great chiefs. They stated that the indiscriminate shedding of blood must cease; that no person could be condemned without trial and without the possibility of appeal to the king; that no life could be taken without the king's prior knowledge and consent; and that for minor crimes fines should be substituted for the death sentence. Quite clearly, their purpose was to restrict the independent authority of the chiefs, and to restore the exclusive power over life and death into the king's hands. The chiefs, naturally, did their best to ensure that the 'laws' remained a dead letter, and carried on doing their best to thwart Cetshwayo's efforts to reverse the trend towards oligarchy in his kingdom.

Cetshwayo, for his part, would henceforth attempt to rule as far as he could with the support and advice of his own favourites, loyal men he had raised up, rather than with that of the magnates of his kingdom, men whose mighty wings he still hoped to clip.[15] Not unnaturally, these great chiefs did their best to obstruct the appointment of the king's creatures to his council, and constantly worked to negate the influence of the likes of John Dunn and Cetshwayo's especial favourite, Sihayo kaXongo, the Qungebe chief.

Sihayo, tall, wiry and urbane, with jovial, flat features, had his chiefdom along the left back of the Mzinyathi opposite Rorke's Drift. He was involved in trade with Natal, and had a fondness for European clothes, especially boots. There were close connections between Sihayo's family and the royal house, and he had been one of Cetshwayo's staunchest supporters in 1856. But this self-important man, who was always receiving land and other gifts from the king, was intensely resented by the well-established members of the council. Such ani-

171

mosities would become of crucial import in the last days before the British invasion of 1879, and would seriously hamper Cetshwayo's ability to deal with the situation.[16]

Even more importantly, the 'laws' were destined to backfire disastrously on Cetshwayo during the mounting crisis preceding the war of 1879. For British officials had come to assume that the 'laws' were intended to restrict the king's right – rather than that of his chiefs – to execute his subjects. From there, it was but a short step to advancing the false claim that Cetshwayo had been crowned king conditional on the 'laws' laid down by Shepstone, and that, if he failed to abide by them, it was Britain's right and duty to depose him.

14

He Who Builds Homes with Spears[1]

While Cetshwayo was staying at emaKheni before his real coronation, he sent people out to find a suitable site for his new great place. They selected a stretch of thorn-country in the Mahlabathini plain between the kwaNodwengu and em-Lambongwenya amakhanda. There a gentle slope allowed for natural drainage down to the Mbilane stream, and the slight elevation above the plain gave scope for cooling breezes and afforded sweeping views of the level countryside and its perimeter of hills.[2] An immediate start was made with clearing the site. Thorn-trees had been felled, brush burned and makeshift shelters already erected before Shepstone came to emLambongwenya to crown Cetshwayo. The new *ikhanda* was called oNdini, the same as Cetshwayo's residence when heir-apparent near the lower reaches of the Mhlathuze. The name was derived from the Zulu word for a rim, as of a bowl, and was also an alternative for the Drakensberg Mountains. The connotation was therefore an assertion of the place's impenetrability.

Once Shepstone had returned to Natal, work went ahead on oNdini with feverish haste. Women busied themselves cutting thatch grass, plaiting grass ropes and fetching good clay for the hut floors. The young men of the uMcijo and iNgobamakhosi *amabutho* went south to the Nkandla forest to cut the saplings for the wicker frames of the huts. *Izangoma*, meanwhile, prepared their magical substances to protect the king's new chief residence from evil influences. Cetshwayo wished oNdini to be an exact replica of Dingane's uMgungundlovu, whose clay hut-floors, baked solid in the conflagration that destroyed his uncle's capital in 1838, would still have been discernible. Likewise, therefore, at the centre of oNdini's *isigodlo* was the 'black' section, which contained the king's private hut, the huts of his wives, and those of the elite of the *isigodlo* girls, who cooked for and waited on the king and royal women. They also served Cetshwayo as concubines, and it was whispered that the reason Cetshwayo produced relatively few royal offspring was that he preferred the maids-of-honour of the *isigodlo* to his official wives.[3]

The two 'white' sections on either side of the 'black' one enclosed the huts of Mpande's widows (the new king's 'mothers'), the royal children and those *isigodlo* girls who had not drawn the king's attention. Cetshwayo himself estimated that there were 400 maids-of-honour at oNdini alone, and a good many more

173

at other *amakhanda* where some of his wives or Mpande's widows lived. Their number was so great because on his father's death Cetshwayo had inherited his *isigodlo*, and all persons of importance regularly presented their daughters to him as a sign of their allegiance.[4] The two great wings of the *uhlangoti*, which housed the *amabutho* at oNdini, contained at least 1 000 huts, and possibly as many as 1 400, arranged by section in three or more rows. The *uhlangoti* surrounded the great parade ground, with the king's special cattle enclosures at the top. An outer palisade constructed of a double row of stout timbers two and a half metres high enclosed the whole complex. Outside it, behind the *isigodlo*, stood two small homesteads, where coppersmiths worked. The king's milch cattle were also kept there, and his grain stored in pits. That was where his women bore their children, whom they did not bring back to the *isigodlo* until they were old enough to walk.

What should be plain from this description is that oNdini was in plan and construction just like any other *ikhanda* or royal residence in the kingdom, except for its unusual size. All visitors were greatly impressed by its sheer magnitude. Contemporary estimations of its extent varied considerably, and the ploughing up in recent years of parts of the *uhlangoti* has not facilitated precise archaeological measurements. It seems clear, though, that oNdini was elliptical in shape, with the major axis of 650 metres and the minor of 507. The outer circumference was of the order of 2 169 metres. The first oNdini, by comparison, consisted of 640 huts (half as many as oNdini), and the nearby emaNgweni of only 310. However, oNdini possessed one unusual, though not quite unique, feature for an *ikhanda*: a house.

At emaNgweni, the principal hut in the *isigodlo* was built in European fashion, showing the hand of the nearby Norwegian missionaries at Empangeni. It consisted of three rooms with glass windows, wooden doors, whitewashed walls and a thatched roof.[5] Similarly, at oNdini, Cetshwayo had a special house of audience constructed in the 'black' *isigodlo*, called the 'black house'. The sun-dried bricks and other materials were supplied by the Revd Ommund Oftebro of the Norwegian Mission Society. His first name reminded the Zulu of their word for a creeper whose bark and roots were used against flatulence. So he was known as Mondi, and his mission on the outskirts of the present town of Eshowe as Kwa-Mondi. The actual construction of the house was undertaken by Johannes ka-Jwangubane of the Ntuli and two other Zulu converts of Oftebro's.

The building was rectangular with four wallpapered rooms and a thatched roof, and boasted features such as two outside doors with locks, glazed windows and verandas at front and back. The rooms contained some European furniture, including a large mirror and a washstand. The king usually spent part of the day in the house attending to affairs of state and consulting his councillors. At night the doors were locked and guarded by two girls of the *isigodlo*. These were members of the king's bodyguard, for John Dunn had instructed the older girls in musketry and armed them with short carbines. Every late afternoon they had target practice at aloes growing near oNdini, and accompanied Cetshwayo when he went in progress from *ikhanda* to *ikhanda*. The intention was that they would protect him whenever the male *amabutho* were away, but they were never actually called upon to defend their lord, and Cetshwayo disbanded them when he fled north after the British burned oNdini in July 1879.[6]

Paulina Dlamini, who was once one of Cetshwayo's maids-of-honour, has left a detailed description of his everyday life at oNdini.[7] At break of day the gatekeeper aroused the sleeping *isigodlo* by calling out the king's praises. When the sun arose the king emerged from his hut, by which time the women had tidied and swept the entire *isigodlo* area. He might then go shooting birds with the sporting guns kept in the black house. While he was away everyone kept indoors and the *isigodlo* seemed deserted. When he returned later in the morning, the king would go to the little enclosure in the royal cattle kraal in front of the *isigodlo*, where he would stand on a stone while he was washed with water brought from the Mbilane stream and rubbed down. The young men who took it in turns to attend the king in pairs were Mehlokazulu, Sihayo's son, Nsizwana of the house of the Xulu chiefs, and Tshanibezwe and Mbulwana, two sons of Mnyamana. While they were busy with the king's toilet, and during the time he subsequently sat on the stone to dry, a breathless silence reigned. Dlamini has left a charming picture of Cetshwayo's inquisitive and naughty young maids-of-honour surreptitiously peeping through the lattice-work of the enclosure to admire their naked king's physique.

Once dry, Cetshwayo put on his clothes and went to his hut to eat. Only the girls from Mnyamana's Buthelezi clan were trusted with preparing his food. The king washed his hands, and two of his *izinceku* would then walk about the *ikhanda* crying out, 'Do not disturb', for no one might cough or sneeze while the king was eating. Sliding on their knees, the girls presented him with a spoon, fly-whisk and a finely woven mat on which they deposited the dishes filled with his food. Cetshwayo would first eat *amasi*, the sour curdled milk, and then his meat. His drinking water came from a cold, bubbling stream on Hlophekhulu mountain to the south-east of oNdini, just on its side of the White Mfolozi. After he had eaten, the king would consume sorghum beer late into the night. He would also hand out food to the young men and women who had attended him, often in quite overwhelming quantities. When Cetshwayo wished to urinate, he did so behind his hut. But when it was cold or wet he used a chamber-pot in the presence of all his attendants, male and female. If he wished to defecate, he put on a black overcoat with red facings, a black hat and shoes and went out to a hillock nearby.

A small mound had been formed behind the fence that separated the white *isigodlo* from the huts of the *amabutho*, from the top of which Cetshwayo could survey the parade ground. From another mound behind his own hut he could watch the *isigodlo* area. Clearly, his presence loomed large over oNdini, which regulated all its activities to his requirements. In this, he was no less a king than Dingane had been, and he dealt out punishments with great severity to keep his attendants in order. Paulina Dlamini recollected many cases of men and women of his household who were sentenced to death for various misdemeanors, sometimes quite petty ones. Once condemned, they were haled off to kwaNkatha, a flat bushy place opposite the uPathe hill on the further bank of the White Mfolozi, presumably named after an individual called Nkatha, just as the similar dread place at uMgungundlovu just outside the main gate had been.[8] Something of the terror Cetshwayo could inspire was graphically recounted by Mtshayankomo of the iNgobamakhosi *ibutho*. When angry, he used to swear the great oath of the royal family, 'By the bones of Nzibe in Soshangane's country!' He would then spit, throw his cloak over his shoulder and cry, 'Let the country become dust this moment!' No one would dare answer, but all would cast down their eyes, and shrivel so in fright that their penis-covers would drop off.[9]

Yet, as we have seen, if Cetshwayo was to resuscitate the awe in which the monarchy had been held in his uncles' time, but which had been dissipated during his and his father's joint rule, it was necessary to inspire fear and sternly impose his will on his subjects. He had tried, with rather limited success, to tame the great magnates through Shepstone's coronation 'laws'. It was perhaps even more crucial that he tighten up on royal control over the *amabutho* and marriage. These were the main buttresses of royal power, the institutions through which the king exerted control over his subjects, and had to be maintained at their full vigour. Cetshwayo did not always find it easy to do so. There is much contemporary evidence of laxity and disobedience, and royal orders for the amabutho to assemble were sometimes ignored or tardily obeyed. Part of the reason was an inevitable reluctance to leave home for the physical discomfort and hunger of the crowded *amakhanda*, and the rather unrewarding labour on their upkeep. But it also seems that some of the greater territorial chiefs, like Hamu and Zibhebhu, were sometimes obstructing the system by trying to keep their young men in service to them, rather than the king.

These difficulties are not evidence, however, that the *amabutho* system was breaking down, and there are many signs that Cetshwayo did succeed in revitalising and strengthening it. Nevertheless, he did not do so without periodic crises. One of the most spectacular occasions occurred in 1876, when he had to take stern measures to enforce obedience to the marriage law.[10]

If the marriage law were broken, Cetshwayo later explained, he 'would be a shadow instead of a king'[11] because through it he regulated the social and economic life of his people. The episode known as the 'marriage of iNgcugce', which became as important a temporal landmark as the 'crossing of Mawa', was therefore of considerable significance. The circumstances were these. At the *umKhosi* in 1875 Cetshwayo gave the iNdlondlo *ibutho*, formed in 1857, permission to put on the headring and marry. They were expected to find brides from the female iNgcugce *ibutho*, born between 1850 and 1853. This made the girls considerably younger than the men, who had been born in 1837.[12] Most of these girls had already given their affections to younger men of the uDloko, uDududu, uMxhapho and uMbonambi *amabutho*, which had not yet received permission to marry, and even to some men of *amabutho* who were so young as to be their near contemporaries, like the iNgobamakhosi. It was customary for girls who had not yet received the king's permission to marry to have several lovers simultaneously from unmarried male *amabutho*. Full penetration, however, did

1. *The proud and self-assured* umnumzane *(married head) of a Zulu* umuzi *(homestead) c. 1879.*

2. *A prospect c. 1890 of* imizi *dotted over the undulating hillsides of the Zulu country.*

3.

3. *A classic Zulu* umuzi *photographed c. 1880 with its inhabitants ranged in front of the cattle-byre.*

4. *A Zulu family c. 1879 with the* umnumzane *standing to the left and his adult but unmarried sons, wives and younger children sitting in front of the hut.*

4.

5. *A Zulu chief and attendants, brought to London for the Great Exhibition of 1851 and photographed there in 1853. One of the extremely early and rare photographs of Zulu preserved in the Prince Consort's own Album at Windsor Castle.*

6. *A Zulu man and woman in ceremonial dress, also posed in London in 1853.*

7. *Zulu artefacts c. 1879, including ceremonial staffs carried by men of high status, shields, spoons, head rests, woven baskets, snuff-horns, knobbed sticks and spears.*

5.

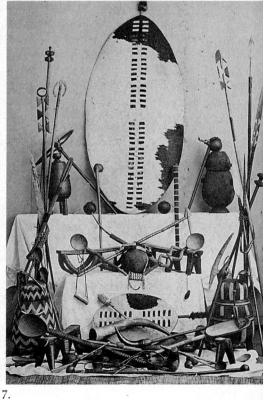

7.

8.

9.

10. **11.**

10. A young Zulu man dressed for courtship.

11. A Zulu warrior decked out in full ceremonial dress, taken in London on 14 June 1853.

12. A member of a married ibutho (age-grade regiment) with headring and carrying a small hunting-shield stands next to a member of an unmarried ibutho in full regalia with a war-shield, c. 1879.

Previous page

8. Zulu women grinding mealies in front of their hut, c. 1880

9. The return of a Zulu war party, c. 1860, driving off cattle from a burning umuzi

13.

13. King Dingane sketched in 1835 wearing both ordinary and dancing dress.

*14. A distant view from the south of uMgungundlovu,
King Dingane's chief royal homestead, sketched in 1835.*

Opposite page

*15. The interior of King Dingane's hut in the isigodlo (royal enclosure) at uMgungundlovu,
sketched in 1835. The king reclines in the fresh air from the doorway close to the scalloped hearth,
attended by the royal women.*

16. The seated King Dingane and one of his pet dogs reviewing his amabutho *in 1835 as they
deferentially file past him on their way to the esiKlebheni* ikhanda

17. King Mpande reviewing his amabutho *in 1847 in the great parade-ground at kwaNodwengu.*

14.

15.

17.

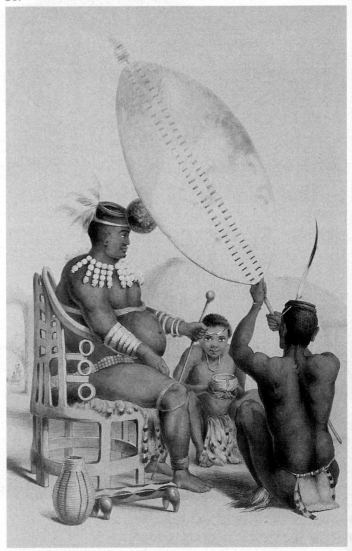

18. *King Mpande in 1847 on his chair of state before the* isigodlo *at kwaNodwengu, his principal residence.*

19. *The deserted emaNgweni* ikhanda, *just before it was burned by the British on 4 July1879. Note the Western-style house in the* isigodlo

Opposite page

20. *Chief Ngoza kaLudaba of the Majozi section of the Cube, who broke away at the time of the battle of Ndondakusuka in 1856 and settled in Natal. He is photographed in about 1865 with some of his young* amabutho *in full festival array.*

21. *Chief Ngoza with senior* amabutho *in war dress, c. 1865.*

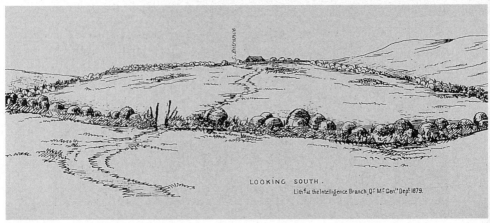

S. Entrance

LOOKING SOUTH.

Lith.d at the Intelligence Branch, Q.r M.r Gen.l. Dep.t 1879.

19.

20.

21.

22.

23.   24.

25.

25. *Prince Dabulamanzi kaMpande, photographed with some of his adherents at Cetshwayo's coronation in 1873. Those at either end carry old-fashioned Tower muskets, while next to them are two men with smaller, muzzle-loading sporting rifles. Dabulamanzi and the man on his right carry breech-loading shotguns.*

26. *White traders trekking into Zululand in the early 1880s*

Previous page

22. *Cetshwayo's coronation on 1 September 1873. The king, wearing his 'crown', is on his chair of state with Theophilus Shepstone seated to his left.*

23. *Cetshwayo's 'crown'. One of its smaller, grey ostrich plumes is still preserved in the Royal Commonwealth Institute Library, Cambridge.*

24. *Prince Sikhota kaMpande (centre) with a wife and induna while in exile in Natal.*

26.

27.

27. *Prince Hamu kaNzibe receiving the advance guard of an ibutho on its return from an expedition. Recorded by the artist Thomas Baines in 1872.*

28. *A view in 1878 of oNdini, King Cetshwayo's chief residence, looking across the great parade ground to the* isigodlo.

Opposite page

29. *Sir Bartle Frere.*

30. *Sir Theophilus Shepstone*

31. *Leaders of the Zulu deputation that heard the British ultimatum on 11 December 1878. Gebula sits on the extreme left, and Vumandaba is third from the left.*

28.

31.

34.

34. *The Zulu army deploying before the British laager at Gingindlovu on 2 April 1879. Drawn by Captain C.P. Cramer, who was present.*

35. *A trophy of Zulu weapons and articles of dress captured by the 91st Highlanders at the battle of Gingindlovu.*

Previous page

32. *Men of the uNokhenke ibutho c. 1879, arrayed as for the hunt or war.*

33. *Chief Ntshingwayo kaMahole, the senior of the joint-commanders of the Zulu army at Isandlwana, who also directed the fighting at Khambula*

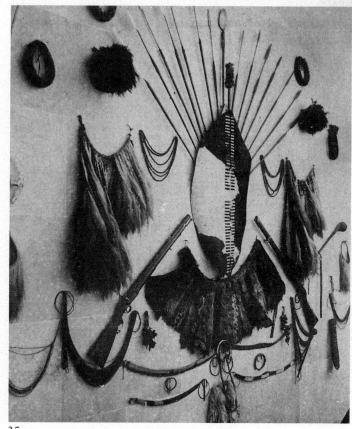

35.

36.

36. *The decomposing Zulu dead left lying on the Gingindlovu battlefield.*

37. *Mbilini kaMswati (right) with his induna Mbambo.*

38. *Prince Makwendu kaMpande after his surrender to the 1st Division on 21 April 1879.*

37.

38.

not take place during intercourse for fear of pregnancy. By the ancient custom of *hlobonga* a man entered only a little way, and when a girl sensed her lover was about to come, she told him to withdraw, crossed and tightened her legs, and allowed the ejaculated semen to run off her. If the girl did by misadventure fall pregnant, she was married to a man who had assumed the headring, and not to her young lover[13].

Thanks to these long-standing carnal relationships enjoyed by the iNgcugce, many members of the iNdlondlo consequently found their offers of marriage refused by girls whose affections were elsewhere. A further complication was that there were too few men of the iNdlodlo to go around the numerous iNgcugce. As the indignant girls put it, 'the necklace is not long enough to fit round the neck'[14] Cetshwayo tried to rectify the problem by allowing the uDloko, who were only a year younger than the iNdlondlo, also to assume the headring and marry during the winter of 1876. But the girls had hoped that the king would give the other, younger, *amabutho* permission to marry as well, and were not mollified. Cetshwayo was furious at this sign of the breakdown of royal control, and took stern action. Armed bands of men from the uMcijo, iSangqu and iNgobamakhosi *amabutho* were sent out across the land to kill any of the iNgcugce girls whom they might find unmarried, and to seize the property of the offenders' fathers. The only way for the girls to save their own lives and their fathers from ruin was to marry a member of the iNdlondlo or uDloko (or some even older *ibutho*) immediately. This most of them did on the strong urging of their fathers and brothers. The young men, to avoid painful scenes of parting from their sweethearts, went off to their *amakhanda* until the marriage business was over. A few of the more besotted couples fled to Natal, but they risked being killed as vagrants and outlaws by the people living along the border. Moreover, the king had given orders that if a young couple were found to be travelling alone, both were to be killed and their bodies placed face to face across the path as a warning to other transgressors.

How many of the girls and their lovers were killed during the operation, which dragged on for five months across the country? Mtshayankomo of the iNgobamakhosi remembered his band killing thirty-one girls in the southern districts, and placing three across the path as ordered. Undoubtedly, there was much consternation in the land, and two *umKhosi* festivals were disrupted on account of general dislocation. Most Zulu, it would seem, were sympathetic towards the members of the iNdlondlo and uDloko, who had nearly been cheated of their rights, rather than towards the young women whose affections had been violated. The king thus had the satisfaction of knowing public opinion was generally behind him, though he had found it disquietening that several of the great territorial chiefs had been less than active in enforcing the marriage law in their districts. This time, though, it was not the northern magnates who proved uncooperative, but some of the major southern chiefs in the broken and wooded country of the Nkandla district along the middle Thukela. In particular, Sigananda kaZokufa, whose Cube people had never been conquered by Shaka, and whose relationship with the crown had therefore remained one more of alliance than subjugation, proved particularly refractory. Cetshwayo not unnaturally considered such reluctance to implement his orders as disloyal, and another sign of how on his guard he must remain if the power of the crown were not to slip away.

Only two years after the marriage of iNgcugce another unfortunate event took place which, by combining the consequences of that crisis with the king's perennial difficulties with disciplining his male *amabutho* and controlling the great chiefs, again confirmed the nature of the internal hindrances to his rule. It was the time of the *umKhosi* in December 1877, and the *amabutho* were gathered in the Mahlabathini plain for the festival.[15] During his reign Cetshwayo always celebrated the ceremony at the new kwaNodwengu he had build just south of his father's old *ikhanda*, and west of the Mbilane stream from oNdini. As was customary, the various *amabutho* were tightly barracked for the festival in one or another of the sixteen *amakhanda* clustered in the Mahlabathini plain and the emaKhosini valley, or were accommodated in temporary shelters. The married uThulwana veterans, of whom Cetshwayo and many of his brothers were members, were barracked as was usual at oNdini. However, Cetshwayo also crammed in the boastful young iNgobamakhosi, who were his favourite *ibutho* since they had been enrolled during his reign, instead of letting them bivouac by the river.

Respect for age was an important aspect of Zulu society, but it was soon obvious that the iNgobamakhosi were not prepared to defer to their elders, who in turn resented the 'boys' being shoved into their huts, especially since, as married men, they were visited there by their wives. For their part, the iNgobamakhosi complained at having to wait outside the huts while the uThulwana were entertaining their spouses. And beneath all this antagonism lay another, more tortured issue. Numbers of the iNgcugce girls had married members of the uThulwana, who were a couple of years older even than the iNdlondlo, in order to avoid punishment in 1876. Some of the iNgobamakhosi had been the girls' lovers, and were thus hardly well disposed towards the married men of the uThulwana.

In the cramped quarters of oNdini raw feelings were chafed daily, and increasingly bitter jibes and insults were exchanged. Eventually, soon after midday on 25 December 1877, trouble broke out when the two *amabutho* formed up at the gate of oNdini to proceed to kwaNodwengu for the *umKhosi*. A stick-fight erupted between the iNdluyengwe, a younger *ibutho* incorporated with the ageing uThulwana to bring them up to strength, and the youthful uVe, who formed the vanguard of the iNgobamakhosi and were only just younger than them in age. The fighting spread throughout the two *amabutho*. The younger *ibutho* had decidedly the better of the encounter and drove the uThulwana back into the *ikhanda*. The humiliated but infuriated older men took up their spears from their huts and went onto the counter-attack in real earnest.

Such action was against all precedent, for it was the accepted custom that in internal quarrels of that sort the king's subjects used only sticks or the shafts of their spears, and never the blades for stabbing. Since the iNgobamakhosi were not carrying spears, as no one brought them to the *umKhosi*, they were now at a severe disadvantage. From kwaNodwengu Cetshwayo caught sight of the fracas, and cried out in agitation, 'My boys are being finished off!'[16] But the fighting proved extremely difficult to damp down, and none of his messengers dared approach near enough to restore control. The uThulwana pursued the iNgobamakhosi across the Ntukwini stream (which runs into the White Mfolozi), drove them through a herd of the king's cattle, which stampeded in fright, and into the open country at the foot of the surrounding hills. The iNgobamakhosi then rallied, and fighting only ended with nightfall, by which time between sixty and seventy men lay dead, with at least twice as many iNgobamakhosi as uThulwana among the fallen.

The king was deeply vexed by this affront to his authority. He forbade the iNgobamakhosi to take further part in the festivities, fined them a beast all round and ordered them to disperse home. But public opinion was largely against him. He was criticised for foisting the iNgobamakhosi onto the uThulwana in their already crowded barracks, and Hamu, the *induna* of the uThulwana, was particularly indignant. He had been badly beaten about the shoulders in the stick-fight, was utterly infuriated by the insult and damage done to himself and his men, and demanded the death of Sigcwelegcwele kaMhlekehleke, the *induna* of the iNgobamakhosi. But Sigcwelegcwele, a chief of the Ngadini near the Ngoye Mountain in south-eastern Zululand, and a fine-looking man in the prime of his life, tall and broad-shouldered with a proud carriage to his head,[17] was a great personal favourite of Cetshwayo's. The king was consequently loath to act against him, and Sigcwelegcwele was allowed to escape to his own district and ultimately to settle the matter with the payment of a fine. This leniency in no way appeased Hamu, and he was further enraged by the king's reproaching him for having given the uThulwana the order to take up their spears in defence. He retired in fury to kwaMfemfe, his homestead in the north, and could not be induced to return to oNdini until Cetshwayo called a royal council in November 1878, on the eve of the Anglo-Zulu War.

What added sinister implications to Hamu's self-imposed exile was the widely held suspicion that he may well have deliberately fomented the fracas at the *umKhosi* as an assertion of his power and independence. To Cetshwayo, it was all further proof that Hamu intended to usurp his throne. Significantly, his response to the situation was to take firm action to reassert his authority over both the *amabutho* and the chiefs. The uVe, who had started the fighting, were separated from the iNgobamakhosi and sent to muster in future at a different *ikhanda*. The chiefs were expressly reminded of the coronation 'laws' which laid down the king's sole powers over life and death.[18] Princes like Hamu might sulk in their own districts and avoid the court, but they were reminded that they were not free to act without the king's sanction. Ultimate power in Zululand, Cetshwayo was determined, must remain in his own hands.

Cetshwayo was realistic in securing power, not only through control of purely Zulu institutions (such as the *amabutho*), but also through contact with the colonial world impinging on his kingdom. If western-inspired innovations brought wealth and strength to the monarchy, then they must be embraced, even if the potential dangers of white interference were also recognised. Missionaries, for example, whose mission stations often came to be regarded by the king's subjects as an alternative to his rule, were tolerated for their skills, but continued to be held in real distrust by a king who, in any case, had little taste for Christian teachings.[19] Likewise, traders might undermine indigenous manufactures with their imported goods, but these items were highly prized among the Zulu elite and were a source of royal patronage.

It was not an unheralded development, therefore, that when negotiating with Shepstone during the 'coronation' of 1873, Cetshwayo struck a pragmatic and significant deal with the Natal authorities over the recruitment of migrant labour for Natal. The Tsonga chiefdoms to the north-east of Zululand had long paid tribute to the Zulu kings, but were not fully subject to them. Cetshwayo agreed that he would permit Tsonga to migrate through Zululand to Natal in return for a fee for every one of them who registered as a worker in the colony. In addition, the king was free to impose what amounted to his own tax on the migrants, for on their return from Natal they were required to give up to him a third of the wages they had received. John Dunn also benefited greatly from the deal. Cetshwayo proposed him as the Amatonga Agent at a salary of £300 a year to ensure that the migrants passed through Zululand unplundered by his subjects, and rendered the king their full dues. From 1874 several thousand Tsonga a year moved through the kingdom, and the revenue they generated became an important source of patronage for the king. Its importance for the crown increased with the depletion by disease of the traditional mainstay of royal wealth, namely cattle, whether the king's own stock or those which he received as tribute.[20]

Tragically, the disastrous spread of lung-sickness among the kingdom's herds was the direct consequence of one of the ceremonies connected with Cetshwayo's genuine coronation. In order to demonstrate his wealth, and to apportion the royal herds anew at the beginning of his reign, Cetshwayo ordered the royal cattle to be brought up from every part of the country and paraded before him. It took more than a week for the 100 000 head to be driven past him as he selected prize stock as gifts for his favourites, and settled at which *amakhanda* or with which honoured individuals they were to be pastured. Unfortunately, this grand review jumbled up herds from every corner of the kingdom and facilitated the transmission of disease from the relatively few infected animals to the rest. The result was the spread of lung-sickness across the entire country, exacerbated by the movements of white traders and their livestock. John Dunn calculated from the number of hides traders carried out of Zululand over the next few years that Zululand's herds were reduced by half during that period. Already poorer than Natal in terms of cattle, Zululand was now relatively impoverished.[21]

Although that was the case, Cetshwayo needed such revenues as he could muster to buy firearms. John Dunn had convinced him that a royal monopoly of firearms in the kingdom was essential for the maintenance of his power against external enemies and internal rivals.[22] A complete monopoly was not possible, however. The independent-minded Zibhebhu, whose chiefdom lay across the route to Delagoa Bay, was heavily engaged in trading for firearms, as was the discontented Hamu in the north-west. Nevertheless, the king, through Dunn, remained the main source of firearms in Zululand.

As we have seen, firearms had entered Zululand in significant quantities from the late 1860s, when Cetshwayo's fears for his succession, combined with threats of Boer encroachment, had compelled him to encourage their importation in order to arm his adherents. The precise number and quality is uncertain. British consular officials reckoned that up to 10 000 guns a year were entering Zululand during the second half of the 1870s.[23] A correspondent to the *Natal Witness* in August 1878 estimated from his observations that there were 20 000 stands of European firearms in Zululand. These consisted of 500 superior British breech-loading rifles, a further 2 500 good rifles like the percussion Enfield, and 5 000 second-hand ones. The balance were inferior weapons, mainly muskets. For with the adoption by European armies in the 1860s and 1870s of breech-loading rifles with metallic cartridges, obsolete firearms were cheaply disposed of and dumped for a solid profit by unscrupulous dealers on the African market. Most were ancient British Tower muskets, often dating back to the 1830s.[24]

Guns reached Zululand from Natal or through the Portuguese possession of Delagoa Bay, though not through the Kimberley Diamond Fields, as very few Zulu had yet become migratory labourers. In June 1875 the Natal government, fearing the threat guns posed to the security of the Colony, prohibited their direct sale in Zululand. Illicit gun-running persisted across the Thukela, nevertheless, with whites dealing mainly in the better quality arms.[25] Traders along the Zulu border carried out a brisk and open business in cartridges, percussion caps and lead.[26] Yet it was the circumvention of Natal's ban by several merchants which provided the main source of firearms in Zululand. Quite legally, they transshipped arms from Durban or Cape Town to Delagoa Bay, where the agents of John Dunn arranged for their transportation by porter to Zululand.[27] It was only by 1878, with the possibility of war looming with the Zulu, that the British decided that the wholesale import of arms through Delagoa Bay must be halted. By an agreement of February 1878 with Portugal, the sale of guns and ammunition to Africans was prohibited – much to the detriment of the local economy[28].

The king also possessed the largest stores of ammunition in Zululand.[29] In time of war he supplied it to his men, though there were quantities of gunpowder, percussion caps, lead and bullet-moulds over much of the country. Moreover, there were Zulu who had learned to make gunpowder from white traders and the Sotho gunsmiths employed by the king.[30] Cetshwayo stored his gunpowder in a deep cave in the side of a cliff in the vicinity of his emLambongwenya and kwaMbonambi *amakhanda*, a few kilometres north-east of oNdini.[31] Nearby, he built a magazine, which was a square, thatched house. His close friend Somopho kaZikhala, an *induna* of the emaNgweni *ikhanda* where Cetshwayo had spent so many years as prince, was his chief armourer and supervised the manufacture of powder.[32]

The power and prestige conferred by firearms was important for Cetshwayo as king, and their possession undoubtedly improved the morale of his *amabutho*, especially when faced with the prospect of war against whites. But, for all that, the ownership and use of firearms was of symbolic, rather than practical, value for the Zulu. They seldom made full use of their firearms or developed new tactics which would have exploited their potential more effectively. In contrast, people such as the Pedi – who were accustomed to take the defensive in their broken terrain against raids by their neighbours – more readily adapted their methods of fighting to the new weapons. The Zulu, like the Ndebele, continued to prefer to rely on the traditional weapons upon which their successful aggressive tactics had been based. They consequently tended to employ their guns only as secondary weapons in place of throwing-spears, to be discharged at a distance and then cast aside in favour of the stabbing-spear as they charged home for hand-to-hand combat.

Perhaps the perceived limitations of the majority of their firearms, besides their inadequate mastery of them, accounts for this practice. After all, most of the older muskets were already condemned, while the barrels of many of the muzzle-loaders were covered in deep-seated rust as the Zulu tended not to keep their guns clean and in working order.[33] Such weapons could be positively dangerous to their users, let alone inaccurate, a problem which was exacerbated by the use of eccentric bullets. Besides stones, it seems that favourite missiles for the muzzle-loaders were the broken pieces of legs from the three-legged cast-iron pots sold in Zululand by traders.[34]

The poor range or penetration of obsolete muskets was not improved by the often inferior quality of gunpowder, nor by the Zulu custom of carrying a single bullock's horn, transformed into a powder-flask, which limited the powder available for a proper charge.[35] Loading such guns was a laborious procedure, limiting the rate of fire, and wet weather could put an end to any firing at all. Nor must it be forgotten that many of the warriors issued with guns had little experience in using them, or mastery over technicalities such as correct range and aim.

There were probably a few hundred men in Zululand who were familiar with modern firearms and proficient in musketry, a skill usually learned while involved in the gun-trade or hunting. Such men would come into their own as snipers in 1879 against small British scouting or foraging parties.[36] But there were neither enough of them, nor a sufficient quantity of superior firearms in Zululand, to modify the traditional tactics of the *amabutho*. For all the resources spent on the acquisition of firearms in the 1860s and 1870s, they never became anything more than an ancillary weapon for the Zulu. Their chief function was to serve as an expression of the king's power and the nation's might, and so as a deterrent to the enemies of either.

During the first five years of his reign, Cetshwayo's foreign relations remained much as they had been before his accession. British support continued to be courted as a counter-weight to Boer expansionism, while Zululand's own ambitions were still focused on the Swazi kingdom to the north. It was along the north-western marches of the Zulu kingdom that the long-standing, but conflicting, claims of the Zulu, Swazi and Boers came most overtly into collision. Already a volatile region during Mpande's reign, it remained an arena for potentially damaging conflict.

For pastoralist Zulu, Swazi and Boer alike, the Disputed Territory was a rich prize.[37] The lovely, red-earthed valleys of the Mkhondo, Ntombe, Phongolo and Bivane rivers cut deep through the terrain, and contrast with the great granite flat-topped mountains and the rugged, broken countryside between. The landscape is open and grassy, with forests crowning some of the higher peaks, and bush filling the kloofs. Summers are warm and reasonably wet, winters dry and cold. Sourveld grasses grow on the sandy highlands, tall sweetveld types in the river valleys, and mixed types between the two. In other words, it is an ideal region for grazing – so long as the free, seasonal movement of cattle is permitted between the various types of pasture. Herds should spend the spring in the high country, and move down to the valley floors for the winter. Effective management of herds, therefore, requires the control of large and varied tracts of land. And therein lay the source of conflict.

The Zulu kingdom of the 1870s was, as has been mentioned, in growing economic difficulties. Population was again increasing after the wars and migrations of previous decades, but cattle herds were severely depleted and natural resources were under strain, not least from the activities of white commercial hunters and recurrent droughts. Territorial expansion or lucrative raids for cattle which might have made good these deficiencies were blocked to the south and west by the existence of Natal and the South African Republic. One possible outlet was the Swazi kingdom north across the Phongolo, the traditional raiding ground of Zulu kings. It also remained the territory on which Cetshwayo fixed his eye, as had his predecessors, in case he were expelled from Zululand and forced to establish a new state elsewhere. But Swaziland, precisely because it had been freed from Zulu attacks since the mid-1850s, had been able to consolidate internally and become a power to be reckoned with across Zululand's trade routes to Delagoa Bay. The Swazi kingdom would therefore prove no easy nut to crack. This consideration aside, Cetshwayo was in any case repeatedly held back from mounting a full invasion in emulation of his father by a complex interaction of factors.[38]

To wash one's spear was a kingly act in Zulu eyes, and many of the restless younger *amabutho*, eager for personal glory and booty, were ardent for a Swazi campaign. So too was Cetshwayo, who saw it as a means of replenishing the royal herds and strengthening his powers of patronage. The great chiefs, on the other hand, recognised all too well how a successful campaign would strengthen the king and his supporters among the younger set, and consistently came out against mounting one. Besides, several of the powerful northern chiefs had independent interests in Swaziland, including marriage ties, and feared the repercussions on their own territories of war with their neighbour. Statesmen among them, like Mnyamana, the king's chief *induna*, were anxious to keep in step with the British, who they hoped would still play a part in the resolution of the boundary dispute with the Boers. And since the Natal government feared the effects on the stability of the region of a Zulu invasion of Swaziland, Mnyamana and other influential councillors were prepared to range themselves alongside the British in dissuading Cetshwayo from attacking the Swazi in 1874, 1875 and again in 1876.

Frustrated in his hopes for a glorious campaign like the one in which he was blooded as a young prince with his companions of the uThulwana, Cetshwayo had to be content with much more modest action against the Swazi. He did manage to seize a number of strategic mountain fastnesses in the Lubombo range on the margins of Zibhebhu's territory from the Nyawo people, among whom Dingane had died. The hope was that they might serve as useful launching pads for later expansion into south-eastern Swaziland. To the north-west, he accelerated the process of cautious expansion across the Phongolo. Since the 1860s Zulu *imizi* had been steadily established in the area, and the idea was that their presence would give concrete weight to Zulu territorial claims.

When all was said and done, however, Swaziland was closed to major Zulu expansion. Cetshwayo was forced to turn his eyes to the rich lands of the northwest, where the boundaries were still unclear, and the grazing good. Here his main competitors were not the Swazi, but the far more dangerous Boers.

The territory of the South African Republic, it will be remembered, formed an arc around north-western Zululand, but the Boers' suzerainty was ill-defined. The fact that there were never enough Boers physically to occupy the land they claimed always made their territorial rights difficult to uphold. By 1878 in the Utrecht District, for example, there were still only 1 352 whites, of whom 375 were men. Despite these tiny numbers, there was almost no free land available that had not already been apportioned out as farms, and the consequent Boer encroachments over the Ncome River into Zululand have been described earlier. North of Utrecht, and abutting both the Zulu and Swazi kingdoms, lay the District of Wakkerstroom. It had not been settled by whites until 1853, but then proved an ideal district for horses and sheep. Boer settlers poured in, and by the 1870s free land was no more available than in Utrecht. As a result, the Wakkerstroomers began to extend their influence in the Swazi kingdom, where they saw scope for settlement, and to spill south-east over the Phongolo, where they came into direct confrontation with the Zulu expanding in the opposite direction.

In 1864 Cetshwayo had angrily repudiated a line of beacons the Boers set up between Rorke's Drift in the south and the confluence of the Phongolo and Bivane in the north to assert their eastern boundary with Zululand. Undeterred, in 1875 the Boers proclaimed a new boundary line that took in a large tract of territory south of the Phongolo, land that had been ruled by the Zulu kings since Shaka's time. To make matters worse, in 1876 officials of the South African Republic began to make good their state's claim to the disputed farms in the northwest of Zululand by trying to levy taxes from the Zulu living there and, when they refused to pay, seizing their cattle. Cetshwayo could naturally not countenance these Boer land claims. He and his councillors insisted that a line running up the Mzinyathi River to its sources in the Drakensberg and along the watershed to the Mkhondo River marked the western limits of the kingdom. In all these regions were people who had *khonza*'d to the king, and the Zulu always considered the boundaries of the kingdom to be determined by the lands occupied by people owing allegiance.[39]

Cetshwayo consequently instructed his subjects to resist by force any attempt by the Boers to tax them or seize their cattle, and sent a large *impi* of several thousand to support them. This military demonstration was enough to persuade the Boers to back off, but it did not solve the dispute. That required a broad-based settlement, and Cetshwayo urgently and repeatedly petitioned the British authorities in Natal to intervene. Such involvement, as before, presented Natal with possibilities to its own advantage, and the Natal government decided to offer to arbitrate between the Zulu and the Boers. Before it could do so, however, its intention was overtaken by the march of great events in southern Africa. On 12 April 1877 Britain annexed the South African Republic to the crown as the Transvaal. At a stroke the whole context of the Zulu-Boer dispute and Anglo-Zulu relations was dramatically transformed. Although the Zulu did not realise it at first, the way was being inexorably prepared for the British to invade and overthrow their kingdom.

15

The Eagle and the Four Hawks

Towards the end of July 1878, a noble eagle soaring above oNdini was attacked and driven off by four hawks in full sight of the king and his councillors below. So obvious a portent filled them with foreboding. Cetshwayo's *izangoma* despondently interpreted the occurrence as a sign that the states bordering Zululand would combine to destroy the kingdom.[1] Yet it hardly required their special powers of divination to come to such a conclusion. Ever since the British annexation of the Transvaal in 1877 the tide had been running high in southern Africa against the gallant but archaic Zulu ship of state. By the middle of 1878 a bewildered Cetshwayo was reluctantly anticipating having to fight the British, his erstwhile and chief support against the Boers' relentless territorial demands.

Such a turnabout on the part of the British had its causes in wide developments as well as in particular events. In general terms, the 1870s were a time in southern African history when policy-makers in London decided to safeguard British interests in the region through firmly establishing their control – by force, if necessary – over the indigenous peoples. Their motives were mixed but complementary. The local economy was in the process of being transformed and stimulated by the mineral revolution. With the development of both mining and capitalist agriculture came increasing demand for labour and land, as well as closer links with the capitalist economy of Europe. British schemes to consolidate their hold on the subcontinent must consequently be understood in part as arising out of a desire to create a settled environment for economic integration and progress.[2]

In this vein, we have already seen how commercial interests in Natal desired to open up a corridor to the interior through Zululand in order to secure markets and an orderly supply of labour.[3] If the existing pre-capitalist Zulu state were overthrown, then the territory would be opened to the developing capitalistic economy of the subcontinent, and a necessary supply of wage-labourers unlocked.[4] In Zululand itself there was some realisation of the implications of these world forces. Many voiced the growing concern that if the old order were overthrown the Zulu, who served only their king, would be reduced to the proletarian level of the abject tax-paying labourers of Natal.[5]

Other impulses besides their general support for the advance of capitalist production motivated those in Whitehall responsible for framing policy in southern Africa. By the 1870s imperial policy-makers were looking to consolidate, rather than extend, the Empire. India, so vital to British commercial interests and her status as an imperial power, remained the key. India's security depended on control of the routes to the east through the Suez Canal and around the Cape. This meant that for essentially strategic, rather than commercial, reasons Britain must remain the supreme power in both Egypt and southern Africa. The difficulty in maintaining Britain's traditional position of dominance in the southern part of Africa lay not so much with the ambitions of rival colonial powers as with the politically and economically fragmented nature of the region itself.

The uncoordinated activities of British colonies, Voortrekker republics and the surviving independent black states, such as Zululand, made for inefficient and incomplete management. Lord Carnarvon, who became Colonial Secretary in 1874, saw in the concept of confederation an answer to this problem. He began obsessively to pursue the chimera of a confederation of the white-ruled states of the region. Ideally, such a confederation would bear the costs of its own administration and internal security, possibly be a base from which to extend British economic and political paramountcy north over much of the rest of Africa, and at the same time provide a firmer link in the British route to India.[6]

Yet, as the London Conference on South African Affairs of August 1876 underlined, the 'native question' was the key to the viability of the confederation project. Carnarvon and white settlers alike perceived the independent black states neighbouring the white colonies and republics as constituting a serious and common danger. Once these black states were under imperial control, however, there would no longer be any possibility of costly and undesired wars between the white colonies and their black neighbours. These financial implications were fully appreciated by the Cape Colony, the largest and richest member of any proposed confederation, and therefore its natural cornerstone. Its leaders were consequently reluctant to be drawn into any confederation until Britain had first subdued the black states along its own eastern borders and those adjoining the Transvaal and Natal.[7]

It was in this context of grand imperial planning that the South African Republic's indecisive war against the Pedi to the east of their territory became so crucial. Sekhukhune, the son of Sekwati, who had been paramount chief of the Pedi since 1861, was dissatisfied with his western frontier with the Boers, where, rather like the Zulu of western Zululand, the Pedi lived side by side with infiltrating white farmers. Hostilities broke out in May 1876 and came to an inconclusive halt in February 1877, underscoring the Cape's fears that in a confederation it would be landed with paying for precisely that sort of unrewarding conflict. To reassure the Cape that this would not be the case, the British government began taking steps to annex the South African Republic. The Republic was a necessary element in the confederation mosaic, though its Boer citizens were naturally reluctant to throw in their lot once more with the British. But their Republic was proving barely viable, and the mismanaged war against Sekhukhune was sapping confidence.

Carnarvon decided to strike while the iron was hot, both to placate the Cape and to bring the Boers into the confederation. To manage the operation, he required an astute man of stature, who believed in the need for confederation, and enjoyed the respect and confidence of the Boers. Carnarvon's choice fell on Theophilus Shepstone, the Secretary for Native Affairs in Natal, and Cetshwayo's patron. Shepstone proved equal to the task. He talked the Boer leaders around, not least with his assurances that annexation would transfer the responsibility for the Pedi war to the British military, who could be expected to make short work of it. On 12 April 1877 Shepstone annexed the Transvaal to the Crown, and stayed on in the new colony as its Administrator.

Carnarvon was encouraged by Shepstone's effortless absorption of the Transvaal to press his confederation plans through to a conclusion. The moment had come to entrust the consummation of the grand design to an imperial statesman of sufficient ability and vision to live up to his elevated role of architect of empire. Sir Bartle Frere, the great Indian administrator, was to be the man. Frere departed for South Africa in March 1877 as Governor of the Cape, High Commissioner for South Africa and Commander-in-Chief of the British forces stationed there. With these very considerable powers he was expected to complete confederation and then to stay on as the first Governor-General of the new South African Dominion.[8]

Frere was the key figure in the prelude to the Anglo-Zulu War, which was to end with the destruction of the kingdom and Cetshwayo's exile. Though he was inevitably influenced by local statesmen, notably Shepstone, he kept the reins firmly in his practised hands, and the great decisions of war and peace were his alone. He believed doggedly in the concept of confederation, so it was a great blow to him when his patron, Lord Carnarvon, resigned in February 1878. Nevertheless, Frere stayed on, determined to complete the task to which he had set his hand. The new Colonial Secretary, Sir Michael Hicks Beach, was so engrossed in crises elsewhere that he was inclined to leave the revered and vigorous proconsul in South Africa to his own devices, especially since the permanent officials in the Colonial Office persisted in considering him the only man capable of bringing confederation about.

Before anything else Frere was an Indian administrator, and had enjoyed a most distinguished career in posts including Chief Commissioner of Sind, Governor of Bombay and member of the Indian Council.[9] He brought his methods and principles intact to the South African situation. Conscientious, ambitious, with informed interests in many practical and scientific fields, he was also a committed evangelical Christian. He had devoted his successful career to improving the material life of the Indians he had governed with projects ranging from irrigation to health care. Trained to act on his own initiative, his prime concern was not whether he would please his superiors, but whether his actions measured up to his own exacting moral standards. He was never afraid of taking vigorous executive action.

Frere believed that it was Britain's high mission to spread the civilising influence of Christian government, and to eradicate barbarous institutions. By enlarging the missionary field and extending British rule over blacks, it would be possible to guide them up the ladder of evolution and improve their standards of living through good administration and economic prosperity[10]. Frere's notion of 'civilisation' was directly related to the advance of capitalist production in that he envisaged putting blacks to 'civilised' labour for wages. The happy consequence would be that they would spend their earnings on European manufactured goods, which would be to the commercial benefit of white colonists, and to their own material advantage. To this high-minded administrator, it was nothing less than a moral failure if the British failed to exert their authority constructively and consistently over their savage neighbours, for his experience in India told him that this dereliction led inevitably to the corruption of indigenous societies and to recurrent border warfare. Confederation, therefore, was a Christian and moral objective, which would bring peace, prosperity and civilisation to all the peoples of southern Africa, both black and white.

When Frere arrived in South Africa in late March 1877, Shepstone was on the verge of clinching the annexation of the Transvaal, so securing the northern component of the developing confederation. The High Commissioner was thus free to turn his attention to other sectors where endemic conflict between white settlers and blacks was jeopardising confederation. In short order, he executed a series of strategic annexations aimed at stabilising the Cape eastern frontier and securing the remaining potential ports along the coasts of southern Africa. However, the Mpondo of the eastern Cape continued a source of unresolved difficulty, as did the Griqua of Griqualand East. The Pedi too proved much more difficult to overcome than had been anticipated, and their confident resistance began to pose a genuine threat to Shepstone's administration and to confederation as a whole.[11] But these problems were as nothing to that of the Zulu kingdom. For Frere had allowed himself to be convinced that until Zululand had been neutralised no solution to the 'native question' could ever be found, which meant in turn that confederation itself hung on the fate of the Zulu kingdom.

Only too aware of these high stakes, Frere employed a variety of arguments – and capitalised on every incident – to convince his superiors in London that Zululand was a savage and barbaric state which, because it threatened the stability of the rest of southern Africa, had to be brought to heel.[12] If challenged, he could always refer for corroboration to the dominant opinion among the white settlers, officials and missionaries. Almost all lived in anticipation of a Zulu invasion abetted by a domestic black uprising, and looked to the imperial government to turn the barbarous Zulu into docile and productive citizens. They characterised the Zulu kingdom as a bloodthirsty despotism where arbitrary executions were the order of the day, and where missionary endeavour (so prized by Frere as the gateway to civilised life) was constantly thwarted. Frere was particularly outraged at the plight of the missionaries, and deliberately invoked their misfortunes as justification for taking steps against the Zulu king.[13] It was the Zulu 'military system', though, which provided him with his most convincing motivation for drastic action against the Zulu monarchy. Disregarding its true nature, he represented it again and again in emotive language as a 'frightfully efficient manslaying war-machine'[14] in the hands of an 'ignorant and blood-thirsty tyrant',[15] which posed a perpetual menace to its neighbours. And to top this lurid characterisation, Cetshwayo was commonly (if hysterically) portrayed in official, military and popular circles as the wicked inspiration behind a burgeoning conspiracy among blacks to rise up together and overthrow white supremacy in southern Africa.[16]

In consequence, Frere could always claim that any action he initiated against Zululand was not only morally justifiable, but actually necessary for the safety of the threatened white colonists. Even so, legitimate and 'legal' grounds were necessary before Frere could actually take steps against the Zulu kingdom. These he found in the so-called 'Coronation Laws' of 1873, which we have already considered, and whose conditions Cetshwayo was taxed with failing to keep. No matter that Cetshwayo was periodically outraged when the Natal government perversely interpreted them as restricting, rather than enhancing, his internal powers, and vehemently repudiated the colony's claims to any form of suzerainty over him.[17] For here was Frere's God-given 'legal' justification for interfering in Zululand's internal affairs.

Intervention was being made imperative by developments in the Transvaal. We have seen how Shepstone, when Secretary for Native Affairs in Natal, had been inclined to side with the Zulu in their smouldering border dispute with the South African Republic, even if only to benefit Natal's specific interests. But now, as Administrator of the Transvaal, he had to take the Boers' part. He was especially concerned to win over those die-hards who remained unreconciled to loss of independence, and planned to do so through a demonstration of the advantages to be gained from British rule. As a priority, this required the successful subjugation of the Pedi. Shepstone believed, though, that Sekhukhune's remarkable obduracy stemmed from the moral support and example of Cetshwayo, the supposed leader of the nebulous 'black conspiracy'.[18] This meant that it had become necessary first to humble Cetshwayo in order to bring Sekhukhune to his senses and to mollify the Boers. The old, vexed issue of the boundary dispute offered a handy means for doing so.

On 18 October 1877, after a series of useful incidents in the border area which nicely brought the dispute back to the boil, Shepstone met a Zulu delegation at Conference Hill, overlooking the west bank of the Ncome River. It was an acrimonious meeting. Chief Mnyamana, who headed the large gathering of councillors and chiefs, insisted that they spoke for the Zulu nation in refusing to abandon their land claims.[19] It is probable that Shepstone actually welcomed this intractable stance, for it graphically underlined the need to take the military action he considered necessary against the Zulu. And, unfortunately for them, the Zulu continued to play into his hands. Over the next few months further border incidents and strained negotiations increased the chance of hostilities, and gave substance to Shepstone's repeated requests to Frere to settle the whole issue by force.[20] What made that deceptively clean solution all the more tempting for Frere was that Shepstone did not consider it would take 'much trouble or much time' to crush the Zulu, whose defeat would eradicate the 'root of all evil' in South Africa.[21] Frere, as we have seen, was of like mind concerning the pivotal nature of the Zulu question in his plans for a confederation, and the war-clouds began perceptibly to darken.

At that tense moment, Sir Henry Bulwer, the Lieutenant-Governor of Natal since 1875, took it upon himself to intervene, so temporarily thwarting Frere's and Shepstone's plans. Bulwer, with his pot-belly, square head of spiky red hair, bushy moustache and incongruous imperial growing on his self-important chin, struck a faintly ludicrous figure. He was undoubtedly a fussy, self-righteous official, but a thorough gentleman withal and an experienced imperial administrator who had served in distant outposts ranging from the Ionian Isles through Trinidad to Borneo. He took his responsibility for the security and prosperity of Natal's people very seriously indeed, which is why he deplored the idea of a full-scale war with Zululand. It was to avoid such a disaster that he sent to Cetshwayo on 8 December 1877, offering to mediate in the dispute. The Zulu king accepted with relief, while the belligerent but chagrined apostles of confederation could not but acquiesce.

Bulwer's Boundary Commission, which was made up from Natal officials, began its sittings at Rorke's Drift on 17 March 1878. It completed hearing evidence in April, and in June handed its scrupulously completed report to Bulwer. Its findings did not affect the disputed area north of the Phongolo River, which had been excluded from the Commission's investigation. However, the report did recognise the Transvaal's rights to the land between the Mzinyathi and Ncome rivers – but, crucially, not to the territory beyond the Ncome where some Boers had settled.[22]

When Frere received the Commission's report on 15 July 1878, he analysed it in terms of its likely effect on the Transvaal in particular, and confederation in general. On both counts it was disastrous to his plans, and he was at a loss as to how to respond. So he passed the report around South Africa soliciting advice on how best to act, and then pondered the alternatives. The process took time, for the Sphinx of the Transvaal proved reluctant to utter, and Frere was loath to come to a decision without Shepstone's approval. At the same time he was being harassed by Bulwer, who feared that a delay in announcing an award would provoke the Zulu to war.[23]

Frere arrived in Pietermaritzburg on 28 September 1878 with the intention of first announcing the boundary award, and then proceeding to the Transvaal to settle that increasingly reluctant colony's affairs.[24] Indeed, the situation there was deteriorating. In April 1878 Shepstone had commenced operations against Sekhukhune but, despite a strong infusion of Imperial troops in August, the campaign was a disaster, and by the end of October the British would have to withdraw from Pedi territory.[25] In these unsatisfactory circumstances, Frere knew that any award which failed to demonstrate Britain's determination to guarantee Boer security against the blacks on their borders could well lead to rebellion. Such an uprising, he greatly feared, might draw in the Boers elsewhere in South Africa, and encourage the Zulu and their fellow members of the 'black conspiracy' to fall upon the whites. Frere began to envisage a dreadful scenario in which the choice lay between risking a Zulu war at once, or bringing about a Zulu war a few months later, preceded by a Boer rebellion.[26]

While Frere pondered how to respond to these combined dangers, a number of incidents occurred in the second half of 1878 along the Zulu border. During July 1878 one of the wives of Sihayo, the Qungebe chief and Cetshwayo's favourite, fled over the Mzinyathi River to the Umsinga Division in Natal with her lover, who had made her pregnant. Another wife, who was also pregnant by a man other than Sihayo, and who stood accused of bewitching her cuckolded husband, likewise escaped to Natal. When Sihayo's sons learned that these miscreant wives were living in *imizi* close to the border, they decided to act. Their leader was Mehlokazulu, Sihayo's chief son. Tall, with an intelligent face and brisk, lively manner, he was a good shot with a rifle, and was looked up to by his fellows as a spirited and dashing warrior. White traders in Zululand, on the other hand, found him too good a businessman for their liking.

On 28 July Mehlokazulu, two other sons of Sihayo and one of the chief's brothers, crossed the Mzinyathi below Rorke's Drift in broad daylight at the head of thirty mounted men, armed with guns, and a large force on foot, mainly carrying spears and shields. They seized one of the wives, intimidating the locals who considered a rescue, and dragged the woman back across the river to Zulu soil, where they struck up a war-song and shot her dead. That night Sihayo's sons collected an even larger following and, crossing once more over the border, dealt with the second woman as with the first. Settler opinion was outraged, and the Natal government demanded the surrender of the ringleaders for trial in the Colony.[27]

In September unusually large and well-armed hunts by *amabutho* opposite the mouth of the Thukela and Rorke's Drift further alarmed settler opinion.[28] The manhandling by Zulu of W.H. Deighton and D. Smith of the Colonial Engineer's Department below Kranskop on 17 September was seen as equally provocative. The Zulu might have had every justification for suspecting that the wagon road the engineers were inspecting in the Thukela valley was intended to facilitate an invasion of their country, but white men could not be stripped and relieved of their pipes with impunity.[29] In the Phongolo region there were similar incidents against white surveyors in November. More serious were the Zulu king's threats against the German-speaking settlers of the Hermannsburg Mission Society settlement at Luneburg, which had been established with Mpande's permission in 1869 three kilometres north of the Phongolo.

Tension in the area was increased by minor raids in October 1878 by the freebooter Mbilini kaMswati, a Swazi prince who had lost a succession dispute and fled to Zululand in 1866. From his caves and rocky fastnesses in the upper reaches of the Phongolo he acted as a useful but unpredictable catspaw of the Zulu kings, raiding both the Swazi and white settlers of the Disputed Territory. But, small and dark, shrewd and notoriously cruel, Mbilini was not easily controlled. His latest raids were inopportune, and resulted in two companies of Imperial troops being despatched to the area in mid-October. White traders, meanwhile, were suffering some harassment in Zululand, as were Tsonga labourers on their way home from Natal. While these incidents were mere symptoms of a tense frontier, and in no way a cause for war, they nevertheless provided Frere with both the excuse and the vital justification to the Colonial Office for taking military action.

Frere's military and naval commanders had preceded him to Natal, and by September were preparing, on a contingency basis, for hostilities against Zululand.[30] Troops had been moved north earlier in the year from the Cape to act against Sekhukhune and to guard against a Boer rebellion in the Transvaal, and they had been deployed accordingly. Now, between September and November, they were being directed to the Zulu border in a steady trickle in order to be in position should war break out.[31] Whatever the misgivings (and Bulwer was particularly indignant that his efforts to achieve a negotiated settlement were being undermined by all the military activity),[32] the truth was that military and much colonial sentiment held increasingly strongly that until the Zulu power was broken there would be no way of permanently settling the 'native question', and that a Zulu war neither could, nor should, be long delayed.

For Frere, it was daily more difficult 'to decline the contest'.[33] How, indeed, could he? He had come to South Africa to effect confederation, and to almost all white observers it was the savage Cetshwayo who stood primarily in the way. Morally and politically it was his duty to proceed against him. Nevertheless, the decision to go to war is perhaps the weightiest a statesman can make. Was it not still possible to break Zulu power by diplomatic means? Frere did not believe it really was.[34] Thus, the ultimatum he set about framing was primarily a means of forcing war on the Zulu, and only secondarily an instrument whereby the kingdom could be emasculated without a struggle.

For the ultimatum, Frere relied mainly upon Shepstone's advice. Yet it is apparent that neither he nor any other official had a sure idea of what demands to make of the Zulu. Frere did insist, though, that the ultimatum be framed to make it quite clear that the British had no quarrel with the Zulu nation as such, but with the 'tyrant' alone. Even more important was his concern that effective security should be required to ensure that Cetshwayo keep his coronation oaths as they were understood by the British.[35] However, Frere realistically doubted whether any verbal undertaking extracted from Cetshwayo would be binding, especially if his military might were allowed to remain intact: a large British force could scarcely be maintained on the borders of Zululand to 'ensure performance' of whatever promises the king might make. So Frere found himself with no choice but to 'draw the Monster's teeth and claws'[36] by ensuring that his military capability was neutralised.

Having at last received Shepstone's tardy comments on the draft ultimatum, Frere and Bulwer finalised the document at the end of November. They decided to present it as soon as possible so as to facilitate military preparations.[37] It fell into two parts. The first dealt with compensation for the recent, but minor, border incidents. Mbilini was to be handed over for punishment for his raid; Mehlokazulu, his two brothers and uncle were to be surrendered for trial and Cetshwayo was to pay a fine of 500 cattle for not giving them up earlier; in addition, a fine of 100 cattle was to be paid in compensation for the Deighton-Smith incident. The remaining demands were of far greater significance. A British

Resident was to be stationed in Zululand; the Zulu army was to be disbanded; all the young warriors were to be granted permission to marry; the king was to observe his coronation oaths regarding the unjust shedding of blood; missionaries were to be readmitted to Zululand; and the king was to undertake not to make war without the consent of the Resident and his Council.[38]

To Bulwer, there was nothing excessive or unjust in these demands, despite the fact that their aim was to subvert the social, political and economic structure of the Zulu kingdom. For, ultimately, he considered them necessary to attain the better government of Zululand and the security of the adjoining British territories. Even Bishop Colenso, the 'ultra philo-Zulu',[39] approved of the terms, which he considered commensurate with Britain's 'civilising mission' and the 'harbinger of better...days for Zululand'. His fear was simply that if it came to war the potentialities for improving 'the social and moral condition' of the Zulu might be negated.[40] Yet Bulwer did not seriously suppose that Cetshwayo would give up his sovereignty without a fight, and neither did Shepstone or Frere. The military certainly thought he had no alternative but to defend himself, and preparations for the invasion of Zululand were complete by 13 December.[41]

Yet why did the Colonial Office, which was increasingly doubtful of the wisdom of Frere's ambitious South African schemes, not step in to restrain their High Commissioner? By October it was clear to the British cabinet in which direction Frere's plans were tending. With a war brewing in Afghanistan and relations strained with Russia, it had absolutely no wish for a campaign in Zululand. Hicks Beach instructed Frere to exercise forbearance, but was unable to reverse the drift to war.[42] As High Commissioner, Frere was entrusted with wide discretionary powers, which were strengthened in a crisis because poor communications meant that the Colonial Office had to depend entirely on the judgement of the man on the spot. It took five weeks in 1878 for a despatch to travel between Cape Town and London, and telegrams had to come by steamer from the Cape Verde Islands, taking at least sixteen days. There is no doubt that Frere coolly exploited this convenient time-lag to manipulate Hicks Beach and to proceed with plans which he knew would not have received his sanction.[43]

Yet Frere suffered from no misgivings concerning his disingenuous conduct and its consequences. It was his intention, once the Zulu army was defeated, Cetshwayo's power broken and the military system dismantled, to ensure the future good government of Zululand according to his principles. To this end, Zululand would not be annexed, but would be subjected on the Indian model to a system of indirect rule by compliant chiefs under a British agent. Taught who was master, the demilitarised Zulu would be easy to manage and civilise. Thus Zululand would be slotted into its assigned place in the confederation rather like an Indian 'subject ally'.[44] Frere was confident that the British government, once presented with this happy conclusion, would condone the high-handed course he had pursued in its realisation.

This triumphant finale depended on a swift, cheap and decisive campaign. Frere had been assured by the military that their strength and skill were more than adequate for the task, and Shepstone had convinced him that under the stress of war existing opposition to Cetshwayo would grow, and that political disarray, compounded by military defeat, would rapidly bring the Zulu kingdom to its knees. These assumptions were to prove ill founded, and the British were to find Zulu military ability greater and political cohesion considerably tighter than they had bargained for.

16

The Whistling of Winds

Shepstone was certainly being unrealistically optimistic when he advised Frere that the Zulu kingdom would come tumbling apart at the first well-directed blow. But, remembering the way in which the kingdom had been put together, and reflecting on its troubled record of internecine conflict, there was genuine room for wondering just how well it would stand up to the threat of a full-scale British invasion. The rulers of Zululand were faced with a stark choice. Either they acceded to the British demands, or they rejected them and risked going to war to preserve their independence. No real choice was thus open to them and, from the moment in mid-1878 when Cetshwayo began clearly to hear the threatening 'whistling of winds',[1] he knew a war for survival was upon him.

The single issue in the erupting crisis which assumed major proportions in Zulu eyes was the demand that the sons of Chief Sihayo of the Qungebe be handed over to British justice for their part in the cross-border incident of 28 July. Cetshwayo's initial response was to play down the culpability of 'rash boys' acting in 'zeal for their father's welfare', and he offered a fine of £50 in restitution.[2] The British dismissed the gesture as adding insult to injury, and at the end of September Bulwer sternly insisted that the offenders be surrendered.[3]

Cetshwayo could not make decisions about how to respond to such British demands and threats without prior consultation with the leading men of his kingdom, in particular with those of his inner council. At the time of the war, the most regular members of this powerful conclave were Mnyamana, Cetshwayo's chief *induna*, Chief Ntshingwayo kaMahole of the Khoza, Chief Godide kaNdlela of the Ntuli, Chief Sekethwayo kaNhlaka of the Mdlalose, Chief Mbopha kaWolizibi of the Hlabisa, and Chief Mvundlana kaMenziwa of the Biyela. Hamu and Zibhebhu, though of the highest standing, were too young to be included.[4]

In one sense, therefore, Cetshwayo was not simply fobbing off the British when he repeatedly stated that he must wait for his council's decision before deciding on the fate of Sihayo's sons. Yet he was also being disingenuous. John Dunn had spoken privately to Bulwer's messengers in late August, warning them that they must never hope that Cetshwayo would ever consent to give up the sons of Sihayo, his favourite at court. So even though a large majority in Cetshwayo's council were in favour of surrendering Sihayo's sons to placate the British, the king was determined to thwart them. He encouraged Sihayo's sons to flee for sanctuary to Mbilini in the north-western marches of the kingdom, out of reach of those chiefs who wished to hand them over to the British.[5] They in turn were greatly incensed, and more determined than ever to undermine Sihayo's influence.

Meanwhile, Cetshwayo, who by September was feeling increasingly hemmed in and threatened by the British military build-up along his frontiers,[6] was being left little alternative but to mobilise his own people. The normal reasons for full or partial Zulu mobilisation were for war, service to the king or participation in the national rituals. When the Zulu king wished to call up his army for a campaign, he sent out orders by runner to the *izinduna* commanding the various district *amakhanda* to collect the local contingents of the *amabutho*, and to proceed with them to the *amakhanda* clustered in the Mahlabathini plain. If hostilities on a smaller scale or in a theatre far from oNdini were intended, the king might then order the local territorial chief or *induna* of the regional *ikhanda* to summon the warriors of the district to muster at and operate from his particular great place or military homestead.

In September Cetshwayo gave orders for a great hunt, to extend from the Ncome River down the Mzinyathi and Thukela to the sea, to be undertaken by the border population south of the Mhlathuze River. While these people gathered, ostensibly to hunt, but really to keep watch on British movements, Cetshwayo at the same time ordered up the uMbonambi, uMcijo and iNgobamakhosi *amabutho* to oNdini for 'war talk' – which included manoeuvres and practice with guns – and to protect his person.[7] Then, late in September, elements of these *amabutho* moved close to the border carrying their war-shields, stabbing-spears and guns. Such a show of force was not normal for a mere hunting-party as regularly organised by the king and, as we have seen, the British construed its activities as a hostile act, especially since its food was being carried by women and *udibi* boys as on campaign.[8] Similar 'hunting' took place at the same time along the Mzinyathi.

The king was aware that the game he was playing was provocative, though necessary to show that he was prepared to defend his frontiers, and at first officially denied all knowledge of the hunts. On being pressed, he tried to explain them away by saying that the usual annual hunts were bigger than normal because of the undeniable scarcity of food and lack of rain that year.[9] But there was no doubt that *amabutho* were indeed being called up, if only to build new *amakhanda* (as was one of their routine functions).

By the end of September the men of standing about the king were becoming anxious concerning the consequences of assembling the *amabutho*, and wished to order them home in the interests of good relations with Britain. Cetshwayo bowed to the pressure, but ordered his *amabutho* to reassemble in a fortnight's time. In making this decision, he was influenced not merely by the younger *amabutho*, who were clamouring for action, but by a quite rational desire not to be caught off-guard by the British, who were persisting in their military preparations. In particular, the movement of British troops from Utrecht to Luneburg in the Disputed Territory on 19 October 1878, in order to protect the settlers from further raids by Mbilini, persuaded the king to take precautions.[10]

By the third week of October the Zulu were again mustering in their *amakhanda* on the king's orders. One concentration was at the kwaGingindlovu *ikhanda* to watch the south-eastern border, and another at kwaNodwengu in the Mahlabathini plain. Every *induna* received orders to provide ten cattle for the commissariat, and it seemed that the Zulu (especially the younger *amabutho*) were this time seriously preparing for war. The response of the Natal authorities was to send a sharp message to Cetshwayo, insisting that British troop movements had been only in reaction to his hostile stance, and untruthfully protesting that aggression against the kingdom was not intended.[11] Cetshwayo, under John Dunn's influence, was himself beginning to consider that he may have been unduly alarmist, and by the end of October he was again permitting his *amabutho* to disperse.[12] For all the war-talk, especially by his younger *amabutho*, it does seem that the king still hoped for a negotiated settlement of the crisis.

Yet there was another reason why Cetshwayo sent his *amabutho* home. With the men all called up, the women had been left alone on the land. It had been an exceptionally dry season. Mealies left over from the previous season were scarce, the young crops which had been planted at the normal time were ruined, and cattle were in poor condition and dying for lack of pasture.[13] There was consequently a general lack of food and little surplus to send as provisions to the menfolk in their *amakhanda*. To feed them, and to keep them occupied, the king had been forced to set them to cultivating the royal gardens and to hunting game near the confluence of the Black and White Mfolozi rivers. Hungry, and thwarted of their expectations of a campaign into Natal, many of the *amabutho* were not waiting to be dismissed, but were dispersing to their homes of their own accord. Though angered at such indiscipline, the king refrained from punishing them, as he could see how some were even dying of hunger at the *amakhanda*.[14] By early December all the *amabutho* were reported to have reached their homes once more.[15]

The lack of discipline among the *amabutho*, as well as the disaffection among many of his council regarding his protection of Sihayo and his conduct of the crisis, were eroding Cetshwayo's authority. By the end of October there were clear indications that a serious rift was opening up within the Zulu leadership. On the one side stood Cetshwayo, apparently swayed by the younger *amabutho* who were keen for a chance to prove themselves in war; on the other were most of the king's brothers and the older men of status in the kingdom, who were beginning to constitute an appeasement, or pro-peace, party.[16] Significantly, the three leaders of this faction, Mnyamana, Zibhebhu and Hamu, were among the most powerful *izikhulu* of the kingdom. Hamu and Zibhebhu, it must be remembered, both had considerable pretensions to local autonomy. In Hamu's case, the clash already described between the uThulwana and iNgobamakhosi at the *umKhosi* in December 1877 had decidedly strained the already uneasy relations between him and the king.

Hamu only reappeared at oNdini in November 1878 to attend the council called by Cetshwayo, when he joined Mnyamana in vehemently opposing the king's policy and demanding the surrender or execution of Sihayo's sons and Mbilini.[17] Yet he was already playing an unscrupulous double game. Clearly convinced as early as September that the British were determined on war against Zululand, he initiated contacts with the civil and military authorities in Utrecht with a view to securing his future. He made it plain that he would not fight with the king against the British, repeatedly begged them to trust his intentions, and on 6 November went so far (with the approval of his *izinduna*) as to undertake that in case of war he would 'run over with all his people to the Government, if Government [would] receive and protect him.'[18]

Cetshwayo did not know of these treasonable overtures. During November he was prepared to hearken to the advice of the duplicitous Hamu and the other members of the peace party. Under their influence he sent out a stream of placatory messages to the British, protesting his peaceful desire 'to sit quietly'.[19] Significantly, the peace party began to risk its own initiatives. On 13 November messengers were sent across the lower Thukela by the highly influential Mnyamana, Ntshingwayo, and Sitshaluza kaMamba, Chief of the emGazini, to convey their disquiet with the shape of events and their desire for peace.[20]

It seems likely that these chiefs decided on their arguably treasonable *démarche* only after a great assembly, called by Cetshwayo to discuss the crisis with his people, had exposed the truly parlous state of affairs. Hamu used the occasion to lead a determined attack on Sihayo, making it clear that his sons should be given up or put to death, rather than that Zululand should go to war on their account.[21] He was backed up by a son of Mnyamana and by Hayiyana kaMaphitha (Zibhebhu's brother), who spat on Sihayo and otherwise insulted and abused him as the root of the crisis with Britain. But throughout that tumultuous and bitter assembly Cetshwayo continued to stand staunchly by his favourite. Not that he could have done otherwise. To have abandoned him then would have been to surrender to Hamu and the other great magnates, forfeiting his authority and prestige.

If surrendering Sihayo's sons could really have deflected the British from their determination to crush Zululand, Cetshwayo might eventually have bowed to his council's wishes. However, mounting British military preparations during November doubtless made it clear to him that the unpalatable sacrifice would have little effect in staving off an invasion. Such conclusions received further confirmation when, towards the end of November, Bulwer sent to Cetshwayo notifying him that Frere was ready to pronounce his award on the boundary question, and that John Shepstone, the acting Secretary for Native Affairs since September 1876, would meet the representatives of the Zulu nation at the Lower Thukela Drift to deliver this and, sinisterly, 'other communications'.[22]

Bulwer's messengers did not actually see Cetshwayo, who was in seclusion after the recent death of one of his children, but conferred with him through Mnyamana. They also held discussions with Hamu, Dabulamanzi, Sihayo and five or six other principal chiefs of the inner circle. Every one of them expressed a strong desire to avoid war. It was obvious that Sihayo was out of favour with all – except the king – for bringing ruin on the country, and that John Dunn was universally blamed for not having warned the king sufficiently strongly of the danger in which the kingdom stood. Indeed, it was noticeable that all were in a state of great apprehension. There was consequently relief that the British still apparently wished to negotiate, and Cetshwayo decided to send a deputation of *izinduna* to the requested meeting. Only then did he summon an enlarged *ibandla* of the great men of the realm to report his decision.[23] But the council apparently broke up in confusion over the persistent issue of whether or not to deliver up Sihayo's sons, and many of the great chiefs were reported to have returned home angry with Cetshwayo for pig-headedly continuing against all advice in protecting them.[24]

John Shepstone, accompanied by a party of colonial officials and four Natal chiefs, reached the Lower Thukela Drift on 9 December 1878. Sir Theophilus's beetle-browed, walrus-moustached, melancholic younger brother had none of Somtsewu's energy and charisma. He related poorly to the black people over whom he was set, was a wretched public speaker and was commonly acknowledged to have succeeded Theophilus as the Acting Secretary for Native Affairs only through his illustrious brother's influence. As it was, the Natal government could never bring itself to confirm him in his post, and he continued to act for eight years.[25] But he had sat on Bulwer's Boundary Commission, and Zululand's fate would be made known through his mumbling lips.

The Zulu deputation of fourteen members and about fifty attendants did not arrive at their side of the river until early on the morning of 11 December.[26] They unhesitatingly accepted the offer to be ferried across the flooded Thukela and stepped onto the Natal side at about 10.30 a.m. The British were pleased to see that the deputation was composed chiefly of elderly and middle-aged men. Their maturity, it was presumed, would predispose them to avoid an open rupture with Britain. However, the British should not have concluded that they necessarily represented the peace party in the king's council. Prominent among them were Vumandaba kaNtati, a royal *induna* and principal *induna* of the uMcijo *ibutho*; Phalane kaMdinwa, *induna* of the Hlangezwa; Muwundula kaMamba, a royal *induna* and brother of the emGazini chief; Mahubulwana kaDumisela, a principal *induna* of the Qulusi; Gebula, an *induna* of the kwaGqikazi *ikhanda* and once a favoured messenger of Mpande; and Mabilwana kaMhlanganisa, *induna* of the kwa-Gingindlovu *ikhanda*. In other words, although trusted elders of rank and distinction, not one was an *isikhulu* with a place on the king's inner council. Rather, they were royal *izinduna*, functionaries raised up through the king's favour and committed to serving his interests. They were in fact typical of the personnel of a Zulu diplomatic mission, and had strict instructions regarding the limits of what they were permitted to discuss.[27] Nor was there anything extraordinary in their having to remember complex and detailed terms. Communications between the British and the Zulu king had almost invariably been conducted through verbal messages relayed with great accuracy.

At 11 a.m. everything was ready for the business of the day, and the two delegations met in the shade of an awning erected under a large Natal figtree on the bank of the river close to the drift. Fort Pearson, a recently built earthwork, commanded the place from the hill above, and an unarmed escort of forty men from the Naval Brigade and twenty-five troopers of the Stanger Mounted Rifles added to the impression of British might. The Zulu sat on the ground in a semi-circle, while a table and four chairs were placed for the British.

Shepstone, in unusually decided tones from under his heavy moustache, first announced the findings of the boundary commission, and his words were translated by F.B. Fynney, the local Natal Border Agent. The response of the Zulu delegates was diplomatically noncommital. The meeting was then adjourned for an hour while the Zulu consumed the ox Shepstone had given them to kill and drank quantities of the sugar-and-water they so relished.

At 2.30 p.m. Shepstone began to present the British ultimatum. He proceeded slowly, recapitulating every point, so ensuring that the Zulu delegates, who listened with increasing indications of concern and anxiety, fully understood the British demands. Although clearly shocked by the terms, the behaviour of the Zulu delegates remained professionally diplomatic. They were visibly disconcerted only when they realised that their picture was being taken by James Lloyd, a photographer from Durban. What they said in reply to Shepstone was spoken calmly and deliberately, without any hint of bravado. Besides defending their king's conduct in dignified terms, they also courteously indicated that thirty days was insufficient time for discussion and decision on the terms of the ultimatum. Their plea for an extension was refused, however. They were also hesitant to deliver the written terms of the ultimatum – set out in English and Zulu – to the king, but legalistically Shepstone insisted. Shortly after 5 p.m. they were ferried back across the river.

Cetshwayo's unhappy deputation had made it plain to Shepstone that they were most reluctant to convey the very unpalatable terms of the ultimatum to their king for fear of his displeasure. Such trepidation did not lend wings to their feet. When they delivered the written copies of the ultimatum at Mangete, John Dunn's great place just north of the Thukela, Dunn, realising to what extent the reluctant deputies were tarrying, sent a messenger in advance to the king with all the details. This messenger returned to Mangete on 18 December, and Dunn forwarded Cetshwayo's initial response to Bulwer. The king agreed to surrender Sihayo's sons and pay the fine, but complained of the short time allowed for compliance and the need for discussion with his council on the more important issues.[28] Meanwhile, the members of the deputation managed to make unusually heavy going of crossing the flooded rivers, and did not succeed in reporting to the king in person until about 22 December. Unaware that Cetshwayo already knew the details, they did not disclose all the terms of the ultimatum at once, and at first suppressed the most unpalatable, thus delaying formal discussion of them in council.[29]

The Zulu leaders could risk no delays, however. The British were determined that, unless Cetshwayo gave in punctually and completely to their demands, the troops would invade the moment the ultimatum expired. Yet in this ultimate moment of crisis the Zulu were not sure how to respond. In order to save the kingdom from being 'spoiled by war', the king's inner council reportedly were prepared to acquiesce to all the terms of the ultimatum – except the fundamental ones relating to the abolition of the *ibutho* system.[30] Both king and councillors were in agreement that those could never be conceded except at the point of the sword. However, the hope remained that the British could still be placated by sufficient concessions to their minor demands.

The king consequently proposed in council that all the chiefs subscribe a number of cattle to make up the number required to pay the cattle fines. But this they resisted. They strongly felt it fitting that Sihayo, the culprit, should first give up all his livestock. Only then were they prepared to make up any shortfall.[31] Cetshwayo accepted this decision, and in late December began to round up Sihayo's cattle and for good measure those of Qethuka kaManqondo, whose Magwaza adherents had assaulted Smith and Deighton. Nevertheless, it is evident that Cetshwayo did not attach sufficient importance to collecting the cattle within the time the British had stipulated, and on 26 December his messengers arrived at the lower Thukela to plead for a further extension.[32] Perhaps this lack of enthusiasm on his part can be explained by Cetshwayo's steadily diminishing faith in the purpose to be served by going through the motions of collecting the cattle fine. Certainly, by the end of December he seems reluctantly to have decided that there was little alternative but to go to war. This was borne out by his increasingly truculent tone, even if his personal demeanour became daily more dejected and tearful at the prospect.[33]

With war now almost unavoidable, it was necessary once again to call up the long-suffering *amabutho* to be ritually prepared to take the field should the last-minute diplomacy fail. This time, however, their mustering coincided with the *umKhosi*, the annual first-fruits ceremony for which they habitually gathered, regardless of whether or not a campaign was in the offing.[34] For weeks before the date set by the king for the 'big' *umKhosi*, which always took place at his kwa-Nodwengu *ikhanda* when the moon was at its full and about to wane in December-January, they gathered at their *amakhanda* to prepare for the festival. As it so happened, the appointed day in 1879 was 8 January – just three days before the British ultimatum was due to expire.[35]

The *amabutho* evinced some reluctance to muster on account of the continuing scarcity of food. Even though the rains had at last come and the people were everywhere taking advantage of the wet conditions to plant their crops, the season was inevitably going to be a late one.[36] The mealie crop, for example, which was later to prove splendid, could not be expected to be ripe until the end of February. Consequently, as in October-November, the king would find it difficult to feed the assembled *amabutho*, or to keep them together for any length of time without employment – such as sending them off on campaign. This prospect suited the young *amabutho*, who were undoubtedly eager to confront the British and confident in their ability to beat them.[37]

To their satisfaction, Cetshwayo clearly had this particular service in mind. When he ordered his *amabutho* to assemble in the Mahlabathini plain, he instructed them to leave the ceremonial dress and ornaments normal for the *umKhosi* at home, and to bring instead their arms and ammunition so as to be prepared for immediate active service.[38] Word had it that the king expected to have to go to war when the new moon was 'still young', or early in January and close to the date set for the *umKhosi*.[39]

Initially, Cetshwayo ordered the fighting men living along the borders with British territory to stay there and watch the threatened frontiers rather than muster at Mahlabathini. The Qulusi, facing the British concentrating at Utrecht, assembled at ebaQulusini, their district *ikhanda*, as did elements of the Mdletshe to the east of the Ncome River. Along the Mzinyathi, opposite Rorke's Drift, Sihayo's Qungebe assembled at Sokhexe (his principal *umuzi*) to oppose a British crossing. Detachments of various *amabutho* were also stationed initially along the Thukela, especially at the drifts. By the date set for the *umKhosi*, however, most of the men guarding the frontier had new orders to assemble with those already at the king's great place. The exceptions were the Qulusi, Qungebe and Mavumengwana's Ntuli opposite the lower Thukela drifts where the British were also massing. Small armed parties elsewhere remained on watch.[40] The king ordered these border units not to resist the British should they advance, lest any last-ditch negotiations be jeopardised.

There seemed little hope of further useful talk, however, and Cetshwayo's inner council and the princes were becoming increasingly dismayed with the drift of events. They began to vent their frustrations on John Dunn, Cetshwayo's main (and obviously imperfect) channel of communication with Natal. Realising that some of them were beginning to demand his death for treason, and knowing full well that his economic and political future in Zululand depended upon extricating himself from a war Britain was bound to win, Dunn decided to abandon his royal patron. He began crossing over into Natal on 31 December 1878 with 2 000 adherents and 3 000 cattle, leaving his *imizi* to be looted and burned by the Zulu, who were disgusted at his betrayal.[41]

Hamu was not far behind Dunn in preparing to desert his king. The British, heartened by his November overtures, opened up direct negotiations with the prince through Herbert Nunn, the white trader who had resided in his district since the 1860s, and on whom he relied for advice, rather as Cetshwayo had on Dunn.[42] Hamu was assured in mid-December that chiefs who collaborated with the British would be placed in the safety of a location in Natal for the duration of the conflict, and that afterwards they would be reinstated in their territory and recognised as independent under the British crown.[43] Hamu was not yet quite prepared to declare himself openly an ally of the British, but he committed himself sufficiently by the end of December for them to believe that once they invaded Zululand he, like Dunn before him, would abandon the Zulu cause.[44]

Cetshwayo's inner council continued to labour under the misapprehension that if Sihayo's sons were surrendered the British would somehow be satisfied and drop their other demands. By early January there were signs that some wished to take it upon themselves to deliver the miscreants over to the British.[45] In the end, they probably refrained because of the strong feeling in the country at large – which, though unsettled and divided, generally supported the king's decision to resist rather than appease the British. Nightmarish rumours were abroad, reflecting people's deep-rooted fears. Many Zulu firmly believed, for example, that under white rule the men would be sent to England to work, that the girls would be married off to white soldiers, and that their cattle would become the property of the government.[46] Not surprisingly, the *amabutho* gathering daily in the Mahlabathini plain were consequently adamant in their aggressive determination not to give in to white demands, and their obvious loyalty to the king made it increasingly risky for his discontented councillors to act openly in opposition to Cetshwayo's wishes.[47]

In the event, the *amabutho* mustered at oNdini that January did not participate in the true *umKhosi* festival, which did not take place after all that year on account of the impending hostilities.[48] Instead, they were 'doctored' for war in rituals that were effectively an abbreviated version of the *umKhosi* ceremonies described previously. It seems that on this occasion two war-doctors were responsible for sprinkling the army, one of whom was a Sotho of special powers. He doctored the firearms with smoke to make the bullets go straight, and smeared *muthi* on the warriors' foreheads, promising that his magic had weakened the British bullets, so that they would be harmless.[49] Ritual challenges between pairs of rival *amabutho* were, as we have seen earlier, an integral part of the ceremonies. In January 1879 the king first called the uMcijo and the iNgobamakhosi (his favourite *ibutho*) into the cattle enclosure to challenge each other. Two or three days later he summoned the uMbonambi and uNokhenke in their turn.[50]

It was also important that the spirits of the king's ancestors should approve of the decision to go to war. In January 1879 the assembled *amabutho* slept the night in the emaKhosini valley near the hallowed esiKlebheni *ikhanda*, and the following day visited the graves of the Zulu kings in order formally to request their favour through the customary sacrifice of cattle. Moreover, cattle were sent to the spirits to ask them to go with the army when it set out, and on this occasion the shades obligingly answered through the loud lowing of the beasts in the darkness of the night. Thus reassured, the king could issue his orders for the coming campaign.[51]

Yet, even at one minute to midnight, Cetshwayo remained uncertain. Sensing the precipice yawning before his people, and the magnitude of his own responsibility for their future, he was under enormous personal strain. It did not help that he felt himself deserted by those councillors on whose broad shoulders he had expected to lean, but who had withdrawn their support on account of the divisive Sihayo issue.[52] And though at one level he appears to have accepted the inevitability of war (after all, he had summoned his *amabutho* with the intention of fighting), at another he persisted in his essentially fruitless negotiations with the British.[53] The latter were not unnaturally convinced that these feelers were no more than a ploy to postpone hostilities until after the harvest was in,[54] but it also seems that Cetshwayo could not quite bring himself to relinquish all hope of a diplomatic settlement.

Thus on 11 January 1879, the very day the ultimatum expired, the British received yet another royal message – the sixth since the king's initial response to the ultimatum – begging for more time to discuss the terms with the people gathered at oNdini for the *umKhosi*.[55] But it was too late. Bulwer replied that if

Cetshwayo wished to communicate, it must in future be solely with Lieutenant-General Lord Chelmsford, whose forces were entering Zululand. Furthermore, no reply short of unconditional acceptance of all the conditions of the ultimatum could be entertained.[56] Zululand was at war with Britain, and compromise was no longer possible.

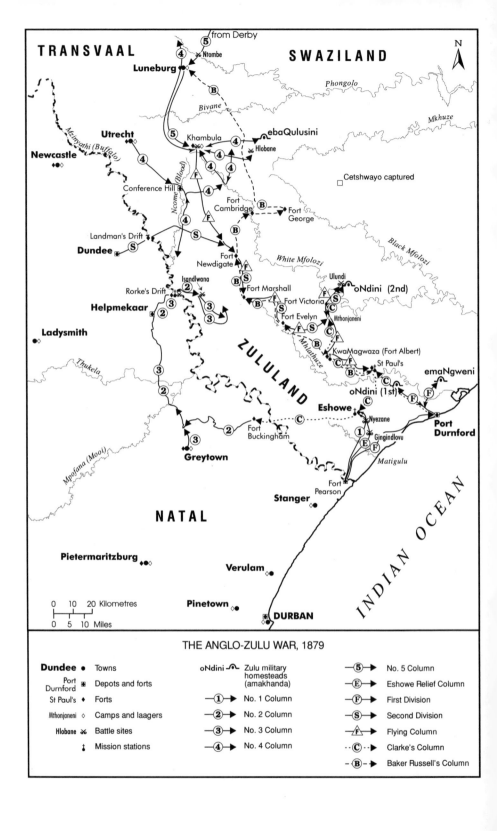

17

'You Will Attack by Daylight'[1]

The British, between 1815 and 1914, waged more colonial campaigns overseas than any other European power besides the French. These 'small wars', conducted not against regular troops trained in the European fashion, but against irregulars inferior in armaments, organisation and discipline, became in themselves an art.[2] The most successful colonial campaigns were those in which the army was best prepared for local conditions of warfare, and where objectives were clear and specific.

The soldier charged with the conduct of the British invasion of Zululand in 1879 was Lieutenant-General Lord Chelmsford.[3] Tall and thin, with a hooked nose to match, he had a pleasant manner and spoke in sharp, jerky sentences. His dark eyes moved restlessly under black, bushy eyebrows, pervading his actions with an anxious watchfulness curiously at variance with his calm air of command. The son of a Lord Chancellor and educated at Eton, he had enjoyed a varied and successful military career, primarily in India. However, it was one with a prosaic emphasis on staff and administrative duties, rather than on practical experience in commanding an army in the field. In this, as in other ways, Chelmsford was typical of many senior officers of the late Victorian army, and was, with them, a product of the privileged, conservative military establishment of the day. His behaviour was unfailingly gentlemanly, courteous and modest, and he was both firm and considerate with his subordinates. Fond of sport and outdoor pursuits, he was a keen participant in amateur theatricals, besides being an accomplished clarinet-player.

Chelmsford had a strong sense of his responsibilities, and always did his best to set an example to his men. He showed calm resolve under fire, and presented himself as a model of moderation (he was a teetotaller), frugality and diligence. Those under his command always appreciated his essential decency, and responded with their loyalty. On the other hand, Chelmsford was unable to delegate successfully, and was prone to frequent vacillation. Besides this, he championed stereotyped military tactics and was reluctant to adapt the well-tried formulae to South Africa conditions. This lack of military flair outweighed his undoubted industry, conscientiousness and bravery, and put him out of his depth in a campaign on the scale and complexity of the Anglo-Zulu War. Historians today find much in his generalship to criticise, and little to commend.

For the Zululand operation, Chelmsford succeeded in putting together an army of 17 929 men, divided initially into five columns, later reduced effectively to three. Of these men, 5 476 were British regulars drawn from regiments in Natal, the Cape and the Transvaal; 1 193 were irregular colonial horse; and 9 350 were black auxiliaries, raised in Natal. The remaining 1 910 men were colonial conductors, drivers and voorloopers necessary to manage transport and supplies.[4] When the blacks called up to defend Natal in various scratch units are also taken into account, it emerges that in 1879 no less than some 16 000 blacks were mobilised on the British side against the Zulu kingdom. Some were Zulu refugees, like the iziGqoza, 273 of whom were to fight courageously at Isandlwana, where 54 would be killed.

The main striking-force of Chelmsford's army was the British regulars. Their numbers were limited, for the professional Victorian army was small, and its manpower and capabilities were constantly overstretched by a multiplicity of commitments, both routine and emergency, across the globe. Consequently, many of the regular troops and officers available to Chelmsford suffered from handicaps of youth and inexperience or inflated professional esteem, and shared his reluctance to adapt to local conditions. As a result, they looked down upon colonial troops, even though they necessarily formed part of any British army campaigning on the margins of the Empire. For British regulars were too scarce to be dispersed on garrison and convoy duty, and in the Zululand campaign they had to be augmented by black levies raised in the Natal Native Reserves and put under white officers. The Natal Native Contingent (NNC), as this force was known, was poorly armed and trained, and was consequently of doubtful morale. A far better fighting force, but unjustifiably underestimated by the British regulars, was the colonial irregular horse, whom the initial lack of regular cavalry made essential for patrol work.[5] Indeed, cavalry retained an importance in colonial war long after it had been lost in European. Vital in pursuit of a broken enemy, it was just as important for reconnaissance and raiding purposes, and the absence of sufficient horsemen was one of the greatest defects in Chelmsford's army.[6]

A potentially more dangerous handicap was the way in which Chelmsford and his staff wholly underrated the fighting ability of the Zulu. There is no doubt that this overconfidence derived from Chelmsford's recent campaign in the eastern Cape. His experiences there misled him and all his men to presume that the Zulu would be an adversary only slightly superior to the easily disposed of Ngqika and Gcaleka Xhosa, and that they too were no more than 'kafirs, who had only to be hunted'.[7] Such misplaced confidence helps explain the strategy Chelmsford adopted for the invasion of Zululand.

To achieve the political objectives of the war, it was necessary to overthrow Zulu military might in the field, and naturally preferable to do this on Zulu, rather than British, soil. An offensive into Zululand would, however, leave the borders of Natal and the Transvaal vulnerable to a Zulu counter-thrust, while Colonel H. Rowland's unsuccessful campaign of 1878 against Sekhukhune meant that a British presence would have to be retained in the north-eastern Transvaal. White settlers generally were in dread of a Zulu raid, and anticipated that the colonial blacks might well rise up in aid of the mobile and merciless Zulu.[8] Chelmsford persuaded the colonial authorities to make some plans for their defence, but even so there were only enough armed men to hold the fortified posts. To dissuade the Zulu from raiding the countryside in between, it was necessary for the colonial government to raise a large field-force of black levies in the border districts and to place Border Police along the river frontiers.

On 11 January, poised to invade Zululand, Chelmsford placed the entire crucial border region under military control.[9] Border defences nevertheless remained pitifully weak, and Chelmsford put more faith in the rivers along the frontier to form a line of defence against anticipated Zulu raids. During the rainy season between January and March they were generally unfordable except at certain drifts, and Chelmsford confidently expected the campaign to be over by the time they subsided.

The seasons determined the timing of the British campaign in an even more fundamental way. Draft-animals subsisted on grazing, and the grass would be at its most plentiful after the late spring rains – precisely in the same early months of the year when the rivers were in flood. This was a vital consideration for Chelmsford because he favoured ox-drawn wagons as the most suitable form of local transport. Firm logistics, the basis for any successful campaign, were built upon the accumulation of necessary supplies and ammunition, as well as upon the organisation of sufficient transport. In this sense, the Zululand campaign exemplified one of the basic features of colonial warfare. For the British, it was a campaign against distance and natural obstacles as much as against hostile man, and problems of supply governed its whole course.[10] Since supplies (except for natural grazing) could not be obtained from the theatre of war, they had to be carried, turning the army into an escort for its food and requiring the establishment of garrisoned depots along its line of advance.

An army's movement is based on the speed of its slowest component. Chelmsford assembled 10 023 oxen, 398 mules, 977 wagons and 56 carts to supply his forces.[11] Wagons, even in the most favourable circumstances, could hardly travel further than nineteen kilometres a day. They required all-round protection on the march, and the larger the convoy the slower it moved. Colonists, especially the Boers, advised Chelmsford to form defensive wagon-laagers when he halted in Zulu territory. But until the dreadful lesson of Isandlwana was administered, the General was reluctant to laager because it was such a time-consuming procedure and his progress was already so painfully slow because of the waterlogged ground.[12]

In planning his strategy, therefore, Chelmsford was faced with certain constraints. When he advanced into Zululand he would leave his own frontiers inadequately protected, while his dependence on slow-moving and vulnerable supply-trains would limit both his flexibility and the size of the columns they were to support. His solution to these problems was to send in a number of relatively small columns to converge on an appropriate point: oNdini. He hoped thereby to move with greater speed and to have more forage at the disposal of each column. The presence of a number of supporting columns was also intended to engross more of the enemy's territory, to reduce the chance of their being out-flanked, and to discourage Zulu counter-thrusts against the British frontiers. With the matter of Zulu raids particularly in mind, Chelmsford selected invasion routes in sectors considered vulnerable to Zulu attack. The advance across the lower Thukela would protect the coastal plain; that across Rorke's Drift central Natal; and that across the Ncome River the Transvaal. Moreover, by invading at several points, he hoped to force Cetshwayo to keep his *amabutho* fully mobilised in order to face the diverse threat, and so to present him with supply problems as great as his own.[13]

Hopelessly unreliable maps and inadequate reconnaissance on account of in-sufficient cavalry meant, however, that Chelmsford had no accurate conception of the terrain over which his columns were to advance.[14] These deficiencies were to handicap the speed of his advance throughout the campaign, and to ren-der the effective execution of his strategy impossible.

An integral element in Chelmsford's strategy was his intention systematical-ly to destroy all the *amakhanda* he could reach. As rallying-points for the *amabutho* and depots for their supplies, their destruction, culminating in that of oNdini, would ensure the reduction of the king's capacity to resist and fatally damage his ability to exercise authority.[15] Unfortunately for the Zulu, the elimination of these 'legitimate' military targets was soon extended to include ordinary *imizi*, and involved the pillaging of grain stores and the capture of livestock. Chelms-ford well understood that one of the most effectual ways of defeating a people such as the Zulu was 'through the stomach', which sanctioned the complete de-struction of the enemy's means of subsistence along the British line of march.[16]

Chelmsford was determined, however, not to allow the campaign to degenerate into protracted, irregular warfare which favoured the more mobile Zulu fight-ing on home ground. Instead, he knew the best way to end a 'small war' deci-sively and swiftly was with a pitched battle where all the advantages lay with prop-erly trained troops.[17] The object, then, was to bring the enemy to battle. This was especially important when, as in the case of Zululand, the war was undertak-en to overthrow a militarily powerful state, whose army was its most potent man-ifestation. Victory in the field was thus necessary to assert ascendancy. Happi-ly for the British strategists, there was every likelihood that a people like the Zulu, with their strong military traditions, would be willing to risk everything in the desperate gamble of a pitched engagement.

Chelmsford's operational gambit of dividing the army into several columns must consequently also be seen as a means of enticing the Zulu into attacking one or more of them.[18] Only when they were committed to battle, the British reck-oned, would the Zulu discover to their cost that the numerical inferiority of the apparently weak columns was more than compensated for by superior fire-power and tactics.

A disciplined British force, once it was properly positioned and handled so as to give maximum effect to the destructive capabilities of modern breech-loading, rapid-firing rifles, Gatling guns and artillery, was normally invulnerable against the poorly armed mass attacks of warriors such as the Zulu. Nevertheless, as appalling as were the effects of this concentrated firepower, Zulu casualties were never to prove quite as heavy as might have been anticipated. This was because casualties depended both upon the range and concentration of fire. For example, at close range (100-300 metres), two minutes' Martini-Henry rifle-fire at six shots per minute would be only ten per cent effective. This would decrease to two per cent effectiveness at long range (700-1 400 metres).[19] The fast-firing Gatling guns would be more lethal, but they were not dependable and tended to jam. Shrapnel bursts from the light 7-pounder mountain guns, which were the only artillery Chelmsford had at first, were not particularly damaging.[20]

Therefore, in order to concentrate fire sufficiently to stem the Zulus' attack, it was necessary for the British to deploy their troops in close order. The most effective way of doing so was to place them in prepared all-round defensive positions, such as fieldworks (whether of earth or stone), or wagon-laagers.[21] Indeed, the Boers had conclusively proved in 1838 that the Zulu were helpless against even hastily arranged and elementarily fortified march-laagers. In their arrogance, however, the British took some time in 1879 to concede that essential fact. Only after the battle of Isandlwana, which demonstrated conclusively that a massed charge could break through or outflank a loose skirmishing line, no matter how superior its armament, did the British abide by the Boers' example.

During the first days following their invasion of Zulu soil, the British were in considerable doubt as to Zulu military dispositions and intentions. King Cetshwayo, by contrast, was apparently well informed as to the strengths of the various invading columns, and their intended lines of advance. The king gained such information from the effective deployment of spies. Spies were no novelty in Zulu society, for the king used them as a means of control, and normally had an 'eyes of the king' at the larger homesteads to keep him informed of what was occurring throughout his kingdom.[22] In time of war, spies were activated on a large scale to gain intelligence on the enemy, and the advancing British were always aware that they were under observation.

Cetshwayo's subjects in every district were expected to keep look-outs and report the enemy's movements to the king, but those along the borders had special obligations. In January 1879 they were ordered to send spies into Natal and the Transvaal, as well as to Delagoa Bay, to collect what information they could.[23] Numbers posing as deserters or refugees managed to infiltrate British military positions, and sometimes were even employed as camp servants. It took some time before the British realised that these apparently harmless individuals were relaying information to the enemy. Civilian authorities became no less suspicious than the military, and the reported movement in January of Zulu spies along the Drakensberg towards Basutoland and Pondoland resulted in Bulwer ordering that any Zulu found in Natal without a refugee pass should be arrested.[24]

The activities of Zulu spies and messengers fuelled the white belief that Cetshwayo was attempting to co-ordinate black resistance in the subcontinent. This fear was no longer entirely groundless. There is no doubt that as the crisis intensified and war loomed, Cetshwayo was in search of allies against the British. Yet his overtures to other chiefdoms were not primarily aggressive in intent, as was supposed by the British, but part of his policy of maintaining contacts and taking what precautions he could. The irony was that in the past Cetshwayo had looked to Britain, as the strongest power in the subcontinent, for aid against his enemies, particularly the Boers. Now he had no choice but to turn to neighbouring chiefdoms for help.[25]

Unfortunately for Cetshwayo, during the years of colonial expansion in southern Africa, African chiefs rarely succeeded in forming large-scale alliances; sectional advantage was ever placed before wider interests. Consequently, there was never any chance, despite some pre-war negotiation, of any help from Swaziland, which for far too long had been a victim of Zulu expansionism, and hoped rather for an end to Zulu military power.[26]

Nor, despite the reported presence of Zulu emissaries in the region of Delagoa Bay, was there any possibility of co-operation with the Mabhudu-Tsonga, the dominant chiefdom across the trade route to Zululand. Although the Mabhudu-Tsonga paid tribute to the Zulu, and Muhena had been regent since 1876 with Zulu support, relations had been poor since the 1860s as both attempted to control the lucrative trade and smaller chiefdoms of the region. The Mabhudu-Tsonga therefore welcomed any diminution of Zulu power. It was rather different with various other chiefdoms to the south and west of them (but still north of the Hluhluwe and Mkhuze rivers), who had a strong cultural and tributary relationship with the Zulu state. Being so thoroughly within the Zulu orbit, men of the more southerly of these chiefdoms were even expected to assist the Zulu in war, though they were not part of the *ibutho* system.[27]

Further afield, Cetshwayo had no similar chance of raising the black chiefdoms under British suzerainty against their overlords. It is certain that he maintained diplomatic contact with certain Sotho chiefs (who, since 1871, fell under the authority of the Cape Colony), and that his emissaries were active in late 1878. But if their purpose was to foment an uprising, they had absolutely no success.[28] Nor did they fare any better in the eastern Cape where, despite some diplomatic contacts, the Mpondo remained quite unaffected by the war brewing against Zululand.[29]

It might have been different with Sekhukhune, the Pedi chief, whom Shepstone accused of acting 'as a kind of lieutenant' to Cetshwayo,[30] and who maintained regular diplomatic contact with the Zulu king. Moreover, the failure by October 1878 of the British campaign against Sekhukhune promised to encourage an anti-British front. There is evidence that Cetshwayo began seriously to pursue the possibility. Even so, no active alliance was ever formed between the Zulu and the Pedi. The latter found it sufficient to pursue their own interests in their relations with the Transvaal administration, and avoided becoming involved in the Zulus' dispute with the British.[31] Consequently, Cetshwayo found that when it came to war he had to face the British alone.

Thus isolated, the defensive became perforce the essence of Cetshwayo's military strategy in 1879. Astutely, he made it conform with his political programme of presenting himself as the pacific victim of an unwarranted attack, prepared only to fight in self-defence within the borders of his own country.[32]

Accordingly, he insisted that his armies, if successful, were not to follow up their victory with an invasion of Natal. He knew well from his white advisers, such as John Dunn, that the British had the resources overseas to continue reinforcing their army in southern Africa until it had won. This meant that the longer the war lasted and the more extensive its scope, the less chance the Zulu would have of winning it. If they violated British territory, they would provoke the British into persevering until Zululand had been crushed in lurid warning to all the other chiefdoms in the subcontinent. The campaign had therefore to be swift and limited, and the hope was that, if the Zulu armies were able through success in the field to menace the borders of Natal, the British would be pressured into concluding a peace favourable to the Zulu before reinforcements could arrive.

The obvious alternative of a protracted, guerrilla-style defensive strategy was not practicable. It could be argued that by withdrawing to traditional strongholds and avoiding conventional engagements, the Zulu might have prolonged the campaign beyond Britain's endurance. Yet that consideration worked equally well in reverse. For how long could the men occupying Zululand's rocky fastnessess have been provisioned? Besides, the nature of the *ibutho* system and the Zulu economy made it imperative that the men be freed at vital times of the year to go about their domestic duties and serve the king; likewise, the prevention of women and boys from planting and harvesting crops, and tending their precious livestock, would swiftly mean starvation and ruin for the entire community. Moreover, the prospect of permitting the British systematically to ravage Zululand was quite unacceptable to a proud and warlike people. Thus, for reasons both material and psychological, only the conventional clash of armies in the open field was possible for the Zulu in 1879.[33] It could not be helped that this strategy played directly into the hands of the British, who also wished to avoid a drawn-out campaign, and sought a swift solution through direct and decisive military encounters with the Zulu.

It is difficult to estimate with any certainty the number of warriors the king had at his disposal. Naturally, the full complement of the Zulu army, which probably did have a nominal strength of about 40 000, would never have been available for active service at a specific moment. Some of the senior *amabutho* were of too advanced an age to fight, while not every member of an *ibutho* could be expected to muster when summoned. When the king's *amabutho* mustered on the eve of the war, therefore, they numbered no more than about 29 000,[34] barely sufficient for the king's strategic requirements. He knew the British intended to invade his territory from widely separated points along the Natal and Transvaal borders to the south and west. He feared besides that they might attempt a sea-borne invasion from St Lucia Bay or Delagoa Bay and, conceivably aided by the Tsonga, advance on the kingdom from the north-east. The Swazi to the north could be relied upon to take the opportunity to attack over the Phongolo.[35] In other words, Cetshwayo faced the risk of attack from every quarter, and had to place his limited forces as effectively as he could.

In the event, he gave priority to his strategy of defeating the British in the field and threatening the Colony of Natal in order to force a peace. This decision

213

required that he concentrate his efforts against the British columns operating from Natal. There are indications that his council did not altogether approve, but the king was fully supported by his military commanders.[36] Since Chelmsford was accompanying the Centre Column, and spies reported it to be stronger than the other columns, Cetshwayo naturally singled it out as the main British force. The king consequently directed the crack *amabutho* of his main army against it. A much smaller force moved off from oNdini at the same time towards the coast to co-operate with local elements of the *amabutho* in impeding the advance of the British Right Column.[37] It seems he also sent some reinforcements from oNdini to support the Qulusi *ibutho* and local irregulars who were preparing to face the Left Column and its Boer allies when they entered Zululand. Local irregulars (and not the large army feared by British intelligence) also collected in the Nkandla forest area in order to repel any advance across the middle Thukela.[38]

Having committed his available forces so thoroughly to the southern and western borders of his kingdom, the king found he had left the interior of Zululand apparently vulnerable to attack from the north and north-east. Certainly, he retained a reserve at oNdini to counter such a threat and to intercept any possible dash by a British mounted force into the heart of the country – not that the British had sufficient cavalry for effective reconnaissance, let alone a venture of that sort. However, this reserve consisted of what had been King Dingane's favourite *ibutho*, the iNdabakawombe, married men of about fifty-eight years of age, who could not have numbered more than 1 000. Elements of the uDlambedlu (izinGwegwe) *ibutho*, only two years their junior, also remained at oNdini, as probably did some other older warriors in their sixties.[39] The inadequacy of this reserve – veterans, for the most part, of the Blood River campaign of 1838 – for countering any real threat indicates that, on balance, Cetshwayo had decided to discount a serious incursion from the sea or across the Phongolo.

Not that he had been unjustified in considering the possibility. The Portuguese had been willing to allow the passage of British troops through Delagoa Bay,[40] and the British had also seriously considered a landing further down the Zulu coast. During the final months of 1878 they had explored the shore at St Lucia Bay, the Thukela mouth and up the coast of John Dunn's chiefdom for likely landing-places.[41] But by January 1879 it was plain that no British landing along the Zulu coast was any longer being contemplated. Nor was there any prospect of the Tsonga initiating hostilities against their Zulu overlords – in fact, the contrary was the case. As war approached, Tsonga labourers in Natal began streaming out of the colony. Some made their way home, but others remained in south-eastern Zululand to fight for King Cetshwayo, their overlord.[42]

If the king was correct in considering that he faced no likelihood of attack from the north-east, he was less confident about leaving his borders with Swaziland exposed. However, despite the Swazis' deep-seated antagonism towards their aggressive Zulu neighbours, nothing would induce them to risk entering a war as allies of the British until they were absolutely certain that they were on the winning side. That was the crux of the matter. Throughout November and December 1878, Norman MacLeod, the Swazi Border Commissioner, made repeated overtures to King Mbandzeni, offering inducements for Swazi intervention in the north of Zululand to protect the left flank of the advancing British and to cut off a possible Zulu retreat to the north.[43] But Mbandzeni would not be drawn, declaring he had still to consult his council. This sort of prevarication intensely frustrated the British, but it allowed Cetshwayo to neglect the Phongolo border and to concentrate on defeating the British advancing from the south.

Zulu strategic thinking has been shown to have been informed and perceptive, well formulated to meet the British threat. Yet what has perplexed many historians is why the Zulu failed at the same time to develop new tactics better suited to confronting the devastating fire-power of the invading British forces, and continued to favour those practised since the time of Shaka.[44] One answer is that it had been forty years since the Zulu had last fought a white army, and though the intervening years had witnessed many battles (the worst being between Zulu factions), all had been fought between forces employing the conventional techniques with some firearms in an auxiliary role. Another answer is that traditional tactics *could* succeed against whites carrying firearms.

King Cetshwayo sent his armies off to war in 1879 in the firm conviction, shared by his people, that they could win if only the British could be forced to give battle in the open field. After all, they had twice beaten the Boers in 1838 when the emigrants left the protection of their wagon-laagers. Not for the Zulu the harassing and oblique tactics employed by other black warriors against whom the British had fought in southern Africa, and which many commentators thought might have been more effective.[45] Their traditions as an aggressive and conquering people demanded the frontal assault, which involved surrounding the enemy and finishing him off without quarter in hand-to-hand combat. Night attacks and ambushes might well be resorted to, but the norm was battle by daylight, in the open,[46] and according to the ordered and predictable formula.

Nevertheless, Zulu tacticians had not completely failed to learn from the lessons of 1838, particularly the disaster of Blood River. They were only too aware of the dangers involved in trying to storm prepared positions such as laagers or forts. The king consequently categorically forbade attacks on entrenchments.[47] Instead, he ordered his generals to bypass British positions. By threatening both their lines of supply and the territory to their rear, this strategy would force the British to come out of their defensive works to fight in their defence. Alternatively, Zulu commanders should surround the entrenched British at a distance (as was later to occur at Fort Eshowe) and attempt to starve them into submission or a disadvantageous sortie.[48]

Sound as this appeared in theory, it did not recognise sufficiently the difficulties involved in supplying a Zulu army in the field, nor the lack of patience and restraint likely to be exhibited by headstrong younger *amabutho* eager for glory. Besides, it was the usual Zulu practice to disperse after action for ritual purification and recuperation. All these factors made compliance with the king's sensible instructions by his generals unlikely, and Zulu success in the field dependent on catching the British in the open. That this should ever have happened was a consequence of the way in which Chelmsford and his staff, fresh from their easy successes in the Eastern Cape, insisted (until taught otherwise) in underrating the Zulu.[49]

18

Bread Smelling of People's Blood[1]

The Zulu army, ritually prepared for war, left kwaNodwengu late in the afternoon of Friday, 17 January.[2] With the uNokhenke in the van, it marched ten kilometres in a great single column to its bivouac across the White Mfolozi in the emaKhosini valley. It was full of confidence, for the king had assured his warriors that it would take but 'a single day' to finish off the whites.[3]

Chief Ntshingwayo kaMahole Khoza and Chief Mavumengwana kaNdlela Ntuli were the joint commanders, with the nearly seventy-year-old Ntshingwayo apparently taking precedence. That was only natural, for the greying *isikhulu* was second only to Mnyamana on the king's council and his great friend. This short, muscular (if slightly stout) magnate, with his strong limbs and massive thighs, and great powers as a public speaker, was, moreover, *induna* of the kwaGqikazi *ikhanda*, and renowned for his abilities in war. Mavumengwana was also a man of great influence in the kingdom. He was the brother of the *isikhulu* Godide, the Ntuli chief and commander of the Zulu army which was to leave the following day to face the British Right Column. Their father, Ndlela, had been King Dingane's chief *induna*, and they had both enjoyed Mpande's favour. Mavumengwana was senior *induna* of the uThulwana and a close friend of the king (they were both in their mid-forties and of the same *ibutho*). Though he had been one of the leading men in the appeasement party before the war, this did not affect the trust the king placed in him.

Sihayo, in whose district the army was to operate, apparently also had some powers of command. His son, Mehlokazulu, who had returned from sanctuary with Mbilini, was present as a junior *induna* of the iNgobamakhosi. Ntuzwa kaNhlaka, the brother of Chief Sekethwayo of the Mdlalose, accompanied the army as the king's 'eyes' to report both on the performance of its commanders and on its success in battle. Various other men of rank and influence who marched with the army included Prince Nugwende kaMpande, Cetshwayo's youngest brother; Muwundula kaMamba, brother of the emGazini chief and *induna* of kwaNodwengu; Vumandaba, who had been prominent among the deputation which had received the ultimatum and was the principal *induna* of the uMcijo; the ambitious Zibhebhu, who was *induna* of the uDloko; and Sigcwelegcwele, the commander of the iNgobamakhosi who had been temporarily disgraced after the fracas with the uThulwana at the *umKhosi* of December 1877.

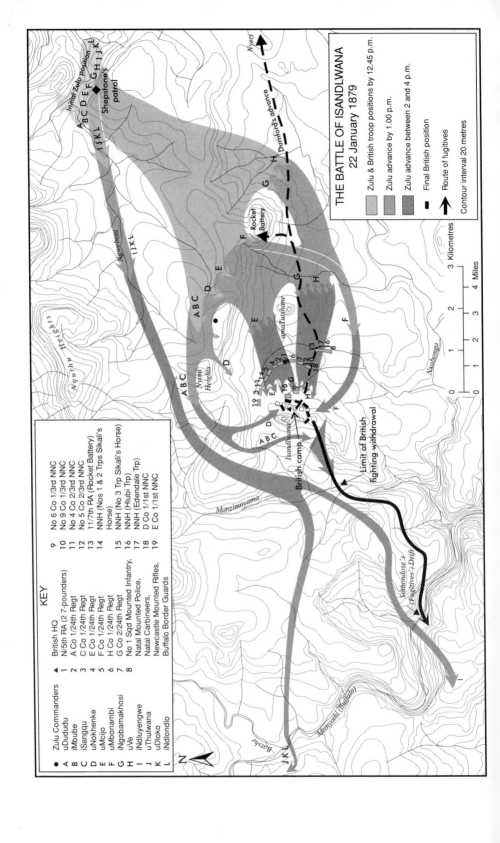

KEY

Zulu Commanders				
A	uDududu	1	N/5th RA (2 7-pounders)	British HQ ▲
B	iMbube	2	A Co 1/24th Regt	
C	iSangqu	3	C Co 1/24th Regt	
D	uNokhenke	4	E Co 1/24th Regt	
E	uMcijo	5	F Co 1/24th Regt	
F	uMbonambi	6	H Co 1/24th Regt	
G	iNgobamakhosi	7	G Co 2/24th Regt	
H	uVe	8	No 1 Sqd Mounted Infantry, Natal Mounted Police, Natal Carbineers, Newcastle Mounted Rifles, Buffalo Border Guards	
I	iNduyengwe			
J	uThulwana			
K	uDloko			
L	iNdlondlo			

9 No 6 Co 1/3rd NNC
10 No 9 Co 1/3rd NNC
11 No 4 Co 2/3rd NNC
12 No 5 Co 2/3rd NNC
13 11/7th RA (Rocket Battery)
14 NNH (Nos 1 & 2 Trps Sikali's Horse)
15 NNH (No 3 Trp Sikali's Horse)
16 NNH (Hubi Trp)
17 NNH (Edendale Trp)
18 D Co 1/1st NNC
19 E Co 1/1st NNC

THE BATTLE OF ISANDLWANA
22 January 1879

Zulu & British troop positions by 12.45 p.m.

Zulu advance by 1.00 p.m.

Zulu advance between 2 and 4 p.m.

Final British position

Route of fugitives

Contour interval 20 metres

Elements of all except the oldest *amabutho* made up the army. No single *ibutho* was present in its entirety, however, since members who lived in the districts threatened by the British Right and Left Columns were kept back to defend their own localities. There is general agreement, though, that the army which set out with such pride and determination on 17 January numbered about 24 000 men.[4]

On the second day of its advance, this great army marched fourteen kilometres to the isiPhezi *ikhanda* near the Mpembeni River. Five months later its track was still evident, the long grass all trodden down in one direction as if a huge roller had passed over it.[5] On 19 January the impi split into two columns which advanced parallel to and in sight of each other. Ntshingwayo commanded the left column, and Mavumengwana the right. Both commanders travelled on foot with their men instead of mounted on horses, thus following Cetshwayo's explicit orders that they did not set a pace which might tire the army. A few mounted men of Chief Sihayo scouted ahead. On this third day the columns traversed much the same distance as on the previous one, and slept on the table-land east of Babanango Mountain. On 20 January the columns proceeded across open country and bivouacked on the northern slopes of Siphezi Mountain, where it rained heavily. During the evening of 21 January the army moved in small detached bodies to the steep and rocky valley of the Ngwebeni stream, which abruptly opens up under the Mabaso heights. Stragglers continued to come up to the bivouac throughout the morning of 22 January.[6]

The Ngwebeni valley, whose floor is sufficiently wide to shelter an army of 25 000 men, is concealed by the Nyoni heights from Isandlwana, a distinctively shaped hill ten kilometres to the south-west, whose Zulu name means 'shaped something like a small house'. Zulu scouts reported the British Centre Column to be encamped at its base.

The mounted men of the 4 700-strong British Centre Column had begun crossing into Zululand at Rorke's Drift at daybreak on 11 January. The following day a detachment stormed Sihayo's Sokhexe homestead in the Batshe River valley and, with little difficulty, put it to the torch.[7] Gamdana kaXongo (a brother of Sihayo) who had been in contact with the British since late December and wished to avoid a similar fate, gave himself up to Chelmsford on 17 January. As it was British policy to encourage chiefs and their adherents to abandon the cause of Zulu national resistance, Gamdana, accompanied by a number of elderly headmen, women and children, was welcomed and relocated for the duration with their cattle in Weenen County in Natal. However, the remainder of Gamdana's adherents, including all the young men, refused to follow him into Natal and, driving their cattle for safety into the deep Mangeni gorge, prepared to resist the invaders.[8]

After the deceptively easy success at Sokhexe, the Centre Column began slowly to advance into Zululand, and on 20 January encamped at Isandlwana hill, which Lord Chelmsford had selected as the next halting place on the road to oNdini. To the British, the mountain resembled a sphinx – which, by some curious chance, was portrayed on the badge of the 24th (2nd Warwickshire)

Regiment, who constituted the column's main striking-force. In the days following, Isandlwana was to take on the most sinister of implications for the British, and the Zulu victory there was to change the whole complexion of the war.

With better vigilance or more experience of Zulu ability to conceal themselves in the folds of the undulating countryside, British patrols should have detected the protracted Zulu movement across open country to the Ngwebeni valley. But one patrol which actually came in sight of a portion of the Zulu army failed to grasp the significance of what it had seen, while Zibhebhu (who superintended the Zulu scouts) drove off another before it came in view of the main force.[9]

Once in the Ngwebeni valley, the Zulu army lit no fires for fear of giving away its position, and remained quiet and under cover, waiting for the morning. The order of the encampment was as follows: on the extreme right were the uNokhenke, uMcijo, uDududu, iSangqu and iMbube of Ntshingwayo's column; the iNgobamakhosi and uMbonambi formed the centre; and the uDloko, uThulwana, iNdluyengwe and iNdlondlo were on the left. The army was in good condition, for it had advanced at a leisurely pace, collecting enough grain and driving in sufficient livestock from the *amakhanda* and *imizi* on the line of march to keep the men well fed. The area was also renowned for an abundance of buck, and numbers of these would have been hunted and killed as well.

The Zulu commanders had left oNdini with the king's instructions to continue negotiations with the British if possible, and to fight only if they remained hostile.[10] That was all very well, but by 21 January the Zulu were being presented with an irresistible military opportunity which, it seems almost certain, they had engineered.

The strategy initially considered by the Zulu commanders had been to advance down the Mangeni valley to the Mzinyathi, and then to fall on the British from behind when they advanced, cutting them off from their base.[11] The obvious choice to have led the army through this broken, difficult country would have been the local chief, Matshana kaMondisa of the Sithole. His grandfather, Jobe, had moved into Natal and made an alliance with the Boers, but had fled back to Zululand when accused by the Natal government of being involved in witchcraft. King Mpande had then settled him and his adherents in the Qudeni bush, southeast of Isandlwana. These circumstances had made Matshana particularly beholden to the royal house, but the other commanders did not trust him. Perhaps it had become known that in late December Matshana (like Gamdana, who had recently defected) had expressed a desire to Fynn, the Resident Magistrate of Umsinga, to side with the British in the event of war.[12] So the commanders devised an alternative plan, but one which made the fullest use of Matshana's knowledge of the local terrain.

While the main army moved from Siphezi to the Ngwebeni valley, Matshana led a small detachment into the hills about the Mangeni valley, where it was reinforced by his own adherents. Subsequently, the British were to have few doubts that his movements were a deliberate ploy, devised by the Zulu high command, to trick Chelmsford into committing the elementary error of dividing and widely separating his force.[13] If so, Matshana played his part to perfection.

Chelmsford was hoping to find a site for his next camp in the Mangeni region. Reports that Zulu were assembling there with the purpose of raiding Natal induced him to send out a reconnaissance-in-force on the morning of 21 January. That day Matshana's men led Major J.G. Dartnell's 150 Mounted Police and Natal Volunteers and Commandant R. Lonsdale's 1 600 NNC a merry chase, gradually retiring before them at a safe distance of about three kilometres.[14] By evening about 2 000 of them were massed on the Magogo heights, nearly twenty kilometres from Isandlwana. When some mounted troops in the valley below attempted to approach them, the Zulu deployed with admirable precision into two horns, and came on in skirmishing order at the double in an attempt to envelop the British. Alarmed at this proficiency, the British withdrew. Dartnell encamped for the night in a hollow square on the Hlazakazi heights, across the valley from the Zulu, in a position he hoped would forestall a Zulu advance in the direction of Isandlwana.

The Zulu lit fires all along their position and kept them going throughout the night. But they were a blind to mislead Dartnell, and when morning came there was not a Zulu to be seen. The fires had succeeded nevertheless in convincing Dartnell's men that a large force was facing them, and during the course of the night they were swept by a couple of demoralising false alarms. The panic among his men convinced the experienced Dartnell (he was a distinguished veteran of the Indian Mutiny and the first commandant of the Natal Mounted Police) that he urgently required reinforcements.

On receipt at about 1.30 a.m. of his urgent message Chelmsford made the fatal decision to lead out a large force to his relief. At 4.30 a.m. on 22 January he marched out of his unentrenched camp with six companies of the 2/24th Regiment under Colonel R.T. Glyn, all the remaining mounted troops, and four of his six 7-pounder guns. He left Colonel H.B. Pulleine in command with orders to defend the camp with its depleted garrison. Pulleine was amiable and efficient, and had proved himself an excellent administrator. But he had never commanded troops in action, and the coming day's events were to find him inadequate for the task.

Chelmsford arrived at Dartnell's bivouac at about 6 a.m. Spotting some Zulu on the Phindo heights to the north-east, he sent Dartnell's men to engage them, while Glyn's force of regulars was sent to secure Silutshana Hill nearby. The Zulu in the latter region conducted an orderly withdrawal north-east in the direction of Siphezi Mountain, drawing Glyn after them, further and further from Isandlwana. Dartnell's men, meanwhile, became involved in a heavy skirmish among the rocks and caves of the Phindo heights, where Matshana had his stronghold, and killed some sixty of the Zulu.[15]

Matshana himself had a close shave. While his men were successfully engaged in luring the British along, he set off for the conference called by the other Zulu commanders at their bivouac in the Ngwebeni valley. He was surprised by mounted Natal Volunteers, and only escaped after a long chase.[16] But his purpose was achieved. The British had split their forces, and while more than half of them marched and counter-marched over the broken terrain of the Mangeni valley region, the remainder were left to hold the camp with numbers only barely sufficient to withstand a determined assault – should it come.

Sunday 22 January 1879 was the day of the new moon. She was to begin her new life at 1.52 p.m., and it was not customary for the Zulu to fight on her 'dark day', nor to undertake any business of importance. For it was a time of *umnyama*, when evil influences would overtake an *impi* to its enemy's advantage. By midday the Zulu bivouacked in the Ngwebeni valley had not yet been prepared for battle through the customary rituals. The warriors had not been drawn up in a circle and sprinkled with medicines to ward off *umnyama*, nor had they been addressed by their commanders.[18] Nevertheless, this does not mean that the Zulu commanders, who were in urgent council, were not intending to fight later that day. After all, the day of the new moon had not prevented Matshana from undertaking his successful diversionary operations, which were clearly part of a concerted strategy. Besides, the Zulu commanders knew their enemy to be at a fatal disadvantage, which could not be expected to persist indefinitely. Nor, as events were to prove, was it likely that so large a force as theirs could maintain the advantage of surprise by keeping its presence hidden for a further day and night, until the more auspicious Monday dawned. However, any Zulu plans for an assault on the British camp later that day were precipitated when a British patrol stumbled on the Zulu bivouac.

Colonel A.W. Durnford, whom Chelmsford had ordered up with a detachment of his No. 2 Column to reinforce the camp in his absence, arrived at about 10.30 a.m. and immediately took command. The joint forces at his disposal numbered 1 768 officers and men, about half of whom were black, poorly trained and inadequately armed. Unfortunately for the British, Durnford was 'as plucky as a lion but as imprudent as a child',[19] and anxious to prove his ability in the field. At about 11.30 a.m. he rode impetuously out of camp with 104 mounted men, a company of NNC and his Rocket Battery in support, to intercept some Zulu in the distance whom he presumed were moving to reinforce Matshana. As he left, he ordered Captain Theophilus Shepstone, Jnr, out with a patrol of Natal Native Horse along the Nyoni heights, to co-operate with him in an encircling movement. His last words to Pulleine were that he expected his support if he got into difficulties.

Since early on the morning of 22 January parties of Zulu foragers had been astir, replenishing exhausted supplies from deserted mealie-fields and abandoned livestock. It was such a group of foragers, driving a small herd of cattle, whom Shepstone and his patrol pursued north-east from Isandlwana, along the Nyoni heights. The foragers fled towards the safety of their bivouac and, together with their pursuers, at about midday came over the edge of the Mabaso heights into sight of the right of the Zulu army, just where the uMcijo were concentrated. The Zulu along the Ngwebeni were already keyed up, for they had been disturbed earlier in the morning by the firing coming from Chelmsford's encounter with Matshana. The uNokhenke had armed and run forward until ordered back to their place, as had the uMcijo, though the iNgobamakhosi had kept their discipline and stolidly gone on cooking their mealies.[20]

When Shepstone's men caught sight of the uMcijo, they were filled with horrified astonishment, but maintained enough discipline to dismount and fire a volley before retiring. This was too much for the already jittery uMcijo, who sprang up and broke away from the control of their commanders, followed by the other *amabutho* who moved up to support them. Thus the uNokhenke, uDududu, iSangqu and iMbube advanced on the right of the uMcijo, and the uMbonambi, iNgobamakhosi and uVe on their left. Ntshingwayo and Mavumengwana did all they could to restrain their men. They succeeded only with the uThulwana, iNdluyengwe, iNdlondlo and uDloko, who had been bivouacked furthest downstream on the Zulu left. The two commanders formed them into the customary circle, where they kept them seated until they had received their instructions. Even so, some of their officers, like the fiery Qethuka kaManqondo, son of the Magwaza chief and an *induna* of the uThulwana, broke away to join the uMcijo.[21]

After quite an interval the two commanders managed to deploy the circle into battle order. With several of the king's brothers in their company, they moved off considerably in the rear of the rest of the army, marching to the north of Isandlwana down the declivity that runs along the Nyoni heights, out of sight of the British. In this way, the Zulu left, as it had been in the bivouac, became the extreme right, while the right became the centre, and the centre the left.[22]

Pulleine learned from Shepstone at about 12.15 p.m. that the Zulu were advancing. Unfortunately, Durnford's ill-considered sortie forced Pulleine to detach units in his support, and so prevented him from concentrating at an early stage on the camp. Pulleine thus forfeited the overwhelming advantage his men's concentrated fire-power would have enjoyed if they had been drawn up in a tight, all-round formation. Instead, he was forced to deploy his troops and two guns about a kilometre to the north and east of the camp in a long, curved, extended firing-line along a slight rise facing the Nyoni heights. This low, rocky ridge commanded the shallow valley through which Durnford would have to fall back before the Zulu advance but, spread out so thinly in open skirmishing order, his men were placed at an unnecessary disadvantage.

The main part of the Zulu army, which advanced at a very fast walking-pace directly on the camp,[23] made their usual dispositions for an attack, and were already in crescent formation as they traversed the Nyoni heights, driving Shepstone's men and their NNC supports before them. Confident in their strength, the advancing Zulu army had at first expected the British to flee without fighting when they saw the overwhelming numbers confronting them.[24] And truly, the Zulu were a marvellous sight as they spilled into the plain below, all the more terrifying for the perfect order and precision of their deployment. For as they became exposed to British fire from the camp, they extended their concentrated formation into light lines of skirmishers, one behind the other, which came on by rushes in the most approved European military manner, making good use of cover. Supports followed close in their rear. The right extremity of the Zulu line was thin, but increased in depth towards the centre and left to between 200 and 300 metres, its constituent ranks of skirmishers varying in number between five and twenty, with ten or twelve perhaps being the mean.

With no untoward hurry or excitement, the Zulu deployed methodically along the entire British front, so that their centre – or chest – went forward steadily against the left centre of the camp, while the left horn engaged and attempted to outflank the right of the British defences. Meanwhile, the right horn moved rapidly round to envelop the British from the rear. Only when the British were outflanked and surrounded did the Zulu finally charge home with the spear. The reserve – or loins – which had followed in the army's wake, was then in position to take up the pursuit. Without doubt, traditional Zulu tactics, expertly executed after discipline was restored following the confusion of the initial encounter, were vindicated that day.[25]

Those Zulu who had firearms kept up a continuous but wild fire at the British as they came on, either firing when still out of range, or aiming too high, as was typical of their defective marksmanship.[26] Yet if Zulu fire did the British little damage, British fire-power all but stopped the Zulu, as numerous and determined as they were. Though 'killed in heaps', the Zulu did not seem to mind, but filled up their gaps in perfect silence, and pressed on with the utmost bravery.[27] Not that they were absurd in their courage. As they rushed forward they threw themselves upon the ground whenever the fire became too hot, and either edged forward on their hands and knees through the long grass, or waited for support before jumping up again. It was easier for them to avoid the shells from the 7-pounders than the rifle volleys. When they saw the gunners stand clear, they either fell down or parted ranks, allowing the shot to pass as harmlessly as wind, and leaving the British unsure as to whether their fire had taken effect or not. They took this evasive action with no hurry or confusion, but as if they had been drilled to it.[28]

As the Zulu attack unfolded, fortunes varied between the two wings and the centre. Some eight kilometres out of camp, towards the Nyezi hill, Durnford encountered the rapidly deploying iNgobamakhosi and uVe of the Zulu left horn, who opened fire at about 800 metres. Durnford retired steadily in skirmishing order, picking up on the way the survivors of his Rocket Battery, which had wheeled left up the Nyoni heights to support Shepstone's men. Just below Itusi peak they had encountered the advance-guard of the uMbonambi, and had only had time to fire an ineffectual rocket before being overwhelmed by a volley from the Zulu followed up by hand-to-hand fighting. Durnford conducted his fighting withdrawal as far as a donga to the east of the camp, where he was reinforced by further colonial mounted units. Here the dismounted force of nearly 200 men held up the Zulu left horn as it attempted to sweep round to encircle the camp.

Although the Zulu left moved in particularly open order, with even two men rarely close together,[29] it began to take heavy punishment. The young and inexperienced uVe, whose fleetness set them in the van, were repulsed, and retired until reinforced by the slower veterans of the iNgobamakhosi. These in turn were pinned down by the rifle fire from the donga, and by the two 7-pounder guns in the centre of the extended British firing-line deployed to the north of the donga. The guns shelled first them and then the uMbonambi on their right, who suffered the more severely. The Zulu responded to the shelling by opening their ranks still further, and a lateral movement to their left by the uMbonambi saved the left horn from stalling in front of the donga. They pushed forward behind and beyond the iNgobamakhosi to complete the intended turning movement around the British right flank, forcing the British to reinforce their right at the expense of their centre.

The Zulu centre – which consisted of the uMcijo, elements of the uMxhapho, and those members of the reserve who had broken away from their generals' command – suffered the heaviest Zulu casualties of the day. Shepstone's mounted men had retired steadily before them, fighting all the way, and – with the support of some advanced companies of the 24th – had managed to fall back to join the British firing line. Thus the Zulu chest, once in the hollow between the Nyoni heights and the rocky ridge, was fully exposed to the musketry and artillery fire from the centre of the British position, where it was at its most concentrated. The chest's attack therefore stalled as the warriors took cover from the devastating fire directed at them.[30]

Meanwhile, the uNokhenke had come down from the Nyoni heights on the uMcijo's right and in line with the British left flank. They massed under cover of an *umuzi* when confronted by the British fire, but scattered when shelled. Quickly recovering, however, they veered back onto the high ground and ran on north of the camp, keeping under the cover of the long grass and the declivities in the terrain. The uDududu, iMbube and iSangqu, who had not attempted to come down into the plain, were already ahead of them, and all raced along in a wide, flanking movement, intending to effect a junction with the Zulu left horn behind the camp. The reserve proceeded more stolidly in the wake of the right horn, and were eventually to make their appearance to the west of Isandlwana, on the wagon road down to Rorke's Drift.

By about 1 p.m. it was evident that the attack by the Zulu centre had stalled, but the situation was saved by the uMbonambi of the left horn. Driving a herd of maddened cattle before them to distract the enemy, they outflanked Durnford's position and began to pour into the camp, together with fleet-footed members of the uVe who had joined them.[31] At much the same time, the right horn completed its turning movement. The uNokhenke began to descend on the camp from the north-west, entering it from the rear, while the other *amabutho* of the right horn passed behind Isandlwana itself, seeking to join hands with the uMbonambi. Durnford's men, seeing they were outflanked, began to fall back on the camp, and so exposed the flank of the infantry on their left to the iNgobamakhosi. Realising that his line had collapsed, and that he was in danger of being surrounded and attacked from the rear, Pulleine ordered a cease-fire and tried to pull his troops back to concentrate on the endangered camp.

The Zulu commanders were, by this stage, stationed on a slight eminence on the Nyoni heights directly north of the uMcijo. When the British suddenly began to fall back on their camp, they grasped that the moment had at last come to encourage the demoralised Zulu centre to advance and support the horns' encirclement. They sent Ndlaka, one of the *izinduna* of the uMcijo, running down the hill to rally his *ibutho*, calling out: 'You did not say you were going to

225

lie down!' and that 'the little branch of leaves that beats out the fire [Cetshwayo] did not order this'. Ndlaka fell dead, shot through the head, but he had succeeded in rousing the uMcijo to charge the retiring British.[32]

To their left, Sikizane kaNomageje, an *induna* of the iNgobamakhosi, was inspired to remind his *ibutho* of its ritual challenge in the presence of the king to the rival uMcijo: 'Why are you lying down? What was it you said to the Kandempemvu [uMcijo]? There are the Kandempemvu going into the tents.' He then shouted: 'Stop firing. Go in hand to hand!'[33] So the iNgobamakhosi took their firearms in their left hands and also fell upon the British.[34] The uVe were similarly roused by one of their *izinduna* to emulate the uMbonambi, who got among the British tents before any of the other *amabutho*.

The Zulu centre did not at first resume their attack at the run, but came on with steady determination at little more than a walking pace. Up to that moment they had been making a low musical murmuring, like a gigantic swarm of bees, but at a distance of about 120 metres from the British they raised the great national cry, 'uSuthu!' and charged home at the double, pouring in a shower of throwing-spears. The British guns fired case-shot to no effect, for the Zulu in the front ranks who might have flinched were pushed on by the force of the numbers concentrating behind. To one of the horrified British survivors, the Zulu seemed to come up like a swarm of bees to get between the retreating British and their camp.[35] They became intermingled with the British soldiers as they drove them back, and the *amabutho* themselves lost formation and became mixed up as they carried the camp.

The uNokhenke had come around the shoulder of Isandlwana and seized its base, which commanded the camp, before the British realised what had happened. The uDududu, iMbube and iSangqu poured into the valley behind Isandlwana, and, drawing themselves into long lines between the camp and the river, cut the wagon road to Rorke's Drift. Their intention was to join the iNgobamakhosi and uVe on the nek, and so entirely block off the British retreat. But many of the uVe and iNgobamakhosi were diverted in pursuit of the mounted units and NNC already in flight towards the river, so that a narrow gap was left open for the British regulars fighting their way back through the camp to attempt a retreat. The uThulwana, iNdluyengwe, uDloko and iNdlondlo of the reserve now made their appearance at the rear of the camp, but seeing it to be in the process of being overrun, decided to continue on their way to Rorke's Drift.[36]

The fighting in the camp became hand-to-hand as the British were rushed before they had time to fire many shots. They were buried by swarms of warriors, so many of them that some of the Zulu were unable to get into the thick of the fight until the very end. Both Zulu and British were blinded by the smoke and dust and, pressed together in the mêlée, struck out wildly on every side.[37] The horror was increased by a partial eclipse of the sun, which was at its greatest extent at 2.29 p.m. It made the dull, cloudy day darker still, and was taken by the Zulu as an omen of *umnyama* and considerable loss of life. Each time a Zulu stabbed one of the British to death, he cried 'uSuthu!' or exclaimed 'This is father's cow!'[38] – a reference to ritual sacrifice which earned the approval of the ancestral spirits.

Numbers of mounted men, divining the likely outcome of the battle, managed early to make their way back to Rorke's Drift. When that way was blocked by the Zulu right horn, others attempted a desperate rush through the narrow gap left in the Zulu encirclement. Since many of them survived, theirs is the tale of the terrible flight down the fugitives' trail to the Mzinyathi. The uDududu, iMbube and iSangqu of the right horn had arrived on the scene too late to be much involved in killing the British in the camp. So lest they be accused of returning without having fought, they joined the iNgobamakhosi and uVe of the left horn in pursuing these fugitives.

The Zulu were all among the mob of flying men and horses, stabbing them as they ran.[39] The ground down to the river was so bad that the Zulu went as fast as the mounted men, killing all the way, while Zulu following closely on the flanks of the fugitives subjected them to a galling fire. Many reached the precipitous banks of the swollen Mzinyathi only to be drowned in the swirling, yellow waters. Nor were those who struggled across in the vicinity of Sothondose's Drift (or Fugitives' Drift as it came to be known) yet safe. Those of Gamdana's adherents who had not submitted to the British joined the fleetest of the *amabutho* in falling upon the fugitives,[40] and fired volley after volley at them as they reached the Natal bank. Some Natal blacks then co-operated with a few of the more determined Zulu who had swum the river in pursuing the exhausted horsemen for a couple more kilometres, killing the stragglers.[41] It was fortunate for the fugitives that most of those Zulu who decided to cross into Natal only did so further upstream, where the drifts were safer.

Yet, full of pathos and dramatic incident as this horrible pursuit was, it was no more than half the story. The places where the British dead were later found were nearly all in and about the camp (especially near the nek) or down the fugitives' path as far as the Manzimnyama stream, nearly two kilometres away. It is plain that most of the regular infantry, having been harried through the camp, managed to rally at the nek. There some made a last stand, shoulder-to-shoulder, while others attempted a disciplined fighting withdrawal towards the Mzinyathi. Shepherded on their left by the Zulu who held the ridge parallel to the line of their withdrawal, and bounded on their right by deep dongas, groups of up to nearly half-company strength were systematically cut off one by one and, out of ammunition, finally destroyed in hand-to-hand fighting. The last of these determined bands died hemmed in on the banks of the Manzimnyama. These professional soldiers sold their lives dearly, and the Zulu admitted suffering an unacceptable number of casualties in quelling them. Even when their ammunition failed and the Zulu could get to grips with them, they preferred to break up the stubborn British formations by throwing their spears, rather than risk coming within striking distance of the deadly bayonets.[42]

The British dead numbered 52 officers, 727 white troops and 471 black. The Zulu, as was their custom, took no prisoners at Isandlwana, and spared no lives despite pleas for mercy.[43] In the heat of battle they stabbed everything living they came across, even at first the highly prized livestock. Some atrocities occurred, and there were incidences of scalping and decapitation.[44] Particularly shocking to Victorian sensibilities was the cruel fate of the little drummer-boys, who were hung up and butchered.[45] Yet what appalled the British most was to find all the corpses of their comrades disembowelled and stripped. They simply could not condone that this had been done in accordance with the usual rituals to remove the contagious pollution that followed homicide and the dangerous identification with death and the other world.

The Zulu left the British dead where they had fallen. Those who had been involved in taking the camp, rather than pursuing the fugitives or making for Rorke's Drift, went on (as was natural in a victorious army) to loot it.[46] The considerable numbers of surviving oxen, as well as the two field guns, were eventually taken to the king, as were four of the wagons – though Matshana also took two and Sihayo four. The tents were cut into convenient lengths and the 'bell' portion of each brought to Cetshwayo. The Zulu carried off to their homes as booty everything else which they personally valued: firearms, cartridges, blankets, waterproof sheets, axes, shovels and the like. Most of the horses were killed, as they were considered 'the feet of the white men' and because the king had not required them. Nevertheless, a number were taken to chiefs like Hamu, who prized them. They also removed watches, money and similar valuables from the slain.

The most prized booty of all, naturally, was the rifles and ammunition. The king later insisted that he be shown the captured weapons, which included about 800 Martini-Henry rifles, but he was wise enough to allow those who had captured them to retain them as personal trophies.[47] The Zulu broke open the ammunition boxes with rocks in their eagerness for the 40 000-odd cartridges they contained. Those who had not managed to seize hold of a rifle tore open piles of cartridges with their teeth to extract powder and ball for their muzzle-loaders. They also found many bottles in the camp, and began indiscriminately drinking their contents, not being able to differentiate by the labels between alcoholic spirits and more harmful liquids like paraffin or chemicals off the veterinarian's wagon. So, while many became very drunk, others fell sick and even died of the effects of the poisons they had drunk.

Perhaps alarmed by these unforeseen effects, the Zulu were suspicious of the more unfamiliar contents of the commissariat stores. Consequently, they carried off the biscuit and maize, but stabbed most of the tinned articles and smashed up boxes of other stores and scattered the contents over the veld. What they did not want they left tumbled about the camp: portmanteaux, camp-beds, boots, brushes, forges, bellows, sponges, books, photographs, gaiters, cricket-pads, papers of every description.

Those Zulu involved in the pursuit of the British or the advance on Rorke's Drift did not return to the plundered camp, but proceeded straight to the king or dispersed to their homes. The remainder retired when, towards evening, they saw Chelmsford advancing in battle order on his stricken camp with the forces Matshana had so successfully lured away that day. They took up with them as much of the plunder as they could carry and, driving the captured livestock before them, fell back in long lines on their bivouac of the previous night, passing in their thousands over the Nyoni heights. The Zulu certainly were in no condition to renew the fighting, but the British had no means of ascertaining their intentions. They consequently spent an appalling night camped amidst the dead and debris of the stricken camp, apprehensively eyeing Zulu watch-fires lit between them and Rorke's Drift, and preparing for a Zulu attack at dawn.[48]

After the battle, those of the Zulu army who did not immediately disperse stayed encamped close to the battlefield for three days, mainly on account of the large number of wounded whom they could not move, many being in a critical condition.[49] There were also the dead to be considered. The only obligation the Zulu had towards those killed in battle was for a friend or relative to cover the corpse with a shield, though on this occasion the victorious army had the opportunity to dispose of most of their dead in decent fashion. They buried large numbers in the mealie-pits of two *imizi* not far off, and in dongas or antbear holes all about Isandlwana.[50]

How many Zulu dead were there? The Zulu considered Isandlwana the worst battle of the war as far as their casualties went.[51] There were certainly not less than 1 000 dead. The only casualties of note who are known were Mkhosana kaMvundlana, the Biyela chief and *induna* of the uMcijo, and Sigodi kaMasiphula, the emGazini chief, whose father had been King Mpande's chief *induna*. The latter died at home of his wounds, but his brother, Maphoko, though severely wounded, recovered. However, two badly wounded sons of Ntshingwayo, the senior of the Zulu commanders, later succumbed.[52] They were typical of the great number of wounded who, although not so badly wounded that they had to be left by the retiring army to die on the battlefield, struggled home only to perish later of their injuries.

Because so many of the even relatively lightly wounded subsequently died, many Zulu imagined that the British bullets were poisoned.[53] However, injuries inflicted by unannointed British bullets were quite sufficiently deadly in themselves. Spear wounds could be healed with the simple treatments the Zulu possessed. Bullet wounds, on the other hand, which smashed bones and caused considerable internal damage, generally required much more sophisticated medical care. Certainly, some Zulu survived the rude amputation of limbs smashed by bullets, and the multiple bullet-wounds and splintered bones.[54] But there is no doubt that hundreds, whom British-style medical attention could have saved, died of their wounds. Bertram Mitford, travelling through Zululand in 1882, was struck by how few of the surviving veterans of the war were men who had been wounded.[55]

229

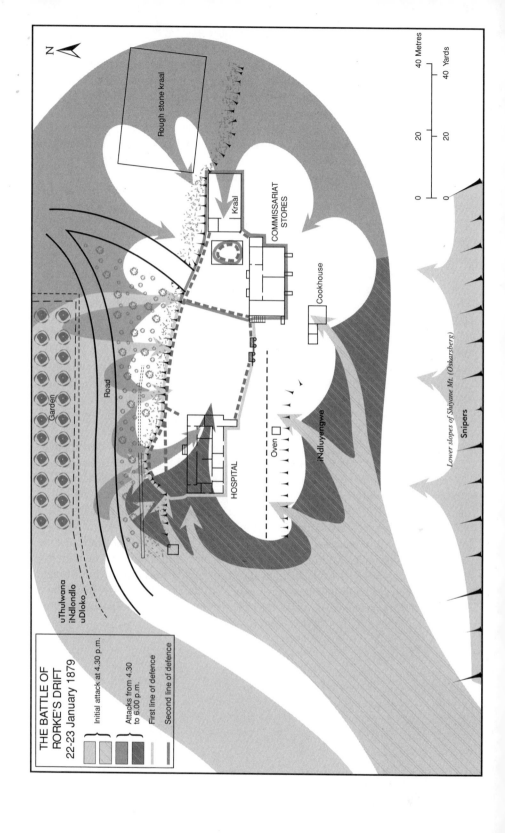

THE BATTLE OF
RORKE'S DRIFT
22-23 January 1879

Initial attack at 4.30 p.m.

Attacks from 4.30
to 6.00 p.m.

First line of defence

Second line of defence

uThulwana
iNdlondlo
uDloko

N

Garden

Road

Rough stone kraal

Kraal

COMMISSARIAT
STORES

Cookhouse

HOSPITAL

Oven

iNdluyengwe

Lower slopes of Shiyane Mt. (Oskarsberg)

Snipers

0   20   40 Metres

0   20   40 Yards

19

The Fight at Jim's

When the British Centre Column advanced into Zululand on 11 January, it left behind a small force to secure its depot at Rorke's Drift on the Natal side of the Mzinyathi. The place had been a Swedish mission station, and the church and house had been converted respectively into a commissariat store and hospital. Not anticipating a Zulu attack, the garrison, which consisted of a company of the 2/24th Regiment, a company of the 2/3rd NNC and various detached personnel, neglected to fortify the post. It was to prove a nearly fatal omission. Shortly after 3 p.m. on 22 January some fugitive horsemen from Isandlwana arrived at the drift below the post with the almost unbelievable but utterly alarming intelligence that the Zulu army had overrun the British camp, and that a large Zulu force was even then making for Rorke's Drift.[1]

Lieutenant J.R.M. Chard, RE, the senior officer present, stalwartly resolved that the garrison must stand and defend itself until it could be relieved. The post was hastily fortified by erecting a breast-high barricade of large ninety-kilogram mealie-bags, which, incorporated with two wagons, connected the barricaded and loopholed store with the similarly prepared hospital, and then ran back along the top of a rocky terrace to a stone-walled cattle-kraal next to the store. Since the Zulu had no artillery, and were inadequately equipped with firearms – and, moreover, would have to face the concentrated Martini-Henry fire from the garrison's all-round defensive position, it was hoped that these improvised fortifications would be sufficient. While this work was in progress, about a hundred men of the Natal Native Horse, who had formed part of Durnford's ill-fated No. 2 Column but had broken out of the Zulu envelopment at Isandlwana, arrived at the drift. Chard positioned them at the river to give warning of and to retard the Zulu advance.

The approaching Zulu force consisted of the uThulwana, iNdlondlo, iNdluyengwe and uDloko *amabutho*. They were the reserve that had not been engaged with the rest of the army in the battle at Isandlwana, but had passed north of the British camp to form up on the high ground above it. Their combined strength was somewhere between 3 000 and 4 000. They did not advance in one unit from Isandlwana towards the vicinity of Rorke's Drift, but in three separate contingents. The younger men of the iNdluyengwe moved in open order in advance of the others around the rear of Isandlwana, following the path of the British

231

fugitives and searching out and killing those making for Sothondose's (or Fugitives') Drift. The other two contingents first went through various disciplinary exercises – dividing, wheeling and reforming – before also moving off at some distance from each other in open order, sweeping the country in the direction of the drifts upstream of Sothondose's.

Their leader was Prince Dabulamanzi, the king's over-confident and aggressive half-brother. He was not actually one of the generals of the army appointed by the king, but his royal status and domineering personality gave him natural precedence over the other officers of the reserve. His undoubted intelligence, as well as his notorious unscrupulousness, showed in his handsome face, which was adorned with a well-cared-for moustache and pointed beard. Indeed, he was a sophisticated man. At ease socially with whites, he liked to wear European clothes, had developed a distinct taste for gin, and was a magnificent shot with the rifle. A vigorous forty years of age, he was finely muscled, though he was fat about the legs, which was typical of the house of Shaka. He was not, however, a general of proven ability.[2] Unfortunately for the Zulu, Zibhebhu, *induna* of the uDloko and unquestionably the most imaginative Zulu commander in the field, seems to have sustained a wound and turned back when the reserve reached the Mzinyathi.

The iNdluyengwe forded the Mzinyathi just up from Sothondose's Drift where great slabs of rock made it possible, and after scaling the precipitous sides of the river gorge, sat down to rest and take snuff on a small hill on the Natal side. The uThulwana, iNdlondlo and uDloko crossed upstream of the gorge where the Batshe runs into the Mzinyathi and the river banks are not steep at all. They spent a long time in the river, cooling down and forming long human chains to assist each other through the water, which was flowing more sluggishly than downstream and only reached up to their waists. When they gained the opposite bank, having brushed aside the foolhardy attempt of some of the Natal Native Horse posted along the river to oppose their crossing, they too sat down to rest on reaching the higher ground. Many used the welcome pause to take snuff and probably *Cannabis sativa* too, for the Zulu often took narcotics before battle.[3]

Cetshwayo had made it very clear to his army that, as the victim of unprovoked British aggression, it was his policy to fight only in defence of Zulu soil, and that Natal was not to be invaded. Perhaps, then, Zibhebhu's wound had been politic, for he was not alone among the Zulu commanders not of the reserve in scrupling to cross the Mzinyathi. The dignified and influential Vumandaba of the uMcijo shouted to the iNgobamakhosi as they were beginning to cross at Sothondose's Drift to come back as they had not the king's permission to invade Natal. Exhausted by the battle and the long pursuit, they were only too relieved to obey him.[4] The uMbonambi were likewise disinclined to prolong their day's fighting, and refused to obey the aggressive exhortations of the domineering Prince Ndabuko, the king's younger full-brother, to join the *amabutho* of the reserve in ravaging Natal. Instead, they turned back to Isandlwana to tend their wounded, setting up the great battle-song of King Dingane as they went.[5]

These contrasting responses by the *amabutho* underlined what had already been made apparent in the opening moments of the battle of Isandlwana: Zulu warriors were only going to obey their commanders if orders coincided with their inclinations. In the case of Dabulamanzi and the *amabutho* of the reserve, they did so perfectly. Dabulamanzi freely admitted that he was chagrined at having missed the fighting at Isandlwana and 'wanted to wash the spears of his boys',[6] as they did themselves. Both he and his men feared that should they return home without fighting at all, they would be the laughing-stock of all Zululand. Yet it is apparent that, tired and hungry after their already long march, they had no plans for a serious incursion into Natal. Their intention was simply to scour the countryside as far as the foot of the Helpmekaar heights, burn the farms and *imizi* they encountered, lift what cattle they could find, and then retire to Zululand with honour vindicated.

However, on 22 January Dabulamanzi's men were diverted from the normal course of a punitive raid into enemy territory when they came up to the little post at Rorke's Drift, known to them as kwaJim after James Rorke, the original white settler at the place. Insignificant, and defended by only a handful of British soldiers, it seemed a tempting and prestigious prize, to be snatched up lightly on the way. Never did they suppose that its determined defence would gradually draw in all their forces in a vain attempt to capture it, and force the Zulu of the reserve to curtail their intended ravaging of the plain.[7]

No sophisticated strategic motives, therefore, such as an attempt to cut off Chelmsford's retreat, should be ascribed to the Zulu attack on Rorke's Drift. To people in Zululand, the affair seemed afterwards to have been both unpremeditated and absurd. As they said, 'You marched off. You went to dig little bits with your assegais out of the house of Jim, that had never done you any harm!'[8]

While the two contingents of older *amabutho* were taking their snuff near the confluence of the Mzinyathi and Batshe, an advance-guard of about ten men of the iNdluyengwe scouted up the valley between Rorke's Drift and the Macembe and kwaSingindi hills to the rear of the post. The main body of iNdluyengwe duly followed them at an easy pace. Meanwhile, some detached sections went about their primary objective of ravaging the plain in the direction of Helpmekaar, and set fire to the farmhouse and huts on E. Woodroffe's farm not far from Rorke's Drift. The first of the two contingents of older men, having rested for about half an hour, set off in its turn. It bore to its left behind Shiyane Mountain, apparently to support the iNdluyengwe in their advance. The remaining contingent sent out a number of scouts, who ran rapidly up the river bank towards the main drift below the post. It then proceeded in their wake, led by two stout chiefs on horseback, one of whom must have been Dabulamanzi, who was a practised horseman. The advancing Zulu forces started rietbuck and duiker, driving them along before them, but no one took any notice,[9] for a far greater prize had come in sight.

At about 4.20 p.m. the British garrison heard the sound of firing coming from behind Shiyane Mountain, which overlooked Rorke's Drift from the south-east. The Natal Native Horse, who were deployed along the river, were apparently skirmishing with the Zulu as they advanced. One of their officers then appeared to report the proximity of the Zulu force, and immediately galloped off with his men to the safety of the heights at Helpmekaar, where there was a strong British post. The company of NNC thereupon followed this craven example. Deprived thus of about 200 of its defenders, the perimeter of the fortified position was now too long to be held by the remaining garrison of 8 officers and 131 men (35 of whom were sick). Chard sensibly ordered it to be reduced by half by building a 1,2 metre-high barricade of heavy wooden biscuit boxes across the position from a corner of the storehouse to the mealie-bags along the stony ledge. But it was still incomplete when the Zulu attacked. Moreover, not all the sick had yet been evacuated from the hospital which would have been left outside the reduced defensive position. So the depleted garrison was forced to try and hold the original perimeter, after all.

At about 4.30 p.m. the iNdluyengwe came in sight of Rorke's Drift around the southern side of Shiyane.[10] Only about twenty appeared at first, formed in a line in skirmishing order, just as the British had been trained to do in similar circumstances. They were rapidly reinforced until they were between 500 and 600 in number, so that their fighting line, formed silently in the classic crescent shape, extended from Shiyane towards kwaSingindi to its south-east. Keeping up a heavy if ineffective fire and staying in formation, the Zulu then wheeled to their right and advanced at a steady trot against the south wall. Stooping with their faces near the ground, they took the fullest advantage of the cover afforded by the many anthills, dongas and steeply banked streams on their line of approach.

The British opened fire at between 500 and 600 metres, dropping many of them. Undeterred, some of the iNdluyengwe rushed on to within fifty metres of the south wall. There they were caught in such a heavy cross-fire from the hospital and storehouse that they could proceed no further. Without stopping, the majority thereupon swerved to their left in search of a less well-defended sector. Those pinned down before the south wall occupied the cook-house ovens and took advantage of the cover provided by numerous banks and ditches on that side of the post.

Those iNdluyengwe continuing to manoeuvre surged around the western end and back of the hospital, and made a rush at the building and the north-western line of mealie-bags as well. This was a much better sector to attack than the southern perimeter, for there was less chance of being caught in a cross-fire, and plenty of cover was available because the defenders had not had time to cut down the bush or trees. The Zulu consequently succeeded in advancing right up to the walls in what was to be one of the three most determined onslaughts of the day. There were a few moments of desperate hand-to-hand fighting before they were repulsed. On falling back they took cover among the bushes and behind the stone wall below the terrace, as well as in the garden of mealies and peach trees.[11] A feature of that brief struggle, which was to have important implications for the further course of the battle, was the Zulu reluctance to face cold steel. It was an inexplicable though oft-repeated feature of Britain's colonial wars (one that we have noticed already at Isandlwana) that the warrior people they encountered, although trained from childhood in the use of spear or sword, nevertheless dreaded the infantryman's sword-bayonet.[12]

Despite their initial repulse, the Zulu persisted in their attack. After all, the first assault had been unsupported, and reinforcements were at hand. The other two contingents of older *amabutho*, who had apparently joined up in the meantime to the east of Shiyane, now came up around the southern shoulder of the mountain. They could scarcely march on and leave the iNdluyengwe to their fate, for the young *ibutho* was by now fully committed to its attack on the post. So, while some lined the ledges of rocks and caves on the mountainside, and from this position, overlooking the British, kept up a constant harassing fire in support of those already firing from the ovens below, the majority moved on to the northwest of the post. They kept further to their left than had the iNdluyengwe, so as to stay out of range of the British fire, and occupied the garden, sunken road and bush on that side.

This considerable reinforcement encouraged the iNdluyengwe already there. Because of the effective cover, they and the new arrivals were able to advance with relative impunity right up to the British defences. They then launched a series of desperate assaults on the hospital and along the wall of mealie-bags as far as the bush reached, which was about up to where the cross-wall of biscuit-boxes began. The Zulu seem not to have thrown their spears at all, but to have kept them for stabbing the defenders once they reached them.[13]

Once the garrison had repulsed each charge in intense hand-to-hand fighting, the Zulu took cover and regrouped in the bush, keeping up their fire on the defenders, and then tried again with great determination. If it had not been for the dead ground to the north-west of the post, the wall and thick bush, it is difficult to see how they could have maintained their position in such dangerous proximity to the post for so many hours. From the dead left upon the ground, the British were able to establish that it was the uThulwana, with whom the iNdluyengwe were incorporated, who must have borne the brunt in this violent second stage of the fighting.[14] Meanwhile, the snipers on Shiyane were taking the British completely in reverse, and though on account of their bad marksmanship the damage was not as great as it should have been, it was serious enough.

At length, at about 6 p.m. as the shadows gathered, the Zulu began to extend their attack further to their left beyond the bush along the more exposed parts of the north-west perimeter. In doing so, they were embarking on what was to be their only night battle of the war. The Zulu did not usually fight at night, but in this case they had unfinished business to complete, and perhaps they hoped that the gathering darkness would compensate for the lack of other cover. In any event, they began to develop their formidable and prolonged third assault. Chard, fearing that in their determination the Zulu would get over the wall behind the line of biscuit-boxes and breach his position, and anxious at the mounting casualties from the snipers on Shiyane, decided to withdraw to the shorter position he had prepared behind the biscuit-boxes. The Zulu immediately occupied the wall the defenders had abandoned and, in emulation of the British, used it as a breastwork to fire over.

At first, a heavy fire from the biscuit-boxes prevented the Zulu from getting over the mealie-bags and into the hospital which its occupants were attempting to evacuate, but at length they succeeded in setting the thatched roof alight at its western end and burst into the building. The hospital garrison retired room by room, gallantly bringing out all the sick they could before the Zulu could kill them.[15]

The capture of the hospital and the retreat of the British behind the line of biscuit-boxes greatly increased the Zulus' confidence. While some looted the abandoned camp of the company of the 24th outside the defences, the majority pressed their attack with renewed vigour. Whenever repulsed, they retired for ten or fifteen minutes to perform a war-dance and work themselves up for a renewed assault. While some attempted (without ultimate success) to fire the roof of the storehouse, others began an assault on the stone cattle kraal which formed the defenders' eastern perimeter. Faced with the real possibility that the storehouse might have to be abandoned and that the line of defences would be breached there and elsewhere, the British set about converting two great heaps of mealie-bags into a sort of redoubt. This redoubt provided a second and elevated field of fire all round, and promised a final line of defence should it come to that, which for a time seemed perilously likely.

Ironically, the glare from the burning hospital, whose flames only died out towards midnight, probably saved the British. When setting it alight, the Zulu had not reckoned on the advantage the light would give defenders with superior firearms whose attackers were thrown up into silhouette. Moreover, by illuminating the whole battlefield, the Zulu lost the advantage of night and the possibility of launching surprise attacks from unexpected quarters.[16] Despite this inadvertent loss of advantage, the Zulu nevertheless managed after several repulses to clear half the cattle kraal of its defenders and to take possession of the wall across its middle. However, the wall was too high for them to fire over effectively, and they were shot down by the British holding the inner wall as soon as they showed themselves.

The capture of half the kraal and subsequent stalemate there marked the turning of the Zulu tide. For as darkness finally fell, the Zulu seemed to pause, and some of the British swore they had just seen redcoats advancing in support down the road from Helpmekaar. Indeed, two companies of the 1/24th had marched towards Rorke's Drift from there, and by sunset their advance-guard was within five kilometres of the post. But on being opposed by a body of Zulu, and seeing the hospital in flames, they incorrectly concluded that the post had already fallen, and retired to secure the depot at Helpmekaar from anticipated attack.[17]

Even so, the Zulu were unsettled by the knowledge that further British troops were moving unpredictably in the vicinity. This, coupled with the uncertainties of night and the awareness of their persistent failure to carry the post despite repeated efforts and heavy losses, made them increasingly reluctant to attempt a fourth full-scale assault. Consequently, although they maintained their positions along the walls the defenders had abandoned, and kept up a heavy fire from all sides until about midnight, they did not actually charge up again in a body after about 9 or 10 p.m. They nevertheless kept the garrison in a state of alarm by every now and again setting up a confused shout of 'uSuthu!' from one side and then another, leaving the defenders in doubt as to where they intended to attack.

They kept up this psychological warfare into the early hours, giving it bite with some desultory fire from Shiyane and the garden and bush on the opposite side. But as the Zulu later admitted, it was no longer fighting, merely an 'exchange of salutations'.[18] Even this ceased at about 4 a.m. The British remained on the alert, however, for they feared that the Zulu would renew their assault at dawn. If only the Zulu had known, the garrison was down to one-and-a-half boxes of ammunition, and could not have defended itself for much longer against a determined attack.[19]

When day broke, the Zulu were out of sight, having retired in the direction they had come, around the southern shoulder of Shiyane. The majority moved back across the Mzinyathi towards Isandlwana, only to encounter Chelmsford's column.

The surviving portion of the Centre Column had spent a dreadful night encamped among the dead at Isandlwana. At first light it had begun to move off towards its threatened base at Rorke's Drift. Once across the Manzimnyama stream and into the more open country that gave way to the Batshe valley, the column came in sight of the Zulu returning from their unsuccessful assault on Rorke's Drift.

The Zulu were south-west of the British, advancing in the direction of the very drift over the Manzimnyama which Chelmsford's men had just traversed. Yet no encounter took place. Although large numbers of the Zulu advance-guard appeared on the right of the road within a few hundred metres of the British rear-guard, they remained squatting, gazing at the British like sightseers at a review, and exchanging a few shouted words. The main mass of the Zulu was moving up the Mzinyathi valley on the British left, but it too avoided a confrontation, so that the two columns moved off harmlessly at angles from each other.[20]

This extraordinary episode can be explained, however. Chelmsford refused to offer battle as reserve ammunition was short and the situation at Rorke's Drift and along the Natal border was unknown. Furthermore, there is no doubt that his forces were in a vulnerable position, strung out on a line of march nearly a kilometre in length, with Zulu to left and right. Indeed, the British feared that they had fallen into a Zulu ambush, and there was great relief when the Zulu passed on. For their part, the Zulu were just as grateful that the British had not attacked, and believed the ancestors had been protecting them. They knew that they would have been able to put up only a feeble resistance since they were exhausted from lack of food and sleep and their crossing of the swollen Mzinyathi, and demoralised after their repulse at Rorke's Drift.[21] There is no need, therefore, to explain their reluctance to fight as the consequence of superstitious apprehensions that the British were the dead redcoats of Isandlwana come back to life.[22] They would have known that part of the Centre Column had not been engaged at Isandlwana, and their main concern (as was that of the British) was to withdraw in order to recoup.

Meanwhile, the garrison at Rorke's Drift, who had no means of knowing that the main Zulu force had retired across the river, and no idea when they were to be relieved, feverishly strengthened their defences against further attack. And duly, at about 7 a.m., a large body of Zulu, who had remained in the vicinity of Rorke's Drift, appeared in growing numbers on kwaSingindi hill to the south-west of the post. The garrison presumed that they were intending to renew the attack, but Chard later came to believe they had gone up to the high ground to observe Chelmsford's advance. Certainly, as Chelmsford's column came in sight of Rorke's Drift at about 8 a.m. the Zulu finally melted away.

Chard had been fairly certain that the Zulu were in no condition to attack again on the morning of 23 January because of the unacceptably heavy casualties they had sustained. And, indeed, the majority of Zulu began their withdrawal from Rorke's Drift while Chelmsford was still encamped at Isandlwana, and posed them no immediate threat. Short of food and sleep, and starkly conscious of their comrades dead in heaps before the British defences, the surviving Zulu would at last have truly understood the lesson of Blood River: prepared defences, manned by determined men armed with modern rifles, were almost impregnable to frontal attack. After their experience before Rorke's Drift, the Zulu flinched at even the suggestion of ever pressing on to Pietermaritzburg. It was sufficient to say: 'There are strongholds there.'[23]

Zulu casualties had indeed been insupportable at Rorke's Drift, somewhere around fifteen per cent of those engaged. In future battles of the war, only half the losses were to prove quite sufficient cause for the Zulu to retire, underlining the extraordinary bravery and persistence of those who attacked Rorke's Drift. When the British inspected the abandoned field that morning, they found the Zulu dead in piles, sometimes three deep. They lay especially thickly in front of the veranda outside the hospital and round the walls on the north-western and north-eastern sides of the post, their heaped bodies sloping off from the top of the barricades.[24] Most were grotesquely disfigured, mutilated by Martini-Henry bullets (often fired at point-blank range) and frozen by death in extraordinary attitudes. About 100 guns and rifles and some 400 spears were also found upon the field, where the Zulu had abandoned them.

If only for hygienic reasons, the British immediately set about burying the rapidly putrefying Zulu dead. However, the NNC, who were assigned the grisly duty, had a deep repugnance to touching the dead for fear of the effects of *umnyama*. So it was arranged that they should only dig the necessary pits, and that the British regulars of the 24th Regiment would move the bodies. But, because there were few carts or draught animals available for the gruesome task, the men of the 24th had to drag the bodies there with the aid of leather *rieme*. The corpses were then burnt with wood cut from the many thorn-trees round about before finally being covered over with earth. The whole awful operation took two days.[25]

Figures vary, but the number buried was about 370. Yet the total number of Zulu dead must greatly have exceeded that. Some of the wounded or exhausted drowned while trying to cross the Mzinyathi,[26] and a further number would inevitably have died of their wounds on their way home or soon afterwards. Many other wounded were too seriously injured even to attempt to withdraw into Zululand. For months afterwards the garrison at Rorke's Drift stumbled across decayed corpses where the wounded had crept away to die in the long grass, in caves or among the rocks a great distance away.

There is an even darker side to the fate of the Zulu wounded, one which the British would rather have suppressed. On the morning after the battle, a further 200 Zulu dead were reported to have been found a way off from those killed near the post.[27] Unfortunately, many of these 'dead' had actually been wounded Zulu lying hidden in the orchard, mealie garden and on Shiyane. They had been systematically finished off with bayonet, rifle butt and spear by British patrols trying to conserve their ammunition.[28] Of course, it must not be forgotten that the British troops had been worked up to an implacable fury by the sight of their own disembowelled dead, and it was the custom of the NNC (as it was of the Zulu too) to kill the wounded. And the Zulu wounded, because they expected no quarter, instinctively fought back when located by the British, their 'treachery' usefully justifying their inevitable despatch.[29] So, in the end, only three wounded Zulu were taken alive, demonstrating how mercilessly thorough the British mopping-up operation had been.

The killing of the wounded brought the probable figure of Zulu casualties at Rorke's Drift up to about 600.[30] British casualties of fifteen men killed and one officer and nine men wounded (two mortally) were comparatively light.[31] Because they had fought behind walls and barricades their wounds were all in the upper parts of the body, and those who died had been hit in the head. If Zulu fire had been more effective, there is no doubt that the British casualty rate would have been much higher.

The Battle of Rorke's Drift presented the British with much-needed propaganda to counter the Zulu success at Isandlwana, and subsequently no fewer than eleven Victoria Crosses were awarded to members of the garrison. The battle also provided the model for all future successful British engagements throughout the remainder of the war, and vividly demonstrated the inadequacy of traditional Zulu tactics against fortified positions. Ordinary Zulu, however, did not necessarily see the implications of the failure to take Rorke's Drift, and jeered at the 'shocking cowards' whom they considered to have been so ignominiously repulsed: 'You! You're no men! You're just women, seeing that you ran away for no reason at all, like the wind!'[32] How unfortunate for Dabulamanzi's men, that they should have marched into Natal to avoid becoming laughing-stocks for missing the battle of Isandlwana, only to become objects of derision for failing to take so apparently weak a position as kwaJim.

After a victory, it was customary for a Zulu army to return in triumph to the king in order to report and share out the spoil.[33] If beaten, an army would scatter, each man making for his home. The fact that after Isandlwana and Rorke's Drift only the *izinduna* and a relatively small part of the army appeared before the king seemed to indicate that the army did not consider itself victorious.[34] The senior women about the king were inclined to blame Cetshwayo for the only partial success of the campaign on account of his failure to perform the necessary rituals wholeheartedly. On the day of Isandlwana, once fleet-footed messengers had brought him word that battle had been joined, he had taken his seat on the *inkatha*. The purpose was to ensure that his influence and that of the royal ancestors would reach out to his warriors, inspiring them not to waver. But against the women's advice he had left the *inkatha* now and then, and the consequences, they claimed, were as they had warned.[35]

Cetshwayo could not immediately confront his warriors on their return. They had first to be purified of the evil and contagious influences of homicide and to ornament themselves correctly before reporting, rejoining their companions or resuming normal domestic life. So for four days, those who had killed or who had ritually stabbed the dead were separated from their companions and, well fed with cattle captured at Isandlwana, underwent the prescribed rituals.[36]

Once they were ritually clean, the warriors presented themselves with their weapons in the cattle enclosure before Cetshwayo. There, with the king seated in their midst, the *amabutho* exchanged accounts of the fighting and renewed the challenges they had made before setting off to war. But already, the king had held the customary extensive discussions to discover who had distinguished themselves in the campaign, or had been revealed as cowards. So Cetshwayo acknowledged the uMbonambi as deserving of the great honour of having been the first to stab the enemy, and rewarded them with cattle. The cowards were publicly humiliated at the same time.[37]

Nevertheless, despite the public ceremonies and reports of victory, Cetshwayo had little cause for satisfaction. Sitshitshili kaMnqandi, one of the king's *izinduna* who had accompanied the army to report on its performance, complained that the commanders had lost control and allowed the army to attack without being properly doctored. Thus no credit was given to either Ntshingwayo or Mavumengwana, for the battle had been fought as a breach of their commands.[38] The unsuccessful attack on Rorke's Drift doubly angered the king, for he had forbidden any forays into Natal. Moreover, he was greatly displeased that his commanders had been unable to prevent so much of his army from dispersing, carrying off home the bulk of the plunder won at Isandlwana before it could be brought up to him for the customary distribution.

Cetshwayo was particularly incensed that the two 7-pounder guns had been abandoned on the field, necessitating their retrieval by the people living in the vicinity. Nor had any British officers had been taken prisoner, to give useful information under interrogation.[39] Above all, he was deeply shocked at the casualties his army had sustained, and alarmed at the way in which the greatly outnumbered British forces at Isandlwana had almost managed to stem the Zulu attack, and had actually done so at Rorke's Drift. The implications were very discouraging.

At first, when the word was shouted from hill to hill that the army had killed the whites at Isandlwana, there was euphoria in Zululand, and people believed that the enemy had been driven out and would be afraid to return.[40] But as news of the ignominious repulse at kwaJim filtered through, and as the wounded straggled home with word of those whom they had left dead on the field of battle, weeping and mourning began to fill the land, and continued for many weeks.[41] Ordinary Zulu were left stricken with grief and cowed by their great losses. The dreadful realisation that further sacrifices would inevitably be required of them filled them with foreboding.

The king showed himself hardly less pessimistic. At oNdini, he told the warriors come to report to disperse to their homes to complete their ritual purification and to recuperate. He bleakly warned them that the British were still coming, and that they must re-assemble in a month's time to resist them.[42]

Isandlwana had been an unsatisfactory victory, and its implications were confirmed by the defeat at Rorke's Drift. The Zulu had been served clear notice that their tactics of envelopment and hand-to-hand fighting could only succeed with great loss, and were altogether ineffective against prepared positions defended with modern weaponry. Mnyamana was prompted to go straight to the king to advise him to make peace while he still had the upper hand.[43] And in this sense Isandlwana had given Cetshwayo hopes of saving his kingdom, for he anticipated that after it the British would be prepared to negotiate.[44] In fact, the opposite was true. The very degree of Zulu success at Isandlwana had ensured that the British would continue fighting until the Zulu army was utterly crushed, and the king had acceded entirely to their demands.

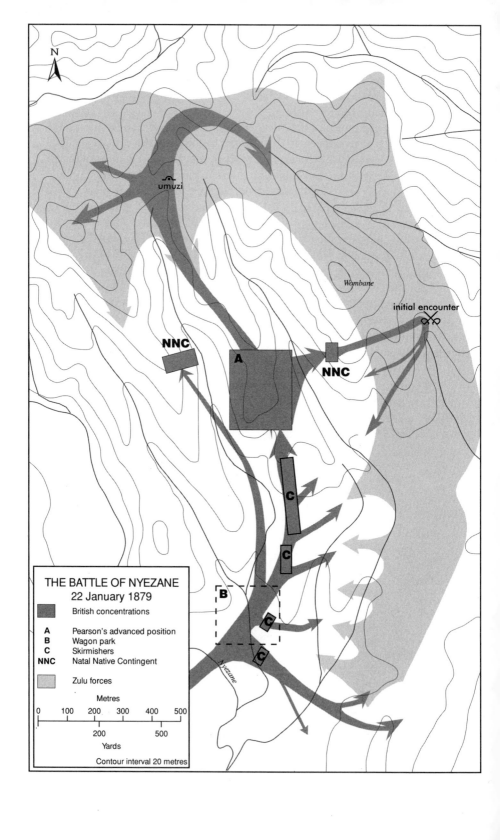

N

umuzi

Wombane

initial encounter

NNC

A

NNC

C

C

B

C

C

THE BATTLE OF NYEZANE
22 January 1879

British concentrations

A   Pearson's advanced position
B   Wagon park
C   Skirmishers
NNC   Natal Native Contingent

Zulu forces

Metres

0   100   200   300   400   500

200   500

Yards

Contour interval 20 metres

Nyezane

20

'The Small Guns Are the Worst'[1]

When the main Zulu army set off from kwaNodwengu on the afternoon of 17 January, a separate, smaller force marched with it. This was the army Cetshwayo intended should confront the lesser threat of Colonel C.K. Pearson's No. 1 Column of 4 750 officers and men, 384 wagons and 24 carts, which began advancing across the lower Thukela drift below Fort Pearson on 13-14 January. The Zulu coastal army was not of the quality of the one pointed towards Isandlwana. Its crack element was the major portion of the uMxhapho *ibutho*, whose members were in the prime of life. The smaller contingents of warriors from the accompanying uDlambedlu and izinGulube *amabutho* were in their mid-fifties, and could hardly be expected to be equally effective on campaign. Nor were the reinforcements they were to pick up as they moved through the coastal region to be of much better quality. These consisted of small local elements of the iNsukamngeni, iQwa, uDududu, iNdabakawombe and other *amabutho* still mustered at the coastal *amakhanda*, as well as numbers of local irregulars. The latter made up about a fifth of the combined Zulu force, which probably numbered between 4 000 and 6 000.[2]

In command was the seventy-year-old *isikhulu* Godide, chief of the Ntuli, *induna* of the uDlambedlu *ibutho*, and elder brother of Mavumengwana, the joint commander of the main army. Godide's lieutenants were, like himself, predominantly powerful men of the coastal region. They included Chief Matshiya kaMshandu of the Nzuzu, the aged Mbilwane kaMhlanganiso, *induna* of the kwaGingindlovu *ikhanda*, Masegwane kaSopigwasi, an *inceku* of the king, and Phalane, a royal *induna*.

On 18 January Godide's force separated from the main Zulu army, and marched south-east, bivouacking that night on the high, open ground at kwaMagwaza. The men were overcome by cold and hunger, and many began to suffer from dysentery, probably brought on by the full meat diet at oNdini after the many months of dearth. Consequently, the army was forced to remain at kwaMagwaza until the morning of Monday, 20 January, when it was sufficiently recovered to resume the advance. On the night of 20 January it slept at Cetshwayo's first oNdini *ikhanda* between the lower Mhlathuze River and Ngoye Mountain, where there would have been supplies and shelter.

On Saturday, 18 January, Pearson divided his column into two mutually supporting sections, and began his march from the newly completed Fort Tenedos across the Thukela from Fort Pearson to the abandoned Norwegian mission station at Eshowe, where he intended to establish a supply depot. The incessant rain of the previous weeks had reduced the tracks to mud and swollen the rivers, so that his progress was considerably slowed. The local people did not oppose his advance, for they had deserted the entire coastal plain and driven their cattle into the hills. Scouts nevertheless observed his movements and signalled his approach with beacon fires.[3] By 21 January the toiling column was only crossing the Matigulu River.

At this stage, Godide was not certain how far Pearson had advanced, and was still intent on marching straight towards the lower Thukela drift to confront him, bivouacking on the way at the kwaGingindlovu *ikhanda* just south of the Nyezane stream. However, when Godide's army reached kwaGingindlovu after dark on 21 January, they found it no more than a smouldering ruin, with the British encamped for the night nearby. The Zulu were appalled. They considered this destruction of the undefended *ikhanda*, which had been the pivot of royal authority in the district, an extremely provocative act which demanded retaliation.[4] And as it happened, they had already chosen the place where they intended to give battle to the presumptuous British and secure their revenge.

It was not Cetshwayo's practice to issue his commanders with precise instructions, and he had left it to Godide to drive back Pearson in the manner he thought best – so long as he did so without fail.[5] However, it seems that in this case the king's familiarity with the terrain where, in 1856, he had campaigned against Mbuyazi and the iziGqoza had led him to suggest the ideal place to ambush the British. Just north of the Nyezane stream, the open plain gives way to a range of hills. The ascent is along a low ridge running up a valley (then thickly overgrown with bush and reeds), between two grass-covered hills which rise steeply either side.[6]

A British column on the march was particularly open to attack on its flanks, which made it imperative that patrols move parallel to it or reconnoitre the broken ground ahead to give ample warning of the enemy. Because of the rapidity and suddenness of Zulu attack, it was also essential that a column keep well closed up. In this case, Pearson's reconnaissance had not been thorough, mainly because the enemy was underrated, and he had allowed the column to string out for eight kilometres. Once it was on the ridge between the hills it would be at its most vulnerable.

At about 8 a.m. on 22 January (the same day as the battle of Isandlwana), Pearson decided to halt for breakfast with the head of his column on the level ground between the Nyezane and the looming hills. He was as yet unaware that the Zulu lay concealed in their strong and well-chosen position, awaiting his approach, so it was unfortunate for them that he noticed some of their scouts on Wombane, the eastern of the two hills before him, and ordered forward a company of the NNC to disperse them.

When they heard the faint buzzing of the uMxhapho *ibutho* lying concealed in the grass, the unhappy NNC being led up the slopes of Wombane knew they were walking into an ambush but could not make their white officers understand.[7] The Zulu leaped up with a great shout of 'uSuthu!', opened fire and routed the NNC. Within a few minutes their attack was fully developed. While the older men of the centre moved cautiously forward, five distinct streams of Zulu who made up the left horn ran straight at the British wagon train at right angles to its length, clearly trying to surround the first part of the column and bisect the line of wagons.[8] Rushing from bush to bush, they skirmished in extended order to within 150 metres of the wagons, firing with great rapidity and retiring under cover to reload, or to receive fresh muskets which had been loaded for them. Their form of attack surprised the British, who had expected to be confronted by great masses of warriors in the open, not men armed with guns and adept at skirmishing.

Unhappy as the consequences were for them, the NNC had provided the signal service of prematurely springing the carefully laid Zulu trap. The precipitate attack of the Zulu left, combined with the cautious lack of movement by their centre, dislocated Zulu strategy, which had aimed at engaging the column in front while sweeping around both its flanks and enveloping it. With Zulu positions and intentions revealed, Pearson was able to take effective counter-measures.

He smartly sent forward the troops at the head of the column – two companies of the 2/3rd Regiment (the Buffs), and two companies of the Naval Brigade, accompanied by two 7-pounder guns, a rocket tube and a Gatling gun – to a knoll close by the road at the base of the pass. From it, the whole Zulu position could be seen and raked with fire. Meanwhile, the convoy began as hurriedly as it could to close up and park. When it was sufficiently concentrated, Pearson directed a further two companies of the Buffs, who were guarding the wagons half-way down the column, to clear the Zulu left horn from the bush. The Zulu in question, already astonished and unnerved at the concentration of British fire, withdrew rapidly but in an orderly manner before the Buffs' determined skirmishing line. They were not yet out of trouble, however, for when their retreat brought them out onto the open hillside they were exposed instead to the shells, rockets and musketry directed from the knoll.

The dispersal of the Zulu left horn enabled the troops who had remained near the Nyezane guarding the wagons to move forward on the Buffs' right and intercept those Zulu trying to retire across the Nyezane further downstream. These Mounted Infantry and Volunteers, as well as a company of Royal Engineers, received the welcome support of two half-companies of the Buffs and the 99th Regiment who were rushed up from the rear column under Lieutenant-Colonel W. Welman. The Zulu, though, were not yet beaten, and exhibited courage, tenacity and a degree of ordered control which the over-confident British had not anticipated. From the bush they continued to direct a heavy fire on the knoll, and seemed to be aiming particularly at the British leaders. Both Pearson and Lieutenant-Colonel Parnell had their horses shot under them.

Soon after the retreat of their left horn, the Zulu attempted rather belatedly to advance their right and outflank the British on the opposite flank. They occupied the high hill to the west of the road and an *umuzi* about 400 metres from the knoll. A portion of the Naval Brigade, supported by some of the NNC, checked this Zulu movement. Forcing the Zulu to evacuate the *umuzi* and setting it alight, they then gained possession of the high ground to the west of the Eshowe road, dispersing the Zulu right horn. Supported by a company of the Buffs, this force next proceeded – despite heavy fire from the considerable numbers of the Zulu centre still in possession – to clear the heights beyond the *umuzi* and take the dominating crest of Wombane. The Zulu, on losing both Wombane and the key to their position, rapidly dispersed in comparatively good order down the far side. Many were too tired to do more than walk, even though under fire from the victorious British. Gun and rocket fire helped break up any groups that re-formed nearby. The last shots died away at about 9.30 a.m.

The old men and the women of the vicinity, who had climbed the hills to see what they could of the battle, were left astounded, for no one had anticipated a British victory[9]. Though the warriors had consequently made no plans for a possible withdrawal, the majority eventually collected on a flat-topped hill 6,4 kilometres away, scaling the sides along different routes in dense files. They remained there shouting, singing and dancing while the British halted to bury their dead and attend to their wounded. Many were surprised to find they were not pursued, but the British dared not do so over the broken, unscouted country, and were indeed apprehensive of falling into a further ambush.[10] Instead, the column re-formed and at noon continued its march, camping for the night eight kilometres short of Eshowe, which it reached the following morning.

Abandoning the fiction that the war was against the king alone, and not his subjects, the British burned all the *imizi* along their route to show their displeasure at being attacked.[11] Of the 95 British officers and 2 687 men (1 660 of them black) who took active part in the engagement, only 2 officers and 6 men of the NNC and 3 men of the Buffs were killed, and 1 officer and 14 men wounded. By comparison, the Zulu casualties were heavy. The British officially estimated these at about 300 killed,[12] but, as at Rorke's Drift, the final count must have been much higher.

What is certain, though, is that the Zulu were impressed with the steady bravery of the British and appalled at the effects of their firepower. This was indeed devastating, despite the better than usual marksmanship required on account of the good Zulu use of cover. The Zulu dead were found lying about in heaps of seven or eight, while in one place ten corpses were found close together, and in another as many as thirty-five. While it seems that the steady Martini-Henry volley-fire and the Gatling gun (employed in action for the first time by the British Army in this battle) had been mainly responsible for the carnage, it was the artillery which had caused the greatest consternation. The rockets especially, even though they did little actual damage, were perceived as lightning called down from heaven by the British, and spectacularly underlined their alarming superiority in armaments. The Zulu learned too that the range of their muskets and other inferior firearms was humiliatingly shorter than that of the British, which meant that for much of the day they had been subjected to a fire they could not effectively return.[13]

It is hardly surprising, therefore, that the out-manoeuvred and out-gunned Zulu were left demoralised and little inclined to resume the fight. Besides, they were fully aware that only part of the British column had been sufficient to defeat them, and that British losses were insignificant compared to their own. All the advantages of a carefully picked position, surprise, and the enemy's lack of preparation had come to naught. Nor was Cetshwayo wrong to read as much as he did into Godide's failure to manage the battle better.[14] Nyezane might have been an unusual battle for 1879, in that it was essentially a running fire-fight during which both sides had exhibited a degree of ineptitude. Yet the decisive difference between them (more even than firepower) was that the British had possessed the discipline to retrieve the situation, and the Zulu had not.

After the battle of Nyezane, the Zulu did not at first disperse as was customary for ritual purification. Expecting Pearson to continue his march north-west towards oNdini, they concentrated in the thorny valley of the Mhlathuze River with the intention of again ambushing him. Instead, however, the British dug in at Eshowe and gave the Zulu some opportunity to recoup before proceeding to blockade the British position.[15]

Pearson's instructions had been to form a supply depot utilising the buildings of the deserted Norwegian Mission, and to fortify it by throwing up earthworks.[16] Work was in progress, and the British confident of soon being ready to advance, when on 28 January a message arrived from Lord Chelmsford informing Pearson of the disaster at Isandlwana, and leaving it to his discretion whether to retire to Natal. At a council of war the decision was narrowly taken to hold fast. It was felt that the continued presence of the column deep in Zululand would have a positive effect on morale in Natal, and tie up Zulu forces which might otherwise be free to attempt an invasion of the Colony. Moreover, a convoy with two months' provisions was close at hand.

It was necessary, even so, to reduce the garrison. Nearly the whole of the two battalions of the NNC and the mounted men were sent back to Natal, leaving only enough for vedette duty. The subsequent lack of mounted men was to be sorely felt. Without regular patrols it was impossible either to learn of the Zulus' movements or to mount punitive raids. The 1 339 white and 355 black soldiers and non-combatants remaining in Fort Eshowe consequently settled down with little positive to do except wait to be relieved. They filled their time constantly improving the fort, making occasional minor forays outside the walls, nursing their dwindling supplies and tending the growing numbers of sick and dying.[17]

Meanwhile, in north-western Zululand too, the British were forced in the wake of Isandlwana to retire on fortified positions. However, in comparison with the coastal region, the initiative remained with them.

As we have seen, the Disputed Territory was a volatile region. Mbilini's raids in October 1878 had been the final straw for the white settlers of the Phongolo region. To dissuade them from abandoning the area to Zulu influence and thus strategically separating the British from the Swazi, with whom they hoped to co-operate, Colonel Evelyn Wood, commander of the British troops stationed at Utrecht, had dispatched a garrison of two companies of infantry to Luneburg.

The soldiers had strengthened their position there and during November had built Fort Clery. As feared, their presence had provoked the Qulusi, who were attached to the ebaQulusini *ikhanda* just to the east of the enormous, flat-topped Hlobane Mountain, half-way up the southern slopes of which Mbilini had his homestead. The Qulusi *izinduna* had come to protest, as had Manyonyoba, a local *induna* who acted as Cetshwayo's representative.

Manyonyoba, who had been much longer established in the region than Mbilini, was equally self-serving and independent-minded. His father, Maqondo, had accepted Shaka's overlordship, so Manyonyoba was considered to owe Cetshwayo his allegiance. His adherents were the debris of various chiefdoms conquered by Shaka and Dingane – Zulu, Swazi, Sotho – who had gone begging for land until permitted to settle north of the Phongolo, in the caves along both steep banks of the Ntombe River. From this fastness Manyonyoba was in the habit of raiding the surrounding countryside. By mid-January 1879 uncertainty as to his intentions, as well as further small raids in the vicinity, had persuaded all the local farmers and their farmworkers to seek refuge in the Luneburg laager.[18]

Early in January the Left (No. 4) Column of 2 278 men assembled near Balte Spruit, and by 10 January it was encamped at Bemba's Kop on the Ncome River awaiting the expiry of the ultimatum. 'Somtseu's *impi*', as the Zulu called it (believing that as it came from the direction of the Transvaal it had been sent by Theophilus Shepstone)[20] was commanded by Evelyn Wood. Short, heavily whiskered, with mournful eyes, the colonel was prey to debilitating illnesses and growing deafness. But he was a tenacious and energetic fighting soldier of real talent. A seasoned veteran of the Crimean, Indian Mutiny and Ashanti campaigns, he had earned the Victoria Cross in India. The Zulu called him 'Lukuni' after the hard wood from which knobkerries were made, a sobriquet which was not only a play on his name, but a tribute to his military abilities and tough character.[21]

Chelmsford's plans for the initial advance of the Centre and Left Columns required that Wood move down the Ncome River and subdue the Zulu to his front and left in order to take pressure off the Centre Column as it crossed the Mzinyathi. The Left Column would also support the Centre Column by covering its left flank and the Transvaal border, and by forming the link between it and Colonel Rowlands's No. 5 Column of 1 565 officers and men to the north.

The No. 5 Column, however, was not (as originally intended) to join the others in the advance on oNdini. As a consequence of Rowlands's unsuccessful operations during September-October 1878 against the Pedi, Chelmsford decided that his column should remain in garrison on the Phongolo frontier to keep Sekhukhune and predatory local chiefs like Mbilini in order, and to protect the Wakkerstroom District from Zulu inroads. Consequently, Rowlands's Column did not advance beyond its posts at Derby and Luneburg except to take part in localised expeditions. When on 26 February the hostile attitude of the Transvaal Boers necessitated the return of Rowlands and his staff to Pretoria, No. 5 Column was attached to Wood's command.[22]

The mobility of the several hundred mounted volunteers and infantry of Wood's Column made them an extremely effective force. Their commander,

Lieutenant-Colonel Redvers Buller, was an inspired leader of men. His powers of organisation might have been poor and his temper uncontrollable, but he was courageous to the point of rashness and a superb horseman. He had a genuine feel for irregular mounted warfare, and led his men in their scouting and skirmishing with considerable flair and dash. During the campaign of January and February, which saw many minor actions but no battles, Wood was able to establish his supremacy in north-western Zululand, ready, like a spider in the centre of its web, to pounce on any hostile force rash enough to penetrate his zone of control.

It was always Chelmsford's hope that the Zulu could be induced to surrender instead of fighting, and he had been encouraged by Hamu's overtures throughout the final months of 1878. Consequently, he had ordered Wood on 16 December 1878 to make every effort to induce the Zulu along his line of advance to come under his protection, and to relocate those who submitted in his rear.[23] In this spirit, Wood had an interview on 9 January 1879 with Bemba, an *induna* of the important Chief Sekethwayo of the Mdlalose, an *isikhulu* in the north-western districts and the *induna* of the kwaNodwengu *ikhanda*. Wood agreed to protect and feed Bemba, who came in the next day with eighty of his adherents and over 800 head of livestock. His people surrendered their arms, and were relocated in the Utrecht District.[24]

Bemba's submission was satisfactory, but it was Sekethwayo's that Wood sought. Because Sekethwayo was much embittered against the Transvaalers for their land claims in his territory, he was logically expected to be firmly against the British and of the war party. But instead, old and infirm, he was inclined to temporise, and Wood proceeded gently in order to reel him in.

On the eve of hostilities, most Zulu across the Ncome from Wood were still living in their *imizi* with their herds and flocks. Only the young men had gone in answer to their king's call to arms. Before he crossed into Zululand, Wood considerately warned the Zulu to his front that the war would begin the following day, and that they must decide whether to be friends or foes. Yet the speed of his mounted men's advance on 11 January to within twenty kilometres of Rorke's Drift caught the Zulu by surprise, so that they had time only to make for the hills, leaving their livestock behind. These the British rounded up, taking about 2 000 cattle belonging to Sihayo, and another 2 000 to 3 000 from the adherents of Sondolosi, Sekethwayo's deceased brother. In addition they drove off some 2 000 sheep, besides goats and horses.[25]

Sekethwayo, thoroughly alarmed, that very day sent word to Wood of his desire to accept the British terms for surrender, and declared that he was prepared to go with his disarmed people to the Transvaal for the duration of the war. Wood instructed him to surrender the next day, and his people by 14 January. In the interim, in order to encourage him, he let Sekethwayo know that the cattle already captured from him would be returned the moment he gave himself up. These negotiations, so promising for Wood, were abruptly terminated on 15 January. An *impi* despatched from oNdini by the king had entered Sekethwayo's territory and brought the errant chief smartly back into line. Disappointed,

Wood sent Sekethwayo's cattle away for sale in the Orange Free State. Even so, by 13 January some fifty of Sekethwayo's adherents had availed themselves of the British terms, and more surrendered on 17 January, having been found by the British in some caves where they had taken refuge. All, however, were women, children or the aged, and there were no able-bodied men among them.[26]

Meanwhile, on 12 January one of Wood's mounted patrols raided and dispersed Mbusa's adherents, who lived on the lower Bivane, killing seven and capturing 538 head of cattle. The Qulusi collected the survivors on 16 January, and returned with them to ebaQulusini. Wood sent a strong reconnaissance patrol after them in the direction of the Batshe River on 15 January, and it became involved in a skirmish with about 500 Zulu. This skirmish was typical of the many running fights that were to ensue during the course of the war. The Zulu tried to draw the British onto unfavourable ground, and sniped at them from the rear and flanks. The British, on the other hand, secured their flanks with mounted men and drove the Zulu back with a line of skirmishers. These were reinforced at the right moment, and broke through the Zulu force. The mounted men completed the Zulu rout, but did not pursue far for fear of an ambush.[27]

Wood, who had marched his force back to Bemba's Kop on 13 January, began an advance on the White Mfolozi on 18 January. During the march some of Wood's Irregulars (black troops raised in the Transvaal) had a successful skirmish across the White Mfolozi near Cerekoma Mountain with a party of Sekethwayo's adherents, and brought in 400 cattle. At this stage, Wood had cause to be content with his progress. He had successfully cleared Chelmsford's left flank, and the discomfited Mdlalose had evacuated their *imizi* with their livestock. Wood spared their huts and standing crops from burning, for he still hoped to accept Zulu as refugees rather than to fight them.[28] And indeed, on 20 January Thinta, Sekethwayo's uncle and chief *induna*, surrendered to Wood, and he and his adherents were relocated in Utrecht. They had been taking refuge in caves, for they expected to be attacked by the Qulusi.[29]

This antagonism by the doggedly loyal Qulusi towards the Mdlalose introduced a new element of potential conflict between those wishing to collaborate with the British and those who were determined to stand by their king. As Wood was to discover, a far more determined foe now faced him in the Qulusi than in the equivocal Mdlalose.

Cetshwayo had ordered the Qulusi to stand against Wood's Column, and all had concentrated at the ebaQulusini *ikhanda* to do so, even those from as far away as the Phongolo valley.[30] Wood realised that he would have to defeat them, especially as they might disrupt his lines of supply. Consequently, he obtained Chelmsford's approval to strike north-east towards ebaQulusini, clearing the Ntendeka range of the Qulusi, before resuming his advance in support of the Centre Column.[31]

On 20 January Buller led a mounted force consisting of eighty-two Frontier Light Horse and twenty-three Dutch Burghers under Piet Uys across the White Mfolozi to reconnoitre the top of Zungwini Mountain, where Mbilini had reinforced the Qulusi. They attacked Mabomba's *umuzi* on the south-eastern spur, killing twelve for the loss of a man wounded. However, the British were prevented from ascending the mountain by a force of about 1 000 Zulu on the summit. These came down the mountain in the conventional formation of three columns, the two horns (which moved in disciplined skirmishing order) quite outflanking the British.

Buller had no option but to make a fighting retreat across the White Mfolozi, where he made a stand on the open ground, driving the Zulu back. This sharp reversal, and two more wounded, was a salutary shock for the British. The Qulusi had proved themselves far more serious fighting men than the Mdlalose. Not only were the majority armed with guns, but they were under regular command and discipline and sure of their skirmishing tactics, which were attuned to the broken terrain of their own territory.[32]

Yet Wood could not allow the Qulusi to retain the ascendancy, even if they did not seem able to make proper use of it by launching an offensive of their own. In the early hours of 22 January he himself led out a strong patrol of infantry as well as mounted men back to Zungwini. A few hundred Zulu on the southeastern summit retired precipitately at the sight of them, abandoning 250 head of cattle and about 400 sheep and goats to the British. From the top of Zungwini, however, Wood experienced a sobering sight. Under Hlobane Mountain, he saw about 4 000 Zulu drilling with great ease and precision, forming squares, triangles and circles.[33] These disciplined warriors would clearly have to be defeated if his column were to regain the initiative.

Consequently, on 24 January Wood led out a patrol between the Ntendeka range and Zungwini Nek, taking about 3 000 Zulu by surprise. Those who attempted a stand were dispersed by the two 7-pounder guns and were pursued and scattered by the mounted men, mainly retiring up Hlobane. About fifty Zulu lost their lives in the affray,[34] including two sons of the prominent Qulusi *induna* Mcwayo kaMangeda, as well as three other *izinduna*.[35] It seems that Msebe kaMadaka, a senior Qulusi *induna* and second cousin of Cetshwayo, had been in charge of the force, which had consisted – besides the Qulusi *ibutho* and local irregulars (including Mbilini's men) – of some members of other *amabutho* who lived in the area.[36]

The Qulusi were greatly disheartened by their ignominious setback, but Wood's position had also suddenly deteriorated. During the course of the skirmish he was brought the astonishing news of the destruction of the British camp at Isandlwana and the consequent collapse of Chelmsford's strategy. Wood at once withdrew to his camp on the White Mfolozi. In order to cover Utrecht from Zulu attack and to maintain communication with No. 5 Column, while remaining in a position to strike at the Qulusi, he moved north-west on 31 January to a strongly fortified camp at Khambula hill, where water and fuel were available. There he intended to stand fast, making his presence constantly felt in a sixty-six-kilometre radius through mounted patrols, until Chelmsford was ready to resume the march on oNdini.[37]

Meanwhile, all Manyonyoba's fighting men, who could not have numbered more than 1 000, were defeated on 26 January south of Luneburg by a patrol from the garrison. Manyonyoba took to his caves with his women, children and infirm, as well as his own cattle, while royal cattle in his care were driven towards oNdini. Commandant Schermbrucker intercepted these at the junction of the Ntombe and Phongolo, capturing 365 of them and some 200 goats besides. Half of Manyonyoba's discomfited warriors joined the Qulusi opposing Wood; the remainder, operating in groups of 100 to 200, kept up raids from the Ntombe caves and made the Luneburg-Derby road unsafe for small parties of British. The garrison at Luneburg was too well fortified for them to attempt to attack it, however, while in turn the garrison was too small to risk assaulting the caves.[38]

In the west, therefore, as on the coast, there was apparent stalemate. This was not on account of Zulu success in these theatres, for they had generally been thoroughly worsted, but rather the consequence of the main Zulu army's victory at Isandlwana. It was this which had quite dislocated Chelmsford's offensive strategy and forced his various columns onto the defensive. Whether the Zulu could take advantage of the situation was, however, another matter.

21

While the White People Were Still Tired

A temporary stalemate succeeded the battles and skirmishes of late January. The British were on the defensive, single-mindedly gathering reinforcements to avenge Isandlwana in the next round, while Cetshwayo was left considering his options. His enemies expected him to take the offensive while 'the white people were still tired'.[1] Intelligence reports reaching the British in the weeks following Isandlwana indicated that the king intended to send a large army to storm Fort Eshowe, before sweeping on to invade Natal.[2] In reality, he found the prospect of resuming offensive operations problematical. Any strategic planning was made exceedingly difficult by the uncertain morale of the Zulu army.

It was normal for the Zulu to disperse after battle for ritual purification, but after their heavy casualties in the first round of battles and skirmishes, discouragingly inflicted by such a numerically inferior foe, his *amabutho* were most reluctant to try conclusions again, and could not be made to muster during February. Moreover, the king's council objected to any further operations until the mealie crop was ripe and more food was available.[3]

Meanwhile, there were threats from the various fronts to consider. Isandlwana had temporarily relieved pressure from across the Mzinyathi, but Pearson was entrenched at Eshowe, right within the kingdom. Exaggerated and unfounded fears persisted that the British were still planning an amphibious landing at St Lucia.[4] The intentions of the Swazi were clearer. Following Isandlwana they remained chary of any commitment to the British until they could be certain which the winning side would be, and preferred to stand on the defensive behind their own borders.[5] Chelmsford consequently had to regard them as 'out of the game',[6] and towards the end of February Cetshwayo tentatively opened negotiations with King Mbandzeni regarding sanctuary should the 'wild animals' who had come against him eventually prevail.[7] Yet if the Swazi presented no threat for the moment, there still remained the untested British No. 5 Column in the Phongolo region. And, most dangerous of all, Wood continued to raid aggressively from Khambula and threaten the whole of north-western Zululand.

What then was the king to do? In the end, he effectively marked time. Along the quiescent frontier with Natal he forbade the border people to make any raids on their own account across the swollen rivers. So, despite settler apprehensions of an imminent invasion, the Zulu living just across the Thukela contented themselves with the odd shot or shouted threat across the flooded river.[8] Those over the Mzinyathi were relatively more aggressive, and did not heed the king's order not to raid. After all, this was the region where Chelmsford had met his defeat, and was an area of chronic frontier disorder. Even so, no major incursions were attempted. Only small raiding parties troubled the plain between the river and the Helpmekaar heights. The British responded with limited counter-raids, and the district continued to witness low-grade military activity until March, when the local warriors began to respond to Cetshwayo's call for his army to reassemble.[9]

The presence of Wood at Khambula was another matter. Until the regular *amabutho* were prepared to come together, the king had to make do with what operational forces he still had in the field to contain him. Accordingly, he ordered the Qulusi to watch him and to attack if the possibility arose.[10] The Qulusi, however, found themselves no match for Wood, who was determined to maintain the initiative. His first strike, in a raid that exemplified the value of rapidly moving mounted troops, was against the ebaQulusini *ikhanda* itself, for he felt that to destroy it would establish his dominance in north-western Zululand.[11]

Buller set off on the morning of 1 February with about 140 Frontier Light Horse and Dutch Burghers for ebaQulusini, some fifty kilometres east of Khambula. The Boers regarded it as impregnable, for it was situated in a basin surrounded by precipitous hills. But Buller's men took the place by surprise, scattering the 100 or so inhabitants and killing 6 of them. They then burned the *ikhanda*, which consisted of 250 huts in a great circle 300 metres wide, before retiring with 270 cattle.[12] As an indication of drooping Qulusi morale, it was significant that parties of between 100 and 300 were seen hovering in the area, but made no attempt to obstruct Buller. For the Qulusi had decided after their series of reverses to abandon the open country, and to take up a strictly defensive position on their mountain fastnesses, such as Hlobane.[13]

Wood had also planned to attack Hlobane, but after the destruction of the Qulusis' rallying-point at ebaQulusini and the damaging blow to their military prestige, he no longer considered it necessary. He contented himself with neutralising the Hlobane stronghold, and on 10 February Buller carried off another 490 head of cattle from its environs.[14] Hlobane, though, persisted as a potential threat. It continued to harbour large numbers of Zulu and their herds, even if by the end of March the grazing was giving out. Cetshwayo, meanwhile, seeing the plight of the Qulusi huddled on the mountains out of reach of Wood's patrols, ordered their women to retire with the cattle out of range, and many fell back east to the Nongoma region.[15]

To Wood's rear, by contrast, the majority of Sekethwayo's hungry adherents were returning home from the mountain tops. The war had swept over them, and they were content to submit so long as they were left in peace.[16] But for the Qulusi it was not so easy. Since they had been involved in actual fighting, they feared that if they gave themselves up they would be killed. Yet they were utterly disheartened by their defeats and wearied by Wood's unremitting raiding. It was becoming imperative that Wood's activities should be curtailed, but as the

Qulusi themselves had no answer to Wood's raids, and were in no position to attack his fortified camp at Khambula, they had no option but to petition the king to send them strong reinforcements of regular *amabutho* for the task.[17]

The situation was less one-sided in the Phongolo region. Although Manyonyoba had seemed increasingly prepared after his January setbacks to open negotiations with the British, he was overborne by his chief *induna*, who wished to intensify the raiding.[18] On the night of 10-11 February, Manyonyoba led as strong a force as he could muster to join a war party, commanded by Mbilini and the Qulusi *induna* Tola kaDilikana, which had advanced from Hlobane. The target of this combined force of about 1 500 was the Christianised blacks *(amakholwa)* and farmworkers of the Ntombe valley. In the course of their audacious raid in the early hours of 11 February, they killed forty-one of the *amakholwa* and farmworkers, burned their houses in the valley, and drove off hundreds of cattle and thousands of sheep and goats to Manyonyoba's caves. Significantly, certain Wakkerstroom Boers who owned farms in the region had entered into a pact with the Zulu, for in return for their co-operation as guides the raiders spared their property.

The British retaliated on 15 February when Buller led a force of 54 mounted men and 517 black auxiliaries from Khambula and Luneburg against Manyonyoba's caves. Buller succeeded in burning five *imizi*, killing thirty-four Zulu (including two of Manyonyoba's sons) and driving off 375 cattle, 254 goats and 8 sheep for the loss of only two black auxiliaries. But though he had evened the score somewhat, he had failed to dislodge Manyonyoba. The raid launched on the same day by Colonel Rowlands was an equally unsatisfactory success.

The constant raiding from Khambula had caused many of the Zulu between Luneburg and Derby to abandon the open country for the relative security of the Ngongama Mountains and the broken terrain at the confluence of the Phongolo and Bivane rivers. One such stronghold was Talaku Mountain, some thirty-two kilometres north-east of Luneburg in the Swazi zone, where some of the Qulusi had taken refuge with their cattle. Rowlands, despite inflicting casualties in a running skirmish and capturing livestock and non-combatants, had nevertheless to leave the Qulusi in possession of the mountain. The story was repeated on 20 February when a patrol from Luneburg attacked Makateeskop sixteen kilometres to the south-east, where Zulu cattle were being driven for safety, and again on 25 February when Rowlands failed in another attempt to dislodge Manyonyoba.

The British were coming to accept that they could achieve no decisive result in the Phongolo region. The most significant indication of their lack of success was the fact that the Zulu continued to command the road between Derby and Luneburg. And as Mbilini was to demonstrate, not even large parties of British were secure from attack.

Supplies for the Luneburg garrison were forwarded from Derby, and on 7 March a company of the 80th Regiment, under Captain D. Moriarty, moved out of Luneburg to meet a convoy of 18 wagons carrying ammunition and supplies, and to escort it in. By 9 March the convoy and escort had reached the north bank of the Ntombe, but the rain-swollen river prevented all but two wagons crossing the drift. While waiting for the river to subside, Moriarty and seventy-one men pitched camp on the north bank and formed a V-shaped laager. A detachment of thirty-five men under Lieutenant H.H. Harward encamped on the south bank.[19] Moriarty's defensive arrangements were inadequate, as gaps were left between the wagons, and the flanks of the laager were not secured on the river.

The soft target Moriarty presented was evidently a sore temptation to Manyonyoba, who called on Mbilini to help him attack it. His appeal came at the right moment, for Mbilini was in any case preparing a fresh offensive, and had been collecting men from all parts of the surrounding countryside.

On the evening of 11 March Mbilini himself is said to have come into the unsuspecting laager and, calmly eating mealies, to have spied out the British dispositions. Before dawn on 12 March, under cover of a thick river mist, Mbilini and a force of at least 800 (though estimations go as high as 9 000) advanced the five kilometres from his fastness, a huge, flat-topped mountain north-east of the sleeping camp. His men approached unchallenged to within sixty-five metres of the laager, when they fired a volley and rushed upon the panicking British with their spears. A detachment crossed the Ntombe to attack Harward's men and to cut off the British retreat from the north bank. Colour-Sergeant Booth managed to rally a few of the fugitives and to conduct a fighting retreat, which caused the Zulu to give up the pursuit after about five kilometres. In the camp they had overrun, the Zulu – as at Isandlwana – ritually disembowelled the dead, killed the dogs, broke open and looted the boxes of ammunition, scattered about mealies and flour, shredded the tents and drove off 250 cattle.

Major L. Tucker, who was in command of the Luneburg garrison, was soon alerted to the attack and marched on the Ntombe with 150 men. However, without mounted troops he was unable to prevent Mbilini's force from loping back in a dense mass to the looming, flat-topped mountain. They were able to carry off most of their wounded, and the British later found only thirty Zulu bodies on the banks of the river. The British themselves had lost one officer and sixty men, a civil surgeon, two white wagon conductors and fifteen black drivers on the banks of that remote little river. Ntombe is an engagement that can be easily overlooked. Yet only the battles of Isandlwana and Hlobane (which was still to come) cost more British lives.

Mbilini returned to his homestead on Hlobane with his captured rifles and ammunition, doubtless well satisfied with his resounding success. In Luneburg the stunned garrison stood in expectation of imminent attack, but despite rumours that Mbilini intended to fall on them in preference to Wood's invulnerable camp at Khambula, the Zulu remained inactive. Meanwhile, on 25 March, in retaliation and to keep spirits up, a mounted patrol from Khambula once more ravaged the *imizi* and mealie fields in the Ntombe valley belonging to Manyonyoba's adherents, and this time encountered no resistance.

The general success of the British No. 4 and No. 5 Columns (leaving aside the Ntombe disaster) in dominating their theatre of operations in north-western Zululand was the consequence of the number of experienced mounted men at

Wood's disposal, and his ability to strike rapidly at great distances from base. This made him a greater immediate danger than the immobile Pearson at Eshowe. This consideration was to persuade the king and his council to send their army, once it had eventually reassembled and they had taken the decision to resume the offensive, against him rather than the Natal border or the Eshowe garrison. In the interim, while the Swazi could be ignored and the Natal border was looking after itself, Pearson remained a thorn in the Zulu side (albeit less sharp than Wood), and the forces still available locally were ordered to do their best to neutralise him.

Indeed, Cetshwayo was exceedingly indignant that Pearson had settled himself down in the middle of Zululand, as if he had already conquered it,[20] but it was more than he could do to turn him out. Rorke's Drift had proved the suicidal folly of storming fortified positions, and Cetshwayo forbade his army to attempt it with Eshowe. The strategy to be pursued was one of blockade. The Zulu investing the fort were charged with cutting the garrison off from all supplies and communication with Natal. The intention was to force the starving garrison into evacuating the fort, and then to attack it in the open.[21] This operation was assigned to men of all the *amabutho* living in the coast country, augmented by local irregulars. About 500 of them, in parties of between 40 and 50, were constantly employed in keeping watch on Fort Eshowe. The remainder, perhaps as many as 5 000, were distributed in small groups at different local *imizi* and *amakhanda*. They were to form an army to prevent Pearson's relief, or to attack him if he made a sortie.[22] Dabulamanzi and Mavumengwana, who lived close by each other in the vicinity of eNtumeni, seem to have been in command.

Because the British in the fort had little information regarding Zulu movements, and were fully employed on the entrenchments, standing guard or foraging in the nearest mealie and pumpkin gardens (much to the sorrow of the women who had raised the crops), they remained almost entirely on the defensive.[23] For their part, the Zulu generally kept a prudent distance, though they watched the fort day and night and subjected it to long-range fire. Scouts would creep up undetected to within a few metres of the earthworks or the unsuspecting outlying vedettes.

These vedettes, unpractised in commando-type operations, were easy prey for the practised Zulu; on a number of occasions they were surprised and suffered casualties. Nevertheless, the garrison's chief anxiety was finding adequate pasturage for their remaining several hundred head of oxen, which would be required to draw the wagons should the column retire or be relieved. The grass close to the fort was soon eaten down, or was deliberately burned by the Zulu, so the British were forced to graze their cattle under strong escort many kilometres from the fort. What surprised them was that, besides a faint-hearted attack on 22 February, the Zulu made no attempt to capture the livestock. This failure was as much a relief and a puzzlement to the British as the relative lack of Zulu activity at night.[24] They never quite understood that the Zulu were merely keeping watch until the British moved out into the open; that the boastful exchanges between the black cattle-guards and the investing Zulu were simple banter, and that the

257

Zulu had absolutely no intention of storming the fort or suffering unnecessary casualties.[25]

To break the dreadful monotony of their situation, and to strike a blow at the base of the parties of Zulu harassing the cattle-guard, Pearson decided to attack eSiqwakeni, the *ikhanda* near eNtumeni of which Dabulamanzi was *induna*. He marched out at 2 a.m. on 1 March with 450 men and a 7-pounder gun.[26] Despite all precautions, the Zulu detected their approach and streamed out of eSiqwakeni to safety before the British arrived at dawn. The disappointed British shelled the fugitives and burned the *ikhanda*, which consisted of fifty huts. Dabulamanzi's own *umuzi* was close by, but Pearson feared he would suffer too many casualties attempting to burn it. He therefore withdrew, destroying three small *imizi* on the way home.

Dabulamanzi, who was recognised mounted on a black horse, directed some 500 Zulu in close pursuit of the withdrawing British, and harassed the column all the way back to Eshowe. The British could not help admiring the expert way in which the Zulu on their flanks skirmished. If their shooting had not been so bad, they would have inflicted considerable casualties. As it was, Dabulamanzi was not completely wrong in his opinion that they had administered a decided reverse to the British expedition.[27]

By early March the garrison was in growing expectation of being reinforced or relieved, and on 7 March set about improving and shortening the road to Nyezane by which their rescuers would come. The Zulu collected every day from the neighbouring *imizi* to fire ineffectually on the work parties from afar. Then, on 11 and 12 March, strong parties of Zulu, many thousands strong, were seen moving towards the Thukela, obviously with the intention of opposing the reinforcements the garrison was expecting daily. However, on 13 March the garrison learned that relief was postponed until 1 April, and so good was Zulu intelligence that on 15 March the Zulu were observed marching back from the direction of the Nyezane to resume position about the fort.[28]

In the first week of March the sole Zulu force assembled had been the one watching Eshowe. There was continuing unwillingness to obey the king's orders to muster, and most men remained at their homes.[29] However, with Chelmsford's palpable preparations in northern Natal for a major military strike, and Wood's train of successes in the north-west, the attitude of the warriors inevitably changed. By the second week of March they were willingly complying with the urgent order going out for the whole army to assemble at oNdini by the new moon on 22 March to be ritually prepared for war.[30] At the muster, the king reviewed his *amabutho* to ascertain their casualties, and consulted with the notables of the kingdom on the best means of prosecuting the war. Dabulamanzi and Mavumengwana, who had been directing the blockade of Eshowe, were among those gathered at the king's side.[31]

Cetshwayo, however, had summoned his *izikhulu* and all the *abantwana* to discuss pressing matters besides purely military ones. Hamu had finally defected to the British in early March, and it was necessary to be assured of the loyalty of the rest of the Zulu leadership. Indeed, Hamu's defection had been a real blow to morale. It was a matter only to be mentioned in whispers, for it was perceived among the Zulu as portending the break-up of the kingdom.[32]

When all Zulu defections up to the end of January are taken into account, they must be seen to be of limited significance. Dunn's flight had been the most serious, though Sekethwayo's, had it not been foiled at the last moment, would have been nearly its equal. As it was, those who had surrendered (Dunn excepted) were merely *izinduna* with limited followings, and only non-combatants had given themselves up with them. Nevertheless, the British continued to pin much hope on Hamu's promised defection.

Yet Hamu was not a free agent. At the outbreak of war he was at oNdini, held there by the king as a hostage for his adherents' co-operation in the struggle. Even so, he contrived to pursue his negotiations with the British. Through his chief *izinduna*, Ngwegwana and Nymubana, who were still in his district, he exchanged secret messages with Wood, plaintively reaffirming his loyalty to the British and asking for advice on how to escape from oNdini. Simultaneously, he continued to treat with the Swazi king regarding sanctuary should he flee Zululand.

Throughout early February Cetshwayo and Hamu were reported to be regularly quarreling over responsibility for the war. Then at last, reportedly at Mnyamana's urging, Hamu managed to slip away from oNdini. Cetshwayo sent after him with a gift of cattle in a vain attempt to appease him, then, on hearing that he was making for the British lines, despatched an *impi* in pursuit. On 17 February two messengers from Hamu arrived at Khambula, urgently desiring Wood's aid in bringing him and his wives to safety. The *impi* (made up of Mandlakazi and ukuBaza) had captured some of his cattle and wagons and was also apparently committing atrocities against his Ngenetsheni. It seems Mbilini also made an attempt to intercept Hamu, but was too late.

Eventually, the harried Hamu took refuge across the Phongolo in Swaziland, whence he was escorted by a British patrol to Khambula, arriving there on 10 March 'in a most awful state of funk'.[33] Over the next few days his adherents continued to trickle into camp, until they finally numbered about 1 300. The fighting men were drafted into an existing unit known as Wood's Irregulars, while the non-combatants, including Hamu and his many wives, were located near Utrecht. Some of his adherents, trying to join him there, were massacred by the king's *impi*. As late as May Ngwegwana, his chief *induna*, reported that forces placed by the king at the drifts across the Phongolo had prevented repeated attempts by some of Hamu's leading *izinduna* and other adherents to escape. Furthermore, to punish these would-be defectors, the king sent men during March and April to help themselves to their mealies and grain-stores, while Mnyamana seized the greater part of Hamu's cattle south of the Phongolo on behalf of the king (though he retained them for his own use). Between them, they succeeded in stripping the district bare,[34] so contributing to bitter animosities that were (as we shall see) to manifest themselves in civil war in the 1880s.

North-western Zululand, where Wood's raiding continued so effectively to demoralise the inhabitants, and which had witnessed Hamu's defection, seemed the region most likely to be detached from its loyalty to Cetshwayo. Sekethwayo's allegiance had only been secured by threat of force, and to the king's concern the Mdlalose chief was steadfastly refusing to attend him at oNdini.[35] Significantly, Msebe, a second cousin of Cetshwayo's and a senior *induna* of the Qulusi, disheartened by his people's plight, began to consider defection.[36] On 22 February, while Hamu was attempting to make his escape, he let the prince know that he too wished to join the British but, being a cautious man and fearing retaliation by those Qulusi who remained loyal, wanted to wait until Hamu had successfully led the way.[37]

However, Mahubulwana, another senior *induna* of the Qulusi, foiled Msebe's plans. Mahubulwana informed the king that Msebe, as well as Mcwayo, also a Qulusi *induna*, were in contact with Hamu and in league with the British. Furious, Cetshwayo ordered their deaths, but spared them on the intercession of Mhlahlo kaKhondlo, a Qulusi *induna*, and instead placed them under surveillance.[38] However, the consequences of their intended treason were grave for their adherents. The hostility of loyalist Qulusi forced them to quit their *imizi*, and to take refuge in caves until their eventual surrender to the British in August.

With such developments in mind, Major H. Spalding of Chelmsford's Head-Quarters Staff optimistically pronounced in early March that Zululand appeared 'to be breaking into fragments'.[39] However, he was reading too much into the implications of the defections and incipient civil war of north-western Zululand. Mnyamana's loyalty might be reported suspect, but there was clearly never any likelihood of his following Hamu's example,[40] and his adherents had been active in attempting to foil the latter's flight. Nor was it probable that Zibhebhu would defect at that stage, despite suggestions by Hamu's adherents that he was contemplating such action.[41] Even so, defections (especially Hamu's) and incipient disloyalty were undoubtedly causing consternation among the Zulu leadership gathered at oNdini, and demanded their urgent attention.[42]

It would be wrong to suppose that the king and his councillors were set on sanctioning a major new offensive, even though the army was being mustered in response to Chelmsford's accelerating military preparations. After all, it had been Cetshwayo's initial intention to force negotiations on the British from a position of strength, and to do so before they were sufficiently prepared to renew their invasion. However, the apparently desirable diplomatic alternative was exploited with neither haste nor great vigour, possibly because it never really seemed feasible. Only on 1 March did two of the king's messengers cross the Thukela and deliver the king's message to his old friend, Bishop Hans Schreuder, then living at kwaNtunjambili, his mission station near Kranskop. In substance, the king begged the British to withdraw their forces from Zululand and to resume talks on a peaceful settlement.[43]

In making this new overture, Cetshwayo probably did not comprehend that, at bottom, the British were not prepared to negotiate.[44] On 17 January Chelmsford had laid down that any further Zulu emissaries must communicate with him only, and that no overtures would be considered which were not 'preceded by...the unconditional acceptance' of all the demands set out in the ultimatum.[45] The British response to the king's latest feeler was consequentially harsh. Chelmsford straightforwardly dismissed Cetshwayo's protestations, and Frere was unprepared to accept anything less than his unconditional surrender and the general disarmament of the Zulu people. Nor was the High Commissioner ready to consider any message that did not come in a form to 'bind' the king.[46] With Machiavellian spirit, though, the British were eager to seize any advantage created by the Zulu willingness to treat. So they coolly proceeded to spin out the spurious negotiations in order to gain time to complete their plans for a renewed offensive.

Cetshwayo's messengers had returned from kwaNtunjambili with 'long faces' to report,[47] but the king and his assembled advisers decided to persevere in their negotiations. On 22 March (the date coincidentally set for the army to reassemble at oNdini) two emissaries delivered the king's latest message to Schreuder and Fannin at Middle Drift. They were frigidly received and sent back with a bald reminder of the terms of the ultimatum. British officials were not unaware of the great warlike muster at oNdini, and can be forgiven for supposing that the king's messengers were nothing other than spies. In like fashion, when on 23 March two other messengers from the king approached Fort Eshowe, they were clapped into irons as spies instead of being accorded the traditional sanctity they expected to enjoy as royal emissaries.[48]

Apparently undeterred by these rebuffs, and at the very moment when they were actually reaching the momentous decision to renew the offensive, the king and his council chose to despatch fresh messengers to the middle Thukela border. Perhaps, after the consistently uncompromising British responses to his earlier feelers, the king was mechanically pursuing his diplomatic initiative without any real hope in the outcome. But, whatever his purpose, the simultaneous but decidedly incongruous despatch of fresh emissaries on the one hand, and his armies on the other, inevitably reinforced the existing British conviction that all Zulu messengers were nothing other than spies.

Consequently, when on 28 March (the very day the battle of Hlobane was fought) three messengers appeared at Middle Drift, they were instantly sent under strict guard to Fort Cherry. One of these messengers was Johannes, a Christian convert from Schreuder's Entumeni mission. The other two, Mfunzi and Nkisimana, were elderly and respected messengers of the king, who over the preceding six years had been sent on many important missions to the Natal government. Although ignominiously treated as spies, and detained in Fort Buckingham pending the successful relief of Eshowe, their message was dignified: Cetshwayo saw no reason for the war against him and asked the Natal government to appoint a place at which a peace conference could be held.[49] But the renewal of out-and-out hostilities had already ruled out such a possibility.

Aside from once wishing to exploit British disarray after Isandlwana to reopen peace negotiations, Cetshwayo had naturally hoped that his victory would impress neighbouring black chiefdoms. The British distinctly feared that Isandlwana had provided the signal for an uprising of all the black chiefdoms around, and would spark off a rebellion among the discontented Transvaal Boers.[50] But, if he had entertained any hopes in this regard, Cetshwayo was disappointed. Nothing at all came of reported contacts with Griqualand West and Kuruman, the Pondo, Sotho, Pedi and even the Ndebele of Lobengula.[51] Even British precautions against communication between Cetshwayo and the Natal border population proved unnecessary, for there was never any chance of his being able to incite them to rebellion. By the time the king had assembled his council in March, it was clear that, as in January, the Zulu would have to undertake any further fighting against the British quite alone.

The major consequence of the great assembly of March was the decision to resume the war with the utmost vigour. In response to the pleas of the hard-pressed Qulusi, the main Zulu army mustered at oNdini was to be sent against Wood at Khambula,[52] while the warriors already in the vicinity of Eshowe were to be reinforced against Chelmsford's relieving column. As the king and his councillors had been compelled to accept, there was indeed no alternative to renewing the struggle, other than capitulation. And the Zulu nation, in its willingness to fight on alone to maintain its independence, was demonstrating (despite defections and other tensions) its essential cohesiveness and continuing loyalty to its king.

22

Breaking the Neck of the Zulu Power

Commandant Schermbrucker, who fought at the battle of Khambula on 29 March, recognised it as the British victory 'which really broke the neck of the Zulu power'[1]. During that long afternoon of desperate fighting at the place the Zulu knew as inqaba kaHawana (or Hawana's stronghold) the morale of their army was irreparably affected. Terrible word of its defeat and heavy casualties 'shook the country',[2] and King Cetshwayo understood at once that the war could no longer be won. Without doubt, Khambula sealed the fate of the Zulu kingdom.[3]

After the Isandlwana disaster Lord Chelmsford exercised extreme caution. The Ntombe debacle of 12 March only reinforced his determination never again to be caught unprepared by the Zulu. He therefore resisted marching to the relief of Eshowe until he had built up sufficient reinforcements and transport to allow him to do so with confidence.[4] Since he supposed the bulk of the Zulu army to be concentrated near kwaGingindlovu to oppose him, he considered it desirable to create some diversions to draw off elements of the presumed force facing him and to secure his flanks.

As a proponent of 'active defence', with its philosophy that it was necessary to maintain the strategic initiative in order to place the enemy at a disadvantage, he decided to put the forces guarding the Natal bank of the Thukela to positive use, and ordered them to mount a number of raids and demonstrations.[5] Major A.C. Twentyman, the commander of the Greytown garrison, began his demonstration on 24 March, and raided across the middle Thukela on 2 and 3 April, burning a few *imizi*. Just how much of a diversion they created in favour of Chelmsford's advance is debatable. The Zulu moved themselves and their cattle out of range, but were sufficiently provoked to threaten retaliatory raids once the opportunity offered. As prophesied by Sir Henry Bulwer, who had always feared the consequences of militarily activating that stretch of border, a cycle of raid and counter-raid had been created.

Downstream, Captain G.A. Lucas demonstrated at the drifts from 27 March, but could attempt no serious crossing because the river was too high. His show of force consequently did no more than frighten the Zulu along the opposite bank into temporarily abandoning their *imizi* and fleeing with their livestock into the hills. Whether this succeeded in distracting or confusing the Zulu to the front of the Eshowe Relief Column is open to doubt. At Rorke's Drift Major W. Black led

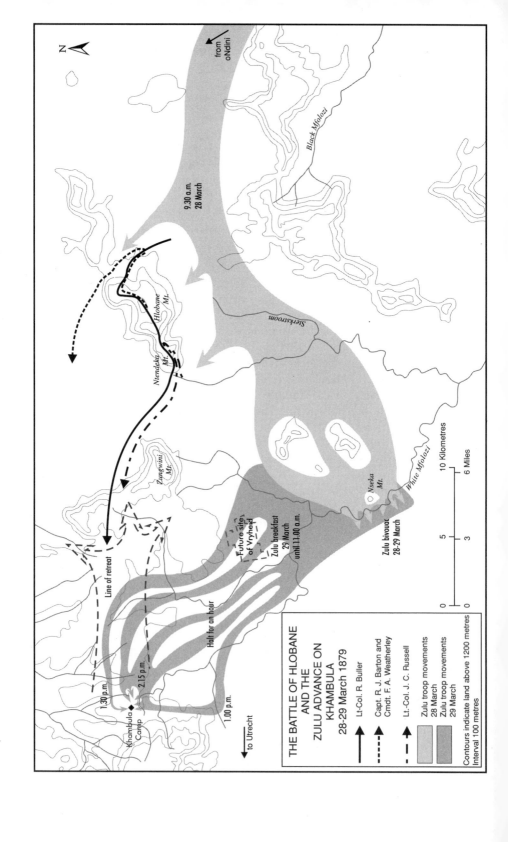

N

from oNdini

Black Mfolozi

9.30 a.m.
28 March

Hlobane Mt.

Ntendeka Mt.

Siertstroom

Zungwini Mt.

Line of retreat

Nseka Mt.

White Mfolozi

Future site
of Vryheid

Zulu breakfast
29 March
until 11.00 a.m.

Zulu bivouac
28–29 March

Halt for an hour

1.00 p.m.

1.30 p.m.

2.15 p.m.

Khambula
Camp

to Utrecht

THE BATTLE OF HLOBANE
AND THE
ZULU ADVANCE ON
KHAMBULA
28–29 March 1879

Lt-Col. R. Buller

Capt. R. J. Barton and
Cmdt. F. A. Weatherley

Lt.-Col. J. C. Russell

Zulu troop movements
28 March

Zulu troop movements
29 March

Contours indicate land above 1200 metres
Interval 100 metres

0   5   10 Kilometres

0   3   6 Miles

an extended patrol sixteen kilometres into Zululand without encountering any Zulu, and obviously without creating any sort of diversion worth the name.

Meanwhile, Wood (whom Chelmsford had given *carte blanche* to take any action he considered suitable to divert the Zulu from his advance)[6] decided to raid Hlobane, the Qulusi stronghold and cattle depot. His purpose was to tie down the local irregulars and prevent them from reinforcing the army Cetshwayo was expected to despatch against Chelmsford. In going ahead with this plan he discounted what was to prove the accurate intelligence that the Zulu intended to move with their fullest strength against Khambula, and to place only secondary forces to face Chelmsford.[7]

By the third week of March the full army had mustered at oNdini, except for the members of *amabutho* investing Eshowe, and was being ritually prepared for war.[8] As commander of this formidable force, the bulk of which was made up of the veterans of Isandlwana, the king appointed Chief Mnyamana, his chief *induna* and the most important man in the kingdom after himself. Mnyamana's command probably numbered at least 17 000 men, made up of the major elements of all the crack *amabutho*. On the march they were to be reinforced by local units, especially the Qulusi *ibutho* and irregulars, who would bring the strength of the combined force up to 20 000 or more. Certainly, this army was as least as large as the one sent against Isandlwana.[9]

Khambula, more than any other battle of the war, was Cetshwayo's own. He gave the most minute instructions to his commanders on how to attack, what ground to occupy, and what dispositions to make. After planning the battle so carefully, he never dreamed that its outcome could be a defeat.[10]

The Zulu had the 'inflating conviction' after Isandlwana that any numerically overwhelming force of theirs must crush the British in the open field.[11] On the other hand, it was equally clear after Rorke's Drift that it would be the utmost folly to attack the British if entrenched. Cetshwayo's strategy accordingly called for his army to draw Wood into the open by harassing his livestock or, if that failed, by threatening white farms and Utrecht to his rear and cutting his line of supply[12]. His final words to his *amabutho* were that they were not to go into the hole of a wild beast lest they got clawed, but must wait until it emerged before falling on it.[13] Yet there seems to have been a fatal gap between the Zulu leadership's intentions and the expectations of the ordinary warriors. The latter presumed a repetition of the circumstances at Isandlwana, and were to be dismayed when they discovered that Wood's position was fortified and could not just be overrun.[14]

The Zulu army set off from oNdini on 24 March. It advanced north-west, covering the ground somewhat faster than in the Isandlwana campaign. As was normal, it lived off the land after the first day or so. Since it was later in the season than at the time of Isandlwana, the supply of food was more plentiful, and the warriors were probably better fed and in stronger condition than on the earlier campaign.[15]

On the afternoon of 27 March Wood's Irregulars, scouting beyond Hlobane, saw smoke and fires to the east, which they correctly assumed to be the campfires of a Zulu army. They refrained from mentioning them to the white mount-

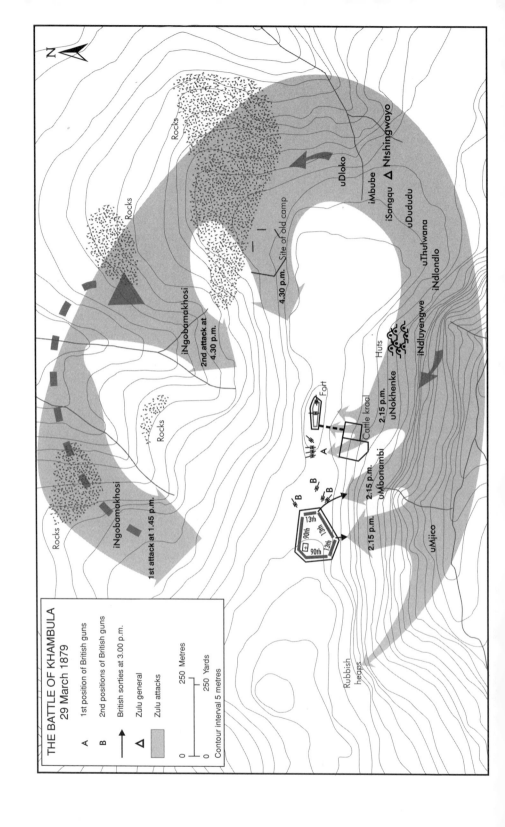

THE BATTLE OF KHAMBULA
29 March 1879

A 1st position of British guns

B 2nd positions of British guns

→ British sorties at 3.00 p.m.

△ Zulu general

Zulu attacks

0   250 Metres

0   250 Yards

Contour interval 5 metres

N

Rocks

Rocks

Rocks

Rocks

Rocks

iNgobamakhosi
2nd attack at
4.30 p.m.

iNgobamakhosi
1st attack at 1.45 p.m.

Site of old camp

4.30 p.m.

uDloko

iMbube

iSangqu △ Ntshingwayo

uDududu

uThulwana

iNdlondlo

iNdluyengwe

Huts

uNokhenke
2.15 p.m.

Fort

Cattle kraal

A

B

B

B

13th
13th
1/13th
90th
90th

uMbonambi
2.15 p.m.

2.15 p.m.

uMijico

Rubbish
heaps

ed troops with them, to whom the campfires would have been equally visible, because they had long since learned that their words were never heeded.[16] Unaware, consequently, of the near presence of the Zulu army, Wood proceeded with his plans to raid Hlobane. Reports that nearly 2 000 cattle had been seen grazing under the mountain spurred him on.[17] At 3.30 on the misty morning of 28 March, Buller and 675 men started to scale the eastern slopes of Hlobane. At the same time the 640 men of Lieutenant-Colonel John Russell's force moved from the west onto the adjoining Ntendeka Mountain. Wood, who exercised overall command, intended that Russell's column would create a diversion in Buller's favour, and draw the defenders away from the eastern side of Hlobane where they were concentrated.[18]

The steep slopes of Hlobane culminate in a belt of sheer cliffs, at the foot of which is a jumble of huge slabs of rock, the gaps and crevices between them forming a kind of cave system. This terrain provided the perfect opportunity for the Qulusi and Mbilini's men – between 500 and 3 000 of them, according to various estimations – to ambush the British struggling up the difficult path. Despite the Zulus' cleverly laid trap, Buller led his men in skirmishing order through a heavy cross-fire with only five killed and gained the summit.[19] Although dismayed at the extent of the enormous grassy plateau stretching before him, Buller extended his force and advanced west across the mountain top. Brushing aside the sniping Zulu, his men rounded up all the 2 000 or so cattle which they found on the southern side of the plateau. Buller's men only halted when they reached the precipitous Devil's Pass at the western extremity of Hlobane. From there they exchanged a hot fire with the Zulu who had built their huts under the krantzes on the north-western side of the mountain.[20]

The British were complacent about their progress. But the Zulu on Hlobane, who knew a great army was approaching from oNdini – indeed, they had been expecting it since dawn and were dismayed that it had not arrived earlier as arranged[21] – were cunningly drawing Buller into a trap. When at about 9 a.m. Buller began to call in his scattered detachments preparatory to descending with his booty, Zulu resistance began steadily to stiffen. Their task was to prevent the British from withdrawing until the Zulu army had appeared in support. To delay them, increasing numbers of Zulu mustered on the higher ground of the northern side of the plateau, and harassed the British as they began to fall back across the summit.

It was then, at between 10 a.m. and 11 a.m., that Buller was stunned by an awesome sight. The enormous Zulu army was sweeping down on Hlobane from the south-east like the shadow of a dense cloud across the grassy plain, its horns thrown out either side of the chest in traditional order of battle.[22] The British would naturally never have gone up Hlobane if they had suspected the main Zulu army to have been so close. Now, their first priority was to get down the mountain again as quickly as possible, not only to save themselves, but for fear that the Zulu army might move directly on Khambula and its depleted garrison in a horrifying repetition of the Isandlwana scenario.

The Zulu commanders had planned initially to advance on Khambula past the southern flank of Hlobane. But, apprised of the situation on its summit by the clear voices of the defenders which carried to their scouts below, they changed direction in support of them.[23] In the event, the army did not have to move up the mountain. Panic overcame Buller's men as the Zulu on the summit determinedly pinched off their flight eastwards and harried many of them in disorderly retreat down the almost sheer Devil's Pass to the west. It was enough to detach a single *ibutho* (either the uMcijo or the iNgobamakhosi)[24] to cut off and engulf those of Buller's horsemen who regained the plain down the eastern side of Hlobane.

Russell's force on Ntendeka withdrew as rapidly as it could, in its craven haste giving little support either to Buller's surviving horsemen, who were making their way down Ntendeka to Khambula, or to the black auxiliaries who were doing their best to bring in the captured cattle. These auxiliaries succeeded in saving about 300 head from recapture, but were most indignant at the way in which the white troops had abandoned them.[25]

The British fell back in disarray on Khambula, leaving fifteen officers and seventy-nine men dead behind them, as well as over a hundred of their black levies.[26] The Zulu took no prisoners, and killed even the officers despite Cetshwayo's orders to bring a few back to oNdini for interrogation. The heavy British casualties can be attributed to a significant factor besides those such as the difficult terrain, panic and Zulu ruthlessness. On this occasion the Zulu displayed far more rapid and accurate marksmanship than in the past. The British were partially right in attributing this to a greater number of modern rifles, many the spoils of Isandlwana and Ntombe.[27] But just as important were the skills of the Zulu irregulars of north-western Zululand. Mbilini's preferred style of fighting was more akin to the Swazis' than the Zulus', and Hlobane was just the sort of running skirmish with which he was most at home.

Hlobane was undoubtedly 'a bad day' for Buller and Wood.[28] Had it not been for the great British victory at Khambula the following day, which drew a veil over the 'really bad business' on Hlobane, both their reputations would have been seriously damaged. Russell's, unredeemed by the considerable personal gallantry displayed by both Wood and Buller, was completely demolished.[29] The only positive aspect for the British in the whole humiliating affair was that by diverting the main Zulu army, it may have delayed its assault on Khambula for a day, thus giving the garrison time to concentrate and prepare. For rather than continuing much further on its march, the Zulu army decided to encamp for the night on the banks of the White Mfolozi, near Nseka Mountain (Tinta's Kop).[30]

Despite their debacle on Hlobane, the British remained confident. The Zulu army's halt gave them time to fall back and consolidate for the coming onslaught. Their position was indeed a strong one, for Khambula camp was manned by a force armed with breech-loading rifles, supported by artillery, and with an almost unlimited supply of ammunition. Wood had under his command 2 086 officers and men. The infantry consisted of eight companies of the 90th Light Infantry (711 men), and seven companies of the 1/13th Light Infantry (527 men). The mounted force, under the command of Buller, was made up of a squadron of Mounted Infantry (99 men), four troops of the Frontier Light Horse (165 men), two troops of Raaff's Transvaal Rangers (135 men), and troopers of Baker's Horse (99 men), the Kaffrarian Rifles (40 men), the Border Horse (16 men), the Mounted Basutos (74 men), and a local commando of Dutch Burghers (41 men). Fifty-eight of Wood's Irregulars remained since the rest, together with many of the Boers, had decamped after Hlobane. In addition there were 11 Royal Engineers and the 110 men of No. 11 Battery, 7th Brigade, Royal Artillery, with their six 7-pounder guns.[31]

This garrison had few preparations still to make, for every man had long been allotted his duties and place behind the defences. The key to the position was the elongated earthwork redoubt on a narrow ridge of tableland. In it were placed two of the guns. The redoubt was connected to the main wagon-laager 20 metres below and 280 metres behind it by the four remaining guns. The wheels of the wagons of the laager were chained together, each wagon-pole was lashed to the wagon in front, and sods were thrown up under the wagons to form a rampart. Bags of provisions were placed along the outside buckrails of the wagons with regular interstices for firing through.

Below the redoubt and to its right was a smaller wagon-laager, connected by a palisade, into which the force's 2 000 cattle were crammed. Its right outer edge, and that of the main laager, stood on the edge of a rocky ravine, affording any assailant a considerable amount of cover. To the left of the position the ground sloped gently away, giving a much better field of fire. The main force was stationed in the laager, with small garrisons in the redoubt and the cattle-laager. All points around the camp had been carefully measured and range markers set up to aid the accuracy of the defenders' fire.[32]

Such preparations minimised the ability of the Zulu ever to charge close enough to the British defences to employ their traditional methods of hand-to-hand fighting. And even if sheer courage and weight of numbers were to prevail in the conventional mass assault, it could only be at the cost of fearful casualties. This being so, it was most fortunate for the British that Zulu tactics at Khambula were not substantially affected by the large number of firearms they were carrying.[33] The likely reason was that the Zulu had little reason to put particular store in them. Most were of very inferior quality. Obsolete muzzle-loaders predominated, as they had at Isandlwana and Nyezane, though a fair number of prized breech-loaders, many of them captured from the British in earlier engagements, had been distributed among the *amabutho*.[34] It is possible to speculate what the cumulative effect might have been had the Zulu been content to harass the camp with long-range fire. As it was, firearms were still only allowed to play a subordinate harassing role to the mass charge. So even though the British were to be subjected to a heavy fire at Khambula, it was wild and ill-aimed and had little apparent effect. Indeed, because the Zulu generally aimed too high, their own men on the far side of the laager – rather than the British within – were more often than not the victims.

When the morning of the 29 March dawned, the Zulu commanders knew they had a most difficult day ahead of them. Much would depend on their ability to conform to the strategy laid down by their king. They had to resist pressure from their warriors to fall directly upon the fortified camp, and had to persuade them to manoeuvre in order to draw the British into the open.

Chief Mnyamana had the direction of the campaign as a whole, though it was as a statesman, rather than as a general, that he had made his considerable mark. Ntshingwayo, the victor of Isandlwana and his great personal friend, would lead the army into actual battle. Nevertheless, Mnyamana was his senior, and it was he who formed the *amabutho* into the traditional circle at their bivouac on the White Mfolozi in order to harangue them.[35] Mnyamana's eloquence had an unfortunately unsettling effect. Doubtless only too conscious of the consequences to the kingdom of an adverse outcome to the campaign, he allowed it to become apparent that he was 'unduly apprehensive and fearful of the results'. So, while stirring up the *impi* to 'burn like a fire', he also left it in a state of alarm.[36]

The British received timely warning of the Zulu approach. Information came from Mbamgulana, an *induna* of Hamu's, who had been fighting with Wood's Column since his chief's defection in early March. To save himself at the battle of Hlobane, he had divested himself of his British insignia and had attached himself to his old *ibutho*. He had marched with them as far as the White Mfolozi, where in the early morning he gave his unsuspecting comrades the slip. He fell in with a patrol of Raaff's Transvaal Rangers, who sent him back with his intelligence to the camp. He told Wood that the *impi* was already on the march, and that he thought it would attack the camp at 'dinner time'.[37] Wood, nevertheless, could not be absolutely certain whether the Zulu intended storming the camp rather than outflanking it. Only events would tell, and he settled down anxiously to see what the advancing Zulu army would do.

Meanwhile, Commandant Raaff's reconnaissance brought him to the edge of the Zungwini plateau. When the morning mist lifted at about 10 a.m. he saw the Zulu army cooking its meal on the banks of the White Mfolozi and a tributary stream (where the town of Vryheid now stands), only a few kilometres north of their overnight bivouac near Nseka Mountain. At 11 a.m. Raaff reported that the Zulu army was advancing north-west against the British camp some nineteen kilometres away. Wood immediately called in all outlying units and prepared to meet an attack.[38]

The Zulu army made its approach in five principal columns at considerable intervals.[39] As their line of advance tended to the west, Wood's heart sank, for it seemed the Zulu intended to bypass Khambula and to march on Utrecht, whose citizens had begged him in vain to garrison their town against such an eventuality. But, to his intense relief, when the Zulu army reached the hills some six kilometres south-east of the camp, it halted. There it stayed in its dense masses for over an hour, in full sight of the anxious British garrison, who could only wait for the Zulu council-of-war to decide on its next move. The British realised that the decision had been reached to attack Khambula when the Zulu army began to deploy in their direction, moving slowly and deliberately so as to conserve the warriors' energy for the struggle ahead.[40] 'We are the boys from Isandlwana!' they shouted threateningly once they came within earshot, hoping to put the fear of death into the hearts of the waiting British.[41]

The Zulu centre stayed where it was, while the left horn resumed the march in column in the direction of Utrecht, until at about 1 p.m. it wheeled to the right and began a rapid advance on the camp, halting about five kilometres away. The right horn, which had further to go, meanwhile spread out to the north of the camp, where it halted about 2,5 kilometres away, just out of range of the guns.[42] Unable to resist a prize, a number of warriors were detached to secure about 200 of the camp cattle which had not been rounded up in time and had strayed.

Wood estimated that when fully deployed the Zulu front stretched for over sixteen kilometres,[43] and a nervous young officer confided to his diary that 'the whole country round was black with the enemy & it seemed as if these legions would swamp us completely.'[44] The Zulu warriors, poised to charge, had discarded all their ceremonial and distinctive regalia for the battle, and wore nothing besides their loincovers and necklaces of charms and medicine wood.[45]

Why, it must be asked, had the Zulu commanders decided to launch an attack on the camp, despite the king's sensible and explicit instructions to the contrary? There are indications that the commanders lost control and were overruled by their young men when they came in sight of the camp. The king himself was convinced that their success of the previous day at Hlobane had greatly elated the warriors, and the prospect of the small and apparently vulnerable British position at Khambula persuaded them that they had another easy victory within their grasp.[46] Moreover, they were greatly encouraged when at 12.45 p.m. Wood ordered the tents to be struck and his men to take up their battle-stations. The Zulu took the sudden striking of the tents as a sign that the British were preparing for immediate flight, and abandoned whatever remaining hesitation they had about attacking the camp.[47]

Expecting to be attacked by the Zulu left, which had been the most active in its deployment, the British were surprised when the Zulu right horn suddenly broke from its stationary line into column, and began to advance at a tremendous pace. The most likely reason for this premature movement by the right horn, which was in closer striking distance of the camp than was the left, lay in the intense rivalry between the crack *amabutho* of the two wings. Hamu's adherents explained to the British that there was a dispute over the question of to whom belonged the honour at Isandlwana of being second among the British tents after the uMbonambi: the iNgobamakhosi or the uMcijo. It had thus apparently been agreed that when the army came upon Khambula the other *amabutho* would look on while the iNgobamakhosi of the right horn, and the uMcijo of the left, settled the issue by vying to be first into the camp.[48]

Possibly, though, this was a rationalisation by the Zulu for what actually occurred, and the iNgobamakhosi only moved forward because they erroneously thought that the rest of the army was in position to attack.[49] But whatever the cause, the advance of the Zulu right horn was a godsend for the British. Their standard manoeuvre against loosely disciplined troops was to entice them into a premature and uncoordinated attack through a feint attack or a simulated retreat. So, when Wood saw the forward movement of the Zulu right horn at 1.30 p.m. he immediately sent out Buller and two squadrons of his mounted men to egg it on into a fully committed but unsupported attack on the camp.

Buller's force rode out of the main laager when the Zulu were just over a kilometre away.[50] Clouds of Zulu skirmishers, fed by supports and reserves, preceded the main body of the right horn. Buller led his force to within good rifle range, and ordered it to dismount and open fire. The sight of this puny body of some 100 men was too much for the mettle of the 2 000 or more iNgobamakhosi. They swept forward, their skirmishers falling back to reveal the more solid line of the dense column. Buller's men remounted, fell back, dismounted and fired again in the style perfected by the Boers, repeating the operation with great precision and coolness, drawing on the iNgobamakhosi with complete success. The Zulu did not comprehend the purpose of Buller's manoeuvre. They simply thought the craven redcoats were running away, and tauntingly called out after them: 'Don't run away, Johnnie; we want to speak to you!'[51]

Buller's action rapidly drew the iNgobamakhosi to within range of the artillery, which opened fire at 1.45 p.m.[52] The guns did not do the damage anticipated on account of the small bursting-charge of the shell and because the Zulu were able to take some cover in the dips and hollows of the ground. But when the right horn came to within effective rifle range some 300 metres from the camp, they were checked by the accurate fire of the 90th Light Infantry and the enfilading fire from the redoubt. Finding this withering fire quite insupportable on the open ground, the iNgobamakhosi were eventually forced to fall back to the cover of some rocky outcrops to the north-east of the camp.[53]

The luring on and subsequent repulse of the Zulu right horn, all within the space of three-quarters of an hour, was a brilliant success for the British. It disrupted Zulu strategy, for the intention of the right horn must surely originally have been to complete a flanking movement along the left of the British position. Eventually, it would have joined up with the Zulu left horn, and so completely surrounded the camp. Such at least were classic Zulu battle tactics, where the flanking horns were sent out in advance of the more slowly advancing chest, one horn generally more extended than the other. Buller's sortie deflected the right horn from its purpose, while its repulse and the devastating blow to its morale ensured that it made no further effort to outflank the camp.[54] Instead, it was content to keep up a fire on the British from the rocky ledges to which it had retired. The result was that for the remainder of the engagement the left and rear of the British position remained unsurrounded and unthreatened, freeing the garrison to face the unsupported Zulu onslaught from the opposite quarter.

As the attack from the Zulu right dwindled away, the heavy masses of the left and centre began at about 2.15 p.m. to develop their own belated assault. The chest moved against the south-eastern side of the redoubt, while the left horn, taking advantage of the cover provided by the steep ridge on the south side of the laager, assembled in the dead ground to attack the position from that direction. Mnyamana, as was the custom with high-ranking Zulu officers, did not come under fire, but watched the battle (which was occurring presumably against his better judgement) from a hill about five kilometres away. Ntshingwayo, who directed the actual fighting, took up position at about 2.30 p.m. about 650 metres from the camp, and remained there under cover of a low hill until his men retreated.[55]

The British who witnessed the waves of the Zulu assault could not but admire their striking courage under fire as they closed up their ranks after each loss and came on at a steady trot.[56] This is not to say that the Zulu were foolhardy, and did not make use of whatever cover was offered. But they had to cross the numerous small streams which form the headwaters of the White Mfolozi, and to traverse at least 700 metres of open ground commanded by the defenders' fire. The left horn could make for the ravine on the right flank of the camp and take cover there, though when they charged out of it they faced the concentrated fire from the laager at a distance of less than a hundred metres. The chest and right horn had to take what little cover they could in the open ground. Some took cover behind the large white marker stones placed by the British, and others carried large stones on their heads, which they threw down to shelter behind. The chest was able to utilise the partially obliterated remains of Wood's previous camp, which he had been forced to relocate on sanitary grounds.[57]

Yet there was inevitably a limit to what even the Zulu could stand. At moments heavy and accurate fire paralysed their movements and sowed panic, while the destructive effect of artillery shells to whole groups proved particularly disheartening.[58] The iNgobamakhosi of the right horn was quite demoralised by such fire. As we have seen, it was first pinned down since 'it could not face the bullets',[59] and then fell back to the shelter of the rocky outcrops. The left horn and the chest who came on after them were 'literally mowed down'[60] until they too had to retire.

This is not to denigrate the extraordinarily courageous endeavour of the Zulu army. As Trooper Mossop later wrote, assaulting a prepared position defended by modern artillery and rifles with spears and inadequate firearms amounted to attacking it with bare hands.[61] And the marvel is that there was even a moment when it looked as if the left horn might carry the laager. Yet the nightmare quality of this desperate effort was expressed in the shocked comment of some Zulu after the battle who, doubtless having seen the pets kept by the British garrison, swore that among the defenders were dogs and apes 'clothed and carrying firearms on their shoulders.'[62]

The sustained attack of the Zulu centre and left, although ultimately unsuccessful, was extremely determined. It went through several phases. To the British onlookers, the *amabutho* of the centre and left appeared to be resting and taking food while the right wing was being repulsed. Then, with a great rattle of shields and spears, they swarmed down the slopes opposite the centre and right of the camp in a series of great waves. Keeping as much as they could to the shelter of the bed of the little stream in the dead ground along the right flank of the camp, they finally charged up in successive lines to assault the British position. The main body remained concentrated in the dead ground, evidently waiting to make a decisive rush once the first waves had gained a foothold on the defences.

The uNdi corps, and notably the uNokhenke *ibutho*, succeeded in getting into the cattle kraal, and eventually drove out the garrison of a single company of the 1/13th. From the vantage of captured wagons they opened fire on the main laager. Encouraged by this success, a column of about 1 000 to 1 500 Zulu (evidently the uMbonambi *ibutho*) formed up west of the cattle kraal for an assault on the main laager. Wood saw some thirty i*zinduna* exhorting their men, while their commander waved them on with a red flag.[63]

To meet this crisis, Wood ordered two companies of the 90th under Major Hackett to counter-attack with the bayonet. This force marched out as if on parade, and took the Zulu greatly by surprise. Their unexpected and determined advance down the slope between the two laagers broke up the Zulu concentration and forced the warriors to abandon the advantage they had previously gained. They retired sullenly to the cover of the stream-bed and to sheltered positions to the right and left of Hackett's force. Once sufficiently down the slope, Hackett's men opened fire, supported by case-shot from the artillery. Fire from the redoubt and the guns also swept the cattle laager, making it untenable for the Zulu.[65]

The two companies of the 90th were then in their turn forced to retire on the main laager, for the Zulu caught them in a most telling cross-fire, kept up by marksmen armed with Martini-Henry rifles positioned in the vacated huts of Wood's Irregulars and behind the camp's refuse dump 330 metres away. At much the same time, Wood was obliged temporarily to withdraw a company of the 1/13th posted at the right rear of the main laager because of the Zulu enfilading fire.[66] The fact that this fire inflicted on the British almost all their most serious casualties of the day, shows what the Zulu might have achieved with proper use of their weapons and with tactics other than the frontal assault. In the end, the British cleared the huts of the Zulu posted there with artillery-fire, while they flattened the rubbish-dumps with volleys of rifle-fire. Sixty-two dead Zulu were found behind them the next day.[67]

At almost the same time as Hackett's sortie at about 3 p.m., a company of the 1/13th was also constrained to advance out of the south-west corner of the main laager to drive off a dense mass of the Zulu left horn at the point of the bayonet. This was the uMcijo *ibutho*, whose impetuous rush brought them near enough to grasp the rifles of the defenders. Altogether, it was a most critical moment for the main laager, for a wagon had to be removed for the sortie, and when the company retired, fresh Zulu who had been in support rushed forward to try and seize the gap.[68]

The temporarily successful Zulu attack on the cattle-laager, followed by the two effective British sorties, marked both the limit of Zulu success that day and the turning-point of the battle. The British sensed accurately that the advantage lay henceforth with the defenders. There followed, nevertheless, some two further hours of fierce Zulu attacks at different points of the camp. At one time the Zulu came almost within grasp of the Artillery horses, which were kept outside the redoubt in the open between it and the laager; at another they came right up to the very trenches along the right flank of the redoubt.

At 4.30 p.m. the Zulu switched the focus of their attack away from the south of the British position, and made a second attempt at the north and north-east faces. Simultaneously, the iNgobamakhosi, from the position among the rocks to which they had retired earlier, and elements of the uNdi corps, from the shelter of the remains of Wood's previous camp, charged the British position. But they came again under a heavy crossfire at about 300 metres from the laager and redoubt and, enfiladed by the guns, had to retire as before.[69]

By about 5 p.m. it was obvious to the British that the Zulu attack was at last beginning to slacken. Within half an hour, as the sun began to go behind the ridge to the west of Khambula camp, it became evident that the Zulu were preparing to retire in defeat. Eagerly noting this, Wood at 5.30 p.m. ordered a company of the 1/13th to clear the cattle-kraal, where some Zulu still crept among the oxen they had been unable to remove. Simultaneously, he advanced a company of the 90th on its right to the edge of the krantz in front of the cattle-laager, where it first pushed the Zulu back with the bayonet, and then poured a heavy fire into the *amabutho* in the stream-bed below. Everywhere the Zulu were now falling back, while a great cheer from the defenders rang in their ears.[70]

At first, the Zulu were able to retire in a most orderly and even leisurely style. But they were not long permitted to do so. The garrison poured its fire into the retreating masses, and the guns discharged cannister-shot. Then bugles sounded to horse, and every mounted man in the laager started out in hot pursuit. One of the chief functions of cavalry is to consummate a victory by turning an orderly retreat into a hopeless rout. This the mounted men at Khambula achieved with complete success. Three columns under Buller's command dashed upon the dispirited Zulu.

Before the fugitives, already on the point of exhaustion after the prodigious physical and emotional efforts of the day, were nearly sixteen kilometres of open country. Behind them, mounted on fresh horses and burning to avenge Isandlwana and Hlobane, were the British.[71] As Major D'Arcy of the Frontier Light Horse exhorted his men, 'no quarter, boys, and remember yesterday!' They responded with a will, 'butchering the brutes all over the place'.[72] The carnage was awful and continued for more than two hours until kindly darkness fell. The last of the mounted men returned to camp only after 9 p.m., having followed the Zulu up to the very foot of Zungwini Mountain.[73]

Once their flight began in earnest the Zulu seemed to lose their capacity to resist, and in their own words the British horsemen 'turned them about as if they were cattle'.[74] It seems Mnyamana made some attempt to rally his men and to persuade them to take advantage of the fact that the British were at last in the open, but Zibhebhu, who was present as one of his senior commanders, dissuaded him. The rout, once begun, was irreversible. Exhausted Zulu soon were unable to move faster than a walk, and were too dazed even to fire in their own defence. Utterly 'done up',[75] many simply dropped to the ground and tried to simulate death or to creep into hiding places such as ant-bear holes, reeds or long grass.[76] But the British infantry and their black auxiliaries followed their mounted men out and scoured the immediate neighbourhood of the camp, killing any Zulu the horsemen had missed. Most met their deaths with silence and valiant stoicism. Some turned to expose their chests to their pursuers, while others just stood waiting to be shot.[77]

It is well that most of the flying Zulu expected no quarter, for they received none. Their pursuers shot them down at point-blank range and lamented the lack of sabres for more efficient killing, since shooting Zulu took 'too much time'. Many made do with captured spears, using them as if 'giving point' with the sabre. Schermbrucker saw Buller at the head of his men, 'like a tiger drunk with blood'.[78] Inevitably, very few prisoners were taken. It was only thanks to Wood's promise to his black auxiliaries of a 'stick' of tobacco for each prisoner brought in that any of the wounded fugitives survived capture.[79]

Harried mercilessly, it was inevitable that the Zulu army should fall into great disorder and begin to break apart in various directions. The general line of flight was eastwards towards Zungwini Mountain, and the main body continued on in the direction of Hlobane, though smaller groups broke off to the north and west. Strong elements remained on Hlobane for the next few days, not fully evacuating it until 3 April, but the main force withdrew towards the south-east.[80] Most, however, did not return to oNdini to report to the king. Considering themselves thoroughly beaten, they mainly dispersed to their own homes despite the efforts of the *izinduna* to keep them together. To Mnyamana's entreaties they replied quite simply that they had had enough. Consequently, it was with only a fraction of the army that the unhappy Mnyamana returned to inform Cetshwayo of the disaster which had befallen the forces under his command.[81]

Zulu losses, whether on the battlefield or subsequently of their wounds, were undoubtedly out of proportion to those suffered by the British. These, considering the length and intensity of the engagement, were light: eighteen NCOs and men killed; eight officers and fifty-seven NCOs and men wounded. It is true that three officers and seven men subsequently died of their wounds, and that a considerable number of unrecorded casualties occurred among the black non-combatants in the camp.[82] Yet, by comparison, the Zulu felt that the casualties they had sustained were at least comparable to, if not greater than, those suffered at Isandlwana.

The general consensus was that 3 000 men were missing after the battle.[83] What was certain, is that 785 dead Zulu (some horribly mutilated by shell-fire) were collected during the two days following the battle in a three-kilometre radius of Khambula, and wagon-load after wagon-load of them were buried 750 metres outside the British lines in pits 60 metres long, 6 metres broad, and 3 metres deep. The ground further off in the direction of their rout remained thickly strewn with bodies, prey to the dogs and vultures. For months afterwards patrols were coming across Zulu corpses at great distances from the battlefield.[84]

These last were the wounded who never regained their homes. The battle had taken place in one of the more sparsely inhabited parts of the Zulu kingdom, so the wounded were compelled to press on for great distances to find succour, and had no means of travelling except by foot. British scouts near Hlobane reported that in the retreating *impi* nearly every two men carried a wounded comrade between them,[85] but there was doubtless a limit to how long they were prepared to do so. A month after the battle British patrols along the line of the *impi*'s retreat were constantly finding bodies buried head-first in ant-bear holes, each covered with a shield.[86]

The impact in Zululand of the lost battle was devastating. Natal Border Police were awed to hear the terrible sounds of lamentation coming from the Zulu home-steads near the junction of the Mzinyathi and Thukela Rivers, a district where almost the whole male population had been called up for the Khambula cam-paign. Two of the most important chiefs of the region, Godide of the Ntuli and Manqondo of the Magwaza, were both reported to have lost a number of sons.[87] What made it worse was that it was the flower of the army which had died, the young men of the crack *amabutho*. The British burying them in the pits near Kham-bula noted their fine physiques and the fact that few wore the head-ring of the married man.[88]

It seems those *amabutho* which suffered the greatest casualties were, in order of the magnitude of their loss, the uMbonambi, uNokhenke and iNgoba-makhosi.[89] The Qulusi, who were less disciplined, lost most heavily in the rout. Among the dead were a great many *izinduna*, more than at any other battle of the war. For, as the king commented, they 'exposed themselves a great deal, at-tempting to lead on their men'[90] – a fact Wood had noted with admiration. Men of the highest status among the dead included the king's own cousin, Ma-dlangampisi kaThondolozi, two sons of Mnyamana, and the sons of various other important chiefs and royal councillors.[91]

Cetshwayo was understandably beside himself when he learned of his proud army's defeat and dispersal. He inevitably attached particular blame to its com-mander, Mnyamana, for disobeying his instructions and countenancing a frontal attack on Wood's prepared position.[92] But what was done could not be undone. Khambula had ruthlessly swept aside any illusions that the war could still be won in the field. The only remaining hope lay in a negotiated settlement with the British. Yet after their decisive victory at Khambula there was little or no likelihood that the invaders would be content with anything short of Cetshwayo's complete sub-mission.[93]

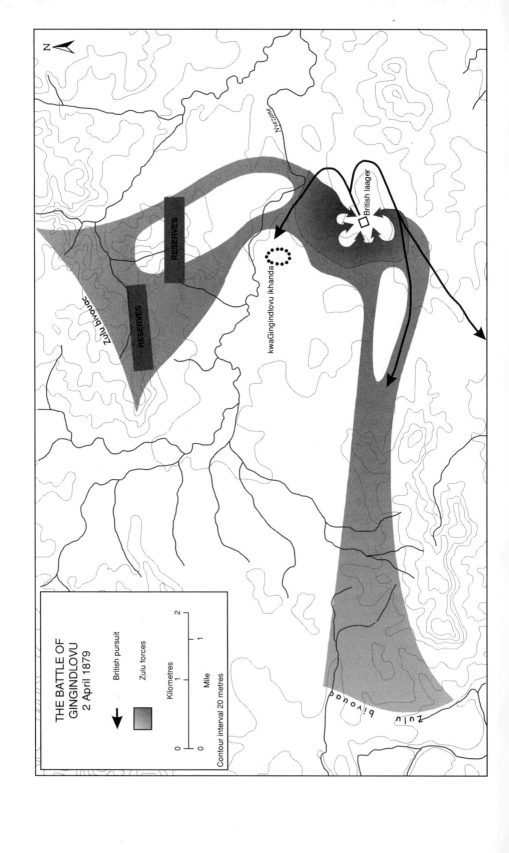

THE BATTLE OF
GINGINDLOVU
2 April 1879

British pursuit

Zulu forces

Contour interval 20 metres

Kilometres
0   1   2

Mile
0   1

British laager

kwaGingindlovu ikhanda

Nyezane

Zulu bivouac

Zulu bivouac

RESERVES

RESERVES

N

23

'The English Burrow in the Ground Like Wild Pigs'[1]

During the last week of March large bodies of Zulu began filing down the distant hills in sight of the Eshowe garrison towards the Nyezane, and their cooking fires multiplied in its valley.[2] They were there on Cetshwayo's orders, for when the king and his council had resolved to send the main Zulu army against Wood at Khambula, they had also decided to reinforce the forces already in the vicinity of Eshowe with more men raised locally, or with the coastal elements of *amabutho* sent back from oNdini.[3] Somopho, senior *induna* of the emaNgweni *ikhanda*, chief armourer to the king and his close personal friend, commanded the forces bivouacked along the Nyezane. They were made up of 3 000 irregulars, mainly Tsonga from up the coast in the region of St Lucia Bay, and of 1 500 local members of *amabutho* connected with the burnt kwaGingindlovu *ikhanda*. Dabulamanzi continued to direct the 1 000 local warriors centred on eNtumeni who were keeping an eye on the fort.

North of Eshowe, 3 000 warriors made up of elements of the iNgobamakhosi, uMcijo, uNokhenke and uMbonambi *amabutho* were barracked at the old oNdini, and 1 500 of the iNdluyengwe were at the isinPuseleni *ikhanda* nearby. They would seem to have been jointly commanded by Sigcwelegcwele, the proud commander of the iNgobamakhosi, and by Phalane kaMdinwa of the Mphukunyoni, likewise a royal *induna*. He was a large, handsome and dignified man with ornaments of beaten brass about neck and ankles, and five-centimetre-long fingernails, white as ivory. The plan was that once Chelmsford marched, this force of 10 000 would concentrate and fall upon his column.

On 28 March the Eshowe Relief Column advanced across the Thukela into Zululand.[5] John Dunn rode with the column to organise effective forward reconnaissance and advise on laagering procedures, for the general was determined to rectify the deficiencies that had led to the Isandlwana disaster. Dunn, whose chiefdom the country had been, suggested a route closer to the coast which, by going for most of the way through open terrain, would reduce the danger of ambush.[6] On 29 March the British formed an entrenched laager at the Nyoni River. Thus far, nothing had been seen of the Zulu except signal-fires burning on the hills, but reports of Zulu movements on 30 March suggested they were concentrating to oppose the invaders.

Chelmsford therefore decided to devote all of 1 April to crossing the swollen

279

Matigulu River with every precaution and to laager just beyond. Meanwhile, Major Barrow and some of the mounted men pushed on some nineteen kilometres towards the Ngoye Forest, close to the Mlalazi River. They saw only small bodies of Zulu, but on the way burned the *umuzi* of Makwendu kaMpande, the king's half-brother, and six other *imizi*. The following day the mounted men patrolled about twelve kilometres inland towards Eshowe, seeing a good many Zulu in the distance.[7] Their patrols were of importance, however. They effectively shrouded the movements of the column from the Zulu scouts, so that the Zulu were left unsure of its strength and movements.

On 1 April the column marched to within two kilometres of the Nyezane stream, just south of the burnt-out kwaGingindlovu *ikhanda*. The undulating and boggy country was covered with very high grass, broken by clumps of palm and undergrowth, which could provide excellent cover for the Zulu. On either side of the Nyezane there was a belt of bush and high reeds. John Dunn selected the best position available for the camp on the summit of a slight knoll.[8] The wagon-laager was made 117 metres square so as to give sufficient room inside for the 2 000 oxen, 300 horses and 2 280 black troops. The 3 390 white troops would advance during combat to the enclosing shelter-trench, which was 144 metres square and about 13,5 metres in front of the wagons. The corners, which were always the weakest sectors of a square, were reinforced by 9-pounder guns, Gatling guns and rocket tubes. Darkness fell before it was possible to cut down the tall grass and bush which came to within 100 metres of the laager, and which would afford the Zulu welcome cover on the morrow. A heavy thunderstorm in the late afternoon and rain during the night made conditions in the crowded and sodden camp most uncomfortable and sleep impossible.[9]

The British were anticipating an attack. Pearson had signalled soon after the column had encamped that a large force of Zulu was on the march towards the Nyezane. Scouts had seen columns of smoke in the afternoon rising from the Zulu bivouacs across the Nyezane, and during the night pickets reported numerous camp-fires on the hills to the north. Although there appeared no immediate danger of attack, tension rose, and at midnight Chelmsford ordered the shelter-trench strengthened. It must have been with relief that the British stood to their arms at 4 a.m., the customary hour before dawn. At about 6.15 the sun rose, breaking through the heavy morning mists. Since earliest dawn an hour before, the mounted scouts and pickets had already been out, and at 5.45 a.m. reported that the Zulu were advancing to the attack.

It made sense that the Zulu should attack the Relief Column at some distance from the fort, for they must have been aware of the danger of being taken in the rear by the garrison. The position of the British, camped out in the open plain, was an added inducement for the Zulu to attack them there using their traditional enveloping tactics, which they deluded themselves the broken terrain at the battle of Nyezane had disrupted.[10]

Some time had been required for the various Zulu forces bivouacked about Eshowe to concentrate, and not all arrived in time for the battle. The more seasoned *amabutho*, who had been in the vicinity of the old oNdini, only reached the main Zulu camp in the hills some eight kilometres north of the Nyezane on the evening of 1 April. It was too late then to probe the British position, and they were in any case tired and hungry. Some of the commanders wished nevertheless to mount an attack immediately, but Dabulamanzi sensibly persuaded them to delay until morning, by which time they would have eaten and rested. So the commanders repaired for the night to a large, makeshift hut, created by covering the drooping branches of a tree with grass.[11]

The Zulu commander-in-chief was Somopho. The many other men of note present acted as his lieutenants. These included not only Dabulamanzi, Sigcwelegcwele and Phalane, who were the local commanders of several of the units stationed around Eshowe, but Masegwane and Mbilwane (the discredited commanders at Nyezane), Mavumengwana (who had been joint commander at Isandlwana), and Sintwangu, a chief of the Cele and an *inceku* of Cetshwayo's.[12] Their army, once all the components had arrived, numbered no more than about 11 000 men. The coastal elements of most of the *amabutho* were present, though local irregulars, especially the Tsonga and neighbouring peoples of north-eastern Zululand, made up a substantial part.[13]

At almost exactly 6 a.m. on Wednesday, 2 April, the Zulu on the far side of the Nyezane and on top of Misi Hill to the west of the laager came into sight of the British. The clouds of skirmishers who masked their advance drove in the British pickets and mounted scouts.[14] The British, however, were quite ready for the rapidly developing attack. The ammunition boxes were open, the shelter-trench was manned two deep, and the tops of the wagons had their load of riflemen. In contrast to Isandlwana, the British were in the ideal formation for repelling a traditional Zulu onslaught. And it was soon apparent that the Zulu were intent on repeating their usual tactics, which were first to surround the enemy before pressing home their attack.

A strong Zulu column divided and crossed the Nyezane, the left division (or left horn) advancing at the north-east corner of the laager, and the right (or chest) at its northern face. Meanwhile, a somewhat weaker column (or right horn) emerged from the bush to the north of Misi Hill and deployed, so that one part confronted the western face of the laager, and the other the southern. All the columns moved in open order at the double, so that within ten minutes of their first being sighted they were formed in the classic crescent shape around three sides of the British position. Reserves (or the loins) waited on the hills beyond the Nyezane, while the large body of women and *udibi* boys carrying food for the army stayed safely away near Eshowe.[15]

Contrary to British expectations, the Zulu did not wear ceremonial dress, but were generally stripped for action to their loincovers.[16] The no-nonsense professionalism of their developing assault matched their dress. Once the enveloping crescent was in position, most of the Zulu broke into three distinct lines, and advanced skirmishing towards the laager in knots and groups of between five and ten men, creeping up under cover of the anthills, bushes and long grass in splendid, disciplined style, keeping up a brisk but inaccurate fire the while, the puffs of smoke alone revealing their positions.

The British noted with relief the characteristically poor Zulu marksmanship, remarking scathingly that they couldn't hit a laager, 'not even a thundering big one'.[17] This could be partially attributed to the inefficient muzzle-loaders carried by most, which fired bullets, old pieces of iron and stones high over the heads of the British. The few casualties they inflicted (two officers and eleven men killed, four officers and forty-four men wounded – of whom one was killed and four wounded in the subsequent mounted pursuit),[18] were mainly caused by the sprinkling of modern rifles in their possession.

The attack of the Zulu left horn and chest on the north-eastern and northern perimeter of the laager developed a little before the more hesitant one of the right horn on its western and southern flanks, where the terrain afforded less cover. The engagement was begun by the Gatling guns at 1 000 metres' range, and when the Zulu closed to within 400 or 300 metres the firing on both sides became incessant. With cries of 'they are encircled!' and 'uSuthu!' the Zulu tried to close in,[19] but despite several desperate charges never succeeded in approaching nearer than within twenty metres of the north-eastern corner of the laager. For even with their extraordinary courage – 'brave to madness'[20] – they were unable to break through the wall of fire set up by the massed rifles, Gatling guns, artillery and rockets. Inevitably too, as they converged on the entrenched laager, their concentrations became denser, and thus more vulnerable. In their grim determination they ceased to shout, and doggedly held their ground, taking cover behind their fallen comrades. But now they were in range of the marksmen on top of the wagons, and subjected to a double tier of fire. No troops in the world could long have stood such punishment. As Sub-Lieutenant Smith-Dorrien put it: 'The poor Zulus hadn't a ghost of a chance.'[21]

This is not to say that the British fire was as effective as it should have been. Many of the soldiers, especially the younger recruits who lacked training and steadiness, had never before been under fire, and were nervous and excited.[22] Their behaviour contrasted adversely with the disciplined Naval Brigade. Yet even among the more experienced soldiers there was a dearth of good marksmen, which meant only controlled volley fire had an effect. Volley fire, though, was not properly suited to stop an enemy rapidly advancing in skirmishing order, and it is clear that the rifles were on occasion incorrectly sighted and firing high.[23]

If the shooting of the soldiers was frankly disappointing, that of the rockets and guns seems to have been little better.[24] Only the Gatlings, serviced by the Naval Brigade, were handled really successfully. During the battle 1 200 rounds were fired from the Gatlings, and about 40 rounds of case and shrapnel from the 9-pounders. The average shots fired per regular soldier was 6,2 (compared to the 7 to 6,4 depending on unit at Ulundi); while the average for the whole force including irregulars was 10. This figure was the normal average for pitched encounters in 'small wars',[25] and shows why, for all its relative ineffectiveness, the British zone of fire was too hot for the Zulu to penetrate.

At 6.40 a.m., when the Zulu chest attacking the northern face of the laager could stand the concentrated fire no longer, and began to retire into the long grass, Chelmsford ordered out the 120 Mounted Infantry and Natal Volunteers under

Major Barrow to keep them on the run. But the Zulu quickly recovered from their momentary loss of nerve, and closed round to cut Barrow off, forcing him to fight his way back into the laager. The chest then executed a change of front, and with perfect discipline circled to their right to reinforce the left division of the Zulu right horn attacking the laager's western face.

Meanwhile, at 7 a.m. the right division of the right horn was only just beginning its assault on the rear, or southern face of the laager.[26] This was to prove the most determined and furious of the whole day. The Zulu were erroneously encouraged by the presence of the NNC inside the rear of the laager to believe that there were not enough British soldiers to man the entire position, and that the southern face must consequently be less strongly held than the others.[27] Dabulamanzi, on horseback, directed this final effort, and he suffered a flesh wound above the left knee as he urged on his men from the thick of the fight.[28]

This attack stalled like the others before the impenetrable British fire, and the disheartened Zulu began to retire to the low ground below the rear of the laager. Chelmsford thereupon directed Barrow and his mounted men, including the Mounted Natives (about 280 men in all), to move out of the laager's unengaged eastern face and open fire on the Zulu right horn's eastern flank. Barrow's well-timed sortie was enough for the wavering Zulu to give up their last hopes of taking the laager. After standing for a few moments and firing at the mounted men, they gave up the effort and commenced their retreat.[29]

Seeing them turn, the NNC advanced out of the laager at 7.15 a.m. in pursuit, though the regular troops were ordered to remain in position lest the Zulu flight be a feint designed to break their formation.[30] Part of Barrow's force charged the Zulu flank with drawn sabre, quite breaking their morale and turning their withdrawal into a rout. In their efforts to escape, the Zulu abandoned weapons and accoutrements. Though some Zulu turned pluckily at bay, most who could not get away threw themselves down (as they had at Khambula) without any attempt to resist. There they were mercilessly speared by the NNC who followed up the charge. One section of Barrow's men pursued the Zulu for about two kilometres towards Misi Hill, some of them breaking off to harry their beaten foe some kilometres southwards towards the Matigulu River. The other part of Barrow's force wheeled north to chase the Zulu who were retiring from the front of the laager, and followed them up towards the kwaGingindlovu *ikhanda*, driving them through the flooded Nyezane.[31]

The two large bodies of Zulu reserves on the hills beyond the Nyezane retreated when they saw the rest of the army put to flight. Fire from the 9-pounder guns dispersed a considerable number of the right horn who, thinking they had gone far enough to be out of danger, had rallied on Misi Hill. After this bombardment, the Zulu made no further attempt at a stand, but dispersed north and west. The manner in which they scattered showed clearly that they had suffered a complete defeat.[32] Long lines of dispirited warriors were seen from Fort Eshowe trekking away northwards along the coastal country towards the Mlalazi River, where they halted for a while before breaking up. Some elements seem later to have rallied further north in the Mhlathuze valley to oppose a possible British advance,[33] but they were the exception. Those who lived further away returned to their homes. The men of the Eshowe region were not so fortunate, and joined their families and cattle where they were already taking refuge in the Nkandla and Ngoye forests.[34]

The British took what could only be described as a sportsman's interest in their bag. Chelmsford reported that 471 Zulu had been buried within 900 metres of the laager, and that another 200 dead had been found near the scene. More of the horribly mangled dead were discovered lying in awful positions within a radius of eight kilometres. The official British tally was 'nearly 1 200',[35] or between a ten per cent and twelve per cent Zulu casualty rate. Nor does this seem an exaggeration. Most of the wounded were abandoned by their comrades who were unable to carry them across the swollen Nyezane.[36] That meant certain death, for the pitiless NNC stabbed every Zulu they came across, dead, dying or wounded.[37] And even if the wounded did succeed in evading the NNC and reaching their homes, most of them eventually succumbed there of their injuries. Only two officers of note, it would seem, died at Gingindlovu, but a great many sons of chiefs and well-to-do men were among the slain.[38]

The morning following the battle, Chelmsford left a garrison with the reduced laager while the remainder of the column marched up to relieve Fort Eshowe. Not a Zulu was seen, though they had partly destroyed the track in two places. Chelmsford had decided to abandon the fort altogether, not least because he considered the coastal route more suitable for subsequent operations. While Pearson supervised the evacuation of the fort on 4 April, Chelmsford accompanied a patrol of 225 men led by Major Barrow to destroy Dabulamanzi's eSulwini *umuzi* at eNtumeni which had escaped burning during the raid of 1 March. A small force of forty Zulu led by Dabulamanzi, who had returned home after the battle and who was typically mounted on a black horse, kept up fire from a neighbouring hill, but were this time unable to prevent the British from completing their vindictive mission.[39]

On 5 April the relieving column and garrison set out from Fort Eshowe for Natal, leaving behind six officers and thirty-five men lying in the little cemetery. The Zulu immediately set fire to the buildings at the abandoned fort, but did not in any way harm the British graves and crosses.[40]

The disastrous defeat suffered by his coastal forces, coming on top of the rout of the main army at Khambula, was a terrible blow for Cetshwayo and his councillors. No wonder that the king furiously castigated his generals for their ineptitude at Gingindlovu.[41] The outcome of the war might even yet have been redeemed had Chelmsford been repulsed before Eshowe, but now that opportunity had been thrown away.

Chelmsford, for his part, buoyed up by the realisation that the initiative was once more wholly his, was determined to allow the Zulu no chance to regain their balance. Consequently, on 7 April he sent orders from Fort Pearson for continued raids to be made across the Natal-Zululand border. The flooded state of the Thukela, however, prevented the border troops from doing more than to hover menacingly at the unfordable drifts, and by the last week of April the Zulu along the river considered it safe to return to their *imizi*.[42]

It was different at Rorke's Drift, where on 9 April Major Dartnell led over 2 000 men on a raid up the Batshe valley and back over Fugitives' Drift. The Zulu had sufficient warning of the raid to be able to drive their cattle and horses eastwards out of range. The British experienced no resistance, leaving them free to burn the crops standing in their gardens as well as three of Sihayo's *imizi* and nine others that had hitherto escaped the attentions of the mounted patrols.[43]

Wood's force remained undisturbed at Khambula after the battle, and his operations were confined to sending out mounted patrols which engaged in several light skirmishes with the few Zulu still in the neighbourhood. By 3 April all of the Qulusi and Mbilini's adherents had gone from Hlobane. They moved north to raid the Phongolo region once more, accompanied by Mbilini, who reportedly travelled in a cart because of a superficial wound to the forehead, sustained either at the battle of Hlobane or at Khambula. Once in the north, they broke into several parties, one of 150 men even raiding as far away as the Mkhondo River valley.

On the night of 4 April several parties, making up a force perhaps 1 200 strong, raided the Phongolo valley opposite Luneburg. They retired rapidly in the direction of Makateeskop with their booty of cattle. On the way they encountered two companies of the 2/4th Regiment on their way to relieve the Luneburg garrison. The British at once formed a laager, and the Zulu, who had learned their lesson well at Khambula, left them unmolested and broke into several small groups which proceeded to ravage the countryside as they went. It was while following up one of these marauding parties that a patrol from Luneburg under Captain Prior became engaged in a skirmish near the Ntombe. They killed Tshekwane, a younger son of Sihayo who had often accompanied Mbilini on his raiding expeditions, and wounded another Zulu horseman. This turned out to be Mbilini himself, who managed nevertheless to make his escape. However, he had been shot in the back through the right shoulder, the bullet coming out below his waist, and died within a few days of his dreadful wound, before he could regain his *umuzi* at Hlobane.

The death of the hyena of the Phongolo, as he was known, and certainly the most gifted guerrilla leader on the Zulu side, left his adherents leaderless and dismayed. They ceased to be a factor in the region, and by May had left Hlobane altogether for the Ngwegwe Hill north of the Phongolo. As for Manyonyoba, constant patrols during May by the Luneburg garrison and by Commandant J.A. Rudolph, whose Burghers operated from their laager on the Bivane River close by Fort Lawrence (which had been built by a company of the 2/4th), kept him bottled up in his caves.

As a result, the British considered that the Zulu of the north-west could safely be contained by the existing garrisons in the area. This was vital, for Chelmsford was preparing his second invasion of Zululand, and Wood's forces – which were required for the renewed advance – could hardly have been employed had this meant leaving the Transvaal frontier open to Zulu raids. Confident, then, that little risk to the frontier communities would be incurred, on 5 May Wood moved south from Khambula to join Chelmsford's force. The men of the Utrecht garrison caught up with him on 28 May, and on 17 June Wood effected his rendezvous with the general.[45] This time, their march on oNdini would be inexorable.

24

I Ask for Peace

Chelmsford returned to Natal on 7 April to find that the main body of reinforcements which he had requested from England had arrived in Durban. He now felt strong enough to launch his long-delayed final thrust into Zululand. It was to take the form of a cautious, two-pronged offensive. The 1st Division of 7 500 men, under the command of Major-General H.H. Crealock, would advance into Zululand from Fort Pearson. The remaining 5 000 men of the assembled force were to concentrate at Dundee as the 2nd Division under Major-General E. Newdigate. This latter Division would co-operate in its advance with the 3 200 men of Wood's command, to be known as the Flying Column. There were various perfectly practical logistical reasons why Chelmsford chose Dundee in preference to Helpmekaar as the 2nd Division's chief depot, but the most potent was an unvoiced one: no one wished to invade Zululand by a road signposted by the dreadful field of Isandlwana and its unburied British dead. Instead, the 2nd Division would advance by an unfamiliar route that would require considerable, time-consuming reconnaissance.[1]

During the first week of May the 2nd Division began to mass at the fortified depot at Landman's Drift on the Mzinyathi. The patrols sent out had more to do than investigate the country ahead, however. Chelmsford wished to prevent the Zulu from attacking the 2nd Division or from raiding the Transvaal to its rear. He considered the best way to achieve this was to deny them bases and supplies in the area of operations by burning the *imizi* and standing crops, and by driving off the livestock.[2]

Accordingly, on 13 May a combined force of mounted men and NNC circled south around Telezeni Hill, a line of fire marking the hundreds of huts they left burning behind them. This was followed up on 16 May with a large mounted raid on Telezeni Hill itself, but the British found that the Zulu had evacuated the vicinity. Then, on 21 May, Major-General F. Marshall, commanding the Cavalry Brigade attached to the 2nd Division, made a reconnaissance in force to Isandlwana. Burning every surviving *umuzi* in its path, his force came to the deserted battlefield.

All was overgrown with grass and sprouting oats and mealies, which concealed most of the skeletal remains of the soldiers, horses and oxen. Skin was still attached to some of the corpses and the facial features of a few of the dead were recognisable. Everywhere was the pathetic litter of torn tents, broken wagons and boxes, scattered meat-tins, bloodstained photographs, books and letters, toilet bags, bottles and a few stray bayonets and spears. Undisturbed except by Zulu signal-fires, Marshall's men commenced the disgracefully delayed burial of the dead in shallow graves before hitching up forty unbroken wagons and returning to Landman's Drift. Finding the missing bodies and burying them properly took some time, and those who carried on with the task did not complete it until March 1880.[3]

Chelmsford could be confident that the country to his front and on his immediate right had been cleared of any Zulu force large enough to threaten the 2nd Division or the Natal border. Meanwhile, in order to draw away any Zulu further east who might later fall upon his right flank or the colony, he ordered a new series of raids to be mounted across the Thukela.

At Middle Drift the river was at last sufficiently low and the drifts passable, and on 20 May Major A.C. Twentyman led across 1 700 men in a three-pronged raid.[4] Resistance was minimal as the Zulu were caught completely off guard. They had time only to drive off their cattle, abandoning their food-supplies and caches of ammunition. The raiders burned an estimated nineteen *imizi* (including that of Godide, the Ntuli chief), destroyed great quantities of grain, and drove off a herd of 150 cattle belonging to the king.

The Zulu gamely responded by raiding the Natal blacks of the Thukela valley that very evening. But they were demoralised. For fear of fresh raids they abandoned those *imizi* near the river which had escaped burning, and withdrew deeper into Zululand with their remaining cattle and food supplies, taking refuge in the Nkandla and Qudeni forests – apparently of no future danger to either Chelmsford or Natal. Further downstream, Captain G.A. Lucas sent in two diversionary raids on 28 May, in which two *imizi* were burned. That was the last raid across the lower Thukela, for the objective of clearing the border had likewise been achieved.[5]

The mounted reconnaissances undertaken during May from Landman's Drift had established that the shortest route for the 2nd Division to follow to oNdini was to the north-east across the Ncome River below Koppie Alleen. A new depot was accordingly established there, and on 31 May the 2nd Division began to cross into Zululand to effect its junction with the Flying Column. The Natal border on his right flank was secure, Chelmsford believed, as was the Transvaal's to his rear. The border garrisons in their chain of forts were left behind to watch drowsily over the deserted Zulu banks of the Mzinyathi and Thukela rivers, where no one laboured in the forlorn mealie-gardens, no smoke arose from the destroyed or abandoned *imizi*, and a profound silence reigned over all.

However, in north-western Zululand the situation (with Mbilini dead and the Qulusi lurking in their mountain fastnesses) was not quite as stable as Wood had supposed when he marched from Khambula to join Chelmsford.[6] It was still necessary to patrol the Transvaal border, but the anti-British Boers of the Wakkerstroom District were unwilling to take the field. The lack of mounted men to defend the region meant that on 4 June a party of fifty Zulu was emboldened to attack the blacks living on a white farm on the Bivane. On 7 June a larger force (quite possibly made up of Qulusi and Mbilini's former adherents) swept the cattle off another farm near Luneburg. Near the Ntombe River they cut off a patrol trying to intercept them. Heinrich Filter, the Lutheran pastor's son, was killed before the horrified eyes of his mother, and six black border policemen died with him.

The depleted Luneburg garrison was too weak to take retaliatory action. The Zulu, for their part, did not risk attacking the fortified post, but retired over the Ntombe with their booty. The local blacks friendly to the settlers took to the mountains and caves, and left the Zulu master of their mealie-gardens. From 7 until 21 June, when they finally passed back across the Phongolo, large forces of Zulu raiders swept with impunity between the Ntombe and Mkhondo, attacking *imizi* in the area and driving off thousands of cattle and sheep. Manyonyoba's men occupied the hills opposite Luneburg, and remained there undisturbed throughout June. It was they who constituted the greatest danger to other blacks in the vicinity, for after these raids no other serious Zulu activity occurred elsewhere in the upper Phongolo region.

Nevertheless, a potential threat from quite another quarter lay over the British and their black dependents along the Phongolo. The Wakkerstroom Boers, rather than aiding the British militarily, were in blatant league with the Zulu against their common imperial foe. Boers of the Mkhondo River region treated with Zulu deputations, and some had reputedly gone to see Cetshwayo. More Boers than usual that June were wintering along the border, some close to the Phongolo among the Zulu *imizi*. The fact that they felt safe to do so confirmed British suspicions of Boer-Zulu collusion, as did reports that during the Zulu raids of June the Boers had again acted as guides to the Zulu, and indicated which farms or homesteads should be spared. The Boers were to remain on the best of terms with the Zulu until August, when the British began to reassert their control of the area. Then, one Conrad Potgieter was reported to be camped among the ruins of one of the Luneburg settler's farms, enjoying excellent relations with Manyonyoba who had burned it, and who still threatened the British garrison.

The activities of the Zulu and Boers in the north-west, though very uncomfortable for the settlers of Luneburg and their black dependents, were ultimately not sufficiently intensive or widespread to threaten Wood's rear or Chelmsford's left flank. Similarly, a sudden and successful Zulu raid on 25 June at Middle Drift, which at a blow reasserted Zulu ascendancy along the Natal border, was not enough to deflect them from their joint march on oNdini.[7]

At daybreak on 25 June, when fog still shrouded the river, a Zulu *impi* of 500 men armed with spears and many firearms crossed at Hot Springs upstream of Middle Drift. They rampaged up to the foot of Kranskop, killing the Ngcolosi people of the valley and setting fire to their *imizi* as they went and driving off livestock. Below Kranskop the *impi* joined up with another force of about 500 which had crossed some 16 kilometres downstream, and had similarly been engaged ravaging the *imizi* of the Hosiyana and Bomvu. The joint force retired by way of Middle Drift, shrugging off the belated attempts at interception by the completely surprised border forces. Zulu strategy had mirrored that adopted much less successfully by the British in their major raid of 20 May. On this occasion, the Zulu burned seventy-three *imizi*, killed thirty of the border population, took captive another forty, drove off 678 cattle and 771 goats and – adding insult to injury – looted £170 intended for the hut-tax.

Quite clearly, the Zulu had gained much the better of the raiding exchange, and the Natal authorities and border population were only too aware of the fact. There was some speculation that Cetshwayo had sanctioned the raid to divert Chelmsford from his advance on oNdini, but it is more likely that the raid was a retaliatory blow of purely local initiative, in which the Magwaza of Chief Manqondo and the Ntuli of Chief Mavumengwana took the lead. In any event, the British border forces were thrown entirely onto the defensive, where they remained until Chelmsford's victory at Ulundi transformed the situation.

When planning his advance into Zululand from Koppie Alleen,[8] Chelmsford naturally feared a Zulu attack on his crawling, extended columns during the day, or against his encampments by night. The latter was the easier to guard against, and he instructed his troops to form wagon-laagers every evening. He hoped, though, that efficient scouting and screening by the cavalry would effectively prevent the Zulu from considering an attack while the columns were on the march. Accordingly, his advance was marked (as his reconnaissances had been) by the systematic burning of homesteads, the destruction of crops and stored mealies, and the capture of cattle. By these means his cavalry created an extensive zone about the vulnerable columns free of sources of supply and shelter for possible Zulu forces.

Of course, the civilian population was the direct victim of this policy, for they lost their homes, possessions and means of livelihood in the process. The war Chelmsford was waging was becoming unmistakably more total in nature, for his deliberate frightfulness was also aimed at sapping the Zulu people's desire to continue with their resistance.

Ironically, an incident at the very beginning of the advance from the Ncome involving a small mounted patrol caused more consternation in Britain than the battle of Isandlwana itself.[9] On 1 June the enthusiastic but reckless twenty-three-year-old Louis Napoleon, Prince Imperial of France and hope of the deposed Bonapartist dynasty, who was serving as an observer on Chelmsford's staff, was killed by a party of Zulu scouts.

In the early afternoon the prince and his patrol, which consisted of Lieutenant J.B. Carey, a Zulu guide, six troopers of Bettington's Horse and six Basuto horsemen, off-saddled for a rest just to the north of the Tshotshosi River near to an *umuzi* belonging to an *induna* called Sobhuza. A Zulu scouting party of between thirty and sixty men, drawn from local elements of the iNgobamakhosi, uMbonambi and uNokhenke *amabutho*, spotted them from Mhlungwane, a round-headed hill across the river, and moved in on the unsuspecting prince and his companions under cover of high river-banks and mealie-fields.

Shortly after 3.30 p.m., just as the British patrol was drawn up ready to remount, the Zulu fired a ragged volley and charged forward shouting 'uSuthu!' A disgraceful *sauve qui peut* ensued, in which the patrol scattered in panic, three of its members nevertheless falling victim to the Zulu. When the athletic prince ran to vault onto Percy, his nervous grey, the saddle-holster he grasped gave way and the rearing horse struck him in the belly, so that he fell back winded. Percy galloped off after the horses carrying Carey and the other survivors to safety, and the prince had no choice but to turn at bay. Seven Zulu, headed by Xabanga, a member of the uMbonambi who was later killed at the battle of Ulundi, caught up with him 150 metres from the *umuzi*.

The prince fired three quick shots with his revolver, and a look of astonishment passed over his face when he realised he had hit no one. He fired twice again, more slowly, but missed once more. He then rushed courageously at Xabanga, who first ran away, then turned, crouched in the grass and threw a spear. It struck the prince in the thigh. He pulled it from the wound and with it determinedly kept his foes at a respectful distance for some moments. Gwabukana then hurled a spear which struck the prince in the chest, high up and to the left, near the shoulder. With that fatal wound he began to sink to the ground, and several other Zulu came up and stabbed him.

Hlabanathunga ritually stripped the prince and slit his stomach. The Zulu did not know who he was, but divined he was an officer of some importance. Once he was dead they plundered the body, breaking his watch open with a stone thinking the humming round box would contain money. Mnukwa, an *inceku* of Cetshwayo's, picked up the Prince's fine sword and carried it to the king.

The tragic event, which extinguished a dynasty's dreams of restoration to the French throne, tarnished Chelmsford's reputation beyond redemption. Unhappily for King Cetshwayo, it also effectively obliterated any residual Zulu hopes for a negotiated end to the war, for Chelmsford was left with a greater need than ever to compensate for his disasters with a brilliant victory in the field.

On 3 June the 2nd Division resumed its advance and crossed the Tshotshosi River behind the Flying Column, which had moved beyond the Nondweni River. On 4 June Baker's Horse reported a large force of several hundred Zulu to their front at eZungeni Mountain across the Ntinini (Phoko) River, where they were mustered in a cluster of four large *imizi*, known as eZulaneni (or Wanderer's Rest), belonging to Sihayo, the Qungebe chief. Baker's men sustained casualties when outflanked in the ensuing running skirmish.[10]

Major-General Marshall and the Cavalry Brigade accordingly started at 4.30 a.m. on 5 June to reconnoitre as far as the valley of the Ntinini. Here they came up to a party of irregular horse from the Flying Column under Buller, who had just routed some 300 Zulu on the small level plain on the eastern side of the Ntinini and chased them through eZulaneni into the thorn bush on the seamed lower slopes of eZungeni Hill. Buller had the situation in control, and put eZulaneni to the torch before beginning an ordered withdrawal. But Colonel D. Drury-Lowe had to demonstrate the mettle of his cavalry. He foolhardily charged with two squadrons of the 17th Lancers and came under heavy fire from the Zulu who had taken cover among the long grass, bushes, dongas and anthills. The Zulu, if they had known how to use their firearms more effectively, might have done considerable damage. As it was, Lieutenant F.J.C. Frith, the Adjutant of the

17th Lancers, was shot dead, and a squadron of the King's Dragoon Guards had to be moved forward to cover the Lancers' withdrawal before they were outflanked.

Buller's men set fire to all the homesteads they came across on their way back to camp, but that could not remedy the fact that the British had suffered a reverse. The ineffectiveness of regular cavalry in broken terrain and irregular warfare was confirmed, as was Zulu skirmishing ability. The following days were not only to reinforce these propositions, but were also to demonstrate how irregular horse, when led by an officer of Buller's ability, could regain the ascendancy.

The difficulty and slowness of Chelmsford's progress, which averaged just three kilometres a day (it would take the British twenty-eight days to advance the 104 kilometres from the Ncome to the Mthonjaneni heights overlooking oNdini), forced the general to halt to establish storage depots and entrenched posts along his line of communications. The 2nd Division built Fort Newdigate on 6 June, and on 7 June moved forward to the left bank of the Ntinini, where it remained until 17 June while supplies were brought up under heavy escort and the tracks improved.

During this period reconnaissances were made by Buller in order to clear the area of the Zulu who had been so successful in the skirmish of 5 June.[11] On 7 June near eZungeni he engaged a force of nearly 1 000 Zulu, consisting of adherents of Sekethwayo, Sihayo and Msebe. Eleven of the Zulu were mounted, and Buller was impressed with their leader's generalship. The Zulu were nevertheless forced to retire, and Buller burnt a number of large *imizi* in the vicinity, which contained equipment evidently looted at Isandlwana. The following day Buller, supported by artillery, outflanked and routed some 400 Zulu at eZungeni, burned some more large *imizi*, and finally drove the Zulu away from the mountain towards the east. On 10 June his active patrols brought in another 300 cattle.[12]

Buller's indefatigable men next crossed the White Mfolozi on 15 June and came to Thabankhulu Mountain forty kilometres north of his camp. Not surprisingly, they caught the Zulu completely unawares. They drove off 300 cattle and 100 sheep, killed twelve Zulu and captured a number more, besides burning twenty-four *imizi*. These far-flung and ruthless patrols by Buller's irregular horse were to clear the country between Conference Hill and Rorke's Drift of all Zulu, whether civilian or under arms, and to drive them away in advance of the British as far as Babanango Mountain.

It was only on 18 June, though, after the combined 2nd Division and Flying Column had built Fort Marshall ten kilometres south of eZungeni and supplies had been secured, that Chelmsford felt free to order a general advance. The following day the combined force reached the Babanango heights, when 45 of Baker's Horse skirmished with 500 Zulu in a thickly populated river valley nearby, probably that of the Mpembeni. The Zulu tried without success to tempt Baker's men into unfavourable terrain by driving past a herd of 3 000 cattle. Meanwhile, the women and children swarmed out of the *imizi*, making for the nearest mountain with their possessions on their heads.[14] Here as elsewhere, the British found the *imizi* which they routinely destroyed near the line of march deserted, though the large supplies of corn which they regularly contained suggested that they had been precipitately abandoned.[15]

The Flying Column built Fort Evelyn on 23-24 June on one of the great spurs of the Babanango highlands, within distant view of the Mahlabathini plain far below, forty-five kilometres to the north-east as the crow flies. Large bodies of armed Zulu were seen keeping watch on the British from the crests of the hills or from the valleys to the north of the Babanango ridge, but were never strong enough to attack.[16] Buller, meanwhile, while reconnoitring on 24 June towards the Mthonjaneni heights, where Pretorius had laagered in December 1838, and where Chelmsford intended to camp before marching down into the plain for his final confrontation with the Zulu army, surprised and dispersed about seventy Zulu. They were burning the drying winter grass along the line of the British advance. This attempt, as well as earlier ones elsewhere, could, if they had been successfully and persistently carried out, have further delayed the advance of the British, who were constantly short of forage. But because the British were well aware of the threat, their mounted patrols were constantly on the look-out for Zulu burning the grass, and were able to prevent it.[17]

Chelmsford had intended Major-General Crealock's 1st Division to play a vital supporting role. Its specified task was to support the 2nd Division and Flying Column in their advance on oNdini by marching up the coast and forcing Cetshwayo to detach fighting men from the main Zulu army in defence of the south-east of his kingdom. That is why Crealock's initial objective was to be the destruction of the emaNgweni and old oNdini *amakhanda*, within sixteen kilometres of each other either side of the Mhlathuze River, for it was presumed that Cetshwayo would not allow them to be burned without making some attempt to protect them. For this ploy to be useful, however, it was essential that Crealock move quickly and anticipate – or at least keep up with – Chelmsford's progress.[18]

Yet speed is what 'Crealock's Crawlers' were quite unable to achieve. Granted, Crealock had to grapple with extremely difficult supply and transport problems,[19] but these were compounded by his cautious and over-methodical approach, which required the construction of numbers of strong and well-supplied advance posts. Disgruntled subordinates scoffed at the 1st Division's dilatory and meaningless advance, and pointed out that it failed even in its primary objective of forcing Cetshwayo to divide his forces.[20]

There were indications that Cetshwayo had initially planned to 'eat up' the 1st Division before turning his attention to Chelmsford's joint force. However, when the king realised that Crealock would never be able to arrive in time to support Chelmsford in his advance on oNdini, he decided to ignore the 1st Division's presence and concentrate on Chelmsford's more immediate threat. Consequently, when he called up his army, he left only a few irregulars living in the coastal country with their families to protect the cattle and, if possible, to drive them out of reach of Crealock's patrols.[21]

It is not certain when Cetshwayo started summoning his *amabutho* against the likelihood of a final stand against the invader. Mobilisation would have taken some time, for it was necessary to send out the order by runner or signal to the far corners of the kingdom. Besides, after the defeats of March and April there was a natural reluctance to face the British again, though many evinced a grim preparedness to do so if it was required of them. Perhaps a factor in their determination – as well as a manifestation of their irrational fears in the face of impending defeat – was the extraordinary rumour sweeping Zululand that, if they were to yield, the whites would take their wives and castrate all the surviving Zulu males.[22] This was corroborated in Zulu minds by the fictitious tale that Gamdana, who had defected in January, had already been mutilated and sent away to an island.[23]

Be that as it may, the *amabutho* resisted calls to muster until they had reaped their crops and stored the grain. The king assented, but on condition that they came up to oNdini during June.[24] And, by early June, the British had positive intelligence that the coastal elements of the *amabutho* were making for oNdini, as were those living along the Natal border and in the upper districts of Zululand. It must have been most disturbing for the king that reiterated commands had been necessary before his *amabutho* would consent to muster, and that there was certainly continuing reluctance to do so. Still, it was of considerable significance that the great majority were proving willing to fight on for their king, despite their undeniably lowered morale.[25]

Since the coastal warriors had gone to join the army before the 1st Division's advance was fully under way, in mid-June, Crealock's men moved through a countryside largely clear of people, except for some concentrations beyond the Mlalazi and around Ngoye.[26] Resistance was consequently minimal, even when the British were at their most vulnerable, crossing rivers. Apart from occasionally cutting the 1st Division's telegraph wire,[27] the only aggressive action the Zulu took was to fire harmlessly every now and again from great range at British forward patrols.

The coastal region nevertheless witnessed crucial developments in a quarter other than the military. In the post-Khambula period it was clear that Zulu allegiance to the king was at last beginning to waver. On 21 April, near kwa-Gingindlovu, Prince Makwendu, with 130 men, women and children, gave himself up to the advance-parties of the 1st Division. He told his captors that it had been the wish of all his adherents to surrender, as they saw the war could no longer be won, but that the king, learning of this intention, had sent an *impi* to intercept part of his following, killing some and taking his cattle.[28]

Makwendu might have been a prince of little influence, who, born of the same mother as Hamu, could have been expected to follow the lead of his elder brother in going over to the British. All the same, the defection of a second member of the royal house must have been as alarming for Cetshwayo as it was encouraging for the British.[29] To the invaders' satisfaction there were persistent rumours that some of the great magnates of the southern coastal region, including Dabulamanzi and Mavumengwana, were also contemplating surrender. There were reports too, from other parts of the country, that some chiefs, with their homesteads full of the wounded and dying, intended to surrender once the British had advanced sufficiently to do so with impunity.[30] Women, not unnaturally, were coming out ever more openly against persevering with a war that was devouring both their menfolk and their homes.

Faced with such waverings, and uncertain how best to prosecute the increasingly disastrous war, in mid-May Cetshwayo had summoned the principal men of his kingdom to give their advice. It was reported that they opposed the continuation of the war and strongly urged peace. Apparently unnerved by the disaffection of his *izikhulu* (not least Zibhebhu's), and himself despairing of fighting off the British, Cetshwayo consented to begin a new peace initiative.[31] However, his *amabutho* were still unwilling to give up without a fight. Cetshwayo consequently assured them that although he was entering into negotiations with the British, he was uncertain if they would have any effect, and was therefore still determined to attack the British if they came on as far as the Mahlabathini plain.[32]

The king's most recent emissaries, Mfunzi, Nkisimana and Johannes, had remained incarcerated at Fort Buckingham until 15 April. They were then informed that should they wish to make any peace proposals they should do so at Wood's camp in Zululand, where they would find Chelmsford.[33] On account of a degree of confusion over who had the authority to permit them to proceed (or perhaps it was a ploy deliberately to delay them), the two messengers remained at Fort Buckingham until 9 May. On 12 June they appeared under flag of truce in Pietermaritzburg, sent on by Fynn, the Resident Magistrate at Rorke's Drift.

It would seem from their conversation with General Clifford in the Natal capital that after leaving Fort Buckingham they had gone, not to Chelmsford, but to consult with the king and his councillors. These had essentially confirmed their previous message calling for peace negotiations, and had sent Mfunzi and Nkisimana back with an injunction to hurry. But the messengers were old and the rains heavy, and Chelmsford's precise whereabouts were unknown to them. This is why they had fetched up at Rorke's Drift. Clifford sent the exhausted messengers back in the direction of Babanango, where he supposed Chelmsford to be.

Before Mfunzi and Nkisimana could locate Chelmsford, they and the message they bore were quite outstripped by events. Besides, in the course of their interrogation by Clifford, they had let slip an observation which pinpointed the fundamental limitation of all Zulu peace initiatives thus far: they admitted they had no authority to talk about the actual terms of peace, only the king's desire to negotiate. This was in accordance with Zulu custom. Messengers were only sent out to make arrangements for a meeting of chiefs who alone had the power to discuss terms.

In any case, on 4 April Frere had directed that 'no overtures of any kind must be allowed to delay military operations', or at least not until 'complete military command' of Zululand had been secured. Then the British would be free to dictate any terms they desired. Complementary to this policy was Frere's authorisation that overtures for peace would be acceptable from any other chief but the king.[34] For as the war turned decisively against Cetshwayo, it would clearly become much easier to detach his chiefs from his cause.

Meanwhile, Major-General Crealock, laying the ground for his laborious advance up the coast, was soon complaining that he was 'in a state of chronic messengers from the king and his indunas'[35] (not that he did any more than to direct them to Chelmsford via Wood, as insisted upon by Frere). On 15 May the first of this series of messengers, Chief Ndwandwe of the Langa in southern Zululand, came into Fort Chelmsford with Cetshwayo's plaintive message: 'What have I done? I want peace – I ask for peace.'[36]

Chelmsford responded to word of this message by evolving fresh terms for surrender over and above those contained in the ultimatum of December. All captured weapons and prisoners were to be surrendered, 10 000 stands of firearms handed over, as well as at least 10 000 cattle or 20 000 sheep: crushing and impossible terms surely designed to elicit resistance until Chelmsford had achieved his desired victory in the field. Frere capped these terms with his harsh directive that the king's messengers were to be informed that unless acts were substituted for 'idle words', and until the Zulu made genuine efforts to comply with the terms, their land would be devastated.[37]

On 27 May Crealock learned that the king was sending him further messengers, and that he had ordered that whites were not to be fired upon during the period of negotiations. There could no longer be any doubt that Cetshwayo was attempting to treat in earnest. The messenger who arrived on 28 May was *inceku* Sintwangu, a well-known emissary who had attended the ultimatum ceremony in December as the king's eyes and ears. In conversation on 31 May with John Dunn, who was now the 1st Division's Chief of Intelligence, he reiterated Ndwandwe's message, and begged the renegade white chief to use his influence to achieve peace.[38] Such pleas were to no avail, and Sintwangu was sent off like the other messengers to negotiate directly with Chelmsford – if he could find him. This was also the fate of Ndwandwe, who reappeared on 7 June with another relay of messengers, purveying what Crealock called his 'peaceful lies from the king'.[39]

Chelmsford, meanwhile, remained obdurate. There could be no permanent peace until the king was deposed, which rendered Cetshwayo's attempts to negotiate with the British advancing from the north-west as futile as his deflected efforts to treat with those slowly moving up the coast.

Three messengers, Mgcwelo, Mtshibela and Mpokitwayo, reached Wood's camp at the Nondweni River on 4 June. They had left Cetshwayo at his em-Lambongwenya homestead on 30 June, and had at first made for Khambula, which the Flying Column had already left. It would seem that they had set out at the same time as Sintwangu had been despatched to Crealock, and Mfunzi and Nkisimana to Rorke's Drift. The three messengers carried a message which Cetshwayo had personally given them in the presence of his chief councillors.

Genuine emissaries though they might have been, they made a bad impression on the prejudiced British, who found them 'villainous-looking scoundrels'.[40] In turn, they were so strongly impressed with the spectacle of British armed might that they assured their interrogators in their preparatory interview that they would 'strongly recommend' on their return that the king come to terms. They also let it be known that Cetshwayo was now prepared to send Mnyamana and other 'officers of state' to treat,[41] as Frere had always insisted they should.

However, in their formal interview on 5 June with Chelmsford, the general laid down conditions which were a preposterous refinement on the additional ones he had evolved in May. Firstly, he made it plain that he no longer believed that the king was being obeyed, and that unless Cetshwayo could provide proof of his continuing authority and desire for peace, the British would rather continue negotiating with his chiefs. He therefore warned that he would continue his advance unless the king, in earnest of his power and genuine intentions, sent in the oxen at his royal homesteads and the two 7-pounder guns captured at Isandlwana, and promised besides that all the other firearms in Zululand would be collected and given up. In addition, an *ibutho*, to be named by Chelmsford, must come into the British lines and lay down its arms. Then, and only then, would he even entertain peace discussions – which, naturally, would be based on the original terms of the ultimatum.[42]

Their mission rendered futile by these astonishing preconditions, the disconsolate messengers left the British camp on 6 June, bearing with them Chelmsford's written statement of his impossible terms. This punctilious sop to correct diplomatic form (for who in the Zulu camp would be able to read his words?) did not disguise the general's transparent cynicism. Cetshwayo had already made it plain that although desperate to negotiate, he could not accede to the demands of the ultimatum. How then could he even consider these outrageous preliminary conditions? How could Chelmsford have ever expected him to?

Clearly he did not. His conditions were merely for the record, since his intention was to fight and win his battle to wipe away the disgrace of Isandlwana. It made not a jot of difference that there were reports of the king calling on his people to send him cattle to help buy off the British and make peace; nor that he did not intend to attack the British unless they continued to advance on oNdini. By way of contrast, Chelmsford's instructions of 16 June laid down that chiefs, on submitting to designated authorities, would be required only to give up their arms and the royal cattle in their keeping. In return, their adherents were to be spared and protected.[43] Only the king could expect no mercy.

Though backed into a corner, Cetshwayo persevered with his peace-feelers. Two new messengers, Ntanjana and Sibungu, arrived at Fort Pearson on the lower Thukela on 25 June, begging that the British stay their advance until negotiations could take place. They explained that if the British continued to march on oNdini, Cetshwayo would have no choice but to resist, 'as there will be nothing left but to try and push aside a tree that is falling upon him'.[44] But these latest messengers, disregarded as were all those before them, left on 29 June.

Sintwangu appeared on a new mission the following day. He came into Crealock's camp at Fort Napoleon on the Mlalazi River bearing an enormous elephant tusk – the symbol of peace and friendship – in earnest of the authenticity of his mission.[45] Haplessly, he created the unfortunate impression messengers seemed now automatically to impress in the minds of the British, one of whom described him as manifesting 'a curious mixture of dogged determination, savage cunning and treachery'.[46] His interview with Crealock did not last twenty minutes, and when directed to address himself rather to Chelmsford, he took the rebuff as if he had expected it – as well he might.

Chelmsford's written conditions, which the two messengers had taken off on 6 June, still required an answer. It had been the general's condition that a reply be returned within eight days. Yet even in this emergency Zulu dignity did not 'permit of hurry'.[47] Moreover, since Cetshwayo could not read the message when it did arrive, it was necessary to summon Cornelius Vijn, the young, lame Dutch trader whom the war had detained in Zululand, to do so for him. Vijn was being kept under watch some distance away, so it was not until about 17 June that he had reached the kwaMbonambi *ikhanda* where the king was resident, translated the note and penned Cetshwayo's response. The king, understandably affronted by Chelmsford's impossible demands, dictated a proud and dignified reply. Despite his perilous situation, he deprecated negotiations while the British were advancing and plundering as they went. This letter never reached Chelmsford. The four messengers to whom it was entrusted were denied entry when they arrived before Fort Marshall on 22 June and, fearing they would be shot, returned with the note undelivered.

Vijn wrote again. The three messengers, Mgcwelo, Mtshibela and Mpokitwayo (who had first carried Chelmsford's written terms to Cetshwayo), were sent with Vijn's letter in a cleft stick, carrying two great tusks of ivory and driving a herd of 150 of the cattle captured at Isandlwana. They were intercepted on 27 June by a British patrol and brought into Chelmsford's camp on the Mthonjaneni heights, which his combined force had reached that day. The tone of this second letter was much more placatory than that of the undelivered one, and probably reflected Cetshwayo's cooler second thoughts. However, it did not come to grips with the conditions Chelmsford had laid down. The general consequently declared that he would continue his advance, and so would not accept the symbolic tusks. Nevertheless, in order to give the king a last chance to comply, he undertook not to cross the White Mfolozi immediately, and condescended to keep the cattle as a sign that he was still willing to negotiate.[48]

With this the messengers had to be content, and left the next day telling the interpreter as they went that they 'would have to fight now' as it was impossible for the king to comply with Chelmsford's terms.[49] For his part, the general remained prepared to 'stop hostilities' only if his conditions were complied with in full.[50] For though he credited Cetshwayo and his councillors with a genuine desire to end the war – their desperate situation required nothing less – he knew well it would still be only on their terms, and never on his.

The king's alarm and desire to negotiate had been greatly increased by political developments in the kingdom, especially in the path of the 1st Division's advance. Members of Chief Ndwandwe's peace delegation to Crealock at Fort Chelmsford on 15 May admitted that more chiefs would already have given themselves up but for fear and jealousy of the others. Spurred on by this intelligence, John Dunn immediately sent messages out to all the chiefs in the vicinity, inviting them to surrender, or to stay with their king and be destroyed.[51]

Two of Dunn's scouts were Mfazi and Fanane. The latter was a half-brother of Sigcwelegcwele, the influential *induna* of the iNgobamakhosi, and the two were sent to him at Ngoye to persuade him to surrender. There they found themselves vying with the king's messengers, sent to summon him to oNdini. Sigcwelegcwele compromised. He refused to go, but at the same time assured Dunn's messengers in public that he could not be the first to desert the king. But his true position (and that doubtless of many like him) came out in a subsequent private interview with his half-brother, Fanane. He vehemently declared the war to have been a great mistake on the part of the king, and professed himself and his people very much in favour of peace negotiations, since they were tired of fighting.[52]

The impression of Zulu war-weariness which the British were gaining was confirmed for other regions besides the coast. Cetshwayo's influence, it seemed ever more certain, was 'passing away'.[53] An example of the king's weakening hold was the response of Muhena, regent of the Mabhudu-Tsonga people to the north-east of Zululand, who had been regent for his nephew since 1876 only through Cetshwayo's support. In May Cetshwayo ordered him and the other chiefs in the region who were in a tributary relationship to the Zulu to join him with their forces as they had for the battle of Gingindlovu. At this stage H.E. O'Neill, the British Consul at Zanzibar, intervened, and persuaded Muhena not to comply with the king's demands. Instead, he ensured that Muhena pledged his support to the British.

Clear considerations in Muhena's decision were O'Neill's threats concerning future loss of independence should he aid Britain's enemies, coupled with promises of commercial advantages if he did not. As weighty, though, was the regent's belief that Cetshwayo must inevitably lose the war.[54] By the end of June his messengers were assuring the authorities in Natal that, far from still being Cetshwayo's ally, he was friendly towards the British and desired their protection against possible Zulu retaliation.

Yet it was further south along the coast that the series of most significant defections occurred, sufficient to deprive the king of his control of the whole southeast of his kingdom. In early June, just before the 1st Division was finally ready to commence its full advance, Dabulamanzi began at last to treat with the British, confirming earlier rumours that he intended doing so. On 8 June his messengers arrived at Fort Pearson, where Crealock maintained his headquarters until 17 June, and stated that he was 'anxious to come in', but that he had been dissuaded so far by messengers from the king who wished him to negotiate peace on his behalf.[55] A further private message towards the end of June from the prince and Mavumengwana assured the British that it was not out of deceit that they had failed to give themselves up. Ever since Prince Makwendu's defection on 21 April they had been closely watched, and were still awaiting a chance to slip away.

While Dabulamanzi and Mavumengwana gingerly negotiated, two other major figures along the coast hearkened to their people's yearning for peace and took positive steps to come to terms. Phalane, one of the commanders at Gingindlovu, and the even more distinguished Somopho, senior *induna* of the emaNgweni *ikhanda* and commander-in-chief at the same battle, sent to Crealock on 5 June admitting they were beaten and asking for terms. They took this step openly, for they also informed Cetshwayo that their men would not reassemble at oNdini, as he had ordered them to do.[56]

These overtures, coupled with a number of defections by minor chiefs along the coast, encouraged Chelmsford to formulate definitive terms for chiefs wishing to submit. He laid down that on surrender a chief, with a small personal following, would be relocated to British territory. They would hand over their arms and the royal cattle in their keeping, and the chief would instruct the *izinduna* left in charge of his adherents to submit once troops entered his district. In return, their people were to be spared and protected.[57]

During the third week of June the 1st Division began to reconnoitre the coast in the vicinity of the open landing-place at Port Durnford, through which it was to draw all its supplies after 9 July. The earlier naval identification of this landing-place had revitalised all the latent Zulu fears of an amphibious landing. On 24 April, when boats from the gunboat HMS *Forester* were taking soundings off Port Durnford, they were fired on from the beach by a large party of Zulu. The gunboat returned fire, killing over thirty cattle which had apparently been driven to the sea's edge to entice the British into landing. On 6 May there was a near repetition of the incident,[58] but by the time two steamers arrived with supplies at Port Durnford on 30 June, the Zulu had abandoned the vicinity.

Once the 1st Division crossed the Mlalazi on 22 June, its patrols became as aggressive as those of the 2nd Division and Flying Column. Successively on 23, 24, 26 and 30 June they scoured the countryside bounded by the Mlalazi, Port Durnford, the Mhlathuze and the foothills of the Ngoye range, driving the Zulu and their cattle into the sanctuary of the Ngoye forest. In the course of these punitive sorties, in which the Zulu made little attempt to resist, but fled leaving their stores of mealies intact and their potatoes sown, the British killed five Zulu and captured many others, besides lifting 378 cattle, 27 sheep and 29 goats. They also destroyed over fifty *imizi*, including the principal ones belonging to Sigcwelegcwele and Phalane. On 4 July a strong patrol under Major Barrow fulfilled one of the 1st Division's official objectives by burning the emaNgweni *ikhanda* and twelve *imizi* in its vicinity, as well as capturing 600 cattle. Ema-Ngweni consisted of 310 huts, and seems to have been unoccupied for some time. On 6 July Major Barrow and his men burned the 640 huts of the old oNdini *ikhanda*. Like emaNgweni, it was deserted and undefended.[59]

Meanwhile, the necessity of destroying the homes and livelihood of the coastal population, which seemed already resigned to submission, began to be questioned.[60] The destruction of the abandoned emaNgweni and the old oNdini did not divert a single warrior to their defence. Indeed, as was pointed out, there was almost no Zulu resistance at all in the coastal zone between the evacuation of the Eshowe garrison and the end of the war. Nevertheless, Crealock was undoubtedly partly right when he attributed the widespread and early submissions of the coastal population to their absolute lack of military success. The battles of Nyezane and Gingindlovu had been disasters, as had the blockade of Eshowe, while since April the Zulu had seen their country progressively occupied by laagers and forts, their *imizi* burned at will by the enemy and their livestock driven off.[61] Yet what probably weighed most heavily in the coastal people's decision to surrender was their sense that their king had turned his back on them. For while he bent all his energies towards warding off the British advance from the west, his coastal subjects were left at the mercy of the 1st Division's ruthless patrols.

On the same day the emaNgweni *ikhanda* was burned, and before the news of the battle of Ulundi could have been known, a number of chiefs surrendered to Crealock with 300 fighting-men, 1 500 women and children and 1 327 cattle.[62] They included Mbilwane, *induna* of the kwaGingindlovu *ikhanda*, and a commander at both Nyezane and Gingindlovu; Manyonyo kaZongolo, an *induna* of John Dunn's and an officer in the iNgobamakhosi (in 1861 he had commanded the detachment which had tracked down and killed Nomantshali, Mpande's favourite wife); and Hobana kaMzwakeli, chief of the Dube and also an officer in the iNgobamakhosi. At the same time, Somopho, Phalane, and the very influential *isikhulu* Chief Somkhele kaMalanda of the Mphukunyoni, a first cousin of the king (and an officer of the uThulwana) who dominated the northern coastal plain, as well as the *isikhulu* Chief Mlandlela kaMbiya of the Mthethwa, a cousin of the king and strongly under the influence of John Dunn, besides several other lesser *izinduna*, all sent word that they were 'coming in', and that the people as far north as St Lucia Bay wished to submit.

On 5 July the chiefs, all wearing a piece of coloured calico flowing loose over their bodies,[63] tendered their formal submissions at an impressive general parade of the 1st Division, where they were astonished at the playing of the bagpipes of the 91st Highlanders. After a harangue by Major-General Crealock, in which they were reminded that they were thoroughly beaten and must give up their allegiance to Cetshwayo, they were issued with passes and sent home.[64]

Crealock's lenient terms, which Frere had given him permission to devise, but which were accompanied by dire threats that *imizi* would be burnt and cattle confiscated if they were not complied with, offered the Zulu their lives and property in return for surrendering their arms and royal cattle.[65] This meant that the local economic and power structures were left minimally disturbed, and persuaded the war-weary people that in submitting they were sacrificing nothing essential. Thus, even before the battle of Ulundi had been fought, or its consequences could be thoroughly felt, and before much of the coastal plain had even been penetrated by the British, the entire region had abandoned the royal cause and come to terms with the invaders.

Yet the coast made up but part of the kingdom. Moreover, the fact that the chiefs of the region were submitting did not mean that the coastal elements of the *amabutho*, who had been mustering at oNdini since early June, would be unwilling to fight once more in defence of their king. During mid-June, the white trader Vijn, who was being held in northern Zululand, saw nothing but great numbers of fighting-men going up continually to join their comrades in the Mahlabathini plain.

By the third week of June the bulk of the Zulu army was assembled once more at oNdini and neighbouring *amakhanda* awaiting the king's instructions. Cetshwayo himself was at oNdini by about 24 June,[66] and his presence confirmed that he was determined to fight the British should they continue their advance.

No options remained save the military if he intended to keep his throne and his people's independence. The days had already passed when, like Mzilikazi, he could abandon Zululand and establish a kingdom to the north. His fate, and that of his kingdom, would be decided in the Mahlabathini plain.

25

What is There to Stop Them?[1]

Curiously, the last pitched battle of the war[2] – normally referred to by the Zulu as the battle of kwaNodwengu, after the *ikhanda* nearest which it was fought, and by the British as the battle of Ulundi, after their version of the name of Cetshwayo's capital – was once equally well known as oCwecweni, the battle of the corrugated-iron sheets.[3] Doubtless, it was the flashing of the bayonets, swords and gun-barrels along the four sides of the compact British formation which gave rise to this impression. The king himself always maintained that the British had fought from behind iron shields,[4] a view genuinely held by many Zulu who had taken part in the battle. Indeed, some went so far as to insist that the British had hung red coats on the iron palings in front of them, off which the Zulu bullets had harmlessly bounced.[5] Perhaps all such tales were necessary for the Zulu to explain why they, having caught the British in the open, away at last from their forts and entrenched laagers, had yet been unable to overcome them.

There is a tendency among historians today to underrate both the intensity and the significance of the battle. The argument is that the British exaggerated the significance of their victory in order to restore the tarnished image of white invincibility among the black people of southern Africa. Whereas, in fact, the swift ending of hostilities after the battle was the consequence not of a decisive victory in the field, but of the desire on both sides to have a rapid end to the war, and of the lenient British peace terms which made submission acceptable to the Zulu.[6] Certainly, there is considerable truth to this argument, but it underestimates the possible repercussions of a military encounter. There is more than enough evidence to show that this final overthrow of his army was fatal for the king's authority and the continued existence of his kingdom.

On 26 June, as Chelmsford's joint force approached Mthonjaneni from Babanango, they came in sight of the *amakhanda* in the emaKhosini valley. Since it was established policy to destroy all such along the line of march, Wood, with a strong mounted force backed up by artillery and the NNC, moved down into the valley with the intention of putting the *amakhanda* to the torch. When the two 9-pounder guns opened fire on the *amakhanda* from long range, a Zulu force of between 500 and 600 men of the uNokhenke and uMxhapho, who had been stationed at esiKlebheni, hastily retired. Before they retreated, they did as their fathers had done with uMgungundlovu, and set three of the *amakhanda* on fire.

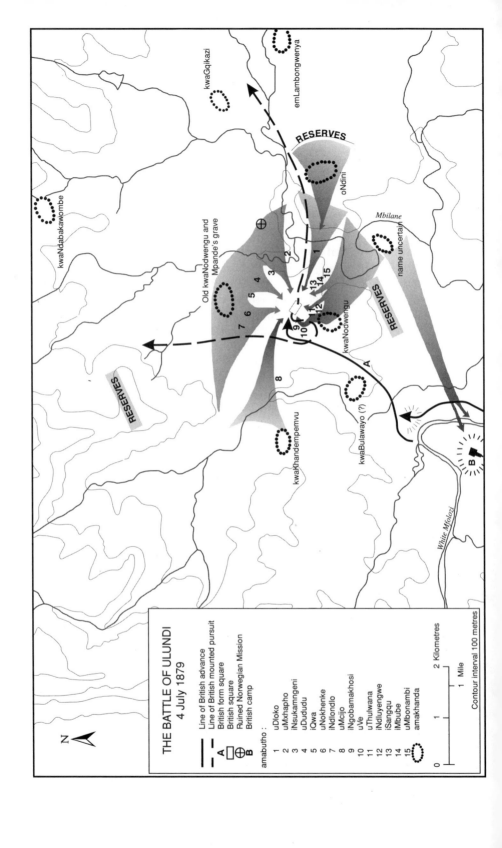

THE BATTLE OF ULUNDI
4 July 1879

Line of British advance
Line of British mounted pursuit
British form square
British square
Ruined Norwegian Mission
British camp

amabutho :

1   uDloko
2   uMxhapho
3   iNsukamngeni
4   uDududu
5   iQwa
6   uNokhenke
7   iNdlondlo
8   uMcijo
9   iNgobamakhosi
10 uVe
11 uThulwana
12 iNdluyengwe
13 iSangqu
14 iMbube
15 uMbonambi
    amakhanda

0   1   2 Kilometres
0   1 Mile

Contour interval 100 metres

N

kwaGqikazi
emLambongwenya
RESERVES
oNdini
Mbilane
kwaNdabakawombe
Old kwaNodwengu and
Mpande's grave
name uncertain
kwaNodwengu
RESERVES
RESERVES
kwaKhandempemvu
kwaBulawayo (?)
White Mfolozi

The British, when they finally reached the scene, burned six more and the immense quantities of mealies stored in them. The burnt *amakhanda*, whose sites are known today, were esiKlebheni, kwaDukuza, kwaKhangela, ezinGwegweni, kwaNobamba, and emaKheni. The whereabouts of the remaining three – oDlabedlwini, oQeketheni and ekuDabukeni – have still to be established.[7]

Unknowingly, Wood had committed a terrible act of the greatest symbolic importance to the Zulu. The *inkatha*, handed down from King Shaka himself, the symbol of Zulu unity and very nationhood, was consumed in the flames of esiKlebheni where it was kept. Its destruction was an unmistakable forewarning of the imminent fall of the Zulu kingdom.

On 27 June, when the flashing light of the British heliograph alerted the Zulu in the Mahlabathini plain to their arrival on the Mthonjaneni heights, preparations were made for the king to retire to the north. His *isigodlo* girls collected all his personal belongings and stored them in a deep cave in Hlophekhulu Mountain, five kilometres to the south-east of oNdini. (After Cetshwayo's capture, the men who had helped hide them retrieved them for their own use.)[8]

Chelmsford, meanwhile, had become painfully aware that he was to be subordinated in his military command to General Sir Garnet Wolseley, whom the British government had sent out to end the embarrassing war in Zululand with speed and honour. The dapper and waspish Wolseley had assured his reputation as a commander in the field during the punitive Ashanti campaign of 1873. He was untiring (if untactful) in his efforts to modernise the British Army, and assembled about him a 'ring' of officers chosen for their distinguished war service or promise, rather than for their seniority in the service.

Wolseley not unnaturally alienated the 'bow-and-arrow generals' (among whom he classed Chelmsford) with his pushy and scornful ways, and they in turn made no secret that they deplored his advanced military ideas and calls for drastic reform. Here was a man under whom Chelmsford could never consent to work, especially since he knew that Wolseley was eager to delay operations until he could arrive at the front to take both personal command and credit for the final defeat of the Zulu. If Chelmsford were to achieve the victory that might wipe out the shame of Isandlwana and the Prince Imperial's death, he would have to act with despatch.[9]

Before he could march down into the plain, however, it was first necessary to prepare a strong base at Mthonjaneni. Three strong wagon-laagers were constructed and garrisoned with two companies of the 1/24th and a unit made up of one NCO and two privates drawn from each company in the joint force.[10] The work was hurried on when large Zulu forces moving about immediately below Mthonjaneni seemed to confirm fears that the base might be attacked once Chelmsford had moved forward with the bulk of his force.

At 8.45 on the morning of Monday, 30 June, Chelmsford led some 5 500 men out of their camp on the Mthonjaneni heights. The men of Wood's more seasoned Flying Column were in advance of those of the 2nd Division. All were lightly equipped, marching without kits or tents, and with rations for only ten days. Supplies were carried in 200 ox-wagons, and there were mule-carts for the regimental reserve ammunition. Cavalry reconnoitring to their front soon spotted three armed bodies of Zulu, each about 5 000 strong, on the move towards the White Mfolozi. Their purpose was clearly to guard the drifts should the British attempt to cross. But the invaders did not proceed beyond the foot of Mthonja-neni. After a difficult march of only eight kilometres through the thick thorn-veld, they halted at about 3.30 p.m. by a small stream on the sandy, bush-covered flats, and there formed their encampment.[11]

At midday, while the British were still laboriously on the move down Mtho-njaneni, the king's footsore messengers, Mfunzi and Nkisimana, finally ran their elusive quarry to ground. These persistent emissaries carried yet a third let-ter penned by Vijn. In earnest of their mission they presented the sword taken from the body of the Prince Imperial, and promised the speedy arrival of the two captured 7-pounders and more cattle.[12] Yet unbeknown to them, Vijn had done the king an evil turn. The letter carried a postscript in which the trader in-formed Chelmsford that it was his opinion that the king and people, if not the princes and chiefs, still intended to fight to the end.

This warning seemed only too likely to Chelmsford and, determined at all costs to have his face-saving battle, he responded to this latest Zulu embassy by modifying his earlier terms. He now declared himself prepared to accept 1 000 rifles captured at Isandlwana in lieu of the surrender of an *ibutho*. Further-more, he announced that Cetshwayo had until noon on 3 July to comply with his conditions, and that his troops would remain on his side of the White Mfolozi up to that moment.

Lest one should be tempted to applaud Chelmsford's apparent magnaminity and readiness to avoid further bloodshed, two things should be noted. His con-cession – only a gesture that could make no difference to Cetshwayo's inability to comply – was calculated to appeal to the British public's sense of fair play. Sec-ondly, and more significantly, the difficult terrain at the foot of Mthonjaneni made it almost impossible for cavalry to operate, and Chelmsford was concerned that the Zulu might attempt to attack his force while strung out on the line of march. Dubious diplomacy would shield the British until they were through that par-ticular danger and had reached the White Mfolozi.

As it turned out, Chelmsford's disingenuous new offer never reached Cetshwayo, for Mfunzi was prevented by the king's councillors from seeing him. The coun-cillors were already 'hopeless and desperate' and had no desire to prolong ne-gotiations which they recognised to be a pointless sham.[13] Nevertheless, the Zulu did not take the opportunity to attack Chelmsford between Mthonjaneni and the river. They were reluctant to attack the advancing column in the thornveld because they anticipated that this would cause the British to form a laager, and they still hoped to be able to attack them when they reached the open.[14]

The British resumed their advance at 7.30 a.m. on 1 July with the Flying Col-umn in the lead, and Buller and his mounted men reached the drift across the White Mfolozi at about 10.40 a.m.[15] From the vantage-point of a small koppie they were able to watch the Zulu army manoeuvring in the plain beyond. These experienced men of the Flying Column realised that the Zulu were not forming up for an immediate attack, but were being drilled and ritually purified and strengthened in preparation for the fighting to come. Some *amabutho*, about 8 000 strong, came chanting and marching in companies from an *ikhanda* in the extreme north-west of the plain (almost certainly kwaKhandempemvu) and filed into the kwaNodwengu *ikhanda* in splendid order. Within half an hour four more *amabutho* were seen on the march from various points to the emLambongwenya *ikhanda* north-east of oNdini, where the king had gone that morning to address his *amabutho*.[16] There they formed up, filling the space in a huge circle, and at about 11.40 a.m., duly prepared, poured out in three long, broad columns, causing even Buller's veterans to fear for a moment that they intended to attack. In fact, the British need not have been alarmed, for Cetshwayo had instructed his *amabutho* to bar any British attempt to cross the river, but not to fire first upon them.

Convinced that the Zulu were not planning an offensive that day, the Flying Column began calmly to construct its laager about a kilometre from the drift. But before it was completed, and while the wagons of the 2nd Division were still on the road, at about 1 p.m. a sudden Zulu movement towards the river caused a panic among the British, especially the less experienced 2nd Division.[17] The Zulu did not take advantage of the invaders' patent state of disarray, and by 5 p.m. the *amabutho* had all retired to their quarters, a possibly great opportunity missed.

That night it poured with rain, and sleep was made no easier for the nervous British by a false alarm which started another demoralising panic.[18] The following morning, 2 July, the 2nd Division moved forward to join the Flying Column, and formed an entrenched double wagon-laager anchored on a small, stone-built fort. The whole position was designed so that a small garrison could effectively defend the position when the main force advanced across the river.

While the British were strengthening their position, Zibhebhu, who was possessed of a keen tactical eye, decided to ignore the king's injunction not to fire on the British until they had crossed the river. He posted marksmen in the rocks on a high bluff overlooking the river just below the drift. From there they opened fire on British details clearing the way down to the crossing-place. They also shot at watering and bathing parties, provoking a lively stampede of naked British soldiers to the safety of their laager. British pickets were hurried up to return the Zulu fire, and soon pinned the Zulu down behind their rocks. One of Mnyamana's sons, who had gone down with other young men to collect wood, was wounded by the British fire.[19] Meanwhile, the British continued with the routine of the camp, and the Zulu were intrigued by the distant sight of companies of soldiers leaving the laagers at regular intervals, squatting down in a row, and then returning. With their own purification rituals in mind, they thought they were witnessing a war-rite, and were disabused only after the war when they had the opportunity to inspect what turned out to be the British latrine trenches.[20]

Feeling more secure as their fortified post took shape, the British ceased to be disturbed by the regular movements of large bodies of Zulu across the river. These conformed to a routine of their own. On 2 July and on the following day, the Zulu advanced on the river in the morning. Having made their show of strength and hopefully deterred the British from attempting a crossing, they then returned at about 9 a.m. to the vicinity of kwaNodwengu to cook a meal before marching off again in the direction of oNdini.[21]

Later on 2 July Cetshwayo made his last attempt to treat with the invader. He ordered a herd of at least a hundred of the royal white oxen to be driven towards the British camp as a peace offering. But the young men of the uMcijo turned them back, declaring that there would be no surrender while there were still warriors left to defend their king.[22] The king was not impressed with the uMcijo's impulsive action, which threatened to take the final decision on fighting out of his and his councillors' hands. In a powerful speech to his *amabutho* gathered at oNdini, he made it clear that he considered the uMcijo's gesture foolhardy, for he was convinced that the British must inevitably win, seeing that the Zulu armies in the past had been unable to halt their advance. Moreover, he voiced his very realistic fear that in defeat his army would disperse, leaving him no option but flight and ultimate capture.

At this, his warriors protested and swore that they would defend him to the last. The king knew better, and sternly warned them that if they did fight, it was against his advice.[23] But seeing that his *amabutho* were determined to offer battle, he issued his instructions. They were not to attack the British when stationary, for that would suggest they had entrenched, and bitter experience had shown the fatal consequences of an attack against a prepared position. And even if they did manage to catch them in the open and defeat them, the *amabutho* were not to pursue the British across the river for fear of the guns in the double laager.

So the final battle was not to be avoided, and that night the anxious British saw all around them the camp-fires of the Zulu, eager to prove themselves against the invader.[24]

Soon after daybreak on Thursday, 3 July, Zulu sharpshooters on the bluff commanding the drift again began firing away at watering-parties and bathers, and sent some shots into the fortified camp. One of these snipers was later found by the British to have made himself remarkably comfortable, with straw to sit on, a bough bent over his head for shade, his snuff in a crevice before him, and a rock conveniently placed on which to rest his rifle.[25] Although a company of the 1/24th answered their fire, the Zulu were too well concealed for this to deter their persistent sniping.

Punctually at noon, when the space Chelmsford had allowed for a reply to his conditions of 30 June had expired, the cattle Cetshwayo had sent in on 27 June as proof of his genuine desire to negotiate were driven symbolically back across the river. Now that all pretence at negotiation was at an end, Chelmsford was free to send a reconnaissance in force under Buller of approximately 500 mounted men of the Flying Column across the river.[26]

At about 1 p.m., while a few shells from two 9-pounder guns distracted the Zulu concealed on the bluff, about a hundred men under Commandant Baker crossed by the wagon drift and made straight for the Zulu position. Buller and the larger part of his force forded the river downstream and wheeled to take the Zulu position from the south. Racing over broken terrain that would have been impossible for regular cavalry, Baker's men were first among the Zulu, who were quite taken off their guard. About thirty of them on the crest of the bluff let fly a volley before fleeing, while the rest bolted in every direction. Baker's men pursued them some way before regrouping.

Noting that the Zulu were rapidly concentrating in some force on the surrounding hills to the west, Baker sent a small party to warn Buller, who was still in pursuit, of the threat to his left rear.[27] But Buller, having achieved his first objective of driving off the Zulu snipers, was intent on completing his second, which was to advance as far as possible along the road to oNdini, both to observe the ground and to decide where the best position would be to fight a battle. From Mthonjaneni he had already singled out the gently rolling country to the west of oNdini as the ideal situation for cavalry action against the Zulu, and was determined to investigate the spot. Though he did not know it, he was about to lead his men into a most cunningly devised ambush, similar to the one into which the Zulu had tempted the Voortrekkers on 27 December 1838.

When Buller's horsemen emerged from the bush near the river into the open grassy plain, they encountered some twenty Zulu scouts who had been deliberately placed to lure them on in the direction of kwaNodwengu – exactly where they intended to go anyway. With great skill and courage the Zulu scouts ran before the horsemen, leading them as far as kwaNodwengu, where other Zulu, driving a large flock of goats, were deployed to draw them towards oNdini. Galloping Zulu horsemen, of whom Zibhebhu was one, then took up the task and brought Buller's force to the valley of the Mbilane stream, where the ambush was prepared.

About 4 000 Zulu, among whom the uMxhapho were prominent (the same who had lain in ambush at Nyezane), were concealed in two lines at right-angles to the British right. The long grass near the banks of the stream had been carefully plaited to trip or impede the horses. But the experienced Buller was beginning to sense a trap, and called a halt when a Zulu presence in the grass was noticed. Upon this, the concealed Zulu rose and poured a great volley at the British at about seventy metres' range. Fortunately for the horsemen, the Zulu fire was as high and inaccurate as ever, and the startled British instantly wheeled about. They were still in grave danger, for two other Zulu forces had been hiding on both flanks as they had passed unwittingly between them, and these two now began to close together to cut off escape back to the laagers.

Buller was saved by his foresight. He had ordered Commandant Raaff to halt near kwaNodwengu with his horsemen as supports, so that when Buller's portion of the force fell back from the ambush, Raaff was able to cover his retreat. Baker's men, who were still near the bluff, supplied cover in their turn, and were supported by fire from the two 9-pounders and from some infantry on the other side of the river. Even so, Buller was lucky to reach the drift before the Zulu could cut him off, with the loss of no more than three killed and four wounded.

The experience had been something of a shock to the British. They could not but admit that the Zulu had shown themselves to be excellent strategists, and that they had been extremely well led. In particular, they had to admire the professional Zulu skirmishing order as they came down the hill to the drift in pursuit of Buller, and the courageous manner in which, despite the storm of fire from the guns and rifles, they had followed the horsemen right to the river's edge. For their part, the Zulu were naturally much elated with their near success, and were encouraged to believe that they could not but have an easy victory should the British venture again into the open.[28] Some Zulu who later came down to the river's edge chaffed the British outposts and with derisive laughs gloated over their victory that day, promising that none would escape should the British again leave the protection of their laager.[29]

Yet the British were well content. Their dangerous sortie had called forth some acts of gallantry which had improved the morale of the army, and Buller had been able to fix on the ideal position for the coming battle. (Ironically, this very spot, just to the north-east of kwaNodwengu, had also been selected by Cetshwayo as the place where the British should be brought to battle.)[30] Moreover, the reconnaissance had had the effect of drawing the Zulu out and so had revealed their points of concentration and given some indication of their numbers. And perhaps most important of all, the Zulu had revealed what tactics they were likely to adopt. Clearly, their intention would be to surround the British and to cut them off from their base on the opposite bank. With this detailed intelligence, Chelmsford was in a position to move with confidence across the river the following day to complete the defeat of the Zulu.

It was a bitterly cold night of bright moonlight. The British were startled at about 11 p.m. by a sound which seemed at first like distant thunder, but was in fact the noise of the Zulu *amabutho* being prepared for their last great battle. The roar of men's voices and the shrill cries of the women as they danced and sang were quite terrifying for the British.[31] Some of the singing came from a large contingent who had arrived that very night from the coast and were greeting the king. Blacks with the British force made out some of the words of the songs, the refrains of which consisted of defiance of the British and laments over the men who had fallen that day.[32]

There was much movement as the Zulu marched from *ikhanda* to *ikhanda*, and at one stage they approached the river, firing off occasional shots. At that point the British thought they were about to be attacked, and went on the alert. But the Zulu did not normally fight at night and, still singing, marched away at about midnight, apparently to take up their positions for the next day. The sleepless British remained in expectation of an attack, at daybreak by the latest. Their nerves were not calmed at the sight of Zulu campfires and signal lights, not only across the river, but behind them as well.[33] They could have no doubt that the Zulu were fully mustered and prepared for the great battle that must finally decide the war.

At 3.45 a.m. on that fateful Friday, 4 July 1879, the British began in bright moonlight to breakfast and form up in column preparatory to crossing the river. The total strength of the force being marshalled was 4 166 white and 958 black soldiers, 12 pieces of artillery and 2 Gatling guns. At 5.15 a.m. the bugles sounded a bogus reveille at the normal hour in a feeble attempt to deceive the watching Zulu into supposing that nothing untoward was in progress. As day broke the British began to cross the river. They left behind them five companies of the 1/24th in the laager and one company of Royal Engineers in the fort, as well as other small detachments – 529 white and 93 black troops in all. Colonel W. Bellairs was in command, and it was his duty to hold the camp should the Zulu attempt to capture the British base once the main force was committed in the plain.

Buller's mounted irregulars crossed by the lower drift at about 6 a.m. and took up position on the bluff overlooking the drift by which the rest of the force was to advance. The Flying Column was over the river by 6.45 a.m. In its rear the 2nd Division had crossed some time after 7 a.m., moving in parallel column. The regular cavalry brought up the rear. As the troops waded across the White Mfolozi they eyed the thickly bushed opposite bank with some apprehension, for although Buller commanded the bluff which he had cleared the previous day of snipers, they still expected the Zulu to oppose them. They need not have been concerned, however. The Zulu plan was to allow the British into the plain and to force them to fight in the open, so they could be destroyed as at Isandlwana. The Zulu commanders feared that if they attacked them at the drift before they were properly across, the British would fall back on their impregnable fortified position.[34]

So the British moved onto the opposite bank without a shot fired. About 2,5 kilometres from the drift, when at 7.30 a.m. they had struggled through the rough and bushy ground into the open country, the Flying Column halted with the great circle of huts of what was probably the kwaBulawayo *ikhanda* to their left. While Buller's men continued to reconnoitre in the direction of kwaNodwengu, the Flying Column formed the front half of a hollow square, which was completed by the 2nd Division marching up behind them. The regular British infantry were ranged four deep, with the guns distributed at the faces and at the angles where the formation was most vulnerable. At this stage all the mounted men continued outside the square, but reserve companies (who might be required to plug a gap), the Royal Engineers, attached Native Pioneers, the NNC, ammunition-wagons, water-carts, stretchers and medical personnel all took up position inside. After arranging the square, Chelmsford drilled the troops for a while in their formation. Shortly before 8 a.m. the square set off towards the north-east, following a route between the kwaBulawayo and kwaNodwengu *amakhanda*.[35]

Chelmsford's square was already an archaic formation in European warfare, devised originally as an infantry tactic for repelling cavalry. Yet this shoulder-to-shoulder formation was finding a new lease of life in colonial warfare, where it was particularly effective in all-round defence against an enemy who sought like cavalry to envelop flank and rear with great rapidity, and then to overwhelm the European invaders with shock tactics and superior numbers. Isandlwana had demonstrated that a widely spaced firing-line (even when equipped with the most sophisticated weapons), though necessary in European warfare against a similarly armed enemy, was ineffective against such an attack. On the other hand, the experiences of Rorke's Drift, Khambula and Gingindlovu had demonstrated conclusively that the Zulu had little chance against disciplined, concentrated fire by well-drilled troops in an all-round position.

An infantry square was naturally not as secure as an entrenched laager or fort, but it possessed their other tactical advantages and its tight formation improved the confidence of the troops. Moreover, once an enemy's attack had broken before the square's disciplined ranks, he would be vulnerable to a devastating counter-attack by cavalry, which had been kept in reserve within the safety of the square. The square's chief disadvantage, which was vulnerability to effective gunfire, did not apply in Zululand. Zulu marksmanship in all the previous battles of the war had proved to be poor, and was not expected to have improved sufficiently to pose any real threat.[36]

But over and above such purely military advantages, there was a decided moral point to be gained by Chelmsford adopting the square. As Wood told the men of the Flying Column on the night before the battle, they were going to form square to prove to the Zulu that they could beat them as thoroughly in the open plain as from behind a fortified laager, so demonstrating that further resistance would be quite pointless.[37]

A square, though, was a clumsy formation to manoeuvre. Thus in unavoidably jerky fashion it proceeded in rather loose formation across the grassy plain. It escaped harassment, for Buller's men were fanned out in advance and about 800 metres away on the flanks to 'touch' the Zulu and keep their skirmishers away. The irregular horse of the 2nd Division, who made up part of the rearguard, set light to kwaBulawayo as they passed. On approaching kwaNodwengu, Chelmsford ordered the square to 'half-right turn', so that the *ikhanda* remained on his right flank and the front of the square now faced oNdini.

The British continued to advance for another ten minutes until, at about 8.30 a.m., the spot Buller had selected the previous day was reached. As the Zulu were now approaching in battle order, the square halted to receive them, manoeuvring slightly to occupy the most favourable part of the ground. The guns were got into position and the ammunition boxes opened. While the men standing in the rear of the four ranks filled the gaps between the men standing in the third, the front two ranks kneeled. All fixed their bayonets. Wood's men began to throw up a slight shelter trench outside their part of the battle formation.

The position was ideal for the battle the British hoped to fight. The ground sloped gently down for several hundred metres on every side from the level top of the slight knoll, providing a perfect field of fire and scope for cavalry pursuit. It was uncommanded from any point, and there was little bush for cover, only the long grass. There Buller's men found the naked corpses of their comrades who had been killed in the reconnaissance of the previous day, and whom the Zulu had ritually disembowelled. The British hastily buried them in the precincts of a ruined Norwegian mission just in front of the square. The mission's remains were then pulled down to open the range.[38]

When at daybreak the Zulu saw the British crossing the White Mfolozi without the great number of wagons necessary to form a defensive laager, they thought the invaders must have taken leave of their senses so to deliver themselves into their hands.[39] The Zulu intention was to surround and annihilate the square once it reached the chosen battleground between kwaNodwengu and oNdini. Perhaps the British were right to have believed that the Zulu would have been wiser to attack them while they were busy forming their square, or were still in the broken ground unsuitable for cavalry – but that was not the Zulu plan. In fact, it was only at about 8 a.m., as they were approaching kwaNodwengu, that the British first saw the Zulu gathering in any strength, and divined that it was their intention (as they had expected it would be) to envelop the square.

To the west an estimated six *amaviyo* were collecting, and twelve *amaviyo* were forming 1 350 metres to the north.[40] These bodies continued to swell as they were joined by warriors streaming out of the *amakhanda*, so that the British were acutely conscious of the dark clusters of Zulu lining the crests of the hill-tops to their left. These Zulu, moving at first in a straggling column parallel to the British square, began to form up in good order for the attack. To the east, in the stream-beds of the thornveld around oNdini, great masses of warriors began to appear through the early morning mists and the smoke from their campfires which had previously obscured them.

The Zulu on the hills and in the thornveld to the left, front and right of the British square first joined up to form the classic crescent battle formation. Then, at about 8.20 a.m., the concentration to the front and right of the square extended at the double to pass around kwaNodwengu to the rear of the square, and so to complete a great circle around the British, over fourteen kilometres in length.

While the British were advancing on kwaNodwengu, two Zulu forces, perhaps about 5 000 strong, were moving out of an *ikhanda* near the river to the right of them (whose name it has not been possible to establish) in the direction of the entrenched camp across the White Mfolozi. It is conceivable that their intention had been to dispute the British crossing and that they had been caught un-awares by their early start. More likely, their purpose was to capture the British base and cut off the square's retreat. At 8.10 a.m. the two forces came close enough to the drift for the garrison of the post to go on the alert,[41] and some Zulu even crossed the river and came to within 450 metres of the laager. However, they never seriously threatened the garrison, and soon melted away to join in the battle developing in the plain.

There, the British watching the Zulu advance could only wonder at the skill and timing which, considering the difficult terrain and the varying distances they had to traverse, allowed the Zulu units to synchronise their envelopment. As the Zulu moved down the hills towards them, they appeared at first to the British to be almost indistinguishable from the aloes that covered the slopes. It was soon apparent, though, that the Zulu were closing in, keeping the most 'splendid order' in loose undulating lines of companies about four deep, with intervals between the *amabutho*, followed by others in file to the rear.[42] They were preceded by irregular waves of skirmishers (just as 'modern tactics' required, the admiring British noted,[43] not for the first time), who opened a desultory fire at a great distance.

In all, the Zulu advance was a revelation to the recent British reinforcements who, unlike the veterans of the Flying Column, had not before met the Zulu in pitched battle, and who had been led to expect a rush from dense, irregular masses rather than the 'beautiful', 'splendid manoeuvering' in half-open order which they were witnessing.[44]

Contemporaries could not agree on the size of the Zulu army converging on the British square. The official British estimation was 20 000,[45] though the figure of 15 000 engaged and between 5 000 and 8 000 in reserve is probably the more accurate.[46] All the *amabutho* were represented.[47] Despite reports to the contrary, the king was not in personal command of his army that day. Having instructed his generals, he had left oNdini on the evening of 3 July, and had travelled east with his *isigodlo* to the emLambongwenya *ikhanda* of his father Mpande. The iNdabakawombe *ibutho* acted as escort.[48] Early the next morning messengers arrived with the news that the British were advancing across the river. On learning this, the king moved further away to his kwaMbonambi *ikhanda*, followed later by his *isigodlo*. He was at kwaMbonambi throughout the battle, and had lookouts posted to give him news of the outcome.[49] Ziwedu kaMpande, his favourite brother and a man of talent and good sense, who stood in status among the princes second only to Hamu (who had betrayed them all), watched the battle from the Mcungi Hill. It was Ziwedu's presence which was popularly mistaken for that of the king.[50]

With Ziwedu were other of the king's brothers and many of the great chiefs. It is not known conclusively who these were. Mnyamana, for example, left the king on the morning of 4 July and rejoined him after the battle, so it is probable but unproven that he was with Ziwedu. As with Mnyamana, it is likely that other close advisers of the king's, such as Ntshingwayo, Sihayo and his son Mehlokazulu, Qethuka, Mtuzwa (the brother of Sekethwayo), and Muwundula (brother of the emGazini chief and *induna* of kwaNodwengu) – all of whom were reported to have attended what was probably Cetshwayo's last formal meeting with his councillors on 2 July – witnessed the battle.[51] Not one of them, though, came to the fore during its course. There was nothing unusual about this, it must be remembered, for it was normal for high-ranking Zulu officers to station themselves at a vantage-point some distance from the battle, and Ntshingwayo's close involvement at Khambula had been most unusual.

There is a degree more certainty over the actual Zulu order of battle. The uDloko *ibutho* came straight at the front of the British square. The encircling left horn consisted of the uThulwana, iNdluyengwe, iSangqu, iMbube and uMbonambi. The Zulu right horn was made up of the uMxhapho, iNsukamngeni, uDududu, iQwa, uNokhenke and iNdlondlo *amabutho*. The iNgobamakhosi and uVe attacked the right rear of the square, and the uMcijo the left rear.[52] It seems too, despite the regent Muhena's withdrawal of his support from the Zulu cause, that some Tsonga were also present. Elements of other *amabutho* either went unnamed because they were few in number, or because they made up the reserves which never fully joined in the attack.

To meet the imminent attack of the Zulu army, the British intended to employ standard tactics. The square was a defensive formation, dependent on develop-

314

ing sufficient fire to mow down an enemy charge and bring it to a standstill before getting close enough for hand-to-hand combat. For fire to be effective, it was essential to ensure that it was accurate and well-disciplined, and that it was reserved until the enemy are well into range, or no further than about 630 metres away.[53] To open fire too early would not only be ineffective, but might have the additional disadvantage of scaring off the enemy before its full effect could be felt. The initial objective then, was to tempt the Zulu into effective range.

The case of Khambula had already demonstrated how effective irregular horse could be as a decoy, especially in provoking uncoordinated charges that could be dealt with most successfully in detail. This successful tactic was repeated, while the regular cavalry of the 2nd Division (the 17th Lancers and the small detachment of Dragoons), who considered the terrain not suitable and the Zulu line too powerful to be charged, entered the rear of the square.[54] Their particular skills would only be of use once the Zulu were in retreat.

Buller's irregular horsemen in advance of the square became engaged with the Zulu between 8.35 and 8.45 a.m. They followed the Boer mode of combat, fighting in two ranks. The front rank remained mounted and ready to dash at a weak spot in the enemy's line, while the second rank dismounted, using their saddles to rest their rifles. As soon as the first rank became too hotly pressed they cantered to the rear, dismounted, and relieved the second rank, who mounted in turn and repeated the procedure.

It was Baker's Horse who first made contact with the Zulu. They advanced towards the left horn of the rapidly closing Zulu formation, who broke up and scattered into skirmishing order when they saw the horsemen coming. Lieutenant Parmenter cantered ahead with about twenty men and poured a volley into the Zulu at the short range of about 180 metres. Furious at being bearded by so small a body, the Zulu fired at random and rushed forward to cut Parmenter off – unsuccessfully.[55]

The greatest admiration of the British infantry was reserved, however, for Captain Cochrane's Natal Native Horse, who were in advance of the right of the square. Slowly and deliberately they fell back, pouring volley after volley into the advancing Zulu. They were, in fact, under the impression that they were to remain outside the square – as some had stayed outside Khambula camp, skirmishing throughout that battle. They consequently only retired reluctantly into the square. But their leisurely withdrawal had the effect of hurrying on the Zulu advance. Irritated Zulu called tauntingly after them: 'Gallop on, but we will overtake you. We are going to kill every one of those red men!'[56]

All of Buller's men in addition to the units already mentioned were soon heavily engaged on three sides, and the various corps retired independently on the square with equal regularity and steadiness, drawing the Zulu behind them.[57] Meanwhile, Shepstone's Horse, who were attached to the 2nd Division, waited to the left rear of the square for the uMcijo to come on in a great column more than thirty deep, firing wildly, waving their shields and shouting 'uSuthu!' Shepstone's Horse opened fire at 270 metres range before retiring slowly into the square before them. As they fell back the artillery opened fire over their heads.[58] Soon all the horsemen were safely back in the square, the front and rear faces of which had wheeled outwards to receive them, before closing again to face the Zulu. The battle was about to begin in earnest.

The 9-pounder guns fired their first shot at 8.45 a.m. when the Zulu were well within range 990 metres away. Soon the guns on all four sides of the square, where they were dispersed to meet the Zulu envelopment, were firing away, at this stage from positions just outside the formation. The Zulu, mainly because they were in skirmishing order, suffered little damage at first, though some were staggered by the bursting shells, and a few scattered.[59]

Perhaps there is some truth in the observation that the shrapnel eventually 'took the dash' out of the Zulu attack,[60] but this was not immediately apparent, for the Zulu instantly rallied with the intention of rushing in. Their great circle surrounding the square contracted to within 270 metres, or close range for the Martini-Henry rifles and Gatling guns, so that small-arm fire joined that of the guns. At 8.50 a.m. the fire from the square became general, though the right face, where the Natal Native Horse had drawn on the Zulu so effectively, came into action a few moments before the other three.

The Zulu advanced into this terrible fire still in skirmishing order, but with large masses behind in support.[61] They closed in steadily and in silence, and only uttered their war-cry, 'uSuthu!' when they were preparing for the final rush. Those who made this desperate charge were stripped for battle of all finery, and were fine, well-made men of the younger *amabutho*. Indeed, the perfect state of their teeth was to be a matter of admiration for the British when they later inspected the dead.[62]

In the main, the Zulu attack brought them no closer than between sixty-three and ninety metres of the British position, or within point blank range. There were individual exceptions, like the young warrior who was shot fruitlessly throwing his spear at six paces.[63] But, generally, the Zulu had learned from their experiences at both Khambula and Gingindlovu, and were acutely familiar with the devastating effect of concentrated British fire at close and point blank range. Nor should there be any doubt that their string of defeats had affected their confidence and shaken their earlier sense of invincibility. Mehlokazulu even stated that the Zulu at Ulundi did not fight with 'the same spirit, because [they] were then frightened'.[64]

Yet, what this evidence amounts to is not so much proof that the Zulu attack was half-hearted,[65] but that the Zulu had acquired a realistic appreciation of what they were up against. They now knew when it was pointless to persist in an attack. As Colonel W.A. Dunne commented, though the Zulu bravery was conspicuous, they were no longer prepared to display the reckless daring so evident in earlier battles.[66] There is overwhelming evidence to show that in the initial stages of the battle, before the hopelessness of their task overcame them, the Zulu came on with enormous pluck, advancing with the 'same intrepidity' as at Khambula and Gingindlovu.[67] Indeed, many of the British were simply astonished at the 'amazing courage' of the Zulu, who repeatedly and unflinchingly attempted to charge through the withering fire. The newspaper artist, Melton

Prior, could only reflect that of all the campaigns in which he had taken part, never before had he come across so courageous a foe, nor one which he could feel more pride in seeing beaten.[68]

The British were confident of their ability to crush the Zulu assault, and the men of the 1/13th Regiment were seen beckoning to the Zulu and shouting, 'Come on, you black devils!'[69] Sheer volume of fire was just as important as the casualties inflicted by it, for if it could be maintained (which it certainly was by the four-deep British formation at Ulundi), that was sufficient to deter the fiercest attack. The Zulu were a hard target to hit because of their open order and their wonderful use of whatever cover was available. Those advancing were seen running in a crouching position behind their shields, while the masses lay in the high grass (the British had only managed to beat down the grass for a few metres outside their square), and afforded no target except the smoke of their firing. This was probably the reason for much high volley-firing from the square, which saved the Zulu casualties.[70] In addition, the volume of smoke aided the Zulu, as the British could not see many metres ahead because of it.

The smoke from their weapons was made worse by the billows given off by kwaNodwengu, which the British had set alight as they passed, and Chelmsford very soon had to order the fire there to be extinguished. Every now and again the bugles had to sound the cease-fire to allow the smoke to clear away, and then the Zulu would take advantage of the lull to creep closer and blaze away at the square, from which deliberate and independent firing at close range was allowed between volleys.[71] Their new weapon, the Gatling gun, employed in battle for the first time during the Zulu campaign, was not as effective as the British might have hoped. The pair in operation were capable of causing havoc among the Zulu only for so long as they did not jam, which they did repeatedly. Their effect was certainly initially demoralising for the Zulu,[72] who suffered heavy casualties before them at point-blank range (Wood counted sixty dead in the long grass sixty-three metres to their front),[73] though some Zulu still managed to get up to within thirty-six metres of them.

In other words, if the Zulu were able to make use of cover to avoid the full effects of British fire at some distance from the square, then they were unable to press with any degree of safety or success into the zone within ninety metres (or point-blank range) of the British firing-line. It was this impenetrable wall of fire the British were able to set up before whatever section of their formation was threatened which was ultimately to deter the Zulu and persuade them to give up their assault.

At first glance, it might seem extraordinary that, in its turn, the British square was not more vulnerable to the energetic Zulu fire. Most of the Zulu had some form of firearm. In total, they probably carried more at Ulundi than the British, though the majority were inferior muzzle-loaders of some sort.[74] But there were small numbers of breech-loaders, including Martini-Henry rifles captured at Isandlwana, Ntombe and Hlobane, and the British square did present an enormous target, with its interior crammed with wagons, draft animals, dismounted cavalry and irregular horse, as well as the NNC. For all that, casualties were very low on account of the usual poor Zulu marksmanship. No sooner had the square taken up its battle position than it had been assailed by a dropping and harmless fire from the distant Zulu who were still out of range, especially those advancing from the direction of oNdini.[75]

When they converged on the square in the wake of the retiring irregular horse, the Zulu fired and pushed forward alternately in their loose, open order. But though the range was less, that fire was equally ineffective, as was the heavy fusillade from their final position around the square, which continued for about half an hour. The fundamental Zulu fault was still that they almost all shot too high. The British supposed they did so because they erroneously believed that by raising their sights so as to fire at long range they would increase the velocity of bullets at short range. Be that as it may, what casualties the British did suffer were mostly in the rear ranks, where men were wounded in the back as a consequence of Zulu fire coming over the heads of the men on the opposite side of the square.[76] Indeed, there were cases – as at Khambula – of Zulu being hit by fire from their comrades on the far side of the British square. There were naturally some Zulu snipers who were more accurate than the mass, though the British were generally able to pick them off, shooting some out of a tree, for example.[77]

The Zulu came nearest to breaking through the cordon of British fire and reaching the square at its right rear corner. The angle of a square is its weakest point because less fire can be developed there, and because there is more likelihood of confusion in the ranks. The Zulu instinctively grasped this fact. Thus, when those advancing against the right face of the square from the kwaNodwengu *ikhanda* were checked by medium-range fire at between 360 and 450 metres, they changed their tactics and made for the right rear corner. (KwaNodwengu, it should be noted, served as a Zulu rallying-point throughout the battle. As it provided good cover close to the British position, crowds of Zulu were constantly rushing into it. Some lined the huts and the stockade facing the square, and kept up a heavy, if ineffective, fire.)

The assault from kwaNodwengu, then, veered left up a depression running along the British rear, which gave them complete shelter to within 134 metres of the right rear corner. Here they rapidly collected, between 2 000 and 3 000 strong and 30 ranks deep. Striking their white shields and shouting 'uSuthu!', they penetrated the cordon of point-blank fire and charged to within twenty-seven metres of the corner, while a few corpses were later found only nine paces from the British line. So close did they come that Battery N, 6th Royal Artillery, had to fire seven rounds of case-shot (which is used only at the closest quarters), and several officers drew their swords or revolvers, expecting a hand-to-hand fight.[78]

The 5th Company, Royal Engineers, was brought up from its position behind the front face to reinforce the corner, though its help ultimately proved unnecessary. Lord Chelmsford was seriously alarmed, and requested the men of the threatened corner to fire faster. The British infantry were still managing to remain as cool as if on parade, and were obeying their officers' orders on sighting and firing in sections. They responded to Chelmsford by developing such a 'solid and well directed' weight of fire that Captain Slade considered that no troops in the world could have stood up to it, and honestly marvelled at the way the Zulu nevertheless persisted as long as they did.[79]

The determined and nearly successful assault by what were mainly the iNgobamakhosi and uVe on the right rear corner of the square was not fully matched by that of their habitual rivals, the uMcijo, on the left rear corner. Shepstone's Horse had retired before their column over thirty men deep, which came up in the most determined manner from a hill to the left rear of the British to the cover of a ridge 270 metres away. There, almost out of close range, they were checked by the British fire and deterred from advancing any further in force, though daring individuals came dashing down the slope and, concealed in the grass, crept forward to snipe.

Meanwhile, the attack against the left side of the square was pushed forward with such vigour that the infantry fixed bayonets in expectation of hand-to-hand fighting. But there too the Zulu were held. At the front face of the square the Zulu developed their attack where a dip in the ground allowed them to form up in comparative safety. Here too they were checked as they appeared at the crest.[80]

At this stage, with the Zulu assault pinned down at every quarter, the main Zulu reserve, a few thousand strong and apparently made up of members of the older *amabutho*, emerged from oNdini. They moved down the slope towards the Mbilane stream in a wide rectangular column fifty deep, beating their shields and shouting their war-cries. The British moved two 9-pounder guns from the left rear to the left front angle (the Gatlings at the front face were jammed), and opened fire at about 2 000 metres with shrapnel. The shells burst in front of the Zulu column, which opened out into two wings. When a shell fell on each of the wings they hesitated, then closed. Two more shells falling on the reunited column caused it to turn and leave the field.[81]

Other reserves posted to the north on the hills to the British left, as well as between them and the river, with the purpose of cutting off the retreat of the square should it break, were consequently not brought up and never came under fire. Their immobility may also be partially ascribed to the reserves' heeding of the king's warning not to fight the British if they were stationary.[82]

The battle in the plain was contested sharply for about half an hour from the time it became general until, at about 9.15 a.m., the Zulu attack began to slacken and then falter. Lieutenant-Colonel Robinson was convinced that this was not from any loss of nerve on the Zulu part, but because they were perplexed that they could find no way around or through the British fire. They had doubtless been confident that working around the faces of the square they would eventually have found some opening (such as the nearly-gained right rear corner) through which to overwhelm the British at close quarters. Yet as success eluded them they began to hesitate: some stopped, while other individuals began to run away. This gradually precipitated a general disorderly withdrawal which was underway by 9.20 a.m., though as yet there was no general rout. For though the Zulu fell back, it was not far, and attempts were made to rally. What must have made their inability to break through the cordon of British fire all the more bitter was their knowledge that they had actually succeeded in their strategy of surrounding the

319

unlaagered invaders in the open plain.[83]

When the British realised that the Zulu were retiring they ceased fire. Wood tried to suppress their jubilation, for he believed that the Zulu would make a last stand at oNdini. But it was not to be, and the sound of British cheering only disheartened some of the Zulu further, for it convinced them that the battle was indeed lost. Yet for others, the British cease-fire was an encouragement. They paused to look back, clearly hoping to see the British formation breaking in pursuit, and so affording them that long-awaited opportunity to close with the invader in hand-to-hand combat. But they were to be disappointed. The left face of the square greeted the momentary Zulu halt at 9.25 a.m. with a short burst of firing,[84] and artillery fire broke up every new concentration. Demoralisation began inevitably to set in and the retreat gathered momentum. It was now becoming a question of escaping unscathed from the hopeless field, and as they fled the Zulu felt acutely that their 'fighting strength was sinking like the setting sun'.[85]

This was the moment the cavalry had long awaited. Regular infantry were unable to deliver an effective counter-thrust against an adversary as mobile as the Zulu, but a well-timed cavalry charge over the open plain was enough to throw the disordered Zulu into a panic, to turn retreat into rout, and to transform a victory into a decisive triumph. At Ulundi, the cavalry's counter-attack was a complete success. The British revelled unashamedly in their exultant pursuit, even if they were constrained to admit that it became 'butchery rather at last'.[86]

At 9.25 a.m., having hesitated for a few minutes to give the order until the Zulu retreat was general, Chelmsford directed Colonel Drury-Lowe to pursue the Zulu. Five troops of the 17th Lancers and twenty-four men of the King's Dragoon Guards under Captain Brewster formed up to the rear of the square. They were met by a heavy fire from a large body of Zulu who had remained hidden in the long grass. Their firing, though, was as ineffective as ever, and the cavalry ignored them, charging initially in the direction of kwaNodwengu.[87] The Lancers, having soon dispersed or killed those Zulu who had been unable to reach the shelter of the *ikhanda*, and discovering that there were too few Zulu in its vicinity to make their presence worth while, halted, and then wheeled right about to confront large numbers of Zulu who were again concentrating to the right rear of the square.

In a furious charge they pursued the Zulu, who scattered in an attempt to reach the lower slopes of the hills about three kilometres away, overtaking and killing the warriors who were running away nearly as fast as the horses could gallop. By the time the Lancers had driven the Zulu to the hills they began to realise that the ground had become too difficult for cavalry. Moreover, the Zulu were now rallying on the hills to receive them and, reinforced by some of the reserves, were setting up a galling fire on the floundering cavalry, whose horses were in any case quite blown. So recognising that the pursuit could not be continued, and having no fresh horsemen in support, the cavalry wisely rallied and retired with some loss out of range of the Zulu.

The Lancers felt they had proved their worth that day, and vindicated the use of the lance – which, although as anachronistic as the infantry square in terms of European warfare, was still invaluable in the colonial context against irregular troops scattered in flight. Despite a tendency to stick in the shield it had penetrated, which had persuaded the cavalry to draw their heavy sabres, it was quickly recognised that only the lance was effective when the Zulu flung themselves flat or sheltered in dongas. Although some of the Zulu avoided the deadly thrusts of the lances in this way, many of the pursued desperately turned and fought for their lives in stubborn knots, never crying for quarter. They dodged among the horses, firing at them, stabbing at their bellies and sometimes seizing a lance in an attempt to drag the horseman from his saddle. The heavy casualties among the cavalry horses – twenty-eight killed and forty-five wounded – attests to Zulu determination.

Meanwhile, Captain Browne and the Mounted Infantry of the Flying Column moved out of the square in support of the Lancers. They fired into the flank of the Zulu retreating before the cavalry, and eventually merged into the Lancer's line. The rest of Buller's mounted men dashed out of the right front corner of the square a few minutes after the Lancers began their charge. Captain Cochrane and the Natal Native Horse, who were in the lead, chased the Zulu beyond oNdini until they reached the Zulu reserve.

The Zulu turned at bay when overtaken by Buller's horsemen, as they had with the Lancers, first firing at them and then using their spears, or crouching down to hide in the long grass. The irregular horse used their carbines pistol-wise, and probably with more deadly effect than the lance or sabre of the cavalry. Like the Lancers, they pursued the Zulu as far as the hills. Once on the hillsides, which were inaccessible to the horses, the Zulu began rallying in groups to fire on Buller's men, who retired in their turn.

The most horrific part of the battle was yet to come. It still remained for the British to flush out and kill those Zulu who had succeeded in concealing themselves in dongas and long grass during the pursuit, or who had feigned death, or who had thought the retreat of their comrades only temporary, and had not joined the flight. Yet whatever their reason for lingering on the fatal plain, they also died hard in the end, fighting to the last and never crying out for mercy. Some of the Natal Native Horse, for example, attacked and killed about seventy Zulu who had been cut off in a donga to the rear of the Lancers as they charged. Others dispatched Zulu who had taken refuge in the pools and under the banks of the Mbilane stream. The regimental mascot of the 17th Lancers, a great crossbred dog, distinguished himself in his regiment's eyes by running about and barking furiously whenever he came upon a living Zulu in the grass.[88]

The Natal Native Horse, in particular, were both thorough and cruel, under no circumstances sparing an enemy, even if wounded. Hours after the battle was over the firing of their carbines told of their horrible work, from which they were not to be dissuaded.[89] Yet even then, the wretched Zulu fugitives, if not too badly wounded, would try to sell their lives dearly. They also fell victim to the NNC, who emerged from the square to spear disabled Zulu and plunder the *amakhanda*. As a consequence of this pitiless activity, of which many British officers were heartily ashamed, only two Zulu prisoners were taken alive that day.[91]

As the main body of Zulu retreated in great masses over the hills to the north, the British moved up their six 9-pounder guns to shell them. They opened fire at 9.40 a.m. on the Zulu who were squatting down in exhausted groups on the hilltops just over four kilometres away, and in a kloof near oNdini. Though out of range, and bursting too high to cause much damage,[92] the shrapnel rapidly caused the resting Zulu to scatter, and after a few rounds they had disappeared over the crests of the hills. It seems that the shrapnel bursts might have caused a few casualties among the women who had been watching the battle from what they had supposed was the security of the hills.[93]

Once the British had finished congratulating each other, attending the wounded and burying the dead where they had fallen, the square moved forward at 11.30 a.m. to the banks of the Mbilane stream. There the men rested and had their dinner. Meanwhile, the mounted men continued to scour the surrounding plain. Besides flushing out Zulu fugitives, the British mounted units were engaged in setting all the *amakhanda* in the plain ablaze, or in completing their destruction. Among those to be burned were oNdini, kwaNodwengu, kwaBulawayo, kwaKhandempemvu, kwaGqikazi, kwaNdabakawombe, kwaMbonambi and emLambongwenya, as well as more distant ones of lesser importance.[94]

At 10.07 a.m. the 9-pounders shelled oNdini and drove out over the hills a large concentration of Zulu who were still sheltering there. Chelmsford then ordered the cavalry and irregular horse, who had returned to the square for a short rest after their pursuit, to go out once more and burn oNdini. So began an irresponsible race between mounted officers for the honour of being the first at Cetshwayo's 'capital'. It was won by the dashing Captain Lord William Beresford. However, the Hon. W. Drummond, Chelmsford's intelligence officer, was killed when he became lost in the maze of huts by a few Zulu still lurking there.[95]

Buller ordered the firing of oNdini at 11.40 a.m. while the infantry relaxed by the Mbilane, and his men moved from hut to hut with flaming torches of grass. It seems, though, that the Zulu themselves, having stripped the *ikhanda* bare, had first set fire to it, though for lack of wind the huts did not burn freely and the British effectively completed their work.[96] There is evidence that the Zulu started the firing of the neighbouring *amakhanda* as well. They had done the same in the emaKhosini valley on 26 June during Wood's raid, and with uMgungundlovu forty-one years before at the approach of the Boers after Blood River. All the *amakhanda*, especially oNdini, made enormous bonfires which smouldered for four days.

It was a 'grand sight' for the victors to see all the *amakhanda* of the plain sending up their columns of smoke.[97] For the Zulu, looking down from the surrounding hilltops, or for those further afield seeing the black haze of smoke covering the country, it was the chilling signal that their power was broken and their kingdom fallen.[98]

At about 2 p.m., after a good rest, the British began their return march to their camp at the White Mfolozi, reaching it by stages between 3.30 and 5.30 p.m. Their leisurely pace can be partially ascribed to the cumber of looted shields and spears shouldered by the men. Everyone was determined to carry away some memento of the battle, especially a weapon. However, the dearth of other, more decorative, 'curiosities' was deplored.[99] The pace of the British march was also slow because of the wounded who had to be carried on stretchers. Yet considering the scope of their victory, British losses had been light. In all, two officers and ten men were killed, another officer died of his wounds on 14 July, and sixty-nine men were wounded. All the serious or fatal wounds were from bullets.

As for the Zulu, their dead lay unburied that night, for they had abandoned the plain and the British had left the Zulu slain where they had fallen. Those who had been hit by shell or rocket fire were terribly mutilated, while those killed by Martini-Henry bullets were only relatively less disfigured, for those soft lead projectiles had left gaping holes.[100]

When later, on 9 August 1879, a British patrol went over the ground, they found no more than 300 skeletons. This indicated not that the Zulu had suffered few casualties, but that in the interval the relatives and friends of many of the fallen had been able to dispose of their bodies and retrieve their weapons. The dead lay in twos and threes for kilometres around, on plain and hilltop, having been killed by shell, rocket, bullet or lance. The greatest concentration was naturally within close firing range of the square, where journalists with the British on the day of the battle marked between 500 and 600 Zulu corpses.[101] Where the fight had been hottest, skeletons still lay in August twelve to fifteen deep.[102] Buller himself estimated that his irregular horse had inflicted a loss of at least 450 in pursuit.[103] The regular cavalry took credit for 150 'kills'. In all, it seems that rather more Zulu died attacking the square than in the rout, and that the official figure of 'not less than 1 500' Zulu dead[104] (or a casualty rate of about ten per cent) is reasonably accurate, especially when it is remembered that the wounded would rarely have survived.

That night the victorious British triumphantly agreed that the Zulu challenge to fight them in the open had been 'fairly answered'.[105] Certainly, that was the view of Lord Chelmsford, who felt that by proving they were capable of victory in the open field, British arms had been vindicated throughout southern Africa.

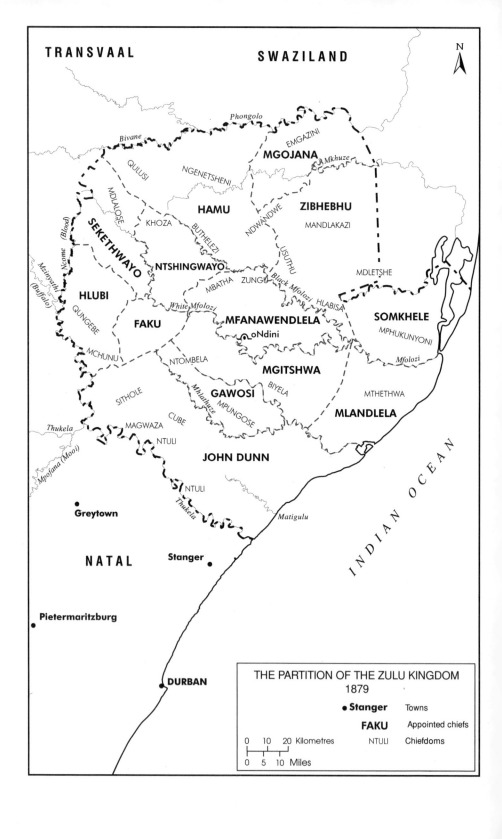

TRANSVAAL

SWAZILAND

N

Phongolo

EMGAZINI

MGOJANA

Bivane

Mkhuze

QULUSI

NGENETSHENI

MDLALOSE

Ncome (Blood)

SEKETHWAYO

KHOZA

HAMU

NDWANDWE

ZIBHEBHU

MANDLAKAZI

BUTHELEZI

Mzinyathi (Buffalo)

NTSHINGWAYO

USUTHU

HLUBI

MBATHA

ZUNGU

Black Mfolozi

HLABISA

MDLETSHE

QUNGEBE

White Mfolozi

FAKU

MFANAWENDLELA

SOMKHELE

oNdini

MPHUKUNYONI

MCHUNU

NTOMBELA

Mfolozi

MGITSHWA

SITHOLE

Mhlathuze

GAWOSI

BIYELA

MTHETHWA

Thukela

MAGWAZA

CUBE

MPUNGOSE

MLANDLELA

NTULI

Mpofana (Mooi)

JOHN DUNN

NTULI

• **Greytown**

Thukela

Matigulu

N A T A L

Stanger •

• **Pietermaritzburg**

INDIAN OCEAN

• **DURBAN**

THE PARTITION OF THE ZULU KINGDOM
1879

• **Stanger**   Towns

FAKU   Appointed chiefs

NTULI   Chiefdoms

0   10   20 Kilometres

0   5   10 Miles

26

We May Now Plough Again[1]

After its defeat at Ulundi the Zulu army speedily dispersed all over the country, and the British, wherever they were in Zululand, detected no organised forces still in the field, though they did notice returning warriors crossing their lines of communication in considerable numbers.[2] For a while the bush in the country to the north and east of oNdini was clogged with the wounded, old men, women, girls, children and cattle, all fleeing from the Mahlabathini plain.

King Cetshwayo himself was one of this number. When the look-outs he had posted reported that his army was defeated he immediately retired northwards from kwaMbonambi, crossing the nek of the Ntabankhulu range into the bush beyond, where he was later joined by Mnyamana and the other important chiefs. Men of the uMcijo *ibutho* followed after the king some way as he fled, but he soon sent them back as he feared their presence would attract attention and alert the British to his whereabouts.[3]

The king travelled on foot with the women of his *isigodlo* and a number of servants. Weighed down by calamity, he spoke hardly a word. The following day he took up Zibhebhu's offer of shelter, and sent his household (including his eleven-year-old heir Dinuzulu) and cattle to seek sanctuary with the Mandlakazi chief in the north-eastern reaches of Zululand. After the king's capture, his full-brother, Ndabuko, insisted that it was proper that he assume the custody of Dinuzulu and Cetshwayo's women. Zibhebhu was greatly affronted and reluctantly complied, but would not yield up the royal cattle. So the seeds were sown for future conflict.[4]

The king himself did not head through Zibhebhu's territory for the natural fastnesses of the Lubombo mountains as Dingane had done and some supposed he might. Nor did he try to reach the Tsonga chiefdoms beyond, where the chiefs had in any case refused his pleas for succour, and were soon to assure the British Consul at Lourenço Marques that they would never allow the king to take refuge with them. Instead, he moved across the Black Mfolozi to Mnyamana's ekuShumayeleni homestead on the Sikhwebezi River, which he reached the third day after the battle. There he stayed for a month, attempting fruitlessly to negotiate with the British.[5]

On the morning of 5 July the victorious British began their withdrawal from their camp on the White Mfolozi, and by the next day all had returned to Mthonjaneni. A storm of bitterly cold wind, rain and hail began that night, and made all further movement impossible until 9 July. Chelmsford's critics seized on his withdrawal south – which, they contended, by not following up the advantage gained by the victory of Ulundi, unnecessarily prolonged the war. Yet if the shortage of supplies, the encumbrance of the wounded, and the need to get his men under better cover made the move desirable to Chelmsford, what made it possible and realistic was his knowledge that the Zulu army had dispersed following its defeat. It was simply not possible for the Zulu to strike another blow against the invader until such time as it reassembled.[6] This was a truth recognised even by Wolseley, Chelmsford's highly critical replacement. And like many another serving officer, Wolseley was aware that the Zulu army was highly unlikely to answer any fresh calls to reassemble. It would not do so because Chelmsford's victory was a decisive one.

After his defeat at Blood River in 1838, King Dingane had set out with his army to beyond the Black Mfolozi, where near the Vuna River he re-established his uMgungundlovu *ikhanda*. It was very different after Ulundi. King Cetshwayo wished likewise to reassemble the iNgobamakhosi, uMcijo, uMbonambi and uNokhenke *amabutho* to build a new *ikhanda* for him north of the Black Mfolozi. But they ignored his orders and stayed at home.[7] They did so because in the eyes of the Zulu people the war was now over and the king's prestige and power gone. All they wanted was to be able to go home to resume the normal course of their lives.[8]

Everywhere was the hope that the British, having made their point, would go home too.[9] And indeed, Wolseley, confident that organised armed resistance by the royal army was over, set about the pacification of Zululand and the capture of the king with drastically reduced forces. On 9 July the Flying Column began its march back to kwaMagwaza and St Paul's to link up with Crealock's 1st Division. It remained for the rest of the month at St Paul's, patrolling the area and being reduced piecemeal until 1 August. The 1st Division began to break up from 10 July and to return to Natal. By 23 July it had ceased to exist. On 10 July the 2nd Division retraced the steps of its earlier advance, and moved back on Fort Marshall, where it was broken up by 27 July. Some troops continued to garrison the line of forts, while the remainder returned to Durban for embarkation.[10]

When Cetshwayo fled north to seek sanctuary with Mnyamana, he ordered his chiefs not to follow, but 'to look out for themselves'.[11] They scarcely needed any urging. In the wake of Ulundi there was a rash of submissions, a regular *sauve qui peut*. Among the most prominent to 'come in' were Dabulamanzi, who at last surrendered himself on 12 July,[12] and Gawozi kaSilwana, chief of a section of the Mpungose and a great favourite of the king's, who surrendered to Wood at St Paul's on 13 July. So when Wolseley, who was determined that not another shot should be fired before peace was achieved, resolved to put the earlier submissions by the coastal chiefs to Crealock on a more formal basis, almost all of them responded to his invitation to meet him at his camp at the emaNgweni *ikhanda*.

On 19 July Wolseley addressed some 250 Zulu near the destroyed emaNgweni *ikhanda*. He announced the end of the Zulu kingdom and, following Crealock's successful formula, required of the chiefs only that they hand over their arms and royal cattle. The surrendered chiefs not unnaturally expressed their satisfaction with these easy terms, while some of the young men were heard to state that they never would have fought for Cetshwayo if they had known that this was all the British would have exacted from them. Spokesmen for the chiefs were even reported to have declared that they never again wished for a black man as king, but wanted a white sovereign, namely John Dunn.[13] It is not improbable, though, that these last sentiments may have been inspired by Wolseley's known wishes, for it was already his intention that Dunn be made chief over the southern districts of Zululand bordering Natal, so that a buffer-zone under a reliable pro-British chief could be created.

Despite the very satisfactory coastal submissions, Wolseley was most concerned that more of the great northern chiefs had not as yet sued for peace.[14] He put this down to the fact that Cetshwayo was still at large; indeed, the coastal chiefs had assured him that as long as the king was at liberty, fears of his possible return to power could well impede further submissions as well as unsettling and discouraging those who had already given up. Privately, Wolseley wished himself rid of this royal stumbling-block, and wrote candidly to his wife that he 'should be quite happy if some kind friend would but run an Assegai through him'.[15]

Furthermore, Wolseley was convinced that Chelmsford's retiring from the Mahlabathini plain after his victory was, if not a military miscalculation, then certainly a political blunder, for it had left the northern Zulu with a false impression of British intentions. To Wolseley's mind, if the rest of Zululand besides the coastal region were finally to be pacified, it was necessary both to reoccupy oNdini and to capture the king. With these intentions, he sent messages to the chiefs concerned to meet him near the burnt-out oNdini on 10 August.[16]

Meanwhile, Wolseley instructed his officers that the chiefs and *izinduna* who had not already submitted were to be offered Crealock's terms and informed that although the *amabutho* system and the monarchy with which it was interwoven were to be abolished, no land or cattle were to be transferred to the whites. The additional proclamation that the kingdom was to be divided into independent chiefdoms under chiefs whose names would be announced at oNdini continued to address their fears and ambitions with unerring accuracy. Those chiefs who had not already submitted were to be invited to do so, and to bring in their arms and royal cattle. Plying the stick with the carrot, they were also to be sternly reminded that if they neglected to surrender by 10 August they would then be treated as enemies and punished.[17]

Wolseley's Zululand policy thus defined, he made the practical arrangements necessary for its fulfilment. From the disbanded 1st Division he created a column under Lieutenant-Colonel C.M. Clarke which was to reoccupy oNdini and send out patrols to capture the king. Wolseley himself was to accompany this column. A second column, made up from Wood's disbanded Flying Column, he put under the command of Lieutenant-Colonel Baker Russell. Russell's objective was the pacification of north-western Zululand, where Wolseley feared the Qulusi and Manyonyoba might attempt a last-ditch resistance.[18]

Wolseley determined that Russell should be supported in his progress from the south towards the headwaters of the Black Mfolozi by a simultaneous advance from the north across the Phongolo by Swazi forces and by British troops from the Transvaal operating through Luneburg, both of whom would clear his front. The Transvaal troops were under the command of Lieutenant-Colonel the Hon. G. Villiers, and were to consist of mounted Burghers and of the adherents of Hamu, who had been living comfortably in Utrecht since his defection in March.

Wolseley put Hamu under great pressure to co-operate. If he were successful in bringing in the king, a reward of 5 000 cattle and independent sovereignty over his own district would be his. However, if he did not play his part fully, his cattle and country would be offered to the Swazi. Hamu's *izinduna* hastily declared themselves willing on those terms to turn out their men and capture the king. While the Swazis' specific objective was to ensure that Cetshwayo did not slip across the upper Phongolo into Swaziland, that of Villiers, as Special Commissioner to Hamu, was to obtain the submission of the turbulent and semi-independent Zulu of the Phongolo frontier.

Besides the north-west, where the royalist Qulusi were concentrated, there was another region where loyalty to the king persisted. This was southern Zululand, along the middle Thukela, a sector the British had never penetrated in any depth.[19] There Godide of the Ntuli, Manqondo and his son Qethuka of the Magwaza, and the blind Sokufa and his son Sigananda of the Cube were loath to submit. During July and August they treated evasively with Natal officials, and stopped short of fulfilling the conditions Wolseley had laid down for submission. It is apparent, though, that their indecision was in part a reflection of divisions among their adherents. The married men were content to accept the British terms, while the younger warriors resented having to give up their arms, and were prepared to carry on the struggle.

Upstream of them, it was different.[20] Mbuzo, a minor Ntuli chief at the junction of the Thukela and Mzinyathi rivers, had put out peace feelers as early as June. After the battle of Ulundi, local officials exploited the changed situation to open negotiations with Chief Ndwandwe kaMhlala of the Langa, Chief Matshana kaSitshakuza of the Mchunu (an *isikhulu* with a long tradition of seeking for greater autonomy), and Chief Matshana kaMondisa of the Sithole (who, like the other Matshana, officials had hoped before the war might throw in his lot with the British). It took some time for these chiefs to conform with Wolseley's terms. Their adherents had taken refuge during the war in caves and forests – particularly as a result of the 2nd Division's punitive patrols during May – and it was necessary that they return to their *imizi* before the requisite guns and royal cattle could be collected. By mid-August it was done, and on 20 August the four chiefs and seven other lesser ones surrendered at Rorke's Drift to H.F. Fynn.

There was no such formal surrender among Sihayo's adherents. He and his son Mehlokazulu were prisoners-of-war, and the Qungebe were in their places of refuge, away from the border and the danger of British raids. Yet by the end of August many were drifting back to their homes, though it was not until October that they were all to return.

By the time, then, that Wolseley set up his camp at oNdini on 10 August, the coastal region had fully submitted, the south-west was well into the process of doing so, and it seemed not unlikely that the south would soon follow suit. In central and even northern Zululand it appeared as if the chiefs were prepared to accept Wolseley's conditions and abandon the king's cause.[21] It is true that none of the important chiefs had assembled at oNdini by 10 August, but Wolseley was not perturbed as he had received word that they were coming in. Zibhebhu was reported still to be in his district, but Wolseley entertained high hopes of his co-operation. He had noted his 'time-serving disposition', and presumed (correctly as it turned out) that the promise of an independent sovereignty under the British settlement would detach him from the king's cause.[22]

By 13 August Zibhebhu had promised to come into Wolseley's camp, as had no less a personage than Mnyamana. To Wolseley, the submissions of Zibhebhu and Mnyamana were of the utmost significance. He was sure they would convince the remainder of the chiefs to follow their lead, and would have the effect of countering messages the king had apparently been sending out, exhorting the chiefs not to give in.[23]

Significantly, the king's messages were in any case largely ignored by chiefs concerned to secure their own future, and he found that few shreds of authority still clung to him. Moreover, the dispersal of his army and his own flight left him few counters with which to negotiate against an enemy who had already achieved his objectives. Now that Zulu military capability was destroyed and royal power shattered, all that he could realistically hope to bargain for was his personal safety and future liberty.

The outcome of Wolseley's meeting of 19 July with the coastal chiefs helped dash Cetshwayo's hopes for continued resistance, and he sent to the southern chiefs urging them to comply with British terms in the hope that his co-operation would soften the British towards him.[24] A suppliant royal messenger duly approached Lieutenant-Colonel Clarke at kwaMagwaza on 26 July. Clarke replied that the king's life would be spared if he surrendered, and directed the envoy to Wolseley.[25] A spate of similar messages and replies were exchanged, until on 7 August Wolseley interviewed an important delegation sent on by Clarke. It was led by the influential Chief Mavumengwana. He had with him yet another letter from the king taken down by Vijn, in which Cetshwayo pathetically declared that he was still collecting cattle which he would send in with Mnyamana, with whom he had taken refuge, and that he would follow in their wake. Meanwhile, 'the English should take pity on him and leave him the country of his fathers'.[26] But they had already determined on his exile, and Wolseley demanded his immediate surrender.

Mavumengwana and his returning delegation fell in with Mnyamana and the promised cattle, and decided to go back with them to Wolseley instead of reporting to the king. Cetshwayo, meanwhile, learning that British patrols were out seeking him, took fright and fled from ekuShumayeleni to the fastnesses of the Ngome forest. When King Dingane had fled to the Lubombo mountains in 1840 after his defeat at the battle of Maqongqo, the Zulu knew his power was broken, as 'a king who left his home and went to the mountains was finished'.[27] So it was with Cetshwayo, who was now being abandoned by all. Vijn, who had come into Wolseley's camp on 10 August with a last message from the king begging to be allowed to stay in Zululand, agreed, on the promise of a reward, to persuade Cetshwayo to surrender. But he could not overcome the king's dread of being sent into exile, and returned empty-handed to Wolseley on 13 August, while the king pushed on deeper into the forest.[28]

On 14 August Mnyamana, Ntshingwayo, Mgidlana and Sukani (two unin-fluential half-brothers of the king's), Sitshaluza (the regent of the emGazini in the north), Melelesi kaManyosi (chief of the Mbatha in central Zululand), and 150 lesser chiefs and *izinduna* presented themselves at Wolseley's camp. All wore only skins and carried sticks.[29] They had with them the 617 head of cat-tle which Mnyamana had collected on the king's instructions. These cattle in-dicated that Mnyamana's overt intention was not to surrender, but to sue for terms of peace on the king's behalf.[30] At last, as the British had for so long insisted, a major chief was to negotiate directly for the king. Yet was it to negotiate, or sim-ply beg? As Ntshingwayo later told Magema Fuze: 'We had gone simply to ask for his head, that he might live and not perish.'[31]

Yet, once assured that the British would not execute Cetshwayo, the chiefs' duty was done, and their thoughts turned to their own future.[32] They soon declared that they had themselves come to surrender, and that they hoped for peace. As they had not met the required terms for submission, Wolseley ordered that the five principal chiefs, including Mnyamana, be held hostage in camp until the nec-essary arms and royal cattle had been collected. On 16 August Cetshwayo's favourite brother, Prince Ziwedu, came in and was also detained. Then, on 26 August, Zibhebhu himself appeared. He had with him as token of submission a number of guns and cattle, and claimed that he had hesitated for so long primarily for fear that he would be killed for the part he had played in the war.

At the same time as these significant developments at oNdini, the people of cen-tral Zululand as far down as the coast, tired of fighting and wishing to bring their families back to the shelter of their homes, were surrendering in great numbers at Fort Evelyn, Fort Marshall and kwaMagwaza.[33] Baker Russell was also achiev-ing success in the north-west, despite the failure of Wolseley's overall strategy for the region. The Boers of Wakkerstroom, not the least surprisingly in the light of their recent record, refused to volunteer for Villiers's force, prevented local blacks from acting as auxiliaries, and even helped the Zulu by forwarding them information of British movements. Hamu's men proved initially unwilling to ad-vance further into hostile territory than midway between Utrecht and Lune-burg. Hamu himself, who was in a 'funk', used stomach pains as an excuse for returning to the safety of Utrecht.[34] As for the Swazi, though they were happy to loot Zulu *imizi* along the Phongolo, they were still too afraid of Zulu power to risk their army in Zululand unless heavily supported, and were eventually called back on 24 August. Their ineffectualness did not much concern Wolseley, how-ever, for by this stage he was satisfied that Cetshwayo was not heading in their direction, and he was in any case reluctant to let loose an army in Zululand which he might not be able to control.

Villiers therefore advanced on the Mkhondo River with the 300 mounted white troops and 700 auxiliaries he had managed to raise. Hamu's men, who had begun to recover their nerve, also started to join him, and wasted no opportunity in looting the countryside as they went. Villiers reached Luneburg on 25 August without having met the Zulu resistance he had anticipated. On 27 August the mounted men of Baker Russell's Column, who likewise had encountered some unfriendliness on their march, but no outright resistance, and had in fact accepted many submissions, pushed ahead and reached Zungwini Mountain.

The Qulusi *izinduna* and Manyonyoba, uncomfortably situated between Baker Russell and Villiers, were in a dilemma whether or not to resist. Following the pattern of southern Zululand, it seems the *izinduna* were predisposed to give up, but the young men wished to continue fighting. The Qulusi knew, to their disgust, that many Zulu on Baker Russell's line of march, especially the Mdlalose, had been clearly relieved that they had not been required to fight (though here too a few of the younger men had shown some disposition to resist), and had surrendered both arms and cattle.

By the end of August the Mdlalose were all back in their homes from their places of refuge in the hills. On 25 August their chief, Sekethwayo, had himself submitted at Fort Cambridge after the confiscation of 300 of his cattle had helped him make up his mind. Baker Russell had ordered him to oNdini, but – most significantly for those Zulu of the north-west still contemplating resistance – had promised him independence in his own district, and the restoration of his cattle. Equally effectively, Baker Russell had also threatened him with the loss of everything should he not co-operate.

The Qulusi seemed at first determined to be more staunch in their loyalty to the royal cause than the Mdlalose. On 22 August Baker Russell's spies reported them to be mustering for war near ebaQulusini under the *induna* Mcwayo. But on 28 August two sons of Msebe, the Qulusi *induna* who had sent out feelers to the British in February and had subsequently been victimised by the other Qulusi, informed Baker Russell that both he and Manyonyoba wished to surrender. Msebe gave himself up the next day and, resentful at his treatment at the hands of the other Qulusi, indicated his desire to join the British in their operations against them.

This proved unnecessary, however. On 28 August Cetshwayo was captured by a patrol in the Ngome forest and this intelligence had an immediate effect on those Qulusi still resisting. At a council held on 30 August they decided to surrender, doubtless influenced by a secret message the captive king is reputed to have sent Mahubulwana (the principal *induna* of the Qulusi and his commander in the field in the north-west), ordering him to disband his men still under arms.[35] On 1 September Mahubulwana submitted on behalf of his people, and Baker Russell resumed his advance on Luneburg.

Manyonyoba, now completely alone in his contemplated resistance and threatened by Villiers's plundering rabble, sent word to Luneburg that he was prepared to lay down his arms on 4 September.[36] This intention, which would have ended the war in the north-west without any further bloodshed – and indeed, concluded the whole post-Ulundi pacification process without a life being lost – was tragically frustrated.

Baker Russell, sceptical of Manyonyoba's intentions and following Wolseley's orders to clear him out, sent a force to the Ntombe valley to ensure his surrender. Many of Manyonyoba's adherents in their caves began to surrender, but the firing of a shot provoked men of Teteleku's Mounted Natives into butchering seven prisoners whom they were guarding. After that act of treachery, Manyonyoba's adherents not unnaturally refused any longer to come out of their caves and give themselves up, while Manyonyoba, his faith in British promises of amnesty dashed, broke off negotiations.

As a consequence, Baker Russell despatched a strong patrol on 5 September to take Manyonyoba's principal cave on the left bank of the Ntombe. Most of his adherents had already slipped away, though the remainder resisted attempts to smoke them out. The next day Manyonyoba's brother and a few adherents were captured, and on 8 September Baker Russell made a determined effort to finish the business. One force proceeded without resistance against the Ntombe caves, which they blew up with dynamite. However, at Mbilini's mountain across the Ntombe, the other force lost two NCOs of the 2/4th Regiment to fire from the caves. In retaliation, the troops blew up the caves with at least thirty people still sheltering in their depths. This act of barbarism ended resistance. Manyonyoba's son, an *induna* and a few others were rounded up, though Manyonyoba himself eluded capture up the Ntombe valley.

With resistance effectively over, Wolseley sent Villiers's disorderly force home and ordered Russell on 10 September to proceed against the Pedi in the Transvaal. Enough troops were left in Luneburg to control the Ntombe valley, and fear of starvation at length compelled Manyonyoba to give himself up on 22 September with his wife and principal *induna*.

Except for the die-hards of the Ntombe valley, the capture of the king was proving, as Wolseley had anticipated, a decisive event, as it took the meaning out of continued resistance. Cetshwayo, initially sheltered by the local population as he moved north from ekuShumayeleni, had succeeded in evading the patrols sent after him. Wolseley, by increasing pressure on the chiefs in whose districts Cetshwayo was reported to be, succeeded in undercutting this aid. Though he long remained frustrated by the general reluctance of the chiefs to come forward and help in the search, he firmly believed that 'in their hearts' they were anxious for the king to be caught.[37] In the end he was proved right.

It was the contention of the apologists of those chiefs who eventually betrayed their king that they had been left no choice. Colenso and Fuze argued that as the country was occupied by the British, the chiefs' adherents were threatened by starvation if they could not return to their homes in safety to plant their crops, for the last harvest had been destroyed by British patrols.[38] Jeff Guy in particular has sustained and popularised this line.[39] Certainly, the king's remaining at large could only have hindered the inevitable settlement on terms dictated by the

British. Yet, by August much of the country directly affected by the war was already pacified, and the people had returned to their fields. Vast areas, especially in the north, had never seen so much as a British patrol. Moreover, British conditions for submission were not of a sort that would disrupt the functioning of the ordinary Zulu *umuzi*. This was widely comprehended. Therefore, the chiefs' position must be regarded as a pragmatic one. There was little point in persistent loyalty to an already fractured polity. Then there was the matter of personal ambitions and survival. Chiefs had to make realistic calculations on how best to enhance their power and independence in a Zululand where the centralised royal state was to be replaced by a number of independent sovereignties. Wolseley worked on these obvious perceptions.

Cetshwayo's capture was only a matter of time. On 23 August Lieutenant-Colonel Clarke left with a strong patrol to put pressure on the neighbourhood where the king was reported to be in hiding. This was a large area, comprising territory which was severally controlled by Mnyamana, Somkhele (the Mphukunyoni chief and Cetshwayo's first cousin, who had submitted on 4 July), by Mgojana kaSomaphunga (the Ndwandwe chief and husband of the king's sister, who came into Wolseley's camp the day Clarke left), and by Zibhebhu (who submitted three days later). It is particularly significant that Wolseley intended to make the last three independent chiefs, but only on condition that they 'behaved well'.[40] The chiefs could not have failed to understand this caveat.

Wolseley used the same tactics with Mnyamana. In a crucial interview on 26 August between John Shepstone and Mnyamana, Shepstone was empowered to threaten the chief that if he did not co-operate he 'should have nothing'. Mnyamana hastily reassured Shepstone that both he and Mgojana were sending messages to their districts ordering their adherents to take the king captive. The former chief *induna* added that since the battle of Ulundi the chiefs had 'lost all regard & interest' in the king, and that having done all that could be required of them for him, Cetshwayo could have 'no further claims' upon their loyalty. Mnyamana reportedly concluded by pointing out that as the Zulu had been afraid to kill neither Shaka nor Dingane, and had only spared Mpande for fear of his white friends, they now had no reason to be afraid of Cetshwayo.[41] He proved as good as his word, as the fugitive Cetshwayo was to discover.

John Shepstone later wrote that Mnyamana came alone to his tent and said merely: 'I have come to tell you that the wind blows from the Ingome forest.'[42] Mnyamana's adherents soon warned the king that their chief had promised Wolseley to assist in his capture, and that he had instructed them to deliver up the king should he seek refuge in any of their homesteads. Cetshwayo was aghast when he heard of what he not unnaturally considered to be Mnyamana's treachery. And indeed, he was almost immediately tracked down in the Ngome forest on 28 August by Major R.J.C. Marter at the remote kwaDwasa homestead of Mkhosana kaSangqana, one of Mnyamana's adherents.[43] Taken by surprise and at the end of his tether, Cetshwayo surrendered with considerable dignity. The following day, on the humiliating journey under escort back to oNdini, two of the king's male attendants were shot as they attempted to make a bolt for freedom.

At 11 o'clock on the morning of 31 August the captive Cetshwayo was brought in a cart into Wolseley's camp at kwaSishwili hard by the burned oNdini, where only ten huts remained standing. Just before reaching the brow of the hills overlooking his ruined capital, Cetshwayo halted in deep dejection and, placing his hands upon the top of his long staff, rested his forehead upon them for a full half minute. Then, resolutely raising his head and summoning up his considerable courage, he entered the British camp with the most perfect dignity, much impressing the troops who all turned out to gawp at him.[44]

However, to his chagrin, he was humiliatingly treated not as a defeated monarch with all the courtesies due to his rank, but as a mere fugitive from justice.[45] Wolseley would not even meet him, but informed him through John Shepstone that, since he had broken his 'coronation' pledges, he was now deposed in the eyes of the British, and his kingdom would be split up among his chiefs. He himself would be kept a prisoner. When John Shepstone told him that there was no possibility of his being allowed to remain in Zululand, the defeated king at last abandoned all hope, and the tears ran down his cheeks.[46]

The next day Cetshwayo set off under escort sadly murmuring, 'I am no longer a King; let me go and live at Pietermaritzburg like any other poor Zulu.'[47] But by the time he and his attendants, who were travelling in an ambulance drawn by ten mules, reached kwaMagwaza, it began to dawn on them that Natal was not to be their destination. To Cetshwayo's mounting dismay he was driven down to the coast and on 4 September taken off by sea from Port Durnford.[48] Cape Town was to be his place of exile, where he would join Langalibalele, the Hlubi chief, who similarly had been banished after his so-called rebellion in 1873 against the Natal authorities. That particularly rankled with Cetshwayo, who did not see why he, a defeated monarch, should be treated in the same way as a mere insurgent.[49]

With Cetshwayo at last a prisoner, and the chiefs relieved of their increasingly embarrassing moral obligation to stand by their defeated monarch, Wolseley could now proceed to his final settlement of Zululand.[50] This entailed the suppression of the monarchy and the dismemberment of the Zulu kingdom into thirteen fragments under appointed chiefs. These were to be formally independent, but had to submit to the arbitration of a British Resident. He signalled his intention to all the great chiefs of holding a meeting on 1 September at oNdini, on which day he would announce which of them would be favoured with independent sovereignties.

Duly, on the appointed day, about 200 Zulu seated themselves in four rows, principal chiefs to the fore, a few paces from the flagstaff in front of Wolseley's tent.[51] They remained in untypical and apprehensive quiet until Wolseley left his tent at half-past four in the afternoon. Then they acclaimed him with upraised hands as if he were indeed a king. Wolseley took his seat close to the flagstaff with John Shepstone, who acted as his interpreter, on his left and the rest of his staff seated behind him. He then condescendingly addressed the assembled chiefs, spelling out the terms of his settlement. The signing of the thirteen separate treaties commenced as soon as he had his say, the illiterate Zulu chiefs simply touching the pen while John Shepstone made the usual cross in place of a signature.

It is hardly any longer a matter for debate whether the boundaries of the chief-doms were ill-conceived, or that the settlement paved the way for disastrous civil war.[52] Wolseley never disguised that in going for 'an economical and speedy peace [he was] thinking of the immediate effect and not of the unfortunate future.'[53] Consequently, what is of particular pertinence to an understanding of that unhappy future is a grasp of the rationale behind Wolseley's division of the kingdom. To see how the existing ambitions of the chiefs (which were so well known to him), coupled with the extent of their collaboration during the war, affected his choice of the thirteen 'kinglets', is to lay out the seeds of civil strife for inspection.

Wolseley's settlement – the details of which the British government had left to his discretion, so long as it ensured the peace and security of the neighbour-ing colonies without involving Britain in any further expense or responsibility for Zululand's affairs – was dictated by strategic considerations. These were in-fluenced by the British school of Indian defence, through which his Chief of Staff, Sir George Pomeroy Colley, had made his reputation.[54] His settlement thus close-ly resembled that which Lord Lytton had intended to impose on Afghanistan, whereby the North-West Frontier of British India would have been secured by breaking Afghanistan into a number of impotent principalities, ruled by chiefs amenable to British control in the form of Residents. So too in South Africa, where Natal and the Transvaal would be made safe through the fragmentation of the Zulu kingdom.

Wolseley turned to local advisers when deciding how Zululand should be di-vided, and who should be set over the pieces. From the eagerly proffered coun-sel of colonial officials and other experts such as Charles Brownlee, ex-Secretary for Native Affairs in the Cape, and Sir Henry Bulwer, he accepted that of Sir Theophilus Shepstone, whose ideas largely coincided with his own because was a leading proponent of the creation of a number of independent chiefdoms. Shep-stone argued that the preservation of the Zulu monarchy would prolong the life of the Zulu military system. Royal authority, he claimed, was actually fragile because the chiefs yearned for the independence their predecessors had enjoyed before the rise of Shaka. The appointment of thirteen chiefs – a number he considered manageable – would ensure that royal influence would be stifled. Whether these chiefs were hereditary, with a tradition of independence, or whether they were new men owing their elevation to the British, they would col-laborate in ensuring that the Zulu monarchy did not re-emerge. In actually choosing the chiefs, Wolseley felt he had found the perfect adviser in John Dunn. An important part was also played by John Shepstone, who obediently reinforced his brother Theophilus's advice. Bishop Schreuder, who prided himself on his knowledge of Zulu affairs, took great umbrage when Wolseley would not heed his counsel.[55]

It went without saying that the reliability of the chiefdoms abutting the Trans-vaal and Natal borders was the most crucial, for they would act as buffer-zones against the conceivably more volatile chiefdoms created to the north of them.

That is why Hlubi of the Tlokwa, whose Sotho-speaking men from over the Drakensberg had fought as irregular horse for the British during the war, was given the strategic territory at the junction of the Thukela and Mzinyathi.[56] He was put over the two Matshanas as well as Sihayo, the erstwhile royal favourite.

Sihayo was now destitute, since Mnyamana, in one of his final acts of authority as the king's chief *induna*, had confiscated 400 of his cattle and 600 from his people. His grounds were that they had been the cause of the war that had destroyed the kingdom and been the death of so many people, including four of Mnyamana's own sons.[57] The two Matshanas had at least shown themselves more amenable than Sihayo by eventually submitting, and Hlubi confirmed them in their chiefdoms. It was because Wolseley considered Hlubi particularly reliable that he decided in October to relocate Manyonyoba and ninety-four of his remaining adherents to his chiefdom. Manyonyoba was permitted to build a new homestead near the site of Sihayo's Sokhexe. His notorious reputation as a freebooter went before him, and his unenthusiastic new neighbours took immediate precautions to safeguard their livestock.[58]

Hlubi was an alien, one who had never been a person of power and status in Cetshwayo's kingdom, and therefore owed his elevation entirely to the British. John Dunn's position was more ambiguous. He had been a chief and favourite of the Zulu king's, yet he had been the first of the leading men of Zululand to desert his cause. He had served the British well during the war and had successfully won Wolseley's confidence.[59] Dunn had no wish to see the king he had betrayed restored, and he already possessed a firm power-base in south-eastern Zululand. So it was that Wolseley restored him to his chiefdom, and more besides. Dunn was entrusted with a territory which, running along the Thukela frontier, was the most significant in Zululand in terms of Natal's security. Wolseley saw it as a buffer between the Colony and the possibly less amenable chiefdoms to the north. As such, it was to serve the same function as Lord Lytton had envisaged for Kandahar, which was to have acted as a bulwark against the more rebellious sections of Afghanistan.[60] It included those chiefs along the middle border whose submissions, even by early September, were still half-hearted and unsatisfactory, and of whom Manqondo of the Magwaza was proving the most recalcitrant.

To bring these chiefs to heel, Wolseley decided on a show of strength, and ordered Clarke's Column to march out of Zululand by way of Middle Drift. Dunn joined the column on 4 September, and patrols were sent out as it advanced, demanding arms and royal cattle, and exacting cattle-fines from those chiefs who did not comply in time. By 20 September all the chiefs of the region had met the conditions for surrender without any attempt at resistance, and Dunn's authority was established. Sensibly he confirmed Godide, Mavumengwana, Qethuka and Sigananda as principal chiefs, so perpetuating their existing local authority.[61]

The area where there was the greatest likelihood of a royalist resurgence was north of the Black Mfolozi, where many of Cetshwayo's most immediate family and adherents had their main homesteads. They were becoming known collectively as the uSuthu. This term, 'uSuthu', from being the distinguishing cry of Cetshwayo's party during the civil war of 1856, and becoming the national cry after his accession, narrowed in the 1880s to become specifically associated with the royalist cause and its supporters.[62] Wolseley deliberately neutralised the possibility of uSuthu consolidation in the north by ensuring that chiefs of great status and local power, who could be relied upon to suppress any such aspirations, were established in authority over them.

Wolseley might have asserted in his typically barbed way that Hamu was not a chief whom he himself would personally have selected, and that he was doing so only to honour the pledges made to him when he defected.[63] In reality, though, there was no one else with the status and hereditary authority capable of controlling the north-west – where, after all, the royalist Qulusi had been among the last to submit. Furthermore, Hamu's long-standing ambitions, which clearly were not satisfied even by the greatly enlarged chiefdom Wolseley awarded him, ensured that he would keep the royalists down. Zibhebhu, thanks to his timely submission, was confirmed in his already quasi-autonomous chiefdom in the north-east, and had his sway extended considerably to take in the homesteads of many of the uSuthu neighbouring him.

Mgojana had not the ambitious record of these two members of the royal house, but he had co-operated in the hunt for the king and was chief of the Ndwandwe, who, before their defeat by Shaka, had been the paramount power in the region.[64] Wolseley hoped that the chiefdom he had created for Mgojana would also serve to keep the royalists in check, as would Mlandlela kaMbiya's, centred as it was on that other great pre-Shakan chiefdom, the Mthethwa. Somkhele, like Mlandlela, had made an opportune submission and had subsequently expressed his antagonism to the king and his regret that he had sent his people to fight in the war.[65] He was, in any case, a chief of considerable power. His grandfather was Velane, *induna* of the Mthethwa chief, Dingiswayo. He lived in great state in a huge homestead with a double row of huts and a central parade ground 200 metres across, surrounded in quasi-royal style by his own *izinduna* and warriors. Fat, smooth-faced and of an easy-going nature, he was entrusted with the most northerly of the coastal chiefdoms.[66] The only other chiefdom on the periphery of Zululand was that created for Sekethwayo. Wolseley might have characterised him as 'a stupid and infirm old man',[67] but he had early attempted to throw in his lot with the British, and so merited his promised reward.

Wolseley, incidentally, by making the northern limits of Hamu's territory the Bivane River, and those of Sekethwayo's the Phemevana, ceded the entire former Disputed Territory between the confluence of the Phongolo and Bivane (including the Ntombe valley and Luneburg) to the Transvaal. This cession at last defined Zululand's north-western frontier, and confirmed the Boer control of the region against which Cetshwayo had struggled for so long.

It is noteworthy that all the chiefs appointed to territories along Zululand's borders or coasts had either materially aided the British during the war, shown themselves to have ambitions to independent sovereignty, or abandoned the royal cause sufficiently early to have at least a degree of trust placed in them by Wolseley. They effectively neutralised the appointed chiefs in the interior of the country, who had not a similar record. Of these, Faku kaZiningo of the Ntombela was a nonentity, though Mfanawendlela kaThanga of the Zungu was an *isikhulu*. Both were likely under the new arrangement to remain under the influence of their more dependable neighbours. Two of the others had been important chiefs, though their submissions had been neither particularly sought nor noticed. They were Gawozi, the self-important Mpungose chief and *isikhulu* who, though a cripple from paralysis, had been a great favourite of the king's;[68] and Mgitshwa kaMvundlana, a younger brother of Mkhosana, the Biyela chief, who had been killed at Isandlwana. Although both enjoyed a developed power-base, they were reputed to have been firmly of the peace party before the war, which was a distinct recommendation. Indeed, Mgitshwa was to prove a determined foe of the royal house.

Only one of the great chiefs upon whose co-operation the British had relied, who was sufficiently powerful in his own right to maintain an independent sovereignty, and to whom Wolseley had promised one as a suitable reward, actually declined the offer. This was Mnyamana. The motives for his refusal (which he rapidly came to regret)[69] were apparently mixed. Some of the Zulu ascribed it to his abiding loyalty to the king;[70] Wolseley supposed it was due to a sense of slight that his designated territory was not as large as he thought his due. Mnyamana himself insisted that it was because he did not wish to be split from the bulk of his adherents, who had been assigned to Hamu's territory.[71] It later came out that another powerful reason for forgoing an independent chiefdom was to curry favour with Hamu, whom he expected the British would reward by making king (as the Boers had done with Mpande in 1839), and whom he hoped would retain him as chief *induna*.[72]

Consequently, Wolseley awarded the chiefdom to Ntshingwayo, the victor of Isandlwana, who, although he had not had a particularly large following in the time of the king, nevertheless had enjoyed a prestige and influence second only to Mnyamana's. Like his old friend, he had submitted in time enough, and the remaindered chiefdom was the reward for his good sense. Wolseley did not go to the trouble of having the treaty already drawn up for Mnyamana's assent redrafted, but simply scratched out the Buthelezi chief's name and replaced it with Ntshingwayo's.[73]

In the final analysis, the Zulu kingdom hung together under the impact of the British invasion of 1879 only so long as the success of British arms did not seem inevitable. In regions where the British military presence was effective over a long period, the pattern was an accelerating one of negotiation and submission. Especially after the repeated defeats of the Zulu armies in the field, and the ever more apparent inability of the Zulu state to continue the struggle at a national level, there was a concerted attempt by the majority of chiefs to preserve or even augment their positions by coming to an arrangement with the British. The British peace conditions facilitated this process: by not disrupting the Zulu homestead economy, they made the fate of the Zulu state as such irrelevant to the majority of ordinary Zulu; while by generally recognising the existing chiefs, and adding appreciably to the powers of a favoured few, they left the influence of the chiefly class undisturbed. Only the power of the king was eliminated with the destruction of the *amabutho* system on which it depended, and that of the royal house curtailed.

The fact that the chiefs, almost without exception, accepted this situation cannot be attributed, as Sir Theophilus Shepstone was to maintain until the end of his life, to the yearnings of the incorporated tribes of the kingdom which Shaka had created to throw off the Zulu monarchy and to 're-enter upon their separate existence'.[74] Rather, it was because the chiefs were pragmatic and ambitious men. The Zulu state had never been so monolithic that they, especially those on the margins of the kingdom and in contact with the whites, had not the ambition – and the relative scope – for greater local autonomy. The war gave these their opportunity, while the others strove to save at least their local positions from out of the debris of the kingdom's collapse. Both these objectives required a degree of co-operation with the British, which transcended any urge for self-defeating sacrifice in the ruined cause of a unified Zulu state under its king.

PART IV

Like Water Spilt on the Ground

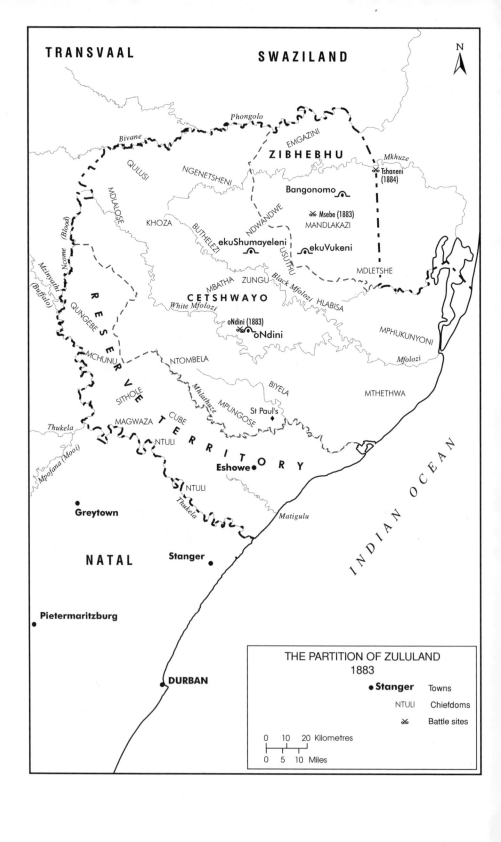

THE PARTITION OF ZULULAND
1883

● **Stanger**   Towns

NTULI   Chiefdoms

✂   Battle sites

0   10   20 Kilometres

0   5   10 Miles

27

Until the Queen Restores Me to Zululand

In the dawn of 15 September 1879 Cetshwayo and his party were conveyed in closed carriages from the transport steamer *Natal* to the Castle in Cape Town.[1] The captive king was wearing a light suit of European clothes, which he had earnestly requested while on board, and a tall dark hat squeezed over his head-ring. Despite the early hour, a large crowd of sightseers had gathered and even attempted to raise a cheer. Cetshwayo, who retained a proper sense of his royal station despite the calamities that had engulfed him, seemed intensely amused and gratified at the eagerness of the people to catch a glimpse of him. As when on board the *Natal*, he continued to do his best to maintain his humour and dignity, and to evince no surprise when driven into what was then the largest and most prosperous city in southern Africa. But overwhelmed by its extent and scale, and struck by the futile presumption of ever having pitted himself and his people against such evident power and prosperity, he could not help himself from moaning, 'I am now a very old man.'[2]

Indeed, it had not always been easy for the royal captive to keep up a front of majestic calm. He had momentarily given way when he had first come into sight of the sea and the waiting ships at Port Durnford, and he had found it impossible to preserve any dignity at all when afflicted by violent sea-sickness moments after stepping into the surf-boat which took him through the wild surf to the *Natal*. During the five days' passage from Port Durnford to Simon's Bay he had suffered miserably again through one rough night off Cape Agulhas. Nor had landfall meant the end of the unhappy journey during which he had spent most of his time secluded in the hut-like wooden structure covered with heavy tarpaulins which had been erected for him and his women on the poop deck of the *Natal*. Legal niceties compelled him to languish on board a further six days until the arrival of his official warrant of delivery permitted him to be put ashore.

As a prisoner of war, he was to remain in the custody of the British military authorities. His appointed custodian was Captain J. Ruscombe Poole, RA, who had conducted him from Wolseley's presence near the charred ruins of oNdini. Poole was a sympathetic man, as was the king's interpreter, Henry Longcast. Long-cast, an orphan of Irish extraction, had been brought up by the Revd Robert Robertson at the KwaMagwaza Mission, so he had known Cetshwayo and other

343

Zulu notables like Sihayo and Dabulamanzi for many years. During the war he had served as interpreter and guide on Chelmsford's staff. Cetshwayo could look upon this straightforward, upright man with his candid blue eyes as a friend, and Longcast did not betray his trust.

Mkhosana kaZangqana, Cetshwayo's longstanding companion and adviser, shared his fallen king's exile. He had been one of Mpande's councillors, and was a man of fine presence and daring outspokenness. A small party of personal attendants tended to the king's needs. It comprised three men including the royal hairdresser, four young women of the royal household (every one the daughter of a great chief) and a female servant. Even their captors admitted the attractiveness of the women, to whose vivacity and good temper the photograph taken of them while on board ship did little justice. Perhaps the reason for its inadequacy was that when the camera was pointed at them the women had found it impossible to stifle their embarrassed giggles until sternly rebuked by Cetshwayo, whereupon they had subsided into uncharacteristic solemnity.[3]

Immured in the Flagstaff Bastion of the seventeenth-century Castle in Cape Town, where he and his attendants were allotted a suite of apartments and a length of parapet where they might take the air and exercise, Cetshwayo resisted sinking into the obscurity intended for him. The Anglo-Zulu War had been too recent and important an event for that, and the king of the terrible Zulu bore an inevitable notoriety. There were also those who saw him as the victim of an unjust war, and they contrived to keep his plight and that of his people in the public eye. Cetshwayo himself was determined to defend his cause and welcomed the attention focused on him. Much of this was merely idle curiosity. While his ship was in Simon's Bay the shore had been thronged with trippers hoping to catch a glimpse of him, and special hoardings had to be erected on the Castle ramparts to protect his privacy. Yet if Cetshwayo discriminatingly kept the gawkers and fashionable snoopers at arm's length, he cultivated those visitors who might help his cause. He was allowed considerable leeway in deciding whom he would agree to receive, and did so with a natural dignity and royal bearing which favourably impressed them all. Those who thronged his quarters included senior imperial officials, Cape politicians, visiting royalty such as Princes Albert and George, the grandsons of Queen Victoria, and committed partisans like Lady Florence Dixie.

Once Wolseley's settlement of Zululand was in place, the British government was advised that Cetshwayo could no longer be held as a prisoner of war. On the other hand, there was no intention that he should be released. He was therefore kept in detention on the strength of a bill enacted by the Cape parliament in July 1880. Not until February 1881 were arrangements to transfer him from military to civil authority at last completed. He was accommodated on the farm Oude Molen on the Cape Flats a few miles out of Cape Town. His neighbour on the adjoining farm Uitvlugt was Langalibalele, the Hlubi chief, who had been held in exile since the suppression of his 'rebellion' against the Natal government in 1873. At Oude Molen the king enjoyed considerably more freedom than at the Castle. He could keep cattle and enjoy outdoor recreations like coursing jackals and rabbits with the deerhound and other dogs he had been given, and hunting birds with his thrown knobkerrie, at which he decidedly surpassed his hunting-companion Langalibalele in skill.

There were other changes too in the conditions of his captivity. Captain Ruscombe Poole had left in December 1880 to serve in the looming First Anglo-Boer War, which culminated in the Transvaal Boers wresting their independence back from Britain. Poole's subsequent death in action caused Cetshwayo considerable grief, for he and his military custodian had become intimate friends. During the tedious days of captivity the king had dictated his invaluable version of the history of the Zulu kingdom to the receptive soldier, who had then published it.[4] Ruscombe Poole's place as custodian was taken by J. Storr Lister, a young Cape official. Longcast, stultified by his own virtual confinement at Cetshwayo's side, also left for the Transvaal and the adventures of a campaign. He was replaced as interpreter by the raw-boned and earnest R.C.A. Samuelson – who, like Longcast, an old acquaintance – had also been brought up at a Zululand mission, St Paul's, not far from KwaMagwaza.

Outings and other diversions helped distract the king who was falling increasingly into a mood of despondency as no end to his captivity seemed in sight, and as disturbing news of burgeoning civil war in Zululand reached him. Samuelson taught him and his women some of the rudiments of reading and writing, and instructed them in Christianity. He went on long walks with the king and accompanied him on carriage rides and excursions by railway. They attended the Theatre Royal in Cape Town for a pantomime called 'The Fair One with the Golden Curls', where the voices and buxom figures of the actresses reminded Cetshwayo irresistibly of the women of Zululand. The king watched the Highland Sports in Rondebosch as the guest of the Governor of the Cape, and was invited to a society dinner-party where he shook hands with all and politely answered the many questions put to him.

But the affairs of Zululand remained uppermost in Cetshwayo's mind, and he sorrowed at the harrowing tales of bloodshed and disorder among the squabbling kinglets set up by Wolseley. In particular, he was affected by the sufferings of his own family. Dinuzulu, his eleven-year-old heir, and his daughter, Beyisile, accompanied by twenty women of the royal household and a herd of a hundred cattle, had taken refuge after the battle of Ulundi with Zibhebhu at his Banganomo *umuzi* in the far north-east of his chiefdom. Zibhebhu saw the obvious advantages, in terms of both political leverage and additional wealth, of keeping them all under his control. But Dinuzulu was, in his father's words, 'a sharp boy',[5] and as a prince greatly resented the humiliations Zibhebhu heaped upon him. He was moreover by nature very short-tempered with eyes that blazed red when he became angry. He quickly developed a deep aversion to Zibhebhu, and resolved to make his escape. Mnyamana managed to spirit him away and handed him over to the care of his uncle, Ndabuko, and his capable mother, Nomvimbi Msweli. Zibhebhu was infuriated, especially since Ndabuko imperiously refused to hand the prince back as though he were an independent ruler, and not merely one of the Mandlakazi chief's new subjects. So Zibhebhu kept the cattle and royal women, and instituted punitive measures against the uSuthu in his chiefdom.[6]

Knowledge of such events deeply disturbed the king, impotent in his captivity, and his sleep was troubled by yearning dreams of a return to Zululand. By way of attempting to influence events in his country, and to further his own tenacious plans to return, he dictated a long apologia to the Governor of the Cape, and patiently answered searching and impertinent questions put to him by the Cape Government Commission on Native Laws and Customs.[7]

In the end, all the energies Cetshwayo devoted while at Oude Molen to recruiting influential people who might help end his banishment paid dividends. Devoted friends and liberal humanitarians like Bishop Colenso and Lady Florence Dixie helped direct the voluminous correspondence he opened up with Cape, Natal and British politicians and officials, public figures, former adversaries like Major-General Sir Evelyn Wood, and even the Prince of Wales and Queen Victoria herself. Samuelson acted throughout as his confidential adviser and scribe. This skilful literary offensive began to bear fruit as Gladstone's Liberal government, which had come to power in April 1880, was increasingly embarrassed by the telling points raised in public concerning the injustice of the king's imprisonment and the disastrous state of affairs in Zululand. The upshot was that Cetshwayo achieved his purpose, which was to be allowed to visit London to plead his cause in person. He was informed on 26 September 1881 that permission had been granted, but a series of delays by unsympathetic officialdom repeatedly prevented his sailing until 12 July 1882. Meanwhile, Cetshwayo remained at Oude Molen for, as he informed the Governor of the Cape with great dignity:

> I was King of the Zulus, had my country invaded by the Queen's troops, tried to defend my country, but was beaten, taken captive and brought down here by the Queen's orders. Here I intend to remain until the Queen restores me to Zululand.[8]

Cetshwayo hoped he could persuade the British government to return him to Zululand as the means of preventing the final ruin of his country. That Zululand was falling into civil war was not an entirely unforeseen consequence of Wolseley's settlement, though it was of little concern to its architects. Wolseley and his advisers had been concerned in an entirely pragmatic way to neutralise any future Zulu threat to Natal or the Transvaal, not through the direct annexation of the kingdom, but through dividing it against itself. In following this course, they anticipated that the more powerful of the thirteen chiefs, especially those on the periphery, like Zibhebhu, Hamu and John Dunn, would continue to align themselves with British interests. Only in this way could they maintain their enhanced power at the expense of the uSuthu who were nursing their hopes for a reunited kingdom under the restored Cetshwayo. Indeed, the elevation of reliable collaborators or 'loyalists' to counterbalance the influence of recalcitrant elements was a common device among imperial administrators such as Wolseley.

Where Wolseley's settlement fell down, even on its own terms, was in its failure to provide a mechanism for containing the spiralling conflict in Zululand, and ensuring that it did not spill over into Natal. The Natal colonists perceived this very well, and their vociferous opposition to the settlement grew daily. Their criticisms, expressed in forthright colonial style in the newspapers and in the Natal Legislative Council, cannot simply be put down to the undeniable disappointment in some quarters that Zululand had not been thrown open to white settlement, nor the Zulu brought onto the labour market. Rather, they were the expression of a sincere belief held by most settlers that Zululand would continue to constitute a threat to the security of Natal until it had been properly annexed and brought under the control of white officials.[9]

The viewpoint of the Natal official establishment concerning the fate of Zululand was consistently and ably expressed over the succeeding years by Sir Theophilus Shepstone, whose ideas on 'native affairs' had (as we have seen) thoroughly permeated the whole colonial administration.[10] Shepstone proposed an alternative to Wolseley's settlement which would be based on the expedient system of indirect rule he had masterminded for Natal's black population. Acutely conscious of the dangers of an over-precipitate transition from indigenous to colonial-style administration, Shepstone favoured leaving hereditary chiefs with certain of their former powers so long as these were exercised under the supervision of white officials. In Natal, this arrangement had gradually undermined and eventually negated the authority of the chiefs since it had progressively dawned on their adherents that the effective source of power no longer resided with their traditional rulers, but with the white officials set over them.

When it came to Zululand, Shepstone envisioned the territory's annexation to Natal and the introduction of an administrative structure of white magistrates set over the chiefs. In other words, Zululand would be turned into an enormous location on the Natal model. Consequently, even if the land were not thrown open to white settlement, it could at least serve to resettle Natal's excess black population. The imposition of a hut tax would, as in Natal, pay for the whole operation, and would have the additional advantage of forcing the Zulu onto the labour market. Yet, crucially, none of this would brutally break continuity with the past. The homestead would still function as the social and economic basis of Zulu life. All that would have changed was that instead of serving the king or his chief, a man's surplus labour and production would be diverted to the colonial government.

Such a transition, Shepstone believed, could easily be achieved in Zululand since Wolseley's settlement had greatly weakened existing political structures while at the same time perpetuating age-old economic and social practices. And, like Wolseley, Shepstone would rely on collaborators during the period of transition. They were particularly necessary in a region such as Zululand, where the partisans of the old order – especially the members of the royal family – were still both powerful and unreconciled, and could be expected to attempt to subvert the new system. Thus, for Shepstone, the basis for any settlement imposed on the Zulu required both the establishment of indirect rule and the neutralisation of the uSuthu through the agency of loyal collaborators raised up by the British and owing nothing to the former royal house.

The Colenso family, Cetshwayo's champions, were diametrically opposed to the extension of the Shepstone system to Zululand and its maintenance through the manipulation of collaborators. Bishop Colenso and his two daughters, Frances and Harriette, consistently warned that any settlement of Zululand which excluded the king and left the country in the hands of the chiefs set up by Wolseley would certainly produce civil war. There is no doubt that they were correct in their prediction, but they were unfortunate in that the first British Resident in Zululand to stick by that thankless and exceedingly difficult task sufficiently long to make himself felt was Melmoth Osborn, a former colleague of Shepstone and a dedicated exponent of his policies.[11] In 1854, at the age of twenty, he had entered the Natal civil service, where Shepstone's influence in 'native affairs' was already paramount. His association with Shepstone had been cemented when, in 1877, he had accompanied him to the Transvaal as Colonial Secretary.

Besides his proven ideological reliability, Osborn also possessed considerable administrative experience, not only through his post in the Transvaal, but as Resident Magistrate of the Newcastle Division in Natal from 1867 to 1876. When William Wheelwright, the former Resident Magistrate of Umvoti County and the first British Resident in Zululand, threw up his undesirable appointment as futile and unrewarding after only two months, Osborn rose to the challenge. With his heavy, bearded features and large, fleshy nose, he gave every appearance of judgement and firmness, and his grasp of the Zulu language and the customs of the people were sufficient at least to impress other whites. Yet for all his apparent attributes as a second Shepstone, Osborn was to prove an inefficient bureaucrat, whose blatant partisanship would detract significantly from his ability to perform his functions as a servant of the state.

Osborn, then, considering his training and preferences, was hardly likely to support the uSuthu in their genuine grievances against the antagonistic chiefs set over them. Indeed, to the contrary, he actively supported Zibhebhu and Hamu in their ill-treatment of the royal family and their close associates such as Mnyamana, for he positively welcomed developments which would destroy the influence of the uSuthu.[12] Consequently, when a deputation led by Ndabuko and Shingana, the king's brothers, walked all the way to Pietermaritzburg in May 1880 to complain of victimisation and to plead for Cetshwayo's return, Osborn threw all his influence behind their oppressors. The colonial authorities were only too content to accept his word in the matter, and the uSuthu deputation returned disconsolate and without redress. A year later, at a meeting held at Osborn's residency at Nhlazatshe in May 1881, the uSuthu fared no better. Far from hearkening to their complaints, Osborn was so outspoken in support of their tormentors that Zibhebhu and Hamu took his words as nothing less than permission to do as they wished with the uSuthu. Within a short space Ndabuko, his brother Ziwedu, and other uSuthu leaders had been driven from their homes in the Vuna valley within Zibhebhu's chiefdom. The triumphant Mandlakazi and Ngenetsheni took possession both of their cattle and of their *imizi*.

Inevitably, the victims drew together to resist and, since Osborn had no armed force at his disposal to keep the sides apart or enforce his authority, the country began to slip inexorably into chaos. Matters reached a crisis on 2 October 1881 when the forces of Hamu and the fiercely royalist Qulusi, who had been consigned to his district but were reluctant to acknowledge his authority, clashed on the right bank of the Bivane River. The Qulusi rapidly broke and took flight and many hundreds fell in the merciless pursuit across the river into Transvaal territory.

Sir Evelyn Wood (who had stepped in as Governor of Natal to replace Sir George Pomeroy Colley, who had fallen on 27 February 1881 in the battle of Majuba during the First Anglo-Boer war) attempted to broker some form of reconciliation between the parties at another meeting at Nhlazatshe on 31 August 1881. Neither snowstorms, illness nor old age prevented almost all the men of note in Zululand from attending, accompanied by about 1 000 followers. But though Wood forced Hamu and Zibhebhu to disgorge some of the cattle they had seized from the uSuthu, he nevertheless upheld their coercive authority, confirmed the banishment of Dinuzulu and his uncles from Zibhebhu's territory, and left Ndabuko, Mnyamana and the others as unreconciled to their hapless lot as before.[13]

These were the circumstances surrounding the British decision to allow Cetshwayo to travel to England. To the officials of the Colonial Office it seemed that the Wolseley settlement was breaking down irretrievably, and that if the undesirable obligation of direct annexation was to be avoided, the only alternative lay in an accommodation with the king of the sort that Colenso had been urging. In any case, as a matter of policy Gladstone's Liberal Party condemned the Anglo-Zulu War begun by the previous Conservative administration as unjust. Lord Kimberley, the Colonial Secretary, was consequently predisposed to be sympathetic to Cetshwayo, who had suffered in defending his righteous cause.

Kimberley's hand was strengthened when Piet Joubert, the Superintendent of Native Affairs in the South African Republic, which had regained its independence from Britain following the First Anglo-Boer War, roundly condemned Wolseley's settlement and, on 25 October 1881 and again on 18 July 1882, urged Cetshwayo's restoration. As Joubert bluntly put it, matters in Zululand were steadily deteriorating thanks to the 'wrong policy' of the British government, and he starkly warned that 'the shedding of blood and barbarities' would increase until the king returned.[14] Wolseley's indignant, but not unreasonable, protests that Cetshwayo's restoration would 'give rise to serious trouble...[and] would be in direct contravention of the guarantee' he had given the thirteen chiefs he had set up[15] consequently fell on deaf ministerial ears.

For their part, the uSuthu leadership did their best to fortify their king's bargaining position. In April 1882 a second deputation of leaders of the royalist cause made their laborious way to Pietermaritzburg to demonstrate their support for Cetshwayo's restoration. Led by Ndabuko, the deputation was 800 strong, and was composed of notables from all over the country. To the satisfaction of the British government at least, it demonstrated that opposition to the appointed chiefs was both widespread and strong. The colonial authorities drew no such conclusion, and put the uSuthu initiative down squarely to Bishop Colenso's 'unauthorized and irresponsible interposition in Zulu matters'.[16] Clearly, the Natal settlers would not easily accept Cetshwayo's return to his kingdom, and on 8 August 1882 a public meeting in Durban recorded its 'solemn protest' at the dismaying prospect.[17] The petition, signed by seven of Durban's most prominent citizens and 389 others, and forwarded to Lord Kimberley, forthrightly stated that Cetshwayo's return would not only revive Zulu 'ideas of military aggression' and impress Natal blacks with the 'weakness and vacillation' of the white government, but, more pertinently, would be 'the signal...for a bloody internecine strife in Zululand'.[18]

Yet only three days before, on 5 August, Cetshwayo had at last arrived in England on the steamer *Arab* accompanied by Mkhosana and a small group of attendants, including his custodian, Henrique Shepstone, a son of Sir Theophilus.[19] The presence of the dusky potentate whose warriors had inflicted such punishment on British arms excited considerable public interest. The king, however, was nothing like the vicious savage conjured up in the vulgar imagination of the British people. His considerable natural dignity and royal ease of manner were irresistibly enhanced in British eyes by his evident familiarity with British ways, which his regular social intercourse with his captors at the Cape had made possible. So, impeccably and fashionably dressed in British style – though still sporting his *isicoco*, that essential indication of his adulthood – Cetshwayo was lionised by fashionable society and (crucial for his cause) met many important public figures. The Queen, whose grandsons he had received in Cape Town, and to whom he had conveyed his pleas to be restored to his kingdom, granted him an audience of a quarter of an hour at Osborne. Their meeting passed off most amiably.

Cetshwayo was much impressed with the magnificence of his surroundings and the evident power and complexity of British civilisation. But of more real significance for his future than the Queen's graciousness or the enthusiasm of the London crowds were the three interviews he had with Lord Kimberley. During their course, the general conditions for his restoration were settled. They were not as liberal as Cetshwayo might have hoped, but only one really disturbed him, though he had little choice but to accept it. He was informed that he was not to be restored to the whole kingdom as it had existed before 1879, and not even to the somewhat shrunken territory making up Wolseley's thirteen chiefdoms.

What the actual boundaries of Cetshwayo's kingdom were to be remained for the present undefined. Yet it was still with high hopes that he landed once more at Cape Town on 24 September 1882. He expected to be allowed to return immediately to Zululand, but his restoration was delayed by the Natal officials who were determined that when the king alighted again in Zululand it should be only with severely clipped wings. They succeeded in persuading the British government that Cetshwayo's authority be confined to the central portion of his former kingdom where he would be under the supervision of a Resident, Henry Francis Fynn, Jnr, the son of the Natal pioneer. He was to be hemmed in to the south of the Mhlathuze River by the so-called Reserve Territory created out of Dunn's and Hlubi's former chiefdoms. The Reserve Territory would act as a military buffer for Natal, and serve as a sanctuary for those wishing to evade the king's reimposed rule. Although nominally to be an independent territory under British protection, it was in fact to be administered by officials recruited from Natal, namely a resident commissioner assisted by sub-commissioners. They would rule through the existing chiefs, and meet the costs of their administration by the imposition of a hut tax. In other words, the full-blown Shepstone system and implied settler control were to be extended over the southern third of Zululand. If the inhabitants did not like it and wished to submit to Cetshwayo's rule, they were given the heartless option of abandoning their homes and moving north to his district.

The safeguards to the north of the king's territory which the Natalians succeeded in securing were even more onerous and pregnant with disaster for the future. Zibhebhu, alone of the thirteen chiefs, was to continue as an independent ruler, and was to have an augmented territory north of the Black Mfolozi precisely in that area where the royalists were particularly strong. In that way he would continue to act as a dependable check to the returning king's ambitions. The Natal officials had learned something from the violence of the previous months, however, and realised that the boundaries of Zibhebhu's territory must be somewhat modified to eradicate some of the causes of the previous conflict. Accordingly, Sir Henry Bulwer, the Special Commissioner for Zululand (and once again Governor of Natal), instructed Osborn on 22 December 1882 that Zibhebhu's boundaries should be readjusted to allow those leading members of the uSuthu cause who had fled from Zibhebhu's territory during the recent conflict to return in security to their homes.[20]

To achieve this, Bulwer suggested that the western and southern portions of Zibhebhu's original territory be excised and added to the country to be placed under Cetshwayo's rule. This would have the effect of removing much of the territory of the king's brothers Ndabuko and Ziwedu from Zibhebhu's jurisdiction, as well as that of the royalist Chief Mbopha kaWolizibi of the Hlabisa, though it would leave that of the uSuthu-aligned Chief Msutshwana kaMfuzi of the Mdletshe still partially under Zibhebhu. This last was an unaddressed problem, and Bulwer compounded it with an additional one of his own making. He proposed that, in order to compensate Zibhebhu for his loss of territory and Mandlakazi *imizi* to Cetshwayo, the land formerly under the appointed chief Mgojana of the Ndwandwe should be made over to him. Equitable as this might have appeared to the distant Special Commissioner in Pietermaritzburg, but the arrangement placed the emGazini people – who, under their regent, Sitshaluza kaMamba, had declined to be put under Zibhebhu in 1879 – into that chief's hands. This was an arrangement that was to prove unacceptable to their new chief, Mabhoko kaMasiphula, who swiftly joined the uSuthu cause.[21]

Despite these considerable flaws, Bulwer hoped to forestall future disputes by having Zibhebhu's new western and southern boundaries properly surveyed and beaconed off. What he intended by this, though, was not a sensitive investigation of the tangled situation on the ground, where *imizi* adhering to different chiefs were often inextricably intermingled. Instead, he commissioned a professionally reputable survey undertaken by a suitably qualified practitioner, and J. Eustace Fannin was chosen for the task. Fannin had worked for many years as a land surveyor, based in Durban, interspersed with spells in the Natal civil service and at the Diamond Fields. In November 1878 he had been appointed Special Border Agent in Umvoti County, with the task of relaying intelligence concerning Zulu activity to the British authorities. He was fluent in Zulu, and performed his commission admirably throughout the Anglo-Zulu War. In August 1879 Fannin's hopes of becoming the first British Resident in Zululand had been dashed when William Wheelwright accepted the job. Now in 1882, he was only too happy in his typically adventuresome way to take up Bulwer's commission.[22]

Superficially, Fannin's task in January 1883 was easier than that which had faced the commissioners who had fixed the boundaries of Wolseley's settlement in December 1879. When making observations with his theodolite, he was able to use many of the beacons they had erected, whether they were cairns built of stones and sods, or great natural rocks chiselled with a 'B' and heaped with stones. In one quaint case Fannin found a large cabbage tree with a great 'B' cut deeply in the bark and piled around the foot with stones. He himself added beacon points that consisted of natural features, such as ponds or hill tops.[23] His work was not facilitated, though, by having to use the map drawn up by Captain James Alleyne, RA, as a base. Although more accurate than any map that preceded it, and drafted while Alleyne was serving on the boundary commission of 1879, Fannin found it nonetheless 'far from perfect, and more or less misleading'.[24]

To compound his difficulties, Fannin realised that he would have to deviate from Bulwer's instructions. The Special Commissioner, displaying a lofty preference for tidy geometrical shapes over messy topographical and social realities, had desired that Zibhebhu's chiefdom be 'a compact territory of a triangular shape',[25] and was to be annoyed when it did not turn out that way.[26] But Fannin found it preferable, as had the previous commissioners in 1879, to create a natural boundary which followed easily recognisable topographical features, rather than to lay down an abstract line on the map. The crucial drawback was that his natural boundary violated the actual situation on the ground no less than would have Bulwer's abstract one. And indeed, as a result of his efforts, the inhabitants of some forty Mandlakazi *imizi* found themselves placed in uSuthu territory. But Zibhebhu did not demur, since he had anticipated losing even more.[27]

Fannin returned to Natal to take up his reward, which was the post of Resident Magistrate of Stanger. He left behind him in Zululand a situation made potentially worse than ever. The king, even before Fannin had begun his work defining Zibhebhu's boundary, had learned with dismay of the compromise worked out between the Natal officials and the Colonial Office. He realised only too well that what was being presented to him as a *fait accompli* was a recipe for continued civil strife. Not only was he being wedged between his arch-enemy to the north and antagonistic anti-uSuthu officials to the south, but he would have to face the deep hostility of the nine deposed chiefs consigned to his own territory – notably that of Hamu. Though he had a large following and various defensible mountain fastnesses, Hamu knew that he would be held accountable for his actions against the Qulusi and Mnyamana's Buthelezi, and undoubtedly was prepared to defend himself. But that at least Cetshwayo had always anticipated. He knew that if he wished ever to return to Zululand he must assent to the conditions placed before him. So on 11 December 1882 he signed, promising reluctantly to keep the peace with Zibhebhu, respect the boundaries assigned his territory and to rule with the advice of the British Resident. More than that, he undertook not to revive the military system, to allow all men to marry when they chose, and to encourage his people to seek work in Natal and the Transvaal.[28]

These conditions fairly represented the triumph of the Natal interest, and served notice to Cetshwayo that he could not hope to be again the truly independent monarch he had once been. Indeed, it was difficult to imagine how he could rule effectively when the main pillar of the old kingdom, namely the military system, had been pulled away – not only by British *fiat*, it should be added, but by the younger *amabutho* themselves, who had made the most of the changing circumstances to take wives without the king's permission.[29] Besides, he no longer possessed the cattle wealth necessary to support his station. Formerly, the royal cattle had covered the country, but the chiefs, particularly John Dunn, Zibhebhu and Hamu, had seized those pastured in their territory as their own. This want of cattle, as Lord Kimberley understood completely, was Cetshwayo's greatest anxiety. A king with empty hands was no king at all. Unless sufficient royal cattle were voluntarily returned to him (which was not very likely), he would have to seize herds to survive – surely an infallible recipe for conflict.[30]

In the first days of January 1883 Cetshwayo set sail from the Cape for Zululand on the *Algerine*. His exile was over, thanks to his tenacity and that of his friends, but his heart can hardly have soared as it should. The conditions he had been obliged to accept, and the intractable difficulties in Zululand he could only too clearly envisage, combined to ensure that he could confront his uncertain future with little other than trepidation.

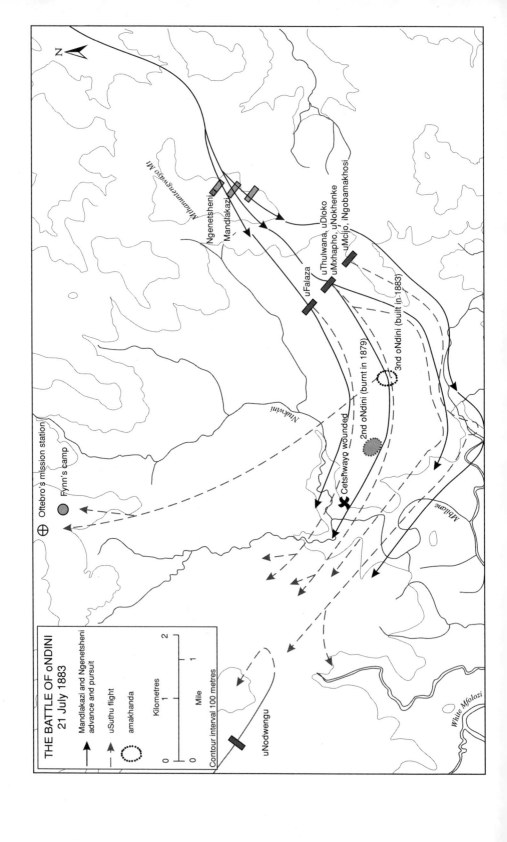

THE BATTLE OF oNDINI
21 July 1883

→ Mandlakazi and Ngenetsheni
advance and pursuit

→ uSuthu flight

⊙ amakhanda

⊕ Oftebro's mission station
⬤ Fynn's camp

Kilometres
0   1   2

Mile
0   1

Contour interval 100 metres

Mhlamamfongwayo Mt

Ngenetsheni
Mandlakazi

uThulwana, uDloko
uMxhapho, uNokhenke
uMcijo, iNgobamakhosi

uFalaza

3nd oNdini (built in 1883)

2nd oNdini (burnt in 1879)

Cetshwayo wounded

Ntukwini

Mbilane

uNodwengu

White Mfolozi

28

Am I to Run Away from my Dog?

King Cetshwayo did not land on the shores of his own territory on the afternoon of 10 January 1883, but at Port Durnford, now in the Reserve Territory.[1] To his disappointed surprise, there were almost no Zulu to welcome him. But when he clambered in a somewhat dazed condition out of the surf-boat on to the beach, he was received by Sir Theophilus Shepstone and a strong detachment of the 6th Dragoons. The grand old sphinx of Natal had been brought out of retirement to supervise Cetshwayo's restoration, and in his typically prudent, if devious, style had kept the date of the king's return after three years of exile a secret to avoid possible demonstrations by his supporters. That would have been an embarrassment to the new Resident Commissioner of the Reserve Territory, no other than John Shepstone. So his wily brother's plan was to escort Cetshwayo to Mthonjaneni in his own territory, where the principal men of Zululand were to assemble to witness his installation and to hear upon what conditions the British were restoring their king to them.

Once at Mthonjaneni on 17 January, where Cetshwayo had waited once before in 1873 to be acclaimed as king by his people, he and his escort had to camp for twelve tedious and anxious days before the chiefs, gathered as ten years before in the emaKhosini valley below, would consent to participate in the ceremony proposed by Shepstone. Zibhebhu came alone up to Mthonjaneni, pointedly not to greet the king, but to pay his respects to Shepstone, his patron. Meanwhile, the chiefs secretly negotiated with Cetshwayo on what policy they were to follow. All were upset that parts of the former kingdom were to be alienated from royal control, and some felt bitterly that they had been tricked into accepting Cetshwayo's restoration at the price of dividing their country. As for the uSuthu, they were aghast that many of their number were to remain under Zibhebhu's tyrannical rule, and were hardly pleased that yet others were to be governed by John Shepstone.

Despite these varied misgivings, the installation ceremony at last took place on the afternoon of 29 January. Ndabuko, Mnyamana and between 5 000 and 6 000 prominent Zulu attended. Zibhebhu had deliberately started a rumour that it was only a waxwork image *(isithombe)* of the king which the British were bringing back with them, and it was not until Cetshwayo advanced and addressed the assembly that all believed it was really their king who had returned.[2] The uSuthu leaders, over forty of them, took the opportunity to deliver in turn a sustained protest, with Cetshwayo's prior approval, at the terms of the king's restoration. Hemulana, Mnyamana's *induna*, led the attack. Inevitably, they succeeded only in enraging Shepstone, who harboured his own uncomfortable memories of the 'coronation' of 1873. In any case, he had no power to alter the conditions devised by the British and Natal governments. Once the unhappy ceremony was over, he and his escort wasted not a moment before riding off for Natal, leaving the king to face his uncertain fate.

Not at all sorry to see the white men's backs, the king, his royal women, their attendants and a large number of supporters of the highest rank all moved down joyfully to the Mahlabathini plain where the king's *amakhanda* had once clustered in all their potency. Nothing save their charred vestiges remained, but the king's adherents immediately rendered him service by starting to build a third oNdini just to the east of the one destroyed in the war of 1879, as well as some of the other royal homesteads. The latest oNdini was somewhat smaller than the previous one, being only 461 metres in diameter, though still consisting of 1 000 huts or more. It was built in the traditional style of an *ikhanda*, with the *isigodlo* at the head, where the customs of the royal household were revived. There Samuelson, Cetshwayo's faithful interpreter, soon found him, seated in a chair, surrounded by many of the Zulu nobility, giving his daughters and some of his wives and maids-of-honour shawls and other glossy items he had purchased in Cape Town.[3]

Undermining such scenes of contentment and royal munificence, however, was the troubling knowledge that not all the great men of the land had come to pay their respects to the king. The most notable exceptions were naturally Zibhebhu, Hamu and some of the other former thirteen chiefs. Mfanawendlela, for example, whose chiefdom had encompassed the Mahlabathini plain, was ashamed to put in an appearance before his former king, especially since he had committed the sacrilege of planting crops on Mpande's grave. When he did come, though, he defiantly seated himself in a chair as if Cetshwayo's equal, instead of crawling into his presence as he would have in the days of the king's past glory.

The hostility of such chiefs proved, as Cetshwayo had feared, an insoluble problem. He had promised the British not to go to war against them, but within days of his restoration uSuthu had begun destroying the crops and *imizi* belonging to Mfanawendlela. The Resident, Henry Francis Fynn, was present in his camp on the hills to the north of oNdini to monitor the king's actions. Fynn had risen through the ranks of the Natal civil service to the post of Resident Magistrate of the Umsinga Division in 1876, had acted as interpreter to the Boundary Commission in 1878, and in January 1879 had served as Chelmsford's interpreter. He had known Cetshwayo ever since 1873, when he accompanied Shepstone's coronation expedition.[4]

Fynn had an extensive knowledge of the Zulu language, customs and institutions, and was credited with dealing with blacks under his jurisdiction with insight and sympathy. They in turn liked and respected him and called him 'Gwalagwala' after the red feather of the lourie which he wore in his hat, and which had associations with heroic qualities in battle. Fynn enjoyed insights into the situation in partitioned Zululand deeper than most other Natal officials and, despite his place in the system, was better capable of empathising with Cetshwayo's difficulties. Indeed, at a personal level, he and the king enjoyed a very close and cordial friendship. But he had a job to do as the representative of the British government, which required that he keep the peace as even-handedly as possible between the king and his antagonists. Cetshwayo was not always capable of appreciating Fynn's attempted neutrality, and expected him to be more overtly partisan. But Fynn's hands were in any case tied. He had to obtain permission for his every action from Natal, and had absolutely no means of coercing any of the parties in Zululand into abiding by the terms of Cetshwayo's restoration. The only weapon he possessed was what Bulwer airily referred to in his instructions as his 'friendly and beneficial influence'.[5]

The king, for his part, had the responsibility of protecting his supporters against the attacks of those who would not accept his rule. Clashes were already taking place in the north-west of his territory between royalist Qulusi and Mdlalose on the one side, and Hamu's Ngenetsheni on the other. In the northeast war was clearly brewing between Zibhebhu and the uSuthu still within his chiefdom. The Reserve Territory to the south posed grave problems of a different sort. John Shepstone was wasting no time in ordering the people either to submit to his authority or to move to the king's territory. The king's many supporters south of the Mhlathuze were thus placed in an impossible position. Most were naturally unwilling to abandon their homes to face the hardships and shortages of establishing new homesteads and cultivated fields, and opted to stay under Shepstone. But they still looked on Cetshwayo as their king. The majority of the chiefs in the Reserve Territory continued to pay him their respects at oNdini, while their young men periodically crossed into his territory to give him service.

Such activities strained Cetshwayo's relations with the officials in the Reserve Territory, but it was to the north that the real danger lay. Zibhebhu, just like John Shepstone, was insisting that his subjects either acknowledge his authority or move out of his territory. On 23 March 1883 he began to back up this requirement with force. When Ndabuko, Mnyamana and other chiefs who hailed from the north learned of this provocative development, they left oNdini, where they had been attending the king, to organise an army with which to finish off Zibhebhu once and for all. It is not clear if they went with Cetshwayo's explicit sanction, for Fynn had certainly warned him that such an aggressive move was guaranteed to antagonise the British.

An army of 5 000 men was assembled near Mnyamana's homesteads on the Sikhwebezi River. It consisted of contingents of Ndabuko's uSuthu, emGazini under Mabhoko kaMasiphula, and Buthelezi led by Mnyamana's son Tshanibezwe.[6] Impatient to come to grips with the Mandlakazi, the hot-headed Ndabuko – who, typically, had wanted to lead his men into Natal after the battle of Isandlwana – refused to heed Mnyamana's sensible advice not to open the campaign until reinforced by the strong contingent promised by the Qulusi. So on 29 March the force already at Mnyamana's ekuShumayeleni homestead, loosely organised into divisions by chief, rather than by *ibutho*, and placed by Ndabuko under the command of Makhoba kaMaphitha (a royalist half-brother of Zibhebhu), advanced east into Zibhebhu's territory between the Msebe and Mkhuze rivers.

The uSuthu marched in a great column thirty men wide and several kilometres long, swollen by the numerous unarmed *udibi* boys who accompanied it. Its objective was Banganomo, Zibhebhu's principal homestead. With vengeful abandon it burned and plundered as it went, destroying *imizi* belonging to the Mandlakazi chief and various members of his family. Morale, however, was not as good as it might have been, for it was rumoured that Cetshwayo had not sanctioned the advance. And it was disquieting to know that a foe with distinctly superior military skills to Makhoba's awaited them,

Spear that destroys men,
White horse that checks the vanguards.[7]

Zibhebhu and the 1 500 men of his well-disciplined army lay in ambush in the Msebe valley, waiting for the disorderly uSuthu to fall into their trap. With them were five or six mercenaries, including Johan Colenbrander, from whom Zibhebhu had traded his all-important firearms. The slopes of the valley's sides are ribbed by water-courses, making it impossible to see any great distance. Moreover, long grass and a scrub of mimosa trees were sufficient to conceal crouching men, and the uSuthu were unaware of the Mandlakazi stretched north to south across their path. Soon after sunrise on 30 March six of Zibhebhu's mounted men fired on the invaders, who were eating looted mealies near the burned Nkunkwini homestead, and drew the uSuthu into the chosen killing-ground. Even thus had Buller's patrol been lured forward on the day before the battle of Ulundi.

'It is now favourably placed. Strike its head,' cried Zibhebhu as he rode along his line of men,[8] and the Mandlakazi fell first on the emGazini of the royalists' left flank, who broke and fled. Because of the nature of the ground the other royalists could not see what was happening to units besides their own, and panic set in. The Buthelezi almost at once followed the emGazini in flight. The uSuthu contingent to the rear initially put up more resistance, but soon joined the others in their desperate retreat over ground that offered little cover, being shot down and stabbed as they ran by the victorious Mandlakazi. Despairing men were heard crying 'Oh, my children!' as they stumbled across the open ground in the direction of the Nongoma hills to the west, or tried to hive off to the north.[9] Most of the uSuthu leadership, who had been placed as was customary to the rear, escaped, though their panic-stricken men were not so fortunate. Gibson thought that in no other battle did a Zulu army ever suffer greater loss of life.[10] The mouldering bones of the slain could still be seen twenty years later, spread widely over the flats. The pursuit went on until sunset, the royalists only occasionally attempting a stand.

Zibhebhu, who at one stage in the battle fell from his famous white horse but remounted in time to charge among the flying uSuthu, picking off his particular enemies with his rifle, intervened only to save and interrogate Ndulunga, a son of Mnyamana's, and Cetshwayo's brother, Sitheku. However, ten other sons of Mnyamana are said to have been killed, and five of Ndabuko's. Zibhebhu reserved his particular vengeance for his brother Makhoba, the hapless royalist general, who was mercilessly sought out and killed in the rout. So too was Mgwazeni of the Zungu, an *induna* and brother of Cetshwayo's mother, who had been prominent in the movement to bring back the king. Only ten of the Mandlakazi were killed, in contrast to the thousands of uSuthu slain. The following day Mandlakazi forces repulsed two contingents of Tsonga who had been advancing over the Lubombo Mountains in support of Ndabuko's drive from the west. As Zibhebhu grimly declared, 'When a man is attacked by wolves he must defend himself and drive them back to the bush they came from.'[11]

When Hamu heard of his ally Zibhebhu's stunning victory, he joined him in harrying the defeated royalists, who fled north over the Phongolo to the South African Republic or back to oNdini. Those who could not make their way out of range took refuge in strongholds in the broken country north of the Black Mfolozi, in the Ngome forest or the mountains of the Hlobane range. The victorious Mandlakazi and Ngenetsheni systematically ravaged the northern districts, destroying standing crops and huts and looting grain and cattle from their opponents in a continuous series of minor skirmishes, leaving their broken foes to face starvation.

The experiences of Paulina Dlamini, once a member of Cetshwayo's *isigodlo* and only just escaped from Zibhebhu's clutches, were typical. She and her people moved into a great cave deep in Ngwibi Mountain that had its own supply of water and was large enough to accommodate their cattle. Though their enemies knew they were there they were afraid to enter the guarded passages and left Paulina's people alone. But they almost perished from starvation because they remained in the caves for nearly a year and were unable to plant or till the fields. All they had to subsist on were edible tubers and berries, and so suffered terrible privations.[12]

The authorities in Natal had no sympathy for the plight they considered the uSuthu had wilfully brought upon themselves. Bulwer put it quite bluntly when he stated that the attack on Zibhebhu had been orchestrated by the 'Ultra-Usutu party' with the king's connivance, and that if Cetshwayo did not intend to abide by the conditions of his restoration, 'he ought never to have returned'. Zibhebhu, by contrast, Bulwer insisted, posed 'no danger to the public peace', and desired only 'to be let alone and keep the word of the Government'.[13] Sir Theophilus Shepstone backed this conclusion to the hilt.[14]

Thus the uSuthu leadership (as Fynn had warned they would) forfeited the confidence of the British without shaking their trust in Zibhebhu, who had emerged as the great power in the land. And not only that, but the extent of their defeat discredited the king and his advisers in the eyes of their demoralised followers. The proud Ndabuko in particular found it hard to escape from under the weight of his great defeat. But it was not enough to repine and, in order to survive at all, the uSuthu had to strike back and attempt to prevent the Mandlakazi and Ngenetsheni from launching a joint attack on the king himself.

It was decided to deal first with Hamu, considered far less tough a nut than Zibhebhu to crack, and by May the uSuthu had succeeded in driving him back into his own strongholds. While the Ngenetsheni were being hard pressed, Cetshwayo remained at oNdini throughout May and June, summoning thousands of men from all parts of the country, including the Reserve, to assemble in the Mahlabathini plain for his protection. Once there, many were sent north to Mnyamana's district, for after their initial successes the royalists were finding it increasingly difficult to finish off Hamu. For their part, the Ngenetsheni resolved on a counter-offensive and, crucially reinforced by the Mandlakazi, repulsed Mnyamana's forces in mid-June. Alarmingly, at that very moment an army of about 3 000 men, which had been doctored for war at oNdini and led out by Dabulamanzi against the Mandlakazi, met an ignominious end. When Dabulamanzi's men reached the Black Mfolozi and were actually confronted by their numerically inferior but formidable enemies, they immediately retired without striking a blow and in such disarray that their stragglers were easily cut off by the Mandlakazi and killed.[15] Cetshwayo delivered Dabulamanzi a blistering rebuke for the ineptness of his campaign, but it was evident that, with morale ebbing away, the tide of war had turned once more against the uSuthu.

Yet the uSuthu could not simply abandon the struggle. The time of spring rains and planting was approaching, and it was essential for those living in the north to regain their lands if they were to survive. Nor could the king admit defeat. It would be political suicide if he were to acknowledge that Zibhebhu and Hamu had got the better of him. And, since Hamu was proving surprisingly difficult to subdue, the king's advisers decided to change their strategy. For months Cetshwayo had been in contact with uSuthu supporters and potential allies living on the borders of Zibhebhu's territory (even including his old enemies the Swazi), and it was hoped to co-ordinate a new, all-out offensive against him. Zibhebhu, through his excellent intelligence, rapidly learned of these preparations. Being the audacious and courageous general he was, he decided to pre-empt them by attacking first.

On 20 July Zibhebhu mustered about 3 000 of his adherents and allies – including five free-booting whites with whom he had trading contacts – at his ekuVukeni homestead on the eastern slope of the Nongoma ridge in the southwest of his chiefdom. When word of this threatening mobilisation reached oNdini reconstruction of the great royal homestead was not yet quite complete, but the uSuthu nobility were all gathered there, and meat and beer were in profuse supply. Cetshwayo and his great council of chiefs decided that Zibhebhu was concentrating his men for a move in support of Hamu against Mnyamana, for the Buthelezi chief was preparing an offensive of his own in the north. Confident that they had read Zibhebhu's intentions aright, the uSuthu leadership took no particular precautions: it was unthinkable that Zibhebhu would be sufficiently audacious to attack the king in his own capital. It was a terrible, fatal underestimation of Zibhebhu's skill and daring as a man of war.

The Mandlakazi came through the broken, thickly mimosa-wooded and stony country of the Black Mfolozi valley during the night of 20 July.[16] It was a

desolate tract of country where there were no living creatures to give the alarm
save wild animals. Zibhebhu's men made one halt on the march about five kilometres south of the Black Mfolozi, where they lit fires to warm themselves since
it was the chilly depth of winter. They then continued on towards oNdini. In one
night they covered nearly fifty kilometres over difficult terrain, a feat the uSuthu
would never have imagined possible. Inevitably, their arduous march left them
drained of energy, and if defeated there would be scant chance that they would
be able to make it all the way back to their homes. But Zibhebhu calculated accurately that the uSuthu, unprepared, demoralised by their recent defeats and
weakened by the absence of so many of their number with Mnyamana beyond
the Black Mfolozi, would put up little fight.

Shortly before dawn on Saturday 21 July, one of the party who had come with
the brother of King Mbandeni of the Swazi to treat with Cetshwayo, and who was
staying at an *umuzi* of Mfanawendlela'a about five kilometres east of oNdini, saw
the advancing Mandlakazi. He got urgent word of their menacing presence to
Cetshwayo shortly after sunrise. Consternation overwhelmed the inhabitants of
oNdini, most of whom had been fast asleep after the carousing of the previous
evening. In alarm, Cetshwayo's many chiefs and councillors began to bicker among
themselves about how best to meet the Mandlakazi attack, but all were agreed
that Cetshwayo should seek his safety elsewhere. 'Am I to run away from my dog?'
the king responded in lordly scorn to their suggestion,[17] and took charge of the
situation. He ordered Ntuzwa, the brother of Sekethwayo, the Mdlalose chief, to
assume command of the *amabutho* stationed at oNdini, and appointed his half-
brothers Sitheku, Dabulamanzi and Shingana his lieutenants. By this stage the
young uFalaza *ibutho* was drawn up outside oNdini, but not under any proper
control. Many of them had already risen to escort their womenfolk, who had
brought food the previous day, back to their homes, but they had hardly been anticipating a desperate life-and-death struggle. The other unprepared *amabutho*
moved out from the front and rear of the *ikhanda* in irregular order. The strong
uNodwengu 'corps' was stationed about thirteen kilometres north-west of
oNdini and was unavailable for its immediate defence. However, Sekethwayo, its
nominal commander, was with the king at oNdini.

One of the reasons for the confusion in the ranks of the *amabutho* was that
they were left to junior officers while their commanders were locked in a panic-
stricken and incoherent council-of-war. At length the chief officers followed
their *amabutho* eastwards along a ridge in the direction from which the Mandlakazi, still out of sight in the folds of the hills, were rapidly advancing. At about
8 a.m., approximately a kilometre and a half east of oNdini, the uSuthu spread
themselves into some sort of disjointed battle-order with the uFalaza on the left
wing, the uMcijo and iNgobamakhosi on the right, and the rest of the *amabutho*
– namely the uThulwana, uDloko, uMxhapho and uNokhenke – jumbled up in
the middle.

All wore white cow-tail decorations, the *imishokobezi*. To *shokobeza* meant to
rebel, and referred originally to those who crossed out of the Reserve Territory
and the white man's jurisdiction to serve Cetshwayo. Thus the *imishokobezi* be-

came the emblem of the uSuthu. For them the other Zulu like the Mandlakazi were the *amambuka*, the deserters or renegades from the king's cause.[18]

The uSuthu dispositions were still far from complete when the Mandlakazi left horn came in sight right over the Mthanuntengwayo ridge, and their menacing silhouettes against the dawn proved sufficient to unman their opponents. The daunted uMcijo and iNgobamakhosi wildly opened fire quite out of range and with no effect at all. Disregarding this useless fusillade, the Mandlakazi gave their terrible battle-cry of 'Washesha!' and swept on in a great outflanking movement without bothering to return the uSuthus' fire. Fearful of being cut off and surrounded, the uMcijo and iNgobamakhosi stampeded south-west beyond oNdini where the terrain was very broken and covered in bush, disregarding runners sent by the king ordering them to stand firm. They were pursued by the Mandlakazi left horn and much of their centre.

The situation was not much different at the uSuthu centre and on their left. Ntuzwa and the other commanders were positioned there, and their men initially made a stand, firing determinedly on the Mandlakazi right and its supporting contingent of Ngenetsheni, known as the Mfemfe after Hamu's principal homestead. Zibhebhu's men did not return fire, but advanced with undeterred determination on the uSuthu. This was too much for the royalists, whose nerve broke even before the Mandlakazi could come to grips with them. They turned and fled westwards at about 8.30 a.m. over the open ground of the ridge past the front of oNdini, scattering like a swarm of bees. So precipitate and general was their flight that very few of them were killed before they got as far as oNdini, and none of the Mandlakazi. Some of the uThulwana attempted to make a stand in oNdini itself, but they were cut off and killed in some sharp hand-to-hand fighting.

When the main body of fugitives from the uSuthu centre and left got just beyond oNdini they turned southwards towards the broken countryside in the direction of the White Mfolozi. However, the Mandlakazi left and centre, who had already pursued the broken uSuthu right horn up the river valley, cut off their retreat. They were thus forced to continue their flight in a more north-westerly direction towards the spot where Chelmsford had defeated the Zulu in 1879, the Mandlakazi pressing them hard. The uNodwengu contingent, which had been hurrying towards oNdini, got caught up in the general rout and unravelled without any attempt at a stand. As the Mandlakazi streamed to the north and south of oNdini, firing among the scattering uSuthu, they set the huts to the right of its entrance alight, and soon the whole *ikhanda* was ablaze. Zibhebhu's men put all the other homesteads they came across to the torch as well, and the dry winter veld caught fire too. Soon the whole Mahlabathini plain was consumed in flame and smoke as it had been in July 1879 when the British ravaged it.

Meanwhile, a mixed force of Qulusi, Buthelezi and northern uSuthu, under the command of Ndabuko, which had set out south across the Black Mfolozi for oNdini when it was learned that Zibhebhu was bent on attacking the king, failed to come to their monarch's aid. Already hobbled by dissension between their leaders, they turned back ineffectually several kilometres short of their objective on hearing of the sacking of the king's capital and the disintegration of his forces.

A number of Cetshwayo's people, women and members of his family, managed to find sanctuary in Fynn's camp in the hills to the north of oNdini. Later, he was able to send them on to safety in the Reserve Territory. Most uSuthu were not so fortunate. Fynn saw Ntuzwa, the uSuthu commander, galloping for his home in the west, but his elderly and infirm brother, Sekethwayo, did not live to reach his. Fynn later stumbled upon his pathetic corpse in the plain west of oNdini, lying with about 500 others scattered over thirteen kilometres of country. Most were men, and very few young warriors. The latter had been spry enough to run from the Mandlakazi, already exhausted after their night march. But the uSuthu leadership, the dignified men of political weight about the king, were more often than not contemporaries of King Mpande or companions of Cetshwayo's youth. Old, or at least fat bellied and unfit, they had been unable to get far. Once the *amabutho* had fled they were left defenceless, and fifty-nine or more men of influence with great followings from every part of the former kingdom were cut down.

Indeed, the list of illustrious dead reads like a roll-call of the old Zulu kingdom. Besides Sekethwayo, once one of Wolseley's appointed chiefs, there was Cetshwayo's close companion, Sihayo, whose sons had lit the match that set the kingdom alight. Ntshingwayo (like Sekethwayo an appointed chief, but one whose death Zibhebhu particularly regretted) and Godide, both of whom had been senior generals in the war of 1879 and were commanders on that disastrous 21 July of the uDloko and uMxhapho respectively, lay dead. So too did Vumanda-ba, whose sensible voice had called back the warriors crossing the Mzinyathi River after Isandlwana, and who fell valiantly defending himself at the last. Ndwa-ndwe, the Langa chief, was among the slain, as were Mbopha of the Hlabisa, a particular favourite of Cetshwayo's, the aged and respected Chief Dilikana of the Mbatha, and Chief Mnqandi of the Sibisa, whose son Sitshitshili helped Prince Dinuzulu escape the slaughter. Hayiyana, Maphitha's eldest son and Zibhe-bhu's sworn rival, who had commanded the uThulwana during the battle in Mnya-mana's absence, was killed fighting for the king. Ngcongcwana, who had trav-elled to London with Cetshwayo, was mercilessly hunted down, as were so many others. Jeff Guy was surely right to conclude that this slaughter of so many of the great men of the kingdom, upon whose established influence Cetshwayo de-pended, marked the true end of the old Zulu order.[19]

As for Cetshwayo, he abandoned his capital as the fight passed over it. Too heavy for the only horse available, which fell under his weight, he made off on foot for the White Mfolozi. Near the junction of the Ntukwini and Mbilane streams, just north of oNdini, he took sanctuary in a cluster of small trees while members of his household proceeded on their way to decoy the Mandlakazi who were hot on their heels. Even so, some of the Mandlakazi came upon Cetshwayo in the trees. The faithful Mkhosana heard the enemy call upon Cetshwayo to stand up before casting four spears at him. Two of them found their mark and wounded the king slightly in his right thigh between knee and hip. Cetshwayo recognised one of his assailants as the young son of the Hlabisa chief who was supported by Zibhe-bhu against Mbopha, the pro-uSuthu regent. Mustering all his considerable dignity despite his pain and overwhelming mortification that a mere youth had wounded him, he sternly called out, 'Do you stab me Halijana, son of Somfula? I am your king.'[20] Aghast at the enormity of having struck their monarch, the overawed Mandlakazi approached him in the correct crouching posture, gave the royal salute and attempted to tend his wounds. Lamely, they explained that they had mistaken him for his brother, Ziwedu. They then let their fallen king go on his way.

Dinuzulu, Cetshwayo's fifteen-year-old heir, managed to escape on horseback, as did Dabulamanzi. The latter had with him his son, Mzingeli, who had trodden on an acacia thorn which had gone through his foot. But Cetshwayo's little boy, Nyoniyentaba, was killed in the arms of his mother, who escaped with only a shoulder wound.

Zibhebhu, who had lost but seven men in the battle, withdrew north the day afterwards. He carried away as prisoners Sitheku, the king's doubly unfortunate half-brother, who had fallen into his hands once before after the battle of Msebe, and various women of the *isigodlo*. Under insistent pressure from Fynn, Zibhebhu later released Sitheku and seventeen women who were actually the king's wives, as well as his six little daughters, but the rest he distributed as booty to his men.

There is a cave in a shallow valley, leading down to the left bank of the White Mfolozi, which Cetshwayo had known ever since he had herded his father's cattle in this secluded spot. There he lurked with four women of the royal household and a young man of Sihayo's until he felt it sufficiently safe on 1 August to proceed on his way to the Reserve, where Melmoth Osborn had taken John Shepstone's place as Resident. His brother Shingana sent him a horse, and on it he journeyed south, conducted by warriors of Sigananda's iron-working Cube people to their traditional stronghold at Manziphambana in the Nkandla forest, between the Thukela and Mhlathuze rivers. There, in the days of their chief Dlaba, they had successfully defended themselves against Shaka. Indeed, with its deep gorges and steep ridges, the rainy Nkandla forest has always been a place of mystery, legend and final refuge.

Surrounded by forest and cliffs, and secure for the moment from further Mandlakazi attack, Cetshwayo settled down in the eNhlweni homestead built for him by Luhungu of the Shezi near secret caves where he could make his final retreat.[21] The king's fortunes had come full cycle. Less than four years earlier he had been a fugitive in the Ngome forest, and had been betrayed. Cast once more from the throne he had worked so hard to regain, not this time by foreign invaders but by *amambuka* – renegades among his own people – he had no choice but to begin again, to attempt to rescue his cause and that of the uSuthu from the miserable depths to which it had sunk. But, for the moment, it was hard not to concede that Zibhebhu had triumphed, he of whom his praises said:

I don't like to name him,
If I named him there would be an outburst of wailing.
He who stalked forth in broad daylight,

For he entered oNdini not when it was dark,
But when it was clear and they saw him,
He finished them off entirely,
Destroyer of the enemy assembly.[22]

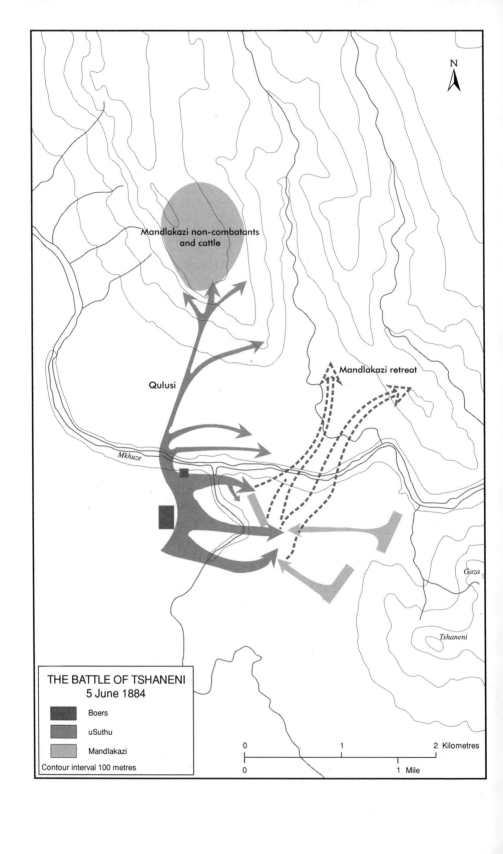

N

Mandlakazi non-combatants
and cattle

Qulusi

Mandlakazi retreat

Mkhuze

Gaza

Tshaneni

THE BATTLE OF TSHANENI
5 June 1884

Boers

uSuthu

Mandlakazi

Contour interval 100 metres

0   1   2 Kilometres

0   1 Mile

29

The Calabash and its Contents Were Shattered

From his refuge in the Nkandla forest, Cetshwayo tried ineffectually to rally his supporters and to negotiate with the British officials to intervene against Zibhebhu on his behalf.[1] The plight of the uSuthu was pathetic. Many from the central districts of his territory, like the king himself, had fled to the Reserve for sanctuary, while the northern uSuthu had taken once more to their strongholds. The Mandlakazi were ravaging the whole region, destroying the foodstocks and huts and carrying off the women and children. Zibhebhu turned his attention in mid-August to the royalists living in the coastal plain, and soon Somkhele of the Mphukunyoni and the emaNgweni were refugees in the disease-ridden swamps and reed-beds.

Although Osborn, the Resident Commissioner, was a committed foe of the royal house and its aspirations, Cetshwayo realised he could achieve nothing without his support. However, no British military aid was forthcoming to put the king back on his throne, and Osborn would only succour him if he placed himself under his protection at Eshowe, where he had established his Residency. Miserably aware that his people needed a settlement to allow them to plant for the coming season, and threatened by Zibhebhu's warlike presence on the borders of the Reserve, Cetshwayo allowed himself to be conducted by Fynn into Eshowe on 15 October 1883.[2]

Cetshwayo was allotted a small house near the site of his father's kwaGqikazi homestead, and there he was visited by his royal brothers and close supporters. For him it was a time of anguish as he contemplated the ruin of all his hopes and the destruction of his adherents at Zibhebhu's hands. Then, on the afternoon of 8 February 1884, at about 2.30, having just eaten, he was suddenly overtaken by a terrible convulsion, collapsed and died.[3] Members of his family present at the time refused a post-mortem, and Surgeon Scott, the military medical officer summoned to the scene, could only declare that he had died of heart disease. However, the uSuthu, and Dinuzulu in particular, were firmly convinced that he had been murdered on Zibhebhu's instructions by means of poison introduced into his beer or mixed with his snuff. The true cause of Cetshwayo's death must remain a matter of doubt, though poisoning seems more than likely, especially since at much the same time a similar attempt was made on Mnyamana's life, which, though made very ill, he survived.

The late king's attendants, following the ancient custom, placed the body in a sitting position tied to the central post of his hut. The hut was then sealed and plastered with mud so that no smell of putrefaction could escape. The unpromising circumstances and the absence of so many of the royal attendants and courtiers meant that much of the appropriate ritual was omitted. His followers wished to bury their king with his ancestors in the emaKhosini valley, but the distance was too great, and Osborn in any case refused permission for fear the uSuthu might use the occasion to make a demonstration. So the body, placed still in its sitting position in a huge coffin, was taken in an ox-wagon belonging to a Christian convert by the name of Hlabangana deep into the Nkandla forest. It was interred there on 10 April near Luhungu of the Shezi's homestead in a valley below the rolling slopes of Bhobhe ridge. Cattle were slaughtered to bring the spirit of the king home, and the assembled mourners, who were all dressed in their ceremonial finery, raised the chant and pointed their sticks towards Mahlabathini, where the shades of the king's ancestors dwelt. Dinuzulu did not stand at the graveside, for he had not yet come of age, but his uncles were all present. The wagon was broken into pieces, for it was not to be profaned by future use, and was laid on the grave.[4] There the king's remains still lie, between the trees of the sheltering grove, watched over to this day by Luhungu's descendants.

When Cetshwayo lay dying at Eshowe, he is said to have spoken these last words to Dabulamanzi, the brother next to him in age in his house, and one to whom he was particularly close:

Dabulamanzi, there is my child; look after him for me. Bring him up well, for I have no other sons. Dinuzulu is my only son. There is your task Dabulamanzi, to look after my child.[5]

Dabulamanzi was shot down in cold blood by Boers on 22 September 1886,[6] quite likely on the instigation of his jealous brothers, and could not long fulfil the king's dying commission. But also present to hear the king's last command, or, in all likelihood, to formulate it after his death, were other brothers, Ndabuko, Ziwedu and Shingana, as well as Mnyamana, his chief councillor. They knew well that, if the uSuthu were to survive the coming months, they could not afford a disputed succession. Cetshwayo's chief wife was pregnant, and if she bore a son his claim might by some be considered superior to that of Dinuzulu, who had been born of a minor wife, Nomvimbi Msweli.[8] So they unanimously rallied round and proclaimed the fifteen-year-old Dinuzulu Cetshwayo's successor.

The adolescent Dinuzulu, wrote Magema Fuze later, was 'clever with the qualities of the young of the Lion'.[9] His royal father knew that to be so, and on hearing while in exile at the Cape that his young son had been given a horse, declared with confident pride: 'Ah! and he'll soon ride it too, he's a sharp boy.'[10] Indeed, Dinuzulu grew up to be a competent horseman and quite a good shot, fond of hunting and pursuing girls. Intrepid, and of fiery and imperious temper, he was very conscious of his exalted position as a king's son and demanding of the respect he considered his due. His looks were those of his family, and at the

39. *Return of King Cetshwayo's ambassadors to Lord Chelmsford's camp on 27 June 1879.*

40. *The* amakhanda *in the Mahlabathini plain, sketched by Lieutenant W.F. Fairlie on 1 July 1879.*

40.

41. *Lord Chelmsford directing the fire of the British square at the battle of Ulundi, 4 July 1879.*

42 *General Sir Garnet Wolseley.*

Opposite page

43. *The ruins of oNdini in the Mahlabathini plain, drawn in mid-August 1879 by Captain C.P. Cramer*

44. *King Cetshwayo's dignified surrender to Major R.J.C. Marter on 28 August 1879 at the remote kwaDwasa homestead in the Ngome forest.*

42.

43.

44.

45. *The captive Cetshwayo was handed over on 30 August 1879 to an escort under Captain Cramer, who drew him (centre, with cloak and staff) on his way from the Black Mfolozi to the British camp near oNdini.*

46. *Cetshwayo on board the* Natal *in early September 1879 on his way to exile in the Cape, managing a pained smile for the camera.*

Opposite page

47. *Cetshwayo's wives on the* Natal, *photographed just after being ordered by the king to comport themselves seriously.*

48. *Cetshwayo's signature done while in captivity in the Cape.*

49. *Samples of Cetshwayo's writing exercises executed while in captivity in the Cape.*

50. *Cetshwayo on the parapet of the Castle in Cape Town. With him, from left to right, are his custodian, Captain J. Ruscombe Poole, RA, Mkhosana kaZanqana, his close adviser, William Longcast, his interpreter, and Mdekeza, an attendant.*

46.

47.

48.

CETYWAYO

Cir BARTLE FRERE
Cir BARTLE FRERE
Cir BARTLE FRERE
Cir BARTLE FRERE
BARTLE FRERE
Cir BARTLE FRERE
Cir BARTLE FRERE
Cir BARTLE FRERE
Car BARTL FRERE

49.

0.

51.

52.

53.

53. *King Cetshwayo in London, August 1882.*

54. *Sir Theophilus Shepstone with officers and men of the military escort which met Cetshwayo in Zululand on 10 January 1883.*

Previous page

51. *John Dunn with his izinduna in 1882.*

52. *Leaders of the first uSuthu deputation to Natal in May 1880. Standing centre in front of the tree and holding staffs are, from left to right, Ndabankulu, Shingana, Ndabuko, Ngcongcwana, Mkhoba and Ndabazimbi.*

54.

55.

55. *Cetshwayo's camp at St Paul's in January 1883 while on the way to his installation as king.*

56. *A photograph of the installation of Cetshwayo as king on 29 January 1883.*

Opposite page

57. *An artist's impression of Cetshwayo receiving a deputation of his relatives during the installation ceremonies on 29 January 1883*

58. *Zibhebhu kaMaphitha, the Mandlakazi chief and bane of the royal house, in later life.*

59. *J.W. Shepstone, Acting Secretary for Native Affairs, Natal.*

56.

57.

58.

59.

60. *A drawing of King Cetshwayo's corpse being prepared for burial in February 1884.*

61. *Dinuzulu kaCetshwayo at about the time of his father, Cetshwayo's, death.*

Opposite page

62. *Harriette Colenso, who tirelessly championed the uSuthu cause.*

63. *Sir Henry Bulwer, Governor of Natal, photographed in 1884.*

64. *The Boers install Dinuzulu as king, 21 May 1884*

61.

62.

63.

64.

67.

67. *Melmoth Osborn, Resident Commissioner of Zululand*

68. *Sir Arthur Havelock, Governor of Natal and Zululand*

69. *Dinuzulu at the time of the British annexation of Zululand*

Previous page

65. *The bones of the slain still littering the battlefield of Tshaneni decades later.*

66. *R.H. (Dick) Addison, subsequently Resident Magistrate of Ndwandwe (left with dog), photographed c. 1885 while serving with Commandant George Mansel (centre) and men of the Reserve Territory Carbineers.*

68.

69.

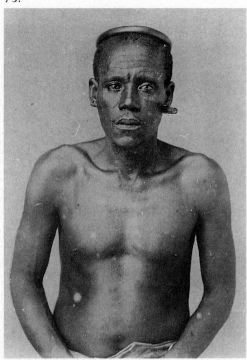

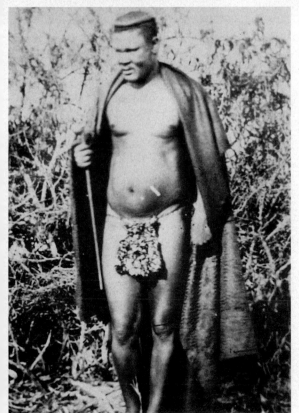

74.

72. *Prince Ndabuko kaMpande, c.1887.*

73. *Mankulumana kaSomaphunga, Dinuzulu's chief* induna. *He governed the uSuthu while Dinuzulu and his uncles were in exile.*

74. *Chief Somkhele kaMalanda of the Mphukunyoni, a first cousin of Cetshwayo, who dominated the northern coastal plain. As a steadfast uSuthu supporter he joined the 'rebellion' in 1888.*

Previous page

70. *Hlubi's Horse (Mounted Basutos) on campaign in Zululand, c. 1888.*

71. *The uSuthu camp at Eshowe during the trials following the collapse of the 'rebellion' of 1888.*

75.

75. Zibhebhu's wives photographed in the late 1880s during their exile in southern Zululand.

76. Dinuzulu in stylish western dress posed shaking hands with R.A. Sterndale, the Governor of St Helena. Ndabuko is on the left in a dark top hat, and Shingana is in the centre wearing a light-coloured one.

76.

time of his succession he was already developing the large hips and thighs of his forebears, though his upper body was still muscularly relatively undeveloped. In later life he would become positively stout and wear a beard.[11]

Ndabuko and Mnyamana, as Dinuzulu's official guardians until he should come of age, took control of the uSuthu in his name. But with the king's death as a refugee the Colensos' plan for bringing order to Zululand through the restoration of the monarchy had clearly foundered. Though Harriette Colenso faithfully continued as a determined and intrepid publicist to support Dinuzulu's cause, it was clearly no longer possible to seat him on the throne of his ancestors. The divisions in Zululand, sanctified by blood calling for vengeance, now ran too deep. Besides, the vested interests of the likes of Zibhebhu were too entrenched, and the influence of Shepstonite officials such as Osborn too strong.

By the time Cetshwayo died the uSuthu were on the brink of a terrible disaster.[12] Zibhebhu's forces already dominated all the territory north of the Mhlathuze, and the uSuthu were threatened with starvation and extinction. In August 1883, even before the king's death, Mnyamana was trying to elicit aid from Natal in brokering a truce between him and Zibhebhu. Clearly at the end of his tether, he even went so far as to attempt to excuse his own military initiatives against Zibhebhu as having been entirely in obedience to 'Cetywayo's orders'.[13] But Zibhebhu refused to allow the Buthelezi to plant their crops, and rejoiced at their degradation. He continued to hunt the uSuthu down through the desolate country, and Mahubulwana, the old Qulusi *induna* and staunch supporter of the royal cause, was killed by Mandlakazi. Not that the desperate uSuthu, perishing in their caves, took their situation passively. They issued out in increasingly brutal raids to terrorise their tormentors and punish those who had not stood staunchly by Cetshwayo. One such was Mfanawendlela, the Zungu chief and former kinglet, whom the Mandlakazi had left suspiciously untouched when they attacked oNdini. On 14 December 1883 he and his family were butchered in their huts on the banks of the Black Mfolozi where they had recently moved in order to be closer to Zibhebhu for protection.[14]

The leaders of the party of their killers were Mankulumana kaSomaphunga, the brother of Mgojana, the Ndwandwe chief, and grandson of the great Zwide, who was destined to become Dinuzulu's chief *induna*, and Ndabazimbi kaTokotoko, a grand-nephew of Maphitha. They were among the new uSuthu leadership which had emerged after the slaughter of the older generation at oNdini on 21 July 1883. All were good horsemen, adept with firearms, and had direct experience of white traders and the colonial world. The vicious fighting since 1879 had left them hardened, and with an uncompromising, burning desire to have their revenge against Zibhebhu. But by the early months of 1884 a self-destructive stalemate had been reached in Zululand. The Natal officials believed that the impasse could be broken if their authority were extended beyond the Reserve. Yet the British government would not sanction such intervention, with its implied increased obligations and expense. After all, the Reserve still functioned perfectly well as a buffer between Natal and the bloody doings to the north of the

Mhlathuze. The Zulu there, it would seem, were to be left alone to destroy themselves.

While Mnyamana and the older surviving uSuthu leadership still looked for some negotiated end to their troubles, the younger men took the initiative. It was a course fraught with the most dangerous of possible consequences. Mehlokazulu, Sihayo's energetic and confident son, and Ndabankulu, the assertive Ntombela chief, reached an agreement with Coenraad Meyer, Veld Kornet Jacobus van Staden and other Boers living on the South African Republic's border to come to their assistance against Zibhebhu and Hamu. Dinuzulu was to be recognised as Cetshwayo's successor and his rule imposed with the backing of Boer fire-power. The Boers, of course, were not risking themselves in a quixotic quest to rescue the Zulu monarchy. Their intervention, which would swing the balance firmly back to the uSuthu, required a reward – and that meant land in Zululand. Since September 1883 they had been taking advantage of the chaos to push forward again into the old Disputed Territory, building houses, laying out farms and driving out the original inhabitants, particularly the Mdlalose. Britain's evident reluctance to become more deeply involved in affairs north of the Mhlathuze inevitably encouraged them to act in this high-handed manner.

Only desperation could have persuaded the uSuthu to barter their patrimony. But desperate they were. When Ndabuko had raised the possibility with Cetshwayo while he was in the Nkandla forest of treating with the Boers, the king had vehemently warned against such a course, foretelling that 'if you once get them into the country you will never get rid of them'.[15] Mnyamana likewise held out against the unholy alliance, but he was isolated and reluctantly fell in with the rest of the leadership. Dinuzulu, who had been sheltering in the Nkandla under Dabulamanzi's tutelage, was spirited away at the beginning of April 1884 to a Boer farm near the Bivane River in the Wakkerstroom District of the South African Republic, and his royal uncles made their way back to the northern districts. They left Dabulamanzi in the Nkandla in charge of the uSuthu in the Reserve. By the end of April word of the uSuthu-Boer alliance was spreading throughout Zululand, giving courage to the uSuthu in their fastnesses and striking dismay into the Mandlakazi.

Dabulamanzi was emboldened to take up a contumacious attitude towards Osborn's attempts to make his administration felt, and mustered over 2 000 men in the Nkandla. Osborn marched to subdue him, but Dabulamanzi was sufficiently confident to attack the Resident Commissioner's encampment on 10 May 1884. Fortunately for Osborn, his Reserve Territory Carbineers, a disciplined and well-armed force of black police under Commandant George Mansel and his white officers, was able to repulse Dabulamanzi with considerable loss. But Osborn fell back on Eshowe in distinct alarm. Regular troops were despatched from Natal to shore up his regime and were posted at Eshowe and Rorke's Drift. Their presence and occasional shows of force were sufficient to pacify the Reserve, and the garrison was reduced in September 1884 to 100 infantry at eNtumeni, 300 infantry and 1 mounted company at Eshowe, and 150 infantry, 1 mounted company and 2 Gatling guns at Rorke's Drift.[16]

Events were also reaching a climax in northern Zululand. Leading Boers from the Wakkerstroom and Utrecht Districts formed the Committee of Dinuzulu's Volunteers and called for recruits for an expedition into Zululand. Since such prominent men as Lucas Meyer, the Landdrost of Utrecht, joined up, it must be supposed that the government of the South African Republic approved of the venture, despite its public disavowals intended primarily to mollify the British. Soon, over 300 volunteers had gathered. Not all were Boers, by any means; adventurous men of British and German extraction were also attracted. Some, like the young Louis Botha, who one day would rise to be the first prime minister of the Union of South Africa, came from as far afield as the Orange Free State. They were no mere rabble of land-grabbers, as Harriette Colenso averred; most were already rich farmers in search of more farms, and were intent on imposing some order on a Zululand where the unrest and flow of refugees was disrupting the seasonal movement of their livestock and threatening their existing holdings.

On 1 May 1884 the commando set out and escorted Dinuzulu into the northwest of Zululand. A laager of seventy tented wagons was established between Hlobane and the Ngome forest at Nyathi Hill, on what is now the farm 'Zalflager'. The hard bargaining then began between the uSuthu and the Boers, both as regards strategy and the compensation the 'Volunteers' were to receive. Mnyamana continued to voice his opposition to Boer involvement, but he was overborne by the majority.

The Boers proclaimed Dinuzulu King of the Zulu on 21 May 1884. Ndabuko, Ziwedu and Shingana had installed him with traditional ritual the day before, but Mnyamana signalled his disapprobation by absenting himself on grounds of ill-health.[17] A crowd of about 9 000 Zulu and 350 Boers assembled at dawn. At about noon the *amabutho* escorting Dinuzulu were met by about fifty mounted Boers who led him to two wagons arranged to form a platform. An upended box served as a throne. Above fluttered a large blue and white flag which, with deliberate symbolism, was similar to the one the Boers had flown when they crowned Mpande forty-five years before, following the battle of the Maqongqo Hills. The coronation platform stood in the centre of the surrounding multitude. The Boers were in two semicircular lines in front of their laager. Directly opposite them, the Zulu dignitaries were seated in rows with the main body of the uSuthu massed behind in a great horseshoe formation.

Very conscious of the significance of the occasion, Dinuzulu mounted the tawdry platform with four members of the Boer Committee, prepared to submit to the improvised and not unludicrous coronation ritual dreamed up by these dyed-in-the-wool republicans. A proclamation confirming Dinuzulu as 'lawful heir and successor of the late Ketewayo...[and] as King of the Zulu nation and of Zululand' was read in Dutch and translated into Zulu.[18] Then Dinuzulu kneeled and the four Boers placed their hands on his head and swore to protect him from his enemies. One of them, Andreas Laas, proceeded next to ape one of the most sacred moments in the European coronation tradition when he anointed the head of the new king with castor oil (since he naturally possessed none of the consecrated oil or chrism commonly applied by a bishop), and the crowd roared out the royal acclamations. Dinuzulu was at least spared the likes of the absurd crown Shepstone foisted on Cetshwayo at his coronation in 1873.

Two days after the ceremony the young king put his mark to a document by which the Boers bound themselves to assist him militarily in return for a tract of land, sufficiently large to establish 'an independent self-government'.[19] Zibhebhu – who, like Hamu, had retired in alarm to his fastnesses – sent urgently to the British requesting aid. At the same time, he was said to have spurned Dinuzulu, contemptuously declaring of the young man that he was no king 'but a dog and when he is hungry he may come to me'.[20] The Natal officials were predictably most sympathetic towards their faithful ally in his predicament, but the British government refused to sanction any form of intervention. This was made public in Natal on 21 May, the day of Dinuzulu's coronation. Effectively assured, therefore, that the British would leave them a free hand, the Boers and uSuthu began their preparations for their advance into Mandlakazi territory. Zibhebhu discovered himself to be isolated, and even most of his erstwhile white allies and trading-partners found it more prudent this time to stay away.

The uSuthu succeeded by the beginning of June in gathering an army near Mnyamana's ekuShumayeleni homestead of some 7 000 men, emaciated though they were from the months spent as refugees in caves, forests and swamps.[21] They were supported by between 100 and 120 Boers (including Louis Botha) under the command of Lucas Meyer, all mounted and armed with modern rifles. Zibhebhu, who could muster only about 3 000 men and a handful of white mercenaries, fell back before the invaders outgunned and outnumbered. Abandoning Bangonomo, his chief homestead, he and his army retreated eastwards towards the Lubombo Mountains with his cattle, women and children.

With the lesson of Msebe fresh in mind, the uSuthu and Boers advanced cautiously, scouting ahead thoroughly to avoid falling into another Mandlakazi ambush. Water for the large joint force was scarce because of the extreme dryness of the winter season. The invading force reached the Vuna River on 2 June, and bivouacked the following night at Msebe, whose painful and humiliating memory the uSuthu hoped soon to avenge. Pressing past Bangonomo, they followed the course of the barely flowing Mkhuze River over flat, arid country for about twenty-two kilometres until in sight of the Mkhuze Poort. This was a gorge worn through the Lubombo Mountains by the river on its way to the sea. It was guarded to the south by the jagged, rocky crest of Gaza Mountain and its more westerly companion, Tshaneni, with its distinctive crown of bare, precipitous rock rising to a slight peak. The mouth of the gorge was an obvious place to lay an ambush, and Commandant Meyer approached with due circumspection on the afternoon of 5 June 1884.

Zibhebhu was a general of considerable experience who knew the terrain intimately, so he made the best of his fundamentally defensive position. To the north of the Mkhuze, along a bush-covered spur above the river, he hid his cattle and non-combatants, all the women, children and elderly men of his following. He positioned his main fighting-force in two detachments to the south of the river, which was thickly overgrown with heavy riverine bush and tall trees. The scored and broken country of the plain and the dense thornbush on the rising slopes of Tshaneni behind would severely impede the manoeuvrability of the mounted Boers. In advance of the main position, close to the river, he placed a small detachment behind a deep donga running south-east down to the Mkhuze and across the track to the Poort. The advancing enemy would be following this path, and the function of the Mandlakazi advance guard was to dispute their progress and draw them into an assault. Once the invaders became fully engaged, the main Mandlakazi forces would fall on their flank, hemming them against the river and neutralising their numerical advantage. That, in any case, was Zibhebhu's intention.

The uSuthu circumspectly approaching the Mkhuze Poort were in the traditional formation of two horns and a chest. Unlike Cetshwayo, who never took part in the fighting of the Anglo-Zulu War (though as a young man he was present at the battle of Ndondakusuka), Dinuzulu would always go out with his army when it took the field against Zibhebhu.[22] The left horn of his force, commanded by Mamese and stiffened by sixteen mounted Boers, advanced along the river bank. The chest, supported to its rear by the main body of Boers under Meyer, who intended that the uSuthu should bear the brunt of the fighting, came directly at the donga held by the Mandlakazi advance guard. The right horn began to cross the donga higher up, to the south. Mamese's left horn ruined Zibhebhu's carefully laid trap by springing it prematurely. It engaged his advance guard before it could embroil the uSuthu chest as was intended, so the centre and the right horn were free to face the main Mandlakazi attack, which had now to come on regardless.

The Mandlakazi had lost the advantage of surprise – and it seems that a nervous or treacherous rifle shot may in any case have given the game away – but they still held the advantage in morale. The uSuthu had suffered so many recent and devastating defeats at their hands that the mere sight of the Mandlakazi, beating their shields with the hafts of their spears and giving their dreaded cry of 'Washesha!' was enough to make them lose all resolve. Many of Dinuzulu's men turned to flee, but on this occasion the Boers on their horses stood between them and home. Meyer's men shouted at the panicking uSuthu to turn and fight on pain of being shot, and fired a fusillade from their saddles more or less over their heads at the charging Mandlakazi, whose left horn was already rolling up the uSuthu right and forcing it back on their centre. Both uSuthu and Mandlakazi fell, shot down indiscriminately, but the Boers' fire had had its intended effect. The uSuthu stood fast as the lesser of two evils. Within ten minutes repeated volleys into the Mandlakazi flanks from the sixty or seventy Boer horsemen actually involved in the fighting had forced even Zibhebhu's doughty men to fall back.

Now the desired moment had arrived for the uSuthu, so long the Mandlakazis' victims, with so many dead, so many hardships and humiliations to avenge. When the Mandlakazi gave way, they made for the river and their cattle and families on the northern side. But the Qulusi contingent got to the ridge across the Mkhuze ahead of them, and cut them off. Retreat turned into rout for the Mandlakazi, and the uSuthu set to, butchering their broken foe with gleeful satisfaction and keeping up the murderous pursuit for many kilometres until darkness fell. The slaughter was particularly heavy along the river banks and deep pools: ironically, the Mandlakazi were penned just where they had intended the uSuthu should be. The number of casualties is unknown, though an indication of the extent of Mandlakazi losses can be gauged from the fact that no less than six of Zibhebhu's brothers, besides other members of his family, were reported to have been killed. Like the field of Msebe, the ground before Tshaneni was still covered with skulls and bones nearly twenty years later. But this time, they were not uSuthu bones. Zibhebhu himself escaped across the Mkhuze on his sure-footed little horse and up the slopes of the Lubombo Mountains. From that eminence he looked down in sorrow upon the destruction of his ambitions and the cruel fate of his people. Truly, as the Zulu saying goes, 'the calabash and its contents were shattered'.[23]

The victors spent the rest of that day and the succeeding two rounding up between 40 000 and 60 000 head of cattle and winkling hundreds of women and children out of their hiding places in the bush and dongas. Numbers of these had been uSuthu captives held by the Mandlakazi, and were overjoyed to rejoin their own people. The Boers made a particular point of looting the wagons of the few white traders who had been foolhardy enough to stay by Zibhebhu. All the cattle were afterwards divided up among the victors, every man getting his share, but the lion's portion went to the uSuthu leaders and the Boers.

The Mandlakazi survivors fled north until they reached the territory of Sambane's Nyawo. These were the very people who had killed the fugitive Dingane, and Zibhebhu did not tarry long. He made the hazardous journey south, and on 12 June, flanked by the two white comrades in whose company he had escaped from the field of battle – Grosvenor Darke and John Eckersley – he rode into Eshowe to report his misfortunes to Melmoth Osborn and to appeal eloquently for British support. The local officials were more sympathetic than ever towards the plight of their loyal collaborator, but the Colonial Secretary, Lord Derby, was adamant that Zibhebhu was not actually a formal ally whom the British were obliged to help (especially if it should come to military operations), but an independent actor. However, Derby was sufficiently alive to Zibhebhu's past services and usefulness to permit him and the remnants of his people to seek asylum in the Reserve.[24] And duly, in September 1884, Zibhebhu led between 5 000 and 6 000 Mandlakazi men, women and children (about a third of his adherents) and thousands of cattle into the safety of a special location set aside for them in the Reserve at Nyoni, near Middle Drift. All were pitifully emaciated and wearied, and the adults carried enormous loads of their belongings on their heads.[25] It was a degrading moment for Zibhebhu, that proud warlord, who had to beg grain from Osborn to feed his starving people, and a spectacle calculated to gladden the heart of many an uSuthu sympathiser.

But the uSuthu had to pay the price for their longed-for victory, and they found it exorbitant.[26] During the weeks after Tshaneni, increasingly tense negotiations took place between the Boers and the uSuthu. Hundreds of white adventurers and landgrabbers, attracted by the possibility of sharing in the spoils, flocked to the Boer laager until there were nearly 800 of them, each demanding a farm. Their determined presence encouraged the Boer leaders to raise their demands. They now had the manpower, they thought, to carve out and hold an extensive republic, stretching from the borders of the South African Republic through the Disputed Territory as far as the Indian Ocean. There would be land aplenty for the original members of the commando as well as the opportunistic latecomers.

Understandably, the uSuthu initially refused to contemplate conceding any reward to the latter undeserving company of vultures, but they were hardly in a position to stand up to Boer demands. They caved in eventually and, on 16 August 1884 at the Boer encampment at Hlobane, Dinuzulu issued a proclamation granting the Boers 1 355 000 morgen (over a million hectares) for the establishment of a Boer state. Furthermore, Dinuzulu conceded that the remaining portion of Zululand north of the Reserve, and all the people living there, would be subject to the fledgling Boer republic.[27] Its first president, Lucas Meyer, then formally proclaimed the New Republic and its protectorate over the Zulu.[28] The members of the original committee were each declared to be entitled to a farm of 2 400 hectares, those who had volunteered before 10 June 1884 to one of 1 600 hectares, and the latecomers to one of 800 hectares each. The members of the committee had the privilege of choosing where they would like their farms to be, and the others were all allocated by lottery.

This was the worst, the most debasing moment ever suffered by the Zulu people, more devastating even than the Wolseley settlement. Then, even though the old kingdom was dissolved and political power fragmented, the land had at least stayed with the chiefs and the people. Now, the choicest grazing lands were in Boer hands, as were the very graves of Dinuzulu's royal ancestors, from which the guardians were driven. Many of the homesteads of the uSuthu leadership were situated on what had become Boer-owned farmland, and some of the royal house's staunchest adherents, such as the Qulusi, Mdlalose, emGazini and part of the Buthelezi found themselves living in the New Republic as tenants on the new Boer farms. It was hardly any consolation that their old enemies, the Ngenetsheni, who had kept up their resistance to the uSuthu even after Tshaneni, also fell under the sway of the Boers. To the south, in the Reserve, Osborn set about strengthening the hold of his administration over the people, levying a hut tax and putting down pockets of opposition by force. Tellingly, even this relatively oppressive regime was preferable to the chaos, expropriation and destitution north of the Mhlathuze, and Osborn could point to the fact that the Reserve was chosen as a haven by a steady stream of refugees from the rest of what had once been Zululand.[29]

The establishment of the New Republic and the extension of a Boer protectorate over the rest of Zululand north of the Mhlathuze quite negated Dinuzulu's position as king and, as far as the British government was concerned, reduced him to 'no more than a nominal ruler in the hands of the Boer invaders'.[30] Certainly, he was powerless, despite his protests, to protect his people from the Boers who fanned out to occupy their farms,[31] often even before the survey had been completed and the boundaries fixed. Driven from their lands, the uSuthu sought refuge once more in the hills and caves, or in those parts of the country not yet apportioned out by the Boers. In mounting anger they began to resist, and the Boers savagely retaliated, burning homesteads, destroying crops and seizing livestock. Even the fourth oNdini, which Dinuzulu had caused to be built at Nhlazatshe, was burned by the Boer authorities. Famine again stalked the uSuthu, who were forced to sell their few remaining cattle to obtain mealies at exorbitant prices from unscrupulous traders. Zululand seemed on the brink of a greater disaster than ever.[32]

The Natal settlers were exceedingly put out at the creation of a Boer republic in what they considered quite definitely their particular zone of interest. Not only would it deprive the colony of the long-desired land and labour of the Zulu, but it would deny access to the new goldfields of the eastern Transvaal and the wealth of the interior.[33] Yet neither these considerations, nor the desperate plight of Zululand and the pathetic uSuthu appeals for help, were sufficient to make the British government intervene. What drove it to act were wider, imperial considerations.

In 1884 Germany, searching for its place in the sun as a new world power, began to take an interest in the coast of Zululand. The British government immediately feared a link-up with the landlocked Boers who sought an outlet to the sea.[34] To forestall such an eventuality, Gladstone's Liberal government reluctantly re-asserted its claims to St Lucia Bay, and the Union Jack was hoisted above its forlorn shores on 21 December 1884. The New Republic's official proclamation of its boundaries on 26 October 1885 next brought British intervention a step closer. The government felt constrained to warn the Boers that their claims to what amounted to five-sixths of Zulu territory beyond the Reserve was regarded as a threat to British interests. It was not, however, until the fall of Gladstone's government and the advent of Lord Salisbury's Conservative administration in August 1886, with its more fully developed concern to safeguard imperial interests in south-eastern Africa as a whole, that Britain began at last to acknowledge that it could not continue to shrug off responsibility for Zululand, and must take direct action.

Bulwer, his term of office as Governor of Natal about to end, recommended in January 1886 in his typically wordy way that British interests could be secured by confining the Boers to north-western Zululand.[35] Sir Arthur Havelock, his successor from February 1886, pushed forward with this idea. The Boers, though, held out for an advantageous settlement. In return for British recognition of their state on 22 October 1886, they agreed to limit its territorial pretensions and to drop all claims to a protectorate over Dinuzulu.[36] Even so, the Zulu lost nearly all the highland grazing and valuable mixed veld in the upper reaches of the great rivers. The Boers ceded control over a block of territory in central Zululand known as Proviso B, but were nevertheless allowed to retain ownership of their farms at a nominal quit rent. This meant that the emaKhosini valley, the sacred heart of the kingdom itself, remained parcelled out into white-owned farms. A Boundary Commission, set up under Melmoth Osborn, completed the task of defin-

376

ing the New Republic's boundaries by 25 January 1887.

The uSuthu were powerless to do more than protest at this arrangement, which left them hardly any better off than before.[37] They would have nothing to do with Osborn's Boundary Commission, and continued to petition the British government against the alienation of so much Zulu territory and the loss of so many royalist adherents to Boer jurisdiction. Besides which, the rump of Zululand, though nominally independent under Dinuzulu, was clearly vulnerable both to renewed Boer expansion and to the vengeful Zibhebhu in the Reserve, constantly agitating for permission to return to his old lands in the north. Zulu living in the New Republic, meanwhile, resistant to undertaking the 'personal service' of quasi-serfs that the Boer farm-owners required of them, flocked into the Reserve Territory to join its already hungry, dislocated and turbulent inhabitants.

Meanwhile, in Natal, determined lobbying for the absorption of Dinuzulu's remnant of Zululand continued in the Legislative Council and elsewhere. The colony, however, hardly possessed the resources to control the territory, which threw the onus onto the British government to assume direct responsibility itself. While Whitehall dithered, Osborn brought matters to a head. Alarmed at the patently deteriorating situation, he simply notified the uSuthu leadership on 5 February 1887 that British protection had been extended over Eastern Zululand, which is what he called the remnant of the country under their nominal rule.[38] To the uSuthu, already viciously battered by forces outside their control, protest seemed futile. Mnyamana at once welcomed Osborn's action, though Dinuzulu and Ndabuko hesitated a few days before signifying their acceptance. The British government, presented with a *fait accompli*, duly agreed to the annexation of central Zululand and the Reserve Territory, which together from 19 May 1887 became the British Colony of Zululand.[39] It was decidedly none too soon for the British to have shouldered the responsibility for their victory of 1879 and its subsequent bitter harvest of endemic civil war, famine, and alienation of two-fifths of the former kingdom to the Boers.

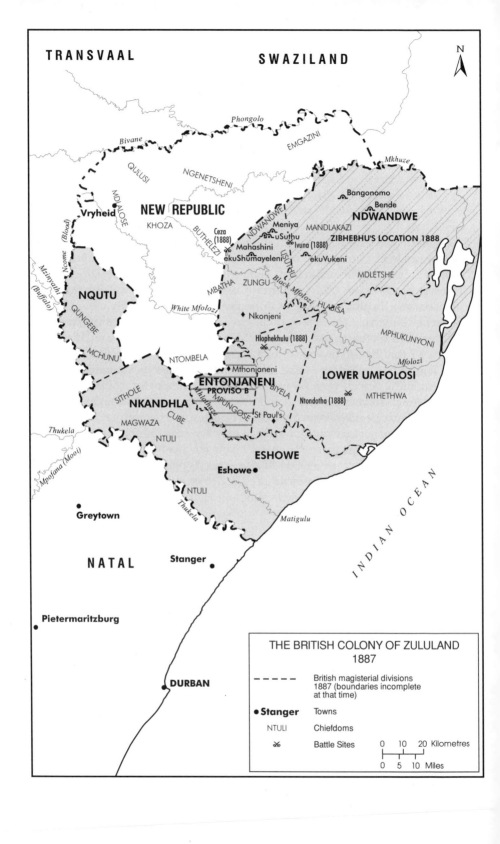

TRANSVAAL

SWAZILAND

N

Phongolo

Bivane

EMGAZINI

Mkhuze

QULUSI

NGENETSHENI

Bangonomo

Bende

NDWANDWE

Vryheid

NEW REPUBLIC

KHOZA

Meniya

MANDLAKAZI

ZIBHEBHU'S LOCATION 1888

Ceza
(1888)

uSuthu

Ivuna (1888)

Mahashini

ekuShumayeleni

ekuVukeni

MDLETSHE

MBATHA

ZUNGU

White Mfolozi

Black Mfolozi

HLABISA

MPHUKUNYONI

NQUTU

QUNGEBE

Nkonjeni

MCHUNU

NTOMBELA

Hlophekhulu (1888)

Mfolozi

Mthonjaneni

ENTONJANENI

PROVISO B

BIYELA

LOWER UMFOLOSI

SITHOLE

NKANDHLA

MPUNGOSE

Ntondotha (1888)

MTHETHWA

CUBE

St Paul's

MAGWAZA

NTULI

ESHOWE

Thukela

Eshowe

Mpofana (Mooi)

NTULI

Greytown

Thukela

Matigulu

NATAL

Stanger

INDIAN OCEAN

Pietermaritzburg

THE BRITISH COLONY OF ZULULAND
1887

- - - - British magisterial divisions
1887 (boundaries incomplete
at that time)

● **Stanger** Towns

NTULI Chiefdoms

✂ Battle Sites

0   10   20 Kilometres

0   5   10 Miles

DURBAN

30

Like a Calf Tied Up
on One Side of the Hedge

On the same day as Zululand became a British possession, 19 May 1887, Sir Arthur Havelock, the Governor of the Colony of Natal, was in addition appointed Governor of the new territory. He used his new powers on 21 June to appoint Melmoth Osborn Resident Commissioner and Chief Magistrate of the Colony of Zululand.[1] The following day Osborn staged a flag-raising ceremony at Eshowe, which was to be the seat of his administration, before some 9 000 assembled Zulu. Eshowe, beginning to develop into a village high up on the misty hills, still had no more than a hundred white inhabitants, including government officials. But a British garrison was stationed at Fort Curtis, and the genteel pleasures of Victorian social and sporting life were beginning to be observed. Ladies held 'At Homes' and flirted with the polo-playing officers of the garrison. Such delights did not detain Osborn from his duties, however. On 7 July he repeated the flag-raising ceremony at Nkonjeni in central Zululand, between the White and Black Mfolozi rivers. Some 600 chiefs and headmen from what had fleetingly been Dinuzulu's 'kingdom' attended that particular occasion and saluted the Union Jack as they were required to do.

Dinuzulu pointedly failed to heed Osborn's repeated summonses to be present, however. And to ensure that his intentional snub of the new authorities would not just be glossed over, he afterwards refused to accept copies of the proclamation of the annexation of Zululand on the disingenuous grounds that he could not read them.[2] Reinforcing the – for want of a better word – ex-king's disturbing gestures of intransigence were the chiefs' loud and bitter complaints about the inclusion of so many of their people in the New Republic. Whatever the British treaty-makers might think, the Zulu clearly did not consider that annexation had closed the unsatisfactory question of the boundaries of their country. Nor, from their bearing, was it certain that they necessarily accepted the new dispensation in Zululand either.[3] Indeed, they had good cause to be wary of it.

Havelock had made his final choice of officials to administer the infant colony by 21 June 1887.[4] In line with the British government's penny-pinching approach to imperial expense, it was understood that Zululand would not become a burden on the British taxpayer. The administration was to be financed by a hut tax (as the Reserve Territory had been), and the official establishment kept to a bare minimum. Thus, besides the governor, who economically doubled up his Natal and Zululand posts, there were only the resident commissioner at Eshowe and his clerk and accountant, who supervised the six assistant commissioners and resident magistrates of the administrative districts into which Zululand was divided, and their clerks. They were expected to enforce their authority through a small paramilitary force recruited from among the Zulu themselves. Styled the Zululand Police, it had originally been the Reserve Territory Carbineers, and was still under the command of Commandant George Mansel, assisted by three young white sub-Inspectors. As a last resort, the small force of imperial troops still stationed in the southern part of the new colony, with Eshowe as its headquarters, could be called upon for assistance.

The character of the Zululand officials is of particular importance in the context of the subsequent uSuthu revolt of 1888. Critics at the time, especially Harriette Colenso, members of the Aborigines' Protection Society and Harry Escombe, the Natal lawyer who defended Dinuzulu against the charge of armed rebellion brought against him in 1889, contended that the uprising was provoked by the ineptitude and maladministration of these very officials. In large measure they were right, and though the very limited number of posts available in Zululand allowed Havelock to exercise some choice in his appointments, the pool of likely candidates was disappointingly restricted.

Havelock did his conscientious best, nevertheless, and the Zululand officials he eventually selected were generally seasoned civil officials, familiar with military command, with considerable experience in the administration of blacks, and fluent in Zulu. They were also prepared to rough it. They had to endure the material discomforts of makeshift dwellings, and to accept long periods of isolation from the company of other whites, and protracted separation from their wives and children. They had to be reconciled to being at the end of extremely uncertain lines of communication, which meant that supplies of necessities ranging from mealie-meal to leg-irons for convicts, ink and official stationery, were constantly being interrupted. They had to cope as best they could with orders and official despatches delayed for days by swollen rivers or garbled by heliographs operating under cloudy skies. Above all, they needed stamina and pluck. Stamina to ride on interminable tours of inspection, to hold court in the open and to hand down judgement, to write long and detailed daily reports and to deal with routine administrative irritants. Pluck to uphold the Queen's law in districts hostile to the intrusion of white officials, supported only by a few Zululand Police or the threat of distant troops, and sustained by whatever aura of authority they could manufacture about themselves. Such were Charles Saunders of the Eshowe District, Andries Pretorius of the Nkandla District, Major Alexander McKean of the Nqutu District, Arthur Shepstone of the Lower Umfolosi District, John Knight of the Entonjaneni District, and Richard Addison of the Ndwandwe District. Their compensation for their sometimes difficult and often unrewarding lives, for it did exist, lay in the splendid shooting, the freedom, and the gratifying exercise of authority over a people who accorded them semi-royal respect.

Besides their shared and necessary positive qualities, these men possessed another fundamental and absolutely essential characteristic. Through birth, service or outlook they were all part of the Natal official establishment, prepared wholeheartedly to adhere to the orthodox official view of the policy to be adopted in the governing of Zululand. And that policy, in a nutshell, was the extension to Zululand of the Shespstone system of Natal, with the concomitant understanding that it was the continuing pretensions of the Zulu royal house which would present the greatest threat to its successful imposition.

What made certain that this perspective would be adhered to by the Zululand officials was not merely the appointment of Osborn, that confirmed Shepstonite, as their superior on the spot, but the fact that Sir Theophilus Shepstone had the attentive ear of the Governor. Shepstone, though in retirement in Pietermaritzburg, had promptly proffered the freshly arrived Havelock his counsel and advice. New to the Zulu question and unsure of his way through its complexities, Havelock had been only too happy to fall back on the wisdom of the person the settlers all acknowledged and revered as the unquestioned expert on the Zulu. Shepstone's most decisive opportunity to influence Havelock came when the Governor was adapting the Code of 1885, which had been adopted in British Bechuanaland, to form the basis of the Laws and Regulations for Zululand. Under Shepstone's tutelage, Havelock's Zululand code emerged as a monument to the elder statesman's concept of indirect rule.[5]

In a magisterial memorandum of 23 April 1887, Shepstone set out his persuasive views for Havelock's edification.[6] The basic objective, he argued from his fund of personal experience, was to make the 'transition from Native rule to civilized administration as gradual as justice and decency permit'. To this end, it was axiomatic that it would be impossible to govern the Zulu without initially co-opting their existing leaders, the chiefs. What would keep them in line were the powers of the 'Supreme Chief', as exercised by the Governor. In Shepstone's view, these were absolute and undefined, and supplanted those supposedly once wielded by the Zulu king. To avoid 'estrangement and discontent' on the part of the chiefs, however, whose powers were to be confined to civil cases and non-capital criminal offences within their chiefdoms, they were to be conciliated by the assurance that they were carrying out the Supreme Chief's behest, even if under the supervision of the white officials.

Yet the whole point of the Shepstone system was precisely that the traditional leaders' authority would indeed be gradually undermined and caused to wither away. This would necessarily take many years, and Shepstone acknowledged that in the meantime the residual power, influence and pretensions of the hereditary chiefs, not least those of the members of the royal house, would continue to counterweight those of the British officials. That is why he considered it absolutely essential to work closely with local collaborators eager to consolidate their positions at the expense of the established Zulu leadership. As early as February 1887 Shepstone had identified Zibhebhu, still tugging restlessly at his leash in the Reserve, as potentially the most effective instrument in this regard. Naturally, those against whom he was most likely to be let loose, who would indubitably be the most intractable in their resistance to the new administration, were the members of the royal house.

Shepstone was convinced that the hold of the royal house over the Zulu was, in fact, very fragile. Referring to the conquests of Shaka and the manner in which the kingdom had been formed, he assured Havelock that the Zulu people, 'composed originally of conquered and incorporated tribes', had in actuality always yearned for 'their ancient separate existence, relieved of the terrible incubus of the Zulu Royal Family'.[7] Consequently, he foresaw no difficulties in bringing Dinuzulu and his uncles to heel, for (as he put it in a subsequent memorandum) the 'rope of sand' with which the Zulu kings had bound their subjects had been crumbling away ever since the war of 1879.[8]

Dinuzulu was hardly likely to accept this interpretation of his situation, and was bound to resent his reduced status in British Zululand. Shepstone recommended, therefore, that to sweeten the bitter draught of loss of power and privilege, the members of the royal house be compensated by annual stipends ranging from £300 for Dinuzulu to £60 for his uncle Ziwedu. And if that did not work, Zibhebhu's leash could always be slipped.

Dinuzulu's uSuthu *umuzi* and Ndabuko's Meniya were close by each other on the upper reaches of the steep-banked and sluggish Vuna River, in which area the uSuthu were heavily concentrated. All fell within the limits of the Ndwandwe District, the largest and, because of their presence, most sensitive and potentially volatile administrative region in British Zululand. For that reason, Havelock took especial care in appointing a resident magistrate who might be relied upon to deal with the disgruntled uSuthu with both sensitivity and firmness. Dick Addison did, on first glance, seem better qualified than most for the post.[9] A scion of the established settler elite, he was an experienced official in the Natal civil service, had seen active service in the Anglo-Zulu War, and since 1883 had been an efficient officer in the Reserve Territory Carbineers. He spoke Zulu well and was a superior horseman. But, above all, he was a thoroughgoing disciple of the Shepstone school. Osborn, after their long and close association in the Reserve Territory, knew Addison could be completely relied upon conscientiously to dampen down the aspirations of the uSuthu, and thought he had the ability simultaneously to prevent their resentment from boiling over into violence. Yet, to the ultimate misfortune of all Zululand, Osborn showed himself a poor judge of men. Addison, although undeniably confirming himself 'a part of Osborn' in Zulu eyes,[10] just as the Resident Commissioner hoped he would, proved lamentably unequal either to soothing or to containing the uSuthu. Ndwandwe consequently became the epicentre of the disturbances that rocked British Zululand in 1888.

Addison selected the site for his future magistracy on the Nongoma hills, which command the open country round about. To the west, the hills fall precipitously away to the Vuna River and the uSuthu *umuzi* only sixteen kilometres away. On the other side, the hills drop gently to the shallow valley of the thickly reeded Mona River, which meanders through the western marches of the territory Fannin had demarcated for Zibhebhu in 1883. Addison did not immediately take up his post on the Nongoma hills, but the isolation, even while he was still based at Nkonjeni some fifty-six kilometres to the south, left him with considerable latitude in the administration of his district. Yet he, like the other resident magistrates, was technically checked from excessively arbitrary action by the Laws and Regulations of Zululand. Consequently, while having jurisdiction over all major criminal cases save capital ones, which were a matter for Osborn and Havelock, any sentences the resident magistrates handed down which exceeded a month in jail or a fine of £5, or involved the infliction of lashes or cuts, had first to receive Osborn's endorsement.[11]

There were other regulations too, novel to the Zulu, which swiftly brought home to them their changed situation under a colonial government. The hut tax was extended from the Reserve Territory to all British Zululand, and was first due on 1 June 1888, when it was expected to yield £17 000. The rates were fourteen shillings per annum for each family's hut, and a further fourteen shillings for each wife and for every hut of unmarried men. The tax was to be paid in sterling coin, or in grain and livestock at the current price at the nearest market. The cost of getting these goods to market, which might be at a considerable distance, was to be borne by the person being taxed.[12] Besides the advent of the tax-collector, in the person of the resident magistrate, the meaning of the Queen's peace made itself evident in the ban on the Zulu possession of firearms. Furthermore, as in a Natal location, a Zulu had to possess a pass signed by the magistrate if he wished to leave Zululand, and had to report his return.[13] This regulation was particularly vexatious since the boundary of the New Republic artificially divided so many chiefs from their adherents and split families asunder. The most dangerous area of potential conflict, however, lay in the twilight zone between the freshly established and alien jurisdiction of white magistrates and the residual powers of existing chiefs. The effective extent to which chiefs' traditional powers had been curtailed had yet to be established in practice, and from the moment the new magistrates took up their posts their authority was persistently probed by the old authorities. Nowhere was this testing more concerted and potentially explosive than in Ndwandwe, where ex-king Dinuzulu still kept up the shadow of his royal state.

On 6 May 1887, just before the official annexation of Zululand, Dinuzulu had 'eaten up' Mfokozana kaBizane of the Buthelezi, killed his wife and carried off twenty-one cattle and two sheep. Dinuzulu had been within his traditional rights, for Mfokozana had committed the crime of 'smelling out' the family of Mankulumana, who was high in the ex-king's favour and would one day be his chief *induna*. Osborn, however, considered that 'energetic steps' should be taken to bring home to Dinuzulu that he could no longer act as if he were an independent ruler. So, at the flag-raising at Nkonjeni on 7 July, he decreed that the absent Dinuzulu and Ndabuko should restore to Mfokozana all his confiscated livestock.[14] Dinuzulu dragged his heels, but before the affair was brought to any conclusion, a fresh but similar one erupted. On the very day of the flag-raising ceremony, a faction-fight exploded involving a number of deaths, and Dinuzulu moved to apprehend and punish the offenders. Addison ordered him not to interfere and instructed the parties to appear before him instead. One of those involved, Zonyama kaMongo, fled to the uSuthu *umuzi* for sanctuary, and Addison's Zululand Police nearly came to blows with Dinuzulu's *amabutho* when trying to apprehend him. Osborn, who wished to avoid a full-scale confrontation over the matter, urged the extremely ruffled Addison to exercise restraint and not to 'resort to forcible measures without instructions'.[15]

Dinuzulu, meanwhile, as the true implications of annexation for his own position were brought home to him, began to make overtures to his old allies – but more recent adversaries – the Boers of the New Republic. On 26 July, without beforehand obtaining the required pass to leave the Colony of Zululand, he met President Lucas Meyer at Hamu's Wasanamuni *umuzi* in the New Republic. Five days of discussion ensued.[16] The Boers were anxious that Dinuzulu should move to the New Republic in order to stem the exodus of uSuthu attempting to join him in British Zululand – though, in fact, Zulu reluctance to render the Boers labour-service was a more potent reason for their emigration than a desire to join their king.

Osborn, when he learned of these negotiations, could not help being overjoyed: Dinuzulu's departure would remove the focus of discontent from British Zululand.[17] But, to his disappointment, Dinuzulu decided in the end to remain on in Zululand to try conclusions with his new masters. He chose the issue of the annual stipend to demonstrate his rejection of the new order. Osborn knew as well as Dinuzulu that it would be an important point gained if the members of the royal house and other chiefs accepted their pensions, for it would be an admission of their subordinate status.[18] On 4 August Dinuzulu and Ndabuko duly refused. But Khilane kaMahohlweni, Addison's *induna*, was a practised negotiator, and he succeeded in opening a rift in the ranks of the resistance.[19]

Mnyamana, ever an astute and moderate adviser to the royal house, clearly perceived the folly and futility of continued opposition to British rule. He therefore, as sign of his loyal submission, consented to accept his stipend. But he insisted on doing so for the moment in secret and, so as not to offend Dinuzulu, handed the money back to Khilane for safekeeping.[20] Despite these precautions, Dinuzulu divined Mnyamana's evident drift. Relations, already strained by mutual recriminations over the responsibility for their loss of independence to Britain, deteriorated further, and Mnyamana began to fear that Dinuzulu would have him assassinated. By the middle of August young warriors of both the uSuthu and the Buthelezi were being doctored for war.[21]

Addison started to panic at these developments, especially when a contingent of Qulusi crossed over the border from the New Republic and swelled the number of warriors already gathered at the uSuthu *umuzi*. Osborn realised he would have to intervene to uphold the authority of his administration. The crux of the matter was that, without sufficient armed backing, Addison would be unable to overawe Dinuzulu and his inflamed followers. Havelock thus allowed himself to be persuaded to sanction the forward movement of troops. On 21 August he ordered Osborn to proceed from Eshowe to Nkonjeni with a company of Mounted Infantry of the 1st Battalion, Prince of Wales (North Staffordshire) Regiment, while a squadron of the 6th (Inniskilling) Dragoons was moved up and stationed in support at Mthonjaneni about forty kilometres to the south.[22]

Osborn and his escort reached Nkonjeni on 26 August, only to discover that Dinuzulu and Ndabuko had left for the New Republic. There, on 27 August, they met Meyer in his capital, the little village of Vryheid. In an extraordinary turnabout, they attempted to place themselves under Boer protection, having concluded that this was a lesser evil than living under British rule. But the New Republicans were becoming cautious, and had no intention of falling foul of the British government by reasserting their claims to paramountcy over one of the Queen's colonies.[23] They declined Dinuzulu's offer, and on 31 August the uSuthu leaders were left to return disconsolately to Zululand to face retribution for their disloyalty – and for their failure to secure passes.

At Nkonjeni, Osborn attempted a fresh, but firm, start and summoned the uSuthu chiefs to appear before him. All except Dinuzulu and Ndabuko obeyed on 3 September, when the Resident Commissioner again explained the new laws of Zululand to them. Then, before the whole assembly, he threw down the gauntlet. Dinuzulu must hand over all the cattle he had seized from Mfokozana, and must pay a fine of thirty head of cattle for his 'contumacy'.[24] Osborn congratulated himself that his determined handling of the uSuthu would scotch further trouble from that quarter, and Mnyamana was certainly convinced by his performance: on 8 September he made known that he had accepted the government's stipend, thus publicly demonstrating his loyalty to the new regime. Dinuzulu, however, refused to hand over any of the cattle required of him, and Osborn, pursuing his tough line, ordered Addison on 8 September to take sixty Zululand Police and seize them.[25]

Addison rode north into the fertile thornveld valley between the Vuna and Black Mfolozi rivers. It was sunset when he came to the uSuthu *umuzi*, built on a gentle slope between rocky outcrops below a wide, open plain. Alarmed at his presence, about 1 500 uSuthu men, some armed with rifles, collected at the *umuzi* to protect Dinuzulu. But Addison was resolute, and warned that if the cattle were not handed over by the morrow, the uSuthu would be 'old people'.[26] True to his word, the next morning he drew up his men in a straight line 140 metres from the *umuzi* with their rifles pointing straight at it. Dinuzulu nevertheless refused to come out when summoned, and sent 400 *izinduna* to parley in his stead. Addison was enraged, especially when he saw Dinuzulu and a few attendants surreptitiously making off through a side entrance of the *umuzi*. For an hour the Resident Magistrate haggled pointlessly, and then, losing his nerve at the prospect of military confrontation, wheeled his force off. It was an ignominious moment. In an attempt to recover some shreds of his authority, he rounded up a herd of Dinuzulu's cattle as he retired, and extracted the number Osborn had demanded in fines and restitution. But that act of cattle-rustling was not at all the same as forcing a gesture of submission out of Dinuzulu. It was only too plain that in his first real confrontation with the authorities Dinuzulu had held his own.

Stern messages from Osborn for Dinuzulu and Ndabuko to appear before him were next contemptuously ignored, and the Resident Commissioner's messengers were even assaulted with sticks.[27] Clearly, other methods would have to be employed – and rapidly – before Dinuzulu's example was emulated by other chiefs and British authority began to be defied throughout Zululand. For, up to that stage, objections to British rule had not been general, and were confined in the main to those who owed particular sentiments of loyalty to Dinuzulu as the heir to the kingdom. The majority of people in British Zululand seemed to be accepting the change with reasonable equanimity, especially those who had lived for years under a modified form of British rule in the Reserve.[28] Even the likes of Somkhele, the influential Mphukunyoni chief in the Lower Umfolosi District, who had close ties to the royal house and had been an uSuthu supporter in the civil war, were (like Mnyamana) coming round to the new order of things. On 9 November he went so far as to come in person to Arthur Shepstone, his local resident magistrate, to assure him of his loyalty and to protest – an acceptable falsehood in the circumstances – that he had 'always been in favour of British rule'.[29]

Nevertheless, in Pietermaritzburg the Governor was mulling over the Dinuzulu problem and the pernicious example he was setting, and was on the verge of a disastrous decision. To his mind, there were two alternatives: either imperial troops must be despatched to reinforce Osborn's hand (an expensive proceeding), or Zibhebhu must be repatriated to act as a counterweight against the uSuthu. Zibhebhu's patrons among the Natal officials had long been urging such an approach, and Sir Theophilus bent all his energies towards convincing the uncertain Havelock, who rightly suspected Zibhebhu's return might well add fuel to the flames, rather than dousing them. Shepstone, in his magisterial memorandum of 31 July 1887, had pointed out that while the small force of Zululand Police could do little more than represent the power behind it, it was inadvisable for a civil administration trying to establish its moral sway to be perceived to be directly dependent on military intervention. The solution, Shepstone had urged, was (in the true spirit of the indirect rule he had ever advocated) to rely on collaborating chiefs to provide 'the real and coercive force'. No one, he had insisted, was better equipped to do so than the loyal but ill-used Zibhebhu. To return him to his district would, Shepstone had triumphantly concluded, 'at once throw the balance of Zulu power into the hands of the Government'.[30]

Even so, Havelock hesitated. What gave him the final push along the fatal road where Shepstone beguilingly beckoned was the treaty signed on 14 September 1887 between the New Republic and the South African Republic, whereby the two states undertook to form a union once their respective *volksrade* had ratified the details.[31] That was not, as it turned out, to be until 20 July 1888, but Havelock at once saw that an enlarged Boer republic was being created, potentially able to give considerably more effective support to Dinuzulu than the weak New Republic had been. The need to be firm was therefore redoubled, but Havelock could take no action as regards the employment of Zibhebhu until permission had been received from London. He duly applied for it, and grudging licence arrived at last in October from the sceptical Colonial Secretary, Sir Henry Holland, who allowed himself to be persuaded (rather against his better judgement) by his man on the spot.[32] Havelock at once notified Osborn that he was prepared to permit Zibhebhu's return if that would help the situation. But the Resident Commissioner, who had been negotiating fruitlessly with Dinuzulu and Ndabuko, nevertheless drew back nervously at the prospect. Closer consultation was clearly necessary before such a crucial decision could be taken, and Havelock agreed to meet Osborn at Eshowe to thrash out a policy.

Havelock intended to come in might to the colony of which he was governor in order to dispel any misconceptions that he was not in earnest about asserting the authority of the Crown. On account of the lack of available imperial troops he ordered Major McKean, the Resident Magistrate of Nqutu, to enrol 200 Mounted Basutos in his district from among Hlubi's adherents, the Tlokwa, and to proceed with them to Nkonjeni, where 75 Zululand Police were concentrated under Commandant Mansel.[33] Calling up the Tlokwa was hardly a politic move, considering that Hlubi's men had fought with the British in 1879, but Havelock knew that they could be entirely relied upon. Havelock also concentrated what white troops he had to hand at Nkonjeni, and a company of Mounted Infantry drawn from the Royal Inniskilling Fusiliers joined the squadron of the 6th (Inniskilling) Dragoons and the company of Mounted Infantry from the 1st North Staffordshire Regiment already there.[34]

Meanwhile, Havelock dealt uncompromisingly on 11 October with a deputation sent by the uSuthu to complain that the Zulu 'have not been used to Magistrates' offices and do not know how to get on with them, and that they are afraid they will not be able to do so'.[35] Dinuzulu's independent authority, he told them, had ended. Undeterred, the deputation put forward a further plaint concerning the unnatural borders of the New Republic cutting Dinuzulu off from his people there, which echoed in its formulation the words of an earlier deputation sent to Osborn on 22 August. Dinuzulu, they had said then, was

> like a calf tied up on one side of a hedge, while its mother is tied on the other side, and constantly lowing for her calf; the calf will fret and keep on tugging until at last the string it is tied up with breaks, and it finds itself rushing through the hedge to its mother.[36]

This homely but moving simile cut no more ice with Havelock than it had with Osborn. The uSuthu leaders, the Governor loftily exclaimed, were all subjects of the Queen and must submit to her laws and dispensations. And to bring this finally home to them, he instructed Osborn to summon Dinuzulu and Ndabuko to appear before the two of them in Eshowe on 1 November. The presence of the Governor in Zululand, backed up by his troops, should finally convince them of the hopelessness of their continued resistance.[37] But Dinuzulu made no reply to the summons, and Ndabuko began to suffer from a convenient cold in the head and a fall from his horse. This time, though, their resolve cracked.

Ndabuko and Shingana did at length set off for Eshowe, albeit days after the date set by Havelock for the meeting, and Dinuzulu himself finally arrived on 13 November. Havelock and Osborn, despite their mounting frustration and irritation at the insult these delays offered their authority, were nevertheless relieved that they had not been forced to go to the lengths they had agreed upon of arresting

Dinuzulu on a charge of 'treason felony',[38] with all the likely consequences of an uSuthu uprising.

Dinuzulu and Ndabuko came before Havelock on 14 November and again the following day.[39] His confrontation with the two recalcitrant uSuthu leaders afforded the Governor considerable personal satisfaction. At their first meeting, he spelled out to Dinuzulu in chilling and unequivocal terms just where the young man now stood:

> Dinuzulu must know, and all the Zulus must know, that the rule of the House of Chaka is a thing of the past. It is dead. It is like water spilt on the ground. The Queen rules now in Zululand and no one else. The Queen who conquered Cetywayo has now taken the government of the country into her own hands.[40]

Since Dinuzulu was no longer a king, but simply a chief over his own 'tribe', subject – like any other chief in Zululand – to the laws of the territory, Havelock firmly informed him and Ndabuko that he was not prepared to overlook their previous misconduct. He therefore sentenced each of them on 15 November to pay a fine of fifty head of cattle, over and above the livestock still to be restored to Mfokozana and the fine of thirty head imposed earlier by Osborn. The Governor's arithmetic seems to have been at fault, for he took into no account the cattle Addison had seized in September from Dinuzulu. But that was a trifle compared with the symbolic import of his sentence, which confirmed that the changeover to the new order was final and irrevocable.

Havelock did not only meet Dinuzulu and Ndabuko in Eshowe. He held another interview on 15 November which contrasted notably in tone with his tense and antagonistic encounters with the uSuthu leaders. The Governor and Osborn had used their days together to decide on their future course. So when the 'loyal' Zibhebhu was brought before him, Havelock informed the deeply gratified chief that he had permission to return to his 'old tribal lands', Not, he was hastily warned, as an independent chief as previously, but as a subject of the Queen. As a special mark of favour and confidence, he was to receive an annual stipend of £240, precisely double that of either Ndabuko or Mnyamana. Asked by the Governor when he would be able to set out to reoccupy his lands, Zibhebhu replied without hesitation, 'I would like to go at once.'[41] After so many months of consultation and hesitation the die was now cast, and Havelock informed the horrified uSuthu on the same day of Zibhebhu's impending return. It was then, wrote Fuze, 'that Dinuzulu became as enraged as a fire that has to be extinguished with water'.[42]

No doubt. Yet Havelock was sanguine that the uSuthu chiefs, humbled by him at Eshowe, and soon to be checked by the neighbouring presence of Zibhebhu, would at last abandon their idle dreams of an independent kingdom and submit. It no longer seemed an unattainable hope. Everywhere else in British Zululand the chiefs and their people were settling down to the new order of things. Even Mnyamana had succumbed, and the uSuthu were no longer putting up a united front. Indeed, in October Shingana, one of Dinuzulu's more influential uncles, who lived in the valley of the White Mfolozi not far from the Mahlabathini plain, had so far broken ranks as to accept his stipend, though secretly.[43]

Havelock had informed the uSuthu on 15 November that Addison would be moving to take up his post on the spot he had selected in July on the Nongoma hills. The advantage of the position was that it was on the very frontier between the uSuthu and Mandlakazi, and would leave Addison well placed to monitor any incidents between them. On 19 November, accompanied by Colonel H. Sparke Stabb, the commander of the British forces in Zululand, and a strong escort, Addison set out for his magistracy, which was to be known as Ivuna. The military stayed on a day to establish a heliograph station and begin construction on a little earthwork fort. It was completed by the garrison of fifty Zululand Police left at Ivuna under the command of Sub-Inspector C.E. Pierce, who had been a junior officer in the Inniskilling Dragoons. He did a very thorough job with the strong little fort. It was circular, with a diameter of fourteen metres, had a sandbagged and loopholed parapet, and around it ran a wide, deep ditch. About forty-six metres from the fort, and surrounding it, was a strong zariba of thornbushes. Within the enclosure, huts for the police and a thatched mess house for the whites soon sprang up. By March 1888 Addison had almost completed the construction of a house with an iron roof and proper doors (all imported laboriously, at his own expense, from Eshowe), where he hoped his wife and children would soon join him. Outside the zariba, Addison began to put up another permanent structure to serve as a magistrate's office.[44]

When Addison took up his post at Ivuna, he found that Dinuzulu had already returned to the uSuthu *umuzi* nearby, filled with foreboding – as were all the uSuthu – at the prospect of Zibhebhu's return. Not only was it up to Addison to keep the peace once he did, but he had also to exact the cattle fines Havelock had imposed. On top of this, he would soon have to make the first collection of the hut tax in Ndwandwe. No wonder that Colonel Stabb, back in Pietermaritzburg, prognosticated that it would be a long time before the various military outposts in Zululand could be withdrawn.[45]

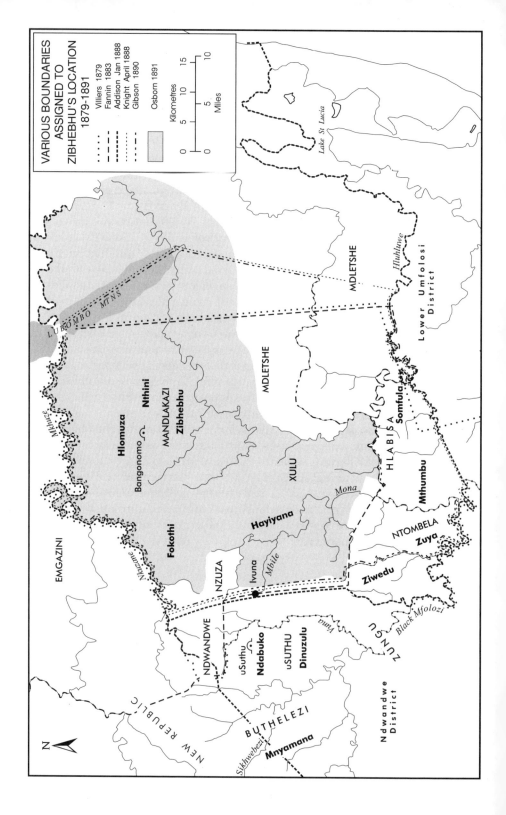

VARIOUS BOUNDARIES
ASSIGNED TO
ZIBHEBHU'S LOCATION
1879-1891

Villiers 1879
Fannin 1883
Addison Jan 1888
Knight April 1888
Gibson 1890

Osborn 1891

Kilometres
0   5   10   15
0   5   10
Miles

Lake St Lucia

LUBOMBO MTNS

Mkhuze

MDLETSHE

Hluhluwe

Lower Umfolosi
District

MDLETSHE

MDLETSHE

Nthini

Hlomuza
MANDLAKAZI
Zibhebhu

Bangonomo

HLABISA
Somfula

XULU

Mthumbu

Mona

Fokothi

Hayiyana

NTOMBELA
Zuya

Ivuna   *Mbile*
NZUZA

EMGAZINI

Nkuze

Ziwedu

ZUNGU
Black Mfolozi

NDWANDWE

uSuthu
Ndabuko

uSUTHU
Dinuzulu

Vuna

Ndwandwe
District

N E W   R E P U B L I C

BUTHELEZI

Sikhwebezi

Mnyamana

N

31

We Cannot Live Together with the Man Who Killed our King

Colonel Stabb was not mistaken in seeing great difficulties ahead in the Ndwandwe District. Before November was out, both Dinuzulu and Ndabuko had sidestepped Addison's demand that they pay their cattle fines forthwith, and fired back a formal protest at Zibhebhu's imminent return. 'His territory', said their messenger, 'is occupied by our people and we cannot live together with the man who killed our King'. But Addison knew that the uSuthu front was not united in steadfast opposition to Zibhebhu, for both Mnyamana and Ziwedu had dissociated themselves from Dinuzulu and submissively declared themselves 'satisfied' with his enemy's return. Thus fortified, Addison gave Dinuzulu and his uncle an ultimatum to pay their fines within seven days and pooh-poohed their fears.[1]

Zibhebhu, in any case, was already on his way. On 25 November he and 700 men (their women and children were to remain behind until they had re-established their *imizi*) marched out of their location in the former Reserve and headed up the coast towards the old Mandlakazi chiefdom.[2] They were accompanied by F. Galloway, a past superintendent of roads familiar with Zululand who, with the aid of four policemen, was to see to their peaceful resettlement. He was an Osborn appointee and a Mandlakazi partisan, but was nevertheless to prove an honest, if ineffectual, broker.

When Zibhebhu and his men entered their old district on 1 December they were on the point of starvation. They immediately began to raid fields cultivated by uSuthu on what they claimed was their territory, and ordered the 'squatters' to clear off. Some, such as Hlomuza kaMaphitha (Zibhebhu's half-brother who had continued living in the district after the Mandlakazi expulsion in 1884), and Nthini (whose adherents came from the Lubombo Mountains) fled spontaneously before him. But the rub was that neither Galloway nor anyone else knew precisely what the Governor had meant when he referred to Zibhebhu's 'old tribal lands', for (as we have seen) their limits had repeatedly been shifted since 1879.[3] All that was certain was that Zibhebhu was received with distinct fear and antagonism by those now settled on the land he might conceivably claim as his own, and it seemed clear that an uSuthu-Mandlakazi clash was in the offing. Naturally, it was hardly Havelock's intention that he should have to shore up the very prop he had introduced to buttress the shaky edifice of British rule in Ndwandwe. But the growing threat of violence left him with no choice but to reinforce

Addison's post at Ivuna with forty Zululand Police under Commandant Mansel.[4]

Addison had not only to patrol the countryside to avert an uSuthu-Mandlakazi confrontation. His ultimatum to Dinuzulu and Ndabuko to pay their fines had not merely expired unanswered, but their cattle were being driven over the border to the safety of the New Republic.[5] Pressed by his superiors to make his will felt, Addison was surprised but gratified when Dinuzulu actually answered a summons to appear at Ivuna on 8 December. Yet it was immediately apparent that his coming was not an act of submission, but an attempt to intimidate the importunate magistrate. He was accompanied by a daunting following of between 400 and 500 men, partly armed with rifles and spears. Dinuzulu expressed his grave dissatisfaction once more over Zibhebhu's return, and left the discomforted magistrate with the distinct impression that he would only ever pay his fines at the point of a gun.[6]

In this case, Addison would require the support of imperial troops, especially since word came that Dinuzulu was making suspicious preparations on Ceza Mountain, a traditional place of refuge for the uSuthu fifty kilometres by wagon-road south-west from Ivuna. Ceza is a great, looming, flat-topped mountain, rising over 300 metres above the Sikhwebezi River basin. It was then mostly within the New Republic, but the boundary with Zululand stretched for a kilometre and a half along its thickly wooded south-eastern face. Dinuzulu, it was confirmed, was having the caves in this natural fortress cleaned and their entrances made defensible. Addison instantly assumed that these preparations were against Zibhebhu, but Mnyamana, whose people were clustered along the Sikhwebezi and its tributaries to the east of Ceza, believed they were directed at him because of his acquiescence in Zibhebhu's return.[7] Either way, the uSuthu were clearly considering a resort to arms.

Zibhebhu, meanwhile, was consolidating his position. On 14 December he was reinforced by 300 men from Swaziland, under the command of his old *induna* Sikizana, who had fled north over the Phongolo with about half of the Mandlakazi after their defeat in 1884. Ominously, they too had left their families behind until it was 'safe' for them in Ndwandwe, and their advent made Zibhebhu's total force of 1 000 fighting men and more a distinct match for the uSuthu, despite their lack of arms and ammunition. With soaring confidence the Mandlakazi set about rebuilding their *imizi* and going on organised hunts for game. These, while serving to feed the men, also doubled as military training manoeuvres.[8]

Having rebuilt Bangonomo, his principal *umuzi*, Zibhebhu demanded of Addison on 18 December that he expel two pro-uSuthu chiefs whose adherents had long lived in the eastern and south-eastern reaches of the Ndwandwe District, but whom Zibhebhu regarded as impinging on his territory. Of the two, Zibhebhu particularly hated Msutshwana kaMfuzi of the Mdletshe who, although his brother-in-law, had refused to *khonza* to him when he had been placed in his territory in 1879, and had been responsible for soliciting Boer aid against him in 1884. The other chief Zibhebhu wished removed was Mthumbu kaMbopha of the Hlabisa, whom he also had every cause to regard as an enemy. Mthumbu's father, Mbopha kaWolizibi, had acted as regent for his minor nephew, Somfula, the rightful chief. But, because of royal favour, Mbopha had consolidated his position at Somfula's expense. In September 1879 the chiefdom fell under Zibhebhu, to whom Somfula gave his allegiance, while Mbopha adhered to the uSuthu cause and was killed by Zibhebhu at oNdini in 1883. Mthumbu continued to dispute Somfula's right to the chieftainship, and in 1884 Somfula was forced to flee to the Reserve.[9] Although they knew Msutshwana and Mthumbu had every right to be living where they were, Osborn and Addison were alienated by the threatened chiefs' strident protestations of loyalty to Dinuzulu, and came to the conclusion that, to mollify Zibhebhu, they 'must think of a plan to bundle the Usutu squatters off Sibebu's sites'.[10]

Dinuzulu too was making preparations against the future. With the Ceza caves prepared as a refuge, he began seriously to muster his support. Without Addison's prior knowledge or permission, and as a direct challenge to Zibhebhu, he called a great kudu hunt in the valley of the Black Mfolozi, bordering on the Mandlakazi location. When, during its course, he asked his men if they would be prepared to rub Zibhebhu out, they shouted in reply, 'give us permission and we will kill him!'[11] Beside such provocation, Dinuzulu was still making clear that he had no intention of paying the cattle fines, and Addison was left pressing Osborn for military support.

Zibhebhu, likewise, was pushing ahead with his agenda. The crops planted by the uSuthu in what had again become his location would, because the season was a dry one, not be ready for reaping until July. But the uSuthu in his district had pits full of corn, and Dinuzulu had forbidden his adherents to let the starving Mandlakazi have any of it.[12] Thus, for Zibhebhu, it was becoming a matter of survival that the 'squatters' be removed and their grain made available. And since the Resident Magistrate hesitated at the practicalities, rather than the morality, of such a course, Zibhebhu decided to take a leaf out of Dinuzulu's book and overawe him with a show of might.

On the afternoon of 2 January 1888 Zibhebhu and about 1 200 of his following arrived at Ivuna in full war costume, and demanded the instant removal of the uSuthu from the Mandlakazi location.[13] To underline their point, the Mandlakazi proceeded to hold a war-dance at the magistracy. These were Addison's supposed allies, and he did his best to put on a welcoming face. But repeated humiliations at the hands of the two factions could hardly be tolerated, and Addison set about finding a way out of his situation. Shortsightedly, he held by his earlier recommendation that the uSuthu 'squatters' should indeed be evicted, and that to effect this in an orderly manner and under legal guise, it was necessary that 'a distinct boundary be defined between the two tribes'.[14] Osborn concurred, and ordered Addison to proceed with marking out a boundary preparatory to removing the uSuthu 'squatters'.[15]

This was a crucial decision, for it removed any lingering doubt from the minds of the uSuthu that the British administration was entirely partial. The apparition of Zibhebhu in battle array at Ivuna on 2 January, only eight kilometres from Ndabuko's Meniya *umuzi*, galvanised the uSuthu leadership. They immediately began mustering their followers from every part of Zululand, and the New Republic as well, and concentrated them at the uSuthu *umuzi*. Even Mnyamana and Ziwedu, who had been distancing themselves from Dinuzulu, intimated they might come to his assistance – if only because they could barely restrain their young men from joining the other *amabutho*. By the afternoon of 6 January there were about 1 500 at the *umuzi* being 'doctored' prior to going to war. They not unreasonably refused Addison's orders to disperse so long as Zibhebhu's men were still in arms.[16]

The Mandlakazi had, by this stage, pulled back to the impregnable stronghold of Bende, about sixteen kilometres south-east of Bangonomo, where, with his force of 15 horsemen and 1 400 footmen, armed with spears and a motley collection of 44 Martini-Henrys, 110 muzzle-loaders, 5 Snider carbines and various other useless and antiquated firearms, Zibhebhu was confident of withstanding anything the uSuthu might throw against him.[17] Unable to regain control of the situation, Addison had no option but to sit tight until rescued by the arrival of the imperial troops whose presence he had been urgently requesting. The attempt to bring Dinuzulu to book through the agency of a loyal collaborator was rapidly proving, in the dry words of the *Natal Witness*, 'a piece of stupid diplomacy, if not worse'.[18] But having once embarked on its misguided policy, the government was bound to do its best to make it work.

On 10 January 1888 a squadron of the Inniskilling Dragoons and a company of Mounted Infantry from Nkonjeni, under the command of Lieutenant-Colonel R.G.R. Martin, arrived to reinforce the eighty-six Zululand Police already stationed at Ivuna. They pitched camp on the banks of the Vuna River, thirteen kilometres equidistant from both Addison's post and Dinuzulu's *umuzi*.[19] As far as the military were concerned, the Governor's decision to send troops forward had come none too soon. Colonel Stabb, for one, was adamant that the so-called Zulu experts had misled Havelock, and that much subsequent trouble could have been avoided if only Zibhebhu had been accompanied north by sufficient troops to cow Dinuzulu into instant submission.[20] His was a typically military approach to a complex problem, but now Lieutenant-Colonel Martin was there to lend Zibhebhu confidence, put some backbone into Mr Addison and give Dinuzulu pause to reconsider his position.

Rather than risk action by Martin's troops, on 13 January Dinuzulu hurriedly rendered up thirty-one cattle to Addison. That left him still owing nineteen head towards the Governor's fine, a further thirty towards Osborn's, and twenty-one to Mfokozana, who was still waiting at Ivuna for restitution.[21] It was at least a start, and Havelock was adamant that Addison must bestir himself and use the temporary presence of Martin's troops to extract the balance, and the fifty owed by Ndabuko too. Addison screwed up his courage to poke his head into the angry hornets' nest that was now the uSuthu *umuzi*, and set off on the morning of 14 January with a small Zululand Police escort. As anticipated, he was in for a not altogether pleasant time. Dinuzulu first degradingly kept him waiting an hour and a half outside the *umuzi*, where the menacing presence of 2 000 emaciated young men of the uFalaza and imBokodwebomvu *amabutho* added to his unease. The three hours of conversation which then passed between the Magistrate, Dinuzulu and Ndabuko were exceedingly strained.

Addison tried to be conciliatory, but the uSuthu leaders would not be mollified and railed against Zibhebhu, forcing the Magistrate to trail home with the gift of a cow and nothing resolved. The return of the troops to Nkonjeni the following day left his position as weak as it ever had been.[22] But his superiors were not going to allow his initiative to collapse. Havelock, who was becoming increasingly alarmed at the way in which Zibhebhu's repatriation, rather than acting as a means of containing the uSuthu, was instead driving them into open resistance, grasped at the idea of preventing armed clashes through the sensitive redefinition of Zibhebhu's location. He accordingly issued specific instructions on 12 January 1888 (relayed to Ivuna on 17 January) by which Addison was strictly to abide. Addison was to allot Zibhebhu 'only such portion of land as may be actually necessary'. He was also to allow as many uSuthu as possible to remain undisturbed within Zibhebhu's redefined location, providing only that they 'submit to Usibebu as their tribal Chief'.

Havelock, himself a man of humanity and good sense, clearly was starting to mistrust Addison's discretion and energy, and though he concluded by charging his subordinate to be firm with all parties, he also urged him to be more conciliatory and forbearing than in the past.[23] Galvanised by such a chastening despatch, on 21 January 1888 Addison submitted his thoughts on the new boundaries he was to draw. He considered that they should be almost the same as Fannin's in 1883, with the exception of Mgojana of the Ndwandwe's territory, which had been cut off by the creation of the New Republic.[24]

Addison had a copy of Alleyn's map of Zululand (the same inadequate map Fannin had been forced to depend on in 1883), on which Osborn instructed him to mark his boundaries in pencil, as Havelock reserved the right to alter them if he was not satisfied.[25] Before he could get into the field to demarcate Zibhebhu's location, however, he had to go through a reprise on the 26 January of his previous performance at the uSuthu *umuzi*. What made a difference this time was the unexpected arrival of Lieutenant-Colonel Martin and a mounted patrol, which put the uSuthu into 'a great fright'. The upshot was that the armed gathering at the *umuzi* began rapidly to disperse, and by 30 January Dinuzulu had disgorged the full fine of fifty cattle required by the Governor, and seven towards Osborn's fine of thirty. Ndabuko also came forward at last and contributed a niggardly seven head. It was marvellous how much more effective were the military than a mere magistrate and his police in persuading the uSuthu leadership to comply with the requirements of the British administration.[26] Stabb clearly had a point.

Addison now scurried off to define Zibhebhu's location, and by 27 January he had fixed his boundary beacons, though in several vital particulars he had deviated from his initially restrained ideas of 21 January. Once in the field he was persuaded to extend Zibhebhu's southern boundary to the Black Mfolozi River, thus incorporating all the Hlabisa people as well as Ziwedu's adherents. He was even more liberal in the east, where he pushed the location to Lake St Lucia, thus restoring to Zibhebhu regions he had controlled before Villiers's boundary of 1879, and which included all the Mdletshe as well as various Tsonga chiefdoms.[27] Dinuzulu was as furious as Zibhebhu was gratified, and declared on 9 February that he could see by Addison's boundaries that 'he wishes Sibebu and myself to fight'.[28]

Addison, meanwhile, was consolidating himself in Zibhebhu's good graces by ordering the removal of uSuthu from the Mandlakazi location he had so lavishly enlarged. By the end of February Msutshwana's adherents, who had initially mustered in arms to resist, were complying with Addison's eviction order and moving into the Lower Umfolosi District, though their chief (whom Addison had briefly detained at Ivuna) was too ill to accompany them. In order to be spared a similar fate, a number of uSuthu headmen in Zibhebhu's location hastened to forsake Dinuzulu and acknowledge their new Mandlakazi chief. These included Mkhonto kaSomfula of the Hlabisa; the family of the late Hayiyana kaMaphitha (Zibhebhu's pro-uSuthu half-brother whom he had killed at oNdini in 1883), now under Nyonyana; as well as several Tsonga *izinduna*. Mthumbu of the Hlabisa refused to obey Addison's orders to remove to the Lower Umfolosi District like the Mdletshe, tore up his pass to do so and fled to Dinuzulu for sanctuary. There he was joined by yet others falling under Addison's eviction orders, presenting the Magistrate with the daunting prospect of having to arrest them there.[29]

Meanwhile, in the vicinity of his magistracy at Ivuna, strategically situated near by Dinuzulu's *umuzi*, Addison proceeded ruthlessly to separate uSuthu and Mandlakazi who were living intermingled. He removed eighteen Mandlakazi *imizi* east of the boundary line (which he left as Fannin had drawn it), and moved considerably more uSuthu *imizi* to the west of it, including that of Fokothi kaMaphitha, another of Zibhebhu's brothers who had refused to *khonza* to him in 1879, and who had returned home in 1884 after his brother's flight to the Reserve.[30] The actual number of uSuthu Addison removed from Zibhebhu's redefined location is a matter for dispute. But no matter how one plays with the contradictory figures, whether in terms of the number of *imizi* affected, or of huts or of their occupants, it seems clear that in 1888 Addison forced close on 5 000, or nearly half of the uSuthu, from their homes.[31] No wonder they came to view him as their determined oppressor.

While the evictions were going on, Addison continued to worry Dinuzulu and Ndabuko over the cattle fines. Dinuzulu genuinely had limited cattle of his own, as even Addison eventually conceded, for those herds captured from Zibhebhu in the civil war had been kept as booty – against custom – by Mnyamana and other chiefs, instead of being made over to him. Thus, the cattle Dinuzulu had paid had actually been contributed by his uncles and the people. Ndabuko, by contrast, still (despite his protestations to the contrary) had great wealth in cattle, and incensed Addison by trickling out only another eighteen towards his fine.[32] Of greater concern to the authorities were Dinuzulu's continuing contacts with the Boers of the New Republic. Dinuzulu crossed the border to hold a discussion with Field Cornet Paul Bester on 15 February and, in the light of growing uSuthu anger at the evictions from Zibhebhu's location, Addison feared that a hostile alliance might be brewing.[33]

His apprehensions were given some substance on 5 March when Dinuzulu appeared before the Ivuna camp with 300 armed young men who were in an ugly and defiant mood. In the confrontational parley that followed, Dinuzulu brushed aside all Addison's attempts to be placatory and made very clear the uSuthu fury at the blatant favouritism he was showing Zibhebhu. Addison was left shaken by his vehemence and convinced that the bitterness between the Mandlakazi and uSuthu had reached such a pass that they were now 'blind to all reason except in trying to do each other as much injury as possible'.[34] Addison therefore decided that where fair words had failed, stern deeds would show the uSuthu who was master. He ordered Sub-Inspector Pierce and his ninety Zululand Police stationed at Ivuna to go out and evict those uSuthu 'squatters' who were sticking fast in the location he had delimited for Zibhebhu. But Pierce and his men found themselves defied and threatened by young uSuthu, and Addison was much shaken by these signs of hardening resistance.[35]

Indeed, Dinuzulu, who was openly sheltering fugitives from British authority at the uSuthu *umuzi*, boasted that the English dared not arrest him there and made contact again with the authorities in the New Republic. On 16 March he and Ndabuko contemptuously brushed aside Addison's renewed demands for the balance of their fines. Addison was convinced that the uSuthu were only waiting until the crops were reaped to commence hostilities, and insisted that the presence of imperial troops was again required to discourage them in their defiance. And certainly, the uSuthu did seem to be making preparations for war. Mnyamana and Ziwedu were in no doubt, and by 22 March both had taken refuge in the Nkonjeni camp itself for fear of an uSuthu attack.[36]

Meanwhile, the uSuthu opened an offensive on another front. Bypassing Addison and Osborn, an uSuthu deputation took the road to Pietermaritzburg to put their case before the Governor. Havelock was in considerable dismay at the slide of events in Ndwandwe towards open resistance, and could no longer ignore the fact that the officials on the spot were at least partly to blame. As he sternly wrote privately to Addison on 18 March, on the eve of his meeting with the uSuthu deputation, who had been earning significant public support for their plight:

> The sooner you and all your people can feel and act as if you are administering a district in one of Her Majesty's Colonies, and not occupying the country of an enemy, – the better it will be.[37]

During the two days of meetings on 19 and 20 March, Havelock could not but be impressed by the uSuthus' credible pleas. He naturally upheld the authority of his officials and took Dinuzulu to task for keeping his men under arms, but, significantly, he undertook to pay the uSuthu compensation for the growing crops and grain they had lost in removal, and agreed to a redefinition of Zibhebhu's location.[38]

In fact, Havelock had already decided that Zibhebhu's location, as delimited by Addison, must be redefined. Even Osborn had recommended that the Governor should not confirm Addison's boundaries of Zibhebhu's location as they were 'unnecessarily large', and that an official not hitherto involved in the case should be put in charge of a boundary revision.[39] Havelock duly appointed John Knight, the Resident Magistrate of Entonjaneni, to the task. Unpromisingly, Knight was an old friend of Addison's, of similar administrative experience and of like mind.[40] On the other hand, his instructions were more specific than Addison's had been, and reflected Havelock's growing unease with the deleterious effects of Zibhebhu's repatriation. The Governor thus laid down that Zibhebhu was not to be allowed to occupy any land which could not be 'shown to have been old tribal lands immediately before the war of 1879', and that the boundary should keep the uSuthu and Mandlakazi from 'coming into dangerous proximity to one another'.[41] He was particularly concerned over the inclusion of Msutshwana's *imizi* in Zibhebhu's territory, and Addison was ordered to take no further steps in removing his people until Knight had completed his task.[42]

On 12 April Osborn arrived with Knight to begin his demarcation, but had to withdraw because of vehement but not unreasonable uSuthu fears that he would influence Knight unduly. Knight therefore proceeded without him, consulting closely with both the uSuthu and Mandlakazi as he set up his beacons. Osborn, in his report to Havelock, insisted that Knight had 'spared no pains or trouble in arriving at a just decision'.[43] Yet Knight exhibited all the anti-uSuthu prejudices one would expect of an official selected by Osborn. His impartiality was fatally discredited when Addison, who undoubtedly knew more about the intricacies of the dispute than any other official barring Osborn, accompanied him on his inspection of the boundaries. His suspect presence damned Knight's delimitation in uSuthu eyes,[44] even though it actually represented a significant departure from Addison's.

Knight made two significant alterations to Addison's line, though in the main he refrained from doing so where the process of eviction was too far advanced to be easily reversed, such as was the case with the Nzuza people just north-east of the Ivuna magistracy. The first alteration involved some 20 000 hectares in the south-west of the location. Knight decided these belonged without doubt to Ziwedu's adherents, thus sparing them the eviction that had threatened. An even more considerable revision withdrew Zibhebhu's eastern boundary to the Lubombo Mountains. This new line affected Msutshwana's adherents, half of whom now found themselves outside the location. Knight recommended that those still left in Zibhebhu's location should move east over the boundary, and that Msutshwana should function as an independent chief over his reunited following. Mthumbu's adherents he reconsigned to Zibhebhu's location.[45] Both Msutshwana and Mthumbu were infuriated by Knight's new line and, rejecting it out of hand, were hardened in their support of Dinuzulu.[46]

Knight finished his task on 20 April. Havelock, on reading his superficially acceptable report of 30 April, could find no overt reasons in terms of his very limited knowledge of the realities of the situation in Ndwandwe not to approve it. Nevertheless, it was a sign of his uncertainty and desire not to exacerbate the situation that he suggested to the Colonial Secretary, Lord Knutsford (as Sir

Henry Holland had become since February 1888) that he wait four months to allow the parties an opportunity to appeal before ratifying Knight's delimitation.[47]

Circumstances rapidly overtook deliberations, however, for those aggrieved with the conditions of Zibhebhu's return were preparing to do more than lodge restrained appeals. On 5 April, even before his delegation returned from Pietermaritzburg with welcome word of the Governor's decision to redraw Zibhebhu's boundaries, Dinuzulu, accompanied by twenty horsemen, had crossed the Phongolo into the New Republic, not to return until 13 May.[48] In the minds of the Zululand officials the purpose of his absence was quite obvious: Dinuzulu had gone to raise forces from his adherents across the border in order to attack not only Zibhebhu, but Mnyamana, Ziwedu and any other who had opposed or betrayed him by collaborating with the colonial administration.[49] And if the uSuthu were seriously considering the desperate option of taking up arms, the Zululand administration was hardening in its resolve to show them once and for all who was the master in the Colony of Zululand.

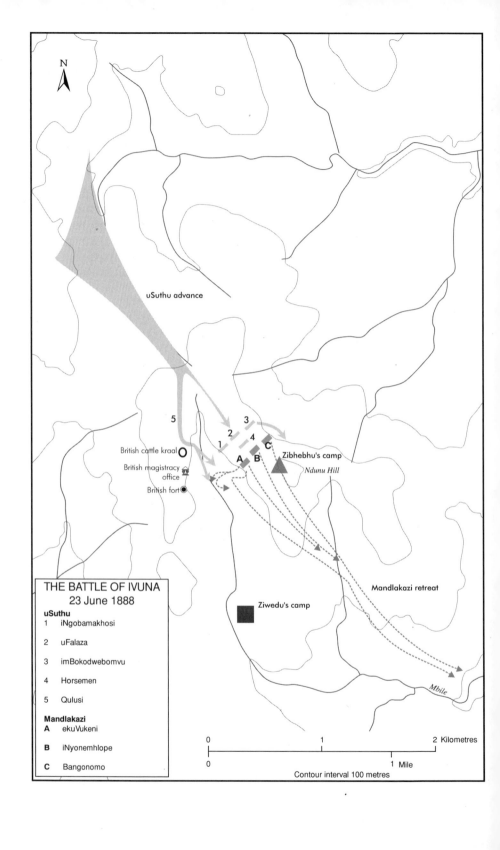

N

uSuthu advance

British cattle kraal ◯

British magistracy office

British fort ◉

5

2   4
1   3

A   B   C

Zibhebhu's camp

Ndunu Hill

Mandlakazi retreat

Ziwedu's camp

Mbile

THE BATTLE OF IVUNA
23 June 1888

uSuthu
1   iNgobamakhosi

2   uFalaza

3   imBokodwebomvu

4   Horsemen

5   Qulusi

Mandlakazi
A   ekuVukeni

B   iNyonemhlope

C   Bangonomo

0   1   2 Kilometres

0   1 Mile

Contour interval 100 metres

32

Applying the Torch of War

Osborn decided to take advantage of his own presence at Ivuna to force Dinuzulu and Ndabuko to pay the balance of the cattle they still owed in fines and restitution. On the morning of 25 April 1888 Addison and the Zululand Police raided Dinuzulu's ekuBazeni *umuzi* and Ndabuko's nearby Meniya. Addison claimed that he seized 'just enough' cattle to pay the balance of the fines, though it is clear that he drove forty-five more than the required seventy back to Ivuna. Encouraged at the success of this *coup de main*, where previous blandishments had failed, Osborn moved next to arrest the four principal fugitives from British justice being sheltered at the uSuthu *umuzi*. They were Mthumbu, the Hlabisa chief who had refused to remove to the Lower Umfolosi District, and three others who had treated Addison's summonses to answer civil claims brought by other Zulu with summary contempt. By no coincidence, all had fallen foul of Zibhebhu and were refugees from his location.[1]

Addison, with uncomfortable memories of his earlier humiliations before the uSuthu *umuzi*, was convinced that the Zululand Police, if unsupported by imperial troops, would be resisted if they attempted to make the arrests ordered by Osborn. But Osborn thought the momentum of his new initiative to be irresistible and ordered the operation to proceed. It was a decision which, in the words of the lawyers who later defended the uSuthu chiefs, 'applied...the torch of war'.[2]

At dawn on 26 April a force of eighty Zululand Police, under the command of Sub-Inspectors Pierce and Jack Osborn (the Resident Commissioner's son), surrounded the uSuthu *umuzi* with military precision.[3] Inside, the alarm was sounded, and some 1 000 *amabutho*, fully armed, in war-dress and shouting their battle cry, *uSuthu!*, rapidly formed up to confront the police. As Addison had once warned, the uSuthu looked upon the Zululand Police 'as merely kafirs and with great contempt', and had not nearly the same fear of them as for Imperial troops.[4] By contrast, the Zululand Police had considerable respect for the defiant *amabutho* who so completely outnumbered them. The white officials therefore dared take no firmer action than to haggle fruitlessly with Ndabuko (Dinuzulu was still away, over the border in the New Republic) before ignominiously retiring. As they fell back, bold and abusive parties of uSuthu followed them for over thirteen kilometres, turning back just short of the fort at Ivuna.

Ill-advised the attempt to execute the four warrants of arrest had certainly been, but Osborn now found himself trapped in the false position of having to proceed – even in the face of armed resistance – if his government's authority was to be vindicated. And Havelock, while certainly regretting Osborn's inept initiative, had no option but to move up troops in support of a fresh attempt to make the bungled arrests.[5]

The uSuthu, meanwhile, had been thrown into a ferment by these events. Men, women and children began to desert their *imizi* and to seek security in their traditional places of refuge, while from the eastern parts of Ndwandwe it was reported that Msutshwana was driving his cattle north-east over the border into the territory of the Nyawo chief, Sambane, who was an uSuthu sympathiser. Word of Dinuzulu's military preparations in Boer territory flew about, and the Mandlakazi began to prepare against an uSuthu attack. By the second week of May Zibhebhu had assembled a 'personal guard' of about 400 men at Bangonomo. For his part, Ndabuko sent his women and cattle safely out of the way and reassembled about 1 000 *amabutho* at the uSuthu homestead, who loudly proclaimed that they would destroy Zibhebhu in spite of his protection by the British official.[6]

Yet, as had happened twice before, uSuthu defiance was deflated by the arrival of the Imperial troops requested by Osborn. On 12 May a squadron of the 6th (Inniskilling) Dragoons, as well as two companies of Mounted Infantry, drawn respectively from the 1st Royal Inniskilling Fusiliers and the 1st North Staffordshire Regiment, all under the command of Captain E.G. Pennefather of the Inniskilling Dragoons, moved forward from Nkonjeni. Like Martin's troops in January, they encamped by the Vuna River some thirteen kilometres from Ivuna.[7] The following day the troops made a reconnaissance towards the uSuthu *umuzi*, only to find that its alarmed inmates, rather than risk a confrontation with real soldiers, had evacuated it during the night and retired into the bush.

Thus far, Ndabuko had avoided any physical confrontation with the government, but it was becoming increasingly difficult to do so in the face of its determination to enforce its sovereignty. Equally taxing was the effort to hold in the uSuthu *amabutho* who were straining to fall upon Zibhebhu, but who would not see that to attack him was to attack the government also. In Mnyamana's striking simile, they had to learn that to strike a dog which the owner was leading by a string was an act of aggression against its master, too.[8]

On 13 May Dinuzulu crossed back into Zululand and was joined by Ndabuko. The two uSuthu leaders, alarmed on 15 May by a patrol of troops and Zululand Police, fell back on their refuge on Ceza Mountain with a force over 1 000 strong. It consisted of about 400 warriors Dinuzulu had raised across the Phongolo, a further 300 from the New Republic, and 400 from his immediate following in British Zululand. Most were members of the uFalalza, imBokodwebomvu and iNgobamakhosi *amabutho*. On the way to Ceza, they raided some of Mnyamana's *imizi* in their path and looted a trading-store belonging to Piet Louw.[9]

Osborn feared that to save themselves from further depredation by Dinuzulu's *impi*, Mnyamana's adherents in the vicinity of Ceza might decide to join him. To forestall such a development, which would surely presage an attack on Zibhebhu, Osborn decided to move swiftly and decisively to dislodge the uSuthu from Ceza. This put him squarely into the hands of the military, who were confident they knew best how to set about the task. They pronounced the terrain between Ivuna and Ceza impracticable for military operations, and insisted that Nkonjeni was better suited as a base for mounting an attack on Dinuzulu's fastness. Osborn could scarcely argue, and on 20 May he moved back with the troops to the Nkonjeni camp. Colonel Stabb did, however, entertain some misgivings over the withdrawal, for he saw that the road between Dinuzulu and Zibhebhu was thereby laid open, and he knew that the Zululand Police garrison at Ivuna would be insufficient to bar the way between them. He decided, nevertheless, that the risk was both justified and small.[10]

The uSuthu on their rocky mountain had to feed themselves, and proceeded to raid those whom they regarded as British collaborators for supplies. On the night of 22 May a party 500-strong ranged as far east as the Nongoma hills, where they captured 181 cattle and 40 sheep from eight of Ziwedu's *imizi* nearby the magistracy itself. Addison, his young clerk, Cuthbert Foxon, and Sub-Inspector Pierce followed up the *impi's* trail with considerable pluck, and even managed to cut about fifty men off from the main body, eventually arresting two of them. These Addison charged with riot and cattle-theft.[11] This was hardly enough to reassure Ziwedu, however, and his adherents moved up with large herds of cattle closer to the protection of the Ivuna fort. He himself took to sleeping every night in the camp at Nkonjeni. Mnyamana and many of his Buthelezi, who had abandoned their *imizi* in anticipation of being raided by the bands of uSuthu roaming the Sikhwebezi valley in search of food, settled down near enough to Nkonjeni to feel secure.[12] Ndukwana, one of James Stuart's informants, was present when Mnyamana addressed his men, all sitting together near the British camp. Explaining to them why he had separated himself from Dinuzulu and given his allegiance to the British, he spoke words to this effect:

> The Usutu leaders say we must go to the Boers because the British killed the king. I refuse to go. We fought against the British and, as we were conquered by them, we cannot now take the country and cede it to the Boers.[13]

The uSuthu, terrorising their neighbours in defiance of their nominal rulers, were also threatening the financial basis of the British administration. The new hut tax fell due for the first time on 1 June 1888, but the unsettled conditions in Ndwandwe made its full and punctual payment unlikely, even by loyalists. Young men who should have been going to Natal to earn money to pay the tax had stayed at home to protect their property. Victims of both uSuthu and Mandlakazi violence, whether Mnyamana and Ziwedu on one hand, or Msutshwana on the other, applied for an extension of the date of payment.

Osborn naturally feared that the effects of uSuthu resistance might spill over into the other districts of the colony, which was all the more reason for putting a swift and effective end to their warlike and lawless behaviour. From Nkonjeni he advised Havelock that the only way to disperse the uSuthu on Ceza was to send the Zululand Police to arrest the ringleaders, supported this time by a strong force of soldiers. Independently, Havelock had reached the identical conclusion, and on 28 May he ordered the arrest of Ndabuko and Dinuzulu on the charge of cattle-theft. Addison, as the appropriate magistrate, drew up the warrants. With them in his pocket, he set out from Ivuna on 1 June escorted by Pierce and twenty Zululand Police. His objective was David Louw's store on the Mfabeni hills, two-thirds of the way to Nkonjeni and in easy striking distance of Ceza, some sixteen kilometres distant. There he was to rendezvous with Imperial troops, more Zululand Police, and black auxiliaries drawn from Mnyamana's adherents. His presence was vital, for the fiction was being maintained that the advance on Ceza was a police action in the execution of civil warrants. The military could consequently take action only if called upon by the magistrate to support his police.[14]

Yet as Addison made ready to leave for the Mfabeni hills, Osborn set the fatal events in train. On 31 May the Resident Commissioner ordered Zibhebhu and his fighting-men to Ivuna to reinforce the depleted garrison and, if necessary, to support Addison at Ceza. Zibhebhu, only too happy at the prospect of action against the uSuthu, arrived at Ivuna just as Addison left, and by the next day his force stood at between 700 and 800 men. In order to preserve the legal fiction that the Mandlakazi were not actually invading uSuthu territory, Osborn ordered Zibhebhu to bivouac just within the boundary of his location in the scrub bush on the slopes of the Ndunu hill opposite the magistracy. In fact, the fiction later turned out to be just that. For when later exactly surveyed, the Ndunu hill, which was separated from the magistracy buildings 830 metres away by the marshy Mbile spruit in its deep, narrow valley, proved to be nearly 100 metres within the uSuthu location.[15]

While Zibhebhu's men set about erecting their temporary shelters on Ndunu hill, the operations against Dinuzulu ensconced on Ceza floundered towards a denouement that was to prove an even greater setback for the authorities than the affair at the uSuthu *umuzi* on 26 April. At 4.30 on the morning of 2 June the sixty-six Zululand Police under Mansel (seventeen mounted), supported by regular troops under Captain Pennefather, consisting of three officers and eighty-one NCOs and men of the Inniskilling Dragoons and seventy-eight Mounted Infantry, left David Louw's store on the Mfabeni hills for Ceza.[16] On the way they picked up 400 of Mnyamana's adherents, who were to act as auxiliaries. Addison lined them up and solemnly warned them not to kill any women or children in the coming encounter. The combined force halted soon after 10.30 a.m. for breakfast at Piet Louw's store, which was about six kilometres east of Ceza, and which the uSuthu had looted on 15 May. While they were eating, they spotted the uSuthu *impi* forming up into a semicircle on the slopes of the mountain to be addressed by its leaders. It then marched towards the flat summit through the encircling bush by two separate paths, both partly within the New Republic. Thinking, correctly as it turned out, that the uSuthu intended bolting for the safety of the New Republic just to their rear across the top of the mountain, Addison decided to execute his warrants in all haste.

As the combined force approached Ceza, two messengers were despatched by the uSuthu leaders to confer with the British. They only managed, however, to catch up with the British rear, and though they reported themselves to Yamela, Osborn's head *induna*, they were unable to have a word with any of the white officials before fighting broke out. For Mansel, and the seventeen mounted Zululand Police under Pierce, who were pushing ahead along the south-western of the two paths up Ceza to make their arrests, became separated from the main body of troops who took the north-eastern path. Suddenly, Mansel's men collided with over a hundred of the uFalaza *ibutho* who were still far down the mountain slopes where the path entered the bush. The uFalaza presented a front, which Mansel considered sufficiently provocative to justify his opening fire. It was immediately returned. The main uSuthu force, hearing the shooting, came streaming down the mountain in support with Dinuzulu himself at the head of the imBokodwebomvu *ibutho*, and threatened to cut off Mansel's little detachment. Addison, seeing the danger they were in, and realising that they were certainly in no position to enforce their warrants, called on Captain Pennefather (whose instructions were to extricate the Zululand Police should they find themselves in difficulties) to take charge of the situation.

With some difficulty, the regular troops managed to cover the retreat of Mansel's Police (one of whom was wounded), themselves losing two men killed and two wounded in the process. Mnyamana's men had prudently declined to advance up the mountain, but were caught up in the retreat. The victorious uSuthu pursued the retiring British forces as far south as the Black Mfolozi, just short of the Mfabeni hills. Only Pennefather's expert handling of his mounted men prevented the uSuthu from again getting within effective striking distance. At one stage he charged with two troops of Dragoons, formed into two single rank squadrons. Their horses were extremely tired and could no longer perform well, but one squadron rode down their pursuers and sabred several of them. That had a considerable effect on morale, and thereafter the Zulu gave up their attempts to surround and cut off the British. Being short of both food and ammunition, the troops did not halt at their camp of the night before, but fell the whole way back to Nkonjeni, which they reached at 10 a.m. on 3 June.

Predictably, settler Natal was absolutely horrified at this blow to British prestige, for Imperial troops, not merely black Zululand Police, had been ignominiously repulsed. As Dinuzulu's praises gleefully proclaimed:

He is the expeller of the rock-rabbit from Ceza,
And he takes up the whole place.[17]

Havelock was dismayed, for he at once understood that the Ceza affair would greatly increase uSuthu confidence and badly unsettle those Zulu who, until then, had remained loyal to the new administration.[18] Certainly, there was an instant collapse of law and order in the Ndwandwe District. The uSuthu redoubled their raids on Mnyamana's people, for his involvement in the expedition against Ceza had put beyond doubt his commitment to the British. In one such incident, a raiding party – allegedly led by Dinuzulu himself – attacked the homestead of Mnyamana's brother Santinga near the Mfabeni hills. He and those with him, including a number of children, were all killed.

On 2 June David Louw, who had thought himself to be on excellent terms with the Zulu, was shot dead at his store near the Mfabeni hills by a young uSuthu, Mbamba, a son of Mbopha the Hlabisa chief, whom he had surprised robbing his premises. His son, Klaas Louw, was shot dead on the afternoon of 6 June at his store across the Vuna River from Dinuzulu's ekuBazeni *umuzi*, only eleven kilometres from the magistracy at Ivuna. The culprits were a party of a hundred uSuthu under Mjongo kaNogwaja. Louw's right ear, eye and brains were removed, clearly for ritual purposes. Owen Roberts, another trader in the locality, had his house near Thokazi Mountain looted and burned and his cattle driven off by uSuthu while he was away burying the younger Louw. A tremendous scare consequently swept the handful of whites trading in Zululand, and for a while it was scarcely safe for them to venture anywhere between Mthonjaneni and the border to the north.[19]

As Havelock had seen it would, the unrest rapidly spread beyond Ndwandwe. On 4 June Dinuzulu's uncle, Shingana, whose *umuzi* now lay in the New Republic, and who had moved to the Mahlabathini plain in Knight's Entonjaneni District rather than live as a tenant on a Boer farm, assembled a small force in support of his nephew on Hlophekhulu Mountain. Hlophekhulu is on the north bank of the White Mfolozi, and in his day Cetshwayo's *isigodlo* women had drawn him water from its pure springs. Shingana's following rapidly grew to 1 000 or more. Like the uSuthu on Ceza, they were soon busy raiding loyal Zulu in the vicinity, and plundering and burning down the store belonging to Alfred Moor. Shingana's messengers, as did Dinuzulu's, boasted far and wide of the uSuthu success on Ceza, and threatened retribution against those who remained loyal to the British once the interlopers retired altogether from Zululand. The Nkandhla District was sliding as a result into a state of unrest, and in the Eshowe District numbers of warriors were seen moving up the valley of the Mhlathuze to join the uSuthu forces. Armed supporters of Shingana in the valley of the White Mfolozi were making the roads so unsafe that wagon-drivers were requiring armed escorts when bringing up supplies from Mthonjaneni to the troops stationed at Nkonjeni.[20]

Havelock, after hasty consultations with Colonel Stabb, concluded that in these deteriorating circumstances there was no option but to call in reinforcements. The Imperial forces in Zululand were therefore raised to a total of 300 cavalry, 120 mounted infantry, 440 infantry, 2 light field guns and 2 Gatlings. In addition, there were presently 160 Zululand Police (25 mounted), and 200 of Hlubi's adherents whom Major McKean had raised in the Nqutu District. To improve the confidence of nervous wagon-drivers, and so ensure the safety of the line of communication, Stabb established posts at St Paul's and KwaMagwaza, whose small garrisons would accompany convoys of supplies. Ammunition issued to the established garrisons at Mthonjaneni and Nkonjeni was doubled, and the number of mule wagons increased to allow them to fall back rapidly if necessary. It was supposed that, supported by the forces Stabb was bringing up,

Addison and Knight would very soon be able to execute their warrants for the arrest of the uSuthu leaders on both Ceza and Hlophekhulu.[21]

But Addison effectively threw cold water on fresh plans for an assault on Ceza. He pointed out that, if attacked, the uSuthu would simply slip over the border to the sanctuary of the New Republic, only to re-emerge when the British withdrew. Stabb could not but agree, and proposed delaying further operations against Ceza until the New Republic could be persuaded to co-operate and disarm and intern the uSuthu on its territory. He insisted at the same time that, when it was possible to mount an attack, black auxiliaries must again be employed.

Stabb's directive raised once more the question of what part Zibhebhu was to play. He and his men were still at Ivuna, nominally protecting the station, but to use him against the uSuthu on Ceza would certainly lead to an escalation of hostilities and most likely provoke otherwise loyal uSuthu sympathisers into violence. On the other hand, his presence at Ivuna seemed to leave him well placed to prevent any link-up between Dinuzulu and Msutshwana and other pro-uSuthu chiefs to the east.[22]

It was one thing for white officers and officials to write Zibhebhu's part for him, but quite another – as they should have realised – for him to consent to play it. Young Cuthbert Foxon, the clerk whom Addison had left in charge of Ivuna while he was with the troops at Nkonjeni, found he simply could not control Zibhebhu at all. Disregarding all injunctions to the contrary, Zibhebhu gaily went off on 'patrols' into the uSuthu heartland, penetrating as far west as Dinuzulu's Mahashini *umuzi* and plundering the deserted uSuthu *umuzi* itself.[23] His unbridled enjoyment was then cut short by bad news from his own location. Msutshwana's and Mthumbu's adherents, emboldened by Dinuzulu's success at Ceza, had begun raiding cattle and women from the Mandlakazi, culminating in an attack on the *umuzi* of Mkhonto kaSomfula, a former uSuthu adherent who had submitted to Zibhebhu in February 1888 rather than be evicted from his location. Three of Zibhebhu's men had died in these encounters.

Msutshwana was to pay dearly for failing to control his young men.[24] Zibhebhu, deeply angered by the fate of his adherents, disobeyed all orders to 'sit down'. On the evening of 11 June he set out from Ndunu hill with about 250 men and at dawn the following day surrounded the *umuzi* of Ntshugu kaKhutshana, one of Msutshwana's *izinduna*, about forty kilometres south-east of the magistracy. Unfortunately for him, Msutshwana was staying there, and he and a few of his adherents were killed in the ensuing Mandlakazi attack. Nearby *imizi* also bore the brunt of Zibhebhu's mission of vengeance, and women were taken and cattle driven off. The terrified survivors fled into the bush.

Reports filtered back to the agitated Foxon that the late Msutshwana's Mdletshe and all the other uSuthu adherents in eastern Ndwandwe and northern Lower Umfolosi were banding together to destroy Bangonomo and then to sweep on to Ivuna itself. Foxon's nerve was cracking under the threat, and Addison returned to Ivuna on the afternoon of 18 June to take charge of the situation. But the reportedly well-disciplined and eager garrison of fifty Zululand Police under Jack

Osborn had no opportunity to do more than strengthen the fort before the uSuthu struck.[25]

Yet it was not the anticipated uSuthu from the east who came, but the forces on Ceza. Messengers had arrived at the mountain bringing word of Zibhebhu's killing of Msutshwana. For Dinuzulu and the other uSuthu leaders, who had suffered so much wrong at Zibhebhu's hands, and in whom deep anger flared, the time seemed to have come to have done with him once and for all. Their spies informed them that Zibhcbhu was back with his men at their camp on Ndunu hill, and that in his arrogance he seemed not to have taken any special precautions against attack.[26] With this knowledge, the uSuthu leaders determined to launch a surprise attack on their mortal foe. Dinuzulu called on a famous war-doctor, Mathanga of the Mthethwa, to doctor his men.

Mathanga possessed a Mandlakazi spear that had been picked up at the battle of oNdini. He bent its twenty-centimetre blade, tied medicines to it and stuck it in the ground. The *amabutho* then filed past and touched it, shouting incantations. The magical intention was to cause the Mandlakazis' spears to be blunt,[27] and who can say the spell did not succeed? With the ritual preparations complete, Hemulana kaMbangezeli of the Sibiya, formerly Mnyamana's chief *induna* and now Dinuzulu's councillor, formed the *amabutho* in a semi-circle and exhorted them to action.[28] The entire armed uSuthu force concentrated on Ceza then stealthily set off just after dusk on 22 June towards Ndunu hill. In July 1883 Zibhebhu's night march had allowed him to fall like a bolt of lightning on unprepared oNdini. The lesson had not gone unlearned in the uSuthu camp; just how well he was soon to discover.

In the early hours of 23 June the uSuthu *impi* bivouacked some six kilometres from the Nongoma hills.[29] Their taxing route had taken them down Ceza, through the valley of the Sikhwebezi, up to the healthy plateau where Dinuzulu kept his horses, and down again into the Vuna valley. Zibhebhu was so far from anticipating an uSuthu attack from the direction of Ceza that he had neglected even to post look-outs. At 5.55 a.m., just before daybreak, when the horns of the cattle first become visible, the Zululand Police sentries at the Ivuna camp gave the alarm that a large armed force was approaching from the north. Apparently the steep western flank of the Nongoma hills dictated the direction of this somewhat oblique uSuthu advance. Through his spy-glass, the hastily aroused Addison recognised the advancing *impi* as an uSuthu force from their distinctive *imishokobezi*, the white cow-tail decorations hanging from neck and elbow. He, with the rest of the garrison, black court messengers, and a number of white traders and transport-riders who had been sheltering at the magistracy since the murder of the Louws, precipitately abandoned the camp and took refuge within the fort.

Within ten minutes of first being sighted, the uSuthu *impi*, which since the morale-building affair on Ceza had swollen to between 3 000 and 4 000 strong, breasted the Nongoma ridge about 1 100 metres from the Ivuna camp. Apparently undeterred by the long march over difficult terrain and a sleepless night, it swept down towards the fort. To those watching apprehensively from behind its earthwork walls, the uSuthu seemed to come on like a great half-moon. Indeed, their battle formation was strictly traditional, with skirmishers to the front of the chest and its curving horns, and reserves in support. Their tactics were traditional too. While the left horn and chest wheeled to the south-east and moved along the slope leading to Zibhebhu's camp, the right horn, of about 1 000 men, came on straight towards the fort.

On the Ndunu hill, Zibhebhu was doing all he could, in the few minutes permitted him, to form up his 700 to 800 men – caught completely off their guard and in considerable disarray – to face the uSuthu onslaught. Numbers of the Mandlakazi ran away at the first sight of the enemy, rather as the uSuthu had done at oNdini in 1883. But the remainder of his badly outnumbered force responded manfully to Zibhebhu's commands. Around the neck or forehead each wore the red ribbon served out to them by Addison to distinguish them as Native Levies in the government's service. (This was a standard practice wherever British auxiliaries looked and were armed like the people they were fighting, and in the Anglo-Zulu war the members of the Natal Native Contingent had each worn a piece of red cloth.) Zibhebhu drew up his best fighting-men, the iNyonemhlophe *ibutho*, in the centre of his line. They were flanked to the left and right respectively by the older ekuVukeni and Bangonomo *amabutho*.

As the Mandlakazi moved to take up position before their camp, Zibhebhu rode before them on his famous little white horse, encouraging them with his indomitable spirit and contemptuous words. 'They are a mere rabble, you could chase them off with sticks,' he cried. Neither side made a sound as they approached each other. At a distance of about 320 metres, the uSuthu charged. Zibhebhu pointed dramatically at them and shouted, 'It is here where the difficulty lies. To the attack!' and the Mandlakazi ran to meet them[30] to a terrific din of cries and counter-cries of *'uSuthu!'* and *'Washesha!'* Though the venerable uSuthu councillor Hemulana, who had commanded at Tshaneni, had devised the uSuthu strategy, Dinuzulu and Ndabuko actively led the attack in person.

Dinuzulu opened the uSuthu offensive by leading his crack force of thirty or forty horsemen – most of whom had firearms – directly against the iNyonemhlope of the Mandlakazi centre. Among these uSuthu horsemen were three or four Boers from the New Republic who had accompanied the *impi* as 'advisers'. These Boers wore the *umshokobezi* in their hats, and their faces and hands were blackened to avoid detection or recognition by the Ivuna garrison. The iNyonemhlope responded by hurling stones and spears at the uSuthu horses, causing them to recoil in complete confusion. But the uFalaza *ibutho* was in close support, followed by the imBokodwebomvu and iNgobamakhosi, and immediately engaged the iNyonemhlope with the stabbing-spear. For a moment the uSuthu wavered and even fell back a few paces in the face of the Mandlakazis' fierce resistance, but their greatly superior numbers soon told. The ekuVukeni and Bangonomo on the Mandlakazi flanks began to crumble while, in a classic manoeuvre, the imBokodwebomvu outflanked the Mandlakazi and took them from the rear. The shattered Mandlakazi flanks thereupon disintegrated completely, and were almost immediately joined in their headlong flight by the iNyonemhlope of the centre, who, in danger of being surrounded, could not alone sustain the overwhelming uSuthu onslaught.

While the uSuthu left and centre engaged the Mandlakazi on Ndunu hill, their smaller right horn continued its advance on the fort. It was made up of Qulusi from the New Republic. In his address before the battle, Dinuzulu had reminded them that their mission was to obliterate Zibhebhu, and not to fight the white people sheltering in their impregnable fort. The uSuthu strategy, which envisaged their right horn cutting off the Mandlakazi line of retreat to the Ivuna camp, demanded that the Qulusi pass close by the fort. That brought them into full range of the garrison, but Dinuzulu had strictly cautioned the Qulusi, even if fired upon, not to retaliate. The Ivuna garrison were naturally not to know of that instruction and were therefore taken considerably by surprise when the Qulusi, instead of launching into a frontal attack on the fort, suddenly wheeled to their left about 550 metres short of their presumed objective and set off in the direction of the battle now raging on Ndunu hill.

Jack Osborn, intending to prevent the Qulusi from joining in the unequal struggle on the hill, ordered the Zululand Police to fire upon them as they changed front. The effect of the well-directed volley was to cause the Qulusi to rush towards the cover offered by the narrow valley of the Mbile stream between the fort and Ndunu hill. Nevertheless, this hasty movement did not interfere with the Qulusi's primary objective, which was to get between the now flying Mandlakazi and the sanctuary of the fort. In that they were fully successful, for they intercepted and killed large numbers of the Mandlakazi in the marshy bed of the Mbile and on the steep slope leading up to the fort. Only the merest handful managed to break through and gain the protection of the fort's walls, when they were almost shot as uSuthu by the Zululand Police.

Zibhebhu himself had retired towards the fort but, gauging that there was no hope of escape across the Mbile, mounted his horse and made good his escape in the opposite direction, evading his pursuers in the thick bush. Most of his surviving adherents were forced by the presence of the Qulusi along the Mbile to take the same direction of flight. Dinuzulu and the uSuthu left and centre pursued them out of sight of the magistracy, across the Mona River eight kilometres away, and only gave up the chase at the Mangwana hill some way beyond.

The victorious uSuthu did not confine themselves to the Mandlakazi. Having routed them and looted and burned their huts, they then turned on Ziwedu's adherents. Since the end of May they had been living on the lower slopes of Ndunu hill, about a kilometre south-west of Zibhebhu's huts, to be under the protection (so they supposed) of the Ivuna garrison. While these unfortunates cowered in caves and holes near the Mbile, the uSuthu rounded up their cattle and other livestock. It was while parties of his men were thus engaged that Dinuzulu ordered his mounted men to take up position on the rocky crest of Ndunu hill, and to open up what turned out to be a desultory and inaccurate fire on the fort. Their intention was apparently to discourage any hostile intervention from that quarter and, if Dinuzulu's later charge is true, also to drive back a small party of mounted Zululand Police who had made a sortie and were 'finishing off' Qulusi lying wounded from the fire earlier directed at them from the fort.[31]

Once they had rounded up a great herd of about 750 cattle, mainly from Ziwedu's people, but also some belonging to Zibhebhu which had been grazing lower down the valley of the Mbile, as well as some from the Police cattle-kraal 300 metres in front of the fort, the uSuthu regrouped. With their booty and prisoners (who comprised several captured Mandlakazi men as well as a number of women and children who had been in their camp) they began to retire along the ridge leading towards the Ndunu hill. The Zululand Police fired on them as they went, and the uSuthu, to avoid possible casualties, passed to the east of Ndunu hill and only turned back in the direction of Ceza one and a half kilometres north of the fort and out of its effective range. Dinuzulu's praises later celebrated the glorious day for the uSuthu thus:

> He who fought bald-headed with the assegai at Dick's.
> The wreath of smoke being the smoke of cartridges,
> Fired off by the Nongqais [Zululand Police],
> At the Fort at Nongoma...
> The swift one like lightning,
> On the occasion he went to Ndunu.
> He who anticipated the sun before it rose
> At Nongoma.[32]

Addison, who had supposed that the Mandlakazi might attempt to take refuge in the ditch surrounding the fort, which was already crammed full with its garrison, had ordered the horses tethered there to be cast loose. They had naturally galloped off in panic, and the Zulu succeeded in rounding up and riding off on seventeen of them. A particularly valuable one belonging to Addison himself bolted back up the wagon road to the fort, throwing its rider, a Qulusi *induna*, and evading recapture by a number of Boers. Addison was less fortunate with his two dogs, a pointer and a greyhound, which, running loose at the time of the attack, were caught and killed by the uSuthu, as was Foxon's retriever.

Once it became apparent that the uSuthu were retiring, Addison ordered out a mounted patrol of eight Zululand Police under Corporal Mathutha to ascertain in which direction they were headed. Mathutha's men followed in the *impi*'s wake along the ridge, occasionally dismounting and exchanging shots with its rearguard. An attempt by some uSuthu horsemen to take them from the rear was foiled by supporting fire from the fort. At length, the intrepid patrol caught up with about 150 of the enemy, all on foot, who had lagged behind the main body since they were driving a herd of captured cattle before them. The nine policemen charged with determination, and the uSuthu fled without attempting to make a stand, abandoning their booty. Since his ammunition was running out, Mathutha decided to retire to the fort with the recaptured cattle. On the way he set his men about collecting stray cattle from the dongas, and in the dry watercourses they came across some eighty of Zibhebhu's and Ziwedu's women, with a number of children, who had been sheltering there during the fighting.

Despite the safe return of Mathutha's gallant patrol with their 200 or so cattle (they had failed to round up any goats or sheep) and the rescued women and children, tension in the fort remained high. Addison doubted his ability to withstand a determined attack, and one seemed not unlikely for some time, as the uSuthu *impi* hovered in sight until late afternoon, when it finally withdrew in the direction of Ceza. Addison's courage revived with its eventual disappearance, and he telegraphed his belief that he could hold the fort if reinforced. He was undoubtedly correct in his perception of the situation, for his withdrawal was guaranteed to have a disastrous effect on the morale of government supporters in Ndwandwe, and would encourage the uSuthu yet further. But Colonel Stabb had the final say, and he persuaded Osborn to put military considerations above the purely political. Not that he did not have cogent enough reasons for withdrawing the Ivuna garrison to Nkonjeni. To detach troops from his small force at Nkonjeni to reinforce, unsupported, a post nearly sixty-four kilometres away across wooded and broken country seemed counter-productive. Not only would they simply be bottled up with the garrison at Ivuna, but the troops left at Nkonjeni would be too weak to mount the projected offensive against the uSuthu strongholds on Ceza and Hlophekhulu. So it was resolved to relieve and instantly withdraw the Ivuna garrison.

At 10 p.m. on 23 June, a column of 516 imperial troops, Zululand Police and McKean's Mounted Basutos left Nkonjeni under Colonel Stabb, who had reached the camp on 9 June. With them went an ambulance and three mule-wagons with which to evacuate Zibhebhu's wounded and his women and children. Some 300 of Mnyamana's men were sent ahead to occupy the dense bush on the banks of the Black Mfolozi where it was feared the uSuthu might attempt to ambush the relieving column.[33]

Unmolested, nevertheless, the column reached Ivuna at about 8 a.m. on 24 June. Besides organising the evacuation of the garrison, the relieving troops had the grisly task of assessing the casualties from the battle of the previous day. No one from inside the fort had suffered the slightest hurt, but Zibhebhu's losses had been heavy. Many of his *izinduna*, including some of his brothers, had been killed. Mgojana, the Ndwandwe chief, who had been one of Wolseley's appointed kinglets, but who had been reduced to a position of little importance under Zibhebhu, was among the slain. Zibhebhu himself estimated that the Mandlakazi had suffered 200 killed and between 50 and 60 wounded, though Commandant Mansel, after a careful examination of the field, put their dead at nearer 300.[34] Many of them had been terribly butchered by spear thrusts, and lay heaped up in piles in the Mbile spruit where the Qulusi had intercepted their flight. Mansel saw forty men lying dead in one line on top of Ndunu hill where the main encounter had taken place, and counted more scattered along the line of the Mandlakazi rout towards the Mona River. Ziwedu's people had lost seven killed and one wounded. Not more than twenty to thirty uSuthu had been killed, and some of these were victims of the fire from the fort.

It was one thing to count and bury the dead – but quite another to remove the living. By the morning of 24 June Zibhebhu had found his way back to the fort, and he was in a fury, bitterly reproaching the government for not allowing him to attack the uSuthu while he held the initiative, and then for tying him to the fort where he had been surprised and defeated.[35] At first he refused to be evacuated to Nkonjeni in the not unreasonable fear that his entire territory would be left to be ravaged by the uSuthu. But Colonel Stabb, who correctly feared that Shingana on Hlophekhulu might take advantage of his absence with such a large force at Ivuna to strike in the Nkonjeni area, would brook no discussion which might delay his withdrawal. So at 1 p.m. Addison and his Zululand Police set off with Stabb's force for Nkonjeni. Knowing that the abandoned post would inevitably be looted, Foxon buried the valuables and documents that could not be taken with them in the ditch surrounding the fort.[36]

Zibhebhu, as Stabb had anticipated, was not prepared to be left behind at the deserted post, and joined the retiring column soon after it set out with his family and some 200 surviving fighting-men. While on the march, the rest of the Mandlakazi women and children (about 1 500 of them), straggled in to join the slowly moving column rather than remain defenseless at the mercy of the vengeful uSuthu.

The column reached Nkonjeni without mishap on 25 June. The Mandlakazi refugees were located in shelters to the rear of the British camp, and the wounded were tended by army surgeons.[37] Stabb discovered that during his absence at Ivuna, on the night of 24 June, Shingana had possessed the temerity to attempt a raid on Mnyamana's cattle, which, with women and children, had been brought for protection into the neighbourhood of the Nkonjeni camp.[38]

The battle of Ivuna promised far-reaching consequences. At a stroke, the Mandlakazi had been eliminated as a factor in northern Zululand, British prestige and authority had suffered another grievous blow, and the uSuthu cause seemed irresistibly in the ascendant. Nevertheless, the uSuthu victory, sweet as it had been, was to prove no more than a transient success.

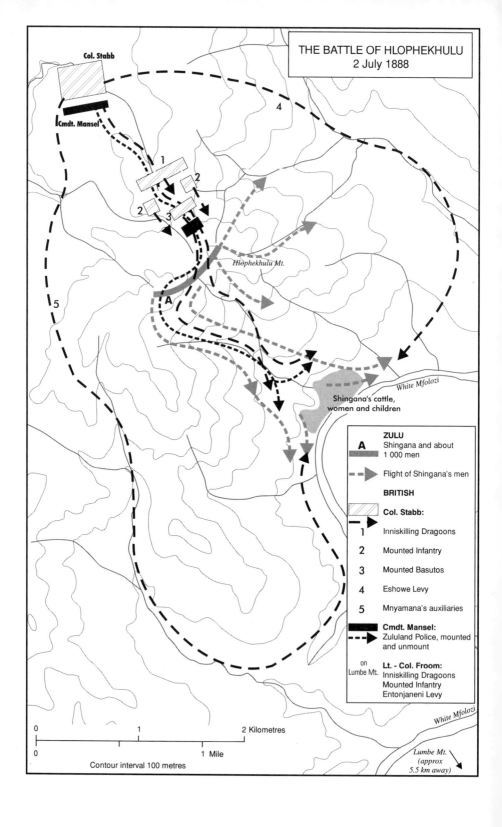

THE BATTLE OF HLOPHEKHULU
2 July 1888

Col. Stabb

Cmdt. Mansel

1

2

2

2

3

4

5

A

Hlophekhulu Mt.

White Mfolozi

Shingana's cattle,
women and children

on
Lumbe Mt.

ZULU

A   Shingana and about
    1 000 men

Flight of Shingana's men

BRITISH

Col. Stabb:

1   Inniskilling Dragoons

2   Mounted Infantry

3   Mounted Basutos

4   Eshowe Levy

5   Mnyamana's auxiliaries

Cmdt. Mansel:
Zululand Police, mounted
and unmount

Lt. - Col. Froom:
Inniskilling Dragoons
Mounted Infantry
Entonjaneni Levy

White Mfolozi

*Lumbe Mt.
(approx
5.5 km away)*

0   1   2 Kilometres

0   1 Mile

Contour interval 100 metres

33

Summoning the Fire Engine

In Pietermaritzburg, Sir Arthur Havelock received word of the battle of Ivuna and the abandonment of Addison's post with fresh consternation, lamenting that untoward events in Ndwandwe were calculated to give 'encouragement and prestige to the rebellious faction'.[1] Nor were the Governor's fears unjustified. Ever since the affair on Ceza Dinuzulu's emissaries had been busy calling upon chiefs and people to join the uSuthu cause. Not only did many make their way to Ceza, but Shingana on Hlophekhulu also received reinforcements, when he was joined by Somhlolo, the regent of the Biyela, and a number of his adherents. Meanwhile, in the Lower Umfolosi District, a full-scale uprising got under way.

Two of the uSuthu emissaries, Nkunzemnyama and Mafukwini, were particularly active in the Lower Umfolosi District among the adherents of the highly influential and pro-uSuthu Chief Somkhele's Mphukunyoni. They moved too among the followers of the equally royalist Somopho, who had been the senior *induna* of the emaNgweni *ikhanda* and the senior commander at the battle of Gingindlovu, and of Bhejana, once Cetshwayo's *inceku*. On about 28 June two traders, Knight and White, were attacked and wounded by the Mphukunyoni and pursued to Andries Pretorius's magisterial post on the lower slopes of Ntondotha hill, which overlooks the Msunduze River eighty kilometres north-east of Eshowe. Ashby, another trader who had been with them, was killed near by their abandoned wagon. Pretorius, for his better protection, hurriedly threw up Fort Andries, which consisted of two small earthworks 370 metres apart flanking his magistracy and offering supporting fire.[2]

On 30 June Pretorius and his garrison of 40 Zululand Police under Sub-Inspector Marshall, and 300 unreliable local levies drawn from the Mthethwa (who lived sandwiched between the Mphukunyoni and emaNgweni and were chronically at odds with them both) found themselves confronted by a large hostile demonstration. Somkhele's people, several thousand strong, and a smaller number of adherents of other lesser coastal chieftains, approached to within 460 metres of the fort and made an attempt to carry off the magistrate's cattle. The Zululand Police resisted, and some shots were exchanged between them and the marauders, who withdrew. But Pretorius was not confident that he would be so fortunate the next time, and for a while his communications with Eshowe were cut off by Somopho and Bhejana. An attempt on 5 July by the Mthethwa levies

415

to open the way to Eshowe ended in a craven rout and the death of forty of their number. Conditions remained very unsafe, and on 3 July a trader named Cecil Tonge, who was quietly proceeding in his ox-wagon towards the Mhlathuze River, was stabbed to death by a party of young warriors.[3]

The correspondent of the *Times of Natal*, travelling from Ivuna to Rorke's Drift, wrote vividly of the renewed breakdown of normal life in Zululand. He 'found the country in a complete confusion, cattle being driven in all directions, women labouring with heavy burdens of food on their heads and their children on their backs making for the strongholds'.[4] Indeed, Mehlokazulu kaSihayo, who had been supplanted in his ancestral lands by Hlubi and his adherents, placed there by Wolseley in 1879, was causing much concern to the authorities in the northern Nqutu District. He had never accepted his loss, and the Tlokwa, surrounded by hostile neighbours and left without the protection of Hlubi and his fighting-men, who were serving under Major McKean, were in daily expectation of being plundered and harried by the disgruntled heir to the Qungebe chiefdom.

As Lieutenant-General H.A. Smyth, the General Officer Commanding in Southern Africa, uneasily expressed it, 'The spirit of rebellion is widespread and growing; the country is generally uneasy and astir with rumours, intrigues, and alarms, and even the well-disposed natives are afraid to show pronounced loyalty.'[5] To forestall the spread of the contagion, the civil officials resorted to some very high-handed action, and interned a number of leading chiefs in the former Reserve Territory (particularly in the Nkandhla District) on the grounds that in 1884 they had led resistance to the imposition of Osborn's administration. Thus Sigananda of the Cube and Qethuka of the Magwaza, with a number of their *izinduna*, were thrown peremptorily into prison in order, as Osborn put it, to re-assure the 'loyal tribes'.[6]

With the country given over to armed bands, violent encounters, looting and trains of refugees, the picture in Zululand was little different from that during the darkest days of the civil war before the British annexation. As such, it was nothing less than a damning indictment of Osborn's administration of the infant colony. To Havelock, it was clear from the reports reaching him that Osborn, demoralised by his all too evident failure to stem the drift towards chaos, was fast losing his nerve. Unable to cope or give a strong lead himself, he was progressively taking refuge in bureaucratic trivia and the brandy bottle, and mounting reports reached the scandalised Governor intimating that the Resident Commissioner was seldom to be found sober after 9 o'clock in the morning.[7] Stabb bluntly stated that the wilting Osborn required 'a strong prop...on whom to lean',[8] by which he meant that the military authorities should take the direction of the affairs of Zululand out of his nerveless hands until the uprising had been put down.

That certainly was the view of Lieutenant-General Smyth. Havelock had been constrained to summon him, as the *Natal Advertiser* irreverently suggested, rather like a fire engine to extinguish the flames of revolt.[9] Smyth arrived in Durban from the Cape on 26 June. Within three days he had concluded that reinforcements must immediately be despatched from Cape Town, and that all operations in Zululand must be put under his unrestricted command. The fiction, he declared, could no longer be maintained that the troops were simply acting in support of the civil power and only on its request, for Zululand had again become a theatre for full-scale operations.[10] The Natal colonists strongly endorsed Smyth's perception of affairs, one forthright correspondent expressing his hope that Dinuzulu would be 'thoroughly whopped'.[11]

Havelock, however, saw that to turn the running of Zululand over entirely to the military would be an unthinkable admission that the civil administration had lamentably failed, and would make it doubly difficult to re-establish its credibility once order had been restored. So he prevailed upon the reluctant Smyth on 1 July to agree upon a compromise. The General, in addition to the regular troops, would command McKean's Mounted Basutos and any other 'native levies' organised along military lines which Osborn succeeded in raising in Zululand. However, Osborn was to retain control over the Zululand Police and any chiefs and their adherents who might be employed as auxiliaries, provided they were deployed in close co-operation with the troops under Smyth's direct command. In that way the civil authorities would retain responsibility for their routine duties of enforcing the law, and would ensure that auxiliaries were not used in an insensitive manner by a military ignorant of political considerations.[12] If nothing else, the disastrous Zibhebhu saga had taught Havelock that lesson.

Before the agreement between Havelock and Smyth could be relayed to the civil authorities in Zululand, they had taken an initiative of their own.[13] In a singularly more successful repetition of his earlier attempt to serve warrants of arrest on Dinuzulu and Ndabuko on Ceza, Addison set out at 6 o'clock on the fine morning of 2 July for Hlophekhulu. He carried a warrant issued by John Knight (the Resident Magistrate of Entonjaneni, in whose district the mountain lay), which he intended to serve on Shingana in accordance with the correct civil procedures. The warrant, though, was nothing more than a judicial fiction, and the authorities were fully prepared for serious military action. Their objective (besides arresting Shingana) was to disperse his adherents concentrated on the mountain, and to seize the cattle they had raided from 'loyal' Zulu.

Addison, as the representative of the civil government, had the purely formal function of requesting the troops standing by to support Commandant Mansel and his force of two officers and seventeen men of the mounted Zululand Police and a further seventy police on foot. Colonel Stabb himself was in command of the regular troops, which consisted of 5 officers and 129 men of the Inniskilling Dragoons under Captain Pennefather, 3 officers and 61 men of the Mounted Infantry under Captain Purdon, and the 1 white officer and 140 Tlokwa of Hlubi's Mounted Basutos under Major McKean. In addition, there were the Eshowe Levy of about 1 000 men raised by Charles Saunders in the Eshowe District with their 5 white levy leaders, and some 400 auxiliaries drawn from Mnyamana's adherents under their 4 white leaders. So in this, the last battle of the uSuthu Rebellion, black fighting-men formed an integral and substantial part of the British force. That had always been the case during the Anglo-Zulu War, but then they had been drawn almost entirely from Natal. Now they were from Zululand, and some had even been part of the uSuthu faction during the civil war. Nothing more clearly demonstrated the degree to which the Zulu north of the Thukela had been politically fragmented and turned against each other by the devastating combination of events since 1879.

Stabb's force was to co-operate against Shingana with another under the command of Lieutenant-Colonel Froom. It was made up of a squadron of the Inniskilling Dragoons, a company of Mounted Infantry, two mountain guns and about 500 dispirited black levies under the Entonjaneni magistrate, John Knight, who had gained some experience in such matters as a levy leader in 1879 in the Umsinga Division of Natal. Their purpose was to prevent the Zulu on Hlophekhulu from retreating across the White Mfolozi when attacked by Stabb's men, or from taking refuge in the thick bush south of the river. Froom's contingent accordingly took up position on Lumbe hill directly facing Hlophekhulu. But during the course of the day they lost touch with Stabb's force and played the entirely negative role of cutting off any possible uSuthu withdrawal to the south.

After several days of fog and rain it was a pleasant sunlit march for Stabb's men, especially since the highlands between Nkonjeni and Hlophekhulu were fairly open and accessible to mounted troops. The long uplands spur they followed eventually terminated in a abrupt rise, which was Hlophekhulu. The opposite, south-eastern face of the mountain, however, falls precipitously to the White Mfolozi below. It was here, among the rocks and thickly wooded kloofs, that Shingana had formed his stronghold, known as Nonkwenkweziyezulu. It overlooked a narrow strip of land, densely covered with bush, between the mountain and the river, where he had collected his cattle, women and children. Because Shingana was anticipating an attack from Froom's force, which had been encamped across the White Mfolozi for two days, many of his 1 000 or so *amabutho* were lying in ambush in the thorn-bush south of the river, and had to be brought back hurriedly to face Stabb's unexpected advance.

Stabb's force arrived at about 11.30 a.m. at an open place a kilometre and a half from Hlophekhulu. Usuthu scouts, some of whom were mounted, watched them from the rocky crest of the mountain. Stabb sent the Eshowe Contingent under Yamela (Osborn's chief *induna*) and the white levy leaders down into a valley to the south-east of the mountain, and Mnyamana's men were similarly despatched to the south-west. The Zululand Police and regular troops were drawn up to the north-west on the grassy spur, and the uSuthu were thus effectively surrounded. Once enough time had elapsed to allow the black levies and auxiliaries to take up their positions in the valleys below the mountain, the police, supported by the Basutos, advanced over the open, narrow nek leading directly to the crest. The Mounted Infantry stayed back on either side of the nek to prevent the Zulu from attempting to outflank Mansel and McKean in their traditional style, while the Inniskilling Dragoons remained behind to back them up in turn.

The uSuthu opened fire with the handful of muzzle-loaders and other generally inferior firearms they possessed. In response, the police deployed into an effective firing-line. Though the uSuthu were concealed by dense bush, only giving their whereabouts away when they fired or moved position, and defended themselves with determined courage, they soon found it difficult to withstand the weight of fire directed at them. Sensing that they were wavering, Mansel decided to clinch the affair by turning their position. He sent the mounted police forward under young Jack Osborn to seize a knoll in advance of the extreme right of the firing-line which commanded the kloof in which Shingana had established his stronghold. But the uSuthu quickly grasped the significance of Osborn's movement, and some thirty of them took up position on the knoll and defended it stoutly, firing from behind the cover of the rocks. After two attempts to dislodge them, Osborn had to retire with a slight wound in his hand and one of his policemen dead. Mansel thereupon resolved to storm the position with his unmounted police. He approached the koppie in extended line and at forty metres his wildly cheering men charged the uSuthu and carried the position at the point of the fixed bayonet. The watching regular troops could only admire the black policemen's superlative dash and courage, which they admitted they could not better themselves.

The dislodged uSuthu scrambled down into a steep kloof closely pursued by the police, who themselves got out of hand as they rushed pell mell with the flying Zulu down the mountainside. Driven from crag to crag, the uSuthu were forced down to the strip of bushy land between the mountain and the river, where they fought desperately among their stampeding cattle. In places the fighting was ferocious and hand-to-hand, with the police abandoning their bayonets for stabbing spears seized from the uSuthu. The Mounted Basutos were now sent forward to reinforce the police, while the Inniskilling Dragoons moved up to take their place. Fire from those uSuthu still on the crest slackened off as they began to disperse in every direction and join their comrades in trying to make good their escape down Hlophekhulu. The fugitives collided with the black levies and auxiliaries in the bushy valleys, particularly the Eshowe Levy, who had rushed in to round up the cattle. Some sharp fighting ensued, and though the levies were at first repulsed with losses, they rallied and completed the rout of the uSuthu.

Since it was now afternoon, Stabb concentrated his troops and withdrew, bivouacking for the night a kilometre and a half from Hlophekhulu. The levies and auxiliaries drove the 1 000 or more captured cattle several kilometres further on to the thornveld of the Mahlabathini plain, irritating the soldiers with their lack of discipline as they abandoned all military formation and streamed away in disconnected groups. It proved impossible to rally them the following day to sweep the valleys for the rest of the uSuthu cattle.

During the night the last uSuthu abandoned Hlophekhulu and Shingana himself escaped on foot to the New Republic. He had lost close on 300 men in the fight. The British had not gone unscathed either. Lieutenant Briscoe of the 1st Royal Inniskilling Fusiliers, who had received his commission in Egypt for gallantry in the field, fell shot through the head by a Zulu concealed in a bush. Two of the Basutos were also shot dead and three were wounded, one by a spear. About sixty of the black levies were killed or wounded. The exertions of the day also proved too much for Mr Trent, a levy leader with the Eshowe Levy, who died of a heart attack.

The effects of the action on Hlophekhulu were almost instantaneous, confirming Havelock's belief about the revolt that 'the whole thing is like a bubble, – only needs a sharp prick to secure a burst up'.[14] True, it would not be until Dinuzulu abandoned Ceza and was captured that the disturbances could be finally settled, but the uSuthu cause had already lost what buoyancy it had ever possessed. After the Hlophekhulu operation, both Stabb and Osborn returned to Eshowe for consultations with Smyth. There it was agreed to maintain the military initiative which Stabb had regained by despatching a column under Major McKean to overawe the fractious Zulu in the Lower Umfolosi District. McKean rapidly accomplished his mission. His column, which consisted of 225 regular troops, 180 Mounted Basutos and a Native Levy of about 2 000 raised by the determinedly 'loyal' John Dunn, left Eshowe on 7 July. McKean relieved Pretorius's post on 9 July and marched as far north as the Mfolozi River without encountering any opposition. Somkhele, who saw the writing clearly on the wall, tendered his unconditional surrender, and McKean expected other chiefs rapidly to follow suit. He and his column were back in Eshowe by 13 July, confident that the coastal plain was pacified.[15]

Addison remained at Nkonjeni to represent the civil authority and to accompany any further troop movements that might be directed against Dinuzulu. The situation north of the Black Mfolozi was still very unsettled, since the British withdrawal with the remnants of Zibhebhu's following had exposed the area to uSuthu depredations. In early July the uSuthu burned Bangonomo, Zibhebhu's principal *umuzi* in the very north-east of his territory, and threatened the stronghold still held by some of his people nearby on Bende hill (though despite their threats and blandishments during the succeeding weeks, they failed to reduce it). On 5 August they captured 360 head of cattle being watered in the Msunduze River nearby, and drove them into the New Republic (or, more correctly, what had formally become the Vryheid District of the South African Republic since 20 July 1888). It was quite clear that the Boers were encouraging the uSuthu in their raiding, which included harvesting Mandlakazi crops as well as rustling their cattle. Several hunting parties from the Vryheid District, taking advantage of the absence of the Zululand Police, were also roaming Zibhebhu's location, burning the grass and killing the large game.[16]

The reproachful figure of Zibhebhu at Addison's elbow at Nkonjeni spurred the magistrate on to urge the military authorities in Eshowe to take energetic counter-measures. Smyth responded on 25 July by sending 50 rifles and 2 900 rounds of ammunition to the defenders of Bende.[17] He next addressed the larger problem of how to pacify Ndwandwe and consolidate the British hold on the coastal plain. His answer was to despatch a fresh column north through the disaffected areas to ensure the promised submission of the local chiefs, and to create conditions in which the people felt safe enough to return home from the fastnesses where they had been driven.

So Major McKean set off again on 23 July from Eshowe at the head of the strong

Coast Column of 312 regulars and the numerous Native Levy indefatigably led by John Dunn himself. McKean's column was performing precisely the same function as had Baker Russell's and Clarke's columns at the close of the Anglo-Zulu War once the big battles had been fought. So he paraded once more through the Lower Umfolosi District and, with John Dunn's help and influence (as in 1879), persuaded many of the chiefs against whom warrants of arrest had been issued for their attack on Pretorius's magistracy to surrender. Somkhele, with various *izinduna* of the emaNgweni such as Lugoyoza, Ndabayakhe, Masekwana and Dlemudlemu abandoned their stronghold in the Dukuduku forest without a fight and tendered their formal surrender on 31 July on the north bank of the Mfolozi River. McKean then continued to Ndwandwe, where he had orders to re-establish Addison's post at Ivuna before co-operating with Stabb's troops at Nkonjeni against Dinuzulu on Ceza. Stabb, meanwhile, set about establishing an advance post on the drift across the Black Mfolozi on the road between Nkonjeni and Ivuna in order to open communication with the Coast Column when it reached Ndwandwe, and to form a base for joint operations against Ceza.[18]

But Havelock was hoping that further military action against the uSuthu would prove unnecessary. He believed that the uSuthu would rapidly disperse to their homes if it were made widely known that those returning would not be molested by the British, and that the government would proceed only against those for whom warrants of arrest had been issued. To persuade them of this essential benevolence, however, it was necessary that the white civil officials take up their posts again and restore an atmosphere of normality.[19] Consequently, in Havelock's eyes, the prime function of the Coast Column was to make it possible for the Zululand officials to resume their civil functions. But as July came to an end, and Dinuzulu remained in arms on Ceza, it seemed that further fighting might become necessary. Havelock was nevertheless determined that every prior attempt should be made to persuade the uSuthu leaders to give themselves up. Addison, despite the deep distrust in which the uSuthu held him, was entrusted with what were likely to prove delicate negotiations, for Ceza was in his administrative district.[20]

Havelock proved justified in his approach, and negotiations proved sufficient to disperse the uSuthu. The decision of Boer officials in the Vryheid District (after some diplomatic prodding by the British) to control the movement of Zulu on their side of the border contributed materially. On 1 August Addison and Field Cornet P.M. Bester met at Hemken's store near Dlebe Mountain, which was on the border between the South African Republic and Zululand sixteen kilometres south of Ceza. Bester promised to prevent the uSuthu from crossing into the Vryheid District should the British again assault Ceza. He also gave Addison the heartening news that the Zulu from the Phongolo region had already left Dinuzulu, and that the Qulusi were beginning to disperse as well. As he wrote in his fractured English, 'Dinizulu's army is alltogether broke. they have no intention anymore to take up there arms again the English'[sic].[21]

Nevertheless, the military movements that had been put in train when McKean's Coast Column set out for Ndwandwe inexorably pursued their course.

On 1 August Smyth moved his headquarters forward to Nkonjeni. A flying column under Colonel Martin was then formed and, accompanied by Addison, set out on 4 August for Ivuna. The idea was that it would rendezvous with McKean's column for the projected assault on Ceza. On 6 August the Coast Column arrived at Ivuna, hot from burning the abandoned *imizi* of still recalcitrant Zulu along the way.[22] That may well have been a standard procedure of the Victorian army against rebellious tribesmen, but it was hardly calculated to restore the atmosphere of civilian rule Havelock was hoping so much to recreate. Addison, arriving the next day, found the magistracy office wrecked and his house, the mess and the police huts within the zariba all burned down. He watched McKean's men strengthen the fort, which the uSuthu had left intact, while he prepared to make contact with Dinuzulu.[23]

Havelock still saw Dinuzulu's surrender as the key to the '*quiet solution*' of the disturbances,[24] but he and his officials were thwarted. Dinuzulu had already left Ceza on the night of 6 August with the remnant of his *impi*, which, while it may have been more than prepared to carry on fighting against Zibhebhu, had no intention after Hlophekhulu of facing regular troops. Dinuzulu and the other uSuthu ringleaders thus became fugitives at large. Those of their adherents who lived in the Vryheid District returned to their *imizi*, but those from British Zululand did not, being unsure of their reception in the colony.[25]

Thus, while the machinery was set in motion to apprehend Dinuzulu and the other uSuthu leaders on the charge of 'public violence', it became Addison's task to encourage the peaceful resettlement of the uSuthu rank and file. In that enterprise the military, still stationed in Ndwandwe, proved more of a hindrance than a help. On 9 August Lieutenant-Colonel Thompson of the 1st Royal Scots had established a post just north of the Mfabeni hills, called the Nsukazi Fort. On 11 August black scouts from the fort and uSuthu raiding from across the border clashed at Dlebe Mountain eleven or so kilometres to the west. Captain R.S.S. Baden-Powell (a dashing young cavalry officer later to achieve fame at the siege of Mafeking in the Second Anglo-Boer War, but at this time better celebrated as an authority on polo and pig-sticking)[26] led out a punitive expedition against the offending uSuthu. In a sharp little skirmish he killed twelve Zulu, took fifteen prisoner, and captured 146 cattle. The problem was that the enterprising future founder of the Boy Scout movement had failed to read his compass correctly, and had violated the territory of the South African Republic in the process. And, to make his error all the more culpable, he had attacked not the uSuthu (as he supposed), but some of Mnyamana's 'loyal' adherents who were sheltering, as they had fondly believed, out of harm's way nearby.[27]

Baden-Powell had made a genuine, if tragic, mistake. McKean's Basutos had no such excuse. Tired of their unvaried rations of beef, they began to take mealies from the surrounding fields. They raided not only the gardens of known uSuthu supporters, who could not well complain, but also of 'loyal' Zulu such as Ziwedu's adherents, who did. To make matters worse, they were not above seizing cattle from uSuthu who had remained in the colony and wished to submit.[28] Such activity ensured that the uSuthu still in their caves and strongholds would not surrender for fear of the Basutos. It was therefore to the relief of the civil authorities that the order came through on 20 August to disband this disruptive force. The reason for their dismissal, though, was not politic but purely military.

Lieutenant-General Smyth and his staff left Nkonjeni on 15 August. A flying column, made up primarily of Native Levies, followed them to Eshowe, marching through the still disaffected districts north of the Black Mfolozi and through Somkhele's country, where the people were delaying paying the considerable cattle-fines (the Mphukunyoni alone owed 2 000 head) which had been imposed on them when they submitted on 31 July. On 23 August a detachment under Colonel Sir F. Carrington undertook a night march of fifty-six kilometres in an attempt to surprise and capture Somopho, who had not submitted with the other coastal chiefs. The force was fired upon as soon as it came in range of the *umuzi* which was its objective. Though Carrington's men rapidly scattered the defenders and captured their cattle, it was discovered that British intelligence had been at fault and Somopho had left some days previously. On the same night McKean set off on an identical march to the Mpembene hills to dislodge uSuthu known to be gathered there in arms under the minor chief Lokothwayo, who, like Somopho, had resisted submission. There too the uSuthu were easily routed and their cattle taken, and Lokothwayo apparently killed. The whole flying column reached Eshowe on 30 August, having finally dispersed all potentially hostile forces in the Lower Umfolosi District. Their mission complete, the Native Levies were disbanded.[29]

The looming departure of the rest of the troops threatened to leave a vacuum north of the Black Mfolozi. To fill it, Addison returned on 29 August to Ivuna from Nkonjeni with an escort of a hundred Zululand Police, bent on receiving the submission of the local chiefs and *izinduna*. Havelock had been emphasising to Osborn and Addison that they should do everything to persuade the uSuthu that they could return home without fear of victimisation, but he did not trust his officials to work that line *'con amore'*.[30] Certainly, the uSuthu were hardly pleased to have Addison back among them, and were reportedly 'very cheeky in their manner'.[31] Nevertheless, Addison made progress. The uSuthu living along the border with the Vryheid District surrendered their arms and received his permission to return home, while Mnyamana and Ziwedu left their refuge among the British troops at Nkonjeni, and by the end of August were rebuilding their *imizi* in their old haunts.[32]

Smyth now considered it opportune to direct that all the advance posts in Ndwandwe be given up by 30 September and the men redistributed to garrisons of regular troops at Mthonjaneni and Eshowe.[33] Well satisfied that their mission was complete, Smyth and his staff sailed for Cape Town on 7 September. As the *Natal Mercury* put it with considerable satisfaction, 'The proper military part of the business is over. Dinuzulu's capture has become a matter of police.'[34] And, to underscore the point that routine civil administration had been restored, Havelock ordered that the people of Ndwandwe should be called upon to pay their hut tax, and be informed that any arrears would be carried forward to the next year.[35]

34

The Queen Alone Disposes the Land

Somcula and five other messengers sent by Ndabuko arrived on 1 September 1888 at Colonel Martin's camp near Ivuna. They wished to treat with the military authorities, rather than with Addison, the civil magistrate who had been so culpably involved in the events leading to the revolt. But the arrest and trial of the uSuthu leaders was to be a civil matter, and Addison intervened to send them away in the unambiguous understanding that while all the common people would be allowed to return home, Ndabuko and Dinuzulu must surrender unconditionally.[1] Ndabuko then appeared without Dinuzulu at Martin's camp on 16 September, intending to make terms on his nephew's behalf. With one bird in the hand and in hopes of securing both, Addison conceived the unscrupulous plan of manipulating Ndabuko in order to snare Dinuzulu. But Colonel Martin developed soldierly scruples at playing such a low trick. Proper legal procedures were consequently adhered to, and Ndabuko was removed in custody to Nkonjeni for his preliminary examination. This procedure, Addison's superiors decided, was too important and public an affair to be left to such an obviously partial magistrate, and to his humiliation it was entrusted instead to Colonel Stabb, who was sworn in as Justice of the Peace in Zululand to maintain the legal fiction that the trial actually was a civil procedure.[2]

Dinuzulu, meanwhile, was in the South African Republic. President Kruger had initially been reluctant to take any action against him besides disarming his following, but pressure brought to bear by the British High Commissioner resulted in Dinuzulu and Shingana being held by the police in the Utrecht District.[3] On 1 November, however, R. Williams, the British Agent in Pretoria, wired that Dinuzulu, hearing he was to be handed over to the British, had broken free of his ineffective custody and fled.[4] On the same day he arrived at his Mahashini *umuzi*, only thirty-two kilometres from Ivuna, in the company of Shingana and the women of his household.

Addison's orders were to arrest him the moment he set foot on British territory, and he sent to him at once requiring his surrender. But if it had been Dinuzulu's intention to give himself up, he lost his nerve when faced with the unpalatable reality and rode off the following day with twenty horsemen in the direction of the Natal border. Infuriated at losing his prize, Addison proceeded in an act of petty revenge to tear down the huts at Mahashini, while his exasperated officials attempted to force Dinuzulu's adherents at gunpoint to disclose his whereabouts. Word of these intemperate acts convinced Dinuzulu that it would be safer to go 'straight to the Governor', rather than to surrender to the thwarted and vengeful Addison.[5]

Shingana decided then to go his own way. He separated from Dinuzulu's party and returned to his stronghold on Hlophekhulu, where he was speedily apprehended on 6 November and taken in custody to Eshowe. But Dinuzulu himself led the Zululand officials, who thought him to be heading for the traditional refuge of the Nkandla forest (where Cetshwayo had fled in 1883) a merry chase before, on 9 November, crossing back into the Vryheid District near Dlebe Mountain. Safely out of Addison's jurisdiction, he and a dozen faithful *izinduna* then rode through the Nqutu District of Zululand and across the Mzinyathi River at Rorke's Drift at 4 o'clock in the morning.[6] Once in Natal, Dinuzulu and his companions boarded the train at Elandslaagte, north of Ladysmith, and travelled sedately to Pietermaritzburg. Arriving at 1.30 on the morning of 15 November, they immediately made their way across the sleeping city to its eastern outskirts eight kilometres away, where they appeared unheralded at first light at Bishopstowe, the home of Harriette Colenso. She, Dinuzulu knew, would take up the burden of his defence once he was arrested. Duly taken into custody by the Natal Mounted Police, he was put into the jail in Pietermaritzburg. Dinuzulu's counsel wished him to stand trial in Natal, away from the presence of the Zululand officials who, they not unnaturally suspected, would intimidate the witnesses. But the authorities were determined otherwise, and in the early hours of 21 November Dinuzulu was secretly put on the Durban train and sent on his way to Eshowe, where he was placed in the hands of the Zululand Police. There, he and the other arrested uSuthu leaders of the collapsed rebellion underwent preliminary investigations before being put on trial.[7]

Both Knutsford and Sir Michael Gallwey, the Attorney-General of Natal, considered that judges in any way connected with the late disturbances could not be regarded as impartial, and recommended that judicial officers other than the officials provided for in the Laws and Regulations of Zululand should be appointed to preside over the proceedings. Consequently, when the trial commenced on 15 November 1888, it was under the guise of a Special Court of Commission under the Presidency of the Hon. Walter Wragg, Senior Puisne Judge of the Supreme Court of Natal. Its other members were G.M. Rudolph, who had been *landdrost* of the Utrecht District at the time of the Anglo-Zulu War, and J.E. Fannin, who had laid down the boundaries of Zululand in 1883.[8] The trial of the ringleaders, which began on 13 February 1889 after an adjournment on 5 December to give the defence time to prepare, and which ended on 27 April 1889, resulted in Dinuzulu, Ndabuko and Shingana being found guilty of high treason and public violence.[9] They were sentenced respectively to ten, fifteen and twelve years' imprisonment without hard labour.

The Special Commissioners, Havelock and Osborn were all of the opinion that the three chiefs should not be held in Zululand or Natal, since their presence would keep the fires of disloyalty smouldering. They recommended to the Colonial Secretary that all should be 'removed to some safe place across the sea'.[10] On 5 December 1889 the Colonial Secretary at last responded, and wrote to Sir C.B. Mitchell, the new Governor of Natal, that it was his decision that the uSuthu leaders be held on the tiny island of St Helena, secure in the mid-Atlantic. Not only would this be wise on political grounds, but it would allow the chiefs a degree of freedom from personal restraint which would necessarily have been denied them if they had continued to be jailed in Natal or Zululand.[11]

So, when their sentences were confirmed on 18 December, the removal of Dinuzulu, Ndabuko and Shingana to St Helena was also ordered. Each was allowed one male attendant, and Dinuzulu's uncles, who were married, were permitted the company of one wife. Dinuzulu, who had not yet taken a wife, was conceded two women from his household. E.R.W. Saunders, the younger brother of the Resident Magistrate of Eshowe, agreed to act as their interpreter. Paul Bontsa Mthimkhulu, an *inyanga* or traditional healer, accompanied the group to look after their health. Rosemary Hall, a large house in spacious grounds six kilometres from Jamestown, the little capital, was selected to accommodate them.

It was made very plain to the prisoners that detention on St Helena, where the great Napoleon had been their unhappy forerunner, was nothing less than a considerable mitigation of their punishment. Even so, there was consternation among the princes and their attendants, for exile (even in relatively comfortable circumstances) is a bitter daily draught to drain.[12] The three princes and their handful of attendants were conveyed under strict security from Eshowe to Durban, where they were embarked on 7 February 1890 on the mail steamer *Anglian*. On 25 February they reached St Helena, that precipitous rock lost in the great wastes of the Atlantic. There, far from the rolling hills and grassy plains of a beloved Zululand, they were to endure their exile. And in their distant homeland, a period ensued, as Gibson demurely concluded his path-breaking history of the Zulu people, 'during which the house of Zulu had no share in the direction of affairs'.[13]

The trial of the Zulu chiefs, as was certainly appropriate, was turned by the defending counsel into the trial of the Zululand administration. As Harriette Colenso squarely put it to the discomforted Governor, 'the appointment of a Special Court constitutes in itself a censure on the present officials, & implies an admission of their incompetence.'[14] Defending counsel was quick to seize upon any evidence which might illustrate official malpractice, for their defence rested upon the contention that 'the violence, wrongly called rebellion, was brought about by...maladministration, and by the wrong acts of officials',[15] in particular through 'the establishment of Usibebu as a power to balance that of the Usutu'.[16] Such argument might have failed to convince the court, but it was swiftly taken up by elements of the press, which began to portray the trial as an exposé of the British administration in Zululand.[17]

No official was more vulnerable to scrutiny than Addison, in whose district the revolt had been centred. Damaging tales of his arbitrary and illegal floggings, and even shootings, began to emerge; awkward questions were asked in the House of Commons on 4 and 20 June and 13 August 1889 by Thomas Ellis, a member of the Aborigines' Protection Society's lobby, and it was all too clear that Addison had become a gross embarrassment to the Zululand administration. But Havelock confined himself to censuring Addison and to transferring him in May 1889 to the Nqutu District, where he languished unpromoted for the next ten years.[18]

Of course, his superiors took no stronger action against Addison since they knew that it would be seized upon as tacit admission of the culpability of the Zululand officials. Knutsford formally refused the Aborigines' Protection Society's request for an official enquiry into the Zululand administration.[19] That is why Osborn escaped even censure for his central responsibility for the late disturbances, and carried on as Resident Commissioner until his retirement with a knighthood in 1893. Not that his past mistakes or those of the other Zululand officials were allowed to fade into oblivion. Harriette Colenso saw to that. All suffered under what Osborn plaintively termed her 'persistent persecution'[20] as she turned out pamphlet after pamphlet remorselessly exposing their shortcomings.[21]

Havelock must have read these pamphlets with rueful acknowledgement of their essential, if sometimes over-didactically expressed truth. Never again would he allow himself to be led astray by the bias of the so-called experts on Zulu affairs. Experienced administrators, sympathetic towards their subjects, but not committed to the cause of any particular group, would be preferred by Havelock over the old Zululand hands in the short time left to him as Governor. Addison's successor in Ndwandwe exemplified the Governor's new direction. J.Y. Gibson (the future historian of the Zulu people) sprang to his mind, not simply because he was a high-charactered gentleman of good education and fluency in Zulu, but because – quite unlike the other officials in Zululand – he had 'never been concerned in the quarrels between the Usutu partizans of Cetwayo's family and Usibebu and his followers'.[22]

Such a person was necessary in Ndwandwe, for Zibhebhu remained an unresolved problem. The uSuthu leaders were in exile, but their adherents still lived in the district, and Zibhebhu was as determined in 1889 as he had been after his first defeat in 1884 to return to his old lands. But the one thing the rebellion of 1888 had achieved was to expose Zibhebhu to the authorities in Britain as the major cause, rather than the solution, of persistent unrest north of the Black Mfolozi. Consequently, even though he continued to enjoy the loyal support of many Zululand officials whose anti-uSuthu programme he had tirelessly served, the decade following the rebellion was to see his removal as an active player as the government deliberately sought a genuine solution to the conflict that had torn Zululand apart since 1879.

Precisely because Zibhebhu was left burning for revenge, Havelock, who was attempting to pacify Zululand, had ordered that he must remain at Nkonjeni, where he had been evacuated.[23] But in August 1888 with the connivance – if not by the deliberate contrivance – of the Zululand officials (Addison and Osborn in particular), Zibhebhu moved back into his location. Havelock was only informed in September by his devious officials that he had done so. Knutsford, faced with an evident *fait accompli*, in November grudgingly sanctioned his remaining there, but only as a conditional 'act of grace' dependent on his behaving himself.[24] But, incorrigible as ever, Zibhebhu set about disrupting the peaceful resettlement of the uSuthu. In late August he fell upon the adherents of Nkhowana kaMfuzi (the late Msutshwana's brother) and Mthumbu, who had been harrying the Mandlakazi around Bende. He killed about fifty men, captured their women and children, and drove the survivors towards St Lucia Bay. The uSuthu responded in kind in early September, but, unlike the Mandlakazi, incurred the still blatantly biased officials' wrath for the deed. Havelock, seeing only too clearly that the settlement of Zululand was being brought into jeopardy, at last overruled the obstructionism of the Zululand officials and himself took Zibhebhu in hand. On 17 November he ordered that he be taken into custody in Eshowe and investigated for his part in the 'unlawful killing' of Msutshwana in June.[25]

Yet Zibhebhu was protected to the last by the Zululand official establishment. On 20 May 1889 C.J.R. Saunders, the Resident Magistrate of Eshowe, who was conducting Zibhebhu's preliminary investigation, which had begun on 16 April, declared that sufficient grounds did not exist for putting him on trial, and discharged him.[26] As R.C.A. Samuelson bluntly (and ungrammatically) put it in his memoirs, 'there were tons of evidence which was available to convict Sibebu of murder and violence', and his exemption from prosecution was 'clear proof' of the 'partiality' of the officials involved.[27] In the end, though, Zibhebhu was not allowed to have it all his own way. On 15 July 1889 he incorrigibly set off with his following for his location in Ndwandwe, only to be recalled almost immediately to Eshowe. Knutsford, whose eyes had at last been opened to the negative and destructive effect Zibhebhu's presence had cast on the settlement of Ndwandwe, decreed on 1 August 1889 that he was not to be allowed to return until a fresh demarcation of his location had been made.[28]

Zibhebhu's friends in the Zululand administration were still prepared to stand behind him. In February 1890 Osborn pleaded with Sir Charles Mitchell, who had replaced Havelock as Governor in October 1889, for Zibhebhu's return to his location, and convinced the new Governor that this time no disturbances would arise.[29] But Knutsford was having none of it. In April 1890 he reiterated his instructions of August 1889, and insisted that, in order to avoid all possible future uSuthu-Mandlakazi conflict, Zibhebhu could not be repatriated until the boundaries of his location had been demarcated, and an uSuthu location laid out.[30] Osborn had no choice but to comply. He informed Mitchell on 14 April that he would instruct Gibson in Ndwandwe to amend Knight's boundary of April 1888 to exclude the Mdletshe under Wombe kaMfuzi (who was regent of the chiefdom following Msutshwana's death). This, he was sure, would finally settle the question, but he would in any case submit Gibson's recommendations for Mitchell's approval.[31]

Gibson, who could be relied upon more than other Zululand officials to be impartial, began his mission by first demarcating the uSuthu location. He recommended that Ziwedu, Dinuzulu's uncle, who had not joined him in the recent rebellion, should be given a separate location.[32] He turned next to Zibhebhu's location, where he found Knight's eastern boundary 'so indefinite' on account of the great distances between beacons that it was impossible to know the position of the line between them. Consequently, he recommended that nothing should be done until the country 'had been properly inspected'. Similarly, he considered that any possible boundaries in the St Lucia area should be left until 'after due inspection of the country and inquiry as to circumstances'.[33]

Gibson's report of 15 May 1890 took some time to work through the system. Osborn eventually found it 'fair and feasible', and agreed with him that it was not realistic to cut out a separate location for Mthumbu since his Hlabisa were too few and were embedded among the Mandlakazi. Mthumbu's choice should be to come to terms with Zibhebhu or remove to Wombe's district.[34] In due course, on 3 October 1890, Knutsford approved Gibson's suggestions concerning both the uSuthu and Mandlakazi locations, and ordered that the final demarcation be completed as soon as possible.[35]

Under Osborn's administration, however, action was seldom swiftly taken. It was left to Colonel F. Cardew, the Acting Resident Commissioner in 1891, to press forward with setting up a boundary commission which would finally settle the matter. But discussion took time, and since Mitchell wished Osborn, whose experience in the affairs of Zululand he valued, to head the commissioners, it was not until August 1891 and the Resident Commissioner's return from leave that Mitchell finally set up a commission. By that stage, his vision had expanded sufficiently to attempt a more comprehensive settlement than Knutsford had envisaged in October 1890. Accordingly, Mitchell instructed the three commissioners, namely Osborn, Cardew and Gibson, to define the boundaries between all 'the various tribes' north of the Black Mfolozi. Unfortunately, his further orders that the commissioners were, as far as was practicable, to select natural features to define the new boundaries,[36] showed that he had not learned from the failure of all previous delimitations, which had failed to take proper cognisance of the actual topography-defying patterns of uSuthu and Mandlakazi settlement.

Nor, it seemed, had Mitchell grasped that for a commission's award to be accepted, the commissioners themselves must enjoy the trust of all parties. Osborn, though President of the Commission, was an avowed and tried partisan of Zibhebhu and opponent of the uSuthu. Gibson had proved himself a more even-handed official since being appointed to Ndwandwe, but he had a commitment to his own proposed settlement of May 1890 to defend. Cardew was recognised by the Zulu as being open-minded, but he had the disadvantages of not understanding Zulu and of not being familiar with the territory under dispute.[37]

Yet Cardew's very lack of partisanship was a decided advantage. Rather than being concerned with pursuing a settlement which would reward or punish either the uSuthu or the Mandlakazi, he was determined to end their protracted and enervating dispute by means of a settlement which would be accepted by all as 'authoritative and final'. This, as he wrote, required that the commissioners 'make a thorough and impartial inquiry into the opposing claims, taking evidence *from both sides on the spot*'.[38] Realistically, moreover, Cardew perceived that to award Zibhebhu his imprecise 'old tribal lands', as had

Havelock in 1887, would only perpetuate the discord. For, as he sagely wrote to Mitchell in July 1891, it would bring under Zibhebhu's control people such as the Mdletshe and Hlabisa who, in the radically changed political circumstances since 1879, had become 'utterly hostile to him'. The answer, therefore, was to lay down a boundary line which would leave no one on either side of it in a position to complain that they had been 'made subject to Chiefs against their will'. And as far as Zibhebhu's possible repatriation was concerned, Cardew was adamant that this should not even be contemplated until the new boundary was determined.[39]

To give the commission the greatest possible weight, Mitchell travelled to Zululand, and on 25 August 1891, flanked by the leading white officials of the Zululand administration, met *izinduna* of the uSuthu and Mandlakazi people at Ivuna. The Governor hoped to ensure that the *izinduna* would send representatives to accompany the commissioners, who were setting off on their task the following day, for he well understood that only if both parties were fully consulted could a final and mutually acceptable settlement be reached. He also comprehended the difficulties involved, for he realised that some *imizi* would inevitably find themselves on the wrong side of the new boundary line – though he hoped to keep the number to a minimum – and would unavoidably have to be relocated. His public admission of this unpalatable reality immediately gave rise to concern among the gathering, and rival land claims began to be aired. But Mitchell repeatedly and firmly made it plain that he had not come to ascertain the causes of the long-standing uSuthu-Mandlakazi dispute, but to find means of preventing quarrels in the future. 'It is because your troubles have not been put to rights', he declared, 'that I am here today'. And to silence further quibble and cynical comment, he sternly reminded the *izinduna* that it was the Queen, not they, who 'had the right of disposing the land'.[40]

The commission duly began its work on 26 August 1891, and concluded proceedings by drawing up its report on 23 September 1891.[41] As a matter of procedure, the commissioners decided that they should take their investigation of the occupation of the country no further back than the period of Wolseley's settlement of 1879, thus forestalling extensive discussion over distant historic claims.[42] They personally visited every locality under dispute, and investigated the claims to every *umuzi* site, whether occupied or vacant.[43] This information was carefully recorded and classified into lists, and formed the basis for the demarcation of the various locations. The commissioners were initially swamped by the hundreds of people who followed the representatives of the concerned parties with whom they were consulting. They found it difficult to control discussion when the presence of numbers of heated young men (whose bitter animosities were rekindled when the old disputes were raked over) promised the outbreak of violence. Consequently, they soon limited the numbers of representatives on each side to twenty. Proceedings thereafter followed with greater smoothness and despatch. The commissioners gave both sides 'full latitude' in making their claims but, once they had reached a decision, put a firm stop to further discussion.

The commissioners' solution was to set aside a separate main location each for the uSuthu and Mandlakazi, and to create a further eight small ones accommodating particular interests. The uSuthu Location No. 1 was westwards of the Mandlakazi Location and bounded on the west and south by that of Chief Mnyamana of the Buthelezi, who had not supported the uSuthu in 1888 and had been raided by them in retaliation. For the same reason, Ziwedu was also given his own location, as Gibson had recommended in his report of May 1890. This had the disadvantage of cutting off a large body of uSuthu loyal to Dinuzulu, and uSuthu Location No. 2 was defined to accommodate them. In turn, this had adverse repercussions on a large number of Mandlakazi under Zibhebhu's *induna*, Zuya, who were separated from the main Mandlakazi Location. They too were given their own location.

These awkward divisions, which isolated elements of both the uSuthu and Mandlakazi from their main locations, had in them some potential for future conflict. But for the first time since they began drawing boundaries north of the Black Mfolozi in 1879, the British officials responsible were taking close note of the actual distribution of *imizi* on the ground, and were allowing this, rather than natural features or partisan considerations, to determine their decisions. And as they had at last come to realise, to have based their boundaries on anything else but the distribution of *imizi* would have involved a wholesale uprooting of people. The consequences of such action, as initiated by Addison in 1888, had been clearly played out in the uSuthu 'rebellion', and the commission was committed to avoiding a repetition. Even so, their new boundaries could not avoid requiring a number of evictions in areas where the uSuthu and Mandlakazi were completely co-mingled, though the commissioners kept the *imizi* affected to the absolute minimum. Nevertheless, this still meant eviction for the inhabitants of 56 Mandlakazi *imizi* who found themselves in uSuthu locations, besides the loss of 20 *imizi* sites to which they had historic claim, while the comparable figures for the uSuthu expelled from Mandlakazi territory were 22 existing *imizi* and 136 *imizi* sites.

The commissioners tried to be as realistic regarding the claims of others north of the Black Mfolozi as they had been with the uSuthu and Mandlakazi proper. The Zungu people, whose animosity to the surrounding uSuthu went back to 1883 when their chief, Mfanawendlela (who had been one of Wolseley's appointees) was killed by them, received their own small location between Ziwedu's and Mnyamana's. Both the Mdletshe and the Hlabisa were at last freed from Zibhebhu's clutches. But while the Mdletshe remained together as one under their acting regent, Wombe, the Hlabisa were divided into two locations because the commissioners could effect no reconciliation between the rival claimants to the chieftainship, namely Somfula, who was a partisan of Zibhebhu, and Mthumbu, a committed uSuthu.

Mitchell was well satisfied with the commission's work, and it was his opinion that 'if a fair adjustment of the questions in dispute' could put an end to the uSuthu-Mandlakazi conflict, then this settlement should do it.[44] Knutsford had some doubts, particularly on account of the way in which uSuthu and Mandlakazi locations remained intermingled. Accepting this as unavoidable, he considered that chances of collision would at least be reduced if the pro-uSuthu Mdletshe and Mthumbu's Hlabisa did not have to depend on the magistrate at Ivuna, from whom they were separated by the Mandlakazi Location. His solution was to put them under a new magisterial district carved out of the eastern half of Ndwandwe and the northern part of the Lower Umfolosi District.[45] Mitchell concurred with Knutsford's assessment, and was able to report in March 1892 that the boundaries of the Hlabisa District had been fixed.[46] On Osborn's recommendation, the Mdletshe people and both Mthumbu's and Somfula's factions of the Hlabisa were included in the new district.[47] Osborn's rationale behind keeping the two Hlabisa factions together was that coherent chiefdoms should not be artificially divided by administrative boundaries, no matter what the current state of their conflicting political affiliations to either the uSuthu or Mandlakazi might be.[48]

Despite Mitchell's optimism, the commission of 1891 seemed initially not to have provided a final and acceptable solution to the Mandlakazi-uSuthu dispute. The reasons were a combination of concrete discontent with the commission's new boundaries and consequent removals, as well as abiding political mistrust of the Zululand administration's intentions, coupled with unrealistic hopes of some sort of restoration of the old order. Thus, while the Mandlakazi continued to express dissatisfaction with the amount of the land allocated to the uSuthu,[49] the uSuthu maintained a 'sullen attitude' towards the British authorities, disliking in particular the way in which separate locations had been set aside for the Mdletshe and Hlabisa in a new magisterial district. It was the implications of this latter development that the uSuthu resented, for they saw it as removing the Mdletshe and Hlabisa from Dinuzulu's nominal authority, which was exercised in his absence by his mother, Nomvimbi Msweli, and his chief *induna*, Mankulumana, both of whom lived at the ekuBazeni *umuzi* just to the west of the Nongoma hills.

Dinuzulu's rights were becoming for them a burning issue, for by 1892, following the commutation of sentence and release in December 1891 of the coastal uSuthu chiefs detained since 1888, rumours were circulating to the effect that Dinuzulu was soon to return from St Helena.[50] Such speculation fanned the hope that he would come vested with the authority of his father, King Cetshwayo.[51] Yet, for his part, Mitchell remained adamant that the question of Dinuzulu's return might not even be considered, and should not be a factor in his plans to 'secure the peace' through the creation of new locations and magisterial districts.[52]

It was not only the agitation over Dinuzulu's return, however, that was thwarting Mitchell's hopes for a final settlement. The possibility of Zibhebhu's repatriation from the Eshowe District to the Mandlakazi Location continued to haunt the uSuthu and destabilise the district. Mitchell, apparently still under the old collaborator's spell, had considered it 'practicable' in October 1891 to sanction Zibhebhu's return once the new locations were firmly established. This would not have occurred until after the next harvest had been reaped, for those *imizi* affected by the new boundaries were not obliged to move until then.[53] The uSuthu, however, were justifiably appalled at the prospect of the reintroduction of Zibhebhu's revengeful presence, and were convinced that the bloodshed would be renewed if 'the spear [Zibhebhu] were to be flung back'.[54] Knutsford, on considering the matter, while not prepared to go so far as to preclude Zibhebhu from ever returning to the Mandlakazi Location,[55] was wise enough not to sanction any immediate action ensuring that he did so.[56] So Zibhebhu's many patrons among the Zululand official establishment were reluctantly forced, as Osborn tartly reported, to inform their old ally that they could not hold out 'the slightest hope' of his being allowed to go back to the Mandlakazi Location.[57]

However, there the matter could not be allowed to rest, because a political solution still had to be found if the 1891 territorial settlement were to become truly viable. The possibility of attempting a new initiative arose with the return in 1892 of a Liberal government to power in Britain and the death the following year of Sir Theophilus Shepstone, who had exercised such a profound influence upon the administration of Zululand. Osborn's retirement as Resident Commissioner provided the opportunity to break with Shepstonite policies, and the government seized it to appoint Sir Marshall Clarke to succeed him on 5 August 1893.

Clarke had been the extremely successful Administrator of Basutoland. He saw his predecessor's tendency to play on factional differences (the essence both of the Wolseley settlement and of the Shepstone system) as a fundamental reason for continuing unrest in Zululand. He consequently advocated the repatriation of both the exiled Dinuzulu and Zibhebhu, hoping they would use their influence to heal uSuthu-Mandlakazi divisions and, by restoring Zulu confidence in the British, help consolidate their administration.[58] But, Clarke counselled, to minimise potential discord Dinuzulu should not come back as paramount chief, but as a 'Government Induna and Adviser' in the administration's employ.[59]

In January 1894 the British government agreed to Dinuzulu's pardon and return. On St Helena he and his uncles were living in a large house south of Jamestown called Maldivia, where they had removed because of the dampness of Rosemary Hall. They were behaving circumspectly and in return were allowed considerable freedom. Thanks largely to Harriette Colenso's efforts, a series of tutors had been appointed for the exiles, and Dinuzulu had learned to speak, read and write English and had taken up both the piano and American organ. He had also adopted western dress with considerable enthusiasm. Many hours were spent riding over the island, for he was an accomplished horseman, and in attending and holding dinner parties for the notables of the island. He also fathered six children from his two *abalobokazi* or 'female attendants'. Silomo was the mother of Solomon Nkayishana Maphumuzana, his future heir, and of Arthur Edward Mshiyeni, later regent for his grandson, Cyprian. Both were christened in the island's Anglican church, and their very names bore witness to their westernised education and upbringing, which were to be of considerable influence when, later in life, they assumed positions of authority in Zululand.[60]

The exiles' promised repatriation was, to their considerable disappointment and dismay, delayed by the intervention of the Natal government, just as Cetshwayo's had been.[61] Since the granting of responsible government to the colony on 4 July 1893, its parliamentary objections had carried greater weight with the home government than they would have in the past. Settler concern over Dinuzulu's return stemmed not only from an understandable reluctance to deal with a possible renewal of civil strife; there was also growing agitation from interests who wanted closer control over Zululand's mineral resources, for it was mistakenly believed that gold and coal were present in exploitable quantities. Farmers and developers continued greedily to eye the coastal belt as they had for decades past as suitable for sugar cultivation. Clarke's policy, it was feared, by conciliating Zulu interests, would maintain the restrictions placed in 1887 on white penetration of Zululand, and foil attempts to open up the country for settlement and exploitation.

While negotiations were in progress, the Liberal government fell in June 1895. The new Conservative administration was more amenable than its predecessor to settler demands. Sir Joseph Chamberlain, the Colonial Secretary, had wide-arching schemes for South African federation, and was prepared in its interests to conciliate settler Natal. An agreement was therefore negotiated whereby Dinuzulu's return was coupled with the annexation of Zululand by Natal.[62] As in 1879, Zululand was again to be sacrificed to imperial expediency and settler interests.

The territory that duly became incorporated on 30 December 1897 as a province of Natal did not of course include the Vryheid District, which had been lost to the South African Republic.[63] However, it did embrace the Ingwavuma District to the north-east, although that coastal stretch had never formed an integral part of the Zulu kingdom and, at most, had been connected in a tributary relationship. Even so, in order to thwart the South African Republic's attempts to reach the sea, Britain had annexed the territory piecemeal in 1888, 1890 and 1895, and had incorporated it into the Colony of Zululand on 15 July 1895. Tongaland (or Amaputaland), which had been fully annexed as a British protectorate only on 30 May 1895, was incorporated into Zululand on 24 December 1897, just in time to be swallowed up with it by Natal. The news of their incorporation into Natal was received for the most part without comment by the Zulu chiefs and without any particular enthusiasm. They could not fully guess the implications for themselves, and as Mankulumana off-handedly said at Ivuna, 'they had always considered Zululand and Natal to be one country' in any case.[64]

With the long-desired incorporation of Zululand achieved, the Natal government had no further reason to resist Dinuzulu's return. On St Helena, Governor Sterndale explained to the former king the position he would occupy in the new Province of Zululand.[65] In line with Clarke's original suggestion, he was to be a Government Induna paid a salary of £500 per annum dependent on his good behaviour. He was required to live near Eshowe and his duties were to involve giving the administration advice on matters of Zulu custom such as, for example, questions of inheritance. He would also be chief over uSuthu Locations Nos. 1 and 2, and subject like other chiefs to the laws of the Natal government.[66]

Dinuzulu and his two uncles, though overjoyed at the prospect of returning to their native land, had certain requests and reservations which they communicated in September 1897 to Chamberlain. They begged that steps be taken to prevent the annual burning of the grass by white farmers over the graves of their royal ancestors in the emaKhosini valley, a 'painful' occurrence which had 'never been done' by the Zulu, who venerated the resting places of their kings and queens. Secondly, they pleaded that the Zulu who were cut off in the South African Republic, not one of whom 'liked the Boers because of their ill-treatment', be reunited under the British crown. Not without good cause, they also feared the implications of unbridled rule by the Natal settlers, and wanted reassurances that the British government could, if applied to, overrule local legislation. And, above all, they prayed that 'our country should not be taken away from us by getting it distributed into farms, because we shall have no place for grazing our cattle and for ploughing'.[67]

Chamberlain replied with the bland assurance that 'due provision will be made for the protection of the interests of the Zulus', though he was emphatic that there could be no question of re-opening the boundary question with the South African Republic.[68] What he did not consider fit to enter into with Dinuzulu and his uncles was the question of the ominous first condition which he had laid down in May 1897 when assenting in principle to Natal's annexation of Zululand. He had required then that for the first five years after annexation the existing system of land tenure in Zululand should be maintained, and that no grants of land should be made to whites. However, he had added that, in the meantime, 'a joint Imperial and Colonial Commission...should mark out sufficient land reserves for native locations' prior to throwing the land open to white settlement.[69]

Sir Marshall Clarke, with his habitual sensitivity to Zulu opinion, eventually succeeded in persuading the Natal government not to proceed with appointing a joint boundary commission until after an interval of a few years. That, he argued, would allow space for the Zulu to have 'thoroughly settled down' under the new regime, and to have become accustomed to 'the new state of things' which lay before them.[70] The upshot was that it was not until August 1902 that a commission was set up, but Dinuzulu's earnest hope that his country would not be carved up like Natal into white-owned farms and black locations was destined to be entirely dashed.

The royal Zulu exiles arrived in Durban harbour on board the steamship *Umbilo* on the evening of 5 January 1898, and landed very early the following morning. Dinuzulu had set his heart on a triumphal entry through the port. But the Natal officials detailed to meet him wished at all costs to avoid public demonstrations in his favour. So they whisked him and his entourage straight off to Eshowe with only a brief and private halt in Durban for Sir Marshall Clarke, who had been succeeded as Resident Commissioner on 1 January 1898 by Charles Saunders, to wish them well. Accompanied by his numerous suits of clothes, drawing-room furniture, books, pictures, ornaments and musical instruments – some forty tons of belongings all acquired in exile[71] – Dinuzulu arrived in Eshowe on 10 January. There he appealed against the condition requiring him to live in Eshowe. The Natal government relented, and Saunders granted him permission to reside among his people in the uSuthu Location No. 1 so long as he regularly carried out his official duties at Eshowe. Dinuzulu's journey north to the uSuthu heartland turned into a triumphal progress as thousands of Zulu thronged the route to acclaim their returning king. But king he was not and could never be again in the eyes of the Natal government. Though he built a new uSuthu *umuzi* at Nongoma, consisting of traditional huts as well as a European-style dwelling, and received chiefs and *izinduna* from all over the former kingdom, his actual powers – such as they were – were firmly confined to the locations over which he was chief.

Zibhebhu was allowed back to the Mandlakazi location at the same time as Dinuzulu. In June 1898 officials of the new administration staged a reconciliation at Eshowe between Dinuzulu and the pitiless scourge of the uSuthu. In the privacy of his office, Saunders extracted a solemn promise from both that they would in future live harmoniously side by side. But even then friction persisted. Not all among the uSuthu and Mandlakazi were prepared to forget and forgive, and Ziwedu made known his deep objections to his nephew Dinuzulu's renewed association with the man he steadfastly believed to have poisoned his brother and king.[72] And truly, so many years of bloodshed amidst the ruins of the Zulu kingdom could not easily be wiped away with a handshake.

EPILOGUE

Towards the New Kingdom

At the turn of the nineteenth century, most Zulu continued as they had ever done to wear traditional dress, to live in their scattered *imizi* and to keep their precious herds of cattle. Loss of political independence seemed superficially not to have radically changed Zulu ways, and J.Y. Gibson could comfortably observe in 1899 of the people of the Ndwandwe District that their 'habits of life' differed 'scarcely in any important respects from those in which their fathers lived'.[1] Yet the reality was rather otherwise under colonial rule, and in many ways a new world was perceptibly dawning in Zululand.[2] Already in 1898, 345 young men left Ndwandwe to seek labour elsewhere to meet payment of the hut tax, and complaints were soon rife among their elders concerning their 'lack of respect' and reluctance to return home.[3] By 1904 17 000 Zulu were at work outside the Province of Zululand, drawn away by the lure of an industrialising subcontinent.[4] Thus the young men of Zululand, who had once laboured in their *amabutho* for their king, were becoming migrant labourers on white farms and in the growing towns and cities.

Not only labour patterns were in a process of uncomfortable modification and redefinition; traditional customs, kinship relationships and regard for the authority of elders and chiefs were as well. Change was accelerated by a series of natural disasters. In 1895-6 immense swarms of red locust swept bare the fields, and returned in 1898, 1903-4 and again in 1906. Between 1895 and 1907 there were six years of serious drought, which made it hardly possible to renew the devastated pastures and fields. Then came the terrible rinderpest epidemic, that highly contagious viral disease of ruminants, which broke out in 1897 and consummated the destruction of the Zululand cattle herds. And, before the herds had any chance to recover, they were struck in 1904-5 by the new and deadly tick-borne disease, East Coast Fever. Cattle were still the basis of the people's social and economic life, and their chief form of storable wealth. The sudden nigh obliteration of their cattle shook the Zulu to their roots.

On top of this crushing, irreparable loss came the brutal injury of white settlement in Zululand. Those Zulu living in what had been the New Republic and which, since its cession on 27 January 1903 at the end of the Second Anglo-Boer War by the South African Republic, had become the Vryheid District of Natal,[5] possessed no land at all. In 1884 they had summarily become tenants of white

437

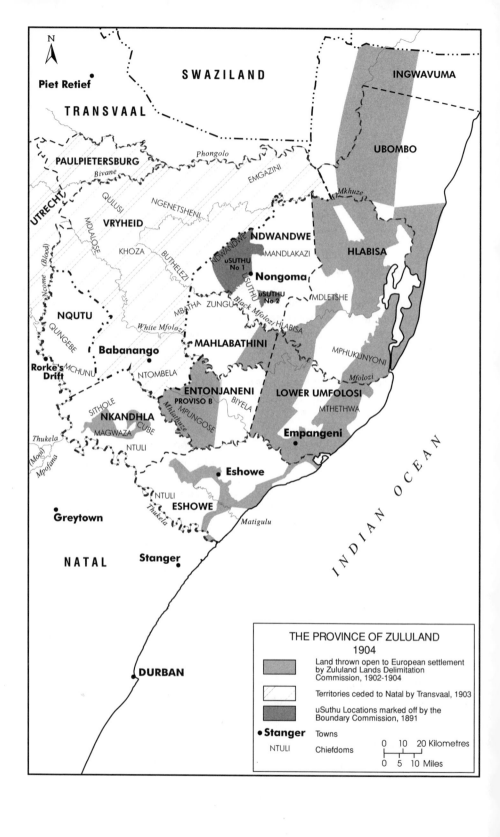

N

Piet Retief

SWAZILAND

INGWAVUMA

TRANSVAAL

UBOMBO

PAULPIETERSBURG

Phongolo

Bivane

EMGAZINI

Mkhuze

UTRECHT

QULUSI

NGENETSHENI

VRYHEID

KHOZA

BUTHELEZI

Ncome (Blood)

MDLALOSE

NDWANDWE

NDWANDWE

HLABISA

uSUTHU
No 1

MANDLAKAZI

Nongoma

NQUTU

QUNGEBE

MBATHA

ZUNGU

Black Mfolozi

uSUTHU
No 2

MDLETSHE

White Mfolozi

HLABISA

Babanango

MAHLABATHINI

MPHUKUNYONI

Rorke's
Drift

MCHUNU

NTOMBELA

Mfolozi

SITHOLE

ENTONJANENI

LOWER UMFOLOSI

PROVISO B

MPUNGOSE

BIYELA

MTHETHWA

NKANDHLA

Thukela

MAGWAZA

CUBE

Mhlathuze

(Mooi)

NTULI

Empangeni

Mpofana

Eshowe

NTULI

ESHOWE

Greytown

Thukela

Matigulu

NATAL

Stanger

INDIAN OCEAN

DURBAN

THE PROVINCE OF ZULULAND
1904

Land thrown open to European settlement
by Zululand Lands Delimitation
Commission, 1902-1904

Territories ceded to Natal by Transvaal, 1903

uSuthu Locations marked off by the
Boundary Commission, 1891

● Stanger   Towns

NTULI   Chiefdoms

0   10   20 Kilometres

0   5   10 Miles

landlords since no areas were set aside for their exclusive occupation in the New Republic. Ever since then they had been required to pay substantial rents or render labour for their tenure. In contrast, no white settlement had been permitted in the British Colony of Zululand, except for a limited number of mission stations and stores. But, it will be remembered, the British government had conceded at the time of the territory's incorporation into Natal that the new Province of Zululand would eventually be thrown open to white farmers. The only proviso laid down was that the Zulu should not be disturbed in their ancient occupancy of the land for at least five years. And duly, on 1 August 1902, the Zululand Lands Delimitation Commission was set up to demarcate 'sufficient land' for 'native locations', and to set aside the rest for grants to whites.[6] The Imperial Commissioner was Brigadier-General Sir John Dartnell (who had commanded the Natal Mounted Volunteers and the Mounted Police in Zululand in 1879, and who had since distinguished himself in the Natal theatre of the Second Anglo-Boer War); the Colonial Commissioner was Zibhebhu's old friend, C.J.R. Saunders, now Chief Magistrate and Civil Commissioner for the Province of Zululand.

In going about their task, the commissioners (R.H. Beachcroft, JP, replaced the ailing Dartnell in 1904) were consciously 'actuated by a desire to exclude from the Reserves, which were to be inalienable, as much land as [they] conscientiously could'. Put in another way, this meant that they identified as reserves regions undesirable in terms of their potential for commercial agriculture and white settlement.[7] The consequence was that in the Commission's final report, submitted on 18 October 1904, 1 057 467 hectares of Zululand (or 40.2 per cent of its total area) were set aside for white purchase and occupation, and 1 573 047 were left for black reserves. In the opinion of the commissioners, the Reserves were quite large enough to accommodate the Zulu population, which the census of 1904 put at 'over 220 000 souls', or one person per 6.88 hectares. Those Zulu who found themselves living on land set aside to be transformed into white privately owned sugar and wattle plantations, and who could not be accommodated as workers on these farms, were reduced to the status of squatters on lands their forebears had sometimes held since the time of Shaka and before, and were made subject to summary eviction to the Reserves.[8] The Native Land Act of 1913 of the new Union of South Africa subsequently confirmed the Reserves in Zululand as they stood.[9] Thus the incorporation by Natal of both the Colony of Zululand and the Vryheid District represented nothing less than the ultimate triumph of Shepstonism. All the people of the former kingdom of Zululand were brought under Natal's administrative system, and the settlers' long-thwarted expansionist aims triumphed at last.

Yet, even though it might have seemed so at the time, that was not to be the end of the Zulu kingdom. All those cumulative disasters – political, natural, economic and social – did not break the Zulu people. On the contrary, the pervasiveness of their distress was eventually to lead in the twentieth century to a renewed sense of national consciousness, pride and unity, increasingly focused on the Zulu royal house, that living link with an independent and powerful precolonial past. And after decades of reverses, humiliations and temporarily blighted hopes – a saga of vicissitudes not a jot less absorbing than the story of the rise and fall of the Zulu kingdom in the nineteenth century – the place of the Zulu monarchy in KwaZulu-Natal was constitutionally recognised and protected by the constitution of the new, post-apartheid South Africa. That tale in all its fullness still awaits its historian.[10] What is certain, though, is that the new, twentieth-century monarchy in KwaZulu-Natal must – despite all the continuities of Zulu tradition – be very different from its historic predecessor and inspiration, the Zulu state founded by King Shaka.

Glossary

In accordance with modern practice, Zulu words are entered under the stem and not under the prefix.

isAngoma (pl. **izAngoma**) diviner inspired by ancestral spirits

iBandla (pl. **amaBandla**) council of state

isiBaya (pl. **iziBaya**) enclosure for livestock (kraal)

umBengo (pl. **imiBengo**) strips of meat

Boer Dutch-speaking white settler

imBongi (pl. **izimBongi**) praise-singer

iButho (pl. **amaButho**) age-grade regiment of men or women; member of age-group; warrior

uDibi (pl. **izinDibi**) baggage boy

iDlozi (pl. **amaDlozi**) ancestral spirit

inDlu (pl. **izinDlu**) hut

Donga dry eroded watercourse running only in times of heavy rain

Drift shallow fordable point in a river

inDuna (pl. **izinDuna**) officer of state, appointed by chief or king to position of command; headman, councillor

isiFuba (pl. **iziFuba**) chest or centre of army

ukuGiya to perform a war-dance

isiGodlo (pl. **iziGodlo**) king's or chief's private enclosure at upper end of his homestead; women of king's establishment

inGxotha (pl. **izinGxotha**) heavy brass armlet conferred as mark of distinction by king

uHlangothi (pl. **izinHlangothi**) wing of *ibutho* or section of *ikhanda* where quartered

isiHlangu (pl. **iziHlangu**) war shield

isiJula (pl. **iziJula**) throwing-spear

iKhanda (pl. **amaKhanda**) royal military homestead where amabutho were stationed

iKhohlo (pl. **amaKhohlo**) left-hand wife, her section of the homestead and her descendants

umKhokha (pl. **imiKhokha**) ritual defilement

iKholwa (pl. **amaKholwa**) Christian

ukuKhonza to pay allegiance to king or chief

umKhosi (pl. **imiKhosi**) annual 'first-fruits' ceremony

isiKhulu (pl. **iziKhulu**) great one in hierarchy of kingdom

umKhumbi (pl. **imiKhumbi**) circular assembly of men

Kloof deep ravine or valley, usually wooded, or gorge between mountains

iKlwa (pl. **amaKlwa**) stabbing-spear (assegai)

Kop prominent hill or peak

inKosi (pl. **amaKhosi**) king; chief

inKosikazi (pl. **amaKhosikazi**) principal wife of king or chief

Kraal enclosure for livestock

Krans overhanging sheer cliff-face or crag, often above a river

Laager defensive formation of parked wagons, but also any defensive enclosure, whether of barricades,

441

masonry, etc.

iLobolo (sing. only) cattle or goods handed over by man's family to formalise marriage transaction

isiLomo (pl. **iziLomo**) courtier; royal favourite

Mealie maize

uMnyama (sing. only) spiritual force of darkness or evil influence

iMpi (pl. **iziMpi**) military force; army; battle

iNceku (pl. **iziNceku**) king's or chief's personal domestic attendant and adviser

umNdlunkulu (sing. only) girls of royal establishment attending king, maids-of-honour

iNkatha (pl. **iziNkatha**) sacred grass coil, symbol of the nation

iNsizwa (pl. **iziNsizwa**) unmarried young man

umNtwana (pl. **abaNtwana**) prince of the royal house, child of the king

umNumzane (pl. **abaNumzane**) married headman of a homestead

iNqadi (pl. **amaNqadi**) right-hand wife, her section of the homestead, and her descendants

iNyanga (pl. **iziNyanga**) traditional healer, herbalist

Pont large, flat-bottomed ferry-boat worked by ropes or cables to convey passengers, animals and wagons across rivers

uPondo (pl.**izimPondo**) horn or wing of army

Riem (pl. **rieme**) thong of softened raw hide used instead of rope

umShokobezi (pl. **imiShokobezi**) cowtail decoration

amaSi (pl. only) sour milk

inSila (pl. **izinSila**) body dirt; king's body servant

ukuSisa to pasture livestock in care of a subordinate

Spruit tributary watercourse feeding larger stream

umThakathi (pl. **abaThakathi**) witch or wizard, user of supernatural forces for evil

Trek to make an arduous journey overland, often involving a permanent move

umuVa (pl. **imiVa**) reserve force of army

Volksraad legislative assembly of a Boer republic

Voortrekker Boer pioneers who, dissatisfied with British rule, left the Cape Colony for the interior of South Africa

iWisa (pl. **amaWisa**) knobbed stick (knobkerrie)

umuZi (pl. **imiZi**) homestead of huts under a headman; people belonging to it

ukuZila to observe ritual abstinence

Notes

PREFACE
1   *Government Gazette of the Republic of
    South Africa*, vol. 346, no. 15681:
    Constitution of the Republic of
    South Africa Second Amendment
    Act, 1994.

PROLOGUE
1   For Shaka's death, see Fynn, *Diary*,
    pp. 156-7, glossed by Gibson, *Story
    of the Zulus*, pp. 40-1; Isaacs,
    Travels, I, pp. 257-8; Bryant,

Olden Times, pp. 659-62; and Fuze,
Black People, pp. 70-1.
2   *JSA* II, p. 93: Magidigidi.
3   *JSA* II, p. 161: Makewu.
4   *JSA* II, p. 295: Maziyana.
5   Maclean, *Ross*, p. 111; *JSA* II, p. 163:
    Makewu; *JSA* II, p. 294: Maziyana.
6   *JSA* I, p. 194: Jantshi; *JSA* II, p. 59:
    Madikane; *JSA* IV, p. 291: Ndwana.
7   *JSA* II, p. 295: Maziyana.
8   *JSA* I, p. 312: Lunguza.
9   *JSA* IV, pp. 232-3: Ndhlovu.
10 *JSA* III, p. 201: Mkebeni.

CHAPTER 1
1   See War Office, *Precis*, pp. 5-22; *Natal
    Regional Survey*, vol. I, part 2; Guy,
    Zulu Kingdom, pp. 4-10.
2   Merrett and Butcher, *Struthers*,
    'Introduction', pp. (28)-(31).
3   Maclean, *Ross*, p. 82.
4   For the daily life of the Zulu and their
    social structure, see Bryant, *Zulu
    People*, especially pp. 74-90, 132-
    204, 253-6, 264-6, 412-54; and
    Krige, *Social System*, especially
    pp. 39-47, 53-60, 184-97, 207-11,
    370-5; and Hammond-Tooke, *Roots
    of Black South Africa*, pp. 45-63,
    101-15, 122-8, 199-213, *passim*.
5   Maclean, *Ross*, pp. 80-1.
6   Webb and Wright, *Zulu King Speaks*,
    pp. 73, 99.
7   Maclean, *Ross*, pp. 68-9.
8   Maclean, *Ross*, pp. 84-5.
9   Delegorgue, *Travels*, p. 84.

10 *Humphrey's Journal*, p. 12: 13 September 1851.

CHAPTER 2

1 This discussion is based on A. Mazel, 'The Stone Age Peoples of Natal' in Duminy and Guest, *Natal and Zululand*, pp. 1-27.
2 Fuze, *Black People*, pp. 2-4.
3 Rycroft and Ngcobo, *Praises of Dingana*, p. 89.
4 For the following discussion, see T. Maggs, 'The Iron Age Farming Communities' in Duminy and Guest, *Natal and Zululand*, pp. 28-48.
5 The account in this and in the following chapter of the rise of the Zulu kingdom is based on J. Wright, 'Power and Conflict', pp. 155-380. See also, J. Wright and C. Hamilton, 'Traditions and Transformations: The Phongolo-Mzimkhulu Region in the Late Eighteenth and Early Nineteenth Centuries' in Duminy and Guest, *Natal and Zululand*, pp. 57-82.
6 See Daniel, 'Geographical Study of Pre-Shakan Zululand', *passim*; Guy, *Zulu Kingdom*, pp. 9-10.
7 See Martin, 'Natal History', pp. 323-5; Taylor, 'Zulu History Rewritten', p. 19.
8 Cope, *Izibongo*, p. 92
9 Maclean, *Ross*, p. 99.
10 Cope, *Izibongo*, p. 128.
11 Cope, *Izibongo*, p. 122.
12 A famous ancestor of the Zulu house.
13 Cope, *Izibongo*, p. 80.
14 Bryant, *Olden Times*, pp. 163-6.
15 Webb and Wright, *Zulu King Speaks*, pp. 1, 3.8
16 Cope, *Izibongo*, p. 76.
17 Cope, *Izibongo*, pp. 171, 174.
18 Account based on Fynn, *Diary*, pp. 12-14, 140.
19 Cope, *Izibongo*, p. 174.
20 Fuze, *Black People*, p. 45.
21 Webb & Wright, *Zulu King Speaks*, p. 4.
22 Rycroft and Ngcobo, *Praises of Dingana*, p. 181.
23 The father of Zulu, the founder of the Zulu clan.
24 Cope, *Izibongo*, p. 172.

CHAPTER 3

1 Fuze, *Black People*, p. 55.
2 Cope, *Izibongo*, p. 96, 116.
3 Bryant, *Olden Times*, p. 126.
4 Webb & Wright, *Zulu King Speaks*, p. 5.
5 Cope, *Izibongo*, p. 150.
6 Fuze, *Black People*, p. 50.
7 Fuze, *Black People*, p. 54.
8 Webb and Wright, *Zulu King Speaks*, p. 7.
9 Cope, *Izibongo*, p. 130.
10 Webb and Wright, *Zulu King Speaks*, pp. 5-6.
11 Cope, *Izibongo*, p. 94.
12 Cope, *Izibongo*, p. 88.
13 Senzangakhona.
14 Samuelson, *Long, Long Ago*, p. 263.
15 *JSA* I, p. 53: William Bazley, who had the story from Henry Francis Fynn.
16 Isaacs, *Travels*, I, pp. 274, 286.
17 *JSA* I, p. 7: Baleka.
18 *JSA* II, p. 248: Mayinga.
19 *JSA* II, p. 163: Makewu.
20 Maclean, *Ross*, p. 135.
21 *JSA* II, pp. 60-1: Madikane; *JSA* III, p. 72: Melapi; Fuze, *Black People*, p. 89; Bryant, *Olden Times*, p. 122.
22 *JSA* I, pp. 189, 195: Jantshi.
23 *JSA* I, p. 8: Baleka. See also, *JSA* II, p. 232: Maquza.
24 *JSA* I, p. 57: Bazley.
25 *JSA* I, p. 195: Jantshi.
26 *JSA* II, p. 248: Mayinga.
27 *JSA* IV, pp. 158-9: Mtshebwe.
28 For the *amabutho* system, see Laband, *Kingdom in Crisis*, pp. 18-22.
29 Maclean, *Ross*, p. 98.
30 Cope, *Izibongo*, p. 178.
31 Laband & Thompson, *Field Guide*, p. 4.
32 For Zulu religion and practices, witchcraft and pollution, see Bryant,

Zulu People, pp. 523-5; Krige, *Social System*, pp. 283-96; A.- I. Berglund, *Zulu Thought Patterns*, pp. 29, 42-3, 53, 94, 120-22, 127 ff., 214-19, 261; Hammond-Tooke, *Roots of Black South Africa*, pp. 149-97, passim.

33 See *JSA* I, p. 9: Baleka.
34 Cope, 'Hamu', p. 8; Krige, *Social System*, pp. 280-335
35 Cope, *Izibongo*, p. 202.
36 *JSA* IV, pp. 277-8: Ndukwana.
37 See Fynn, *Diary*, pp. 83-5; *JSA* I, p. 194: Jantshi; *JSA* II, p. 93: Magidigidi; p. 161: Makewu.
38 Webb and Wright, *Zulu King Speaks*, p. 6.

CHAPTER 4
1 For the first white penetration into Natal, see Brookes and Webb, *History of Natal*, pp. 17-22; and C. Ballard, 'Traders, Trekkers and Colonists' in Duminy & Guest, *Natal and Zululand*, pp. 116-19.
2 Maclean, *Ross*, pp. 52-3, 63-4.
3 Maclean, *Ross*, pp. 149-50.
4 Maclean, *Ross*, pp. 62-3.
5 Fynn, *Diary*, pp. 123-8
6 For the problems related to Fynn's account of his time at Port Natal, see Pridmore, 'James Stuart, Douglas Malcolm and The Diary of H.F. Fynn' in Edgecombe, Laband and Thompson, 'Debate on Zulu Origins', passim.
7 This account of the Zulu army is based on Laband, *Kingdom in Crisis*, pp. 38-40, 60-2, 65-7, 88, 109-10.
8 See Ngubane, *Body and Mind*, pp. 77-8, 81, 86, 131, 133.
9 *JSA* IV, p. 373: Ndukwana. Baleni kaSilwana agreed substantially with Ndukwana, though according to him the ritual vomiting only took place when an army left on the king's initiative. When attacked, as in 1879, the ceremony was not observed (*JSA* I, p. 41: Baleni).

10 For full descriptions of doctoring at time of war, see *JSA* I, p. 124: Dunjwa; *JSA* IV, pp. 296-300, 306: Mpatshana; and Callaway, *Religious System*, pp. 437-40. For the significance of the ceremonies, see Ngubane, *Body and Mind*, pp. 109-10, 119,126, 129-30, 152. The last occasion on which a ceremony on this scale was held in Zululand was in the spring of 1934, when some 10 000 warriors were ritually cleansed at Mahashini after the death of King Solomon. See Birkby, *Zulu Journey*, pp. 70-2.
11 *JSA* III, pp. 123-4: Mgudeni.
12 *JSA* IV, p. 291: Ndukwana.
13 *JSA* IV, p. 77: Mtshapi; p. 146: Mtshayankomo.
14 The most comprehensive recent discussion on Zulu war-dress is in Knight, 'Uniforms and Weapons', pp. 38-41. See also Laband and Thompson, *Field Guide*, p. 4; and Knight, *The Zulus*, pp. 6-7.
15 See the descriptions of ceremonial dress in Fynney, *Zulu Army*; and Samuelson, *Long, Long Ago*, pp. 238-9. For modern representations, see McBride, *Zulu War*, illustrations between pp. 24-6; and McBride's excellent new set of illustrations in Knight, *The Zulus*, between pp. 32-45. *The Zulus* also contains many rare photographs of items of Zulu dress and equipment.
16 Samuelson, *Long, Long Ago*, p. 239.
17 Fynn, *Diary*, p. 285
18 Samuelson, *Long, Long Ago*, pp. 238-9.
19 Maclean, *Ross*, p. 127.
20 Hallam Parr, *Kafir and Zulu Wars*, p. 113; Fynney, *Zulu Army*, p. 4. See Knight, *The Zulus*, p. 47.
21 H.C. Lugg Papers, File I, MS 1405 b: List of weapons, 9 March 1942. See also Smail, *Land of the Zulu Kings*, p.23.
22 Blair Brown, 'Surgical Notes', pp. 6-

7; *JSA* II, p.242: Maxibana; *Natal Mercury*, Special Supplement, 22 January 1922: recollections of Gumpega Gwabe; Knight, 'The Zulu Army, 1879', in Knight, *There will be an Awful Row*, p. 41.

23 Plant, *Zulu in Three Tenses*, p. 29.

24 H.C. Lugg Papers, File I, MS 1405 b: List of weapons, 9 March 1942; Bourquin, 'Zulu Military Organization', p. 149; Knight, 'Zulu Army', pp. 41-2.

25 *JSA* I, p. 41: Baleni; *JSA* III, p. 317: Mpatshana; *JSA* IV, p. 297: Ndukwana. For the extraction of iron and the forging of metal, see Ndukwana above and James Stuart Collection, File no. 87, KCM 53320 & 53321, MS translation by E.R. Dahle of *uVusezakithi* (London, 1938) by J. Stuart, chapter 28: 'The Forging of Metal in Early Zulu Times' and 'The Working of Iron'.

26 James Stuart Collection, File no. 85, MS translation by E.R. Dahle of *uThulasizwe* (London, 1936) by James Stuart: chapter 16, 'The Cutting Out of War Shields'.

27 Smail, *Land of the Zulu Kings*, p. 24; Knight, 'Zulu Army', p. 38.

28 Anstruther Letters: Col. P.R.Anstruther's Letter-Book, 12 August 1879; Knight, 'Zulu Army', p. 38; Bourquin, 'Zulu Military Organization', p. 149; Laband and Thompson, *Field Guide*, p. 4.

29 Maclean, *Ross*, p. 123.

30 *JSA* II, p. 243: Maxibana; *JSA* III, pp. 318-9: Mpatshana; Knight, 'Zulu Army', p. 38.

31 *JSA* IV, p. 92: Mtshapi.

32 War Office, *Precis*, p. 113; Zulu Tribal History Competition, 1950, file 24, KCM 64795: Vivian Maphanga, 'The Life of a Male from Birth to Marriage', p. 2.

33 *JSA* IV, p. 380: Ndukwana.

34 Fynney, *Zulu Army*, p. 6.

35 *Times of Natal*, 3 March 1879.

36 Laband, *Kingdom in Crisis*, p. 100.

37 Laband and Mathews, *Isandlwana*, p. 21.

38 Colenso, *Zulu War*, p. 408.

39 Cato Papers, no. 1, MS 1602a: G.C. Cato to Richards, 2 February 1879.

40 *JSA* III, pp. 316-7: Mpatshana; TS 38: G. Cato to H.C. Shepstone, 12 February 1878.

41 *JSA* IV, pp. 331-2: Ndukwana; Zulu Tribal History Competition, 1950, file 24, KCM 64795: V. Maphanga, 'The Life of a Male from Birth to Marriage', p. 2.

42 Fynney, *Zulu Army*, p. 6; Mitford, *Zulu Country*, pp. 91, 312-3.

43 Fynney, *Zulu Army*, pp. 6-7; Carl Faye Papers 8: Diagram illustrating formation of attacking Zulu impi; Hallam Parr, *Kaffir and Zulu Wars*, p. 201; Ludlow, *Zululand and Cetewayo*, p. 47; War Office, *Precis*, pp. 113-14.

44 *JSA* I, pp. 312, 322: Lunguza; *JSA* IV, p. 352: Ndukwana.

45 See, for example, Harrison, *Recollections*, p. 140.

46 *JSA* I, p. 35: Baleni.

47 Samuelson, *Long, Long Ago*, p. 237.

48 See Maclean, *Ross*, p. 68.

49 Isaacs, *Travels*, I, p. 128

50 Laband, *Kingdom in Crisis*, p. 91.

51 *JSA* III, p.317: Mpatshana; Maclean, *Ross*, pp. 113-14.

52 Webb & Wright, *Zulu King Speaks*, p. 31; *JSA* III, pp. 302-4: Mpatshana; Ngubane, *Body and Mind*, p. 121.

53 Fuze, *Black People*, p. 53.

54 *JSA* III, pp. 141, 305, 307: Mjobo and Mpatshana; *JSA* IV, pp. 147-8: Mtshayankomo; Zulu Tribal History Competition, file 25, KCM 64795: Vivian Maphanga, 'The Life of a Male from Birth to Marriage', p. 2. For the punishment of cowards, see *JSA* IV, pp. 88-9: Mtshapi.

55 Cope, *Izibongo*, p. 100.

56 Cope, *Izibongo*, p. 170.

57 Maclean, *Ross*, p. 111.

58 *JSA* I, pp. 56-7: Bazley.
59 Fuze, *Black People*, pp. 60, 63.
60 *JSA* IV, pp. 292-3: Ndukwana.
61 Webb and Wright, *Zulu King Speaks*, p. 97.
62 Fynn, *Diary*, p.139.
63 For the internal and external situation of the Zulu kingdom during the last two years of Shaka's reign, see Wright, 'Power and Conflict', pp. 338-71.
64 Cope, *Izibongo*, p. 180.
65 Cope, *Izibongo*, p. 94.
66 Webb and Wright, *Zulu King Speaks*, p. 8.
67 *JSA* I, p. 307: Lunguza
68 *JSA* III, p. 206: Mkebeni.

CHAPTER 5
1 Rycroft and Ngcobo, *Praises of Dingana*, p. 87.
2 See Bryant, *Olden Times*, pp. 666-7, 671; Fynn, *Diary*, pp. 157-8; Webb and Wright, *Zulu King Speaks*, p. 97; Samuelson, *Long, Long Ago*, p. 291; *JSA* III, p. 108: Mgidhlana; *JSA* IV, p. 360: Ndukwana.
3 Lugg, *Historic Natal*, p. 111.
4 Fuze, *Black People*, pp. 71-2; JSA II, p. 217: Mangati; Bryant, *Olden Times*, p. 667.
5 For the situation following Shaka's assassination, see Wright, 'Power and Conflict', pp. 371-80.
6 Bryant, *Olden Times*, pp. 668-9; Fynn, Diary, pp. 158-60.
7 Fuze, *Black People*, p. 72.
8 Rycroft and Ngcobo, *Praises of Dingane*, p. 107.
9 *JSA* I, p. 6: Baleka. See also *JSA* I, 195-6: Jantshi; Fynn, *Diary*, pp. 160; Bryant, *Olden Times*, pp. 669-70.
10 *JSA* I, p. 6: Baleka.
11 Fynn, *Diary*, 161-2; Webb and Wright, *Zulu King Speaks*, p. 8.
12 Webb and Wright, *Zulu King Speaks*, pp. 97-8; *JSA* IV, pp. 291-2: Ndukwana.
13 Fynn, *Diary*, p. 174; *JSA* I, p. 196:

Jantshi; *JSA* II, p. 49: Madikane.
14 *JSA* I, p. 196: Jantshi.
15 Fuze, *Black People*, p. 72; Webb and Wright, *Zulu King Speaks*, p. 10; Bryant, *Olden Times*, p. 670; *JSA* IV, p. 346: Ndukwana.
16 Bird, *Annals*, I, pp. 282-3: Capt. Gardiner, February 1835; Fynn, *Diary*, p. 241.
17 Webb and Wright, *Zulu King Speaks*, p. 10
18 Fuze, *Black People*, pp. 73-4; *JSA* II, p. 272: Maziyana; Wright, 'Power and Conflict', pp. 371-80.
19 Bird, *Annals*, I, p. 289: Capt. Gardiner, February 1835.
20 Fuze, *Black People*, p. 84.
21 See Fynn, *Diary*, pp. 257-9.
22 Fynn, *Diary*, p. 209.
23 Bryant, *Olden Times*, pp. 670-1; Fynn, *Diary*, pp. 162-3; Webb and Wright, *Zulu King Speaks*, p. 10; Fuze, *Black People*, pp. 72-3; *JSA* I, p. 194: Jantshi.
24 Cope, *Izibongo*, p. 186.
25 *JSA* I, pp. 329-30: Lunguza; Bryant, *Olden Times*, p. 670.
26 *JSA* I, p. 196: Jantshi.
27 *JSA* I, p. 29: Baleni.
28 *JSA* I, pp. 314-15: Lunguza.
29 Rycroft and Ngcobo, *Praises of Dingana*, p. 75.

CHAPTER 6
1 Rycroft and Ngcobo, *Praises of Dingana*, p. 95.
2 Bryant, *Olden Times*, pp. 674-5; Rycroft and Ngcobo, *Praises of Dingana*, p. 1.
3 Bird, *Annals*, I p. 289: Gardiner in February 1835; Gibson, *Story of the Zulus*, p. 51.
4 Rycroft and Ngcobo, *Praises of Dingana*, p. 83.
5 *JSA* I, pp. 318, 321: Lunguza.
6 Rycroft and Ngcobo, *Praises of Dingana*, pp. 75, 89, 91.
7 Brownlee, *Reminiscences of Kaffir Life*, pp. 100-1. See also the typical

comment of Barrett, *Fifteen Years among the Zulu and Boers*, p. 20: 'A Zulu chief is of all men the most despotic; having absolute power over any of his subjects.'

8 Webb & Wright, *Zulu King Speaks*, p. 67.

9 The following discussion is based on what is arguably the best literature in this field: Gluckman, 'Kingdom of the Zulu', pp. 28-55; Lugg, *Life under a Zulu Shield*, pp. 31-6; Guy, *Zulu Kingdom*, pp. 21-40; Colenbrander, 'The Zulu Political Economy on the Eve of the War' in Duminy and Ballard, *New Perspectives*, pp. 78-97; Guy, 'Production and Exchange in the Zulu Kingdom' and J. Wright, 'Control of Women's Labour in the Zulu Kingdom' in Peires, *Before and After Shaka*, pp. 33-48 and 82-99; Hammond-Tooke, *Roots of Black South Africa*, pp. 65-87, passim.

10 Grout, *Zulu-land*, p. 118; Lucas, *The Zulus*, p. 111; Moodie, *John Dunn*, pp. 56-7; Webb and Wright, *Zulu King Speaks*, p. 78; *JSA* IV, pp. 311-12, 315: Ndukwana.

11 For a full description of the *ukusisa* practice, see *JSA* IV, pp. 269-70: Ndukwana. See also Webb and Wright, *Zulu King Speaks*, p. 90.

12 It seems probable that some men were dependent on the monarchy in that it was through service in the *amabutho* that poorer individuals were able to acquire some of the cattle necessary to marry and to set themselves up as young heads of households.

13 Webb and Wright, *Zulu King Speaks*, pp. 80-83, 93; Mael, 'Problem of Political Integration', pp. 130-38; Cope, 'Political Power', pp. 19-20, 25. It was common in Africa for kings to consult with a council of elders (Mair, *African Kingdoms*, p. 106). Note the apposite comparison Bishop Colenso drew

between King John constrained by his barons and Cetshwayo by his great chiefs (Colenso Collection 2: Letter Book, 1872-82, p. 236: Colenso to Frere, 14 January 1879).

14 Bryant, *Zulu People*, pp. 458-9.

15 Mair, *African Kingdoms*, p. 73.

16 See Webb and Wright, *Zulu King Speaks*, pp. 80-82, 84, 94; *JSA* I, p. 315: Lunguza; and *JSA* II, pp. 257-8: Mayinga.

17 Webb and Wright, *Zulu King Speaks*, p. 99.

18 *JSA* IV, pp. 357-9: Ndukwana; Samuelson, *Long, Long Ago*, pp. 394-5.

19 Webb and Wright, *Zulu King Speaks*, pp. 80-2, 90-1.

20 Webb and Wright, *Zulu King Speaks*, p. 93.

21 Lugg, *Life under a Zulu Shield*, pp. 32-3.

22 *JSA* IV, pp. 300-1: Ndukwana; Bryant, *Zulu People*, p. 461.

23 *JSA* IV, pp. 318, 328: Ndukwana; *JSA* III, p. 257: Mmemi; p.179: Mkando.

24 Webb and Wright, *Zulu King Speaks*, pp. 82-4.

25 Webb and Wright, *Zulu King Speaks*, pp. 74, 82.

26 Owen, *Diary*, pp. 45, 93.

27 *JSA* II, p. 248: Mayinga.

28 Maclean, *Ross*, pp. 129-30.

29 Maclean, *Ross*, pp. 112, 136.

30 Owen, *Diary*, p. 180.

31 See Dlamini, *Two Kings*, pp. 29, 34-5, 41; *JSA* I, pp. 40-1: Baleni; *JSA* II, pp. 211: Ndhlovu; pp. 281-2, 373: Ndukwana; Bryant, *Zulu People*, pp. 475-8; Lugg, *Historic Natal*, 112-14.

32 For the *umKhosi*, see Bryant, *Zulu People*, pp. 509-23; Krige, *Social System*, pp. 247-60; KCM 64805, File 24: Zulu Tribal History Competition, 1950: M. Mhlongo, 'The Feast of the First Fruits'; Webb and Wright, *Zulu King Speaks*, pp. 84-5, 95-6; Fuze, *Black People*, pp. 90-2;

Dlamini, *Two Kings*, pp. 36-43.

33 Dlamini, *Two Kings*, p. 28.

34 A. Koopman, 'The Place of the Elephants?' in Laband and Haswell, *Pietermaritzburg*, p. 44.

35 Much of this information is synthesised in Stuart Collection 83: J. Stuart (E.R. Dahle (tr.)), *uKulumetule* (1925), chapters 2-4; and Natal Provincial Museum Service, *uMgungundlovu* (n.d), pp. 2-5, 8-9. See also, Owen, *Diary*, pp. 43, 56, 60-1, 88-9; Bird, *Annals*, I, pp. 283-95: Captain Gardiner's first interview with Dingane, February 1835. See also, Bryant, *Zulu People*, pp. 472-5, 478-84 and Krige, *Social System*, pp. 233-41.

36 See John Dunn's description and discussion of the causes of a fire at one of Cetshwayo's *amakhanda* in 1872 (Moodie, *John Dunn*, pp. 46-9.

37 Delegorgue, *Travels*, pp. 86-7.

38 Bird, *Annals*, I, pp. 292-4: Capt. Gardiner, February 1835.

39 Delegorgue, *Travels*, pp. 91-3. See also Maclean, *Ross*, pp. 127-8, who saw a very similar dance performed before Shaka.

CHAPTER 7

1 Rycroft and Ngcobo, *Praises of Dingana*, pp. 7, 202-3; *JSA* IV, p. 107: Mtshayankomo.

2 *JSA* IV, p. 316: Ndukwana.

3 The following account of Dingane's foreign relations is based upon P. Colenbrander, 'The Zulu Kingdom, 1828-79' in Duminy and Guest, *Natal and Zululand*, pp. 86-9; Ballard, 'Traders, Trekkers and Colonists', pp. 118-21; Wright, 'Power and Conflict', pp. 371-5; Okoye, 'Dingane', pp. 223-34; and L. Thompson, 'Co-operation and Conflict: The Zulu Kingdom and Natal' in Wilson and Thompson, *Oxford History*, I, pp. 351-4.

4 Bryant, *Olden Times*, pp. 392-8.

5 Jones, *Swaziland*, p. xix; Bryant, *Olden Times*, pp. 321-3.

6 Bryant, *Olden Times*, pp. 398-9.

7 Maclean, *Ross*, pp. 71-3, 170; Fynn, *Diary*, pp. 179-89, 196-8, 208.

8 Fuze, *Black People*, p. 74.

9 Owen, *Diary*, p. 51.

10 Bryant, *Olden Times*, pp. 675-7; Lugg, *Historic Natal*, pp. 21-2; N. Etherington, 'Christianity and African Society in Nineteenth-century Natal' in Duminy and Guest, *Natal and Zululand*, pp. 275-7.

11 Bird, *Annals*, I, pp. 377-8: William Wood.

12 For the Great Trek, see T.R.H. Davenport, 'The Consolidation of a New Society: The Cape Colony' in Wilson and Thompson, *Oxford History*, I, pp. 292, 310, 355-9; J.T. du Bruyn, 'The Great Trek' in Cameron and Spies, *Illustrated History*, pp. 127-32.

13 I. Pols, 'The Voortrekker Museum' in Laband and Haswell, *Pietermaritzburg*, pp. 163-4.

14 Cope, *Izibongo*, p. 132.

15 See Cobbing, 'Evolution of Ndebele Amabutho', pp. 607-31.

16 For the defeat of the Ndebele by the Boers, see L. Thompson, 'Co-operation and Conflict: The High Veld' in Wilson and Thompson, *Oxford History*, I, pp. 403-5, 411-12; Summers and Pagden, *The Warriors*, pp. 57-65; R. Edgecombe, 'The Mfecane or Difaqane' in Cameron and Spies, *Illustrated History*, pp. 124-6; Smail, *Monuments and Trails*, pp. 4-8. Bulawayo became the centre of a new kingdom which the Ndebele carved out at the expense of the Shona people, and which survived under Lobengula, Mzilikazi's successor, until destroyed by the forces of the British South Africa Company in 1893.

17 Bird, *Annals*, I, pp. 359-60: Retief to Dingaan, 19 October 1837.

18 Pols, 'Voortrekker Museum', p. 164.

19 Delegorgue, *Travels*, p. 87.

20 See Owen, *Diary*, pp. 61-8; Bird, *Annals*, I, pp. 364-5: letter from Retief in *Graham's Town Journal*, 18 November 1837.

21 Owen, *Diary*, p. 175: Hulley.

22 Bird, *Annals*, I, pp. 361-2: Dingaan to Retief (witnessed by Owen), 8 November 1837.

23 Owen, *Diary*, pp. 167-8: Revd D. Ellenberger.

24 Bird, *Annals*, I, p. 362: Retief to Dingaan, 8 November 1837.

25 Owen, *Diary*, pp. 61, 64.

26 Owen, *Diary*, p. 158: Joseph Kirkman's story.

27 Owen, *Diary*, p. 89.

28 Delegorgue, *Travels*, p. 174.

29 Bird, *Annals*, I, pp. 368-9: D.P. Bezuidenhout's narrative; Owen, *Diary*, pp. 100, 168-70: Revd D. Ellenberger's account.

30 Bird, *Annals*, I, pp. 401-2.

31 Owen, *Diary*, p. 93.

32 Owen *Diary*, pp. 100-1.

33 Owen, *Diary*, p. 105.

34 Owen, *Diary*, p. 108.

35 Owen, *Diary*, pp. 175-6: Hulley.

36 For accounts of the death of Retief, see Owen, *Diary*, pp. 104-12, 116-17, 157-9, 169, 176-9; Bird, *Annals*, I, pp. 379-81: William Wood.

37 *JSA* III, p. 258: Mmemi.

38 Bird, *Annals*, I, p. 366: cession to the Boers by Dingaan, 4 February 1838.

39 Gibson, *Story of the Zulus*, p. 64. On enquiry at the beginning of this century, Gibson discovered that Mnwana kaCelo was a 'private servant', and that Magonondo kaKondlo was a 'medicine man in attendance'. He could not trace Juliwane.

40 Dlamini, *Two Kings*, p. 13.

41 *JSA* III, pp. 205-6: Mkebeni; *JSA* IV, p. 112: Mtshayankomo; pp. 276, 347: Ndukwana; Fuze, *Black People*, p.170, note 5.

42 *JSA* I, pp. 318-19: Lunguza.

43 *JSA* III: pp. 257-8: Mmemi.

44 Bird, *Annals*, I, p. 380: William Wood.

45 The arms were piled beneath two euphorbia trees that stood near the main gate, one of which marked the burial place of Nkosinkhulu, a distant ancestor of Dingane (Gibson, *Story of the Zulus*, p. 64).

46 Dlamini, *Two Kings*, p. 13.

47 *JSA* I, pp. 319-20: Lunguza.

48 Zulu testimony has it that one Boer broke away and ran for his life, and was not overtaken and killed until he reached the Thala mountain 24 kilometres away in the direction of the Boer encampments (Gibson, *Story of the Zulus*, p. 65).

49 Bird, *Annals*, I, p. 381: William Wood.

50 *JSA* I, p. 312: Lunguza.

51 Owen, *Diary*, p. 176: Hulley.

52 Owen, *Diary*, pp. 108, 112, 117.

53 Owen, *Diary*, p. 177: Hulley.

CHAPTER 8

1 Bird, *Annals*, I, p. 381: William Wood.

2 For a general account of events between February 1838 and January 1839, see Walker, *Great Trek*, pp.166-89; Brookes and Webb, *History of Natal*, pp. 31-5; Thompson, 'Co-operation and Conflict' in Wilson and Thompson, *Oxford History*, I, pp. 362-3. For the Weenen 'massacre', see Bird, *Annals*, I, pp. 233, 241-3, 351, 370-74, 403-8, 463-4; Smail, *Land of the Zulu Kings*, pp. 56-60; Nathan, *The Voortrekkers*, pp. 216-28.

3 Bird, *Annals*, I, p. 413: J. Boshof, 31 July 1838.

4 For the *Vlugkommando* see Owen, *Diary*, pp. 134-7; Bird, *Annals*, I, pp. 233-4: W.J. Pretorius; p. 243: C. Celliers; p. 374: D.P. Bezuidenhout; pp. 408-12: J. Boshof; Fuze, *Black*

People, p. 75; *JSA* II, p. 92:
Magidigidi; Nathan, *The Voortrekkers*,
pp. 230-6; Smail, *Land of the Zulu
Kings*, p. 61.

5 For the battle of the Thukela and the
sack of Port Natal, see Owen, *Diary*,
pp. 126-34, 137-8; Holden, *Colony of
Natal*, pp. 63- 74; Bird, *Annals*, I,
pp. 383-7: William Wood; pp. 551-2:
D.C. Toohey; Bryant, *Olden Times*,
p. 495; Fuze, *Black People*, pp. 76-7;
JSA II, p. 272: Maziyana; *JSA* III,
p. 223: Mkotana; Smail, *Land of the
Zulu Kings*, pp. 62-3.

6 Fuze, *Black People*, p. 76.

7 For the battle of Veglaer, see *JSA* I,
p. 77: Christian Cane; p. 322:
Lunguza; Bird, *Annals*, I, pp. 234:
W.J. Pretorius; Lugg, *Historic Natal*
p. 69; Nathan, *The Voortrekkers*,
pp. 241-5; Smail, *Land of the Zulu
Kings*, p. 64.

8 For the most recent account of Blood
River, see G. Chadwick, 'Blood River'
in Van Lingen, *Battlefields*, pp. 18-23.
See also Bird, *Annals*, I, p. 234: W.J.
Pretorius; pp. 245-7: C. Celliers; pp.
374-5: D.P. Bezuidenhout; pp. 438-
50: Journal of the expedition against
Dingaan, November-December
1838; pp. 453-5: despatch by A.
Pretorius, 22 December 1838;
Delegorgue, *Travels*, pp. 109-10;
Fuze, *Black People*, pp. 77-8; *JSA* I,
pp. 312-13, 320: Lunguza; *JSA* II,
p. 81: Magidi; Nathan, *The
Voortrekkers*, pp. 252-60.

9 Bird, *Annals*, I, p. 246: C. Celliers.

10 For the sack of uMgungundlovu and
the discovery of the bones of Retief's
party, see Bird, *Annals*, I, p. 234: W.J.
Pretorius; pp. 247-8: C. Celliers;
p. 370, 375: D.P. Bezuidenhout;
pp. 450-1: Journal of the Expedition
against Dingaan; Nathan, *The
Voortrekkers*, pp. 260-3.

11 Bird, *Annals* I, pp. 13-15, 111 (note
8).

12 Dlamini, *Two Kings*, pp. 13-15, 111

(note 8).

13 For the battle at the White Mfolozi,
see Bird, *Annals*, I, pp. 235-6: W.J.
Pretorius; pp. 248-9: C. Celliers;
pp. 451-2: Journal of the Expedition
against Dingaan; pp. 456-7: letter by
A. Pretorius, 9 January 1839;
p. 492: Maj. Charters to Sir G.
Napier, 5 January 1839; Gibson,
Story of the Zulus, pp. 72-6; Bryant,
Olden Times, p. 493; Samuelson,
Long, Long Ago, pp. 215-16:
Autobiography of Cetywayo; Fuze,
Black People, pp. 78-9; *JSA* III,
p. 129: Mini; *JSA* IV, p. 177:
Ndabambi; p. 276: Ndukwana;
Nathan, *The Voortrekkers*, pp. 263-5;
Smail, *Land of the Zulu Kings*, p.71.

CHAPTER 9

1 For Dingane's withdrawal
northwards, see Gibson, *Story of the
Zulus*, pp. 76-7.

2 R. Haswell, 'Pieter Mauritz Burg: The
Genesis of a Voortrekker
Hoofdplaats', in Laband and Haswell,
Pietermaritzburg, pp. 24-7.

3 Bird, *Annals*, I, p. 516: Jervis to
Napier, 30 March 1839.

4 Bird, *Annals*, I, p. 496: Maj. Charters
to the Boers.

5 Lugg, *Historic Natal*, p. 35.

6 Bird, *Annals*, I, pp. 497-8: Shepstone
to Charters, 7 February 1839.

7 Bird, *Annals*, I, pp. 516-19: Jervis to
Napier, 30 March 1839; pp. 523-4:
Napier to Glenelg, 15 April 1839.

8 Bird, *Annals*, I, p. 575: 'Journal of
Commando', 10 February 1846.

9 *JSA* IV, p. 276: Ndukwana.

10 *JSA* II, pp. 91-2: Magidigidi; *JSA* IV,
pp. 276-7, 345: Ndukwana; Jones,
Swaziland, p. xx; Bonner, *Swazi State*,
pp. 42-4.

11 See Kennedy, 'Mpande', pp. 24-30.

12 *JSA* IV, pp. 314, 321: Ndukwana.

13 For a comprehensive analysis of
Mpande's flight, see Colenbrander,
'Zulu Kingdom', pp. 93-6.

14 *JSA* I, p. 197: Jantshi; *JSA* II, pp. 200-1: Mangati; *JSA* IV, p. 67: Mtshapi.
15 Bird, *Annals*, I, p. 537: minutes of the Volksraad, 15 October 1839.
16 *JSA* IV, p. 140: Mtshayankomo: his father Magolwana's praises of Mpande.
17 Fuze, *Black People*, pp. 92-3.
18 See Delegorgue, *Travels*, pp. 82-95 for an account of Mpande in Natal.
19 *JSA* I, p. 109: Dinya; Webb and Wright, *Zulu King Speaks*, p. 13.
20 Delegorgue, *Travels*, p. 96.
21 Bird, *Annals*, I, pp. 538-40: minutes of the Volksraad, 15 October 1839.
22 For the Boer deputation to Mpande, see Bird, *Annals* I, pp. 540-4: Report of the Landdrost of Tugela, October 1839.
23 Delegorgue, *Travels*, pp. 85, 87-8.
24 *JSA* IV, p. 74: Mtshapi; Gibson, *Story of the Zulus*, p. 111.
25 *JSA* I, pp. 46-7: Baleni.
26 *JSA* II, p. 237: Maquza.
27 *JSA* I, p. 197: Jantshi.
28 *JSA* IV, p. 191: Ndabazezwe.
29 Delegorgue, *Travels*, p. 95.
30 Bird, *Annals*, I, pp. 600-2: Jervis to Napier, 8 December 1839.
31 Delegorgue, *Travels*, pp. 98-9; Brookes and Webb, *History of Natal*, p. 35.
32 For the 1840 campaign, see Delegorgue, *Travels*, pp. 101-27; Bird, *Annals*, I, pp. 576-99: Journal of the Commando against Dingaan; Gibson, *Story of the Zulus*, pp. 85-91.
33 For the battle of the Magongqo hills, see Delegorgue, *Travels*, pp. 109, 115, 116; Bird, *Annals*, I, pp. 585, 587; *JSA* II, p. 90: Magidigidi; *JSA* IV, p. 70: Mtshapi; Fuze, *Black People*, p. 82; Gibson, *Story of the Zulus*, p. 86.
34 Stuart Collection 84: Stuart, *uKulumetule*, chap. 20, p. 2.
35 *JSA* III, p. 123: Mgundeni.
36 *JSA* III, p. 204: Mangati.
37 *JSA* III, p. 128: Mini.
38 *JSA* III, p. 123: Mgundeni.
39 Dlamini, *Two Kings*, p. 112, note 10.
40 *JSA* III, p. 201: Mangati.
41 *JSA* I, p. 172: Hoye.
42 Ibid.
43 Delegorgue, *Travels*, p. 114.
44 *JSA* II, p. 202: Mangati; Gibson, *Story of the Zulus*, p. 88.
45 Delegorgue, *Travels*, pp. 116-17.
46 Bird, *Annals*, I, p. 591.
47 *JSA* III, p. 123: Mgundeni.
48 For Dingane's death, see *JSA* III, pp. 260-1: Mmemi; *JSA* IV, p. 68: Mtshapi; Gibson, *Story of the Zulus*, p. 90; Bryant, *Olden Times*, pp. 325-6; Fuze, *Black People*, pp. 82-4; Lugg, *Historic Natal*; pp. 162-8; Bonner, *Swazi State*, p. 44
49 See Bird, *Annals*, I, pp. 375-6: D.P. Bezuidenhout.
50 Fuze, *Black People*, p. 83.
51 *JSA* IV, p. 68: Mtshapi; pp. 107-8: Mtshayankomo; p. 298: Ndukwana.

CHAPTER 10

1 For the Boer negotiations with Mpande, see Bird, *Annals*, pp. 591-6: Journal of the Commando against Dingaan, 9-14 February 1840.
2 Delegorgue, *Travels*, pp. 120-1.
3 Bird, *Annals*, I, p. 376: D.P. Bezuidenhout; p. 596: Journal of the Commando against Dingaan. Each Boer on the commando received at least 20 cattle as his share of the booty (Delegorgue, *Travels*, p. 127).
4 For recent accounts of Mpande's reign up to 1856, see Colenbrander, 'The Zulu Kingdom', pp. 97-103; Kennedy, 'Mpande', pp. 31-8. See also Gibson, *Story of the Zulus*, pp. 92-101, and J. Wright and R. Edgecome, 'Mpande kaSenzangakhona' in Saunders, *Black Leaders*, pp. 45-59.
5 For the transition of Natal from Boer republic to British colony, see Ballard, 'Traders, Trekkers and Colonists', pp. 122-8; Brookes and Webb,

History of Natal, pp. 35-75; L. Thompson, 'Zulu Kingdom and Natal' in Wilson and Thompson, Oxford History, I, pp. 364-81.

6 Fuze, Black People, p. 80.

7 Bird, Annals, II, p. 397: H. Cloete to J. Montagu, 14 June 1844.

8 For Cloete's visit to Mpande, see Bird, Annals II, pp. 290- 99: Cloete to Montagu, 28 October 1843.

9 Bird, Annals II, pp. 299-300: Articles of a Treaty, 5 October 1843.

10 For the Klip River Republic, see Walker, Great Trek, pp. 361- 2; Brookes and Webb, History of Natal, p. 63.

11 Webb and Wright, Zulu King Speaks, pp. 79-80, 93-4.

12 Journal of William Humphreys, p. 12: 13 September 1851.

13 For Masiphula, see JSA II, p. 208: Mangati; JSA IV, pp. 318, 350, 378: Ndukwana; Fuze, Black People, p. 92.

14 JSA III, pp. 180-1: Mkando.

15 Journal of William Humphreys, p. 12: 13 September 1851.

16 Webb and Wright, Zulu King Speaks, p. 14.

17 See Fuze, Black People, pp. 94-5.

18 Bird, Annals, II, pp. 198-9: Major Smith to Sir G. Napier, 26 June 1843; p. 316: Smith to Montagu, 14 November 1843; JSA II, p. 216: Mangati; Gibson, Story of the Zulus, pp. 98-9.

19 For Mpande's involvement in Swaziland, see Bonner, Swazi State, pp. 49-64, 93.

20 Bryant, Olden Times, p. 306; JSA II, p. 142: Mahungane and Nkomuza.

21 Webb and Wright, Zulu King Speaks, p. 15.

22 Webb and Wright, Zulu King Speaks, pp. 13-14.

23 Webb and Wright, Zulu King Speaks, p. 15.

24 For Schreuder, see Laband and Thompson, War Comes to Umvoti, p. 29.

25 Journal of William Humphreys, p. 9: 29 August 1851.

CHAPTER 11

1 Cope, Izibongo, p. 178.

2 JSA III,p. 223: Mkotana.

3 For the background to the civil war and Cetshwayo's early career, see Colenbrander, 'The Zulu Kingdom', pp. 103-6 and Laband and Wright, King Cetshwayo, pp. 1-4.

4 N. Etherington, 'Anglo-Zulu Relations 1856-1878' in Duminy and Ballard, New Perspectives, p. 15.

5 JSA II, p. 165: Makuza.

6 Webb and Wright, Zulu King Speaks, p. 13; JSA II, p. 165: Makuza; pp. 215-16: Mangati; Fuze, Black People, p. 61

7 JSA IV, p. 301: Ndukwana.

8 JSA II, p. 162: Makewu; p. 243: Maxibana; JSA IV, pp. 198-9, 218: Ndhlovu; Cope, Izibongo, p. 209; Fuze, Black People, pp. 60-1.

9 Fuze, Black People, p. 101.

10 JSA IV, p. 212: Ndhlovu.

11 JSA III, p. 291: Mpambukelwa; JSA IV, p. 359: Ndukwana.

12 JSA II, p. 241: Maxibana; Webb and Wright, Zulu King Speaks, p. 15.

13 Gibson, Story of the Zulus, p. 102.

14 Fuze, Black People, pp. 61, 98.

15 Samuelson, Long, Long Ago, p. 218.

16 Fuze, Black People, p. 101; JSA IV, p. 301: Ndukwana.

17 For Mnyamana, see Times of Natal, 27 August 1879: correspondent near Ulundi, 15 August 1879; Vijn, Cetshwayo's Dutchman, p. 162: Colenso's notes; JSA IV, p. 83: Mtshapi; pp. 300-1, 357, 377: Ndukwana; M.G. Buthelezi, 'Early History of the Buthelezi Clan' in Argyle and Preston-Whyte, Social System, pp. 34-5.

18 For Cetshwayo's appearance and personality, see Moodie, John Dunn, pp. 44-5; Samuelson, Long, Long Ago, pp. 228-31; Laband and

Wright, *Cetshwayo*, pp. 6-7; Cope, *Izibongo*, p. 210; Dlamini, *Two Kings*, pp. 46-7; Vijn, *Cetshwayo's Dutchman*, pp. 179-81: Colenso's notes; Fuze, *Black People*, p. 109; Mitford, *Zulu Country*, pp. 299-300, 303; Colenso and Durnford, *Zulu War*, p. 161; *Graphic*, 1 November 1879; Colenso, *Digest*, series 1, part 2, pp. 632-3.

19 *JSA* III, p. 203: Mkebeni.

20 *JSA* I, p. 36: Baleni.

21 *JSA* II, p. 244: Maxibana.

22 *JSA* II, p. 244: Maxibana.

23 *JSA* III, p. 232: Mkungu.

24 *JSA* III, p. 291: Mpambukelwa.

25 *JSA* III, p. 292: Mpambukelwa. For the mock hunt, see also *JSA* II, pp. 223-4: Mangoya; p. 241: Maxibana; *JSA* III, pp. 105-6: Mgidhlana; p. 232: Mkungu.

26 Webb and Wright, *Zulu King Speaks*, p. 16.

27 *JSA* IV, p. 380: Ndukwana.

28 *JSA* IV, p. 359: Ndukwana.

29 *JSA* II, p. 227: Manyonyana.

30 Cope, *Izibongo*, p. 216.

31 The fullest modern account of the battle of Ndondakusuka is by Torlage, 'War of the Children', pp. 2-5. See also, Webb and Wright, *Zulu King Speaks*, pp. 15-16; Moodie, *John Dunn*, pp. 3-8; *JSA* II, pp. 223-4: Mangoya; pp. 241-4: Maxibana; *JSA* III, pp. 292-4: Mpambukelwa; *JSA* IV, pp. 165-7: Mvayisa; C. Ballard, 'The Transfrontiersman', pp. 61-5; Kennedy, 'Fatal Diplomacy, pp. 125-30.

32 Webb and Wright, *Zulu King Speaks*, p. 16.

33 Cope, *Izibongo*, p. 222.

34 *JSA* IV, p. 301: Ndukwana.

35 *JSA* III, p. 293: Mpambukelwa.

36 *JSA* II, p. 190: Mandhlakazi.

37 *JSA* IV, p. 61: Mtshapi.

38 Moodie, *John Dunn*, p. 7.

39 Cope, *Izibongo*, p. 216

40 Cope, *Izibongo*, p. 218.

41 *JSA* I, p. 358: William Lyle.

42 Cope, *Izibongo*, p. 220

43 *JSA* III, p. 106: Mgidhlana.

44 *JSA* II, p. 243: Maxibana.

45 Samuelson, *Long, Long Ago*, p. 4.

CHAPTER 12

1 'Truly, you have set up a young tiger who will shortly tear & rend within yr territory unless means are taken to restore the power of Panda before it is too late' (SNA 1/1/2: D.C. Toohey to the Colonial Secretary, Natal, 13 November 1862).

2 Gibson, *Story of the Zulus*, p. 107; Kennedy, 'Fatal Diplomacy', p. 165.

3 For the period in Zululand between 1856 and 1872, see Laband and Wright, *Cetshwayo*, pp. 4-8; Colenbrander, 'Zulu Kingdom', pp. 106-7; Gibson, *Story of the Zulus*, pp. 105-11; Kennedy, 'Fatal Diplomacy', pp. 163-235.

4 *JSA* IV, pp. 106, 109-10, 117-18: Mtshayankomo; p. 301: Ndukwana; Moodie, *John Dunn*, p. 44; Fuze, *Black People*, pp. 93, 100; Gibson, *Story of the Zulus*, p. 106; Cope, 'Hamu', pp. 34-40, 45-7.

5 Quoted in Cope, 'Hamu', p. 46.

6 Kennedy, 'Fatal Diplomacy', pp. 165, 168.

7 *JSA* IV, pp. 86-7: Mtshapi.

8 *JSA* IV, p. 284: Ndukwana.

9 Kennedy, 'Fatal Diplomacy', pp.134, 139, 144-5, 166, 182. Sothondose settled on the south bank of the Mzinyathi, just downstream from Rorke's Drift, within hailing distance of Zululand.

10 For Bishop Colenso, see Etherington, 'Anglo-Zulu Relations', p. 16; Brookes and Webb, *History of Natal*, pp. 105-12; Guy, *Zulu Kingdom*, pp. 89-91. The best modern study of Colenso's life is Guy, *The Heretic*.

11 For the Utrecht District, see Laband and Thompson, *Buffalo Border*, pp. 2, 19-20; Kennedy, 'Fatal Diplomacy',

pp. 105-7,181.

12 For the Mthonga affair, see Kennedy, 'Fatal Diplomacy', pp.188-190; *JSA* II, pp. 189-90: Mandhlakazi; pp. 207-8: Mangati; *JSA* III, pp. 106, 110: Mgidhlana; Webb and Wright, *Zulu King Speaks*, pp. 16-17; Fuze, *Black People*, pp. 61, 99; Gibson, *Story of the Zulus*, pp. 105-6.

13 *JSA* II, p. 190: Mandhlakazi. See also, *JSA* III, p. 106: Mgidhlana.

14 Ibid.

15 *JSA* II, p. 207: Mangati.

16 Binns, *Last Zulu King*, pp. 47-8.

17 For the boundary dispute between the South African Republic and Zululand, see Webb and Wright, *Zulu King Speaks*, pp. xi-xiv.

18 Somtsewu, or Somtseu, is a hybrid word, derived from Xhosa, Zulu and Sesotho. It literally means 'father of the white man', that is, a pioneer.

19 For T. Shepstone and his policies, see Brookes and Webb, *History of Natal*, pp. 56-60; Gordon, *Shepstone*, chaps. 10-21, pp. 304-9; N. Etherington, 'The "Shepstone System" in the Colony of Natal and beyond the Borders' in Duminy and Guest, *Natal and Zululand*, pp. 170-181; J. Laband and P. Thompson, 'The Reduction of Zululand, 1878-1904', in Duminy and Guest, *op. cit.*, pp. 207-8; Thompson, 'Co-operation and Conflict' in Wilson and Thompson, *Oxford History*, I, pp. 375-7.

20 Quoted in Gordon, *Shepstone*, pp. 304-5.

21 Quoted in Brookes and Webb, *History of Natal*, p. 57.

22 Lugg, *Historic Natal*, p. 37: Shepstone's praises.

23 Etherington, 'Anglo-Zulu Relations', p. 17.

24 For Shepstone's visit to Mpande in 1861, see Kennedy, 'Fatal Diplomacy', pp. 190-1, 201-2; Etherington, 'Anglo-Zulu Relations',

pp. 18-20, 45; *JSA* II, pp. 165-6: Makuza; Fuze, *Black People*, pp. 102-4; Binns, *Last Zulu King*, pp. 48-51; Gordon, *Shepstone*, pp. 240-2.

25 Fuze, *Black People*, p. 103.

26 Cope, *Izibongo*, p. 196.

27 Haggard, *Cetywayo*, p. 10.

28 Kennedy, 'Fatal Diplomacy', pp. 226-8; Webb and Wright, *Zulu King Speaks*, p. 17.

29 Etherington, 'Anglo-Zulu Relations', pp. 16-17.

30 See Ballard, 'The Transfrontiersman', chapter 3, *passim*.

31 Moodie, *John Dunn*, p. 12.

32 Dlamini, *Two Kings*, pp. 42-3.

33 Moodie, *John Dunn*, p. 33.

34 Moodie, *John Dunn*, p. 28.

35 *JSA* I, p. 32: Baleni; p. 199: Jantshi; *JSA*, IV, p. 191: Ndabazezwe; p. 293: Ndukwana.

36 *JSA* I, p. 171: Hoye.

37 *JSA* III, pp. 200-2: Mkebeni.

38 Gibson, *Story of the Zulus*, p. 108.

39 For the 'invasion scare' of 1861, see Kennedy, 'Fatal Diplomacy', pp. 202-6, 212-13.

40 Kennedy, 'Fatal Diplomacy', p. 218.

CHAPTER 13

1 Kennedy, 'Fatal Diplomacy', p. 268, note 5.

2 For Mpande's death and burial, see Dlamini, *Two Kings*, pp. 26-7, 114-15: notes 33-6; Webb and Wright, *Zulu King Speaks*, pp. 17-18, 97; *JSA* I, pp. 42-4: Baleni; *JSA* III, p. 108-9: Mgidhlana; p. 261: Mmemi; *JSA* IV, pp. 290-1, 360: Ndukwana; p.121, 125: Mtshayankomo; Binns, *Last Zulu King*, pp. 54-7; Samuelson, *Long, Long Ago*, pp. 291-2, 369; Bryant, *Zulu People*, pp. 468, 470, 526-9; Krige, *Social System*, pp. 171-4.

3 Colenso, *Digest*, series 1, part 2, p. 672.

4 Etherington, 'Anglo-Zulu Relations', pp. 26-7.

5 Coghlan, 'Natal Volunteer Movement', pp. 65-6.

6 Cetshwayo's first, or real, coronation is described in detail in Moodie, *John Dunn*, pp. 33-43, 50; Gibson, *Story of the Zulus*, pp. 122-4, 129-30; and Dlamini, *Two Kings*, pp. 28-31.

7 See Laband, *Kingdom in Crisis*, p. 30; Fuze, *Black People*, p. 117.

8 *JSA* IV, pp. 344-5: Ndukwana.

9 *JSA* III, p. 312: Mpatshana.

10 Moodie, *John Dunn*, p. 55.

11 *JSA* IV, p. 301: Ndukwana.

12 Dlamini, *Two Kings*, pp. 60-2. Dlamini had been let into the secret of the poisoning by the women who had performed the deed. She recalled that John Dunn had provided Cetshwayo with the poison, but the truth of this allegation cannot be established. See also *JSA* IV, p. 127: Mtshayankomo.

13 For the coronation by Shepstone, see *BPP* (C. 1342), enc. in no. 1: Report of the Expedition sent by the Government of Natal to instal Cetywayo as King of the Zulus, August 1873 by T. Shepstone; Cope, 'Political Power', pp 11-31; Etherington, 'Anglo-Zulu Relations', pp. 21-37; Binns, *Last Zulu King*, pp. 59-75.

14 *JSA* IV, p. 127: Mtshayankomo.

15 *JSA* IV, p. 341: Ndukwana.

16 E. Unterhalter, 'Confronting Imperialism' in Duminy and Ballard, *New Perspectives*, p. 99; *JSA* IV, pp. 341, 357: Ndukwana; Colenso, *Digest*, series 1, part 2, p. 632; Mitford, *Zulu Country*, p. 149; *Natal Witness*, 6 September 1879.

CHAPTER 14

1 Cope, *Izibongo*, p. 226.

2 For descriptions of oNdini, see Rawlinson, 'Ondini', *passim*; Dlamini, *Two Kings*, pp. 31-4, 117-18, notes 46-9, 52.

3 *JSA* IV, p. 338: Ndukwana.

4 Webb and Wright, *Zulu King Speaks*, pp. 98-9; *JSA* III, pp. 151-2: Mkando.

5 *Natal Witness*, 22 July 1879: Special correspondent at Port Durnford, 5 July 1879; WO 32/7772: Maj. Barrow to Maj.-Gen. Crealock, 5, 8 July 1879.

6 *JSA* III, p. 328: Mpatshana; Dlamini, *Two Kings*, p. 54.

7 *JSA* III, pp. 43-6.

8 *JSA* III, pp. 60-6, 118: note 51.

9 *JSA* IV, p. 117: Mtshayankomo.

10 See *JSA* IV, pp. 78-9: Mtshapi; pp.132-5: Mtshayankomo; pp. 272-5, 333-4, 349-52: Ndukwana; Gibson, *Story of the Zulus*, pp. 133-5; Cope, 'Political Power', pp. 21-3; Laband and Wright, *King Cetshwayo*, pp. 10-11.

11 Webb and Wright, *Zulu King Speaks*, p. 72.

12 See Krige, *Social System*, pp. 406-7.

13 *JSA* IV, pp. 299-300, 338: Ndukwana.

14 *JSA* IV, p. 132: Mtshayankomo.

15 For the uThulwana-iNgobamakhosi clash, see SNA 1/4/2, confidential no. 9: H. Fynn to Secretary for Native Affairs, 9 January 1878; *Times of Natal*, 18 January 1878: Biggarsberg correspondent, 14 January 1878; *Natal Witness*, 26 January 1878: *Mercury* correspondent, 14 January 1878; *Natal Witness*, 21 March 1878: *Mercury* correspondent, 25 February 1878; *JSA* I, pp. 31-2: Baleni; *JSA* IV, pp. 183-5: Ndabazezwe; pp. 294-5: Ndukwana; Moodie, *John Dunn*, pp. 61-7; Fuze, *Black People*, pp. 105-7; Gibson, *Story of the Zulus*, pp. 133-5.

16 *JSA* IV, p. 295: Ndukwana.

17 Mitford, *Zulu Country*, p. 211.

18 *Natal Witness*, 21 March 1878: *Natal Mercury* correspondent, 25 February 1878.

19 Webb and Wright, *Zulu King Speaks*, p. 92; Etherington, 'Anglo-Zulu Relations', pp. 28-30, 37-8.

20 Laband and Wright, *Cetshwayo*, p. 11; Moodie, *John Dunn*, pp. 49, 53.

21 Moodie, *John Dunn*, pp. 56-8; Gibson, *Story of the Zulus*, pp. 129-30.

22 Moodie, *John Dunn*, pp. 27-8, 58; Vijn, *Cetshwayo's Dutchman*, pp. 57-8; Ballard, *John Dunn*, pp. 85-6.

23 Guy, 'Note on Firearms', p. 560; Harries, 'Ingwavuma', p. 16, note 71.

24 *Natal Witness*, 22 August 1878: Letter from 'Rufus'. The Zulu had specific names for the various types of guns. See *JSA* I, p. 63: Bikwayo; Strachan, *European Armies*, pp. 76-7; Guy, 'Note on Firearms', p. 55; Ballard, *John Dunn*, pp. 116-17; Harries, 'Ingwavuma', p. 15.

25 *Natal Colonist*, 7 December 1877: Letter from 'Rifleman'; *Natal Witness*, 7 November 1878: Biggarsberg correspondent, 2 November 1878.

26 *Natal Mercury*, 20 December 1877: Letter from 'One who has something to lose in case of an outbreak'.

27 The merchants were the firms of Lipperts & Deutzelman, A. Bennet, Beningfield & Sons, Randles Bros. and Hudson & A. Fass.

28 CO 179/131, p. 466: R.E.D. Morier to Lord Salisbury, 16 February 1879; Harris, 'Ingwavuma', p. 16; Ballard, *John Dunn*, p. 118.

29 Magwaza, 'Visit to King Ketshwayo', p. 431.

30 SNA 1/6/11, no. 11: J.L. Knight to H.F. Fynn, 18 November 1878; Vijn, *Cetshwayo's Dutchman*, pp. 10-11; Ludlow, *Zululand and Cetywayo*, p. 133.

31 In August 1879 the British found 1 100 lbs of powder stored in 178 barrels in the cave.

32 WO 147/7: Wolseley's Journal, 18 August 1879; *Natal Witness*, 22 July 1879: Correspondent at Port Durnford, 7 July 1879; Norris-Newman, *In Zululand*, p. 237.

33 *Natal Colonist*, 21 January 1879: Correspondent from Zulu side of the Tugela Drift, 14 February 1879.

34 *Times of Natal*, 7 March 1879: Notes by 'a gentleman well acquainted with the Zulus'.

35 Blair Brown, 'Surgical Notes', p. 6.

36 Guy, 'Note on Firearms', pp. 562-3.

37 For a recent discussion on the Disputed Territory, see J. Laband, 'Mbilini', in Laband and Thompson, *Kingdom and Colony*, pp. 183-5.

38 Webb and Wright, *Zulu King Speaks*, p. 25; Moodie, *John Dunn*, pp. 58-9; Cope, 'Political Power', pp. 23-4.

39 *JSA* IV, p. 316: Ndukwana.

CHAPTER 15

1 *Natal Witness*, 2 August 1878.

2 See Atmore and Marks, 'Imperial Factor', pp. 121-7.

3 See especially Etherington, 'Labour Supply', pp. 236-45.

4 See Guy, *Zulu Kingdom*, especially pp. 41-51.

5 Cope, 'Civilization and Proletarianization', p. 24.

6 Goodfellow, *Confederation*, pp. 208-9.

7 W.R. Guest, 'The War, Natal and Confederation' in Duminy and Ballard, *New Perspectives*, p. 67.

8 See Benyon, *Proconsul and Paramountcy*, pp. 144-8.

9 For Frere's career, see Mason, *The Men Who Ruled India*, pp. 186-7, 189-93.

10 For Frere and the civilising influence of Christian rule, see Emery, 'Geography and Imperialism', pp. 346-8.

11 Benyon, *Proconsul and Paramountcy*, pp. 153, 161-2.

12 See *BPP* (C. 2222), enc. 1 in no. 42: Memorandum by Frere, 6 December 1878, in which he sets out a comprehensive list of his official reasons for moving against Zululand.

13 See *BPP* (C. 2252), no. 4: Frere to Hicks Beach, 30 January 1879, enclosing depositions by missionaries recounting Zulu

violence against them.

14 CO 879/14: *African Confidential Print* 166, p. 5: Notes by Frere, 3 February 1879.

15 CO 879/14: *African Confidential Print* 162, p. 515: Frere to Hicks Beach, 28 October 1878.

16 See, for example, CO 879/14: *African Confidential Print* 164: Memorandum on the Zulu Question by T. Shepstone, n.d. 1878.

17 'Do I come to Natal and dictate to him [the Lieutenant-Governor] about his laws?' (SNA 1/7/13, p. 17: Message from the King, 2 November 1876).

18 TS 68: Shepstone to Carnarvon, 11 December 1877.

19 Cope, 'Shepstone and Cetshwayo', pp. 226-34, 237-9.

20 Cope, 'Shepstone and Cetshwayo', pp. 242-5, 251, 261, 274, 282-96.

21 TS 68: Shepstone to Carnarvon, 11 December 1877; Shepstone to Frere, 18 December 1877.

22 H.C. Shepstone Papers 9: T. Shepstone to H. Shepstone, 21 August 1878.

23 TS 34: Frere to T. Shepstone, 26 October 1878; 2 November 1878; 29 November 1878.

24 A Boer deputation had already gone to London to plead unsuccessfuly for the restoration of the Transvaal's independence, and Frere knew that agitation could only increase. See BPP (C. 2144), no. 70: T. Shepstone to Hicks Beach, 9 May 1878.

25 War Office, *Narrative*, pp. 6-10.

26 See, for example, GH 600: Frere to Hicks Beach, 5 September 1878.

27 Laband and Thompson, *Buffalo Border*, pp. 30-1, Laband and Mathews, *Isandlwana*, p. 40; Gibson, *Story of the Zulus*, pp. 149-51.

28 See *Times of Natal*, 18 September 1878.

29 Laband and Thompson, *Umvoti*, p. 23.

30 TS 31: Thesiger to T. Shepstone, 21 July 1878; *BPP* (C. 2222), enc. in no. 46: Commodore Sullivan to Admiralty, 12 August 1878.

31 War Office, *Narrative*, pp. 12-15.

32 Bulwer Letters: Bulwer to Edward Bulwer, 8 December 1878.

33 Martineau, *Frere*, II, p. 253: Frere to Hicks Beach, 8 December 1878.

34 Martineau, *Frere*, II, p. 267: Frere to Hicks Beach, 5 November 1878.

35 TS 34: Frere to T. Shepstone, 7, 15 and 20 November 1878.

36 TS 34: Frere to T. Shepstone, 30 November 1878.

37 WC II/2/2: Chelmsford to Wood, 10 December 1878.

38 SNA 1/6/3, n.n.: Original draft of the ultimatum, signed by Bulwer on 4 December 1878.

39 Martineau, *Frere*, II, p. 264: Frere to Hicks Beach, 23 December 1878.

40 Cox, *Colenso*, pp. 496-7.

41 TS 35: Chelmsford to T. Shepstone, 13 December 1878.

42 *BPP* (C. 2220), no. 92A: Hicks Beach to Frere, 17 October 1878; CO 879/14: *African Confidential Print* 162, p. 478: Hicks Beach to Frere, 21 November 1878.

43 Webb, 'Lines of Power', pp. 31-6.

44 Martineau, *Frere*, II, pp. 259-60: Frere to Hicks Beach, 28 October 1878; p. 264: Frere to Hicks Beach, 23 December 1878; *BPP* (C. 2222), no. 54: Frere to Hicks Beach, 14 December 1878.

CHAPTER 16

1 SNA 1/4/2, confidential no. 91: Message from Cetshwayo to Fynney, 28 November 1878.

2 GH 1399, pp. 105-7: Message from Cetywayo to Bulwer, 30 August 1879.

3 *BPP* (C. 2260), sub-enc. 29 in 1 in no. 6: Reply of Bulwer to messages from Cetywayo, 28 September 1878.

4 *JSA* IV, pp. 306-7: Ndukwana.

5 GH 501, no. G67/a/79: Declaration of Mehlokazulu in the Pietermaritzburg gaol, 18 September 1879; Webb and Wright, *Zulu King Speaks*, p. 27.

6 *BPP* (C. 2260), sub-enc. 19 in enc. 1 in no. 6: Message to the Lieutenant-Governor of Natal from Cetywayo, King of the Zulus (signed by John Dunn), 20 September 1878.

7 From among the many reports, see SNA 1/4/2, no. 30: Statement of Ndabinjani, taken by Fynn, 4 November 1878.

8 SNA 1/4/2, no. 49: Report of ASNA on report of Border Agent, Lower Tugela, 28 September 1878.

9 *BPP* (C. 2260), sub-enc. 19 in enc. 2 in no. 6: Reply of Cetywayo to message from Lieutenant-Governor of October 1878 (translated by J.W. Shepstone), 29 October 1878.

10 *BPP* (C. 2367), enc. 5 in no. 39a: Minute by Bulwer, 28 October 1878; enc. 6 in no. 39a: Memorandum by Frere, 29 October 1878.

11 *BPP* (C. 2260), sub-enc. 23 in enc. 2 in no. 6: Message to Cetywayo from the Lieutenant-Governor of Natal (signed by J.W. Shepstone), 30 October 1878.

12 SNA 1/6/11, no. 8: John Dunn to ASNA, 28 October 1878.

13 *Natal Witness*, 19 September 1878: Lower Tugela correspondent.

14 See, among many similar reports, *Natal Colonist*, 7 December 1878.

15 *BPP* (C. 2308), enc. 2 in no. 7: Statement of Umlunge and Umlamula (taken by C.B.H. Mitchell), 6 December 1878.

16 GH 1399, pp. 237-41: Fynney to ASNA, 30 September 1878; *Natal Mercury*, 25 November 1878: Utrecht correspondent, 19 November 1878; Vijn, *Cetshwayo's Dutchman*, pp. 16-17.

17 SNA 1/6/11, no. 11: J. Knight to Fynn, 18 November 1878.

18 AU 25: Hamu to Landdrost of Utrecht (letter signed 'Home'), recd. 6 November 1878.

19 SNA 1/4/2, no. 31: Message from Cetywayo to Fynney, conveyed by Ruqu, Umlamula and Unyumbana, 7 November 1878.

20 SNA 1/4/2, no. 79 (confidential): Message from the chiefs of Zululand to Fynney, conveyed by Mavwanga and Ugodi, 13 November 1878.

21 AU 25: Gwegwana, Hamu's messenger, to Rudolph, 6 November 1878.

22 *BPP* (C. 2308), enc. 1 in no. 7: Message from Bulwer to Cetywayo, 16 November 1878.

23 *BPP* (C. 2308), enc. 2 in no. 7: Statement of Umlunge and Umlamula to Colonial Secretary, 6 December 1878.

24 CSO 1925, no. 4624/1878: Robson to Colonial Secretary, 5 December 1878.

25 Gordon, *Shepstone*, pp. 310-17.

26 For the ultimatum gathering, see *BPP* (C. 2308), enc. 2 in no. 7: Report by J.W. Shepstone, 19 December 1878; *BPP* (C. 2222), enc. 3 in no. 53: Brownlee to Frere, 12 December 1878; *BPP* (C.2222), enc. in no. 56: Brownlee to Littleton, 16 December 1878; Norbury, *Naval Brigade*, pp. 205-14.

27 Raum, 'Zulu Diplomacy', pp. 34-5, 41.

28 *BPP* (C. 2222), enc. 1 in no. 59: Dunn to SNA, 18 December 1878; Moodie, John Dunn, pp. 91-2.

29 CSO 1925, no. 250/1879: Fannin to Colonial Secretary, 12 January 1879; Webb and Wright, *Zulu King Speaks*, p. 28.

30 *BPP* (C. 2242), enc. 5 in no. 4: Schreuder to Littleton, 23 December 1878.

31 SNA 1/1/31, no. 66: Fynney to ASNA, 23 December 1878.

32 SNA 1/1/31, no. 69: Message from

Cetywayo to Fynney, 26 December 1879.

33 *BPP* (C. 2242), enc. 8 in no. 4: Dunn to SNA, 30 December 1878; Moodie, *John Dunn*, pp. 71-2, 74.

34 *JSA* I, p. 32: Baleni; *JSA* IV, p. 35l: Ndukwana.

35 CSO 1925, no. 5024/78: Robson to Colonial Secretary, 25 December 1878; *Natal Almanac, Directory and Register*, 1879, p.13: moon's phases.

36 CSO 1925, no. 4533/1878: Fannin to Colonial Secretary, 2 December 1878; SNA 1/3/31, no. 66: Fynney to ASNA, 23 December 1878.

37 CSO 1925, no. 343/79: Fannin to Colonial Secretary, 15 January 1879.

38 *BPP* (C. 2242), no. 5: Frere to Hicks Beach, 6 January 1879.

39 *BPP* (C. 2242), enc. 3 in no. 4: Capt. E. Woodgate to Col. R. Glyn, 19 December 1878. The new moon was on 23 December 1878.

40 Among the myriad of reports, see *BPP* (C. 22242), enc. 3 in no. 20: Report to Schreuder and Fannin (taken by G. Shepstone), 8 January 1879.

41 Ballard, *John Dunn*, pp. 114, 129-30, 133-4, 138.

42 Wood Papers, KCM 51088: Thesiger to Wood, 31 October 1878.

43 WC II/2/2: Chelmsford to Wood, 11 December 1878.

44 *Times of Natal*, 24 January 1879: Correspondent, 17 January 1879.

45 SNA 1/1/34, no. 85: Statement of Sihlahla to J. Shepstone, 3 June 1879.

46 Vijn, *Cetshwayo's Dutchman*, p. 15.

47 JSA IV, p. 209: Ndhlovu.

48 CSO 1925, no. 250/1879: Fannin to Colonial Secretary, 12 January 1879; *JSA* IV, p. 183: Ndabazezwe.

49 *JSA* III, pp. 296-7, 313: Mpatshana; *Natal Mercury*, 30 January 1879: Wounded *induna* captured after the battle of Nyezane.

50 *JSA* III, pp. 306-7: Mpatshana. See also, *JSA* IV, p. 89: Mtshapi; and p. 371: Ndukwana.

51 *JSA* IV, p. 77: Mtshapi; p. 146: Mtshayankomo.

52 CSO 1925, no. C6/1879: Fannin to Colonial Secretary, 8 January 1879.

53 See SNA 1/4/1: Messages from Cetywayo to Bulwer, 1 January and 5 January 1879.

54 See BPP (C. 2242), no. 5: Frere to Hicks Beach, 6 January 1879.

55 CSO 1925, no. 221/1879: Fynney to ASNA, 11 January 1879.

56 SNA 1/4/1: Message from Bulwer to Cetywayo, 12 January 1879.

CHAPTER 17

1 Cetshwayo's instructions to his army in January 1879, quoted in Laband, *Fight Us in the Open*, p. 10.

2 See Callwell, *Small Wars, passim.*

3 For Chelmsford, see Laband, Lord *Chelmsford's Zululand Campaign*, pp. xix-xxv.

4 War Office, *Narrative*, pp. 145-6; Mathews, 'Chelmsford', pp. 89-90.

5 Laband and Thompson, *Field Guide*, pp. 9, 13-14.

6 Ashe & Wyatt Edgell, *Zulu Campaign*, pp. 188-9.

7 AC, p. 27: Clery to Alison, 13 April 1879.

8 Hallam Parr, *Kafir and Zulu Wars*, pp. 166-8, 171.

9 Laband, *Lord Chelmsford's Zululand Campaign*, pp. xxx-xxxi.

10 Bailes, 'Technology and Imperialism', pp. 89, 103.

11 War Office, *Narrative*, p. 146. By the end of the campaign, the British had used 27 152 oxen and 4 633 mules for transport services (War Office, *Precis*, p. 58).

12 Mathews, 'Chelmsford', pp. 105-6.

13 CP 24: Memorandum 'F'. Chelmsford's review of the strategical conduct of the campaign, n.d.; Wood Papers, file 7, KCM

51074: Thesiger to Wood, 13 November 1878.

14 Mathews, 'Chelmsford', pp. 85-6.

15 *Illustrated London News*, 24 October 1879, p. 314: Sir E. Wood on the Zulu Campaign.

16 St Vincent Journal: 29 May 1879.

17 TS 35: Chelmsford to T. Shepstone, 28 November 1879.

18 Strachan, *European Armies*, p. 83.

19 Whitehouse, *Battle in Africa*, p. 35.

20 For detailed discussion on the characteristics of these various weapons, see Laband and Thompson, *Field Guide*, pp. 10-11.

21 For description of the various types of fortification and prepared defence employed by the British during the war, and their specific function, see CP 26, no, 88: Molyneux, *Hasty Defences*, pp. 1-9; Plé, *Les Laagers*, pp. 1-15.

22 Molyneux, *Campaigning*, pp. 196-7.

23 Webb and Wright, *Zulu King Speaks*, p. 30.

24 GH 1421: Minute, Bulwer to Colonial Secretary, 29 January 1879.

25 Monteith, 'Cetshwayo and Sekhukhune', pp. 119, 133, 175-6.

26 Bonner, *Swazi State*, pp. 147-52.

27 Harries, 'Ingwavuma', pp. 12-13, 17, 21-2.

28 Benyon, *Proconsul and Paramountcy*, p. 120.

29 GH 1326, no. 127: Bulwer to Frere, 19 August 1878.

30 Martineau, *Frere*, II, p. 235: T. Shepstone to Frere, 30 April 1878.

31 Monteith, 'Cetshwayo and Sekhukhune', pp. 173-6; Delius, *Pedi Polity*, pp. 236, 238.

32 Webb and Wright, *Zulu King Speaks*, pp. 29-31; Vijn, *Cetshwayo's Dutchman*, pp. 31, 96-7.

33 Laband and Thompson, *Field Guide*, pp. 18-19.

34 CSO 1925, no. 488/1879: Fannin to Colonial Secretary, 21 January 1879.

35 Webb and Wright, *Zulu King Speaks*, p. 55.

36 TS 38: Rudolph to Henrique Shepstone, 16 February 1879: Statement of the refugee Ncagyama.

37 Webb and Wright, *Zulu King Speaks*, p. 32

38 CSO 1925, no. 488/1879: Fannin to Colonial Secretary, 21 January 1878.

39 Webb and Wright, *Zulu King Speaks*, p. 30, 32.

40 CO 879/14: *African Confidential Print* 162, no. 227: Confidential, Hicks Beach to Frere, 9 October 1878.

41 CO 879/14: *African Confidential Print* 162, enc. in no. 248: Capt E. Baynton to Commodore F. Sullivan, 23 August 1878.

42 *BPP* (C.2454), enc. 5 in no. 55: H.E. O'Neill to Frere, 2 June 1879.

43 Bonner, *Swazi State*, pp. 151-2.

44 N. Etherington, book review of *Kingdom in Crisis*, *Journal of Imperial and Commonwealth History*, 21, 2 (May 1993), pp. 466-7.

45 See, for example, Emery, *Marching over Africa*, p. 83: Lt.-Col. H.F. Davies to his son Harry, 1 June 1879.

46 *JSA* III, pp. 301, 325: Mpatshana.

47 CP 8, no.49: Report by Bishop Schreuder on conversation with Ulankana, 10 February 1879.

48 Vijn, *Cetshwayo's Dutchman*, p. 39.

49 AC, p. 23: Clery to Alison, 18 March 1879.

CHAPTER 18

1 Four days after Isandlwana, the young Muziwento and friends visited the battlefield to witness the devastation. One of the boys took some biscuit to eat, but Muziwento declined to share it, saying, 'Sit there if you please, with your little bits of bread smelling of people's blood!' (Quoted in Laband, *Fight Us in the Open*, p. 21.)

2 There are several recent and

comprehensive descriptions of the battle of Isandlwana, notably those in books by Ian Knight (see the bibliography). For a succinct account, see Laband and Mathews, *Isandlwana*, pp. 16-69, *passim*.

3 *JSA* IV, p. 87: Mtshapi of the uMcijo.

4 Whybra, 'Main Zulu Impi', pp. 13-16.

5 Molyneux, *Campaigning*, p. 171.

6 Norris-Newman, *In Zululand*, p. 254: Cetshwayo's testimony.

7 War Office, *Narrative*, pp. 26-7.

8 *BPP* (C. 2260), enc. 2 in no. 4: Chelmsford to Frere, 17 January 1879.

9 Gibson, *Story of the Zulus*, p. 175: Testimony of Ndabuko kaMpande (Cetshwayo's brother) and Zibhebhu; Webb and Wright, *Zulu King Speaks*, p. 57.

10 WO 32/7717: Fannin to Colonial Secretary, 1 March 1879; Vijn, *Cetshwayo's Dutchman*, p. 116: Colenso's notes.

11 H.F. Fynn, Jnr Papers, file no. 26031: 'My Recollections of a Famous Campaign and a Great Disaster', pp. 8, 13.

12 SNA 1/4/2, no. 4 (confidential): Fynn to SNA, 31 December 1878.

13 J.W. Shepstone Papers, vol. 10: 'Reminiscences of the Past', p. 107: conversation with several of the chiefs on the late war; *BPP* (C. 2260), no. 10: Statement of Ucadjana, 3 February 1879.

14 For Dartnell's reconnaissance, see Mathews, 'Chelmsford', pp. 135-7, 140-8.

15 WO 32/7731: Report by Lt.-Col. J.C. Russell, 1 April 1879.

16 Colenso, *Digest*, series 1, part 2, p. 549.

17 *JSA* III, pp. 323-6: Mpatshana.

18 *BPP* (C. 2260), enc. 2 in no. 13: Umtegolalo's statement, 23 January 1879.

19 TS 37: T. Shepstone to Offy Shepstone, 6 February 1879.

20 Colenso, *Zulu War*, p. 409: Testimony of 'Zulu Deserter'; p. 411: Testimony of Uguku.

21 *JSA* IV, p. 83: Mtshapi.

22 Colenso, *Zulu War*, p. 409: Testimony of 'Zulu Deserter'.

23 *Natal Mercury*, Supplement, 22 January 1929: Nzuzi's account.

24 *Natal Mercury*, 7 April 1879: Kambula correspondent, 26 March 1879: Testimony of Hamu's warriors who had fought at Isandlwana.

25 *Historical Records of the 2nd Battalion, 24th Regiment*, p. 14.

26 WO 33/34, enc. in no. 70: Capt. Essex's evidence, 24 January 1879.

27 Commeline Letters, D1233/45: Commeline to his father, 31 January 1879.

28 Montague, *Campaigning*, p. 91.

29 Hattersley, *Later Annals of Natal*, p. 153: Brickhill's account.

30 Mitford, *Zulu Country*, p. 220: Testimony of Vumandaba, *induna* of the uMcijo.

31 *JSA* III, p. 307: Mpatshana.

32 Mitford, *Zulu Country*, p. 91: Testimony of Warrior of the uMbonambi.

33 *JSA* III, p. 307: Mpatshana.

34 *Natal Colonist*, 11 February 1879: Account of four black wagon-drivers, told on 26 January 1879.

35 Emery, *Red Soldier*, p. 101: Sgt W. Morley to his family, 1 February 1879.

36 *BPP* (C. 2260), enc. 2 in no. 13: Statement of Umtegolalo, 23 January 1879.

37 *Natal Witness*, 2 October 1879: Mehlokazulu's account.

38 *Natal Colonist*, 11 February 1879: Account of four black wagon-drivers, 26 January 1879.

39 WO 33/34, enc. in 70: Lt. S. Curling to J.N. Crealock, 26 January 1879.

40 *Natal Colonist*, 11 February 1879: Account of four black wagon-drivers,

26 January 1879.

41 *Natal Mercury*, 22 January 1929: Memoirs of C.M.F. Sparks, N.M.R.

42 Norris-Newman, *In Zululand*, p. 83: Mehlokazulu's account.

43 *BPP* (C. 2454), enc. 1 in no. 32: Statement of Sibalo, 1 June 1879.

44 Norris-Newman, *In Zululand*, p. 84: Mehlokazulu's account; Emery, *Red Soldier*, p. 114: Archibald Forbes's description.

45 Emery, *Red Soldier*, p. 95: Pte W. Meredith to his brother and sister. See also Mason Papers, KCM 55067: Mason to Cary, Mary and Charley, 8 February 1879: '...the black buggers got the boys and tied them up by the hands to the waggons and butchered them cut there privates of and stick them in there mouth' (sic).

46 Colenso, *Zulu War*, p. 410: Zulu Deserter's account.

47 War Office, *Narrative*, p. 48; *JSA* III, p. 318: Mpatshana.

48 AC, p. 19: Clery to Harman, 17 February 1878 [9]; Child, Henry Harford, p. 33.

49 SNA 1/1/34, no. 73: Statement of Sibalo, son of Ribana taken by J.W. Shepstone, 1 June 1879; Webb and Wright, Zulu King Speaks, p. 31.

50 Webb and Wright, *Zulu King Speaks*, pp. 31, 37; Vijn, *Cetshwayo's Dutchman*, p. 29.

51 *Natal Colonist*, 14 June 1879: Statement of Zulu messengers; Webb and Wright, *Zulu King Speaks*, p. 36.

52 FC 2/5: Fannin to his wife, 5 March 1879; Webb and Wright, *Zulu King Speaks*, pp. 31, 37.

53 CSO 1926, no. 1185/1879: Fannin to Colonial Secretary, 23 February 1879: Statement of two Christians from Ntumeni; CP 7/32: Fynney to Col. Law, 8 March 1879: Statement of Magumbi.

54 Child, *Henry Harford*, p. 73; Molyneux, *Campaigning*, pp. 195; Tòmasson, *With the Irregulars*,

p. 130.

55 Mitford, *Zulu Country*, p. 241.

CHAPTER 19

1 For the battle of Rorke's Drift, see J. Laband, '"O! Let's Go and have a Fight at Jim's!" The Zulu at the Battle of Rorke's Drift' in Laband and Thompson, *Kingdom and Colony*, pp. 111-30; and Knight, *Nothing Remains but to Fight*, pp. 73-116.

2 *Natal Witness*, 19 July 1879: Correspondent with General Crealock, 13 July 1879; *Graphic*, 11 October 1879, p. 350; 186; Norbury, *Naval Brigade*, pp. 298-9; Mitford, *Zulu Country*, pp. 179-81; *JSA* IV, p. 373: Ndukwana.

3 *Natal Mercury*, 7 April 1879: The Defence of Rorke's Drift by an Eye-Witness; *Illustrated London News*, 8 March 1879, p. 218: Narrative of the Revd Mr Witt.

4 *Natal Colonist*, 11 February 1879; Vijn, *Cetshwayo's Dutchman*, p. 97: Colenso's notes.

5 *Natal Colonist*, 11 February 1879: Account of four black wagon-drivers, 26 January 1879; *Natal Witness*, 2 October 1879: Mehlokazulu's account.

6 Ludlow, *Zululand and Cetewayo*, p. 61.

7 TS 37: H.C. Shepstone to T. Shepstone, 9 September 1879; J. Shepstone Papers 10: 'Reminiscences of the Past', pp. 109-10; Mitford, *Zulu Country*, p. 161: Warrior of the Undi's account.

8 Webb, 'Zulu Boy's Recollections', pp. 12-13.

9 Carl Faye Papers 8: Statement of Lugubu Mbata kaMangaliso (who had fought with the NNC) taken by Faye on 4 November 1938.

10 The basis of the following account of the battle is drawn from WO 32/7737: Lt. Chard's report on the defence of Rorke's Drift, 25 January 1879 (Chard's Report); Holme, *Silver*

Wreath, p. 50-3: Major Chard's account of January 1880 (Chard's Account); and Paton, Glennie and Penn Symons, *Historical Records*, pp. 251-4: Revd G. Smith's account, 3 February 1879 (Smith's Account).

11 Zulu War, file 2, KCM 42358: Letter from R.J. Hall to the editor of the *Natal Witness*, 25 October [?].

12 Callwell, *Small Wars*, p. 399.

13 *Natal Mercury*, 7 April 1879: Defence of Rorke's Drift by an Eye-Witness.

14 H.F. Fynn, Jnr. Papers, file no. 26031: 'My Recollections of a Famous Campaign and a Great Disaster', p. 16.

15 For details of the defence of the hospital, see Holme, *Silver Wreath*, pp. 64-5: Pte. A. H. Hook's account.

16 Emery, *Red Soldier*, p. 134: Gunner A. Howard's account.

17 War Office, *Narrative*, p. 47.

18 Webb, 'Zulu Boy's Recollections', p. 12: comment of Munyu, who fought at Rorke's Drift.

19 WC II/1/6: A.F. Pickard to Wood, 14 October 1879.

20 H.F. Fynn, Jnr. Papers, file no. 26031: 'Recollections', p. 16; Child, *Henry Harford*, p. 35; Jones, John Maxwell, pp. 6-7; Norris-Newman, *In Zululand*, p. 64; Hattersley, *Later Annals of Natal*, p. 148: Trooper F. Symon's account.

21 Colenso, *Zulu War*, p. 406: Dabulamanzi's testimony.

22 Hamilton-Browne, *Lost Legionary*, p. 142; Child, *Henry Harford*, p. 44.

23 Webb, 'Zulu Boy's Recollections', p. 13.

24 H.F. Fynn, Jnr. Papers, file no. 26031: 'Recollections', p. 17; *Natal Mercury*, 7 April 1879: The Defence of Rorke's Drift by an Eye-Witness.

25 Jones, *John Maxwell*, pp. 7, 9; Hallam Parr, *Kafir and Zulu Wars*, p. 261; Laband and Thompson, *Buffalo Border*, p. 44.

26 H.C. Lugg, 'Short Account of the Battle of Rorke's Drift' (1 September 1944, typescript in Natal Archives).

27 FC 2/4: Fannin to his wife, 23 January 1879.

28 Hamilton-Browne, *Lost Legionary*, p. 152; Hattersley, *Later Annals of Natal*, p. 150; Symons's account.

29 Hallam Parr, *Kafir and Zulu Wars*, p. 263-4.

30 TS 37: Henrique Shepstone to T. Shepstone, 9 February 1879.

31 War Office, *Narrative*, p. 158.

32 Webb, 'Zulu Boy's Recollections', p. 12.

33 *JSA* I, p. 125: Dunjwa.

34 *BPP* (C. 2260), no. 10: Statement of Ucadjana, 3 February 1879; Webb & Wright, *Zulu King Speaks*, pp. 31-2.

35 Dlamini, *Two Kings*, pp. 69-70.

36 Webb and Wright, *Zulu King Speaks*, p. 31; *JSA* III, pp. 302-4: Mpatshana.

37 *JSA* III, pp. 141, 305, 307: Mjobo and Mpatshana; *JSA* IV, pp. 147-8: Mtshayankomo.

38 *JSA* IV, p. 147: Mtshayankomo; Gibson, *Story of the Zulus*, p. 188.

39 Webb and Wright, *Zulu King Speaks*, p. 32.

40 TS 38: Rudolph to H. Shepstone, 16 February 1879.

41 *BPP* (C. 2260), no. 10: Statement of Ucadjana, 3 February 1879.

42 CP 8, no. 49: Letter from Bishop Schreuder, 10 February 1879; CSO 1926, no. 1346/1879: Fannin to Colonial Secretary, 3 March 1879.

43 Vijn, *Cetshwayo's Dutchman*, p. 126: Colenso's notes.

44 *Natal Colonist*, 25 September 1879: Cetshwayo's comments from the *Cape Times*.

CHAPTER 20

1 Sihlahla of the uMxhapho describing the effects of British fire at the battle of Nyezane (*BPP* (C.2454), sub-enc. in enc. 1 in no. 34: Statement of Sihlahla taken by J.W. Shepstone, 3 June 1879.)

Notes

2 Inevitably, there is lack of clarity in the sources (which are based on information drawn from Zulu spies and prisoners as well as hearsay) on the precise composition and size of this Zulu army.

3 *BPP* (C. 2242), enc. 5 in no. 20: Pearson to DAG, 15 January 1879; Norbury, *Naval Brigade*, pp. 220, 222.

4 WO 32/7717, enc. in Fannin to Colonial Secretary, 1 March 1879: Message of two Ntumeni natives from Cetshwayo.

5 Webb and Wright, *Zulu King Speaks*, p. 30; *Times of Natal*, 5 February 1879: Correspondent with Pearson's Column, 24 January 1879.

6 Today, the hills are being covered by commercial timber plantations, though the lower ground is relatively unchanged.

7 Cato Papers I, Ms 1602 a: Cato to Richards, 2 February 1879.

8 The description of the engagement at Nyezane is based, among others, upon the following sources: *BPP* (C. 2260), enc. in no 3: Pearson to Hallam Parr, 23 January 1879; WO 32/7708: Report by Commander Campbell, 24 January 1879; WO 32/7708: Lt. T.W. Dowding to Capt. A. Campbell, 23 January 1879; War Office, *Narrative*, pp. 23-4; Moodie, *British, Boers and Zulus*, pp. 259-62; Norbury, *Naval Brigade*, pp. 229-32; Hart-Synnot, *Letters*, pp. 107-13, 148. See also, Laband and Thompson, *Field Guide*, pp. 38-9. The most recent account is in Castle and Knight, *Fearful Hard Times*, pp. 57-73.

9 *Natal Mercury*, Supplement, 22 January 1929: Chief Zimema's account.

10 Turner Papers: Turner to Ellis, 30 January 1879.

11 *Times of Natal*, 5 February 1879: Correspondent, 24 January 1879.

12 War Office, *Narrative*, p. 24.

13 CSO 1926, no. C19/1879: Statement of Unxakala and Udhlozi, 4 February 1879; SNA 1/1/34, no. 85: Statement of Sihlahla, 3 June 1879; *Natal Mercury*, Supplement, 22 January 1929: Chief Zimema's account.

14 CSO 1926, no. 1147/1879: Fannin to Colonial Secretary, 20 February 1879.

15 CP 8, no. 49: Bishop Schreuder's despatch, 10 February 1879; *Natal Mercury*, Supplement, 22 January 1929: Chief Zimema's account.

16 AC, p. 153: MacGregor to Hume, 14 February 1879: No. 5: Eshowe Fort. For details of the fortifications, which were daily improved, see J. Laband, 'British Fieldworks of the Zulu Campaign of 1879 with Special Reference to Fort Eshowe' in Laband and Thompson, *Kingdom and Colony*, pp. 68-77.

17 WO 32/7730: Pearson to Hallam Parr, 9 April 1879; War Office, *Narrative*, pp. 53-4.

18 J. Laband, 'Mbilini, Manyonyoba and the Phongolo River Frontier' in Laband and Thompson, *Kingdom and Colony*, pp. 190-3.

19 War Office, *Narrative*, p. 145.

20 Vijn, *Cetshwayo's Dutchman*, pp. 84-5.

21 Wood, *Midshipman*, II, p. 54 (note).

22 War Office, *Narrative*, pp. 8-10, 20, 143-44.

23 WC II/2/2: Chelmsford to Wood, 16 December 1878.

24 Woodgate's Military Diary: 10 January 1879.

25 Woodgate's Military Diary: 5, 11 January 1879; *Times of Natal*, 17, 31 January.

26 Woodgate's Military Diary: 11, 12, 14, 15, 17 January 1879.

27 *BPP* (C. 2252), no. 20: Wood to Military Secretary, 18 January 1879.

28 *BPP* (C. 2260), enc. 3 in no. 4: Wood

to Military Secretary, 20 January
1879.

29 WO 32/7712: Journal of Operations
of No. 4 Column, 20 January 1879.

30 Webb and Wright, *Zulu King Speaks*,
pp. 32-3.

31 Wood, *Midshipman*, II, p. 30.

32 *BPP* (C. 2260), enc. 2 in no. 13:
Report by Buller, 21 January 1879;
Wood Papers 7, KCM 51124: Buller
to Wood, 20 January 1879; *Times of
Natal*, 31 January 1879.

33 *BPP* (C. 2260), enc. 2 in no. 13:
Wood to DAG, 23 January 1879;
Times of Natal, 7 February 1879:
Wood's report, 23 January 1879.

34 WO 32/7708: Wood to Chelmsford,
25 January 1879; Woodgate's
Military Diary: 24 January 1879;
Fairlie's Zulu War Diary: 24 January
1879.

35 CP 9, no. 12: Lloyd to Wood, 29
January 1879; *BPP* (C. 2260), no.
10: statement of Ucadjana, son of
Matendeka, 3 February 1879.

36 *BPP* (C. 2374), enc. in no 9:
Wheelwright to Colonial Secretary,
18 February 1879: statement of
Undobolonkwana.

37 *BPP* (C. 2260), enc. 3 in no. 4: Wood
to Military Secretary, 25 January
1879.

38 CP 9, no. 10: Schermbrucker to
Wood, 26 January 1879; Fairlie's
Zulu War Diary: 26, 27 January
1879; *Natal Mercury*, 17 February
1879: Luneburg correspondent, 6
February 1879.

CHAPTER 21

1 *BPP* (C. 2374), enc. in no. 9:
Wheelwright to Colonial Secretary,
30 January 1879.

2 WO 32/7717: Chelmsford to
Secretary of State for War, 2 March
1879.

3 CSO 1926, no. C18/1879: Fynn to
Colonial Secretary, 3 February 1879.

4 *Natal Colonist*, 4 February 1879.

5 Bonner, *Swazi State*, pp. 152-3.

6 WC II/2/2: Chelmsford to Wood, 3
February 1879.

7 CP 9, no. 30: Memorandum,
MacLeod to Wood, 24 February
1879.

8 Laband and Thompson, *Umvoti*,
pp. 23-4, 35-41.

9 Laband and Thompson, *Buffalo
Border*, pp. 58-61.

10 *BPP* (C. 2260), no. 10: Statement of
Ucadjana, 3 February 1879.

11 *BPP* (C.2260), enc. 3 in no. 4: Wood
to Military Secretary, 25 January
1879.

12 CP 9, no. 19: Buller to Military
Secretary, 1 February 1879
Woodgate's Military Diary: 1
February 1879.

13 *Times of Natal*, 10 March 1879:
Correspondent at Kambula Camp, 3
March 1879.

14 All this captured livestock had to be
disposed of in a regular fashion to
prevent freebooting. Consequently, it
was either sold to the commissariat
or auctioned off in Natal and the
Transvaal.

15 TS 37: H.C. Shepstone to T.
Shepstone, 2 February 1879.

16 TS 38: Rudolph to H.C. Shepstone,
16 February 1879.

17 CP 8, no. 49: Bishop Schreuder's
Report, 10 February 1879.

18 See Laband, 'Mbilini' in Laband and
Thompson, *Kingdom and Colony*,
pp. 194-8, for the Phongolo region
during February and early March
1879.

19 For accounts of the Ntombe
engagement, see Laband, 'Mbilini' in
Laband and Thompson, *Kingdom and
Colony*, pp. 198-9; War Office,
Narrative, pp. 69-72; Moodie, *British,
Boers and Zulus*, pp. 263-69; Emery,
Red Soldier, pp. 157-62; *Marching
over Africa*, pp. 74-7; Laband and
Thompson, *Field Guide*, pp. 84-5.

20 CSO 1926, no. 1185/1879: Fannin

to Colonial Secretary, 23 February 1879; AC, p. 79: J.N. Crealock to H.H. Crealock, 2 March 1879.

21 CSO 1926, no. C19/1879: Statement by Unxakala and Udhlozi, 4 February 1879; BPP (C. 2374), enc. in no 9: Statement by Fokazi and Umpothlo, 7 February 1879. For a recent and full account of the blockade of Eshowe, see Castle and Knight, *Fearful Hard Times*, pp. 74-163.

22 CP 7, no. 32: Fynney to Law, 8 March 1879; Webb and Wright, *Zulu King Speaks*, p. 33

23 WO 32/7730: Pearson to Military Secretary, 9 April 1879.

24 WO 32/7730: Pearson to Military Secretary, 9 April 1879; Norbury, *Naval Brigade*, p. 252.

25 Lloyd, 'Defence of Ekowe', p. 21.

26 WO 32/7730: Pearson to Military Secretary, 9 April 1879; Ashe and Wyatt Edgell, *Zulu Campaign*, pp. 77-84; Norbury, Naval Brigade, 253-5; Wynne, *Memoir*, pp. 46-9.

27 So Dabulamanzi later told Lt. Lloyd.

28 Norris-Newman, *In Zululand*, pp. 150-1; Norbury, *Naval Brigade*, pp. 260-1; Lloyd, 'Defence of Ekowe', p. 24.

29 *Natal Colonist*, 8 March 1879: Fort Bengough correspondent, 24 February 1879; *Natal Mercury*, 22 March 1879: Kambula correspondent, 12 March 1879.

30 CP 14, no. 8: L.H. Lloyd, Political Assistant: report of three spies, 24 March. Submitted by Wood to Military Secretary, 27 March 1879.

31 CSO 1926, no. 1669/1879: Fannin to Colonial Secretary, 22 March 1879.

32 CSO 1926, no. 1346/1879: Fannin to Colonial Secretary, 3 March 1879. For the defection of Hamu, see J. Laband, 'The Cohesion of the Zulu Polity under the Impact of the Anglo-Zulu War' in Laband and Thompson, *Kingdom and Colony*, p. 10.

33 TS 39: H.C. Shepstone to T. Shepstone, 23 March 1879; 30 March 1879.

34 WO 32/7779: Journal of Col. Baker Russell's Column, 14 August 1879; BPP (C. 3182), no. 34: Wood to the Earl of Kimberley, 23 June 1881.

35 WO 32/7715: Diary of Operations, 10 March 1879.

36 CP 9, no. 12: Lloyd to Wood, 29 January 1879.

37 CP 9, no. 26: Memorandum by Lloyd, 16 February 1879.

38 CP 14, no. 9: Wood to Military Secretary, 27 February 1879.

39 WO 32/7715: Diary of Operations, 10 March 1879.

40 CSO 1927, no. 2702/1879: Fannin to Colonial Secretary, 30 May 1879.

41 CP 9, enc. in no. 37: MacLeod to Wood, 1 March 1879.

42 CP 7, no. 32: Fynney to Col. Law, 8 March 1879.

43 CSO 1926, n.n.: Fannin to Colonial Secretary, 1 March 1879.

44 For Anglo-Zulu negotiations during March 1879, see J. Laband, 'Humbugging the General? King Cetshwayo's Peace Overtures during the Anglo-Zulu War' in Laband and Thompson, *Kingdom and Colony*, pp. 49-52.

45 BPP (C. 2252), no. 20: Lord Chelmsford's Order of 17 January 1879.

46 BPP (C. 2318), enc. 2 in no. 9: Frere to Chelmsford, 3 March 1879.

47 FC 2/5: Fannin to his wife, 10 March 1879.

48 Still in irons, they were brought into Natal after the relief of Eshowe, and only released in early April after interrogation by Lord Chelmsford.

49 CSO 1926, no. 1761/1879: Fannin to Colonial Secretary, 28 March 1879.

50 Littleton Papers, no. 91: Littleton to Ciss, 14 February 1879.

51 See Monteith, 'Sekhukhune', pp. 149-51, who has noted and discussed all these contacts.

52 Huw Jones has recently argued that the principal reason for sending the army into the area where Mbilini and the Qulusi were operating was to secure a line of retreat for Cetshwayo northwards across the Phongolo to a bolt-hole in the broken country beyond. See Jones, 'Why Khambula?', pp. 18, 21.

CHAPTER 22

1 Schermbrucker, 'Zhlobane and Kambula', p. 337.

2 SNA 1/1/34, no. 73: Statement of Sibalo, taken by J.W. Shepstone, 1 June 1879.

3 For a detailed account of the Khambula campaign, see J. Laband, 'The Battle of Khambula, 29 March 1879: A Re-examination from the Zulu Perspective' in Laband and Thompson, *Kingdom and Colony*, pp. 80-110.

4 Mathews, 'Lord Chelmsford', pp. 244-7.

5 J. Laband, 'Bulwer, Chelmsford and the Border Levies: The Dispute over the Defence of Natal, 1879', in Laband and Thompson, *Kingdom and Colony*, pp. 154-7.

6 WC II/2/2: Chelmsford to Wood, 14 March 1879; 19 March 1879.

7 Woodgate's Military Diary: 15 February 1879; CP 14, no. 7: Officer Commanding Luneburg to Staff Officer, No. 4 Column, 27 March 1879.

8 CSO 1926, no. 1669/1879: Fannin to Colonial Secretary, 22 March 1879; Wright and Webb, *Zulu King Speaks*, p. 33.

9 *Natal Colonist*, 10 April 1879: Kambula correspondent, 31 March 1879.

10 *Natal Colonist*, 20 September 1879: Report by *Natal Mercury*

correspondent on the march with the king to the coast.

11 CP 8, no. 49: Schreuder to Chelmsford, 10 February 1879.

12 Webb and Wright, *Zulu King Speaks*, p. 33.

13 Knight, '"Kill Me in the Shadows"', p. 12: Witness Mamboola, 29 May 1936; p. 16: Luke Sofikasho Zungu, 17 December 1935.

14 Vijn, *Cetshwayo's Dutchman*, p. 36.

15 Gibson, *Story of the Zulus*, p. 197.

16 TS 39: H. Shepstone to T. Shepstone, 30 March 1879.

17 *Natal Mercury*, 7 April 1879: Kambula correspondent, 26 March 1879.

18 Schermbrucker, 'Zhlobane and Kambula', p. 342; Mitford, *Zulu Country*, p. 262.

19 Moodie, *British, Boers and Zulus*, pp. 276, 279, 283; Schermbrucker, 'Zhlobane and Kambula', p. 342.

20 Buller Papers, WO 132/1: Buller to A.G., 30 March 1879.

21 Woodgate's Private Diary: 21 April 1879.

22 Buller Papers, WO 132/1: Buller to A.G., 30 March 1879; Woodgate's Military Diary: 27 March 1879.

23 Gibson, *Story of the Zulus*, p. 196.

24 Woodgate's Military Diary: 29 March 1879. It is quite possible that elements of both *amabutho* were involved.

25 Buller Papers, WO 132/1: Buller to A.G., 30 March 1879; Schermbrucker, 'Zhlobane and Kambula', pp. 346-7; Moodie, *British, Boers and Zulus*, pp. 284-5.

26 War Office, *Narrative*, p. 160.

27 TS 39: Piet Uys Jnr's statement, 29 March 1879; Wood, *Midshipman*, II, p. 50.

28 Buller Papers, WO 132/1: Buller to A.G., 30 March 1879.

29 AC, p. 45, Clery no. 19: Clery to Alison, 18 July 1879.

30 Wood, *Midshipman*, II, p. 53.

31 War Office, *Narrative*, p. 161.
32 Wood, *Midshipman*, II, p. 59; War Office, *Narrative*, p. 79; Norris-Newman, *In Zululand*, p. 163.
33 Schermbrucker, 'Zhlobane and Kambula', p. 376.
34 Woodgate's Military Diary: 30, 31 March 1879.
35 Woodgate's Military Diary: 29 March 1879.
36 *JSA* III, p. 314: Mpatshana.
37 Schermbrucker, 'Zhlobane and Kambula', p. 376; Gibson, *Story of the Zulus*, p. 197.
38 Wood, *Midshipman*, II, pp. 57-8.
39 Woodgate's Military Diary: 29 March 1879.
40 *Natal Colonist*, 10 April 1879: Kambula correspondent, 31 March 1879; Ashe and Wyatt-Edgell, *Zulu Campaign*, p. 136.
41 Moodie, *British, Boers and Zulus*, p. 290.
42 *Natal Colonist*, 10 April 1879: Kambula correspondent, 31 March 1879. The maximum range of the 7-pounder was 2 790 metres.
43 Emery, *Red Soldier*, p. 176: Wood to Sir A. Horsford, 6 April 1879.
44 Slade Papers: Slade to his Mother, 29 March 1879.
45 Holden, *British Rule*, p. 159: *The London Times*, 23 May 1879.
46 Webb and Wright, *Zulu King Speaks*, p. 33.
47 Wood, *Midshipman*, II, p. 64.
48 TS 39: H.C. Shepstone to T. Shepstone, 30 March 1879; Mitford, *Zulu Country*, p. 278: Warrior of the Tulwana.
49 Vijn, *Cetshwayo's Dutchman*, p. 114: Mehlokazulu's testimony.
50 Not all the mounted men were stationed in the main laager during the battle. Wood permitted the Mounted Basutos under Maj. Cochrane to fight in their own fashion outside the camp, hovering on the extremes of the Zulu horns,

harassing them whenever possible.
51 Montague, *Campaigning*, p. 263. The Zulu had picked up this term for the British from the BaSotho.
52 Schermbrucker, 'Zhlobane and Kambula', pp. 377-8.
53 Wood, *Midshipman*, II, p. 60.
54 Vijn, *Cetshwayo's Dutchman*, p. 114: Mehlokazulu's testimony.
55 CP 14, no. 21: Wood to DAG, 3 April 1879.
56 Moodie, *British Boers and Zulus*, p. 298.
57 SNA 1/1/34, no. 85: Statement of Sihlahla to J.W. Shepstone, 3 June 1879; McToy, *13th Regiment*, p. 50.
58 Mitford, *Zulu Country*, p. 160: Two Warriors of the Undi and One of the Tulwana.
59 SNA 1/1/34, no. 85: Statement of Sihlahla to J.W. Shepstone, 3 June 1879.
60 McToy, *13th Regiment*, p. 51.
61 Mossop, *Running the Gauntlet*, p. 75.
62 Vijn, *Cetshwayo's Dutchman*, p. 38.
63 Wood, *Midshipman*, II, p. 61.
64 Ashe and Wyatt Edgell, *Zulu Campaign*, p. 139.
65 Norris-Newman, *In Zululand*, p. 164.
66 Wood, *Midshipman*, II, p. 62.
67 KCM 53791: Trooper Hewitt to Annie, 3 January 1879.
68 Schermbrucker, 'Zhlobane and Kambula', p. 379.
69 Ashe and Wyatt Edgell, *Zulu Campaign*, p. 142.
70 Norris-Newman, *In Zululand*, p. 164.
71 Emery, *Red Soldier*, p. 172: Letter by Sgt. E. Jervis, 5 September 1879.
72 Moodie, *British, Boers and Zulus*, p. 279: Capt. C. D'Arcy to his Parents.
73 Buller Papers, WO 132/1: Buller to A.G., 30 March 1879.
74 SNA 1/1/34, no. 73: Statement of Sibalo to J.W. Shepstone, 1 June 1879.
75 Moodie, *British, Boers and Zulus*, p. 275: Correspondent to a Natal

newspaper.

76 *Natal Mercury*, 16 April 1879: Young Natalian's account.

77 Mossop, *Running the Gauntlet*, p. 74; Emery, *Marching over Africa*, p. 79: Letter by Pte. E. Fowler, 28 April 1879.

78 Emery, *Marching over Africa*, p. 65: letter by Schermbrucker, 1 May 1879.

79 Wood, *Midshipman*, II, pp. 67-8.

80 Woodgate's Military Diary, 30, 31 March, 1, 3 April 1879.

81 Woodgate's Military Diary: 21 April 1879; SNA 1/1/34, no. 73: Statement of Sibalo, 1 June 1879; SNA 1/1/34, no. 85: Statement of Sihlahla, 3 June 1879; Vijn, *Cetshwayo's Dutchman*, pp. 36-7.

82 War Office, *Narrative*, pp. 81, 161.

83 *Natal Mercury*, 9 April 1879: Kambula correspondent, 1 April 1879; *Natal Colonist*, 14 June 1879; Webb and Wright, *Zulu King*, p. 36.

84 Mossop, *Running the Gauntlet*, pp. 74-5.

85 *Natal Colonist*, 24 April 1879: Kambula correspondent, 2 May 1879.

86 *Times of Natal*, 9 May 1879: Kambula correspondent, 2 May 1879.

87 CSO 1926, no. 1939/1879: Fannin to Colonial Secretary, 9 April 1879.

88 *Natal Colonist*, 10 April 1879: Kambula correspondent, 31 March 1879.

89 SNA 1/1/34, no. 73: Statement of Sibalo, 1 June 1879; SNA 1/1/34, no. 85: Statement of Sihlahla, 3 June 1879; Knight, '"Kill Me in the Shadows"', p. 16: Luke Sofikasho Zungu, 17 December 1935.

90 Webb and Wright, *Zulu King Speaks*, p. 37.

91 Woodgate's Military Diary: 30, 31 March 1879; CP 14, no. 21: Wood to DAG, 3 April 1879.

92 SNA 1/1/34, no. 85: Statement of Sihlahla, 3 June 1879.

93 *Natal Colonist*, 25 September 1879: Cetshwayo's comments taken from the *Cape Times*.

CHAPTER 23

1 '...we have never fought with men who were so much afraid as these. They are continually making holes in the ground and mounds left open with little holes to shoot through. The English burrow in the ground like wild pigs.' (Vijn, *Cetshwayo's Dutchman*, pp. 40-1.)

2 WO 32/7730: Pearson to Military Secretary, 9 April 1879.

3 For Zulu dispositions and numbers, see CP 7, no. 38: Drummond to Chelmsford, 27 March 1879: Report of spy Magumbi.

4 Ludlow, *Zululand and Cetewayo*, pp. 71-2.

5 For the British advance and the battle of Gingindlovu, see WO 32/7727: Chelmsford to Secretary of State for War, 10 April 1879. For a recent and thorough account, see Castle and Knight, *Fearful Hard Times*, pp. 186-214.

6 Moodie, *John Dunn*, p. 101.

7 Stainbank Diary: 31 March, 1 April 1879.

8 Moodie, *John Dunn*, p. 101.

9 Mathews, 'Chelmsford', pp. 251-4.

10 Anti-Slavery Society Papers, G 12: statement of one of the Native Contingent to Colenso: testimony of prisoners.

11 Norbury, *Naval Brigade*, pp. 278-9.

12 Webb and Wright, *Zulu King Speaks*, p. 37.

13 Vijn, *Cetshwayo's Dutchman*, p. 40.

14 CP 7, no. 50: Report of Major P. Barrow.

15 Norris-Newman, *In Zululand*, pp. 137-8.

16 Hutton, 'Recollections', p. 70.

17 FC 2/5: Barton to Fannin, 16 April 1879.

18 War Office, *Narrative*, p. 163; CP 7, no. 50: Major Barrow's Report.
19 Anti-Slavery Society Papers G 12: statement of one of the Native Contingent to Colenso.
20 Conductor in the Transport Division's Diary, p. 24: 2 April 1879.
21 Smith-Dorrien Papers, SMD/1: Scrap-Book, unnumbered pages.
22 Mynors, *Letters and Diary*, p. 30: 2 April 1879.
23 Moodie, *John Dunn*, pp. 102-3.
24 Dawnay, *Private Journal*, p. 13.
25 Ashe and Wyatt Edgell, *Zulu Campaign*, p. 170.
26 CP 7, no. 50: Major Barrow's Report; Ashe and Wyatt Edgell, *Zulu Campaign*, pp. 168-9.
27 *Natal Mercury*, 10 April 1879: Eyewitness to Gingindlovu.
28 *Natal Witness*, 19 July 1879: Correspondent with Crealock's Column, 13 July 1879.
29 The following account of the Zulu rout is based, among many other sources, on CP 7, no. 50: Major Barrow's Report; WO 32/7727: Chelmsford to Secretary of State for War, 10 April 1879.
30 Molyneux, *Campaigning*, p. 136.
31 Vijn, *Cetshwayo's Dutchman*, p. 40.
32 Moodie, *John Dunn*, p. 103
33 CSO 1926, no. 2051/1879: Fannin to Colonial Secretary, 17 April 1879.
34 SNA 1/1/34, no. 10: Fynney to ASNA, 8 April 1879.
35 War Office, *Narrative*, p. 65.
36 Mynors, *Letters and Diary*, p. 34: 6 April 1879; Hutton, 'Recollections', p. 73.
37 Conductor in the Transport Division's Diary, p. 21: 2 April 1879; Molyneux, *Campaigning*, p. 139; Hutton, 'Recollections', p. 73.
38 Conductor in the Transport Division's Diary, p. 54: 20 April 1879: Makwendu kaMpande's report; Webb and Wright, *Zulu King*

Speaks, p. 37.
39 Ashe and Wyatt Edgell, *Zulu Campaign*, pp. 179-82; Molyneux, *Campaigning*, pp. 141-3.
40 Norbury, *Naval Brigade*, pp. 299-300.
41 CSO 1926, no. 2051/1879: Fannin to Colonial Secretary, 17 April 1879; SNA 1/1/34, no. 85: statement of Sihlahla, 3 June 1879.
42 Laband and Thompson, *Umvoti*, pp. 50-1; P. Thompson, 'Captain Lucas and the Border Guard: The War on the Lower Thukela 1879' in Laband and Thompson, *Kingdom and Colony*, pp. 172-4.
43 Laband and Thompson, *Buffalo Border*, pp. 63-5.
44 For operations in the Phongolo region during April and May 1879, see Laband, 'Mbilini' in Laband and Thompson, *Kingdom and Colony*, pp. 201-2.
45 War Office, *Narrative*, pp. 100-3.

CHAPTER 24
1 See Mathews, 'Chelmsford', pp. 263-91.
2 Laband and Thompson, *Buffalo Border*, pp. 67-9.
3 Laband and Thompson, *Buffalo Border*, pp. 70-3.
4 See Laband and Thompson, *Umvoti*, pp. 56-67.
5 Thompson, 'Lower Tugela' in Laband and Thompson, *Kingdom and Colony*, pp. 174-5.
6 For events in the Phongolo region during late May and June, see Laband, 'Mbilini' in Laband and Thompson, *Kingdom and Colony*, pp. 202-4.
7 For a full account of the Zulu raid of 25 June, see Laband and Thompson, *Umvoti*, pp. 67-7
8 For the advance of the 2nd Division and the Flying Column, see Mathews, 'Chelmsford', pp. 293, 297-8, 301-2, 312-14.

9 See in particular WC II/1/2:
   Statement of evidence elicited at
   Ityotyosi River, 26 May 1880:
   testimony of Umbooza, Umparlarz,
   Luabagazi and Dabayan; Vijn,
   Cetshwayo's Dutchman, pp. 145-6:
   Colenso's notes: testimony of
   Mnukwa; Mitford, *Zulu Country*,
   pp. 124-5: Sabuza's testimony; and
   Knight, '"Kill Me in the Shadows"',
   pp. 16-17: statement of
   M'Wunuzane.
10 See Laband, '"Chopping Wood with a
   Razor"', pp. 5-9.
11 WO 32/7749: Chelmsford to
   Secretary of State for War, 9 June
   1879.
12 St Vincent Journal: 10 June 1879.
13 Milne Papers, MLN 202/2, Naval
   Diary: 15 June 1879; Woodgate's
   Private Diary: 15 June 1879; BPP (C.
   2454). enc. 1 in no 51: Buller to
   Marshall, 16 June 1879.
14 *Natal Witness*, 10 July 1879:
   Ibabanango correspondent, 19 June
   1879; Tomasson, *With the Irregulars*,
   pp. 131-4.
15 For a graphic description of the
   routine burning of *imizi* along the
   British line of advance, see
   Montague, *Campaigning*, pp. 213-17.
16 Malet, *Diary*, pp. 21-2.
17 Ashe and Wyatt Edgell, *Zulu
   Campaign*, p. 328; Harrison,
   Recollections, p. 181.
18 WO 32/7728: Memorandum for
   Guidance of Major-General Crealock,
   C.B. by Chelmsford, 12 April 1879.
19 Mathews, 'Transport and Supply',
   pp. 111-16, 121, 136-7.
20 AC, p. 43, Clery no. 18: Clery to
   Alison, 12 July 1879.
21 Webb and Wright, *Zulu King Speaks*,
   p. 34; CP 35, no. 16: Summary of
   information by Faenane, 28 May
   1879.
22 CSO 1927, no. 2090/1879: Fannin
   to Colonial Secretary, 21 April 1879.
23 CSO 1926, no. 1957/1879: Fynn to

Colonial Secretary, 11 April 1879.
24 SNA 1/1/33, no. 11: Fynn to SNA,
   10 May 1879: Statement of
   Mabotyobana, wife of Voboza; CP 9,
   no. 52: Wood to Military Secretary:
   Statement of scouts from the Zulu
   Country, 10 May 1879.
25 CSO 1926, no. 2076/1879: Fannin
   to Colonial Secretary, 19 April 1879.
26 SNA 1/1/134: Fynney to ASNA, 24
   May 1879.
27 WO 32/7754: 2nd Brigade, 1st
   Division, Diary ending 15 June: 12
   June 1879.
28 AC, p. 87, Crealock no. 19: Col.
   Crealock to Alison, 20 April 1879.
29 GH 1424, no. 338/1879: Maj.-Gen.
   Crealock to Bulwer, 28 April 1879.
30 Woodgate's Private Diary: 21 April
   1879.
31 CP 9, no. 52: Wood to Military
   Secretary, 16 May 1879: Statement
   of Scouts from Zulu country; Webb
   and Wright, *Zulu King Speaks*, p. 34.
32 CP 16, no. 40: Drummond to
   Assistant Military Secretary, 16 June
   1879: Statement of Zulu prisoner
   Umgaunsi.
33 For Zulu peace initiatives during
   April, May and June, see Laband,
   'Humbugging the General?' in
   Laband and Thompson, *Kingdom and
   Colony*, pp. 52-8.
34 CP 13, no. 5: Minute by Frere, 4 April
   1879.
35 AC, p. 113: Maj.-Gen. Crealock to
   Alison, 31 May 1879.
36 WO 32/7750: Diary of the 1st
   Division, 15 May 1879; WO
   32/7740: Telegram, Maj.-Gen.
   Crealock to Chelmsford, 16 May
   1879.
37 BPP (C. 2374), enc. 10 in no. 32:
   Telegram, Frere to Chelmsford, recd.
   30 May 1879.
38 WO 32/7747: Correspondence
   regarding peace: summary of the
   conversation between John Dunn
   and the king's messenger Usitwangu,

31 May 1879.

39 AC, p. 115: Maj.-Gen. Crealock to Alison, 7 June 1879.

40 Harness Letters: Harness to his sister Co, 4 June 1879.

41 CP 13, no. 40: Notes by Drummond on the report of the king's peace messengers, 5 June 1879.

42 CP 13, no. 37: Chelmsford's message to the Zulu king, 4 June 1879, with the amendment of 5 June 1879.

43 *BPP* (C. 2454), C in enc. 7 in no. 51: Message from Chelmsford to the Zulu Chiefs, 16 June 1879.

44 SNA 1/1/34, no. 117: Translation of a message from Cetywayo by Fynney, 25 June 1879.

45 The tusk was subsequently forwarded to Queen Victoria.

46 Ashe and Wyatt Edgell, *Zulu Campaign*, p. 317.

47 Gibson, *Story of the Zulus*, p. 209.

48 CP 13, no. 54: Message from Cetywayo to Chelmsford, 26 June 1879; and message to Ketchwayo from Chelmsford, 27 June 1879.

49 WO 32/7761: Gen. Newdigate's Diary for the week ending 29 June 1879: 28 June 1879.

50 WO 32/7751: Telegram, Clifford to Secretary of State for War, 3 July 1879.

51 CP 35, no. 5: Telegram, Maj.-Gen. Crealock to Chelmsford, 16 May 1879.

52 CP 35, no. 16: Telegram, summary of information by Fanaene, 28 May 1879; *BPP* (C. 2374), enc. 7 in no. 37: statement of Umfazi, 28 May 1879.

53 WO 32/7747: Correspondence regarding peace: summary of conversation between John Dunn and the king's messenger, Usitwangu, 31 May 1879.

54 CO 179/131, no. Natal/12358: O'Neill to Lord Salisbury, 7 June 1879.

55 CP 15, no. 4: Telegram, Maj.-Gen. Crealock to Military Secretary, recd. 8 June 1879.

56 CP 16, no. 40: Drummond to Assistant Military Secretary, 16 June 1879: Statement of Zulu prisoner Umgaunsi; BPP (C. 2454), enc. in no. 33: Report of three messengers to Drummond, 5 June 1879.

57 *BPP* (C. 2454), enc. 7 in no. 51: Message from the Lieutenant-General...to the Zulu Chiefs, 16 June 1879.

58 AC, p. 105: Maj.-Gen. Crealock to Alison, 1 May 1879; WO 32/7750: proceedings, 'Forester', 6 May 1879; Norbury, *Naval Brigade*, pp. 294-5.

59 WO 32/7772: Maj.-Gen. Crealock to Wolseley, Memorandum of Operations of the First Division, 18 April to 7 July 1879; WO 32/7772: Maj. Barrow to Maj.-Gen. Crealock, 5 July and 8 July 1879.

60 See the remarks in *The Cape Times* quoted by Colenso, Zulu War, pp. 461-2.

61 WO 32/7772: Maj.-Gen. Crealock to Wolseley, Memorandum of Operations of the First Division, 18 April to 7 July 1879.

62 *Natal Witness*, 8 July 1879: Maj.-Gen. Crealock's report, 5 July 1879.

63 *Times of Natal*, 9 July 1879: Port Durnford correspondent, 6 July 1879.

64 WO 32/7772: Memorandum of Operations of the First Division, Maj.-Gen. Crealock to Wolseley, 4 and 5 July 1879.

65 WO 32/7772: Report of Operations of First Division, Maj.- Gen. Crealock to Wolseley, 21 July 1879.

66 Vijn, *Cetshwayo's Dutchman*, pp. 43-4, 49.

CHAPTER 25

1 On 2 July 1879 Cetshwayo asked of his assembled *amabutho*: 'If the white men keep advancing when so many of them have been killed, and when

so many of us have been killed, what is there to stop them?' (*JSA* IV, p. 72: Mtshapi).

2 For a very detailed account of the battle of Ulundi, see Laband, *Battle of Ulundi*, pp. 1-48, *passim*.

3 Gibson, *Story of the Zulus*, p. 213.

4 Carle Faye Papers 7: 'How We Captured Cetywayo' by Martin Oftebro, p. 1.

5 Montague, *Campaigning*, p. 311.

6 For the most persuasive expression of this line of argument, see Guy, *Zulu Kingdom*, pp. 58-9. It has since been hallowed by S. Marks in 'Southern Africa 1867-1886' in Oliver and Sanderson, *Cambridge History of Africa*, 6, pp. 392-3.

7 *BPP* (C. 2482), no. 47: Wood to DAG, 27 June 1879.

8 Dlamini, *Two Kings*, pp. 70-1.

9 Mathews, 'Chelmsford', pp. 316-17.

10 War Office, *Narrative*, p. 111; Molyneux, *Campaigning*, p. 177.

11 *BPP* (C. 2454), enc. in no. 55: Telegram no. 2, Chelmsford to Officer Commanding Landman's Drift, 5 July 1879.

12 For these last-minute negotiations, see Laband 'Humbugging the General?' in Laband and Thompson, *Kingdom and Colony*, pp. 58-9.

13 Colenso, Digest, series 1, part 2, pp. 593a-593b. Magema interviewed Mfunzi in October 1879 and was shown the still unopened letter.

14 *Times of Natal*, 13 July 1879: statement of Undungunyanga, son of Umgenane, a prisoner taken at the battle of Ulundi.

15 *BPP* (C. 2454), enc. 1 in no. 55: Telegram no. 2, Chelmsford to Officer Commanding Landman's Drift, 5 July 1879. For his detailed report on the final march to Ulundi and the battle itself, see *BPP* (C. 2482), enc. in no. 32: Chelmsford to Secretary of State for War, 6 July 1879.

16 Vijn, *Cetshwayo's Dutchman*, p. 52.

17 WO 32/7767: Newdigate's Diary for the week ending 6 July: 1 July 1879.

18 Molyneux, *Campaigning*, pp. 181-2; Harrison, *Recollections*, pp. 184-5.

19 Webb and Wright, *Zulu King Speaks*, p. 58.

20 Faye Papers 7: 'When the English Took Cetywayo', told by Mapelu Zungu and set down by Carl Faye in about 1964, p. 1.

21 *Natal Colonist*, 12 July 1879.

22 Vijn, *Cetshwayo's Dutchman*, pp. 50-1, 144: Colenso's notes; Webb and Wright, *Zulu King Speaks*, p. 58.

23 *Natal Colonist*, 20 September 1879: Cetshwayo's statement on his march to the coast; Vijn, *Cetshwayo's Dutchman*, p. 51; *JSA* IV, p. 72: Mtshapi.

24 WO 32/7767: Newdigate's Diary for the week ending 6 July: 2 July 1879.

25 Tomasson, *With the Irregulars*, p. 158.

26 For descriptions of Buller's reconnaissance and the Zulu ambush, see WO 32/7764: Wood to DAG, 5 July 1879; *Natal Witness*, 17 July 1879: Correspondent with Wood's Division, 7 July 1879; Tomasson, *With the Irregulars*, pp. 160-4; Mossop, *Running the Gauntlet*, pp. 88-9.

27 Malet, *Diary*, pp. 25-6; Tomasson, *With the Irregulars*, pp. 157-60.

28 *Times of Natal*, 13 July 1879: statement by Undungunyanga.

29 *Illustrated London News*, 26 July 1879, p. 78: Archibald Forbes's report, 3 July 1879.

30 *Times of Natal*, 13 July 1879: Statement by Undungunyanga.

31 Hotham Papers: Hotham to Ella, 7 July 1879; Malet, *Diary*, p. 26.

32 Moodie, *British, Boers and Zulus*, p. 355: Melton Prior's account.

33 WO 32/7767: Newdigate's Diary for the week ending 6 July: 3 July 1879.

34 AC, p. 141: Robinson to Maude

Lefroy, 6 July 1879; Commeline Letters: Commeline to his Pater, 18 July 1879.

35 WO 32/7764: Glyn to Assistant Adjutant-General, 5 July 1879; War Office.

36 Callwell, *Small Wars*, pp. 190, 256-67, 386-7, 414.

37 McToy, *13th Regiment*, p. 84.

38 Moodie, *British, Boers and Zulus*, p. 360: Account by Archibald Forbes; Tomasson, *With the Irregulars*, pp. 175-6.

39 *Times of Natal*, 13 July 1879: Statement by Undungunyanga.

40 Harrison, *Recollections*, p. 186.

41 Stabb's Zulu War Diary: 4 July 1879; WO 32/7753: Telegram, Maj.-Gen. Clifford to Secretary of State for War, recd. 23 July 1879.

42 St Vincent Journal: 4 July 1879.

43 AC, p. 127, Russell no. 2: Russell to Alison, 6 July 1879.

44 WO 32/7767: Newdigate's Diary for the week ending 6 July: 4 July 1879; St Vincent Journal: 4 July 1879; AC, p. 141: Robinson to Maude Lefroy, 6 July 1879.

45 War Office, *Narrative*, p. 117.

46 Ashe and Wyatt Edgell, *Zulu Campaign*, p. 350; Norris-Newman, In Zululand, p. 213.

47 Webb and Wright, *Zulu King Speaks*, p. 34.

48 Vijn, *Cetshwayo's Dutchman*, p. 144: Colenso's notes.

49 Webb and Wright, *Zulu King Speaks*, pp. 34-5; Dlamini, *Two Kings*, pp. 70-1.

50 Vijn, *Cetshwayo's Dutchman*, p. 52; Webb and Wright, *Zulu King Speaks*, p. 35.

51 Woodgate's Military Diary: 7 July 1879; *Times of Natal*, 13 July 1879: statement of Undungunyanga.

52 Woodgate's Military Diary: 7 July 1879.

53 At long range, or between 630 m and 1260 m, fire was only 2 per cent

effective; at medium range, or between 270 m and 630 m, it was 5 per cent effective; at close range, or between 90 m and 270 m, it was 10 per cent effective. At point blank range, or between 0 m and 90 m, it was 15 per cent effective (Whitehouse, *Battle in Africa*, p. 35).

54 WO 32/7764: Col. Drury-Lowe to Assistant Adjutant-General, 6 July 1879.

55 Tomasson, *With the Irregulars*, pp. 177-9.

56 Tomasson, *With the Irregulars*, p. 183.

57 WO 32/7764: Buller to Assistant Adjutant-General, 5 July 1879.

58 TS 41: Offy Shepstone to William, 17 July 1879.

59 AC, p. 141: Robinson to Maude Lefroy, 6 July 1879; *Natal Mercury*, 11 July 1879: letter from Wood's Column.

60 Mitford, *Zulu Country*, p. 237: account of Eye-Witness in the *Port Elizabeth Telegraph*, 12 August 1879.

61 Moodie, *British, Boers and Zulus*, p. 356: Melton Prior's account; Ashe and Wyatt Edgell, *Zulu Campaign*, p. 347.

62 TS 41: Offy Shepstone to William, 17 July 1879.

63 AC, p. 141: Robinson to Maude Lefroy, 6 July 1879; Cpl. Roe's Diary: p. 68; Malet, Diary, p. 29.

64 Norris-Newman, *In Zululand*, p. 85: Mehlokazulu's statement.

65 Guy, *Zulu Kingdom*, pp. 58-9.

66 Bennett, *Eyewitness in Zululand*, pp. 104-5.

67 *Illustrated London News*, 23 August 1879, p. 182: account by *Natal Witness* correspondent.

68 Moodie, *British, Boers and Zulus*, p. 356: Melton Prior's account.

69 Moodie, *British, Boers and Zulus*, p. 366: Account by *Natal Colonist* correspondent.

70 AC. p. 141: Robinson to Maude

Lefroy, 6 July 1879; Tomasson, *With the Irregulars*, p. 188.

71 TS 41: Offy Shepstone to William, 17 July 1879; Tomasson, *With the Irregulars*, p. 188; Fripp, 'Zulu War', p. 558.

72 Mitford, *Zulu Country*, p. 238: Testimony of an *induna* of the kwaNdabakawombe *ikhanda*.

73 Wood, *Midshipman*, II, p. 81.

74 TS 41: Offy Shepstone to William, 17 July 1879.

75 Ashe and Wyatt Edgell, *Zulu Campaign*, p. 345.

76 *Graphic*, 13 September 1879, p. 246.

77 Malet, *Diary*, p. 29.

78 AC, p. 141: Robinson to Maude Lefroy, 6 July 1879.

79 Slade Papers: Slade to his mother, 6 July 1879.

80 Fripp, 'Zulu War', pp. 558-60.

81 Molyneux, *Campaigning*, pp. 187-8.

82 Vijn, *Cetshwayo's Dutchman*, p. 143: Colenso's notes.

83 Hotham Papers: Hotham to Ella, 7 July 1879.

84 Stabb's Zulu War Diary: 4 July 1879; Fripp, 'Zulu War', p. 560.

85 Carl Faye Papers 7: 'When the English took Cetywayo', told by Mapelu Zungu kaMkhosana, p. 2.

86 TS 41: Offy Shepstone to William, 17 July 1879.

87 For the mounted pursuit see WO 32/7764: Col. Drury-Lowe to Assistant Adjutant-General, 6 July 1879; St Vincent Journal: 4 July 1879; WO 32/7764: Buller to Wood, 5 July 1879; Ashe and Wyall Edgell, *Zulu Campaign*, pp. 348-9.

88 Tommason, *With the Irregulars*, p. 197.

89 Malet, *Diary*, p. 29; Montague, *Campaigning*, p. 235.

90 *Natal Mercury*, 11 July 1879: letter from Wood's Column; Tomasson, *With the Irregulars*, p. 199.

91 AC, p.141: Robinson to Maude Lefroy, 6 July 1879.

92 The maximum range for a 9-pounder firing shrapnel was about 3230 m.

93 Tomasson, *With the Irregulars*, p. 206.

94 Stabb's Zulu War Diary: 4 July 1879; *JSA* IV, p. 73: Mtshapi.

95 Norris-Newman, *In Zululand*, p. 215; Tomasson, *With the Irregulars*, pp. 199-200; Moodie, *British Boers and Zulus*, p. 358: Melton Prior's account.

96 Colenso Papers 27, no. 224: Colenso to Chesson, 25 July 1879; *BPP* (C. 2482), enc. in no. 51: Fannin to Colonial Secretary, [?] July 1879.

97 Moodie, *British, Boers and Zulus*, p. 367: Account by correspondent of the *Natal Colonist*.

98 *JSA* IV, p. 73: Mtshapi.

99 AC, p.141: Robinson to Maude Lefroy, 6 July 1879.

100 Tomasson, *With the Irregulars*, p. 198.

101 Norris-Newman, *In Zululand*, p. 213.

102 *Natal Witness*, 21 August 1879: Correspondent with Clarke's Column, 11 August 1879; *Times of Natal*, 22 August 1879: Ulundi correspondent, 12 August 1879.

103 WO 32/7764: Buller to Wood, 5 July 1879.

104 War Office, *Narrative*, p. 117.

105 Moodie, *British, Boers and Zulus*, p. 358: Melton Prior's account.

CHAPTER 26

1 Zulu near Fort Evelyn greeted the news of King Cetshwayo's capture with these words (Stabb's Zulu War Diary: 29 August 1879).

2 WO 32/7767: Precis of Diaries of Officers Commanding Posts on Frontiers and Lines of Communication: Fort Newdigate, 6-9 July; Fort Evelyn, [?] July; Conference Hill, 7-9 July 1879.

3 Webb and Wright, *Zulu King Speaks*, p. 35; Fuze, *Black People*, pp. 114-5;

JSA IV, p. 73: Mtshapi.

4 Dlamini, *Two Kings*, pp. 71-2; *JSA* IV, p. 192: Ndabazezwe.

5 Webb and Wright, *Zulu King Speaks*, p. 35.

6 *BPP* (C. 2482), enc. 2 in no. 23: Telegram, Chelmsford to Wolseley, 6 July 1879; Harness, 'Zulu Campaign', pp. 483-4.

7 Vijn, *Cetshwayo's Dutchman*, p. 53.

8 AC, p. 101: Lt.-Col. Crealock to Alison, 11 July 1879; Natal Mercury, 22 August 1879: Fort Evelyn correspondent, 14 August 1879.

9 Montague, *Campaigning*, p. 281.

10 War Office, *Narrative*, pp. 119-125.

11 WO 32/7760: Wolseley to Secretary of State for War, 10 July 1879. See also Webb and Wright, *Zulu King Speaks*, p. 35.

12 For Zulu coastal submissions after Ulundi, see Laband, 'Zulu Polity' in Laband and Thompson, *Kingdom and Colony*, p. 15.

13 *Natal Mercury*, 26 July 1879: letter from one of Sir Garnet's Staff.

14 For Wolseley's negotiations near oNdini, see Laband, 'Zulu Polity' in Laband and Thompson, *Kingdom and Colony*, p. 16.

15 Wolseley Papers, Letters 2: Wolseley to his wife, 10 July 1879.

16 WO 32/7756: Wolseley to Secretary of State for War, 21 July 1879.

17 WO 32/7786: Brig.-Gen. G. Pomeroy Colley: Minute for the guidance of all officers commanding posts and all political officers dealing with the Zulu people, 26 July 1879.

18 For the pacification of north-western Zululand, see Laband, 'Mbilini' in Laband and Thompson, *Kingdom and Colony*, p. 204.

19 For the pacification of the middle border, see Laband and Thompson, *Umvoti*, pp. 79-82.

20 For the pacification of the Mzinyathi frontier, see Laband and Thompson, *Buffalo Border*, pp. 78-81.

21 For the submission of central and southern Zululand, see Laband, 'Zulu Polity' in Laband and Thompson, *Kingdom and Colony*, pp. 18-19.

22 *BPP* (C. 2482), no. 27: Wolseley to Secretary of State for Colonies, 18 July 1879.

23 WO 32/7775: Wolseley to Secretary of State for War, 13 August 1879.

24 Webb and Wright, *Zulu King Speaks*, p. 59.

25 For Cetshwayo's negotiations with Wolseley, see Laband, 'Humbugging the General?' in Laband and Thompson, *Kingdom and Colony*, pp. 59-60.

26 Vijn, *Cetshwayo's Dutchman*, p. 54.

27 *JSA* III, p. 123: Mgundeni.

28 Vijn, *Cetshwayo's Dutchman*, pp. 58-62; Webb and Wright, *Zulu King Speaks*, p. 35.

29 WO 147/7: Wolseley's Journal: 14 August 1879; *Times of Natal*, 27 August 1879: Correspondent near Ulundi, 15 August 1878.

30 Colenso Papers 27, no. 230: Colenso to Chesson, 13 September 1879.

31 Vijn, *Cetshwayo's Dutchman*, p. 160: Colenso's notes.

32 See Laband, 'Zulu Polity' in Laband and Thompson, *Kingdom and Colony*, pp. 18-19.

33 For the pacification of the Mdlalose and Qulusi, see Laband, 'Mbilini' in Laband and Thompson, *Kingdom and Colony*, pp. 204-5.

34 AU 14, no. 301: Rudolph to Lt.-Col. Villiers, 6 August 1879.

35 Webb and Wright, *Zulu King Speaks*, p. 30.

36 For Manyonyoba's subjugation, see Laband, 'Mbilini' in Laband and Thompson, *Kingdom and Colony*, pp. 205-7.

37 Wolseley Papers, Letters 2: Wolseley to his Wife, 26 August 1879.

38 Colenso Papers 27, no. 230: Colenso to Chesson, 13 September 1879;

Fuze, *Black People*, p. 115.

39 See Guy, *Zulu Kingdom*, p. 59.

40 WO 147/7: Wolseley's Journal: 23 August 1879.

41 WO 147/7: Wolseley's Journal: 26 August 1879; *BPP* (C. 2482), no. 82: Wolseley to Secretary of State for Colonies, 27 August 1879.

42 John Shepstone Papers 10: 'Reminiscences of the Past', p. 103.

43 For the capture of the king, see War Office, *Narrative*, pp. 132-6; and Carl Faye Papers 7: M. Oftebro, 'How We Captured Cetywayo', *passim*.

44 Marter, *Capture of Cetywayo*, p. 18.

45 Special Reporter, *Cetywayo*, p. 15.

46 John Shepstone Papers 10: 'Reminiscences of the Past', p. 104.

47 Special Reporter, *Cetywayo*, p. 15.

48 Special Reporter, *Cetywayo*, pp. 15-16; Binns, *Last Zulu King*, pp. 174-7.

49 Special Reporter, *Cetywayo*, p. 16.

50 For the settlement of Zululand, see Laband, 'Zulu Polity' in Laband and Thompson, *Kingdom and Colony*, pp. 22-4.

51 For a description of the formal proceedings on 1 September, see *Natal Mercury*, 8 September 1879.

52 See Brookes & Webb, *History of Natal*, p. 147; Guy, *Zulu Kingdom*, p. 76.

53 Littleton Papers, no. 107: Littleton to his Mother, 11 July 1879.

54 Preston, *Wolseley's South African Journal*, pp. 2-3; C. Ballard, 'Sir Garnet Wolseley and John Dunn: The Architects and Agents of the Ulundi Settlement' in Duminy and Ballard, *New Perspectives*, pp. 130-1.

55 TS 42: G. Cato to T. Shepstone, 29 September 1879; Ballard, *John Dunn*, pp. 147-8.

56 For the thirteen appointed chiefs, see Guy, *Zulu Kingdom*, pp. 72-5. For the boundaries of the chiefdoms, see ZA 19, enc. in St. L. A. Herbert to Melmoth Osborn, 24 February 1880: Report of the Zululand Boundary Commission by Lt.-Col. G. Villiers,

Capt. J. Alleyne and Capt. H. Moore, 5 December 1879.

57 CSO 1927, no. 4162/1879: Robson to Colonial Secretary, 8 September 1879.

58 SNA 1/1/35, no. 73: Robson to SNA, 9 October 1879; ZA 21, enc. in G.728/79: Report on the Relocation of Manyonyoba, 15 October 1879.

59 Ballard, 'Wolseley and John Dunn' in Duminy and Ballard, *New Perspectives*, pp. 137-9.

60 Preston, *Wolseley's South African Journal*, p. 318 (note 53.22).

61 WO 32/7785: Journal of Clarke's Column, 4-5, 8, 11-20 September 1879. All the chiefs who submitted are listed. See also Laband and Thompson, *Umvoti*, pp. 84-6, 89.

62 Colenso Collection 73: H. Colenso to Sir A. Havelock, 26 September 1888; F. Colenso, *Ruin of Zululand*, II, pp. 384-5.

63 *BPP* (C. 2482), no. 179: Wolseley to Secretary of State for Colonies, 11 November 1879.

64 Mgojana was a descendent of Zwide, the great Ndwandwe chief, through a secondary wife.

65 J. Home Thompson Papers: Report by Thompson, 3 September 1879: Interview with Somkhele, 20 August 1879.

66 Child, *Henry Harford*, pp. 69-73. Harford visited Somkhele in July 1879 and was impressed by his evident power.

67 *BPP* (C. 2482), enc. 2 in no. 93: Wolseley to Villiers, 9 September 1879.

68 *JSA* IV, pp. 341, 378: Ndukwana.

69 *Times of Natal*, 3 November 1879: *Natal Mercury* correspondent at Ulundi, 18 October 1879.

70 *JSA* IV, p. 300: Ndukwana.

71 WO 147/7: Wolseley's Journal: 1 September 1879. Indeed, there ended up being more adherents of Mnyamana in Hamu's territory than

of the Ngenetsheni chief himself.

72 *BPP* (C. 3182), enc. in no. 34: Minute, Osborn to Wood, 30 May 1881.

73 Original Zulu War Treaties: Treaty with Tshingwayo, Ulundi, 1 September 1879.

74 Shepstone, *Native Question*, p. 6.

CHAPTER 27

1 For Cetshwayo's captivity at the Cape, see Special Reporter, *Cetywayo*, pp. 18-22, 29-30; Samuelson, *Long, Long Ago*, pp. 97- 116; Laband and Wright, *Cetshwayo*, p. 21; Webb and Wright, *Zulu King Speaks*, pp. xvi-xxi; Guy, *Zulu Kingdom*, pp. 124-47.

2 Special Reporter, *Cetywayo*, p. 30.

3 Special Reporter, *Cetywayo*, pp. 20-2.

4 See Webb and Wright, *Zulu King Speaks*, pp. 1-38: 'Cetywayo's Story of the Zulu Nation and the War', *Macmillan's Magazine*, February 1880.

5 Binns, *Dinuzulu*, p. 3.

6 Dlamini, *Two Kings*, pp. 71-4; *JSA* III, p. 310: Mpatshana; *JSA* IV, p. 194: Ndabazezwe; Binns, *Dinuzulu*, pp. 1-5.

7 See Webb and Wright, *Zulu King Speaks*, pp. 41-63: Cetshwayo to Sir Hercules Robinson (translated and written by R. Samuelson), 29 March 1881; pp. 65-101: Cetshwayo's evidence to the Cape Government Commission on Native Laws and Customs, 6-7 July 1881.

8 Samuelson, *Long, Long Ago*, p. 105.

9 Pridmore, 'Reaction of Colonial Natal', ch. 2 *passim*.

10 For a summary of Shepstone's and the Colensos' conflicting views, see Laband and Thompson, 'Reduction of Zululand' in Duminy and Guest, *Natal and Zululand*, pp. 207-8.

11 Laband, 'Zululand Administration', pp. 64-6.

12 For events in Zululand between 1879 and Cetshwayo's restoration, see Gibson, *Story of the Zulus*, pp. 221-8.

13 See *BPP* (C. 3182), no. 65: Wood to Kimberley, 31 August 1881.

14 *BPP* (C. 3466), annex. 2 in no. 63: P.J. Joubert to S.J.P. Kruger, 18 July 1882.

15 *BPP* (C. 3466) no. 1: Wolseley to Colonial Office, 23 March 1882.

16 *BPP* (C. 3466), no. 42: Bulwer to Kimberley, 30 June 1882.

17 *BPP* (C. 3466), no. 45: telegram, Bulwer to Kimberley, 8 August 1882.

18 *BPP* (C. 3466), enc. in no. 109: Petition of the inhabitants of the Colony of Natal to Kimberly, n.d.

19 For the negotiations surrounding Cetshwayo's restoration and his time in England, see Laband and Thompson, 'Reduction of Zululand' in Laband and Thompson, *Natal and Zululand*, pp. 209- 11; Gibson, *Story of the Zulus*, pp. 232-9; Binns, *Last Zulu King*, pp. 188-99; Guy, *Zulu Kingdom*, pp. 148-66; Laband and Wright, *Cetshwayo*, pp. 25-6.

20 For Bulwer's instructions relating to the modification of Zibhebhu's territory, see *BPP* (C.3174), enc. 1 in no. 153: Bulwer to Osborn, 22 December 1882.

21 *BPP* (C. 3174), no. 36: Bulwer to the Earl of Derby, 9 May 1883.

22 Laband and Thompson, *Umvoti*, pp. 20-2, 84, 89.

23 *BPP* (C. 3705), enc. 1 in no 36: Survey of new boundary line of Usibebu's territory, Zululand, made by J.E. Fannin in January 1883.

24 *BPP* (C. 3705), enc. 4 in no. 36: Fannin to Bulwer, 17 April 1883.

25 *BPP* (C.3174), enc. 1 in no. 153: Bulwer to Osborn, 22 December 1882.

26 *BPP* (C.3705), enc. 3 in no. 36: Bulwer to Fannin, 14 April 1883.

27 *BPP* (C. 3705), enc. 1 in no. 36: Fannin to Osborn, 14 January 1883; enc. 4 in no. 36: Fannin to Bulwer, 17 April 1883.

28 *BPP* (C. 3466), enc. 2 in no. 61:
Terms, Conditions and Limitations of
Cetywayo's Restoration.
29 *JSA* IV, p. 86: Mtshapi.
30 *BPP* (C. 3466), no. 72: Kimberley to
Bulwer, 7 September, 1882.

CHAPTER 28
1 For the events of 1883 up to the
battle of oNdini, see Pridmore, 'Diary
of Fynn', 1, pp. 92-113; Gibson,
Story of the Zulus, pp. 239-54; Guy,
Zulu Kingdom, pp. 167-200; Laband
and Wright, *Cetshwayo*, pp. 27-31.
2 *JSA* III, p. 310: Mpatshana.
3 Samuelson, *Long, Long Ago*, pp. 118-
19.
4 For Fynn's career, see Pridmore,
'Diary of Fynn', I, pp. 13-25.
5 *BPP* (C. 3293) enc. 1 in no. 161:
Bulwer to Fynn, 8 January 1883.
6 For the battle of Msebe see Pridmore,
'Diary of Fynn', II, pp. 73-3: 4 April
1883: statement of Ntangweni son
of Nobengula; *BPP* (C. 3705), enc. 1
in no. 3: statement of Nsaba, 10
April 1883, and statement of
Marwanqa and Matiya, 12 April
1883; enc. in no. 39: statement of
Thomas Edwin Peachey, 27 April
1883; *BPP* (C. 3864), enc. in no. 9:
statements of Maqondiyana,
Lagatyana and Nongai, 14 June
1883; Gibson, *Story of the Zulus*,
pp. 247-9; Guy, *Zulu Kingdom*,
pp. 191-3.
7 Cope, *Izibongo*, p. 206.
8 Lugg, *Historic Natal*, p. 150.
9 Gibson, *Story of the Zulus*, p. 248.
10 Gibson, *Story of the Zulus*, p. 249.
11 *BPP* (C. 3864), enc. in no. 9:
statements of Maqondiyana and two
other messengers from Zibhebhu, 14
June 1883.
12 Dlamini, *Two Kings*, pp. 75-9.
13 *BPP* (C. 3705), no. 4: Bulwer to Lord
Derby, 23 April 1883.
14 *BPP* (C. 3705), no. 48: Shepstone to
Colonial Office, 12 May 1883.

15 *BPP* (C. 3864), no, 29: Bulwer to
Derby, 16 July 1883.
16 For the battle of oNdini, see
Pridmore, 'Diary of Fynn', II,
pp. 140-1, 145, 148, 150-1, 155,
161-4, 166: 21, 24, 30 July, 2, 10,
23, 27 August 1883; *BPP* (C. 3864),
enc. in no. 71: Fynn to Bulwer, 23
August 1883; Samuelson, *Long, Long
Ago*, pp. 120-1; *JSA* I, p. 125:
Dunjwa; III, pp. 203-4: Mkebeni; IV,
pp. 185-6, 188-9, 193: Ndabazezwe;
Fuze, *Black People*, pp. 116-19;
Gibson, *Story of the Zulus*, pp. 255-8;
Guy, *Zulu Kingdom*, pp. 200-4.
17 Samuelson, *Long, Long Ago*, p. 120.
18 *JSA* IV, p. 189: Ndabazezwe.
19 Guy, *Zulu Kingdom*, p. 204.
20 Pridmore, 'Diary Fynn', II, p. 145: 24
July 1883. See also Dlamini, *Two
Kings*, pp. 76-7.
21 Guy, *Zulu Kingdom*, pp. 205-6.
22 Cope, *Izibongo*, p. 206.

CHAPTER 29
1 For Cetshwayo's last months and
death, see Gibson, *Story of the Zulus*,
pp. 259-67; Guy, *Zulu Kingdom*,
pp. 204-18; Laband and Wright,
Cetshwayo, pp. 31-2;
2 See Pridmore, 'Diary of Fynn', II,
pp. 186-91: Fynn to Osborn, 16
October 1883.
3 For Cetshwayo's death and burial,
see *BPP* (C. 4037), no. 40: Bulwer to
Derby, 12 February 1884; *JSA* III,
pp. 200-4: Mkebeni; IV, pp. 144-5:
Mtshayankomo; Fuze, *Black People*,
pp. 119-21; Binns, *Last Zulu King*,
pp. 211-12, 225-9; Binns, *Dinuzulu*,
pp. 8, 13-17, 259-60.
4 Its pieces lay on the grave until
removed to the KwaZulu Cultural
Museum at Ulundi for safekeeping.
5 *JSA* III, p. 202: Mkebeni.
6 See Binns, *Dinuzulu*, pp. 86-9.
7 See *BPP* (C. 4037), enc. in no. 44:
Statement by Undabuko and others
of the words alleged to have been

spoken by Cetywayo in the forenoon of the day upon which he died, 11 February 1884.

8   A son, Manzolwandle, was indeed born posthumously to Cetshwayo by his chief wife.

9   Fuze, *Black People*, p.123.

10 Colenso, *Ruin of Zululand*, I, p. 57.

11 Binns, *Dinuzulu*, pp. 3-5.

12 For the period between Cetshwayo's death and the battle of Tshaneni, see Gibson, *Story of the Zulus*, pp. 267-70; Binns, *Dinuzulu*, pp. 13-33; Guy, *Zulu Kingdom*, pp. 218-225; Dominy, 'Etshaneni', pp. 27-8.

13 *BPP* (C. 3864), enc. 1 in no. 65: Statement by Umdudwa, a messenger from Umyamana to the Secretary for Native Affairs, 22 August 1883.

14 *BPP* (C. 3864), no. 161: Bulwer to Derby, 24 December 1883.

15 Samuelson, *Long, Long Ago*, p. 122.

16 War Office, *Precis*, pp. 94-6.

17 For Dinuzulu's coronation, see *Natal Witness*, 29 May 1884; *BPP* (C. 4191), no. 54: Bulwer to Derby, 31 May 1884; enc. in no. 54: A.L. Pretorius to Bulwer, 25 May 1884; Binns, *Dinuzulu*, pp. 28-32.

18 See *BPP* (C. 4214), no. 4: Proclamation signed by Dinizulu (his mark) and A. Shiel, 21 May 1884 (translation).

19 *BPP* (C. 4645), enc. 1 in no. 21: Bulwer to Stanley, 18 August 1885.

20 *Natal Witness*, 26 June 1884.

21 For the battle of Tshaneni, see *Natal Witness*, 26 June 1884; *BPP* (C. 4191), enc. in no. 70: statement by Usibebu, 13 June 1884; Fuze, *Black People*, pp. 123-4; Gibson, *Story of the Zulus*, pp. 270-2; Binns, *Dinuzulu*, pp. 34-8; Guy, *Zulu Kingdom*, pp. 226; Dominy, 'Etshaneni', pp. 28-31.

22 *JSA* III, p. 317: Mpatshana.

23 Fuze, *Black People*, p. 124.

24 *BPP* (C. 4191), no. 82: Derby to Bulwer, 19 August 1884.

25 *BPP* (C. 4214), Bulwer to Derby, 15 September 1884; *BPP* (C.4274), no. 10: Maj.-Gen. Sir L. Smyth to Secretary of State for War, 19 September 1884.

26 For the formation of the New Republic, see Gibson, *Story of the Zulus*, pp, 273-4; Binns, *Dinuzulu*, pp. 39-66; Laband and Thompson, 'Reduction of Zululand', in Duminy and Guest, *Natal and Zululand*, pp. 213-15; Dominy, 'The New Republicans', pp. 87-94; Dominy, 'Etshaneni', pp. 31-2.

27 *BPP* (C. 4214), enc. in no. 44: Bulwer to Derby, 26 August 1884.

28 See *BPP* (C. 4214), enc. in no. 56: Proclamation of the New Republic, 16 August 1884.

29 Guy, *Zulu Kingdon*, pp. 231-2.

30 *BPP* (C. 4214), no. 66: Colonial Office to Foreign Office, 10 October 1884.

31 See, for example, *BPP* (C. 4274) Message from Dinuzulu, Ndabuko and Mnyamana to H.C. Shepstone, 11 May 1885.

32 Binns, *Dinuzulu*, pp. 66-7.

33 *BPP* (C. 4587), Bulwer to Derby, 12 January 1885.

34 For British intervention and annexation, see Gibson, *Story of the Zulus*, pp. 275-85; Guy, *Zulu Kingdom*, pp. 233-7; Binns, *Dinuzulu*, pp. 68-100; Laband and Thompson, 'Reduction of Zululand' in Duminy and Guest, *Natal and Zululand*, pp. 214-16.

35 *BPP* (C. 4913), no. 1: Memorandum on the situation in the Zulu Country beyond the Reserve territory by Bulwer, 6 January 1886.

36 *BPP* (C. 4980), no. 42: Havelock to Stanhope, 24 October 1886.

37 See *BPP* (C. 5143), enc. 1 in no. 2: Dinuzulu, Ndabuko, Mnyamana, Shingana and Mahanana to Havelock, 26 November 1886.

38 *BPP* (C. 5143), enc. 1 in no 10: Osborn to Havelock, 8 February

1887.

39 *BPP* (C. 5143), enc. in no. 28: Proclamation of the Annexation of Zululand, 14 May 1887.

CHAPTER 30

1 ZA 5, no. R595/87: Havelock to Osborn, 21 June 1887.

2 NLB I, pp. 8-9: Addison to Osborn, 23 July 1887.

3 GHZ 845: Osborn to Havelock, 13 July 1887; ZA 41, no. 13: Osborn to Havelock, 16 July 1887.

4 See Laband and Thompson, 'Reduction of Zululand' in Duminy and Guest, *Natal and Zululand*, p. 216.

5 See *BPP* (C. 5331), enc. 1 in no. 2: Laws and Regulations for the Government of Zululand (Zululand No. II, 1887), promulgated on 21 June 1887.

6 See *BPP* (C. 5331), enc. 3 in no. 2: Memorandum by Shepstone, 23 April 1887.

7 *BPP* (C. 5143), enc. 3 in no. 10: Memorandum on the Zulu Situation by Sir T. Shepstone, 17 February 1887.

8 *BPP* (C. 5143), enc. in no. 13: Memorandum by Shepstone, 12 August 1887.

9 Laband, 'Zululand Administration', pp. 68-9.

10 Stabb Papers 6, no. 2/2/80: Stabb to Havelock, 5 September 1888.

11 Laws and Regulations of Zululand, articles 7, 13, 22.

12 ZA 5, no. R856/87: Proclamation (Zululand No. III of 1887) of 30 August 1887.

13 Laws and Regulations, articles 47, 48, 69.

14 ZA 41, no. 49: Osborn to Havelock, 8 May 1887; GHZ 845: Osborn to Havelock, 13 July 1887.

15 Addison Papers, Osborn to Addison, 7 August 1887. See also, NLB I, pp. 11-12: Addison to Osborn, 23 July 1887.

16 NLB I, pp. 14-16: Addison to Osborn, 31 July 1887.

17 NC: Osborn to Addson, 12 August 1887.

18 Addison Papers: Osborn to Addison, 7 August 1887.

19 NLB I, pp. 17-19: Addison to Osborn, 8 August 1887.

20 NLB I, pp. 24-6: Addison to Osborn, 20 August 1887.

21 NLB I, pp. 20-2: Addison to Resident Commissioner, 14 August 1887.

22 GHZ 845: Havelock to Osborn, 21 August 1887.

23 ZA 5, enc. in no. R855/87: D.J. Esselen to Havelock, 1 September 1887.

24 GHZ 821, no. 40: Havelock to Holland, 14 September 1887.

25 GHZ 845: Osborn to Havelock, 9 September 1887.

26 Colenso Collection, Box 106, 'Dinizulu's Statement, 22 December 1888', p. 7: Mpwapuna's statement.

27 GHZ 845: Osborn to Havelock, 12 September 1887.

28 Gibson, *Story of the Zulus*, pp. 289-90.

29 BPP (C. 5331) enc. in no. 36: A. Shepstone to Osborn, 9 November 1887.

30 GHZ 704, enc. 4 in no. ZA149/87: Memorandum by T. Shepstone, 31 July 1887.

31 GHZ 707, enc. in no. Z227/87: Telegram, State President of the South African Republic to the High Commissioner, 23 September 1887.

32 GHZ 707, no. Z238/87: Holland to Havelock, 12 September 1887.

33 GHZ 845, Havelock to McKean, 17 October 1887.

34 War Office, *Precis*, p. 98.

35 Colenso Collection, Box 101: Message to Havelock from Dinuzulu, Umnyamama, Undabuko and the Heads of the Zulu people, 11 October 1887.

36 *BPP* (C. 5331), enc. 1 in no. 15: Message from Dinuzulu, Ndabuko, Siwetu, Umnyamana, and all the Zulu headmen to Osborn, 22 August 1887.

37 GHZ 845: Havelock to Osborn, 24 October 1887.

38 *BPP* (C. 5331), no. 33: Havelock to Holland, 1 November 1887.

39 For the Eshowe meetings, see *BPP* (C. 5331), no. 37: Havelock to Holland, 22 November 1887, and enclosures 1-6.

40 *BPP* (C. 5331), enc. 2 in no, 37: Memorandum read by Havelock to Dinuzulu and Ndabuko, 14 November 1887.

41 *BPP* (C. 5331), enc. 1 in no. 38: Notes of an interview between Havelock and Usibebu, 15 November 1887.

42 Fuze, *Black People*, pp. 124-5.

43 CSCZ, p. 34: Addison's evidence, 17 November 1888.

44 GHZ 845: Stabb to Havelock, 23 November 2887; CSCZ, p. 159: Foxon's evidence, 1 December 1888; Addison Papers: Addison to Havelock, 18 March 1888.

45 Stabb Papers 5, no. 2/2/68: Stabb to General Sir H. Torrens, 30 November 1887.

CHAPTER 31

1 NLB I, pp. 55-6: Addison to Osborn, 30 November 1887.

2 GHZ 845: Osborn to Havelock, 25, 30 November, 6 December 1887.

3 Addison Paper: Galloway to Addison, 15 December 1887.

4 NC: Osborn to Addison, 6 December 1887.

5 NLB I, pp. 66-7: Addison to Osborn, 6 December 1887.

6 NLB I, p. 70: Addison to Osborn, 8, 9 December 1887.

7 NLB I, pp. 91-4: Addison to Osborn, 20 December 1887.

8 Addison Papers: Galloway to Addison, 15 December 1887; NLB I, pp. 83-6: Addison to Osborn, 18 December 1887.

9 NLB I, pp. 83-6, 88-90: Addison to Osborn, 18, 19 December 1887.

10 Addison Papers: Osborn to Addison, 19 December 1887.

11 NLB I, pp. 95-8: Addison to Osborn, 23 December 1887.

12 NLB I, pp. 102-5: Addison to Osborn, 27 December 1887.

13 See NLB I, pp. 113-20: Addison to Osborn, 2, 3 January 1888.

14 NLB I, pp. 113-14: Addison to Osborn, 2 January 1888.

15 NC: Osborn to Addison, 3 and 4 January 1888.

16 NLB I, pp. 117-20, 127-9: Addison to Osborn, 3, 6 January 1888.

17 NC: Galloway to Addison, 8 January 1888.

18 *Natal Witness*, 10 January 1888.

19 GHZ 821, no. 5/88: Havelock to Holland, 18 January 1888.

20 Stabb Papers 5, no. 2/2/71: Stabb to Torrens, 11 January 1888.

21 NLB I, p.148: Addison to Osborn, 13 January 1888.

22 NLB I, pp. 145-6: Addison to Osborn, 15 January 1888.

23 ZA 5, no. R105/88: Havelock to Osborn, 12 January 1888.

24 NLB I, pp. 159-61: Addison to Osborn, 21 January 1888.

25 NC: Osborn to Addison, 26 January 1888.

26 NLB I, pp. 165-6, 168-9: Addison to Osborn, 24, 28 January 1888; Stabb Papers 4, no. 2/2/17: Martin to Stabb, 25 January 1888.

27 NLB I, pp. 167-8: Addison to Galloway, 27 January 1888.

28 NLB I, pp. 189-91: Addison to Osborn, 9 February 1888.

29 Laband, 'Dick Addison', pp. 102-3, 243.

30 *BPP* (C.6684), enc. 6 in no. 1: List B

31 See Laband, 'Dick Addison', pp. 238-41: Appendix E: The incidence of

expulsions from Zibhebhu's location, 1887-88.

32 NLB I, pp. 203-6: Addison to Osborn, 18 February 1888.

33 NLB I, pp. 215-19: Addison to Osborn, 26 February 1888. 10

34 NLB I, pp. 225-6: Addison to Osborn, 6 March 1888.

35 NLB I, pp. 236-9: Addison to Osborn, 10 March 1888.

36 NLB I, pp. 236-9, 240-2, 252-5, 263-4: Addison to Osborn, 10, 12, 17, 19, 22 March 1888.

37 Addison Papers: Havelock to Addison, 18 March 1888.

38 *BPP* (C. 5522), enc. 2 in no. 6: Reply of the Governor to Umtokwana and other messengers from Dinuzulu, 20 March 1888.

39 GHZ 710, no. Z136/88: Osborn to Havelock, 5 March 1888.

40 For Knight's career and orthodox official views regarding the need to suppress uSuthu aspirations, see Laband, 'Zululand Administration', pp. 67, 69.

41 ZA 6, no. R443/88: Havelock to Osborn, 10 March 1888.

42 NC: Osborn to Addison, 19 March 1888.

43 *BPP* (C.5522), enc. in no. 49: Osborn to Havelock, 11 May 1888.

44 GHZ 712, no. Z413/88: Statement of Sifo and Soni, 9 July 1888.

45 See ZA 21, enc. in no. R777/90: Knight's Report on the Boundaries of Usibebu's Location, 30 April 1888. For his further elucidation of his proceedings, see *BPP* (C.5892), enc. 3 in no. 34: Report by Knight to Osborn, n.d.

46 GHZ 716, no. Z791/88: Kilane's deposition to Addison, 16 October 1888.

47 *BPP* (C.5522), no. 49: Havelock to Knutsford, 22 June 1888.

48 CSCZ, p. 355: Addison's evidence, 12 February 1889.

49 GHZ 821, no. 35/88: Havelock to Knutsford, 25 April 1888.

CHAPTER 32

1 GHZ 711, no, Z249/88: Osborn to Havelock, 26 April 1888; CSCZ, p. 359: Addison's evidence, 12 February 1889; CSCZ, pp. 156-7: Foxon's evidence, 1 December 1888.

2 GHZ 721, no, Z398/89: Escombe and Dumat to Knutsford, 13 May 1889: Report on the 'Trials of the Zulu Chiefs'.

3 For the incident, see GHZ 711, enc. in no. Z249/88: Report by Sub-Inspector Osborn, 26 April 1888; GHZ 712, no. Z413/88: Statement of Sifo and Soni, 9 July 1888.

4 NLB I, pp. 282-4: Addison to Osborn, 2 April 1888.

5 ZA 6, no. R741/88: Havelock to Osborn, 3 May 1888.

6 NLB II, pp. 17-18, 20, 22-3: Addison to Osborn, 4, 9, 12 May 1888.

7 GHZ 716, no. Z767/88: Stabb to Assistant Military Secretary, Cape Town, 19 October 1888 [henceforth Stabb's Report].

8 Gibson, *Story of the Zulus*, p. 302.

9 GHZ 711, annexures A and B in no. Z305/88: statements of Hanis-ka-Bensa and Baleni-ka-Jojo, 16, 17 May 1888; CO 879/30, *African Confidential Print* 370, enc. in no. 48: Osborn to Havelock, 4 September 1888.

10 Stabb Papers 5, no. 2/2/74: Stabb to Havelock, 20 May 1888; Stabb's Report.

11 NLB II, pp. 29-32: Addison to Osborn, 23, 24 May 1888.

12 ZA 41, no. 64: Osborn to Havelock, 25 May 1888.

13 *JSA* IV, p. 292: Ndukwana.

14 *BPP* (C. 5522), no. 27: Havelock to Knutsford, 28 May 1881; NC: Osborn to Addison, 31 May 1888.

15 NC: Osborn to Addison, 31 May 1888; CSCZ, p. 356: Addison's evidence, 12 February 1889.

16 The fullest accounts of the fighting

on Ceza are GHZ 711, no. Z322/88:
Mansel to Osborn, 3 June 1888; and
GHZ 712, no. Z327/88: Captain
Pennefather to Staff Officer, Eshowe,
6 June 1888. See also Stabb's Report
and GHZ 712, no. Z413/88: state-
ment of Sifo and Soni, 9 July 1888;
JSA III, p. 317: Mpatshana; and
Gibson, *Story of the Zulus*, pp. 304-5.

17 Samuelson, *Long, Long Ago*, p. 286.
18 *BPP* (C. 5522), no. 35: Havelock to
Knutsford, 6 June 1888.
19 NLB II, pp. 44, 46: Foxon to Addison,
7, 8 June 1888; GHZ 712, no.
Z413/88: Report by Addison, 4
August 1888; Gibson, *Story of the
Zulus*, pp. 305-6.
20 GHZ 712, no. Z338/88: Osborn to
Havelock, 12 June 1888; *BPP* (C.
5522), no. 53: Stabb to Osborn, 17
June 1888; Stabb's Report.
21 GHZ 712, no. R1058/88: Havelock
to Osborn, 6 June 1888; Stabb's
Report.
22 GHZ 712, no. 345/88: Stabb to
Havelock, 15 June 1888; GHZ 712,
no. Z345/88: Stabb to Osborn, 16
June 1888.
23 NLB II, pp. 42-3, 46: Foxon to
Addison, 5, 6, 8 June 1888.
24 GHZ 716, no. Z791/88: Depositions
taken before Addison, 7, 8, 12
October 1888.
25 NLB II, p. 58: Addison to Osborn, 18
June 1888; GHZ 716, no. Z791/88:
Depositions before Addison, 12
October 1888.
26 CSCZ, p. 184: Foxon's evidence, 4
December 1888.
27 *JSA* III, p. 321: Mpatshana.
28 Fuze, *Black People*, p. 126.
29 For a full account of the battle of
Ivuna, or Ndunu hill, see Laband,
'The Battle of Ivuna', pp. 16-22.
30 Lugg, *Historic Natal*, p. 150.
31 See Colenso Collection, Box 106,
'Dinuzulu's Statement', p. 34.
32 Samuelson, *Long, Long Ago*, p. 285.
33 *BPP* (C. 5522) Stabb to Deputy

Adjutant-General, 28 June 1888;
Stabb's Report.
34 GHZ 712, no. Z377/88: Addison to
Osborn, 26 June 1888; CSCZ, p. 195:
Mansel's evidence, 23 January 1889.
35 *Natal Mercury*, 7 July 1888.
36 NLB III, p. 377: Foxon to Addison, 11
April 1889.
37 GHZ 712, enc. in no. Z374/88: Stabb
to Havelock, 26 June 1888.
38 Stabb's Report.

CHAPTER 33
1 ZA 6, no. R1025/88: Havelock to
Osborn, 3 July 1888.
2 War Office, *Precis*, p. 154.
3 *BPP* (C. 5522), enc. in no. 67:
Osborn to Havelock, 6 July 1888;
War Office, *Precis*, p. 101; Gibson,
Story of the Zulus, pp. 310-11.
4 *Times of Natal*, 12 July 1888.
5 *BPP* (C. 5522), enc. 1 in no. 60:
Smyth to the Adjutant- General of
the Forces, London, 2 July 1888.
6 *BPP* (C. 5522), enc. in no. 67:
Osborn to Havelock, 6 July 1888.
7 Stabb Papers 5, no. 2/2/49: Havelock
to Stabb, 19 September 1888.
8 Stabb 5, no. 2/2/75: Stabb to
Havelock, 1 July 1888. Private and
confidential.
9 *Natal Advertizer*, 27 June 1888.
10 GHZ 713, no. Z485/88: Smyth to
Havelock, 21 July 1888.
11 *Natal Mercury*, 20 July 1888.
12 ZA 6, enc. 3 in no. R937/88:
Havelock to Smyth, 1 July 1888.
13 For the battle of Hlophekhulu, see
BPP (C. 5522), no. 54: Havelock to
Knutsford, 4 July 1888; enc. 1 in no.
66: Addison to Osborn, 5 July 1888;
enc. 2 in no, 66: Knight to Osborn, 7
July 1888; enc. 3 in no. 66: Mansel
to Osborn, 6 July 1888; enc. 4 in no.
66: Osborn to Havelock, 11 July
1888; enc. in no. 75: Stabb to Chief
of Staff, Eshowe, 6 July 1888.
14 Stabb Papers 5, no. 2/2/31: Havelock
to Stabb, 10 July 1888.

15 *BPP* (C. 5522), enc. in no. 55:
    Havelock to Knutsford, 1 August
    1888.
16 NLB II, p. 74, 86-8, 90-2, 96-7, 134-
    6 : Addison to Resident
    Commissioner, 6, 17, 21, 29 July, 12
    August 1888.
17 NC: Windham to Addison, 25 July
    1888.
18 CO 879/30, *African Confidential Print*
    370, enc. 2 in no. 2: Smyth to
    Havelock, 25 July 1888; War Office,
    Precis, pp. 101-2.
19 ZA 6, no. R1216/88: Havelock to
    Osborn, 19 July 1888.
20 NC: Osborn to Addison, 30 July
    1888.
21 NC: Bester to Addison, 2 August
    1888.
22 *BPP* (C. 5892), enc. 3 in no.9: C.
    Saunders to Osborn, 9 August 1888;
    GHZ 716, enc. in no. Z767/88: Stabb
    to AMS, 16 October 1888.
23 GHZ 713, enc. in no. Z562/88:
    McKean to Smyth, 7 August 1888.
24 Stabb Papers 5, no. 2/2/36: Havelock
    to Stabb, 7 August 1888.
25 NLB II, pp. 134-6: Addison to
    Osborn, 12 August 1888; GHZ 714,
    no. Z578/88: H.E. Colenso to
    Havelock, 25 August 1888.
26 Robinson, *Celebrities of the Army*, p. 4.
27 NLB II, pp. 137-40: Addison to
    Bester, 14 August 1888; Addison to
    Osborn, 15 August 1888.
28 NLB II, p. 146: Addison to Col.
    Martin, 16 August 1888.
29 Stabb's Report; War Office, *Precis*,
    pp. 102-3.
30 Stabb Papers 5, no. 2/2/40: Havelock
    to Stabb, 24 August 1888. Private.
31 *Natal Mercury*, 29 August 1888.
32 NLB II, pp. 165-6: Addison to
    Osborn, 30 August 1888.
33 Stabb's Report; War Office, *Precis*,
    p. 103. These garrisons were in turn
    reduced in late November to normal
    levels once Dinuzulu had been
    apprehended.

34 *Natal Mercury*, 5 September 1888.
35 ZA 7, no. R1573/88: Havelock to
    Osborn, 7 September 1888.

CHAPTER 34
 1 Stabb Papers 6, no. 2/2/80: Stabb to
    Havelock, 5 September 1888.
 2 Stabb Papers 5, no. 2/2/51: Martin
    to Stabb, 16 September 1888; NC:
    Osborn to Addison, 23 September
    1888.
 3 For Dinuzulu's vicissitudes in the
    South African Republic between 7
    August and 1 November 1888, see
    van Zyl, 'Dinuzulu se Flug', pp. 12-
    32.
 4 *BPP* (C. 5892), enc. 3 in no. 60:
    Williams to High Commissioner, 1
    November 1888.
 5 NLB III, pp. 130-1, 137-42, 146-7,
    154: Addison to Osborn, 1, 3, 4, 6
    November 1888; Colenso Collection,
    Box 106, 'Dinuzulu's Statement',
    p. 41.
 6 For Dinuzulu's journey through
    Natal and arrest, see Binns, *Dinuzulu*,
    pp. 133-7.
 7 *BPP* (C. 5892), nos. 70 and 76:
    Havelock to Knutsford, 14, 20
    November 1888.
 8 GHZ 714, no. Z385/88: Report on
    the constitution of the court for the
    trial of the prisoners in Zululand by
    Sir M.H. Gallwey, 27 August 1888;
    ZA 7, enc. in no. R1884/88:
    Proclamation (Zululand IV, 1888),
    16 October 1888.
 9 For an account of the trial and the
    removal of the chiefs to St Helena,
    see Binns, *Dinuzulu*, pp. 137-49,
    274-8.
10 *BPP* (C. 5892), no. 162: Havelock to
    Knutsford, 27 May 1889.
11 *BPP* (C. 5893), no. 2: Knutsford to
    Mitchell, 5 December 1889.
12 Fuze, *Black People*, p. 131.
13 Gibson, *Story of the Zulus*, p. 316.
14 Local History Museum, Durban, File
    no. 65/1001: H. Colenso to

Havelock, 20 October 1888.

15 ZA 8, enc. in no. R465/88: Escombe to Havelock, 8 March 1889.

16 GHZ 715, no. Z701/88: Escombe to Havelock, 10 October 1888.

17 See the editorials in the *Times of Natal*, 25 October 1888, and the Natal Advertizer, 23 November and 4 December 1888.

18 Laband, 'Dick Addison', pp. 199-212.

19 CO 879/32, *African Confidential Print* 390, no. 34: Colonial Office to Aborigines' Protection Society, 14 April 1889.

20 Addison Papers: Osborn to Addison, 28 November 1890.

21 See, for example, Colenso, *The Zulu Impeachment of British Officials*, *passim*.

22 GHZ 821, no. 89/89: Havelock to Knutsford, 10 May 1889.

23 For Zibhebhu's activities during August-December 1888, see Laband, 'Dick Addison', pp. 181-94.

24 GHZ 717, no. Z874/88: Knutsford to Havelock, 1 November 1888.

25 CO 879/30, *African Confidential Print* 370, no. 104: Havelock to Knutsford, 19 November 1888.

26 *BPP* (C. 5892), no. 190: Mitchell to Knutsford, 31 July 1889; and enclosures 9-19.

27 Samuelson, *Long, Long Ago*, p. 126.

28 *BPP* (C. 5892), no. 181: Knutsford to Mitchell, 1 August 1889.

29 ZA 10, enc. 2 in R731/90: Osborn to Mitchell, 27 February 1890; and enc. 3 in R731/90: Mitchell to Knutsford, 3 March 1890.

30 ZA 10, enc. 1 in no. R731/90: telegram, Knutsford to Mitchell, 10 April 1890.

31 GHZ 728, no. Z268/90: Osborn to Mitchell, 14 April 1890.

32 GHZ 729, no. R900/1890: Gibson to Osborn, 30 April 1890; and no. R1023/1890: Gibson to Osborn, 17 May 1890.

33 GHZ 729, no. R996/1890: Gibson to Osborn, 15 May 1890.

34 GHZ 729, no. R996/1890: minute by Osborn, 13 June 1890.

35 ZA 11, enc. 2 in no. R1916/1890: Knutsford to Mitchell, 3 October 1890.

36 *BPP* (C.6684), enc. 4 in no. 1: Mitchell to Osborn, 25 August 1891.

37 *BPP* (C. 6684), no. 12: Harriette Colenso to Knutsford, 5 February 1892.

38 *BPP* (C. 6684), enc. in no. 1: Cardew to Mitchell, 24 April 1891.

39 *BPP* (C. 6684), enc. 2 in no. 1: Cardew to Mitchell, 4 July 1891.

40 *BPP* (C. 6684), enc. 7 in no. 1 (M): Notes by W. Windham, Secretary for Zululand, of an interview between Sir C. Mitchell and the uSuthu and Mandlakazi people at Ivuna, 25 August 1891.

41 *BPP* (C. 6684), enc. 6 in no. 1: Journal of the Commission, 26 August-23 September 1891.

42 The following account of the Commission's proceedings and decisions is based on *BPP* (C. 6684), enc. 5 in no. 1: Report of the Commssion by Osborn, Cardew and Gibson, 24 September 1891.

43 See *BPP* (C. 6684), enc. 6 in no. 1: Journal of the Commission, Appendices A1 to L.

44 *BPP* (C. 6684), no. 1: Mitchell to Knutsford, 27 October 1891.

45 *BPP* (C. 6684) no. 5: Knutsford to Mitchell, 23 December 1891.

46 *BPP* (C. 6684), no. 22: Mitchell to Knutsford, 22 March 1892. For Knutsford's rapid approval, see *BPP* (C. 6684), no. 23: Knutsford to Mitchell, 30 April 1892.

47 Their numbers were not great. Gibson estimated (*BPP* (C. 6684), enc. in no. 19: Gibson to Osborn, 5 February 1892) that the Mdletshe occupied 475 huts, Mthumbu's Halbisa 146, and Somfula's 100: a

total (at the rate of 5 to a hut) of 3 605 people.

48 *BPP* (C. 6684), enc. 1 in no. 22: Osborn to Mitchell, 11 March 1892.

49 *BPP* (C. 6684), enc. in no. 3: report by Osborn, 19 November 1891.

50 *BPP* (C. 6684), enc. in no. 14: Report by Osborn, 7 January 1892.

51 *BPP* (C. 6684), enc. in no. 16: Osborn to Mitchell, 4 February 1892.

52 *BPP* (C. 6684), no. 14: Mitchell to Knutsford, 11 January 1892; no. 16: Mitchell to Knutsford, 9 February 1892.

53 *BPP* (C. 6684), no. 1: Mitchell to Knutsford, 27 October 1891.

54 *BPP* (C. 6684), enc. 2 in no. 2: Mubi Nondenisa to Harriette Colenso, 16 September 1891.

55 *BPP* (C. 6684), no. 13: Edward Fairfield to the Aborigines' Protection Society, 5 February 1892.

56 *BPP* (C. 6684), no. 5: Knutsford to Mitchell, 23 December 1891.

57 *BPP* (C. 6684), enc. 1 in no. 17: Osborn to Mitchell, 2 February 1892.

58 Edgecombe, 'Sir Marshall Clarke', pp. 43-53.

59 *BPP* (C. 8782), no. 1: Marquess of Ripon to Sir W.F. Hely Hutshinson, 4 April 1895.

60 Binns, *Dinuzulu*, pp. 151-2; Fuze, *Black People*, pp. 132-5; Ballard, *House of Shaka*, pp. 80-2.

61 *BPP* (C. 8782), no. 1: Ripon to Hely-Hutchinson, 4 April 1895. For the incorporation of Zululand into Natal, see Laband and Thompson, 'Reduction of Zululand' in Duminy and Guest, *Natal and Zululand*, pp. 219-21.

62 See *BPP* (C. 8782), no. 10: Chamberlain to Hely-Hutchinson, 26 August 1896 and nos. 11, 14, 15: Hely-Hutchinson to Chamberlain, 9 October 1896, 20 and 22 January 1897.

63 *BPP* (C. 8782), annexures to No. 50: Letters Patent passed under the Great Seal of the United Kingdom, for annexing the British Possession of Zululand to the Colony of Natal, 1 December 1897; Proclamation by Hely-Hutchinson, 29 December 1897. By Natal Act 37 of 1897, Zululand was annexed to Natal on 30 December 1897.

64 *BPP* (C. 8782), no. 45: Hely-Hutchinson to Chamberlain, 19 November 1897.

65 For Dinuzulu's return, see Binns, *Dinuzulu*, pp. 158-63; Ballard, *House of Shaka*, pp. 82-3.

66 See *BPP* (C. 8782), no. 53: Conditions describing the position which Dinuzulu will hold on his return.

67 *BPP* (C. 8782), enc. in no. 27: Dinuzulu, Ndabuko and Tshingana to Chamberlain, 4 September 1897.

68 *BPP* (C. 8782), no. 32: Chamberlain to Governor Sterndale (St Helena), 29 October 1897.

69 *BPP* (C. 8782), no. 19: Chamberlain to Hely-Hutchinson, 4 May 1897.

70 *BPP* (C. 8782), enc. 1 in no. 37: Hely-Hutshinson to Prime Minister of Natal, 8 October 1897.

71 As the Governor of St Helena had put it, to arrange for their departure from the island was 'no slight matter: they came here savages in karosses; they are leaving with Gladstone bags and packing cases' (*BPP* (C. 8782), no. 46: Sterndale to Chamberlain, 23 November 1897).

72 *JSA* III, p. 201: Mkebeni.

EPILOGUE

1 *Natal Blue Book on Native Affairs, 1898*, p. C 44: Report on Ndwandwe by Gibson, 4 January 1899.

2 For a discussion on changes to the Zulu way of life by the beginning of the twentieth century, see Laband and Thompson, 'Reduction of

Zululand' in Duminy and Guest, *Natal and Zululand*, pp. 221-4.

3 *Natal Blue Book on Native Affairs, 1898*, p. C 43: Report on Ndwandwe by Gibson, 4 January 1899.

4 *Zululand Lands Delimitation Commission*, p. 44: Final Report.

5 Natal Act 1 of 1903, 27 January 1903.

6 *Zululand Lands Delimitation Commission*, p. v: Commission issued by the Governor of Natal to the Imperial and Colonial Commissioners, 1 August 1902.

7 *Zululand Lands Delimitation Commission*, pp. 269, 271: Annexure A by C.R. Saunders to the Final Report, 11 May 1900.

8 *Zululand Lands Delimitation Commission*, p. 44: Final Report, 18 October 1904; *Natal Government Gazette*, no. 3558, 14 August 1906: Governor's Proclamation No. 107, 1906: Rules and Regulations for the Disposal of Crown Lands, other than Crown Reserves, Special Reserves, and Township Lands.

9 Brookes and Hurwitz, *Native Reserves of Natal*, p. 13. See p. 21: Table 4, The Zululand Reserves, 1953.

10 The story has been partially told in Ballard's well illustrated *House of Shaka*, pp. 83-131. Cope, in his recent and masterly study, *To Bind the Nation*, has examined the period 1913 to 1933 in detail. Taylor, in *Shaka's Children*, pp. 263-374, has provided the most comprehensive account to date.

Picture Acknowledgements
and Sources

Select Bibliography

Only documents and works which have been referred to in the footnotes, or which have been directly material to the writing of this book, have been listed below.

MANUSCRIPT SOURCES

Private papers

GREAT BRITAIN

THE BRITISH LIBRARY, LONDON
Hutton Papers

THE BUFFS REGIMENTAL MUSEUM, CANTERBURY
Album of the 2/3rd Regiment

THE BRYNMORE JONES LIBRARY, UNIVERSITY OF HULL
Hotham Journal and Letters

HOVE CENTRAL LIBRARY
Wolseley Papers

NATIONAL ARMY MUSEUM, CHELSEA
Anderson Letters
Anstruther Letters
Chelmsford Papers: 7-36
Cookson Album
Cooper Album
East Scrap-Book
Fairlie Diary and Album
Floor Album
Hume Album
MacSwiney Letters
Mills Album
Roe Diary
Slade Letters

NATIONAL MARITIME MUSEUM, GREENWICH
Hamilton Journal
Milne Letters and Naval Diary
Smith Dorrien Service Scrap-Book

PUBLIC RECORD OFFICE, KEW
Buller Letters
Wolseley Journal

RHODES HOUSE, OXFORD
Anti-Slavery Society Papers: G12
Colenso Papers: S. 1285-6

THE ROYAL ARCHIVES, WINDSOR CASTLE
Ashanti and Zululand Album
Calotypes II
South African Campaign Album, 1879

ROYAL COMMONWEALTH SOCIETY LIBRARY, CAMBRIDGE
Redwood Album
Curtis, H. 'A First List of the Regiments Stationed in Natal, South Africa, 1838-1914' (compiled 1930)

SHERWOOD FORESTERS MUSEUM, NOTTINGHAM CASTLE
Crealock's Watercolours and Drawings

SOMERSET MILITARY MUSEUM, TAUNTON CASTLE
Album of the 1/13th L.I.

THE SOUTH WALES BORDERERS AND MONMOUTHSHIRE REGIMENTAL MUSEUM OF THE ROYAL REGIMENT OF WALES, BRECON
Zulu War Boxes: 1-3

COLLECTION OF DR G. KEMBLE WOODGATE, ST PETER'S COLLEGE, OXFORD
Woodgate Military Diary and Private Diary

SOUTH AFRICA

COLLECTION OF MR R.H. ADDISON, KLOOF
Addison Papers

THE AFRICANA LIBRARY, JOHANNESBURG
Conductor in the Transport Division's
  Diary
MacLeod Letters
Stabb Diary

THE BRENTHURST LIBRARY, PARKTOWN
Alison Collection
Bulwer Letters
Harness Letters
St Vincent Journal

KILLIE CAMPBELL AFRICANA LIBRARY, DURBAN
Cato Papers: 1
Clarke Papers
Colenbrander Papers: 1
Colenso Papers: 6, 9, 13-17, 25-9
Commeline Letters
Cramer Album
Dinuzulu File
Dunn Papers: 1-2
H.F. Fynn, Jnr. Papers
Goatham Letters
Lugg Papers: 1-3
Mason Letters
Peace Scrap-Book
Reminiscences of the Zulu War 1879:
  1-2
Shepstone Papers: 6
Stainbank Diary
Stuart Collection: 79-88
Watson Letters
Wood Papers: 4-5, 7, 9
Zulu Essay Competition, 1942
Zulu Tribal History Competition, 1950

LOCAL HISTORY MUSEUM, DURBAN
Turner Letters
Vause Diary

NATAL ARCHIVES DEPOT, PIETERMARITZBURG
Colenso Collection: 1-2, 6, 8, 23-7, 72-3,
  100-1, 106-9; C.1278/14-15,
  C1279/6, 12
Fannin Collection: 2/4-6, 8
Faye Papers: 7-8
H.F. Fynn Snr Papers: 18
Home Thompson Papers

Lugg Papers: 1
H.C. Shepstone Papers: 9
J. Shepstone Papers: 1, 9-10
T. (Offie) Shepstone Papers: 2
Sir T. Shepstone Papers: 11, 25, 31-42,
  52-7, 68-74, 95
Stabb Papers, 4-6
Sutton Diary
Wood Collection: II/1-5

WILLIAM CULLEN LIBRARY, UNIVERSITY OF THE
WITWATERSRAND, JOHANNESBURG
Booth Papers
Parke Jones Letters
Littleton Papers: 53-116
Original Zulu War Treaties, September -
October 1879

Unpublished official papers

GREAT BRITAIN

PUBLIC RECORD OFFICE, KEW
Colonial Office: CO 179/126-32
War Office, Papers Relating to the Anglo-
  Zulu War: WO 32/7708-93

SOUTH AFRICA

KILLIE CAMPBELL AFRICANA LIBRARY, DURBAN
Wolseley Letter-Book

NATAL ARCHIVES DEPOT, PIETERMARITZBURG
Archives of the Nongoma (Ndwandwe)
  Magistracy: 2/9/2-4, 11
Colonial Secretary's Office, Natal:
  CSO 625-734, 1925-7, 1969-75,
  2094-99, 2479, 2552-3, 2610,
  2617, 2621, 2629-31, 2700
Government House, Natal:
  GH 142-8, 500-1, 528, 568-9, 600-1,
  789, 1054, 1220-1, 1300, 1326,
  1381, 1398-1402, 1410-1413,
  1421-4, 1730
Government House, Zululand:
  GHZ 696-729, 820-1, 824, 830-2,
  844-5
Secretary for Native Affairs, Natal:
  SNA 1/1/2, 30-5, 1/2/4-6,
  1/3/31, 1/4/1-2, 1/5/1, 1/6/3, 11-
  16, 1/7/11-13, 1/9/6-7
Zululand Archives:
  ZA 4-11, 19, 21, 41-2

TRANSVAAL ARCHIVES DEPOT, PRETORIA
Argief Utrecht: 1, 13-14, 25
Argief Wakkerstroom: 4-5, 43-4
Staatsekretaris, Transvaal:
SS 236, 281, 283, 286, 291, 292,
295, 298, 306, 314, 316, 318, 346,
348-9, 352, 358

OFFICIAL PRINTED SOURCES

CO 879/14: *African Confidential Print*
158, 162, 164-2, 168-9
CO 879/15: *African Confidential Print*
170-3, 181a, 187, 190-1, 196
CO 879/16: *African Confidential Print*
202
CO 879/30: *African Confidential Print*
370, 373
CO 879/33: *African Confidential Print*
398
British Parliamentary Papers:
C. 1342, C. 2000, C. 2079, C. 2100,
C. 2144, C. 2220, C. 2222, C. 2234,
C. 2242, C. 2252, C. 2260, C. 2269,
C. 2308, C.2316, C. 2318, C. 2367,
C. 2374, C. 2454, C. 2482, C. 2505,
C. 2584, C. 3174, C. 3182, C. 3247,
C. 3270, C. 3293, C. 3466, C. 3616,
C. 3705, C. 3864, C. 4037, C. 4191,
C. 4214, C. 4274, C. 4587, C. 4643,
C. 4645, C. 4864, C. 4913, C. 4980,
C. 5143, C. 5331, C. 5522, C. 5892,
C. 5893, C. 6070, C. 6684, C. 7780,
C. 8782
Colony of Natal, Ministerial Department
of Native Affairs, *Blue Book on Native
Affairs*, 1898 (Pietermaritzburg,
1904)
Fynney, F. *The Zulu Army and Zulu
Headmen. Published by Direction of
the Lieut.- General Commanding*
(Pietermaritzburg, April 1879)
*Government Gazette of the Republic of
South Africa*, vol. 346, no. 15681
Intelligence Branch of the War Office,
*Narrative of the Field Operations
Connected with the Zulu War of 1879*
(London, 1881)
Intelligence Division of the War Office,

*Precis of Information Concerning
Zululand* (London, 1895)
Natal Government Gazette, XXX, XXXI,
XXXIX, XL
WO 33/33: *Isandhlwana*, 1879
WO 33/34: *Zulu War, Miscellaneous*,
1878-9
*Zululand Lands Delimitation
Commission, 1902-1904. Reports by
the Joint Imperial & Colonial
Commissioners (with Annexures and
Maps* (Pietermaritzburg, 1905)

**UNOFFICIAL CONTEMPORARY
PRINTED SOURCES**

Newspapers and periodicals

Graphic
Illustrated London News
*Natal Almanac, Directory and Yearly
Register*
Natal Mercantile Advertizer
Natal Colonist
Natal Mercury
Natal Witness
Punch
Times of Natal
Zululand Times

Articles

Brown, Surgeon D. Blair 'Surgical Notes
on the Zulu War, *Lancet*, 2 (5 July
1879)
Colenso, Bishop J.W. 'Cetywayo's
Overtures of Peace', *The Aborigines'
Friend: A Journal of the Transactions
of the Aborigines' Protection Society*,
new series, 5 (June 1879)
Forbes, A. 'Lord Chelmsford and the Zulu
War, *The Nineteenth Century*
(February 1880)
Fripp, C.E. 'Reminiscences of the Zulu
War, 1879', *Pall Mall Magazine*, 20
(1900)
Harness, Lt.-Col. A. 'The Zulu Campaign
from a Military Point of View', *Fraser's
Magazine*, 101 (April 1880)
Hutton, Lt.-Gen. Sir E. 'Some
Recollections of the Zulu War', *The*

Army Quarterly, XVI (April 1921)
Magwaza, M. 'A Visit to King Ketshwayo', MacMillan's Magazine, XXXVII (November 1877 - April 1878)
Montgomery, A.N. 'Isandhlwana: A Visit Six Months After the Disaster', Leisure Hours Magazine, (1892)
Ross, Capt. J. 'Through the Zulu War with General Wood's Flying Column', Canadian Military Institute: Selected Papers, 5 (1893-4)
Schermbrucker, F. 'Zholbane and Kambula', The South African Catholic Magazine, III, 30 & 31 (1893)
'The Zulu War: With Colonel Pearson at Eshowe: By One Who Was There', Blackwood's Edinburgh Magazine, DCCLX, CXXVI (July 1879)

Pamphlets

Bird, J. An Inquiry into the Causes of the Zulu War (Pietermaritzburg, 1880)
Chesson, F.W. The War in Zululand: Brief Review of Sir Bartle Frere's Policy, Drawn from Official Documents (Westminster, 1879)
Colenso, H.E. Mr Commissioner Osborn as One Cause of the Confusion in Zulu Affairs (London, n.d.)
— The Zulu Impeachment of British Officials 1887-8 Confirmed by Official records in 1892 (London, 1892)
— The Present Position Among the Zulus (1873). With Some Suggestions for the Future (London, 1893)
— Cases of 6 Usutu (other than the exiles at St. Helena) Punished for Having Taken Part in the Disturbances of 1888 (London, 1893)
Dawnay, G.C. Private Journal of Guy C. Dawnay. Campaigns: Zulu 1879; Egypt 1882; Suakim 1885 (printed for private circulation)
Durnford, Lt.-Col. E. Isandhlwana, 22nd January, 1879: A Narrative, Compiled from Official and Reliable Sources (London, 1879)
Escombe, H. and Dumat, A. A Remonstrance on Behalf of the Zulu

Chiefs (London, 1889)
Hartley, W. Natal, Transvaal and Zululand (Leeds, 1879)
'H' [Heron-Maxwell, W.] Reminiscences of a Red Coat (London, 1895)
Historical Records of the 2nd Battalion, 24th Regiment, for the Campaign in South Africa, 1877-78-79; Embracing the Kaffir & Zulu Wars (confidential, Secunderabad, January 1882)
Mann, R.J. The Zulus and Boers of South Africa: A Fragment of Recent History (London, 1879)
Marter, Lt.-Col. R.J.C. The Capture of Cetywayo, King of the Zulus (private, 1880)
Martineau, J. The Transvaal Trouble: How it Arose (London, 1896)
Molyneux, Maj. W.C.F. Notes on Hasty Defences as Practised in South Africa (private circulation of notes made in 1879)
Montgomery, A.N. Cetywayo, Natal, Zululand (n.p., August 1882)
Mynors, A.C.B. Letters and Diary of the Late Arthur C.B. Mynors, Lieut. 3rd. Batt., 60th Rifles, Who Died at Fort Pearson, Natal the 25th of April, 1879 (Margate, 1879)
Plé, J. Les Laagers dans La Guerre des Zoulous (Paris, 1882)
Shepstone, Sir T. The Native Question: Answer to President Reitz (reprinted from the Natal Mercury, January 29, 1892)
Special Reporter of Cape Times [Murray, R.W.] Cetywayo, from the Battle of Ulundi to the Cape of Good Hope (Cape Town, 16 September 1879)
The Zulu War: Correspondence between His Excellency the High Commissioner and the Bishop of Natal, Referring to the Present Invasion of Zululand (Durban & Pietermaritzburg, 1879)
Tulloch, Lt.-Col. Natal and the Zulus (Natal, 1885)
Wynne, W.R.C. Memoir of Capt. W.R.C. Wynne, R.E. (for private circulation, Southampton, n.d.)

Books: General Accounts; Autobiographies; Memoirs; Reminiscences

Ashe, Maj. W. & Wyatt Edgell, Capt. the Hon. E.V. *The Story of the Zulu Campaign* (London, 1880)

Barrett, A.J. *Fifteen Years among the Zulus and Boers* (Hull, 1879)

Blood, Sir B. *Four Score Years and Ten: Bindon Blood's Reminiscences* (London, 1933)

Brownlee, Hon. C. *Reminiscences of Kaffir Life and History and Other Papers* (Lovedale, 1896)

Callaway, Rev. Canon *The Religious System of the Amazulu* (Leipzig, reprint, 1884)

Callwell, Col. C.E. *Small Wars: Their Principles and Practice* (London, 3rd edit., 1906)

Clairemont, E. *The Africander: A Plain Tale of Colonial Life* (London, 1896)

Colenso, F.E., assisted by Durnford, Lt.-Col. E. *History of the Zulu War and its Origin* (London, 1880)

Colenso, F.E. *The Ruin of Zululand* (London, 1884-5)

Colenso, Bishop J.W. and Colenso, H.E. *Digest of Zulu Affairs Compiled by Bishop Colenso and Continued after his Death by his Daughter Harriette Emily Colenso* (Bishopstowe, 1878-88), series no. 1, parts I & II (December 1878 - April 1881)

Cox, Sir G.W. *The Life of J.W. Colenso* (London, 1888)

Deleage, P. *Trois Mois chez les Zoulous et les Derniers Jours du Prince Imperial* (Paris, 1879)

Durnford, E. (ed.) *A Soldier's Life and Work in South Africa, 1872-1879: A Memory of the Late Colonel A.W. Durnford, Royal Engineers* (London, 1882)

Frere, Sir B. *Afghanistan and South Africa: Letters* (London, 1881)

Gardiner, Capt. A.F. *Narrative of a Journey to the Zoolu Country in South Africa, Undertaken in 1835* (London, 1836)

Gibson, J.Y. *The Story of the Zulus* (London, 1911)

Grout, Rev. L. *Zulu-Land, or, Life among the Zulu Kafirs of Natal and Zulu-Land, South Africa* (London, n.d. [1861?])

Haggard, H. Rider *Cetywayo and his White Neighbours; or, Remarks on Recent Events in Zululand, Natal and the Transvaal* (London, 1888)

Haggard, Sir H. Rider *The Days of My Life: An Autobiography* (London, 1926), I

Hallam Parr, Capt. H. *A Sketch of the Kafir and Zulu Wars* (London, 1880)

Hamilton-Browne, Col. G. *A Lost Legionary in South Africa* (London, 19[?])

Harrison, Gen. Sir R. *Recollections of a Life in the British Army* (London, 1908)

Holden, W.C. *History of the Colony of Natal* (London, 1855)

— *British Rule in South Africa: Illustrated in the Rule of Kama and his Tribe, and of the War in Zululand* (London, 1879)

Holt, H.P. *The Mounted Police of Natal* (London, 1913)

Jenkinson, T.B. *Amazulu: The Zulus, their Past History, Manners, Customs and Language* (London, 1882)

Laurence, W.M. *Selected Writings* (Grahamstown, 1882)

Lucas, T.J. *The Zulus and the British Frontiers* (London, 1879)

Ludlow, Capt. W.R. *Zululand and Cetywayo* (London and Birmingham, 1882)

Mackinnon, J.P. and Shadbolt, S. (comps.) *The South African Campaign, 1879* (London, 1882)

Malet, T. St. Lo. *Extracts from a Diary in Zululand* (Upper Norwood, 1880)

McToy, E.D. *A Brief History of the 13th Regiment (P.A.L.I.) in South Africa during the Transvaal and Zulu Difficulties* (Devonport, 1880)

Mitford, B. *Through the Zulu Country: Its Battlefields and its People* (London, 1883)

Molyneux, Maj.-Gen. W.C.F. *Campaigning in South Africa and Egypt* (London, 1896)

Montague, Capt. W.E. *Campaigning in South Africa: Reminiscences of an Officer in 1879* (Edinburgh & London, 1880)

Moodie, D.C.F. (ed.) *The History of the Battles and Adventures of the British, the Boers and the Zulus in Southern Africa, from 1495 to 1879, Including Every Particular of the Zulu War of 1879, with a Chronology* (Sidney, Melbourne & Adelaide, 1879)

Moodie, D.C.F. (ed.) *John Dunn, Cetywayo and the Three Generals* (Pietermaritzburg, 1886)

Mossop, G. *Running the Gauntlet* (London, 1937)

Norbury, Fleet-Surgeon H.F. *The Naval Brigade in South Africa during the Years 1877-78-79* (London, 1880)

Norris-Newman, C.L. *In Zululand with the British throughout the War of 1879* (London, 1880)

Paton, Col. G., Glennie, Col. F. & Penn Symons, W. (eds.) *Historical Records of the 24th Regiment from its Formation, in 1689* (London, 1892)

Plain Woman *Alone among the Zulus* (London, n.d [1866?])

Plant, R. *The Zulu in Three Tenses: Being a Forecast of the Zulu's Future in the Light of his Past* (Pietermaritzburg, 1905)

Richards, W. *Her Majesty's Army: A Descriptive Account of the Various Regiments Now Comprising the Queen's Forces, from their First Establishment* (London, 188[?])

Robinson, Cmdr. C.N. *Celebrities of the Army* (London, 1900)

Samuelson, R.C.A. *Long, Long Ago* (Durban, 1929)

Shooter, Rev. J. *The Kaffirs of the Natal and Zulu Country* (London, 1857)

Smith-Dorrien, Gen. Sir H. *Memories of Forty-Eight Years Service* (London, 1925)

Tomasson, W.H. *With the Irregulars in the Transvaal and Zululand* (London, 1881)

Vijn, C. (tr. from the Dutch and edited with preface and notes by the Rt. Rev. J.W. Colenso, D.D., Bishop of Natal) *Cetshwayo's Dutchman: Being the Private Journal of a White Trader in*

Zululand during the British Invasion (London, 1880)

Wood, Field Marshal Sir E. *From Midshipman to Field Marshal* (London, 1906), II

LATER EDITED, ANNOTATED AND PRINTED CONTEMPORARY SOURCES

Ballard C. (ed.) and Feist, H. (tr.) 'On a Tough Missionary Post in Zululand: The Life Experiences of the Missionary Friedrich Volker according to the Notes of his Wife (1928)', *Natalia* 9 (December 1979)

Bennett, Lt.-Col. I.H.W. *Eyewitness in Zululand: The Campaign Reminiscences of Colonel W.A. Dunne, CB: South Africa, 1877-1881* (London, 1989)

Bird, J. (compiler) *The Annals of Natal 1495-1845* (Cape Town, facsimile reprint, 1965), I and II

Bourquin, S. (compiler) *The First Six Months of the Zulu War of 1879 as Reported in 'The Graphic', January-June 1879* (Durban, 1963)

— *The Concluding Stages of the Zulu War of 1879 as Reported in 'The Graphic', July-December 1879* (Durban 1965)

Bourquin, S. and Johnston, T.M. (compilers) *The Zulu War of 1879 as Reported in 'The Illustrated London News' during January-December 1879* (Durban, 1971)

Butterfield, P.H. (ed.) *War and Peace in South Africa 1879-1881: The Writings of Philip Anstruther and Edward Essex* (Melville, 1987)

Cope, T. (ed.) and Malcolm, D. (tr.) *Izibongo: Zulu Praise-Poems Collected by James Stuart* (Oxford, 1968)

Child, D. (ed.) *The Zulu War Journal of Colonel Henry Harford, C.B.* (Pietermaritzburg, 1978)

— *Portrait of a Pioneer: The Letters of Sidney Turner from South Africa, 1864-1901* (Johannesburg, 1980)

Clarke S. (ed.) *Invasion of Zululand 1879: Anglo-Zulu War Experiences of Arthur*

Harness; John Jervis, 4th Viscount St
Vincent; and Sir Henry Bulwer
(Houghton, 1979)
— *Zululand at War 1879: the Conduct of
the Anglo-Zulu War* (Houghton, 1984)
Delegorgue, A. (Webb, F. (tr.), Alexander,
S.J. and Webb, C. de B. (intro. and
index))*Travels in Southern Africa*
(Durban & Pietermaritzburg, 1990), I
Dlamini, P. (Filter, H. (compiler),
Bourquin. S. (tr. and ed.)) *Paulina
Dlamini: Servant of Two Kings* (Durban
and Pietermaritzburg, 1986)
Emery, F. *The Red Soldier: Letters from the
Zulu War, 1879* (London, 1877)
— *Marching over Africa: Letters from
Victorian Soldiers* (London, 1986)
Fannin, N. (ed.) *The Fannin Papers: Pioneer
Days in South Africa* (Durban, 1932)
Fuze, M.M. (Lugg, H.C. (tr.) and Cope,
A.T. (ed.)) *The Black People and Whence
They Came: A Zulu View*
(Pietermaritzburg & Durban, 1979)
Fynn, H. (Stuart, J. and Malcolm, D.
(eds.)) *The Diary of Henry Francis Fynn*
(Pietermaritzburg, 1969)
Hart-Synnot, B.M. (ed.) *Letters of Major-
General Fitzroy Hart-Synnot C.B.,
C.M.G.* (London, 1912)
Hattersley, A.F. *Later Annals of Natal*
(London, 1938)
Holme, N. (compiler) *The Silver Wreath:
Being the 24th Regiment at Isandhlwana
and Rorke's Drift* (London, 1979)
Isaacs, N. (Herman, L. and Kirby, P. (eds.))
Travels and Adventures in Eastern Africa
(Cape Town, 1970), I and II
Jones. L.T. (ed.) *Reminiscences of the Zulu
War by John Maxwell* (Cape Town,
1979)
Knight, I. (ed.) *'By the Orders of the Great
White Queen': Campaigning in Zululand
through the Eyes of the British Soldier,
1879* (London, 1992)
— (ed.) '"Kill Me in the Shadows": The
Bowden Collection of Anglo-Zulu War
Oral History', *Soldiers of the Queen*, 74
(September 1993)
Laband, J. *Fight Us in the Open: The Anglo-*

Zulu War through Zulu Eyes
(Pietermaritzburg & Ulundi, 1985)
— (ed.) *Lord Chelmsford's Zululand
Campaign 1878–1879* (United
Kingdom, 1994)
Lloyd, Lt. W.N. 'The Defence of Ekowe',
Natalia, 5 (December 1975)
Maclean, C. (Gray, S. (ed.)) *The Natal
Papers of 'John Ross'* (Pietermaritzburg,
1992)
Merrett, P. and Butcher, R. (eds.) *The
Hunting Journal of Robert Briggs
Struthers, 1852-1856: in the Zulu
Country and the Tsonga Regions*
(Durban and Pietermaritzburg, 1991)
Owen, F. (Cory, G.E. (ed.)) *The Diary of the
Rev. Francis Owen, Missionary with
Dingaan in 1837-38, together with
Extracts from the Writings of the
Interpreters in Zulu, Messrs Hulley and
Kirkman* (Cape Town, 1926)
Preston, A. (ed.) *Sir Garnet Wolseley's
South African Journal, 1879-1880*
(Cape Town, 1973)
Pridmore, J. (ed.) *The Journal of William
Clayton Humphreys in the Zulu Country,
July-October 1851* (Durban and
Pietermaritzburg, 1993)
Rycroft, D.K. and Ngcobo, A.B. (eds.) *The
Praises of Dingana (izibongo
zikaDingana)* (Pietermaritzburg, 1988)
Webb, C. de B. and Wright, J.B. (eds.) *A
Zulu King Speaks: Statements Made by
Cetshwayo kaMpande on the History and
Customs of his People* (Pietermaritzburg
& Durban, 1978)
— *The James Stuart Archive of Recorded
Oral Evidence Relating to the History of
the Zulu and Neighbouring Peoples*
(Pietermaritzburg & Durban, 1976,
1979, 1982, 1986), I-IV
Webb, C. de B. (ed.) 'A Zulu Boy's
Recollections of the Zulu War',
Natalia, 8 (December 1978)

LATER PRINTED SOURCES

Articles

Atmore, A. and Marks, S. 'The Imperial

Factor in South Africa in the Nineteenth Century: Towards a Reassessment', *Journal of Imperial and Commonwealth History*, III, 1 (1974)

Bailes, H. 'Technology and Imperialism: A Case Study of the Victorian Army in Africa', *Victorian Studies*, 24, 1 (Autumn 1980)

Ballard, C. 'The Political Transformation of a Transfrontiersman: The Career of John Dunn in Zululand, 1857-1878', *Journal of Imperial and Commonwealth History*, VII, 3 (May 1979)

— 'John Dunn and Cetshwayo: the Material Foundations of Political Power in the Zulu Kingdom, 1857-1878', *Journal of African Studies*, 21 (1980)

— 'Natal 1824-44: The Frontier Interregnum', *Journal of Natal and Zulu History*, V (1982)

— 'The Historical Image of King Cetshwayo of Zululand: A Centennial Comment', *Natalia*, 13 (December 1983)

— '"A Year of Scarcity": The 1896 Locust Plague in Natal and Zululand', *South African Historical Journal*, 15 (1983)

— 'The Role of Trade and Hunter - Traders in the Political Economy of Natal and Zululand, 1824-1880', *The International Journal of African Historical Studies*, 3 (1986)

Benyon, J.A. 'Isandhlwana and the Passing of a Proconsul', *Natalia*, 8 (December 1978)

Bourquin, S. 'The Zulu Military Organization and Challenge of 1879', *Military History Journal*, 4, 4 (January 1979)

Burroughs, P. 'Imperial Defence and the Victorian Army', *Journal of Imperial and Commonwealth History*, XV, 1 (October 1986)

Cloete, D. 'From Warriors to Wage Slaves: The Fate of the Zulu People since 1879', *Reality*, XI, 1 (January 1879)

Cobbing, J. 'The Evolution of the Ndebele Amabutho', *Journal of African History*, XV, 4 (1974)

Colenbrander, P. 'An Imperial High Commissioner and the Making of a War', *Reality*, XI, 1 (January 1979)

— 'External Exchange and the Zulu Kingdom: Towards a Reassessment' in Guest, B. and Sellers, J. (eds.), *Enterprise and Exploitation in a Victorian Colony: Aspects of the Economic and Social History of Colonial Natal* (Pietermaritzburg, 1985)

'Colloquium: The "Mfecane" Aftermath: Towards a New Paradigm', *South African Historical Journal*, 25 (1991)

Cope, R.L. 'Political Power within the Zulu Kingdom and the "Coronation Laws" of 1873', *Journal of Natal and Zulu History*, VIII (1985)

Daniel, J.B. 'A Geographical Study of Pre-Shakan Zululand', *South African Historical Journal*, 55, 1 (1973)

Davenport, T.R.H 'The Fragmentation of Zululand, 1879-1918', *Reality*, XI, 5 (September 1979)

Dominy, G. 'The New Republicans: A Centennial Reappraisal of the "Nieuwe Republiek", 1884-1888', *Natalia*, 14 (1984)

— 'In the Aftermath of the Anglo-Zulu War: The Battle of Etshaneni 5 June 1884', *Soldiers of the Queen*, 74 (September 1993)

Edgecombe, R. 'Sir Marshall Clarke and the Abortive Attempt to "Basutolandise" Zululand', *Journal of Natal and Zulu History*, I (1978)

— 'Bishop Colenso and the Zulu Nation', *Journal of Natal and Zulu History*, III (1980)

Emery, F. 'Geography and Imperialism: The Role of Sir Bartle Frere (1815-84)', *The Geographical Journal*, 50, 3 (November 1984)

Etherington, N. 'The Origins of "Indirect Rule" in Nineteenth Century Natal', *Theoria*, 47 (October 1976)

— 'Labour Supply and the Genesis of South African Confederation in the 1870s', *Journal of African History*, XX,

3 (1979)

— 'The Great Trek in Relation to the Mfecane: A Reassessment', *South African Historical Journal*, 25 (1991).

Gluckman, M. 'The Kingdom of the Zulu of South Africa' in Fortes, M. and Evans-Pritchard, E. *African Political Systems* (London, 1940)

— 'The Individual in a Social Framework: The Rise of King Shaka of Zululand', *Journal of African Studies*, I, 2 (1974)

Guy, J. 'A Note on Firearms in the Zulu Kingdom with Special Reference to the Anglo-Zulu War, 1879', *Journal of African History*, XII, 4 (1971)

— 'The British Invasion of Zululand: Some Thoughts for the Centenary Year', *Reality*, XI 1 (January 1979)

Harries, P. 'History, Ethnicity and the Ingwavuma Land Deal: The Zulu Northern Frontier in the Nineteenth Century', *Journal of Natal and Zulu History*, VI (1983)

Jackson, F.W.D. 'Isandhlwana, 1879: The Sources Re-Examined', *Journal of the Society for Army Historical Research*, XLIX, 173, 175, 176 (1965)

— 'The First Battalion, Twenty-Fourth Regiment, Marches to Isandhlwana', *Soldiers of the Queen*, 16 (February 1979)

— 'Isandhlwana Revisited: A Letter to the Editor', *Soldiers of the Queen*, 33 (July 1983)

Jones, H.M. 'Why Khambula?' *Soldiers of the Queen*, 74 (September 1993)

Kennedy, P.A. 'Mpande and the Zulu Kingship', *Journal of Natal and Zulu History*, IV (1981)

Knight, I.J. 'The Uniforms and Weapons of the Zulu Army, 1879', *Soldiers of the Queen*, 16 (February 1979)

— 'The Zulu Army 1879' in Knight, I.J. (ed.) *There Will Be an Awful Row at Home about This* (Shoreham-by-Sea, 1987)

Lambert, M. 'Ancient Greek and Zulu Sacrificial Ritual: A Comparative

Analysis', *Numen*, 40 (1993)

Laband, J.P.C. 'The Battle of Ivuna (or Ndunu Hill)', *Natalia*, 10 (1980)

— 'The Establishment of the Zululand Administration in 1887: A Study of the Criteria behind the Selection of British Colonial Officials', *Journal of Natal and Zulu History*, IV (1981)

— '"Chopping Wood with a Razor": The Skirmish at eZungeni Mountain and the Unnecessary Death of Lieutenant Frith, 5 June 1879', *Soldiers of the Queen*, 74 (September 1993)

— 'British Boundary Adjustments and the uSuthu-Mandlakazi Conflict in Zululand, 1879-1904', *South African Historical Journal*, 30 (May 1994)

Marks, S. 'Harriette Colenso and the Zulus, 1874-1913', *Journal of African History*, 4 (1963)

Martin, G. 'Identity and Interaction: A Defence of Natal History', *Journal of Imperial and Commonwealth History*, 22, 2 (May 1994)

Morris, D. 'Isandhlwana', *Soldiers of the Queen*, 29/30 (Summer 1982)

Okoye, F. 'Dingane: A Reappraisal', *Journal of African History*, X, 1 (1969)

Potgieter, F.J. 'Die Verstigting van die Blanke in Transvaal (1837-1886) met Spesiale Verwysing na die Verhouding tussen die Mens en die Omgewing', *Archives Year Book for South African History, 1958 (II)* (Pretoria/Cape Town, 1958)

Raum, O.F. 'Aspects of Zulu Diplomacy in the Nineteenth Century', *Afrika und Übersee*, LXVI (1983)

Reynecke, G.J. 'Utrecht in die Geskiedenis van die Transvaal tot 1877', *Archives Year Book for South Africa, 1958 (II)* (Pretoria/Cape Town, 1958)

Taylor, S. 'Zulu History Rewritten and Rerun', *The Times Higher Educational Supplement*, 1 November 1991

Torlage, G. 'Impi Yaba Ntwana: The War of the Children', *Soldiers of the Queen*, 74 (September 1993)

Tylden, Maj. G. 'The Waggon Laager',

Journal of the Society for Army Historical Research, 41, 168 (1963)

Van Rooyen, T.S. 'Die Verhouding tussen die Boere, Engelse en Naturelle in die Geskiedenis van die Oos Transvaal tot 1882', *Archives Year Book, 1951 (I)* (Cape Town, 1951)

Van Zyl, M.C. 'Dinizulu se Vlug na die Suid-Afrikanse Republiek in 1888', *Communication of the University of South Africa*, C30 (1961)

Verbeek, J.A. and Bresler, V. 'The Role of the Ammunition Boxes in the Disaster at Isandhlwana, 22nd January, 1879', *The Journal of the Historical Firearms Society of South Africa*, 7, 6 (December 1977)

Webb, C. de B. 'Lines of Power: The High Commissioner, the Telegraph and the War of 1879', *Natalia*, 8 (December 1978)

Whybra, J. 'Contemporary Sources and the Composition of the Main Zulu Impi, January 1879', *Soldiers of the Queen*, 53 (June 1988)

Wright, J.B. 'Pre-Shakan Age-Group Formations among the Northern Nguni', *Natalia*, 8 (December 1878)

Wylie, D., 'A Dangerous Admiration: E.A. Ritter's Shaka Zulu', *South African Historical Journal*, 28 (1993).

Books

Acocks, J.P.H. *Veld Types of South Africa* (Pretoria, 1951)

Argyle, J. and Preston-Whyte, E. (eds.) *Social System and Tradition in Southern Africa* (Cape Town, 1978)

Ballard, C. *John Dunn: The White Chief of Zululand* (Craighall, 1985)

— *The House of Shaka: The Zulu Monarchy Illustrated* (Durban, 1988)

Barthorp, M. *The Zulu War: A Pictorial History* (Poole, 1980)

Becker, P. *Rule of Fear: The Life and Times of Dingane, King of the Zulu* (Great Britain, 1964)

Belich, J. *The New Zealand Wars and the Victorian Interpretation of Racial Conflict* (Auckland, 1986)

Benyon, J.A. *Proconsul and Paramountcy in South Africa: The High Commission, British Supremacy and the Sub-Continent, 1806-1910* (Pietermaritzburg, 1980)

Berglund, A.I. *Zulu Thought-Patterns and Symbolism* (Uppsala, 1976)

Binns, C.T. The *Last Zulu King: The Life and Death of Cetshwayo* (London, 1963)

— *Dinuzulu: The Death of the House of Shaka* (London, 1968)

Birkby, C. *Zulu Journey* (London, 1937)

Booth, A.R. *Swaziland: Tradition and Change in a Southern African Kingdom* (Boulder, Colorado, 1983)

Bonner, P. *Kings, Commoners and Concessionaires: The Evolution and Dissolution of the Nineteenth-Century Swazi State* (Johannesburg, 1983)

Braatvedt, H.P. (Mqangabodwe) *Roaming Zululand with a Native Commissioner* (Pietermaritzburg, 1949)

Brookes, E.H. and Hurwitz, N. *The Native Reserves of Natal* (Cape Town, 1957)

Brookes, E.H. and Webb, C. de B. A *History of Natal* (Pietermaritzburg, 1965)

Bryant, A.T. *Olden Times in Zululand and Natal* (London, 1929)

— *The Zulu People as They Were before the White Man Came* (Pietermaritzburg, 1949)

— *A History of the Zulu and Neighbouring Tribes* (Cape Town, 1964)

— *Zulu Medicine and Medicine-Men* (Cape Town, 1966)

Bulpin, T.V. *Shaka's Country: A Book of Zululand* (Cape Town, 1956)

— *Natal and the Zulu Country* (Cape Town, 1966)

Cameron, T. and Spies, S.B. (eds.) *An Illustrated History of South Africa* (Johannesburg, 1986)

Castle, I. and Knight, I. *Fearful Hard Times: The Siege and Relief of Eshowe, 1879* (London, 1994)

Cope, N. *To Bind the Nation: Solomon kaDinuzulu and Zulu Nationalism 1913-*

1933 (Pietermaritzburg, 1993)

Coupland, Sir R. *Zulu Battlepiece: Isandhlwana* (London, 1948)

Davenport, T.R.H. *South Africa: A Modern History* (4th edition, Basingstoke, 1991)

Delius, P. *The Land Belongs to Us: The Pedi Polity, the Boers and the British in the Nineteenth Century Transvaal* (Johannesburg, 1983)

Drooglever, R.W.F. *The Road to Isandhlwana: Colonel Anthony Durnford in Natal and Zululand* (London and Novato, California, 1992)

Du Buisson, L. *The White Man Cometh* (Johannesburg, 1987)

Duminy, A. and Ballard, C. (eds.) *The Anglo-Zulu War: New Perspectives* (Pietermaritzburg, 1981)

Duminy, A. and Guest, B. (eds.) *Natal and Zululand from Earliest Times to 1910: A New History* (Pietermaritzburg, 1989)

Edgerton, R.B. *Like Lions They Fought: The Zulu War and the Last Black Empire in South Africa* (Great Britain, 1988)

Featherstone, D. *Weapons and Equipment of the Victorian Soldier* (Poole, 1978)

French, Maj. the Hon. G. *Lord Chelmsford and the Zulu War* (London, 1939)

Goodfellow, C.F. *Great Britain and South African Confederation, 1870-1881* (Cape Town, 1966)

Gordon, R.E. *Shepstone: The Role of the Family in the History of South Africa, 1820-1900* (Cape Town, 1968)

Guy, J. *The Destruction of the Zulu Kingdom: The Civil War in Zululand, 1879-1884* (London, 1979)

— *The Heretic: A Study of the Life of John William Colenso 1814-1883* (Johannesburg & Pietermaritzburg, 1983)

Hammond-Tooke, W.D. (ed.) *The Bantu-Speaking Peoples of Southern Africa* (London, 1974)

— *The Roots of Black South Africa* (Parklands, 1993)

Hattersley, A.F. *The British Settlement of Natal* (Cambridge, 1950)

Hurst, G.T. *Short History of the Volunteer Regiments of Natal and East Griqualand: Past and Present* (Durban, 1945)

James, L. *The Savage Wars: British Campaigns in Africa, 1870-1920* (Great Britain, 1985)

Jones, H.M. *A Biographical Register of Swaziland to 1902* (Pietermaritzburg, 1993)

Junod, H.A. *The Life of a South African Tribe* (Neuchatel, 1912), I (The Social Life)

Knight, I.J. (ed.) *There Will Be an Awful Row at Home about This* (Shoreham-by-Sea, 1987)

— *The Zulus* (London, 1989)

— *Brave Men's Blood: The Epic of the Zulu War, 1879* (London, 1990)

— *Zulu: Isandlwana and Rorke's Drift 22nd - 23rd January 1879* (London, 1992)

— *Nothing Left But To Fight: The Defence of Rorke's Drift, 1879* (London, 1993)

Krige, E. *The Social System of the Zulus* (Pietermaritzburg, 1974)

Laband, J.P.C. *The Battle of Ulundi* (Pietermaritzburg and Ulundi, 1988)

— *Kingdom in Crisis: The Zulu Response to the British Invasion of 1879* (Manchester and New York, 1992)

Laband, J.P.C. and Haswell, R. (eds.) *Pietermaritzburg 1838-1988: A New Portrait of an African City* (Pietermaritzburg, 1988)

Laband, J.P.C. and Mathews, J. *Isandlwana* (Pietermaritzburg and Ulundi, 1992)

Laband, J.P.C. and Thompson, P.S. *War Comes to Umvoti: The Natal- Zululand Border, 1878-9* (Durban, 1980)

— *Field Guide to the War in Zululand and the Defence of Natal 1879* (Pietermaritzburg, 2nd revised edition, 1983; reprinted with minor revisions, 1987)

— *Kingdom and Colony at War: Sixteen Studies on the Anglo-Zulu War of 1879* (Pietermaritzburg and Constantia, 1990)

Laband, J.P.C. and Thompson P.S. with Henderson, S. *The Buffalo Border*

1879: The Anglo-Zulu War in Northern Natal (Durban, 1983)

Laband, J.P.C. and Wright, J. *King Cetshwayo kaMpande (c. 1832-1884)* (Pietermaritzburg and Ulundi, 1983)

Lamar H. and Thompson, L. (eds.) *The Frontier in History: North America and Southern Africa Compared* (New Haven and London, 1981)

Lehmann, J.H. *All Sir Garnet: A Life of Field-Marshal Lord Wolseley* (London, 1964)

Lugg, H.C. *Historic Natal and Zululand* (Pietermaritzburg, 1949)

— (compiler, revised by Cope, A.T.) *Zulu Place Names in Natal* (Durban, 1968)

— *Life under a Zulu Shield* (Pietermaritzburg, 1975)

Mair, L. *African Kingdoms* (Oxford,1977)

Marks, S. *Reluctant Rebellion: The 1906-8 Disturbances in Natal* (Oxford, 1970)

Marks, S. and Atmore, A. (eds.) *Economy and Society in Pre-Industrial South Africa* (Hong Kong, 1980)

Marks, S. and Rathbone, R. (eds.) *Industrialisation and Social Change in South Africa: African Class Formation, Culture and Consciousness, 1870-1930* (London, 1982)

Martineau, J. *The Life and Correspondence of the Right Hon. Sir Bartle Frere, Bart., G.C.B., F.R.S., Etc.* (London, 1895), II

Mason, P. *The Men who Ruled India* (London, 1985)

Maylam, P. *A History of the African People of South Africa: From the Early Iron Age to the 1970s* (Cape Town, 1989)

Moberly, G.S. *A City Set on a Hill: A History of Eshowe* (Pietermaritzburg, 1970)

Morris, D.R. The Washing of the Spears: *A History of the Rise of the Zulu Nation under Shaka and its Fall in the Zulu War of 1879* (London, 1966)

Natal Regional Survey, Vol. I: Archaeology and Natural Resources of Natal (London, 1951)

Nathan, M. *The Voortrekkers of South Africa* (London, 1937)

Ngubane, H. *Body and Mind in Zulu Medicine: An Ethnography of Health and Disease in Nynswa-Zulu Thought and Practice* (London, 1977)

Oliver, R. and Sanderson, S.W. (eds.) *The Cambridge History of Africa* (Cambridge, 1985), VI

Omer-Cooper, J.D. *The Zulu Aftermath: A Nineteenth Century Revolution in Bantu Africa* (Great Britain, 1966)

Peires, J.B. (ed.) *Before and after Shaka: Papers in Nguni History* (Grahamstown, 1981)

Reader's Digest Illustrated History of South Africa: The Real Story (Cape Town, 3rd ed., 1994).

Ritter, E.A. *Shaka Zulu. The Rise of the Zulu Empire* (London, 1957)

Roberts, B. *The Zulu Kings* (London,1974)

Robinson, R. and Gallagher, J. with Denny, A. *Africa and the Victorians: The Official Mind of Imperialism* (London, 1961)

Samuelson, L.H. (Nomleti) *Some Zulu Customs and Folklore* (London, 19[?])

Saunders, C. (ed.) *Black Leaders in Southern African History* (London, 1979)

Smail, J.L. *Historical Monuments and Battlefields in Natal and Zululand* (Cape Town, 1965)

— *Monuments and Trails of the Voortrekkers* (Cape Town, 1968)

— *With Shield and Assegai* (Cape Town, 1969)

— *From the Land of the Zulu Kings: An Historical Guide for Those Restless Years in Natal and Zululand 1497 to 1879* (Durban, 1979)

Spiers, E.M. *The Army and Society 1815-1914* (London and New York, 1980)

Strachan, H. *European Armies and the Conduct of War* (London, 1983)

Summers, R. and Pagden, L.W. *The Warriors* (Cape Town, 1970)

Taylor, S. *Shaka's Children: A History of the Zulu People* (London, 1994)

Theal, G. McC. *History of South Africa from 1795 to 1872* (1892, facsimile,

Cape Town, 1964), II

— *History of South Africa from 1873 to 1884* (1919, facsimile, Cape Town, 1964), I

Thompson, L. (ed.) *African Societies in South Africa* (London, 1969)

Van Lingen, G. et al. *Battlefields of South Africa* (Parklands, 1991)

Walker, E.A. *The Great Trek* (London, 1934)

— (ed.) *The Cambridge History of the British Empire: South Africa* (Cambridge, 1963), III

— *A History of Southern Africa* (London, 1968)

Welsh, D. *The Roots of Segregation: Native Policy in Colonial Natal, 1845-1910* (Cape Town, 1971)

Wilkinson-Latham, C. *Uniforms and Weapons of the Zulu War* (London, 1978)

Wilson, M. and Thompson, L. (eds.) *The Oxford History of South Africa* (Oxford, 1971), I and II

Whitehouse, H. *Battle in Africa, 1879-1914* (Mansfield, 1987)

Worsfold, W.B. *Sir Bartle Frere* (London, 1923)

UNPUBLISHED THESES AND CONFERENCE AND SEMINAR PAPERS

Ballard, C.C. 'The Transfrontiersman: The Career of John Dunn in Natal and Zululand 1834-1895' (Ph.D. thesis, University of Natal, 1979)

Cobbing, J.R.D. 'The Ndebele under the Khumalos, 1820-1896' (unpublished Ph.D. thesis, University of Lancaster, 1976)

Colenbrander, P.J. 'Some Reflections on the Kingship of Mpande' (paper presented to the Conference on Natal and Zulu History, University of Natal, Durban, July 1985)

Cope, N.L.G. 'The Defection of Hamu' (unpublished B.A. Hons. thesis, University of Natal, 1980)

Cope, R.L. 'Shepstone and Cetshwayo

1873-1879' (unpublished M.A. thesis, University of Natal, 1967)

—'Civilization and Proleterianization: The 'New Native Policy' of the 1870s' (paper presented at the Wits History Workshop on the Making of Class, Johannesburg, February 1987)

Dominy, G.A. 'Routine of Empire: The Use of Force to Maintain Authority and Impose Peace as a Principle of Imperial Administration: the Cases of Waikato 1863 and Zululand 1879' (unpublished M.A. thesis, University College of Cork, 1983)

— 'Awarding a "Retrospective White Hat"? A Reconsideration of the Geopolitics of "Frere's War" of 1879' (paper presented at a workshop on Natal in the Colonial Period, University of Natal, Pietermaritzburg, October 1984)

Edgecombe, D.R., Laband, J.P.C. and Thompson, P.S. (eds.) 'The Debate on Zulu Origins: A Selection of Papers on the Zulu Kingdom and Early Colonial Natal' (Pietermaritzburg, 1992)

Etherington, N.A. 'The Rise of the Kholwa in Southeast Africa: African Christian Communities in Natal, Pondoland and Zululand, 1835-1880' (unpublished Ph.D. thesis, Yale University, 1971)

Guy, J. 'The Destruction of the Zulu Kingdom: The Civil War in Zululand, 1879-1884 (Ph.D. thesis, University of London, 1975)

Hamilton, C.A. 'Ideology, Oral Tradition and the Struggle for Power in the Early Zulu Kingdom' (unpublished M.A. thesis, University of the Witwatersrand, 1986)

Hedges, D.W. 'Trade and Politics in Southern Mozambique and Zululand in the Eighteenth and Early Nineteenth Centuries' (unpublished Ph.D. thesis, University of London, 1978)

Hernaes, P. and Simensen, J. 'The Zulu

Kingdom and the Norwegian Missionaries 1845-1880' (paper presented at the Conference on Natal and Zulu History, University of Natal, Durban, July 1985)

Kemp, B.H. 'John William Colenbrander: A History of the Times, People and Events with which He was Associated, 1879-1896' (unpublished Ph.D. thesis, University of Natal, 1962)

Kennedy, P.A. 'Fatal Diplomacy: Sir Theophilus Shepstone and the Zulu Kings, 1839-1879' (unpublished Ph.D. thesis, University of California, 1976)

Laband, J.P.C. 'Dick Addison: The Role of a British Official during the Disturbances in the Ndwandwe District of Zululand, 1887-1889' (unpublished M.A. thesis, University of Natal, 1980)

— 'Kingdom in Crisis: The Response of the Zulu Polity to the British Invasion of 1879' (Ph.D. thesis, University of Natal, 1990)

— 'The Zulu Strategic Response to the British Invasion of 1879' (paper presented at a workshop on Natal History in the Colonial Period, University of Natal, Pietermaritzburg, October 1990)

— 'An Assessment of the Cohesion and Resilience of the Zulu Polity under the Impact of the British Invasion of 1879' (paper presented at the 58th Annual Meeting of the American Military Institute, Duke University, Durham, North Carolina, 1991)

Mael, R. 'The Problem of Political Integration in the Zulu Empire' (unpublished Ph.D. thesis, University of California, 1974)

Mathews, J. 'Lord Chelmsford and the Problems of Transport and Supply during the Anglo-Zulu War of 1879' (unpublished M.A. thesis, University of Natal, 1979)

— 'Lord Chelmsford: British General in Southern Africa, 1878-1879' (unpublished D. Litt. et Phil. thesis, University of South Africa, 1986)

Monteith, M.A. 'Cetshwayo and Sekhukhune 1875-1879' (unpublished M.A. thesis, University of the Witwatersrand, 1978)

Pridmore, J. 'Reactions of Colonial Natal to Sir Garnet Wolseley's Settlement of Zululand, June-December 1879' (unpublished B.A. (Hons.) thesis, University of Natal, 1983)

— 'The Diary of Henry Francis Fynn, Jnr: 1883' (unpublished M.A. thesis, University of Natal, 1987), I and II

Rawlinson, R. 'Ondini: Royal Military Homestead of King Cetshwayo kaMpande, 1872-1879' (paper presented at the Conference on Natal and Zulu History, University of Natal, Durban, July 1985)

Slater, H. 'Transformations in the Political Economy of South-east Africa before 1840' (unpublished Ph.D. thesis, University of Sussex, 1976)

Van Wyk, A.J. 'Dinuzulu en die Usutu-Opstand van 1888' (unpublished M.A. thesis, University of the Orange Free State, 1972)

Wright, J. 'The Dynamics of Power and Conflict in the Thukela-Mzimkhulu Region in the Late 18th and Early 19th Centuries: A Critical Reconstruction' (unpublished Ph.D. thesis, University of the Witwatersrand, 1989)

Index